THE WIZARD AND THE TYPHOON

David J Reynolds

*Dedicated to Eric Stanley Tomkins, the grandson of Tom Bulch.
A true gentleman, without whose friendship and contribution this
book would have been much diminished.*

About the Author
Dave Reynolds was born in the County Durham market town of Bishop Auckland in England. After a basic secondary education he attained further education qualifications in Design, and followed a career path to become a Business Analyst for a major UK telecommunications company. More recently he served two terms of public service as a Town Councillor, in his now home town of Shildon not far from where he was born. He claims to have has a life-long passion for history, for which he firmly blames his mother. This has led him to become a founding Director of the Shildon Heritage Alliance CIC, and a champion for the Shildon Railway Institute, which was founded in 1833, becoming a world first. When not knee-deep in history he's quite fond of gardening, keeping an allotment, filmmaking or making music.

Foreword and Acknowledgements
The journey to producing this book began in 2018, not long after I'd become a Town Councillor. I attended a training course for new councillors at the Town Hall in Barnard Castle, County Durham, a town best known now as the controversial eye-test destination for one-time Prime Ministerial Advisor, Dominic Cummings. Setting that sleight aside, I was impressed by a display board they had depicting famous sons and daughters of the town. I later remarked to my partner, Kelly, that it was disappointing that we did not have such a display for Shildon. I should add at this point that though Shildon is a small town, it is world renowned as the 'cradle of the railways,' having been the point of origin of the world's first steam hauled passenger rail journey, and the world's first industrial railway town. It was once the home of a good few pioneering engineers. Kelly, who is a fine musician and was some decades ago a youth member of Shildon Town Band, pointed out that such a board should really include George Allan, and showed me a commemorative stone in the town centre that somehow I had failed to notice before. That was a trigger, I wanted to know a little more, not realising that it would be the first step of a four year journey; so I'll offer my thanks to Kelly for setting me away on a journey in which I'd encounter some tremendous people and make some new friends across the globe, some of whom I will mention in a few moments. It was also one in which I was astounded to find that

there would be not one main character but two, and that those two lives would have so much in common that it would have been a total injustice to write about one without its counterpart. George Allan and Tom Bulch are like two sides of a coin forged in the the mint that was Victorian Shildon. In terms of personality they are 'yin and yang' to one another but theirs is without doubt one single tale to tell,

I don't consider my approach to this book to be 'academic' and didn't want a section of references at the end, the pages of which would never see light of day. I have however attempted to be transparent throughout as to the sources I have used. I have also unashamedly included many direct quotes of newspaper articles and documents rather than paraphrasing. This has been deliberate as I wanted the reader to see situations that evolve through Victorian eyes, and expressed as they would have been at the time. It's part of the character of the narrative. I would also confess to having, in places, included more on individual band contests than may have been necessary, however as so many of the bands mentioned have long since dissolved I felt it important to allow their ghosts some space in this narrative. I'll absolutely forgive the reader for skipping over anything that appeals less to their curiosity or interest.

I think this is a book for anyone hoping to get insight into the aspirational working classes of the Victorian and Edwardian eras. It's a tale of attainable adventure with many lessons that still hold true today. I can't deny, however, that I'd love it to be read by bandsmen and women worldwide in the hope that the next time they dust off "Knight Templar," "The Senator," or "The Wizard" perhaps at the Whit Friday` Contests or Durham Miners Gala, or perhaps dig out one of Tom Bulch's greater works, they might keep something of either man, and what they went through, in mind while playing their hearts out.

The most important person I'd like to acknowledge and thank is Kelly for setting me off on a journey of discovery unlike any I've been on before, and for tolerating my obsessions with it over four years and patiently listening to me talk of each new discovery that came to light. I hope I haven't been too unbearable. I'd also like to thank bandmaster and composer Steve Robson for his enthusiasm and friendship throughout my research after I contacted him to ask about his discovery of several original George Allan self published pieces of music in the attic of the old Shildon Town Band bandroom. Also, Brian

Yates of the Northern Regional Brass Band Trust for his interest and passing on any findings he happened across. Thanks are additionally extended to former bandsman Bob Wray of South Shields for his assistance and for sharing his notes and investigations from the nineteen-eighties which included correspondence with Dorothy Allan, George's grand-daughter. I'd like to express appreciation for the generous encouragement in my work expressed by fellow historical writer Gerald Slack and information kindly shared with me by another Shildon historian whom some locally know by the name Mia Thomas. Thanks are due also to the much respected Bob Pattie, a bandsman, writer and music historian of Ballarat without whose kind help and friendship I'd have learned far less than I came to, especially about the music and banding scene in Ballarat and Victoria. Thanks also to my dear old mum for casting a critical eye over my draft manuscript. There are many others that have offered help or encouragement, sometimes indirectly, along the way, but I reserve my final and biggest thanks for Eric Tomkins, through whose family insight, own genealogical writing and correspondence I felt I was able to feel several steps closer to the true persona of his grandfather, Tom Bulch. Eric, I hope you find that my account does your grandfather's achievements justice.

Finally, an appeal to any bandsmen or women who might be reading this. Please, please do ask your band librarian to have a look through the band library and if there are any pieces by either George Allan or Tom Bulch then please encourage them to reach out to let me know through the contact details on our website www.wizardandtyphoon.org

We are really keen to understand any gaps in our understanding of what these musicians created, and build a definitive collection. The website is a useful resource for readers as we have published there some of the music you will see mentioned throughout the book. Thank you.

© Dave Reynolds 2022

The Wizard and The Typhoon

How do we choose, from the myriad untold life stories that surround us, which ones we ought to explore and tell? By weighing up the comparative fame and cultural worth of an individual's contribution to their society? So many documented stories of men and women that have come and gone before us pertain to those who were, became, or entertained the wealthy. Others relate to individuals who overcame adversity to do great and unique things. In many ways those stories are among the easier to tell, as those people mattered sufficiently during their lifetimes for documentary evidence to have been produced, and to endure.

Sometimes the decision is based upon some individual remarkable factor. Was the subject, for example, the first to reach an achievement, or to discover something significant that would make a difference to the lives of many people? In this way, we see historical biographies predominantly based upon the lives of kings and queens, dukes and duchesses, earls, bishops, politicians (good and bad), eminent scientists, engineers, military commanders, tyrants, villains, murderers and, of course, the greatest composers of classical music.

Most, but not all, subjects would be figures of some wealth, that being the surest means to become prominent, or notorious, enough to matter. Few storytellers elect to tell the stories of the relatively poor, for who cares enough about the lives of such people for their stories to matter enough to be heard? There are so many of them; too many to tell. Who, besides ourselves, would want to read of the day-to-day struggles and key moments in the lives of our own grandparents or great-grandparents? Looking ahead a hundred and fifty years, who might want to read about how our own relatively ordinary lives were lived?

In this book I have chosen to explore, and share with you, a story of comparatively ordinary, yet surprisingly remarkable people. Two working-class Victorian musicians, Tom Bulch and George Allan. That they were both born within fifteen months of each other into similar circumstances, and barely two streets apart in distance, makes for an interesting start. What makes it more compelling is perhaps that throughout their lifetimes they gradually set themselves a series of near-identical goals, then, driven by contrasting personalities, went about achieving those goals as differently as could have been possible for two young men of their time. We will follow their two threads through the rich tapestry of the social history of the early age of the popular brass band movement, interweaving through global historic events and bound by occasional coincidences. What follows is consequently, in my humble opinion, a tale of unique interest, and one certainly worthy of telling.

Though these two men become neither wealthy beyond their wildest dreams, nor famous household names, their endeavours were to bring pleasure and opportunities to so many people in ways that, as we shall learn, still resonate today. Whilst I have found that times, fashion, culture and technology have changed there are still lessons within this story that hold true and appear relevant to our lives in the present.

I feel it important to start by setting a context in which the story I am going to tell is set. It will help us to fully understand something of the nature and personality of its two principal players and their motivations.

We commence this journey at the beginning of the nineteenth century in the town of Shildon, County Durham, England. A place traditionally thought of as being at the eastern edge of the South Durham Coalfields which in turn would become, particularly during the Victorian era, vitally important to Britain's strength and wealth. By the time of King George IV's reign as British monarch and on through the reign of William IV, Britain had entered an industrial age that increasingly required energy and heat in huge quantities, and coal was the most reliable and prolific fuel available. It therefore became essential to extract it from the earth and rock, and to transport it to wherever it was needed as quickly as possible.

Unlike many of the other towns and villages of the North-East of England, it would not entirely be true to say that Shildon solely owes its existence to the presence of coal; however, it does owe much of its fame in part to the coal industry. As the meaning of its original name 'shield hill' suggests, the original small and ancient market town of Shildon was situated on the crest of a hill that once overlooked valleys and hills to the west under which, to the frustration of the coal owners, much of the coal lay. The landscape eastward between this town and the coast was, by comparison, quite flat.

At the beginning of the nineteenth century, engineers were engaged to find the quickest ways to get coal to the coast, from where ships could transport it to buyers within and outside the British Empire. Much has been written of the outcome of this study which I will not attempt to replicate here, but suffice to say that the usual solution of creating a canal was considered and dismissed in favour of a more recent technological development. By 1819 the investors had been persuaded that the solution was to create a railway powered by horses, static steam powered engines, ropes and steam locomotives. This wasn't an entirely new concept. Other parts of the North-East of England had achieved this already with varying degrees of success, but this would be by far the most ambitious railway project to date.

The Stockton and Darlington Railway Company was thus founded, and a route surveyed and mapped by which the coal would be transported. At the western extreme of the flattest part of the route a new settlement was established, which quickly became the world's first proper railway industry town. On account of its proximity to the older town up on the hill, this was called New Shildon, and the older settlement was prefixed to become Old Shildon. Its inhabitants were initially almost exclusively workers brought in to support the Stockton and Darlington Railway Company's operations, some of these people had been engaged in the construction of the route. Estimates prior to the coming of the railway suggest that the original population of the area where the new town was founded had fluctuated between ten and twenty persons for centuries. Suddenly it had become an attractive destination for ambitious mechanics and engineers and their families.

Like the pioneer towns of the western United States of America, or the goldfield towns of Australia, New Shildon was a place to which an entirely new set of people were drawn from all directions in search of opportunities created by the fledgeling industry it hosted. There are very few New Shildon families that can trace a lineage specifically within the town beyond the early to mid-nineteenth century.

By the beginning of the 1860s, the decade in which our subjects Tom Bulch and George Allan were born, the population of New Shildon had swelled just short of 1150. Many were still new to town and were outsiders, interlopers and opportunists. It was a young community brought together by a Victorian imperative to survive and strive for personal betterment.

Before exploring the lives of George Allan or Tom Bulch in this setting, we need to understand the influence of one other man. A person who, along with his sons, would take these two young men under his wing and unlock skills and aspirations that would set them on their way to creating their own lasting cultural impact on the world.

Francis Dinsdale

Francis Dinsdale, who, if asked, would have provided his name as Frank, was born on 28 September 1813 at Burtersett, Hawes in Wensleydale; one of the Yorkshire Dales. Burtersett was little more than a hamlet, though its roots go back to the years just after the Norman Conquest of Britain at which time it became a clearing to house a Norman 'forester' or gamekeeper. By the time of Francis's birth, Burtersett had evolved to be a scattering of farmsteads. His parents were Anthony Dinsdale and his wife Margaret, née Sill, of whom little beyond the outline of their lives is known. Francis was born before the peak of the lead mining industry in the Yorkshire Dales, so with little prospect of employment the family moved to the market town of Thirsk, where Francis was soon joined by a brother, Anthony, on 2 June 1816. A further brother, James, was born in 1819.

There is not much documented detail to be found concerning Francis's early life, though we understand that childhood in the era was brief, and education for the poorer classes limited. Sunday Schools existed to teach the reading of the Bible. Schools of Industry and Monitorial Schools were rare and existed to give elementary instruction on basic skills or prepare pupils for specific industries. General Infants Schools and Elementary Schools were gradually introduced from the 1820s onwards. Whether Francis Dinsdale received any formal education, we can only speculate. We do know that at some time before 1835, and probably looking for employment opportunities himself, Francis moved to Darlington where he married an eighteen-year-old Mary Burnside from Shincliffe. The couple's first child Elizabeth was born during a brief period after they had relocated to Stockton- on-Tees, but, by 1837 they were back in Darlington and over the next few years six more children followed, two of which did not survive infancy.

Around the year 1848, Francis and his family moved to Strand Street, in New Shildon, and here their wanderings ended. The family expanded further, though one child, a son named Watson Dinsdale did not survive, passing away on the day he was born in 1858. By 1851 Francis Dinsdale had secured work as a railway telegrapher.

Telegraphy was a means of conveying messages over medium to long distances that had begun with manual visual signalling based systems in the 18th century and gradually developed into electrical telegraphy in the early to mid-1800s. It was a key technology necessary to operate a railway network and an indispensable tool in conveying the movement of rail traffic and goods enabling avoidance of collisions and line blockages.

One other particular thing that we do know about Francis Dinsdale is that somewhere through his early years, and on his journey to New Shildon, he received tuition in the principles of music to a sufficient degree of expertise as to be able to conduct a band. The Durham Chronicle of 14 September 1855 tells readers of a game of cricket played at Shildon against a team from Yarm on Monday, 3 September. The report on the game adds the following:

> "The West Auckland Brass Band, ably conducted by Mr F Dinsdale, of New Shildon, attended on the occasion, and played several popular airs during the day, which gave zest to the day's amusement."

Francis would have been around forty-two years of age at the time of that performance. We don't know how long Francis might have been involved at West Auckland, other than what we know about his having arrived in New Shildon in 1848, but the first evidence we have been able to discover concerning the West Auckland Brass Band appears in the Durham Advertiser of 2 July 1852. With the town of West Auckland being only around four miles away from New Shildon, it would have been a relatively easy distance for Francis to travel to lead rehearsals. Nevertheless, to establish something a little closer to home would have been a more convenient prospect. It wasn't long before Francis did precisely that, becoming one of the founders of the New Shildon Saxhorn Band.

Though the earliest 'brass band' in Britain is believed to have been formed late in the first decade of the nineteenth century, the specific Saxhorn range of valved bugle instruments, from which this new band derived its name, was developed during the 1830s. They were first exhibited in 1844 and then patented, by their creator Adolphe Sax, in 1845. Thus we can conclude that a Saxhorn band exclusively using this specific range of instruments anywhere in Britain is unlikely to have emerged before that period. Sax did not invent the keyed bugle, and at no point did he ever claim to have done so, but his patented Saxhorn was instead perceived to be an instrument of a much higher quality than its predecessors. They were popularised by the distinguished Distin family of performers and instrument manufacturers who toured Victorian Britain and Europe during the mid-nineteenth century.

It was this Distin family that, through their travels, are now believed to have had the most significant influence on the growth and expansion of the Victorian brass band movement. John Distin and his sons George, Henry, William and Theodore, were all excellent and accomplished players of the keyed bugles. Consequently they were treated as celebrities by press and public alike and from this there also grew to be much interest in their use of Sax's instruments.

An example of this interest can be found in the Durham Chronicle from Friday 15 March 1850:

"THE DISTIN FAMILY. - We hear that the Messrs Distin, the celebrated performers on their Sax Horns, who have just returned from America, after a highly successful tour, have intimated their intention of again visiting this city."

The use of Saxhorns, often expressed as Sax-Horns, is emphasised in almost every newspaper mention of the ensemble, conveying something of the perceived novelty surrounding these instruments. The Distin family were true to this expressed intention of returning to Durham and from 28th to 30th October, following a tour in Scotland where they had entertained Queen Victoria for a sixth time at Balmoral, they gave three consecutive theatre performances in Durham. The Chronicle explains how one concert was received.

"There was a large gathering at the Music Hall, on Monday evening last, to hear the Distin Family. Indeed a full house is certain whenever they appear. Their performance on the Sax Horns was in their usual brilliant, unequalled style. Their operatic selections were very beautiful and exceedingly well executed. That from the "Daughter of the Regiment" was most enthusiastically and deservedly encored. Of their singing we cannot speak so flatteringly. However it gave variety to the evening's entertainment and in this respect it was cheerfully tolerated."

On 5 November, the family gave a similar concert at Darlington of which little is reported barring the 'respectable' nature of the makeup of the audience. It's worth noting, though, that it is very possible that someone as enthusiastic about music as Francis might well have made particular effort to see the Distin family on this, or some other, occasion, and doing so may perhaps have been the inspiration for his choice form a brass band exclusively of Saxhorn players. If so, it wasn't a unique decision. Other bands across the country were doing likewise. Shapcott's Saxhorn Band, the Stockton Corporation Saxhorn Band, Halberts Saxhorn Band and Mossley Saxhorn are but a few examples from the 1850s.

Of earlier bands in New Shildon specifically, we do know that there was a Railway Works Band of sorts during the 1840s. The Durham County Advertiser of 8 January 1847 tells us of an annual 'soirée' of the Shildon Mechanics Institute at which a party of six hundred inhabitants of the town sat down to dinner in the long room for tea, coffee and Christmas cake and to receive addresses from Timothy Hackworth and other grandees of the local railway industry. We are told that:

> "The Shildon Brass Band was in attendance and played at intervals in a style that reflected credit on them."

A further newspaper report in 1848 noted that another such engagement was supplying music at a similar social function which included influential people such as the pioneering rail engineer and founder of the town, Timothy Hackworth, and Darlington's great railway owner, investor and politician Henry Pease.

Starting up a brass band in this still new and rapidly expanding town would be influential in keeping a young community together, but getting one started was no mean feat and required certain commitments from the outset. It would take time to negotiate a place to rehearse, attract bandsmen in sufficient numbers, secure funding for instruments and, ideally, uniforms. Though privately-run bands did exist, most were run by committee, and the creation and maintenance of that element alone could be challenging. Securing a sound financial start would, of course, be made easier if the band were sponsored by a local organisation, corporation or industrial board. We've seen no evidence of whether the New Shildon Saxhorn Band received support from a local coal mine owner or the railway company, but if any such support were received it could most likely have come from the latter source.

The initial set of bandsmen would very probably have been possessed of varying degrees of quality from experienced players to enthusiastic beginners. Though the arrangement of brass music allows for varying degrees of competence, with parts of varying complexity for most of the instruments, it might still have taken Francis time to forge an operable line-up and to tutor those performers lacking in basic skills.

The mid to late 1850s saw an emerging trend of brass band contests being arranged, usually as part of a wider social gathering such as a horticultural, agricultural or sporting event. These were seen by the banding community as good ways to encourage improved quality but also delivered benefits to communities in terms of pride and solidarity. The practice was enabled by the ongoing expansion of the railway networks. This allowed bands to quickly visit contests at connected towns in the hope of returning home with honours and a prize. Such contests were initially very popular with the public, and the organising committees of the various types of show could usually count upon a greatly bolstered attendance by simply offering a prize and opening an invitation for bands to compete. For the bands themselves there were varying degrees of satisfaction to be had in the early years of amateur band contesting. There was little consistency in how they were run or judged until standard procedures were later adopted. The quality of the judges' decisions was also reportedly variable.

In this context it should not be too surprising to discover that our earliest known reported instance of the New Shildon Saxhorn Band appearing in public was of their attending a contest held at Bishop Auckland on 4 September 1857, though it appears they were not yet ready to compete. The Teesdale Mercury tells us that:

> "The Shildon band were also upon the ground, but being lately formed, they did not compete for the prizes."

We can conclude from this that the band may have been formed sometime either early 1857 or else late 1856. The timing is appropriate as prior to 1856 it was extremely rare for brass or military bands in the United Kingdom to play in public parks on Sundays, though societies had been established to campaign to secure the right to do so. Spokespeople for the various Christian sects were outspoken against it in the newspapers, but nonetheless concerts were organised in an attempt to demonstrate that such entertainments would not lower the moral standard of the nation.

Some of the earliest notable examples were those arranged in 1855 at the Crystal Palace, scene of the 1851 Great Exhibition, and then at London's Kensington Gardens where even the Dean of Durham was reported as enjoying the spectacle. These Sunday instrumental concerts were originally introduced by Sir Benjamin Hall, London's First Commissioner of the Works after whom the 'Big Ben' bell in the clock tower of the Houses of Parliament is believed to have been named. The Queen and Parliament were subsequently petitioned by incensed clergymen requesting that the concerts be ceased, and a general disagreement carried over into 1856. Supporters of the notion argue that such concerts had not destroyed the moral fabric of other nations such as Switzerland and the Netherlands where Sunday concerts were plentiful, and arranged further demonstration concerts. Another example on 1 May 1856 was arranged informally by supporters of the Sunday band movement including Sir John Shelley and the then Member of Parliament for Leicester, Sir Joshua Walmsley, a vocal champion of Sunday recreations for the masses. They had been advised that a stage had been erected for a Wednesday concert by the Band of the Second Life Guards, and having quietly been given permission to use it saw their chance. The movement had arranged for a private military-style 'people's band' to give passers-by a programme of marches and dance music. The Times, on the Monday after the concert, described that the occasion had proceeded as the organisers had hoped:

"The greatest order prevailed throughout the afternoon, and the moment the band had concluded the people quietly dispersed."

Lord Palmerston, considering petitions of religious groups such as the Wesleyans and figures, such as the Archbishop of Canterbury, who saw the labour of the bandsmen, police and park- keepers in facilitating the Sunday concerts as an embodiment of evil and an assault on the English Sabbath, despite his personal convictions that the practice carried no harm, nonetheless instructed Sir Benjamin's concerts to cease.

Though the newspapers proclaimed this as a great victory for the nation, the huge attendances at those concerts reveals their popularity with the wider public whose voice seems characteristically absent from the press. Orderly demonstration concerts by the Sunday band movement continued with increasing frequency the length of the country, including one in Newcastle on Sunday, 15 June at which between twenty and thirty thousand people assembled on the Town Moor and quietly left after the music concluded. Public appetite was not dissipating and it seems that despite the order to cease them a general tolerance by the authorities was setting in. In London the Sunday Bands Committee held its final concert of the season in Regents Park on Sunday, 7 September by which point 200,000 people were estimated to have attended that year's Sunday concerts there and in Victoria Park, but the committee continued to meet in order to plan how to further the campaign.

Such instances carried on in a similar manner into 1857. Interestingly the committee of the People's Subscription Band who had been performing at London's Victoria Park had started gathering money from ticket and programme sales, and attempted to donate their first eight guineas of proceeds to the nearby Hospital for Diseases of the Chest, and later the Queen Adelaide's Dispensary at Bethnal Green. Both refused the money on grounds of disapproval of Sunday bands, so the money was donated to the poor-boxes of the Thames and Worship Street Police Courts who both accepted graciously. This is significant in that it demonstrated another way in which the Sunday concerts could be deemed benevolent. It appears that the notion continued to cause controversy and, though there is little evidence of intervention to prevent them, the acceptance of public instrumental concerts on Sundays was very gradual.

Robert De Lacy

Francis Dinsdale was not the only major influence on the early development of the New Shildon Saxhorn Band: the other key figure in that period was Robert De Lacy. De Lacy, had been born in York in early February 1831 to a family of bookbinders that later settled in Sans Street in the north-eastern coastal town of Sunderland. As a young man he had received a thorough musical instruction, becoming a bandmaster and composer, and may have first come to the attention of Francis Dinsdale and his band while leading the Wear Royal Yacht Club Band at the aforementioned Bishop Auckland contest in 1857.

So far as we can tell, De Lacy was something of a roving bandmaster and was never resident in New Shildon. This musician, a solo cornetist, would proffer his services wherever they were deemed needed, occasionally with more than one band at a time. Perhaps engaging an experienced and inspiring professional conductor for one or more contests might have been thought to give a band an edge whilst that band's regular conductor also benefited from their presence.

For the individual bandsmen, the opportunity to take part in contests not only helped them, through the preparations, to improve and attain a higher standard but also enabled more interaction with the world outside the confines of their home town or village. For industrial patrons, contributing towards costs for travel to contests helped sweeten the relationship between management and workforce. Some even felt it contributed to a reduction in strike activity following some troubled decades early that century. The Newcastle Daily Chronicle of Tuesday 25th May 1858 reports of one such band contest on Whit Sunday two days prior:

> "A new feature of the present times to which the wonderful invention of railway communication has given birth, was witnessed in this town yesterday, when eight brass bands from towns some of which are separated by a hundred miles, were gathered together in the Northumberland Cricket Ground, Northumberland Street, and afforded a great amount of gratification, and the means of healthy recreation, to several thousands of pleasure seekers, to whom the festive season of Whitsuntide had afforded a temporary respite from labour."

The New Shildon Saxhorn were joined at this contest by bands from Staindrop, Morley, Allendale, River Wear Royal Yacht Club, Mirfield, Darlington and Helmsley. Other bands that had entered from Tibthorpe, Nafferton, Sheffield, Victoria, York, Batley and Castleford failed to arrive. The New Shildon Saxhorn Band, on this occasion under the baton of conductor Francis Dinsdale, were first to perform the test piece of "The Venetia Waltz" shortly before three o'clock, followed by a piece of their own choice, for which they chose "The Fairy Polka." The observing reporter said they "went through the waltz with care and skill. The performance was heartily applauded." Robert De Lacy and his River Wear Royal Yacht Club Band played fifth choosing a selection from "Attila" as their own choice contest piece.

After each band had given their contest performances, all eight bands massed to play "Rule Britannia" and the National Anthem before settling down to await the judge's decision which was that De Lacy's band had performed best, followed by the band from Morley. The judges, three military bandmasters from the 5th Dragoon Guards, 9th Regiment and Northumberland Light Infantry respectively, asked the New Shildon, Darlington and Staindrop bands to play again to see who would take third place. Following that second set of renditions they decided that the Darlington band was the best of the three, followed by Staindrop, which left New Shildon Saxhorn fifth and missing out on one of the cash prizes. A grand firework display ended the occasion.

The next encounter between De Lacy and the Saxhorn Band occurred two months later, on Saturday 24th July, at a reportedly chaotic band contest and horticultural fete in Darlington. Again, Francis conducted the New Shildon band while De Lacy held the baton over the River Wear Royal Yacht Club. Thirteen bands took part in that contest and once again between Dinsdale and De Lacy it was the latter that achieved the most impressive result, coming third. Whether impressed by his prowess, or perhaps on the basis of a friendship having formed at these contests, this seems to have been the point where Francis Dinsdale decided upon an alliance with De Lacy for at the New Shildon Saxhorn band's next contest appearance at the Barnard Castle Contest held at the end of August 1858, they were conducted by De Lacy. The band played the "Hallelujah Chorus" and "Il Trovatore" that day, and certainly achieved an improved result on that occasion, coming second, after Darlington, from a pack of six bands which included a short-lived rival band, the New Shildon Philharmonic Band. One reporter wrote of the Saxhorn Band:

> "They performed the task with extreme care and in a manner which clearly showed that they had undergone diligent training."

Another reporter in the Durham County Advertiser, published on 3rd September 1858, stated that:

> "One could not but notice the performance of the Darlington and Shildon Sax-Horn Bands, which was fully up to the mark to which their long practice should bring them. The announcement of the result was given amid breathless suspense."

Some evidence of the measure of respect for De Lacy at that time is perhaps shown in the fact that it was under his conductorship that, at the end of the contest, all of the bands present united to play the National Anthem. As you may have gathered by now, that practice was something of a tradition, but conducting it was usually an honour reserved for the most notable conductor present. The flurry of appearances at that year's band contests continued with one taking place in Sunderland on Monday, 13 September. De Lacy stood once again before the New Shildon Saxhorn Band to conduct, with the outcome that they were placed fourth, two places behind his River Wear Royal Yacht Club whom he also conducted to second place that day. Straight afterwards the New Shildon band made a presentation of a silver tankard to De Lacy "as a mark of esteem for him as their master and instructor". Another gift was to be bestowed upon Robert De Lacy in appreciation of his services in improving the band's results as the Durham Chronicle of Friday, 17 September 1858 reported:

> "PRESENTATION. The New Shildon Saxhorn Band presented Mr De Lacy, their tutor and leader, with a handsome vase, on Tuesday last, as a mark of their esteem and regard for him personally, and as a musical teacher. Mr P Robinson, of Bishop Auckland, furnished the testimonial."

You would think, from these reports, that the lives of bandmaster and bandsmen were now solely focused on the stream of contest opportunities that punctuated the summer months each year. There were, however, many more social and ceremonial occasions at which the presence of the band was requested. One such is mentioned in the Kendal Mercury of Saturday 11 December 1858 explaining how the New Shildon band featured as part of an evening of celebration at the Railway

Hotel (now the Old Well) in Barnard Castle following the opening of the Deepdale Railway Viaduct. This 161-feet high cast iron lattice bridge on the route between Barnard Castle and Kirkby Stephen had been designed by the railway engineer Thomas Bouch, brother of the New Shildon railway works manager William Bouch.

A new band contest season commenced in spring of the following year, and the New Shildon Saxhorn's first such appearance was at a contest at Polam Grounds, in Darlington on 31 May. Francis Dinsdale was the named band leader, a senior position within the band itself, while once again Robert De Lacy conducted. This time the New Shildon band came only fourth. This appears to be the point at which De Lacy and the New Shildon Saxhorn part company. We can only speculate as to why, and there are a full range of plausible possibilities. Francis and his band may have felt that they were ready to go forward without De Lacy, or it may be, as the next report we see implies, that once again De Lacy received a better offer elsewhere. A good bandmaster with a strong reputation would have been in demand, and even with an improving railway network to transport him around the region, could not serve many bands at once.

Travels

The Newcastle Daily Chronicle on 7 June 1859 tells readers of a Grand Brass Band Contest and People's Festival at the Northumberland Cricket Ground, Newcastle-upon-Tyne, on Whit Monday. De Lacy is named on that occasion as the conductor of the Allendale Town Saxhorn Band. The New Shildon Saxhorn Band also featured among the sixteen bands competing at that contest, for which a prize of fifteen pounds and a silver medal for each band member was offered. They had returned to being under Francis's conductorship, with a bandsman, Mr John Gornal, named as band leader.

Within months De Lacy's services were also courted by the Stanhope Band, though his ties with the New Shildon Saxhorn were not entirely severed, suggesting that relations with the band and its master continued to be amicable. De Lacy conducted the New Shildon band one more time at the annual Barnard Castle contest in September 1859. They did not finish among the prize placings, while De Lacy's other band at the time, Stanhope, took first prize.

The bandsmen of Shildon were, in that period and through their involvement in the band, privileged to have been able to witness, and participate in, spectacular events in places many miles away from their hometown. Much more so, it would seem, than they were able to in subsequent decades, when the never-ending cycle of band contests had lost some of its early glamour and become more commonplace, resulting in the band's later travels becoming limited to more localised band contests. The Derbyshire Courier reported on 2 July 1859, for example, that the New Shildon Saxhorn participated at a "Monster Brass Band Contest and Gala" at the Chesterfield Recreation Ground on Monday 11 July 1859. This huge event featured twenty-five bands, within which there were reportedly around 390 performers:

> "After the First Part of the Contest the whole of the bands will form an immense circle and perform 'Rule Britannia' and ' The National Anthem'. Also promised was 'Illumination at night by various coloured lights.'"

Arguably the grandest occasion of all however, required the bandsmen of New Shildon to travel south almost to the nation's capital and was anything but a convenient day trip. Enderby Jackson's 'Great National Contest' was held at the famous Crystal Palace, Sydenham, between the tenth and eleventh of July 1860. It was a hugely ambitious national band contest that featured one-hundred bands from all over the country. This was to be a musical spectacle on a scale never seen before.

Jackson, born in the Mytongate area of Kingston-upon-Hull, was one of the great 'characters' of the Victorian music scene. Coming from a family with a business of candle-making and soap-boiling, he chose instead to pursue a career in music. He learned to play a variety of instruments and joined a band playing popular dance music of the day. It was for his organisation of band contests, however, that he would be best remembered. Having organised his first in Hull in 1851 he developed the art and year by year his events grew in reputation and size of spectacle. The Crystal Palace contests were the pinnacle of his achievement. He had already been engaged there in 1858 to organise a contest for handbell ringing ensembles but for 1860 the management at the Crystal Palace determined that brass bands should be the subject. The contest comprised six preliminary rounds, mini-contests in their own right, in which the bands would perform in zones around the grounds outside the palace itself. The winning bands from the preliminary stages would then be invited to play in the finals inside the Palace. An exceptional array of prizes was offered which included cash payments, band journals and new musical instruments.

The New Shildon Saxhorn Band competed on Tuesday the tenth, though unusually this time under the leadership of 'T. Dinsdale'. Excluding the possibility that this might be a misprint, this would be Tony Dinsdale, Francis's son who would have been around twenty-three years old at the time. Robert De Lacy was also present on that same day conducting the Stanhope Band. Between De Lacy and Dinsdale it would be the former whose band's performance was deemed to be sufficiently good from the qualifying round as to be admitted to the grand finals within the Palace itself. The Saxhorn Band, having failed to qualify, had the rest of the day to enjoy the event and surroundings before travelling homeward by train. De Lacy, and Stanhope, finished outside the five prize places, though it would still have been considered a worthy outcome to have returned home as one of the best twelve bands from one hundred on the day.

Such contests, where bands from across the nation gather in one place, may well seem commonplace in the modern era where the finals of the National Brass Band Championships are held annually at the Albert Hall. At the beginning of the 1860s it would have been an unprecedented, spectacular and national sensation event, once again only enabled by the popularisation and relative affordability of rail travel. Nonetheless, the cost, and organisation necessary, to take a whole brass band to the Crystal Palace would not have been insignificant. We've no idea how funding was attained but it's unlikely that it could have been done without the benevolent patronage of either New Shildon-based townspeople, business or industry. Additionally, securing permission for those bandsmen involved to be absent from their respective workplaces for the two days of that contest would have been a challenge, and this might possibly have been the explanation for why it appears Tony Dinsdale, rather than his father Francis, conducted the band. Perhaps the Stockton and

Darlington Railway Company felt unable to spare a telegrapher, a key role in managing traffic flow on their routes.

Enderby Jackson continued with his annual brass band contests at the Crystal Palace, though with a reduced field of entrants, until 1863. The event recalled above would be the first and only appearance by the New Shildon Saxhorn Band.

As we've seen, the Saxhorn band wasn't the only ensemble to be set up in New Shildon during this period. We saw evidence of others in some of the contest reports, such as the New Shildon Operatic and Philharmonic bands, though they seem to have been short lived. Another such short lived band was the Shildon Works Teetotal Drum & Fife Band. The Durham Chronicle of Friday, 19 August 1859 mentions them and does explain something of the part the railway played in the transportation of bands:

"Concert at Waskerley. The third annual concert of the Shildon Works Teetotal Band took place on Thursday last, in the house of the Fire-horse (engine shed), Waskerley, when about 700 persons from Berry Edge, Tow Law, Stanhope, &c., who had been brought by special trains were present. During the day many friends beguiled by the beauty of the 'brown heather,' which is in full bloom now, and the fineness of the day, rambled with pleasure across the moor, regretting that they were a day too soon for a lawful shot at the numerous convoys of birds, which muster strong both in numbers and in wing; whilst other parties indulged in athletic games, the pleasure of which will be long remembered. Bountiful supplies of the creature comforts were provided by Mrs Bouch, of Shildon, aided by a number of fair and willing young ladies, to which ample justice was done by the invited guests. The temporary music hall was tastefully decorated with the products of the moor; and when nature was scant in her gifts, the deficiency was supplied by artificials, flags or various devices &c. Dependent lamps reminded the spectator of those wonderful fairy scenes so often read about in youth. The members of the band are all teetotallers, and their performances on this occasion proved very satisfactorily that it needs not the stimulating cup to enable any to appreciate and execute first class music. Through the kindness of Mrs Bouch, this band have for some time been under the care and training of Mr W W Woodhams, bandmaster of the North York Rifles, and have attained a most surprising degree of efficiency during the past six months. The programme was well selected, and the whole of the pieces were given with good taste. The National Anthem brought proceedings to a close."

This appears to be the only mention we have seen of the Shildon Works Teetotal Band, so this may have been a short-lived project in the town or may have evolved directly into one of the Temperance movement bands we shall return to later.

After 1859, Francis Dinsdale and the bandsmen of New Shildon appear to have had little further to do with Robert De Lacy, who continued on his own journey and eventually spent a distinguished lifetime in music with many achievements. I offer only a summary overview here as aspects of this will become relevant later.

One of the first things we learn about De Lacy after his involvements with Shildon is that on 24 October 1861 he joined the Palatine Lodge 97 of Freemasons, listing his profession as Professor of Music. Looking at this lodge's records, they appear to have a number of such professors as members. At some point before 1871, he relocated from Sunderland to London where he set up home with his wife Eliza, in the borough of Lambeth. The couple had a son, Charles John, and a daughter Rosamond, both of whom had been born in Sunderland. Eliza died in 1879 leaving Robert a widower living with his daughter Rosamond. By 1881 a thirty-year-old widow, Louisa Hill from Bath, had moved into their home as a boarder. In time Robert married Louisa. While in London De Lacy established the London Brass Journal, which we've seen advertised as early as 1866 where it was being published in, and distributed from, Southwark and later from his music shop in Brixton, London. This journal evolved to become the London Brass and Military Band Journal, and was widely advertised in the banding papers of its day. De Lacy was one of the principal composers featured within, and as such was fairly prolific without being a significant composer with enduring appeal.

De Lacy's Music Shop would have been a convenient outlet through which to sell his journal which would ensure that his name would be well known throughout the banding community. There was, however, another way in which the De Lacy name was distributed among bandsmen, which was that it was for a time stamped on his own branded range of brass instruments, all purchasable from his shop. The full brass range became available with 'R. DE LACY, MAKER, 84 HOLLAND ROAD, BRIXTON, LONDON.' imprinted on the bell. Where I have enquired as to how likely it was that he was making these and what skills and facilities he would have required, I've been advised that it was a common practice at the time for some manufacturers to offer unbranded pieces that could be marked by the seller in this way. Furthermore, one of the De Lacy instruments we have seen was a 'ventil-horn', now deemed quite archaic, but which had been patented by the Distin family and was only manufactured by them.

Above: Maker's imprint from the bell of a De Lacey horn.

One further thing we understand about Robert is that he was a fine singer of some significant ability. Throughout his years in London he would advertise his services as a bass singer for ensembles and he was also, for many years, one of the twelve Vicars Choral at St Paul's Cathedral. Robert De Lacy died on 20 December 1908 while he was living at the Holland Road shop address. His estate, totalling seven hundred and seventy two pounds, was bequeathed to his wife Louisa who, despite being far younger than her husband, only survived him by two years, passing away on 8 February 1910. Remarkably, by the time of her death her estate was valued at over five thousand pounds.

Robert's son, Charles is worthy of remark in his own right in that he went on to be one of the foremost British marine artists of his period, known especially for his warship imagery. He was trained at The National Gallery and the Illustrated London News was one of his patrons. He exhibited at the Royal Academy in 1889.

We referred briefly to De Lacy's London Brass and Military Band Journal. As such journals will play a part in this story it's worth taking a moment to understand what we mean by them. The term 'journal' would in any other context relate to a newspaper or magazine, quite often with a specialism or relating to a particular profession. Usually when you see the word you would conjure up a paper with lots of text and written articles. Band journals differed somewhat in that they were serialised publications produced by music publishers that would contain all of the band parts for multiple pieces of music.

For these the publishers would usually invite subscriptions for a minimum period, a year for example, during which each issue of the journal would be sent to the band at the published intervals. In many cases this was monthly. This ensured a steady stream of revenue for the publisher, but also encouraged and enabled them to engage composers to create the pieces to publish. It became the most common way for bands to accumulate a library of music. Rather than seek out band sets for individual pieces of music, though this was still possible, the bandmasters would receive all the pieces included in each issue of the journal, and would then decide which to play and which to ignore. This trend created a demand for new pieces of brass band music for the bands to play, and particularly music that had specifically been created for that format of band and the dance preferences of the day. In the earliest days of the brass band movement, much of the music available to a brass band was adapted from church music, among the most widely distributed music at the time. Other pieces were converted from a wealth of classics and opera to brass band format by a musical arranger. Some more martial pieces, including many of the early marches, would have been introduced via the military banding tradition of the armed forces and local militias.

Then early in the 1850s, we see the emergence of this phenomenon of the journals. Many were monthly publications started by enterprising composers or publishers usually with a sufficiently respected background and reputation. Often they tried to cater for both the brass and military formats, by including additional reed instrument parts. At the beginning of 1852 Boosey and Sons of 28 Holles Street, London, launched their Boosey's Brass Band Journal, one of the earliest and most successful. This journal, produced in London, was one of the first to be advertised and available nationally. London was certainly initially the dominant city in terms of distribution and publication of such journals. These included Chappell's, published from around 1860 by the well-known music merchants Chappell and Co; Distin's, from about 1862 onwards; Davidson's, also starting in 1862; Sidney Jones's, also in 1862 which was arranged by its namesake, one time bandmaster of the Essex Rifles and the Universal Brass Band Journal from 1860. There were journals published from the regions too, such as Mr R Smith's Brass Band Journal from Leeds, reputedly favoured by the Leeds Model Band, The Champion Brass Band Journal published by Richard Smith of Hull, and Tidswell's, also of Leeds. Brandon's was published by a musical instrument retailer, Mr T Brandon, of Barnard Castle.

Over the space of a few years it became a congested and highly-competitive market in which the numerous titles jostled for subscribers and supremacy. Those that attracted the very best or most popular composers would do well, as would those that advertised strongly and created the best distribution network. Many publishers sought to become involved in the premier contests of the age, sponsoring prizes to raise awareness or offering journal issues as prizes in the hope that bands might subscribe and become loyal followers. Some, such as Wright and Rounds Brass Band Journal, based in Liverpool and promoted ceaselessly through its sister newspaper Wright and Round's Brass Band News, would flourish and evolve. Other journals without money, influence and presence fell by the wayside.

Interestingly the format and instrumental line-up of the brass band had not been standardised by the time journals began to be published, so it seems that some bands structured their players to suit the makeup of the music provided, making it difficult to switch between journals on account of each having a slightly different formula of players and instruments. It was otherwise necessary to transpose or adapt published pieces to suit the players and instruments that you had. That may well have been a skill a bandsman or bandmaster may have had to acquire en route to becoming a composer in their own right.

Returning to New Shildon and the Dinsdale family, whom as we mentioned had originally taken residence in the town's Strand Street, we know from census records that at some point between 1851 and 1861 they moved but a few feet west to a newly built terrace, Adelaide Street. This consisted of some ninety-five new houses principally for the accommodation of railway workers. There were two engineering works sites. One, the Soho Works founded by the engineer Timothy Hackworth, after ending his employment by the Stockton and Darlington Railway Company, to develop locomotives, marine engines and industrial engines and boilers many of which were sold to his former employer. The other had been the Stockton and Darlington's Railway's own Shildon Works, building locomotives and rolling stock until 1871 whereafter locomotive production ceased and production became an exclusive specialism in wagon building and repairs for the North Eastern Railway.

The houses in the streets between these works were home to engine drivers, engine 'feeders' (an old term for the railway firemen), engine smiths, railway agents, joiners, works clerks, iron turners, boilersmiths, blacksmiths, brass moulders, railway gatekeepers, joiners, wagonwrights and cartwrights. Their wives fulfilled demanding roles running crowded homes and tending large families in an era of little convenience. Some brought in a small second income by putting skills such as dressmaking into practice. Working-age children were sometimes drafted by the surrounding mines as colliery screen boys (opening and closing ventilation traps down in the mines), or more often apprentices and general labourers. That designation of being of 'working age' arrived much sooner than for children today.

Adelaide Street, of which only a stub-end of seven properties remains today, was possibly named to honour Princess Adelaide of Saxe-Meiningen, the spouse, and queen consort to King William IV, who had passed away in December 1849, twelve years after her husband. Worthy of note that in the 1850s the influential Pease family opened an Adelaide Colliery to extract coal from the opposite side of the hill upon which Old

Shildon sat, again possibly a dedication to the former Queen Consort. Yet another perhaps more likely possibility exists which is that it may have been named so after Timothy Hackworth's steam locomotive "Adelaide." There were other streets in New Shildon that shared their name with locomotives such as Magnet Street mirroring Hackworth's "Magnet." Whatever the reason, by receiving this name Adelaide Street shared something in common with the capital city of the state of South Australia. The city of Adelaide was founded in 1836 after South Australia was officially proclaimed a British colony.

The connection was probably not lost on Francis Dinsdale, as his brothers Anthony and James had been émigrés to Australia, probably as part of an incentivised emigration scheme. There are many reasons that British nationals left their homeland for Australia during the mid-nineteenth century. Deportation of convicts under penal transportation continued to be a practice until 1868, though later there was also voluntary emigration in significant numbers, particularly during the 'gold-rush' period that began in 1851. This particularly attracted workers with backgrounds in mining or engineering. During the 1840s and 1850s, there was also an Assisted Immigrants Scheme, and prior to that a Bounty Scheme, both of which provided incentivised emigrants to Australia providing they met certain criteria to address labour shortages. Overall though there was a desire on the part of the Government to boost the British population of the colony and thus keep it dominant.

James Dinsdale was the first to go to Australia, sailing in 1848 and setting up as a poulterer and fruiterer in Adelaide. Anthony Dinsdale, like his brother Francis, had moved several times to find work, taking his wife and young family, and by 1851 had settled briefly in Bradford, close to the mills. Within four years of that year's census he, as James had before him, had decided that to spend the rest of their lives in Australia offered a better prospect. The family travelled to Liverpool to board the Nashwauk, bound for Australia, and embarked on 13th February 1855. To have travelled without incentive would have been expensive for there was Anthony, his wife Anne, and children: Thomas, aged seventeen; Margaret aged fifteen; Esther, twelve; John, eight; and Isabella, just six years old.

However uncomfortable their experience of the cramped conditions during the voyage had been, it was the family's arrival in Australia that was destined to be the most traumatic. On what was, according to the ship's log, the 89th day of the voyage, the Nashwauk, a 762-ton, Canadian-built, wooden ship that was only eighteen months old at the time, crashed into the shoreline south of the mouth of the river Onkaparinga, south of Adelaide. This collision occurred at three o'clock in the morning on 12 May 1855. It's likely to have been a complete shock to passengers and the bulk of the crew alike. Local people living nearby helped to remove the stranded passengers from the vessel and took care of them until a local steamer 'Melbourne' and a schooner 'Yatala' arrived to take them north to Adelaide. Understandably many of the travellers were reluctant to take to the water again and were transported instead by carts hauled by bullocks and suchlike.

A newspaper reporter from the South Australian Register attempted to determine, and report, the cause of the tragedy. According to his account the ship's captain had been below deck, having taken watch the previous two nights, leaving the second mate at the helm. The second mate claimed to have mistaken a light onshore for a lightship. The ill-fated Nashwauk remained in its distressed state until a northwesterly gale broke its ruin against the rocks on 26th May, and sadly Anthony Dinsdale did not fare any better. Whether as a consequence of the collision, or some other cause potentially worsened or triggered by that event, Anthony Dinsdale died less than a month later in Adelaide on 7 June 1855, his Australian adventure having been brought to a premature and tragic end. He was buried at the city of Adelaide's West Terrace Cemetery by his widow and children, who now faced an uncertain future.

Back in England, Francis and his sons worked hard to strengthen and improve the brass band he had helped to establish. As well as championing the town's reputation at brass band contests across the region, they ensured that the Saxhorn band was a reliable source of entertainment for any, and every, public occasion in the vicinity of the Shildons. Any local sports meeting, parade, horticultural show, religious festival or opening of a new facility worth its salt would be no spectacle at all without a brass band to 'wow' the attending crowds with their musical soundscapes.

For more prestigious events or occasions, organisers with sufficient means would secure the services of a military band from Britain's armed forces. These were deemed a superior source of musical entertainment. Britain has long had a strong military band tradition to provide both marching and field music, as well as ceremonial and funerary pieces when such occasions demanded it. Though it seems remarkable and possibly even impractical now, military bandsmen once played a key role on the battlefield in the direction and control of troops and troop formations. In a global context the idea of a military band is a very old one, though in Britain such use was not made official until 1762. That's not to say that there weren't older British military bands: the oldest extant one is considered to be the Royal Artillery Band which can trace its unofficial roots back to the 1550s. Such military bands differ from brass bands partly by virtue of the array of instruments used. A military band typically includes more drums, added percussion and woodwind instruments. The clarinet and piccolo add to the upper end of the aural spectrum in military arrangements. Another key difference would have been that military bandsmen in the armed forces would be professionally tutored, musical performance being an essential part of their 'job'. Thus they were perhaps more respected publicly for their art than the evening hobbyists of the industrial communities.

In addition to the formal military bands assigned to official units of the armed forces there were, nationally, an array of militia bands following a similar format, but comprising members of non-professional soldiers drawn from the civilian population and held in military reserve. Though different to the brass bands, these bands would still influence the brass band movement through the migration of players back and forth between the two types.

The members of local amateur brass bands such as the New Shildon Saxhorn Band had long, and often very physical, working days to complete before music was even a consideration. Excepting the most fortunate individuals, or most passionate and dedicated, the liberty to convene to play music together was a rare pleasure, an escape, and possibly even a welcome distraction from an otherwise crowded home. Membership of a band brought another form of camaraderie, different to that established in the workplace, though it was likely to have strengthened workplace bonds too.

Given the speed of emergence of the brass band scene and the scarcity of authoritative local judges some early brass band contests employed a military bandmaster, should one be available, to adjudicate. They were considered more qualified to make judgement on quality and execution of performance. In a reflection of military values, on such occasions points might be awarded for the presentation of physical appearance, uniform and regularity of marching as well as for how the music was played. The press of the period reveals something about the gulf in how the two types of bands were initially regarded. This example from the Durham Chronicle of 10 September 1858, which refers to two Shildon bands, is a telling example:

> "A band contest was one of the minor features of the show. This came off between four and six o'clock when the Artillery Band had left. The entry of competitors was small and the interest attached to their performances was not very marked. Coming as they did after so splendid a musical treat, the public was naturally in an unsympathetic mood, and therefore the contest was – except to friends and acquaintances of the men engaged – a somewhat flat affair. The order of playing was, as usual, decided by lot and the bands went onto the 'rostrum' in the following order: 1st Shildon Philharmonic; 2nd Stanhope; 3rd Shildon Saxhorn; 4th Auckland. Haydn's 'Heavens Are Telling' was the test piece – a noble composition as all ecclesiastical musicians declare, and having a Handelian suitability for orchestral power. We cannot say much for either performance. There was however a marked superiority in that of the Stanhope men – so marked that Mr Smyth's award only confirmed a conclusion already arrived at in the public mind."

Shildon Saxhorn came third to Shildon Philharmonic and subsequently, for whatever reason, noble or otherwise, returned their prize to the event committee.

The typical selection of music that one might hear at a concert performance by a military band might be considered surprising. Professor Stephen Martin, in his research into the Bishop Auckland Flower Shows of the Victorian era, discovered that the programmes of music contained significantly sophisticated pieces being performed by the likes of the Band of the Coldstream Guards and of the 2nd Light Infantry. Where the article mentioned above refers to a 'splendid musical treat' it's unlikely to be an exaggeration and more a justifiable reaction to a demonstration of musical skill that might only be achieved through dedicating one's life to its improvement. Little wonder then that the masters of such bands, men such as Charles Godfrey, one-time bandmaster of the Coldstream Guards became influential and revered figures among amateur brass bandsmen. Such military bands would, however, only be available for occasions of a certain stature. There were plenty of events, occasions and parades in the annual calendar of a growing town like New Shildon to keep the amateur bandsmen of Shildon busy. The more they played, the more they would improve. As they improved they gave great pleasure to their community. A report, from 1862, of the New Shildon Saxhorn Band, expresses some of this:

> "The celebrated band, giving vent to their musical talents, came out in Saturday January 18th, to cheer the villagers with their strains of music. They played choruses and selections from Mozart, Handel, Verdi and other eminent authors, with such precision and brilliancy, that much credit is due to their talented leader, Mr F. Dinsdale. After playing they formed in promenade, to the house of Mr Thomas Thompson, Bay Horse Inn, New Shildon, where they, with other respectable gentlemen of the neighbourhood, partook of an excellent supper, which was served up in grand style, and which reflects great credit upon worthy host and hostess. After doing justice to the repast, the cloth being removed, vocal harmony being the order, which was efficiently applied by Messrs. Dinsdale, Harrison, Spark, Robinson, and others of the band. After playing, 'Rule Britannia,' and the, 'National Anthem,' they separated, each to their respective homes, highly delighted with the night's entertainment."

The New Shildon Saxhorn Band could be engaged by organisations within the near and surrounding community to lead a variety of parades, for example as the Durham County Advertiser of 11 August 1865 tells us when the St John's Lodge of Oddfellows Manchester Union celebrated their twenty-fifth anniversary on Saturday, 5 August, it was the New Shildon Saxhorn Band that marched at the head of the procession with the banner of the order, from the lodge room at the Talbot Inn, West Auckland, to the church for a sermon. Throughout the Victorian era many friendly and mutual beneficial societies such as these Oddfellows, the Foresters and the Druids emerged. This was a time before the welfare state and such organisations gave an opportunity for people to join and contribute to a common fund while they were able on the assurance that when they found themselves in need the society would aid them.

An Accident

As the years went by, Francis's Dinsdale's children began to grow up and start families of their own. On 28 November 1857 Francis's eighteen-year-old daughter Margaret Dinsdale married twenty-one-year-old Thomas Bulshey, originally from Catterick in Yorkshire. Thomas's family had moved to Darlington where he had worked briefly as a tailor before finding employment on the railway as a fireman. Though the marriage took place at St John's Church in Old Shildon it's probable that the couple had met whilst in Darlington. The young couple set up a home on New Shildon's Strand Street and by the time of the 1861 census they gave their surname as Bulch. Why the family surname changes from Bulshey to Bulch is something we can't be certain about but seems a deliberate decision. The surname Bulshey appears on other documents for family members prior to the 1861 census, but the name Bulch is used consistently thereafter.

Thomas and Margaret wasted no time in starting a family. Their first child Mary Jane was born in 1859, followed by Ellen in 1860 and then Francis, likely named after his grandfather, in 1861.

Thomas appears to have enjoyed growing flowers, and in August of 1860 he exhibited dahlias at the Bishop Auckland Flower Show which was a major event on the regional calendar at that time. Specially arranged excursion trains came into Bishop Auckland from all directions, Leeds, Newcastle, Darlington, Sunderland, Barnard Castle and Durham in a complex logistical exercise conducted by the railway companies. The show took place in the Bishop of Durham's park, adjacent to his palace, with the gates opening at ten o'clock to admit the masses. The Royal Artillery Band from Woolwich, with its ensemble of seventy performers, gave a grand promenade concert. Marquees, for exhibiting flowers and vegetables, were erected in a valley by the gently bubbling River Gaunless. Thomas's entry of six varieties of best dahlias won him third prize in the cottagers class, which included a five shilling cash payment.

We mentioned that Thomas was employed on the Stockton and Darlington Railway, the first passenger railway company in the world, as a fireman, or 'engine-feeder'. It's an archaic but understandable term. Locomotives had essentially replaced horses in their duty, and as those horses ate grass and hay the locomotives might be perceived to similarly consume coal and require feeding. The company's employment records show that Thomas was accepted into the role during February of 1854. It involved standing on the footplate of a locomotive with the driver of the train transferring coal by shovel into the firebox evenly in the correct quantity to ensure that sufficient steam continues to be produced to keep the locomotive in motion at the correct speed. It would be hot and physical work but also usually a step as part of a career progression to eventually becoming a locomotive driver.

One late summer day in 1861, after seven years spent as a locomotive crewman, Thomas was involved in a great tragedy. In 1861 the Directors of the Stockton and Darlington Railway were celebrating a new venture partnership and the opening of a new branch line. The South Durham and Lancashire Union Railway had been created by the S&DR to connect Bishop Auckland in County Durham with Tebay, enabling onward travel to the Lake District and Cumbrian towns. Work had commenced on this route in 1858, extending a track south-west from Bishop Auckland through Barnard Castle and Bowes then, taking a detour around the Duke of Cumberland's holdings, over the moorland into Cumbria via Stainmore. The route required the building of four new viaducts along the way, at Tees Valley, Deepdale, Belah and Smardale Gill.

Interestingly, Thomas's father-in-law Francis Dinsdale and his New Shildon Saxhorn Band had entertained at the celebrations that followed the opening of the 161 feet high iron lattice Deepdale viaduct in December 1858. The celebration itself took place at the Railway Hotel (now The Old Well) in Barnard Castle.

Using aerial maps and photography you can still see the embankments and cuttings of South Durham and Lancashire Union line if you trace the landscape westward from Bowes, or north from Barnard Castle. It's a landscape which has changed little since 1861. Parts of the route are now preserved as public footpaths and there has been an attempt at the village of Stainmore to revive a stretch of the railway in a 1950s style reflective of the era before Dr Beeching's decimating effect on the British railway network. Otherwise it is as bleak and rough a landscape now as it was during Queen Victoria's reign. Initially the primary function of the Stockton & Darlington Railway's operations had been the movement of minerals and goods but over the decades since it's inaugural journey there was an increasing demand for, and moneymaking potential from, passenger services. This meant there was also a demand for suitable locomotives to haul them.

Two new 4-4-0 locomotives had been commissioned to be built by the railway company's directors specifically to operate passenger traffic on this line. Named "Brougham" and "Lowther" they were designed by William Bouch, a former apprentice of Timothy Hackworth at Shildon who had risen to become Chief Superintendent of the Stockton and Darlington Railway's operations. They were built at Robert Stephenson's locomotive works on Tyneside, but despite their introduction a number of only slightly older Panther Class 0-6-0 mineral locomotives such as "Gazelle," "Zebra," and "Fox" were also used for passenger services.

Above: Line drawing of a Panther Class locomotive on which Thomas Bulch senior would have worked as fireman

The route was famed for its harsh and inhospitable weather and the locomotive crews, over time, revelled in their resulting reputation as being 'hard men' for bearing it with little but a turned up collar and an open cap to protect them from the wind, sleet, snow and rain. Even so, locomotives built specifically for this route incorporated extra cab protection for the footplate crew. Though not as open as the footplates of the very early locomotives, the crew were still far more exposed to the elements than those in later decades.

The new route had been traversed by mineral trains since the July of 1861, though the formal opening ceremony of the South Durham and Lancashire Union Railway did not take place until the 7 August. Passenger traffic commenced, promptly, the following day.

The incident of specific interest to us occurred three weeks after the opening of the line. On Thursday, 29 August, the locomotive No. 149 "Fox" crewed by Thomas Bulch, and driver Robert Aaron, set out on a passenger excursion from Darlington. This locomotive had been built in April 1860 by R & W Hawthorn to a William Bouch design. Bouch as superintendent would have been personally acquainted with the crew. The engine, weighing just under 50 tonnes, was another built especially for this route though not specifically for passenger traffic, and equipped with the more complete cab to protect the crew from the bleak weather. What happened that day was reported, most ably, by the Durham Chronicle on Friday, 6 September. I include here the accounts as reported as they convey the drama, in the spirit of the times, so effectively:

> "ALARMING ACCIDENT ON THE SOUTH DURHAM AND LANCASHIRE RAILWAY – On Thursday week, about half-past seven o'clock in the evening, an accident occurred on the South Durham and Lancashire Union Railway, which, it will be remembered, was opened on the 7th ult. It appears that an excursion train, under the auspices of the Darlington Mechanics' Institute, had been at Windermere, and were returning. A correspondent furnishes the following account of the accident –
>
> The first pleasure trip to the lakes was taken on Thursday, the 29th ult., over the new line from Barnard Castle to Tebay, and accommodated about 400 excursionists from Darlington and Barnard Castle. The train steadily driven to its destination at Windermere, the journey was fully enjoyed, the weather being delicious throughout, and the scenery beyond Winston an uninterrupted succession of ever-changing beauty. Amid Wordsworth's favourite haunts the party spent eight merry hours, rambling over mountains and glens, gathering ferns, and listening to the echo of "the post horn." No happier day till 5:30 p.m., when the train started punctually from Windermere, was ever passed.
>
> During the return journey, especially on this side of Kirkby Stephen, many of the passengers, and among them Mr Geo. Brown. the secretary of the new line, observed a recklessness of pace; the gradients being somewhat hazardous, the way perhaps

not consolidated, and the curves extreme, excited general alarm. All at once, close by a cattle creep or bridge, near Low Spittal, three miles west of Bowes, the engine got off the line, and ploughing down the embankment, jerking, shuddering, so to say, bounded into a peaty field, there stuck fast flat on her side.

This happened in a shorter time than it takes to write it. The hour, 7:45 p.m., was closing on the lovely day, with thick gathering clouds and hurrying darkness. There was but one first class carriage which, and another covered, with the last van, maintained their position. The five others were pitched athwart, in odd directions, and many of them smashed, but the coupling chains kept entire. After the first pause in excitement, in which men live their lives again, all that could escape bolted through windows, the doors being locked.

One man, Mr Fortune, states that before he came to his senses he was spanbowed through the window, such the violence of the concussion. The others, stupefied in heaps, or stunned dotted here and there, were hauled out, some with superhuman effort and incredible difficulty; some were silent, others tumultuous, and the scene altogether beggars description.

Had this untoward affair occurred a few yards on either side of its point, by nothing but a miracle could a single individual have escaped. As it was, taking into account the terrible shaking and horrible alarm, all suffered; for many feeling themselves wonderfully right on Friday, had to call in advice and keep prudently quiet afterwards. Mr Foggett, of the High Row, was found with his collar bone fractured; Mr Ridley, whitesmith, a similar catastrophe, and internal injuries; Mr Michael Watson, builder, who bled profusely, had his head cut; Mr Fortune, his wrist and chest injured; Mr Railton, his wrist dislocated; Mr. Dunning, shoemaker; Mr. Dunning, of the George Inn; Mr. Harrison, silversmith; Mr. Spence, seedsman; Mr. Lee, bookseller; Mr. Maitland, Mrs Wallis, Mrs Edmondson; Mrs Crabtree, and Mrs Wray, all of Darlington; Mr and Mrs Smith, and Mr and Mrs Moore, all of Cockerton; and old people; were hurt, some seriously. Many had black eyes, others were cut in various parts; one his teeth knocked down his throat, and some suffer internally. But these were trifling, though bad enough.

Dr Torbock, the only surgeon present, and prepared with all the means and appliances necessary, attended to his unexpected patients at once. To the horror of everyone, it was also discovered that the engine-man and stoker were actually buried under the engine; their position seemed hopeless, such was the nature of the ground; the awful weight and ponderous mass above them struck every one with the idea that any attempt to extricate them, without the aid of mechanical contrivances, would be futile. The wounded cared for, to the praise of a few – only a few alas – for many there were who refused to help, skulking away unconcerned, a prey, it is to be hoped, to their own remorse – the utmost energy was directed to those poor fellows.

The gloom of the blackest night, intensified by a furious howling wind and pelting rain, which Stainmore knows well to show, added to the baffling difficulties of every one. Fence rails torn up, splinters of carriages gathered together mixed with hay from a neighbouring stack, soon made a prodigious crackling blaze, and the sparks darted along with the angry wind, a distance between the High Row and the church gates. Under the fire, cinders raked from the coal-box fell upon the victims, and any attempt to slake it only added to the horror of the steam which scalded, and the styth which affected them. What a scene this for Salvator or Van Schnendel, or our own wondrous Turner!

If there was leverage enough the weight could be easily raised, but the difficulty was a fulcrum. Big plates were brought from the line, and hard work it was; for in uncertain light and intense darkness, boggy holes lay treacherously in the way; but good hearts never give in.

Plank after plank, and stone after stone, sank down, and then at length the engine was moved; but only unfortunately to increase the poor men's pain, and add fresh anguish to their hopeful friends. Struggling thus till 11:30 p.m. – what a time it was! – the night seemed like three.

By some unaccountable blundering with the telegraph at Bowes, whence stupid, selfish, contradictory messages went home, the lateness of the hour, and the awkwardness of a single line, it was not until the opportune time help came from Darlington, when exhaustion seemed almost to have worked its inexorable will.
From that time nothing was wanting – the chief secretary, with heads of various departments, and their workmen, took the matter in hand. The fireman, Bulsh, whose case is the far more serious of the two, was rescued before the brave excursionists departed. Aron, the other man, buried for 8 hours, was not got out till after 3 a.m. Both were taken to their homes at Shildon;

and each lies very ill – burnt, and scalded, and crushed. The special trip came cautiously back – arriving at Darlington between one and two; the excitement being intense.

This is the first great accident that ever happened on any line under the direction of the oldest and best managed railway company in the kingdom; and it is to be hoped the fullest investigation into its cause will be made. Contradictory assertions have been confidently bruited about by interested parties. On the one hand, the pace at which the train was driven is considered the sole cause; on the other, the condition of the way, and the weak girders of the cattle creep, "where the engine always jumps;" but all agreed that, had it happened elsewhere, every one would have been smashed; and the extraordinary escape of so many, as it is, is due in a great measure to the soundness and excellence of the carriages. Thus ended a day full of hope, and more than half full of pleasure, to the committee of the institution and their friends – some of whom, loitering behind in Westmoreland, were no little astonished on their return next morning, in passing the end of the disaster, where the line had been remade, to discover the awful danger they had escaped."

The Yorkshire Gazette of 7 September adds:

"With the engine-men things had not fared so well, and they were found jammed under the engine in such a manner as to prevent the possibility of extricating them without sending to Darlington for a crane; and as this was the work of several hours, the poor fellows were compelled to endure great suffering. Intelligence of the catastrophe was immediately telegraphed to Barnard Castle and Darlington, and a special train came on to take away the passengers. An efficient staff of workmen commenced operations, and, after a lapse of seven or eight hours, the engine-man and stoker were released. The former was severely scalded and otherwise hurt, but it is thought not dangerously. The fireman's was found to be the worst case, for he was scalded all over his side and had his leg broken. The van and carriage next the engine were smashed, and it is the greatest wonder how the passengers in them escaped."

On 13 September, the Newcastle Journal published an update, thus:

"South Durham Railway Accident – The engine-man who received serious injury in this accident died on Sunday afternoon; his name was Robert Aaron and he was 35 years of age. The stoker, Thomas Bulch, is dying; Dr Torbock, who has been in daily attendance on the poor fellow, holds out no hopes."

The official Board of Trade report of 14 September written by the accident investigator, Captain Tyler, read in part:

"The driver and fireman were found under a heap of coke, which had fallen on them from the tender, with their legs jammed in between the quadrant of the reversing lever and a cover provided on the engine to shelter them from the weather.

They could not be extricated from their position for eight hours, and were so much injured and burnt, that the driver has since died, and the fireman is not expected to recover. A third person, also a fireman in the service of the Company, was thrown off to the right on the grass, and stunned; but he escaped without serious injury."

The Newcastle Journal of 20 September describes some of the inquest proceedings:

"THE ACCIDENT ON THE SOUTH DURHAM RAILWAY —CAPTAIN TYLER'S REPORT. The adjourned inquest the body of Robert Aaron, who died on Sunday the 8th instant, in consequence of injuries received in this accident, was held at Shildon, on Tuesday, before Mr Trotter, coroner. Deceased, who was the driver of the engine, was found buried beneath the coke, and his legs were held fast by the engine, which was thrown its broadside.

Captain Tyler (from the Board of Trade), who came down from. London to inspect the scene of the accident, stated before the coroner his opinion as to the cause of the accident. He said the original construction of the line at this particular point was defective. He had learned that the inspector of the permanent way had ordered the repair of the defect on the day previous to the accident. The plate layers, however, had mistaken the instructions given them, and, instead of making the way more safe, increased the play in some longitudinal beams which span the cattle creep at the spot. Those beams were not fastened in the girders of the bridge, and did not fit in them accurately, and there was some degree of shake in the girders, owing to their not having been perfectly buried in the masonry of the abutments of the bridge, and owing to the masonry having settled, to some extent, since the construction of the bridge.

The reason why so little injury was done to the passengers, and why the carriages were so little damaged, considering the serious nature the accident, was partly because the carriages were of considerable length, strongly built, and stiffened with timber placed vertically at the ends. But the principal reason was because very powerful brakes, of Mr. Newell's pattern, were employed the tail of the train but for which there would probably have been good many passengers killed. The Jury arrived the conclusion that the deceased came to his death by the engine accidentally running off the line; but what caused the engine to run off they could not say. The Coroner expressed his surprise at the verdict, whereupon A Juryman said there had been various causes stated, and they could agree none of them.

The Coroner requested them reconsider their verdict. The Jury again retired, and after the lapse of a quarter of hour returned similar verdict, stating, that how the engine came to run off the line there was no evidence to satisfy them."

Then as part of a piece in the York Gazette of the 28 September 1861, the following extract makes acknowledgement to the fact that Thomas Bulch appeared to be pulling through after his injuries:

"The wounded taken care of to the praise of a few — only a few, alas! — for many there were who walked away unconcerned — the utmost energy was directed to those poor fellows, (the deceased engine-man Aaron and the stoker Bulsh, who is recovering.) The country people seemed more than half savage. The gloom of the blackest night, intensified by a furious wind and the most sweeping rain added to the difficulty of every one. No help, by some unaccountable ignorance of the telegraph, reached the spot from head quarters for a long painful interval, and the men remained buried for eight hours, when they were brought home to Shildon."

And thus, despite the broken leg, the scalding and burning and eight hours spent crushed beneath the locomotive, Thomas Bulch lived. Being so grievously injured could well have seriously affected Thomas's employability and also detrimentally affected the wellbeing of his wife and their two young daughters in the longer term. All this happened several decades before the existence of a welfare state. It was a time when anyone suffering from such a devastating industrial accident might find themselves surplus to requirements and falling back upon the charity, goodwill and benevolence of family members to sustain and nourish them. Those with a little foresight and money to spare might have subscribed to a friendly society, whereby for a weekly or monthly contribution they might, in such circumstances, receive either a funeral payment or sickness benefit until well enough to work.

This wasn't what the future had in store for Thomas Bulch. Gradually, day by day, he recovered much of his physical health. Despite this, he would never return to working on the footplate of a steam locomotive. Considering the possible psychological experiences of his trauma and the physical rigour demanded of his former occupation that is perhaps quite understandable. Instead, whether through his own initiative, personal connections at the Shildon Works or maybe the intervention of the works manager William Bouch himself, he secured a new role. The employment records from the Stockton and Darlington Railway Company's Shildon Works, held at the National Archives in Kew, show that on the 10 March 1862 Thomas entered into a new position of 'Timekeeper' there. The post was not especially well paid, earning four shillings and four pence per week, certainly not as much as a locomotive driver. He was however, working and able to provide for himself and his family.

Throughout Thomas's recovery from his injuries, he may well have been able to hear his father-in-law rehearsing the New Shildon Saxhorn Band nearby to keep them ready for public engagement. The Teesdale Mercury gives us an example of their activity in this period:

> "New Shildon Saxhorn Band. This celebrated band, giving vent to their musical talents, came out on Saturday, January 18th, to cheer the villagers with their strains of music. They played choruses and selections from Mozart, Handel, Verdi and other eminent Authors, with such precision and brilliancy, that much credit is due to their talented leader, Mr F Dinsdale. After playing they formed in promenade, to the house of Mr Thomas Thompson, Bay Horse Inn, where they with other respectable gentlemen of the neighbourhood, partook of an excellent supper, which was served up in a grand style, and which reflects great credit upon the worthy host and hostess. After doing justice to the repast, the cloth being removed, vocal harmony being the order, which was efficiently supplied by Messrs Dinsdale, Harrison, Spark, Robinson, and others of the band. After playing "Rule Britannia" and the "National Anthem,"

they separated, each to their respective homes, highly delighted with the night's entertainment."

Births

On the thirtieth of December eighteen hundred and sixty two, at the family home on Strand Street, New Shildon, Margaret Bulch brought another baby boy into the world. With his father's name in mind, as was often the tradition with so many families, the couple named him Thomas Edward Bulch. Had Thomas senior not survived his experiences during the previous year this baby would not have been conceived and born, and we'd not be telling this story.

Above: Long demolished houses on Strand Street, New Shildon where Tom Bulch was born in 1862.

Just under fifteen months later, and two streets away on Chapel Street, on the twenty-first of March eighteen hundred and sixty-four, the second important subject of this story, George Allan came into the world. George was the third child of John James Allan and his wife Hannah, née Longstaff. John Allan had been born in Ellerton on Swale, in Yorkshire, to parents William and Martha. His own journey to the gradually expanding town of New Shildon been via Crakehall, near Catterick, where he appears to have met and married Hannah, and started a family. George's older brother William was born there in 1859. George also had an older sister, Eleanor Mary, who had been the first member of the Allan family to be born at New Shildon, close to one month before the taking of the 1861 census. That census reveals that when it was taken the Allan family were being visited by an Eleanor M. Buck, and it seems possible that young Eleanor Mary Allan was named after this lady. However the unfortunate infant only survived until the spring of 1862. Surviving infancy in the mid-nineteenth century was a struggle in itself.

John had started his working life as a farm servant at St Giles' Catterick before he became fifteen and the 1851 census had been taken. Somehow, between that year and the following census in 1861 he had been educated in the profession of Tailoring. It was in this occupation that he found work at New Shildon. John wasn't the only member of his family to seek his fortune in the town. The 1861 census shows John's older brother, Ralph, living alone on neighbouring Adelaide Street and employed as a shoemaker. Ralph, George Allan's uncle, married and settled in the town for the long term. He and his wife, also called Hannah, had five children; Martha, Alfred, Ralph William, Sarah Hannah and Emily Ann. This meant that through his early life George would have cousins living nearby.

Wherever it was that the Allan brothers had learned their trades, it seems they came to the town not to work on the railway or in engineering, but to provide clothing and footwear to the growing workforce. By the time of the 1871 census, John James Allan's occupation is stated as Master Tailor suggesting either completion of an apprenticeship, marked by the production of an assessed 'master-piece', or else being under his own employment.

The world into which Thomas Edward Bulch and George Allan were born was quite different to that we recognise today. It is probably worth taking a moment to set a context. Globally the early eighteen-sixties was an era of turmoil, discovery, invention and innovation well above and beyond what was going on with the expansion of steam passenger transport which, of course, first happened within metres of the very place these lads were born.

Between 1861 and 1865 for example the States of America were absolutely not 'united', with groups of states and the families that lived in them locked into a terrible and destructive ideological civil war. Abraham Lincoln was President of the union of northern states, and would be famously assassinated just over a year after George Allan's birth. Closer to home, in Europe, there was also war between Denmark and Prussia. In New Zealand British colonial forces waged the New Zealand War on the indigenous Maori population as part of a British Empire land-grab, while the Second French Empire vied for control of Mexico. When George Allan was born, Queen Victoria was enjoying her 26th year as British monarch. A Liberal Prime Minister, Viscount Palmerston oversaw the British Government in a parliament elected only by male adults over twenty-one years of age that held property. By the early 1860s, only around 1.43 million Britons could vote from a total population of thirty million. The rest had no voice concerning who governed the nation, nor in whose interest they did so. What's more, the lack of secret ballots resulted in open voting: voters could be, and often were, offered bribes or subjected to intimidation to persuade them to vote a certain way.

The Clifton Suspension Bridge in Bristol was completed around that time, now still an enduring memorial to its innovative designer, Brunel. Charles Dickens's 'Our Mutual Friend', one of his most sophisticated works, combining savage satire with social analysis was being serialised in the newspapers. In science, John Alexander Reina Newlands produced the first periodic table of chemical elements. In Paris, the first 'true' bicycle, with a cranked front wheel, was created and the early flames of a Victorian craze for cycling was kindled.

There was also a significant social change in this period in that the proportion of the population that could be considered middle-class was growing. Across Britain these middle-class men now managed factories, traded stock, wrote in ledgers, oversaw building sites, and sparred in the law courts. Fortunes were made, rather than inherited, as these aspiring Victorians tested their mettle through competition with colleagues and rivals alike. Even before Charles Darwin's ideas about natural selection began to circulate in the 1860s, the middle class of the mid-nineteenth century experienced life as one long competition. Victorians fostered the belief of it being possible for any man to succeed in the world through his own efforts no matter how humble his origins. Self-help literature, manuals of etiquette and moral standard and aspirational novels such as "Great Expectations" were widely read. To fail to reach one's potential in such times was deemed to be a flaw in the character of an individual, rather than the society as a whole, with the desolation of the workhouse awaiting those too lazy, extravagant or proud, to avoid poverty.

In these times, and this context, New Shildon and the surrounding area had, not unusually, a reputation for hard drinking and disorder. The construction of the railway infrastructure and the town itself had continued to draw tough, physical, workers, and pay them comparatively well. Many of these men had a characteristic thirst for ale, and trouble. After Robert Peel's Metropolitan Police Bill of 1829 an emerging series of various police forces grew nationally and by the mid-1800s there was a local police presence that would attempt to keep order on behalf of 'the establishment' and suppress petty crime.

In doing so they were as likely to be physically attacked in return. Throughout the childhood of Thomas Edward Bulch and George Allan, local newspapers speak of of robberies, theft, domestic abuse, physical assaults on both men and women in the home, ale-houses and on the streets.

A variable approach to personal health and safety in the local heavy industries resulted in injuries and fatalities. It would often take only a mishap or slight distraction for a railway worker to find themselves crushed and injured or killed by rolling stock. The industries presented a hazard not only to the workers, but also the local children. In one New Shildon newspaper story of 1869, when Thomas would be around seven years old, and George a little younger, a one-year-old girl called Mary Ann Bell was killed as a result of an accident when children had been riding in a 'bogie' and she reportedly fell out fatally injuring her spine. Another example, of 1863 tells of eight-year-old John Thompson, crushed to death after falling off rail wagons he had been riding.

Other infants' lives were shortened through poor health and unsanitary domestic conditions. The Allans, and the Bulch family, both lost young children. It was not that parents were necessarily negligent in looking after their children. Mothers did their best to protect their offspring, but a lack of essential facilities made it an uphill struggle. For example, in our comparatively privileged times we see washing and bathing as a basic necessity, however a supply of running water was not provided to New Shildon until 1866. Both Tom Bulch, and George Allan, survived their earliest years without it.

Childhood

Thomas Edward Bulch was christened at St John's church in Old Shildon on 28 January 1863. The day was a double celebration for the family as the Reverend C S Ellwood also had the happy duty of christening Thomas's aunt, Sarah Anne Dinsdale, the daughter of Thomas's grandfather Francis Dinsdale and his wife Mary. Over a year later, on 10th April 1864, at that same venue, George Allan was christened by William Hayton. It would not be until 1868 that New Shildon would have a church of its own.

At some indeterminable date between 1862 and 1871, the Allan family moved from Chapel Street to Adelaide Street. Thus, for a while, and certainly when the 1871 census was taken, the Bulch family, the Allan family and the Dinsdales all lived in closer proximity. As infants, it is highly likely that the young Tom and George knew each other and probably spent time in each other's company.

It would have been a small but noisy town. To the north-east was a brick and tile works, conveniently placed to support the building work underway as the town expanded in almost all directions. To the east, behind the cottages where the pioneering railway engineer Timothy Hackworth had once lived, were the Soho railway works, gasworks and a reservoir which existed to service the railway rather than provide water for the townspeople. At the south end of Adelaide and Strand Streets was a busy crossing where railway tracks crossed the main through road for rail traffic entering or leaving the Shildon Works.

Both boys would owe some gratitude in part to the railway companies for the facilities used in, and quality of, their early education. The British School, located at the junction of Station Street and Cross Street, was built in 1841 by the Stockton and Darlington Railway Company to provide schooling for the children of the area. When the North Eastern Railway company acquired the Stockton and Darlington in 1863, it inherited responsibility for the upkeep of the school until the latter became self-sufficient. Like most of the town's earliest buildings it was stone built, and consisted of two large classrooms. Capacity-wise, this mixed gender school was of sufficient size to accommodate three-hundred pupils. A second school, the 'National School', was built in 1875 uphill, and and eastward of the town, to accommodate the children of the growing population. The year before Thomas Edward Bulch was born the population of New Shildon was 1142. Within ten years, when George Allan reached seven years of age, the population had boomed to 1667. By then, however, Tom and George would be close to finishing their early education.

Above: The British School in New Shildon at which Tom and George would have received their education, with the Mechanics Institute to the right of the picture

A basic education did not become a mandatory requirement in Britain until the 1870 Education Act was passed and effected, so Tom and George had a comparatively fortunate, though not unique, start. Victorian childhood was shorter than that of twenty-first century British children. Children were often thought of more as 'small people', and owners of industries up to that time usually found ways to deploy their labour as soon as they were physically able. In many communities around the North East of England children fulfilled roles in mines or factories from the age of five years, and certainly by age of eight. Though legislation was introduced in the nineteenth century to curb the use and working hours of children, industrial leaders often found ways to circumnavigate such legislative rules.

The owners of the North Eastern Railway required more of their workforce than the ability to undertake basic labour so understood the benefit and value of an education that might provide essential skills as a good foundation for the work they expected to be done. Though some of those children might take what they learned in company supported schools elsewhere and use it in in other industries, such provision was deemed a worthwhile investment until a basic education became more widespread.

When not at school the young Tom Bulch, guided by his father, grandfather Francis Dinsdale and uncle, Edward Dinsdale, had an additional education in the principles of making and understanding music. Being surrounded by a musical family it was almost an inevitability. Eric Tomkins's Bulch family history, which includes some stories passed down through his family, explains that Tom's father had also been a bandsman. There's no information to explain what instrument he played, or for how long. The closest to any other documented evidence suggesting any connection between Thomas and the band is a newspaper article in the Durham Chronicle that explains how on the 7 August 1868, on a Friday evening at the Commercial Hotel, Thomas Bulch senior. played a key part in the presentation of a special 'contre bass' horn to the then secretary of the New Shildon Saxhorn Band, Mr James Robinson. That Tom's father had been engaged to present the instrument, and that he made a speech, suggests he at the very least occupied some position of respect or relevance among the assembled bandsmen.

Young Tom would probably have seen a great deal of his grandfather's Saxhorn Band as he grew up, and seen how his grandfather, uncle and others were involved, conducted themselves and led their bands. We're told, though, that It was the pianoforte that was to be Tom's first instrument.

In the mid nineteenth century, many in the middle classes were desperate to adopt and demonstrate their cultural credentials. I'm not suggesting that the Bulch family were, in any way, middle-class, but there there were many among the working classes with aspirations to attain that status. In Victorian Britain, ownership of a piano was, for the lower middle classes of the day, a sign of status, as well as a form of entertainment during long evenings in the years before radio or television became the default focus of our attentions. Its proper name of 'pianoforte' being derived from the Italian words for soft and loud, the piano was a versatile instrument and the perfect accompaniment to singing in the home. The importance of possessing a piano in one's home might perhaps be equated to the early twenty-first century imperative to have the latest flat screen television set on display. Changes in design and technology, including the use of cross-stringing where one longer set of piano strings, enabling the deeper low notes, could be placed in the same space across a first shorter set for the high notes, enabled more compact and convenient upright models that might fit into a corner of a room in a modest terraced house whilst still producing a respectable richness of tone. The piano was much more than a musical instrument.

With a cabinet required to conceal the stringed frame and soundboard as well as the mechanical workings of the keyboard, the piano was a fully fledged piece of furniture, styled to suit whichever aesthetic trend was prevalent at intervals throughout the Victorian era. Music shops sprang up around the region, selling a range of pianos, organs, harmoniums and other instruments, as well as a broad range of sheet music to play upon them. Some such localised shops, including Brotherton's Music, established in Bishop Auckland in 1842, would go so far as to offer their own branded range of piano.

Tom Bulch also learned to play the violin. Though learning the piano and violin would have required a great deal of concentration and practice from the young Thomas, it would give him an early understanding of the principles of polyphony (simultaneous melody), monophony (singular melody) and homophony (where a dominant melody is accompanied by chords), which would be a great foundation for his later evolution into a composer of music for ensembles of instruments.

The demand for, and improving technological capability to mass produce, printed sheet music enabled the professionalisation of music. This was an idea that would catch the attention of the young Thomas Bulch as he grew up. Eminent musicians once limited to performing, composing and teaching also saw new opportunities. As Tom learned to play he would have access to a wider variety of traditional and new music.

Gradually Tom was guided to embrace brass instruments, though his love of the piano stayed with him throughout his whole life as we will see. We don't specifically know which brass instrument Thomas Edward began with but we do know that he learned how to play, and look after, a cornet and that would be his principal brass instrument of choice throughout his many years as a bandsman, musician, and bandmaster.

George Allan's arrival at brass band music appears to have taken a slightly different path. Bob Wray, a former bandsman in the North East of England, who conducted his own research into Allan's life during the nineteen-eighties and nineteen-nineties, had the rare pleasure of asking George's then only remaining, grandchild, Dorothy Allan. From those exchanges Bob learned a few things about his life that weren't otherwise formally documented. According to Dorothy, though there were members of the Allan family with musical ability, George was initially self-taught. His cited influences from articles published later in later in his life, make references to pianists, suggesting that, as with Tom Bulch, he had learned piano. This is also echoed in the account told to Bob by a former Shildon bandsman named Jack Kitching who began playing in brass bands in 1926 when George was still alive and influential on the local music scene. Though Jack had admitted he didn't know George Allan personally, he was able to remember being told by fellow bandsmen and musicians more closely acquainted that George could play piano or organ.

As to how George became a bandsmen, we have a more detailed account in the form of partly-retrospective article printed in a band music paper, The Cornet, on 14 November 1896. This informs the reader that George had, as a child, been a member of the church choir. This was most certainly at All Saints Church, New Shildon, which was completed and opened in 1868 when George would have been four years old, and with which the family had ongoing connections throughout his life.
The church was built, for the people of New Shildon, on land gifted to the church by John Scott, the 3rd Earl of Eldon and was, in a demonstration of gratitude, named after the saint's day closest to the Earl's birthday.

According to that article previously mentioned, George was, like millions of other children of that generation, taught to sing using the Tonic Sol-Fa method. This was a means of learning devised by an English music educator called Sarah Glover. It was then then developed and popularised, following a commission by a conference of Sunday School teachers, by a minister named John Curwen. The method's advocates believed that all social classes of people, and all ages, should be able to learn music, and that this method simplified that process and made the principles easier to understand. Using the sol-fa method, a competence in musical literacy could be achieved by graduating through three phases. Beginners commenced by reading the special sol-fa notation only and then progressed, via an interim stage, to a state of being able to read the musical notation directly from the music staff. Though many learned this through singing; for example in a choir, this would have been a useful skill when the time came to make a transition to a musical instrument. Though the method was originally created to improve Sunday School singing, it was recognised for its effectiveness and adopted in 1860 by the English education authorities. Given this, George may well have initially started to learn through this method at Sunday School, regular school, or perhaps even both.

His choirmaster in the church choir recognised a musical talent in young George and, as the 1896 article from The Cornet explains, had presented a question: "What can you learn in a brass band as to theory etc?" George took it upon himself to find out. We have clues as to the identity of that choirmaster who set George on a path that would later see him compose brilliant brass marches such as Knight Templar and The Wizard. Church records tell us little, but a newspaper report in January of 1870, at which time George would have been six years old, tells us that the choirmaster at All Saints Church was Mr William Dodds. Dodds had been born in Darlington in 1820 and had worked as a railway agent and later insurance agent resident at St John's Road, New Shildon. He also had connections to the choir at St John's Church in Old Shildon prior to the building of All Saints. The Durham Chronicle of Friday, 10 August 1855 tells us of a 'pleasure trip' to Redcar for the church choir, which had been laid on by the Rev James Manisty, M.A. and says:

> "Although the weather was rather unfavourable the party enjoyed themselves, and returned home highly pleased with their treat. The singing of the services in this church has been of late greatly improved by the superintendence of Mr Wm. Dodds, late of Darlington, who has exerted himself in bringing the choir to its present state of excellence."

He was also the conductor of the Old Shildon Choral Society, so actively engaged in singing activities within the community. We know also from membership books that he was a subscribing member of the New Shildon Mechanics Institute, which George would also join when he was able. Though he lived, worked and spent time socially in New Shildon and as choirmaster of All Saints church, he felt a stronger tie to St John's church, returning as a parishioner and in later life became a warden there. He was found dead in his office, adjoining his house on St John's Road, by his daughters on 29 of September 1897 and was buried at St John's on 2 October.

New Shildon Juvenile Band

Throughout his childhood George, even prior to his choirmaster's suggestion to find out about what could be learned from a brass band, would have seen the New Shildon Saxhorn Band. They were present at, and associated with, almost all of the major events in the town. For example when, in July 1866 when Tom and George were little more than toddlers, the Saxhorn Band led a procession of townspeople through the streets celebrating the Weardale and Shildon Water Company's successes in attaining Parliamentary approval for plans to bring a water supply to the town. The Teesdale Mercury gives a description of the merriment:

> "The bells of St John's Church and various public works were set in motion, and rang merry peals until late in the evening. The public works many of the locomotive engines, as well as many of the private dwellings, were decked with flags and mottoes being testimony to the success of the new company. Orders were given at the various works that the men should cease working; this being done the workmen to the number of upwards of seven hundred, formed a procession in their working clothes headed by the Shildon Saxhorn Band, and marched through the town in order. Presenting a very novel appearance. Numerous guns, fog signals etc. were fired almost incessantly through the day."

The mentions of guns is reminiscent of scenes from old Hollywood western movies though in this case, fortunately, the guns mentioned were safely in the hands of the 4th Durham Rifle Volunteers under the command of Lieut. Davison, who marched outside the home of William Bouch, the works manager, and offered volleys in salute. The article also mentions how workmen watered the garden of a man connected to the water company to demonstrate the lifting of their "fear of indulging too freely on the present meagre supply of water at this place." It's easy to understand how in an overcrowded new town with questionable sanitation the prospect of the arrival of a new fresh water supply could cause such celebration, and also easy to imagine that days like this would stay in the memories of the young children that might witness it.

The Dinsdale family, wanting to ensure an ongoing supply of capable musicians for their Saxhorn Band, formed and maintained a juvenile band in which young prospective bandsmen could be tutored. With little to no exception, brass bands generally were the exclusive preserve of men and boys. Though girls were encouraged to sing, and to play the piano, they were excluded from access to the inner-sanctum of the bandroom and what went on there. Perhaps this traditional gender split was a carry over from the military band tradition, or it may have been felt that the presence of the ladies might prove a distraction. It may even have been the case that some of the men may have genuinely believed that the ladies were incapable of producing such musical skill as was required. If that were true then those doubters would surely have been shocked and surprised to see the modern brass bands in which women players excel, and without whom many bands would have long discontinued.

We don't know exactly when the Juvenile Band was started but it is probable that it was either at the same time as, or just after, the Saxhorn Band. Equally we don't know exactly from when, or for how long, Tom Bulch or George Allan were included in its ranks. From their respective ages we can speculate with some certainty that it would have been within a similar timeframe, and that the two would have played alongside each other in this band. Tom eventually graduated, and may have been groomed by his uncle, to occupy the solo cornet player's position, and George, though he would later also move on to play cornet, became its solo tenor horn player. Contemporary newspaper reports also tell us that the Juvenile Band was not always confined to rehearsing in the band room. On parade days and other local civic and societal occasions such as the Heighington Flower Show, at which the Shildon Saxhorn Band made a regular appearance through the 1870s, it's likely that members of the Juvenile Band would have been encouraged to attend. Sometimes, the Juvenile Band would be able to be seen performing in its own right separately to the senior band. Gradually, and subject to their abilities, members of the Juvenile Band would have migrated to a position in the senior band.

While Tom and George were growing up, and pursuing their musical apprenticeship under Edward Dinsdale, the New Shildon Saxhorn Band continued to develop its reputation in, and away from, the town. There are reports telling of just a few of the engagements they attended during this period which offer a flavour of the role and value of a brass band in the mid-Victorian working class communities of England. Tom in particular, with his family connections, might well have attended, if not performed at, some of the later performances during these years. Some of what he saw could have influenced his own perception and vision of what made a first-rate brass band, and what role it should play in the community. In 1862, the year Tom was born, the Durham Chronicle tells us, on June 13, of an appearance of the Shildon Saxhorn Band wherein the band had, on the previous Saturday, headed a procession of the Ancient Order of Foresters, Willington, from the Commercial Inn, Willington to Willington Hall. The Saxhorn band "ably performed their duties, and gave great satisfaction to the officers and members of the court, and musicians." At Willington Hall, following a sermon, the band played "God Save The Queen" and then the procession moved on to Burn Hall and back to their court room for dinner at which members of the band sang for those in attendance. The following year, 1863, the same newspaper, on the May 1, reports:

> "A miscellaneous concert was given in the Mechanics Hall, New Shildon on the 22nd ult, by the Saxhorn Band under the leadership of Mr F Dinsdale, assisted by the Bishop Auckland Serenaders under the tutor of Mr A Boyd. It being their first debut, the hall was well filled, and the programme was varied and well selected."

The same report goes on to say that:

> "The instrumental part of the programme was delivered with good taste and brilliancy, and was highly appreciated by the lovers of good music."

The Durham County Advertiser of 23 June 1865 tells us:

"Under the auspices of the New Shildon Saxhorn Band a picnic was held at Newton Cap Park on Tuesday evening, when about 200 young people attended and enjoyed the merry dance to the lively strains of the band. Numbers, however, seemed to prefer to race for a kiss, in the numerous games which were indulged in in various parts of the ground."

Then both the Newcastle Journal of 7 September 1865 and the Newcastle Guardian and Mercury of 9 September 1865 tell us that at a band contest in Crook as part of the Crook Agricultural Society Annual Exhibition the Shildon Saxhorn Band came second to the Fourth Durham Rifles Band. Other competing bands were Crook Saxhorn and Witton-Le-Wear bands. Later that same month, according to the Durham County Advertiser, the Shildon Saxhorn Band was engaged to lead a procession, with the banner, of the St Johns Order of Oddfellows from their lodge room at the Talbot Inn, West Auckland to the church for a sermon.

Being in charge of a brass band from a working town at social events where alcohol was made available presented specific difficulties as this story from the Durham County Advertiser of 21 July 1865 attests.

"Picnic at Brusselton. A Picnic and gala under the auspices of the New Shildon Saxhorn Band, was held on the grounds at Brusselton Folly, on Monday, when upwards of 500 attended and amused themselves in the different games provided for their entertainment, consisting of cricket, turzey, etc. but the chief attraction seemed to be dancing, which was joined in and kept up till dark. Refreshments including intoxicants were provided on the grounds, the latter of which we regret to say having been rather too freely indulged in by the band and officials, so much so that towards the latter part of the day, many of them got intoxicated and their conduct became of the most disgraceful character. The bandmaster getting enraged at one of his party, addressed him in the most violent terms, and using the most inelegant language he could choose (to the disgust of all present), threatened to leave the platform, taking with him his books, but on secondary consideration returned, and the dancing was resumed. The day was beautifully fine, and had the affair been properly conducted, and intoxicating drinks excluded, a most pleasant afternoon might have been spent."

This description feels quite reminiscent of the scenes in the film Brassed Off where Pete Postlethwaite's character of bandmaster Danny Ormondroyd is left outraged and incensed after his fictitious Grimley Colliery bandsmen gradually fall into a drunken state at the famous Whit Friday Contests at Saddleworth. You can imagine the similar frustration of Francis Dinsdale on that day at, the now long demolished, Brusselton Folly.

The attendance of the Saxhorn Band at revelries and processions continued into 1866 where the Newcastle Daily Chronicle of 9 July 1866 tells of the Shildon Lodge Colliery Reading Room Gala, held in connection with Messrs. Bolckow and Vaughan and Co's Colliery where an "excellent tea was provided for upwards of 500 people, presided over by ladies interested in the welfare of the institute." The Shildon Saxhorn Band was in attendance and dancing was kept up till dark. Another Durham Chronicle article reported on Friday, 14 August 1868, covers an event referred to earlier which took place when Tom, would have been about six years old. The Mr Bulch referred to here, therefore, was his father.

"PRESENTATION AT NEW SHILDON – The members of the New Shildon Saxhorn Band, under the superintendence of their much respected bandmaster, Mr F Dinsdale, met at the house of Mr Wm Bushby, Commercial Inn, Shildon, on Friday last, for the purpose of presenting a new monstre circular contrabass to their hon. sec., Mr James Robinson, as a mark of their esteem and respect for his long services in that capacity.

The instrument is a splendid piece of workmanship, and for brilliancy of tone cannot well be surpassed, and was supplied by the firm of Mr Jos. Highan, Manchester, one of the oldest and most renowned manufacturers in the world. The chair was taken by Mr J Spark, the leader of the band, who called upon Mr Bulch to present the instrument. Mr Bulch said it gave him great pleasure to be amongst them on such an occasion. The present section of the members showed that a good feeling existed among them. He had known their secretary for a number of years and hoped that he would enjoy health and strength to use the large instrument he had presented to him through the members of the band. Mr Robinson responded in a few appropriate remarks, and the meeting separated."

Then, during 1870, The Northern Echo announces:

"The New Shildon Mechanics Institute will hold a Gala Day at Stanhope Castle on Tuesday July 12th 1870, when the New Shildon Saxhorn Band will be in attendance"

During those years of the 1860s and early 1870s Thomas Bulch senior appears to have been one of the volunteers making up the part-time 4th Durham Volunteer Rifle Corps that we saw mention of a moment ago where they were participating in celebrations relating to provision of a water supply. These, largely autonomous, part-time precursors to the Territorial Army were formed following a communique in 1859 by the Secretary of State for War to the respective Lord Lieutenants of the English Counties, and were intended to be mobilised in the event of an invasion by aggressor nations. The 4th were one of eighteen corps in County Durham and were inaugurated on the 24 May 1860. Volunteers were required to pay for their own firearms, though all were acquired through the War Office to ensure consistency. As a result of having to pay for one's own rifle and uniform the Rifle Volunteer Corps tended to attract a more middle-class volunteer. The working class, unable to afford the cost of basic equipment and annual subscription fee, remained with the older local Militias. Thomas's involvement in Rifle Volunteer Corps activities would have taken place outside of his working hours. The volunteers would meet at the Newton Cap Rifle Range just to the west of the neighbouring town of Bishop Auckland. At some point during his service as a volunteer, Thomas was elevated to the rank of Sergeant and also took part in a number of rifle shooting contests in the Bishop Auckland area. Improving accuracy was a key developmental requirement of a volunteer part-time soldier, and these contests encouraged the men to practice. In 1871 Thomas Bulch senior won the Helmington Challenge Cup, a prize donated by Mrs Spencer of Helmington Hall and awarded to the volunteer achieving the highest score three times in succession. This was given with an accompanying cash prize of one pound and fifteen shillings.

Returning to the Saxhorn Band, two further engagements are described during 1872. An August issue of the Durham County Advertiser tells us that the Shildon Saxhorn Prize Band was engaged to perform at the Tudhoe Floral and Agricultural Society annual show, one of the oldest shows in the county the article states, to attend in uniform and perform a choice selection of music. What's interesting about this is that it's the

the first mention we see, anywhere, that the band performed in uniform. In our time spent researching this story, one thing that has eluded us is a photograph of the Saxhorn Band. There are a number of images we have seen around the turn of the century onwards that show Shildon bands playing in working clothes with traditional cloth caps, but it is only in later pictures that we see any Shildon bands in uniform. Then, on the 13 September that same year, the Durham County Advertiser informs us that the New Shildon Saxhorn band was engaged for the Sedgefield Flower and Pigeon Show and on that day "enlivened the scene by playing lively selections of music during the show".

The Northern Echo of Monday, 28 July 1873 reports upon a picnic held the previous Saturday afternoon at which the miners of New Shildon gathered on a field owned by their employers. Prior to that, they had marched through the streets with two "splendid" lodge banners in a procession headed by the New Shildon Saxhorn Band. Later all kind of amusements were partaken of including foot-racing, wrestling, kiss in the ring, dancing, Aunt Sally, turzey etc. Later that year at a band contest at the Tow Law Flower Show the Shildon Saxhorn Band, under the baton of Francis Dinsdale, came third.

In a report of the Annual Shildon Show which took place on Saturday, 21 August 1873, we learn something new about Thomas's father. Thomas Bulch senior seems to have been quite skilled as a maker of scale models. At this show we see him demonstrating his skill through his entry of a "careful model of a screw steamer that featured everything from rigging to the man at the ship's wheel." This model earned him third prize in the mechanics category.

The Northern Echo of 28 September 1875 then tells how the Shildon band took part in the 50th Anniversary Railway Jubilee celebrations, held in the presence of the Lord Mayor of London, accompanying a group of stonemasons to Darlington's Bank Top Station with their stonemasons' banner which was reported to be 'the most gorgeous exhibited'. The occasion was a huge celebration of the progress of the railways since that day in 1825 when the first very steam hauled passenger journey set off from New Shildon on its way to the coal docks on the south bank of the Tees at Stockton. An exhibition of locomotives from across the five decades had been set up at the North Eastern Railway Company's Faverdale works for the amusement of the Lord Mayor and other dignitaries. A parade of various trades and guilds led the way to the exhibition through streets festooned with bunting and garlands of flowers.

For June 1876 the Echo describes the "Grand Attraction" of a Whit Monday, Order of Druids Annual Brass Band Contest and Gala at Woodlands at which the New Shildon Saxhorn Band were competing. This is followed in August by a report of the band once again having entertained at the Heighington Flower Show.

A report from 1877 in the South Durham & Cleveland Mercury includes a suggestion that a young Tom Bulch may have played a part in a concert involving his grandfather's band:

> "Co-operative Hall, Old Shildon. – A concert of vocal and instrumental music was given in the above hall on Monday night, under the auspices of the Shildon Saxhorn Band (conductor Mr F Dinsdale), which played popular selections of music, assisted by the following artistes:- Miss Sallie Dargue, Miss Costello, Miss and Master Bulches, Mr. Sant and Mr. H Hopper."

It's most probable that Tom, by then age sixteen, is the Master Bulch referred to. In August of that same year, the band reportedly returned to entertain again at the Heighington Flower Show with Francis Dinsdale, as always, holding the conductor's baton. During this period, the young Tom also seems to have engaged in musical activities away from the brass band and appears to have been just as comfortable as part of a concert orchestra. In October of 1879, when he would have been almost eighteen years old, Tom was one of the entertainers at a concert at the Town Hall in Richmond, North Yorkshire. The event had been organised for the benefit of a Mr. John Race, who reports tell us had taught music and singing to the poorer classes gratuitously for over twenty years, and was held under the patronage of the Earl and Countess of Zetland, the Borough Member, the Mayor, magistracy, and gentry of the locality. Tom is listed as one of the vocalists featured during the evening, as was his sister Mary Jane, who in July of the previous year had married a William Summerbell of Richmond. Perhaps Mary Jane's having married into a Richmond family explains the pair's involvement at that particular engagement in that town. Her new husband, was a wine porter at the Spirit Vault in Barnard Castle and the couple had moved in with William's mother, a china dealer in the town. As well as singing, Thomas also played second cornet in the orchestra that evening.

All the while, through this colourful swirling carousel of fetes, parades, celebrations, contests, horticultural and agricultural shows, dances and galas, the New Shildon Saxhorn Band had been the darlings of the town with their repertoire of popular tunes. The brass band movement had so ingrained itself into the fabric of the working class society that to hold such an event without a band in attendance to brighten the day would be almost unthinkable. Being a member of a band was one way to ensure that one would be able to, and often be assisted to, attend some of the most enjoyable social events on the calendar. Yet all was not quite well with the bandsmen of Shildon and by the end of the 1870s there was a change in the general mood in the town that would introduce competition and rivalry to New Shildon and see Tom and George veer in different directions.

Temperance

Victorian public houses were one of the main meeting-up places for the working classes nationally, particularly for men. New Shildon was no exception, and for so small a town it boasted a good many such public houses and inns. The rise of trade union activism increased opportunity for the workers to spend time in pubs, and that increased opportunity and consequent drinking of alcohol was felt to be the cause of perceived issues in social conduct and health.

It's not clear exactly when 'temperance' came to the two Shildons. There are reports of temperance events in the area going back to June 1834 of reportedly well attended open-air temperance meetings in Old Shildon and there is evidence of influencers from the Temperance movement living in New Shildon at work as far back as 1840, such as one Mr Calvert Spenceley who appears in a report explaining that he was delivering lectures on teetotalism as far away as the Temperance Hall in Barnard Castle. The report explains that he was being listened to "by a large, and respectable, audience, after which several persons signed the teetotal pledge." Calvert's endeavours to convert people to the temperance cause were not always appreciated, and there was a tension between the opponents of alcohol and some of those that imbibed, as a story in the York Herald of 8 February 1840 reveals:

> "Guy Fawkes the Second.— About ten days ago, whilst Mr Spenceley, of Shildon, and Mr John Rogers, of Barnard Castle, were advocating the total abstinence cause to a crowded audience in a room used by the Primitive Methodists in the village of Cockfield, in the county of Durham, a labourer, whilst in an intoxicated state, took from his pocket a parcel containing 2lbs of powder, (commonly used for blasting stones) went into a dwelling room below where the meeting was being held, and with imprecations on the abstinence society declared he would blow them all up, and he accordingly threw the parcel containing the powder on the fire. A female in the room promptly snatched the parcel from the coals and thus prevented the awful consequences which must inevitably have attended so diabolical and wicked an act."

The earliest Temperance Movement is thought to have formed in Belfast, inspired by Presbyterian minister John Edgar and later John Livesey. Temperance initially and specifically targeted the drinking of spirits, but over time took to including ale on the list of prohibited beverages. Policy wise, the movement veered between demanding a ban on such drinks by law, and encouraging the desired behaviour through principles of moral persuasion. Regular Temperance meetings were established in the Shildons by 1857. The Durham Chronicle of the 20 March 1857 gives us some insight as to the atmosphere at such events:

> "On Friday last a meeting was held at New Shildon, where addresses were delivered Wm. Johnson, John Brown, and Job Walmsley. The meeting was a very lively one. The temperance band and vocalists were attendance, by whom some fine pieces were executed, and several melodies sung. At the close, two signed the pledge. These meetings are held monthly in the British school-room on the pay-day, the object being to induce the men employed at the works to spend their hard-earned money for the benefit of themselves and their families. Already great good has resulted from these meetings, and the friends of temperance anticipate happy future for the working men at this place."

A further pair of reports of April 1858 tells of a combined meeting and tea party of the Shildon and South Church Temperance Societies convening in Bishop Auckland marketplace. There "working men connected with the societies addressed the audience." After the addresses, the members formed a procession back to the National School at South Church "to partake of the abstinence cup". The procession included bands carrying banners and an unnamed band from Shildon. On this occasion, as there is no evidence available to support the existence of a brass band specifically aligned to the temperance cause, it is supposed that this band mentioned could be one that was mentioned in another news article from the Durham Chronicle of 24 September of the same year:

> "New Shildon. —On Friday evening, the 17th inst., temperance meeting was held in the British school-room, Mr John Pickering in the chair. Addresses in the cause of total abstinence were delivered by Mr Wm. Johnson, agent of the Darlington Ladies Temperance Association, and Messrs Daniel McKenzie and Robert Russell. Several melodies were sung by Messrs Bowes and Berald. The Shildon Works teetotal drum and fife band was in attendance, and enlivened the meeting by playing several popular airs. Several persons signed the pledge at the close of the meeting. After the usual vote of thanks to the chairman and to Mr Johnson, the meeting broke up an early hour, highly delighted with the evening's entertainment."

In September 1858 the North of England Temperance League was inaugurated, strengthening the structure of the movement:

> "The provisional formation of which took place in Newcastle some months ago was formally inaugurated yesterday by conference of delegates from the various societies enrolled as members of the league, and by a public soiree held in the evening, in the Temperance Hall, Nelson Street, Newcastle."

It is perhaps easy to see where the clergy and members of 'polite society' might be drawn to abstinence; however as to why ordinary working men felt drawn to temperance, there is a terrific piece of reporting in the Durham Chronicle from nearby Old Shildon of 25 June 1859 where the writer captured the essence of the speaker's reasons for taking the pledge, and for how long they have adhered to the principles therein.

"TEMPERANCE DEMONSTRATION AT SHILDON. In the long room of the Temperance Hotel at Old Shildon (formerly known as the Black Lion Hotel), a large meeting was held on Saturday evening, the 17th inst. Through the kindness of Joseph Pease, Esq., the above room has been set apart for the use of the temperance society of Shildon, and it must be highly gratifying to that gentleman to know that working men of Shildon duly appreciate the boon. A mental improvement society has been formed, in which reading, writing, arithmetic, reciting, singing, and discussion is carried forward; the room is supplied with temperance literature, and library is about to be established. When working men learn to depend on themselves, and to cultivate those talents with which their Creator has endowed them, we may anticipate the speedy arrival of "the good time" about which so much has been said and sung.

J. M. Browne, missionary, from Pease's West, presided, and in his opening address urged the working men help themselves. "and then they would find others ready and willing to help them."

Robt. Jacques, a turner, from Shildon Works, had been a teetotaller three years, and felt bound to give it a good word. Ever since he left off drinking, he had been better mind, body, and pocket. Public-houses were injurious to the working man's interests, and he believed the working-classes would never have their rights until they became sober.

Thomas Dixon did not feel as if had much to say, but thought he would come forward to show which side belonged to. He had tried teetotalism, and having derived much benefit from it, he thought he should be very foolish give it up.

John Tinkler, a smith, had been a member the temperance society two years. He could not say that drinking had done him much harm, but he believed teetotalism to be infinitely better. If a man could work down the pit without drink he could do without it, too. Drink only excited a man, and took away the little bit of sense he had. It was a dangerous thing to begin with a single glass — he was sure there was nothing good to be learned in a public-house. Example was more powerful than precept, it was, therefore, the duty of every man to his best to banish drink.

Robert Millett had abstained nine years. He had not been in the habit of addressing public meetings, but was willing to do the best he could. Many died young in consequence of drinking, and though but a young man, eternity alone could tell what evils teetotalism had saved him from. Many of his youthful companions had derided him because he would not go with them to the public-house; but he was proof against scoffs and sneers. His head, heart, and hands should all be employed to put down the drinking system—that system which made widows, orphans, criminals, and paupers.

Robt. Martin, fitter, was sorry could not say that be had been nine years a teetotaller. He had been in Russia, and had travelled for a fortnight together in the cold. He had tried both spirits and tea, and always derived more warmth from the latter than from the former. He had seen men frozen to death while under the influence of spirits; he often wondered he had not been nipped to death. He had lost his senses and his money too, going into the public-houses. If he had been a teetotaller aa long as some in Shildon, he should, like them, have had two or three houses of his own. He was happy to say that he had the whole of his wages in his pocket; and he felt more comfortable under the new dispensation than under the old.

Isaac Haigh, fitter, believed drink unnecessary as beverage, and would leave the doctors to deal with the physic. He formerly worked In Upleatham mines, and before becoming a teetotaller he never weighed more than nine and a half stones. He had lost a leg: and after trying teetotalism one year and a half, he could bump down ten stones without his leg. They talked about landlords bagging-out, but was the use of bagging out with bad stuff. He didn't bag-out, and yet weighed heavier than before.
Getting drink to help them to work, was something akin to the wagoner who took drink drive the horses, and gave the horses water to help them pull the load.

Jno. James – joiner, and a teetotaller of long standing, was pleased find his brethren going forward in everything good. In reading Adam Clarke he met with a sentence which said, "A knowledge of Ignorance the beginning of knowledge." There were many things going on the world of which he had no knowledge, and he determined to get to know, and for that purpose he had joined the "dry company." He felt disposed to remain a teetotaller. It had done him good – he had money in his pocket. It always afforded him pleasure to attend a temperance meeting. It was not much that he could say, but he was willing to say all he could.

An interesting dialogue between the publican and the teetotaller was given by John Stephenson and William Alder. During the evening, songs and melodies were sung the temperance choir, assisted by the Philharmonic Society, and at the conclusion seven signatures were obtained to the temperance pledge."

Later that year, that same building on Chapel Row where the Old Shildon Temperance Society met, formerly the Black Lion was re-designated as a temperance hotel, becoming known as the Temperance Lecture and Reading Room. Just down the hill in New Shildon the Temperance Society did not have a dedicated building, so continued to meet for some years in the British School during hours when the children were not receiving tuition.

After 1860, when a dedicated building was provided to the members of the New Shildon Mechanics Institute by the Stockton and Darlington Railway Company only a few feet away from the school, that Institute was deemed a more appropriate meeting place for Temperance Society meetings and lectures. The Darlington & Stockton Times tells, on the on 21 February 1863, of one such meeting:

"Temperance at New Shildon – A temperance meeting was held at the Mechanics Institute, on Station Street, New Shildon, and addresses delivered by Messrs. Browne, Guisbrough, and Johnson, Darlington, on Friday night week. Mr Hannay presided. At the close several signed the pledge."

The Temperance Movement drew support and strength from a variety of religious organisations, especially non-conformist Methodists, Quakers and Salvation Army, who collectively and separately lobbied parliament to restrict alcohol sales. A church of England Temperance Society was founded in 1862 and reconstituted in 1873 and the Catholic League of the Cross, proclaiming total abstinence from alcohol, was founded in 1873.

We know from, among other examples, the New Shildon bandsmen's behaviour at Brusselton Folly in 1865 mentioned already that, as working-class men of the day, they enjoyed the opportunity to imbibe an alcoholic drink or two, and that there were times when the indulgence was perceived to have been taken a little too far from in the view of their bandmaster, his sons and of the public. As more of the men from New Shildon signed up to the Temperance Pledge, there's likely to have been a perception by those bandsmen that no longer partook of alcohol that a band consisting solely of like-minded players might render a better performance. The mood and attitude of the band as a whole may have shifted, or been guided, as time went on. In August of 1870, and again in 1871, the New Shildon Saxhorn Band had provided entertainments at a Grand Temperance Gala at Brinkburn and Pierremont in Darlington which was reportedly attended by several thousand persons. It would not necessarily mean that the members of the band would have had to be adherents of "the pledge" to perform at this event, though it would be highly improbable that ales or spirits would be found there.

Other brass bands around the North were either establishing themselves as, or declaring themselves to be, aligned to the Temperance Movement. Though the New Shildon Saxhorn was not to be one such band, the articles contain an insinuation that the Dinsdale family had begun to form a connection to the Temperance movement. Then, towards the end of the 1870s the ideological split in New Shildon's bandsmen fully materialised. It was a rift that would not only split the bandsmen into two groups, but also divide the Dinsdales. An early report that confirms this appeared in the Daily Gazette for Middlesbrough on 8 August 1878 which tells of a band contest and flower show at the town's South Bank district on the shores of the River Tees:

> "The greatest attraction during the afternoon, as the weather was delightful, was the band contest. The prizes offered in this department were £10 for the first, £5 for the second, and £3 for the third. In consequence of some misunderstanding the following four bands only put in an appearance:— The Skelton Brass Band; Milburn's Model Band, Middlesbrough; Blair and Company's Band; and the New Shildon Juvenile Temperance Band, and they after their performance were placed in the above order. Immediately after the competition of the bands a ten guinea cornet was given to the best player on that instrument. After a keen competition by four competitors, Mr H Milburn, conductor of the Model Band, was awarded the prize."

New Shildon's Juvenile Band, under Edward Dinsdale, had rebranded itself as allied to the principles of temperance. On precisely why, there is insufficient documented information available to explain. Perhaps Edward may have taken the temperance pledge himself, or was keen to promote the wholesome values of the movement to the young bandsmen in his charge. Perhaps there was some incentive to do so, or some opportunity to be derived from it. This break away from the Saxhorn Band was not, however, limited to the younger bandsmen. The earliest found mention of a New Shildon Temperance Band at a senior level is a record of a contest appearance by them on 24 June 1879 where they were placed second at the Lofthouse-in-Cleveland Contest, earning a prize of four pounds. This implies that the Temperance band was formed long enough before that date to have acquired a full complement of players, equipped, and rehearsed well enough to have been placed at contest.

Perhaps Edward Dinsdale felt that enough members of his juvenile band had developed and aged to the point of qualifying to be a senior band. Or perhaps between the members of both Temperance Juvenile and adult Saxhorn Band, there were sufficient members having taken the temperance pledge and in frustration with their alcohol drinking counterparts forced an agreement to break into two camps. Whatever the reason, New Shildon's bandsmen did become two groups. The young bandsmen in the Bulch family along with Edward Dinsdale aligned themselves to perceived moral superiority. Presuming why the young George Allan opted to remain with the Saxhorn Band would be speculative, but there is one story from his life that we shall come to later which implies that he wasn't averse to, nor saw any issue with, enjoying an alcoholic refreshment.

The split would eventually lead to important developmental opportunities for both Tom and George.

By the August of 1879 the Temperance Band also seems to have begun to supplant the more established Saxhorn Band as the 'go to' source of entertainment for the Heighington Flower Show. This was perhaps enabled by connected parties having moved to the new band, or perhaps a desire on the part of the show organising committee for assurance of a well behaved and sober unit of men. We're told the following about this occasion:

> "The New Shildon Temperance band were engaged and performed several choice selections, but their services in the way of providing dance music were not largely in demand, the rain having rendered the field totally unfit for 'tripping the light fantastic.'"

Another significant report in that same month printed by the York Herald, was that the Temperance Band also appeared at the famed annual Shildon Show, with Edward Dinsdale once again wielding the baton. They came third in the band contest, behind the Leeds Model Band.

One Saturday in July 1880 the Temperance Band played at a Primitive Methodist Gala at Darlington and took their place at the head of a procession from the North Road Institute to Southend Grounds. Then on 20 August they played, according to the Darlington & Stockton Times of the following day, at the Barnard Castle Flower Show band contest where they came third behind Milburn's Model Band.

During this short time, the New Shildon Temperance Band began to occupy a special place in the hearts and minds of the people of the Shildons. On Friday, 10 September the Eastern Daily Press described how the New Shildon Temperance Band played again at a contest at the Shildon Horticultural and Agricultural Show. It quoted from another report in the Northern Echo that:

> "The stand upon which the competing bands played for the valuable prizes offered was completely hemmed in all day by those of the spectators (and there were evidently many) who took a delight in music. The playing occupied several hours, during which the judge, Mr William Mann (who has performed a similar duty at Shildon on a previous occasion, and who was late bandmaster to the Royal Cumberland Militia) occupied as usual an enclosed tent."

It goes on to say that:

> "For the New Shildon Temperance Bad there was no fourth prize, a fact which the judge regretted, for the playing was good – a remark which elicited hearty applause."

Work

Of the two young men at the heart of this story it was Tom Bulch that was the first to reach the age where he was expected to work to earn a living. Having a father employed at the Shildon Works, whilst not being a guarantee, did enhance a lad's chances of being accepted to work there. Tom's brother Frank chose not to follow this path and had become a coal miner, but Tom opted to pursue an apprenticeship at the works. He was later followed by his younger brother Jeremiah. We don't have an exact date for Tom Bulch's acceptance into the Shildon works, but it certainly happened before the taking of the 1881 census.

Though Hackworth's original Soho Works was in decline and close to closing, labour at the Shildon Works was still very much in demand. The entrance to this site was just at the end of the street, a very short walk for Tom and his father. He'd have grown up hearing its clank and clatter daily, and heard endless tales of what happened there from the men around him. He might even have watched the activity there from the outskirts feeling a certain sense of inevitability. Whether Tom had a mechanical, or engineering, mind is uncertain. One thing we do know from records held at the National Archives is that in 1876, when Thomas would have been around fifteen years old, he and brother Frank joined the local Mechanics Institute. Frank joined in April, paying the subscription fee for the quarter of nine pence. Thomas joined in May. Both renewed their membership for the quarter in July of that year, but afterwards, let their membership lapse. Neither re-joined. Their grandfather Francis, recorded in the membership book as Frank, had been a member from 1871 to 1872, but he too allowed his membership to lapse. These brief periods of membership may have been as part of a quest for basic engineering knowledge as the Institute served an educational purpose, but may just as equally have been with a view to accessing some of the other facilities on offer.

The Gala

The year 1871 brought a number of changes politically and culturally that would lead to the inauguration of an annual event that would, over the years that followed, prove to provide influence and inspiration to George Allan. It would also become a ritual occasion of tremendous importance to the working communities of County Durham, and a key dates in the calendar for members of the brass bands in the region to this day. It was the the year that saw the passing of the Trade Union Act, which gave legal status to the unions representing bodies of workers. Unwilling to relinquish too much influence to workers the then Liberal government tempered this recognition of the right to join a Union with a Criminal Law Amendment Act that made picketing punishable by imprisonment.

The coal mining communities of the North East of England had long been discontent with their treatment and conditions, not least of which was the binding ties between the worker and the colliery that employed them that prevented miners from moving to where more favourable pay and conditions might be offered. Non-compliance with a coal owner's terms of employment would sometimes result in intervention by units of the military. From the mid 19th Century activists had travelled the villages building support for a county-wide union of mine workers. Earlier attempts at a union had been made but had been quickly stifled. The Durham Miners Association had been formed in 1869 and initially grew to comprise of around four thousand members, though confidence quickly waned with the membership. By 1871, with the passing of the Trade Unions Act, there was now a growing genuine belief that a Union could survive and was the only path that would lead to genuine change. To promote this end, word was communicated out to the men of the mining communities of County Durham to convene in Durham City on 12 August.

Early that morning, miners and their families, on foot or in carts, tramped along the narrow roads from their villages toward Durham. The folk of Durham itself were alarmed, for they were of different ilk to these sinewy mining men. Across the city there was a pervading fear of rioting. As people arrived at the gathering on the field at Wharton Park the event began as something akin to a country fair, and as was becoming the tradition with such gatherings, arrangements had been made for sporting and athletic competition, and of course a band competition. In the afternoon though, the proceedings turned to political speeches with spokesmen presenting appeals to miners to agitate for the passing of a Mines Inspection Bill through parliament and condemnation for the Criminal Law Amendment of that year.

This formation of the Durham Miners Association, in part through the demonstration of strength exposed through the success of that first Gala yielded results. The following year, the Durham Coal Owners Association met the Miners Association and agreed to end the bonding of miners to collieries and pits.

For George though, what mattered was an aspect that had been something of a sideshow at the 1871 Gala but developed by the same time the following year to becoming one of the most notable features of the annual Gala demonstration. When the miners of each pit or colliery in County Durham arrived in Durham City on 15 June 1872 there was a new pride on display in the manner of their arrival. They marched through the city from various directions in columns headed not only by their brightly coloured banners, featuring mottos from religion and heroes and slogans of the union movement, but also each had a brass band. According to a report printed in the Northern Echo, seventy brass bands took part in the Gala that year, all playing rousing marches in a manner for which the occasion is still famed today. Almost a hundred and fifty years since that Gala the idea of the Big Meeting without the sound of brass music is simply inconceivable. The city would have been alive with colour and music in a spectacle the like of which may never have been experienced before. Just as now, the bands and procession would pass by the balcony of the County Hotel on their way to the racecourse where the meeting was held.

For anyone with an interest in brass band music, Gala day would become a rare opportunity to take in so much brass music in one sitting, and even today the sound of it evokes that real sense of the hope, solidarity and aspiration of the Durham Miners that it can cause surprisingly emotional reactions. In an age without television or radio and without recorded music being commonplace, this would be an incomparable opportunity to hear the music the bands were playing. Marches old and new, great or simply beloved, would reverberate through the tall narrow streets giving new rhythm to the step of pitmen's boots. From a good vantage point it would be the best place in the world for a common civilian to hear new marches and get a feel for what made the best marching music.

In the years that followed, George Allan would become most famed for his mastery of the march format. Though he would of course create many other pieces in various dance formats as well as more complex selections and overtures, there is a quality to his marches that transcend his attempts at the other formats and could only be born of a deep love and understanding of what makes a great march piece.

We have one piece of information passed on that elaborates on the emotional connection that George made with the Miners Gala. As we mentioned before, the historian and one-time bandsman, Bob Wray, seeking to find out more about George from any surviving peers, entered into a series of exchanged letters with Mr Jack Kitching, the former Shildon bandsman. Jack recalled for Bob that George would sit at the entrance to the field where the gala was hosted and listen to each band in turn march in. The overall effect would, it was said, inspire him to write another new march for the following year's Gala. We don't know when George attended the Miner's Gala for the first time. It would be nice to imagine that as a lad he'd have been there in 1872, though it's more likely that he was not and that his first Gala would have been as a bandsman a few years later. Both New Shildon bands were usually engaged to accompany their banner by one of the collieries in the vicinity. There are few clues to confirm the place and value of the Gala in the mind of George Allan but there are items in his catalogue of compositions that are reminiscent of Gala day, such as the march entitled "With the Banner."

The ability, and desire, to compose and arrange music was something that George and Tom had in common from early adulthood if not before. For the greater majority of bandsmen the skill to be able to interpret their own part in an arrangement and play it competently under the direction of the conductor was sufficient a challenge to satisfy their ambitions: for these two lads it was not enough. The two boys must have realised, or been advised of, the importance of capturing their compositions so that they could be shared. I'd expect as well that some tutoring or mentoring in composition must at some point have been provided, though if so it is unclear whom by and when. Maybe Tom's grandfather, Francis, had told stories of Robert De Lacy, his time with the Saxhorn Band, and how he had progressed to establish a shop in London and found a band journal that included his own compositions. We don't know whether De Lacy and Francis Dinsdale stayed in touch at all, but his band journal was widely advertised and available.

Evidence suggests that Tom was the first of the two to achieve a published composition. Being around a year and a half older than George he was always the first to reach all the milestones through their musical careers. According to the account of Tom's life produced by his grandson Eric, he composed his first published contest march "The Typhoon" at age of seventeen years old. It's hard to prove exactly when his composing activity truly started without a dated manuscript, but this certainly seems plausible. The early unpublished compositions of students of music would have been handwritten and in this case have not survived to the best of our knowledge. We do, however, know something of "The Typhoon" and can place it's publication within an approximate time-window. Whether the published version of "The Typhoon" is as Tom first produced it as a teenager, or whether he evolved and refined it, we'll never know.

Above: Soprano Cornet part from Tom Bulch's first published composition, "The Typhoon."

For a first published march though, and a 'contest march' at that, it is a very fine effort indeed and was deemed good enough for bands in Britain and Australia to still be playing it at concerts over thirty-five years later. It's first reported appearance was in September of 1883, where it was played by Tom's own New Shildon Temperance Band, and at that time Tom would have been twenty-one years old. The following year we see that it had been played by both the Band of the 2nd Durham Artillery Old Battery on the band of the River Wear and the Sunderland Constabulary Band as part of a programme of music rendered in that city's Roker Park.

How did these bands come to possess, and ultimately perform Tom's march? Simply by purchasing or subscribing to the "Amateur Brass (and Military) Band Journal." Bands commonly acquired music through such serialised journals, as we have already observed. There were publishers in various parts of the country. The above journal was published by T. A. Haigh of Hull, was well distributed and became very popular from the late 1870s onwards.

Thomas Albert Haigh, an interesting figure in his own right and influential in this story, had been born on 19 November 1843 at Uppermill, Saddleworth, Greater Manchester, an appropriate location for a publisher of brass music as by the mid 1880s Saddleworth would became one of the centres for the now famed Whit Friday Band Contests. Uppermill held its first Whit Friday Band Contest on 6 June 1884. He was married in 1873, at the parish church in nearby Dobcross, to Irish born Ellen Stephens, the daughter of a shoemaker. At that time he had been working as a warden at an asylum. By the time of the 1881 census, the Haighs had installed themselves at a new home at number 1 Cranbourne Villa, Newington in the borough of Hull, and Thomas Haigh had set up business as a music publisher. He was a bandsman, contest adjudicator, composer and arranger in his own right, though not prolific in the latter two it would seem. His publishing interests extended beyond brass and military style music as he also created a journal for string bands and another for fife and drum ensembles. Haigh started publishing his 'Amateur Brass and Military Band Journal' somewhere between 1877 and 1879, and it went on to regularly include pieces by many of the principal brass composers of the era including William Rimmer, James Ord Hume and Edwin Swift; all of whom remain familiar to bandsmen of all ages today.

Haigh would also became a high ranking Freemason and an examiner for the Tonic Sol-Fa College, being by reputation a good singer in his own right. It's remotely possible therefore that Tom and George may have become acquainted with him through their singing studies as much as their brass band involvements. It's more likely that Tom would have seen the Haigh's journal at band rehearsal and submitted his own piece for consideration to the publisher's address that was printed conveniently and prominently on every sheet of the journal. Having received Tom's manuscript for "The Typhoon," Haigh was sufficiently impressed to publish it as piece number 263 in his journal. Tracing the serial numbering of published pieces back from later ones we've been able to date and using the frequency of the journal we can approximately place publication of the piece to somewhere between 1880 and 1881.

That both Tom and George were published by the same music publisher raises interesting, but probably unanswerable, questions as to how or why. For example, did Tom introduce George to Haigh in some way, or suggest that George contact Haigh? Or did George see Tom's success in being published and think to try to emulate the same approach? The nature of how connections were made is a tantalising mystery.

George Allan, yet to attain the achievement of having become a published composer, continuing his musical development under the tutelage of Francis Dinsdale, moved seats within the Saxhorn Band, to become solo cornet player. It's likely that he took up the cornet rather than tenor horn some time before this, but also possible that this opportunity may not have arisen had so many members of the band not left to start up the Temperance Band.

In the brief biography we mentioned previously which appeared in The Cornet in 1896 it is explained how his early musical influences had included the romantic church music of Sir John Stainer. There is an interesting coincidence in this statement which is that the former Shildon bandmaster Robert de Lacy, with his reportedly fine bass voice, was at that time one of the twelve Vicars Choral at St Paul's Cathedral where Stainer was the resident organist. George also professed his admiration for the work of the Italian born British pianist and composer Muzio Clementi.

George's early compositions would probably also have been shaped by the musical choices and tastes of Francis Dinsdale as his bandmaster, and those composers emerging specifically to create secular music for the growing brass band scene. Tom and George as two composers navigating music in an era before the availability of recorded music or radio, would be strictly limited to knowledge of music which they had the opportunity to see performed directly.

Emigration of the Malthouse Family

From about 1878 Tom Bulch and George Allan, as we now know, no longer played alongside each other as they had in the Juvenile Band but had become members of separate brass bands. George kept allegiance with Francis Dinsdale's New Shildon Saxhorn Band and Tom was part of the group that broke away to become his uncle Edward Dinsdale's New Shildon Temperance Band.

There were others in that new band that were family members and friends with whom he had graduated from the ranks of his uncle's Juvenile Band. Of Tom's brothers, we know that older brother Francis, or 'Frank,' was a bandsman and one newspaper report also names a "J Bulch" which may have been John or Jeremiah, as a euphonium player. It's possible that other brothers may have been involved. As these latter brothers were younger than Tom it's possible that they might not have graduated from the Juvenile Band until later.

Tom also had friends from his peer group in the new Temperance band. These included Samuel Lewins, James Scarff, Joseph Garbutt and John Malthouse with whom, later evidence suggests, Tom appears to have been particularly close. John was one of four brothers, all of whom had learned to play a brass instrument under the Edward Dinsdale's tutelage. Other Malthouse brothers involved were Thomas, Robert and George. It would be John, however, who would prove to have a persuasive influence on the path Thomas Edward Bulch would follow.

John had been born in April 1860 and was ten months old by the time of the 1861 census, making him over a year older than Tom Bulch. His parents, George Malthouse, born in 1839 and Ann (née Applegarth), three years her husband's junior, were married at St Michael's Church, in Heighington, a village not far from Shildon, on 29 October 1859. George, the son of a family of farm labourers with roots in Yorkshire, was born at Aycliffe, and after his rudimentary education had learned the skills of boilersmithing in the railway engineering industry, and hence was drawn to New Shildon. Ann was a native of Heighington, which was perhaps why the couple had married there. Robert Malthouse followed John into the world in 1861, then Thomas in 1863, George in 1864, William in 1866 and a sister, Jane Ann in

1867. The older lads were very much contemporaries of both Tom Bulch and George Allan. All would have been educated together at the small British School on Station Street. As infants they probably made up games together in the shadows of the two rail works in the town or the steam mill that ground corn to feed townspeople, the gas works, the reservoir, the brick and tile works or the fringes of building sites that supplied building materials as street after street was built to accommodate more workers and their families.

Above: Alma Road, New Shildon, where the the young bandsmen of the Malthouse family once lived.

As was so often the case in that period of our past, the Malthouse family was fragile. Three of the children died before reaching adolescence. Robert, William and Jane Ann all passing away in 1868. A further baby son, Robert William, joined the family in 1869 before George Malthouse senior died on 31 October 1870 leaving Ann a widow with four sons to raise. The family had lived in Alma Road, but by In 1871 had moved to Soho Street and widowed Ann tried to provide for her children by taking in lodgers and selling toys and sweets. Taking in lodgers, where space permitted, was common practice and not difficult as the demand for labour locally outstripped the availability of accommodation. Most houses in the small clutch of streets sitting between the town's twin railway works were small and overcrowded. It would have been a difficult existence.

By the time of the 1871 census one of Ann's sons, George, was no longer living at New Shildon with his brothers but instead, aged only six, was living away from the family as a lodger at Great Lumley with the family of John Cowens, a farmer who also ran the Wheatsheaf public house. It's not at all clear why. Perhaps some arrangement had been made to enable Ann to have the space she needed to take in a paying lodger. It must have been a difficult decision for Ann to separate this one child from the family, and it may possibly have made an impression on the lad and been a contributing factor towards why, in later years, George Malthouse led a troubled life. We'll return to that later.

On 26 April 1873, Ann Malthouse married again, to John Abdale Gascoigne at the still relatively new All Saints Church in New Shildon. John thus became a step-father to the surviving Malthouse boys. John, a general labourer, had been born in the nearby market town of Darlington and had come to New Shildon after a spell of time working in the rural town of Wolsingham, in Weardale. His mother, like Ann, was a widow too. He initially lodged on Railway Terrace with his sister Hannah who had married Joseph Fleming, an engine driver. All four of the Malthouse lads were young bandsmen. The band, most probably funded through donations, entry charges at concerts and perhaps some sponsorship from the railway company, was an opportunity open to even the boys from the poor families. It was with John Malthouse, however, that the young Tom Bulch built up a particular camaraderie throughout this childhood.

In June 1879, the Malthouse family made a decision that would interrupt that friendship. Finding life in Shildon difficult, they decided to seek their fortune in the Australian territories. There were opportunities to be had in that country, and the government of the day were keen to strengthen the British presence there. Whether the Malthouses were incentivised is unclear, though it would have cost a significant amount for the family of six to make the journey. On 30 June 1879, John Gascoigne, his wife and the four boys all travelled to London where they boarded a steamer 'City of London' as steerage passengers to travel to Australia via Plymouth and St Vincent.

The 'City of London' had been built in 1863 to be operated by the Inman Fleet as part of the Liverpool and Philadelphia

Steamship Company transporting passengers to the United States. From 1853, this company had been the first to offer transport to steerage passengers at a cheaper rate, though such passengers were expected to take their own food for the journey. Steerage passengers gradually made up eighty percent of the Inman line's custom. After a decade and a half in the service of the Inman Line she was sold, in 1878, to William Ross and Company and fitted with new steam engines. This sale led to being repurposed to transporting passengers and cattle to and from the US and Australia. Whilst trying to imagine what such a long-haul ocean crossing might be like, I came across a report on The City of London arriving into New York in the year it was launched which describes the vessel in excellent detail:

> "She is constructed on the most approved principles, with all the recent improvements as to both build and machinery, measuring 355 feet in length on deck, by a breadth of 40 feet 4 inches in beam, with a depth of 26 feet. She is about 2,466 tons gross measurement, and is 1,678 tons register, and is propelled by an engine, of 550 horse power, which can be worked up to 1,500.
> The motive steam is raised by four boilers, heated by twenty furnaces, fitted athwart-ships from the centre, the furnace and engine-rooms being kept cool and sweet by an admirable system of ventilation. It is calculated that these twenty furnaces will consume about sixty tons of coal per day, by which agency it expected that the vessel will attain a speed of about fourteen knots an hour.
>
> The City of London is very strongly framed, and is divided into six water-tight compartments by five strong iron bulkheads, which extend from the keel up to the upper deck, thus receiving great additional strength, and being secured in a high degree from dangerous accident from either water or fire. She is further strengthened by steel water-tight deck stringers, which extend in breadth from the bulwarks to the house on deck, throughout the whole length of the vessel; and besides this security, still greater firmness and tension are insured by her sheen strake being of double steel plates from stem to stern.
>
> Besides her powerful propelling machinery, she is also fully equipped as a sailing vessel, having three tall masts, is ship-rigged, carrying large square as well as fore and aft sails. On deck she has a wide and lofty house, which extends from the stem right aft to the stern, the roof of which forms a spacious and magnificent promenade deck. To the extreme aft of this is

the wheel-house. Immediately in front of the wheel-house are the Captain's cabin and first officer's room, and between the officer's rooms and the engine-room is the saloon or main cabin, an exceedingly elegant and beautiful apartment, sixty feet long by eighteen feet wide, very fully lighted and ventilated by side lights, and fitted up in a style of luxurious and tasteful elegance.

Directly forward of the saloon are the steward's pantry and bar, which are furnished with a profusion of elegant and beautiful silver-plate, porcelain and crystal. The staterooms for the saloon passengers, 52 in number, capable of accommodating 120 passengers, are under the main-deck – spacious, well lighted, and, like every other portion of the vessel, most carefully ventilated, by side openings and air shafts. The portion on this deck, forward from the engine-room, is devoted to sleeping apartments and mess-rooms for the second and third class passengers. These apartments also are well lighted and admirably ventilated. The closet and other sanitary appliances of the ship are ample and complete.

The ship is supplied with eight life and other boats, two very large ones being fitted with Clifford's lowering apparatus. She has also numerous life-buoys and apparatus for preventing and extinguishing fires."

She sounds a rather grand vessel, though it would be fair to say that the four-hundred-and-fifty third class 'steerage' passengers of which the Malthouses were part would have experienced little of ships finer points during their fifty-four days on board. When the ship finally did arrive at Melbourne, at around midnight on the 23 August after what was reportedly an agreeable passage, passengers were quarantined for a period, during which a number of cases of measles broke out. The City of London, however did not stay in Melbourne but moved on to the terminal point for the voyage which was the port of Sydney to the east in the territory of New South Wales. An interesting detail at this point is that around two years later in November of 1881, the City of London disappeared at sea along with forty-one people, whilst making a return passage to London. It's clear that, even in the steam powered age, with all the technological advances it brought, such long journeys by sea still involved an element of risk to life.

The family endeavoured to set up a home in the Allandale district close to Creswick in the Victorian goldfields north of the city of Ballarat. Though the industry that had caused these gold-mining towns and villages be built differed to the that which had similarly caused the birth of New Shildon, bringing the relatively new and growing communities together presented similar challenges and perhaps unsurprisingly ideas from the mother country re-emerged in Australia. This included the notion of forming brass and military bands. The Malthouse lads weren't the only musicians in the district and were able to maintain their interest in brass band music. In the handful of years following their arrival, a brass band seems to have sprung up centred around Allandale, increasing is size to nineteen players by September 1883. By the time John Malthouse was twenty-four years old he had become its bandmaster.

1881

By the time of the 1881 census, taken when Tom Bulch was eighteen years old, the family had moved to 40 Adelaide Street, New Shildon. Thomas senior and his wife Margaret had been joined by five more children: Christopher, Sarah, Minnie, Ada and six-month-old infant Frederick. Of these Minnie had been born with a twin sister Melinda who had not survived infancy. When you look at the terraced houses today in the short stretch of Adelaide Street that remains un-demolished since those days it's hard to imagine how a family of fourteen people aged between six months and forty five years could peacefully coexist within. All the more so when you imagine most of them being at different stages of learning or practicing a musical instrument. Though participation in the brass band was a boys only activity, there was nothing to prevent the girls from learning to play or sing at home. The houses consisted of two rooms on the ground floor and two rooms for sleeping on the upper. Front doors opened directly into the pavement outside, and to the rear of most properties was a small yard for storing coal, washing and drying laundry in warmer months and importantly an outside toilet often referred to as a 'netty' which would be used not only as a lavatory but also a place to dispose of ash from the coal fires which not only heated the home but were also a source of heat for cooking. Bathing, where possible, was done in conditions that offered little privacy.

At times it was most likely as far from a being a peaceful setting as you could imagine. If you were to apply the thinking of early twenty-first century social standards to the situation, you might have considered the Bulch family to be 'neighbours from hell'. These were very different times. Not, it's important to understand, that the families might not have chosen more spacious accommodation had they been able. However when building houses for workers in industrial communities the owners and builders had little intention beyond providing basic space and function. Families therefore, and particularly large ones like the Bulches, were close. Privacy would have been a fleeting luxury, and beds crowded. Neighbours too were generally closer and likely to have an 'open door' policy where each freely visited the others houses with little formality applied. High infant mortality, questionable life expectancy, and limited availability of birth control were certainly factors and in an age without a welfare state and where life was hard and work took its toll on the body, it's easy to see how having a large family to fall back upon in later life might be an insurance policy of sorts for a married couple.

In this environment young Tom would, we are informed by his grandson, not only learn to play and understand every instrument in the brass band but also piano and violin. He would also sing and had a reputation within the family of being a very good whistler. For younger members of the family a crowded home might have seemed normal, even fun. For the adults and teenagers it was probably an impractical and stressful space to be at times.

In the summer of 1878 Tom's older sister Mary Jane had married William Summerbell of Richmond so had already moved out from the family home to live with her new husband and start a family of her own, having had two young children already. As for Tom the limitations of an apprentice's wage would mean that he'd need to stay at home a little longer. The long working days of the industrial Victorian era would afford him little time to spend on musical compositions, or with the Temperance Band but despite this, as a determined lad he did find that time. This may even have been a factor in his choice to adopt the Temperance Pledge seeing time spent drinking in the public houses of Shildon as just another barrier to his art. When he did have time to give to furthering his music it's possible that being part of a musical family to interact with may have helped. 1879 brought the death of Tom's paternal grandfather, Jeremiah Bulch who passed away on the 10 August at his home on North Road, Darlington.

While the Bulch family had moved to Adelaide Street during the 1870s, the Allans had moved away from there to 23 Redworth Road, a newer street that was part of the town's eastward expansion. The move would have taken them closer to All Saints Church with which the family had some associations. By 1880, George's father, John James Allan, had become one of the two churchwardens there; a part-time volunteer role taking responsibility to assist the clergy in the upkeep of the parish. As with the Bulches, the Allans had expanded to a family of eight; William, George and James having been joined by John Henry, in 1873, Ada, in 1875 and Ralph in 1879. George's older brother William had followed his father into the family trade of tailoring, while George, old enough to work, had found basic employment as a labourer. Though George was comfortable with manual and physical work he, like Tom, had an inquisitive mind and some intelligence. In January of 1881, George Allan became a member of the Mechanics Institute, which was based in a building just across the road from Tom and George's old school on Station Street.

The Mechanic's Institute had been founded in 1833, initially as a "Society for the Promotion of Useful Knowledge" by the Stockton and Darlington Railway company. This was during the era of Timothy Hackworth's influence as the manager of railway manufacturing at Shildon, and as such it also holds the distinction of being the world's first such institution founded in connection to the railways. Hackworth and his colleagues saw it as as a means of stimulating and cultivating a high quality workforce through education and opportunity. Starting life as little more than an idea and a shelf of books, this Institute had over time occupied a number of locations in various buildings around the town until a bespoke building was built to house it by the railway company, in 1860. The Institute's record books show that the first caretaker, following completion, was Tom Bulch's grandfather, briefly mentioned above, who at that time lived in the house adjacent. This new and attractive facility contained reading rooms for which a library of over two thousand books had been acquired by 1890. It also featured a lecture theatre to seat 400, a recreation room and billiard room as well as a stock of magazines and newspapers of the day to which the Institute had subscribed. These included journals in engineering, politics and also the Musical Times which may have attracted George's attention. The Institute wasn't solely there to enrich mechanical and technical understanding. It was used to nurture cultural interests too, having an Institute band and science and art departments as well as clubs participating in various games and pastimes. Membership of the Institute also enabled participation in occasional excursions, events, lectures and galas onsite and offsite. There was a wealth of opportunity to feed a curious mind as Tom Bulch and his brother Frank had also discovered back in 1876. Francis Dinsdale had also been a member, as was William Dodds, the choirmaster who had encouraged George to explore brass music. The Institute's half-yearly report book tells how Francis and the New Shildon Saxhorn Band would perform at the organisation's occasional entertainments as well as at the 'penny reading' sessions held in the early years of the new building. Dodds remained a member for many years, with the Institute acquiring insurance through his services, so either of these men may have influenced George's decision to become involved. So far as we can tell from the Institute's membership record books, neither George's father or older brothers joined. A subscription to the Mechanic's Institute cost nine pence per quarter-year when George joined, and considering he would only have been about seventeen at the time it's probable that this fee may have been paid from the wages of his first labouring job. He remained a member for many years thereafter, though his membership was not always continuous. There were perhaps times when it was necessary for him to prioritise paying other costs over paying his Institute membership fee.

The two ideologically split brass bands of New Shildon, though connected by the DNA of a single family, were now operating separately to one another. The comparatively new Temperance Band, with a point to prove about the advantages of abstinence, worked hard to improve upon, and supplant, the more established Saxhorn Band as the darlings of their community. For their endeavours, they were rewarded with offers of engagements and put themselves forward for contests. They were also doing so without their founder, and original tutor and mentor. Edward Dinsdale, was no longer living in New Shildon by the time of the 1881 census. He, and wife Mary Ann, whom he married in 1868 when they were both eighteen years old, had moved their home to Farrer Street in Stockton, toward the opposite end of the former Stockton and Darlington Railway route, where Edward had secured employment as a boilermaker.

His successor for the post of bandmaster was Tom Bulch. Despite his youth the young man had probably been groomed and trained for this moment, and with the reputation of being an aspiring composer of brass music, he was probably the most natural fit to assume the role. In spite of the Temperance Band having taken the moral high-ground over abstinence from alcohol and its improving effect on conduct in daily life, things didn't always go smoothly for the band. The band had entered a contest at Loftus in Cleveland that was scheduled to occur on Thursday 23 June 1881. They were reported afterwards as absent from the contest not having been able to attend. Whether that was as a consequence of being unable to raise the funds for the whole band to make the journey by train, or that too many of the members were unavailable owing to having to spend that day working, is unclear.

On Saturday, 20 August of that same year however, a contest took place that these young men of limited means could not possibly have defaulted on. It was a band contest held in conjunction with the thirteenth annual Shildon Show. The show was described by the Northern Echo as "the largest, most popular, and most representative of its kind in the North," and conveniently being located right on his doorstep its band contest offered an tremendous opportunity for Tom to prove his prowess as a master of the town's premier brass band. Under pleasant weather conditions the specially arranged excursion trains from all quarters of the region arrived at New Shildon's station, which was much maligned in its way for its inconvenience of location as being set away from the town. Even on this occasion the Northern Echo could not help to offer a dig, sparing two words to describe the station as "somewhat uninteresting." Visitors progressed from there to the grounds of the vicarage, taking in the spectacle en-route, which the same newspaper described thus:

> "The town itself, even to the church tower, was festive with bunting; some hundreds of stalls and tents, reminding one of the departed glories of Bartlemy Fair, were pitched outside the show in much admired disorder; whilst shooting ranges, swings, steam roundabouts and shows, from which the noise of rival barrel organs, cymbals and drums was simply indescribable. If

there was a fault - though we can hardly apply such a word here - it was that the attractions were too numerous."

The interesting mention of "Bartlemy Fair" was a reference to an annual fair, once notorious for its excess, held at St Bartholomew's Priory, Smithfield on the feast of St Bartholomew, August 24th. Hugely popular since the middle ages, the potency of that fair was gradually eroded by the Victorian morality of the authorities until its eventual extinction by the 1850s. Contests in most skills imaginable were on display: baking, drawing and painting, model making, smith-work, rug making, tapestry, engineering, needlework and penmanship among them, not to mention a vast array of horticultural classes and livestock. At the centre of this show-field stood a large platform on which the band contest, as a centrepiece to the occasion, was to be played out. The famed Charles Godfrey junior of Her Majesty's Horse Guards, son of the legendary Coldstream Guards bandmaster by the same name, was present to act as adjudicator and the generous prizes on offer had attracted three of the cream of Yorkshire's bands: Meltham Mills, Black Dyke and Linthwaite, to compete against the New Shildon Temperance Band and Blair and Company's Engine Works's Band of Stockton. Even in those days the Black Dyke Band and their ilk were considered to be among the best brass bands going, so there was something of the 'David and Goliath' about this contest. This does also tell us something as to how important Shildon Show was regarded at that time: a significant event on the region's show calendar, being hosted in one of the North's prospering industrial towns, sufficient to draw in large crowds and top class entertainment. Though the press reports do not confirm this, barring the possibility that Edward Dinsdale returned for the occasion the New Shildon Temperance Band were most probably conducted by Tom as their new bandmaster. At the announcement of the results they had been placed fifth after the Meltham Mills, Black Dyke, Blair's and Linthwaite bands in that order. Undeterred the young local band played a programme of music to entertain the attendees for the remainder of the evening. The Saxhorn Band were not present, though it's likely its members attended the show individually to enjoy the spectacle, and perhaps observe the band contest itself with more than a little envy.

1882

In fact there are few reports of activity of the New Shildon Saxhorn Band during the first years of the Eighteen-eighties. It's not clear whether the function of the band was affected in any way by the split of bandsmen into two groups: for example whether more bandsmen joined the Temperance Band leaving the other short handed. One occasion in the Northern Echo appears in April of 1882 wherein:

> "The brethren of the Rose of Sharon Lodge of the United Order of Oddfellows paraded the principal streets of the Shildons accompanied by the New Shildon Saxhorn Band, they afterwards dined at the Dun Cow Inn, Old Shildon."

In June of that year, the Newcastle Courant reports on the New Shildon Temperance Band's appearance at the grand band contest at the Newcastle Temperance Festival on the Town Moor. On this particular occasion it is documented that they competed under the baton of Tom Bulch, and had entered in two classes of the four available. Once again the band found itself under the scrutiny of Charles Godfrey junior as one of the 'go to' senior band contest adjudicators of his generation. Class 1 of this contest invited Temperance Bands of Northumberland and Durham to compete, and Class 2 was specifically restricted to Local Temperance bands. In that first class, the New Shildon band failed to impress and didn't feature in the the top placings. Their points total placed them fifth, behind the band of the 7th Lancashire Rifle Volunteers, Blackhill Teetotal, Boarshurst and Blair & Co Engine Works of Stockton. In the class Class 2 contest, though, New Shildon Temperance did better and finished second to the Blackhill band beating five other competing bands. The band returned home with a prize of five pounds, which doesn't look to be a great amount of money if you look at it as what five pounds are worth today, but in terms of comparative purchasing power that amount might have bought, in 1882, roughly the same as you would get for about four hundred and twenty-five pounds in 2018. This would represent a tremendous first contest success for the New Shildon bandsmen, away from home and at a 'respectable' contest. A fine result in what would be a relatively successful year for the Temperance Band.

At the end of July 1882, we learn from the Durham County Advertiser that a South Durham Colliery Sports event was held at a field near Eldon Colliery westward and downhill from Old Shildon. This festivity brought together amateur sportsmen from the community around the South Durham Colliery to compete against each other for honours and to engage socially. What's interesting to us is that both the New Shildon Saxhorn Band and the New Shildon Temperance Band were engaged. Though not a contest, you can imagine that this would be an opportunity for the two bands to test their mettle against each other, particularly as both bands were entered into the band contest at Shildon Show the following month. There is a slight implication that as both had been engaged for the day's revelries that any rivalry between the bands may well have been amicable. For the sake of the family ties involved: the two bandmasters being grandfather and grandson, we would hope so. The day started well enough with fair weather for the sporting events which included a cricket match between the South Durham Cricket Club and eleven members of the New Shildon Saxhorn Band, which could have included George Allan though newspaper reports don't confirm it. As the event went on it was reportedly disrupted by torrents of rain. Both bands remained undeterred from entertaining the miners and the families and each of them played a choice selection of music.

It would not be long before the two bands turned out alongside each other again. 19 August 1882 saw these two bands go head to head, in front of a large audience sprinkled liberally with friends and family members. This time the two groups of bandsmen were part of a broader field of competing bands at the Vicarage grounds for what was to be the fourteenth annual Shildon Show. In such a setting and with high expectations, which band would leave with the local honours? Unlike the previous year's contest which pitted the Temperance Band against a cluster of the North's strongest brass bands, the organisers had either recognised the need to, or been advised to, make new arrangements for the sake of fairness. The applications from competing bands were, therefore, split the into two classes grouping bands of more comparable ability. Both New Shildon Saxhorn and New Shildon Temperance had entered the second class contest. Once again, Charles Godfrey junior had been engaged to act as judge, and having recently impressed him at the Temperance Festival in Newcastle, New

Shildon Temperance would surely have relished the chance to do so again. Unfortunately, by the time the Class 2 contest commenced Godfrey had not arrived, so Edwin Swift, with sound reputation as current conductor of the Linthwaite Band was drafted as a replacement. At the conclusion of the contest, after each band had played the test pieces and the points earned had been announced, the New Shildon Temperance Band were placed second, behind Whitworth. This achievement earned them a prize purse of ten pounds: a sum roughly equivalent to winning eight hundred and fifty pounds at the time of my writing this account and might perhaps be put to use replacing uniforms, broken instruments or improving the band's facilities in some other way.

The New Shildon Saxhorn Band, with George Allan in its ranks and performing under the baton of Tom Bulch's grandfather, finished fifth behind all the other bands. They had been fairly and squarely bested in front of their friends, relatives and neighbours. This made it a good day for the advocates of abstinence from alcohol, reinforcing their worldview that succumbing to the temptation to partake of the 'demon drink' impairs the capability of the individual. For Francis Dinsdale, New Shildon's grand old bandmaster, it must have been a bittersweet moment. He might surely have felt disappointment at having his Saxhorn Band bested by the young upstarts his son Edward had tutored and developed, but also an element of pride in how his young grandson was growing in capability. The musical legacy of his family looked safe in this young man's hands.

Of course brass and military bands did not exist solely to compete against each other for money. In the Victorian era no public event would be complete without music for the people, and the bands would be engaged to add that touch of magic to a diverse variety of gatherings. Some, like the horticultural shows and sports days were commonplace and repeated annually. Other treats were of a more unusual and bespoke nature and, given the imaginative creativity and eccentricity of the era, may never have been seen before, or since. In the September of 1882, the New Shildon Temperance Band were engaged to entertain at an odd and distinctly visual spectacle described in some detail in the Newcastle Journal of Friday, 8 September 1882 as follows:

"NOVEL GAME CHESS AT HEIGHINGTON. The Vicar of Heighington (the Rev C C Chevalier) hit upon novel mode of affording public entertainment and at the same time raising to provide bells for the parish church, by arranging for a game chess to be played in Redworth Park by living players who were dressed to represent the different pieces on the chess board.

The day was extremely fine and a large and fashionable company was yesterday attracted from Darlington, Bishop Auckland; and other parts of the district. A tent had been erected providing refreshments, while the New Shildon Temperance Band played selections during the day.

The novel chess game, though played some years ago, it is stated, at Perth in the same manner, is quite new in this country, the only approach to it at all being that a game played by living players some years since in a Durham drawing room. From this the enterprising vicar, the Rev C C Chevalier took the idea which he embodied so successfully on Thursday by the aid of his parishioners, who lent themselves to the representation, and allowed themselves to be dressed in the most fantastic guise.

The game did not commence till nearly half-past four o'clock. There was a considerable space of green-sward roped off in the Park, which was laid out in squares of grass, intersected with white material. The band escorted the opposing forces, who marched in procession and presented most picturesque appearance in their 15th century costume.

The prevailing colour of the the costume of the players one side was green intersected of course with varicoloured hats, streamers, &c., and on the other red. The pawns were dressed as pages of the the 15th century, with long pointed shoes and tights. The castles were imitations of the castles known in chess, consisting of canvas in which four young ladies were enveloped. The bishops appeared in bishops' costumes, those red being the cardinals.

In the drawings for the costumes the Rev C C Chevalier was assisted by Mr Etton, of the Darlington School of Art, and Mr Thompson. The coup d'oeul of the knights with the helmets and spears, the bishops and cardinals with their wands of office, and the highly coloured dresses, had quite a spectacular effect, and carried the mind back to scenes of the long ago.

The two gentlemen who directed the players were the Rev C C Chevalier and Mr Johnson of the Heighington School. The moves were faultlessly made, showing that the players had been well drilled. Afterwards, an impromptu game was undertaken between the Rev W H G Stephens and the Rev H Spurrier. Worthy of note that the existing bells of the parish church are years old, being of the date 1430. They require repair, and besides this money is required to hang the three new bells presented by Mr H. E. Surtees, Mrs Tyzack and Miss Hodgson. To-day there will be continuation of the proceedings."

This description surely offers the kind of eccentricity we typically associate with the Victorian era. Echoes of this news story appeared in various papers across England and Scotland: the Yorkshire Gazette, Bury and Norwich Post, Berkshire Chronicle and Manchester Evening News to name but a few.
The Northern Echo also made mention of the New Shildon Temperance Band's services being employed as well as naming several notable persons present on the day including Mr T Fry MP and his wife. The newspaper, clearly tickled, suggested a repeat of the event, but relocated to Darlington Cricket Field.
When the contest was re-staged again the following day the attendance was much reduced, the novelty of the moment having worn off. As it happens the Heighington chess players did continue with their sport and in the following year made an appearance in Durham on the grounds occupied by the Archery Club, though on that occasion the musical effect was provided by the band of the 4th Durham Light Infantry.

December 1882 created a new opportunity for George Allan. The North Eastern Railway company were hiring at their Shildon Works and, on the eighteenth, only a few days before Christmas, George was accepted onto the books as an apprentice. Though the wage of an apprentice was modest, it was a great step forward for him. The wages book from the NER Shildon Works, today held at the National Archives at Kew, explains the pay scale as set in 1879 for Apprentices at the works. Apprentices were taken on from the age of fourteen onwards, and an apprenticeship lasted seven years. The working week was fifty-three hours over six days which would be a time commitment that would leave little time for musical pursuits. This new commitment might also account also for why George's membership of the Mechanics Institute lapsed in 1883, after he fell nine pence in arrears. He would later rejoin.

Based on those 1879 rates, in the first year, an apprentice would earn eight pence per day or four shillings for the week. This rose to sixteen shillings a week by the end of the seventh year. Wages in most industries at the time, rose or fell on the say of the employing industry and their perception of their economic state and when George was apprenticed as a Blacksmith's Striker it was at a rate of three shillings and sixpence per week. Tom Bulch was already much further into his apprenticeship in the same department, so most probably earned more than this. The Blacksmith's Striker was an assistant, whose job was to swing a larger hammer, when required, in forging operations as directed by the Blacksmith. In practice, the blacksmith would use tongs to hold the hot iron at the anvil and show the striker where the iron is to be struck by tapping it with their smaller hammer. The striker would then provide the heavier blow with the sledgehammer. This was physical work in a hot environment. While it is pure conjecture to imagine this, it is very easy to imagine young George, and Thomas, creating tunes in their minds to accompany the rhythmic hammering in the forge.

Above: The blacksmith's forge at Shildon Railway Works where Tom was employed as apprentice blacksmith and George an apprentice blacksmith's striker.

In his fact-based novel for boys, published in 1871 and entitled "The Iron Horse: or Life on the Line," the author R M Ballantyne describes a tour of a railway works offered to one Mrs Marrot, a locomotive driver's wife, and her son Bob who, like George, was to enter service there. The tour includes an atmospheric vignette of the blacksmith's department which, though based upon the author's experiences at Swindon and Glasgow, would have been as true of the facility at Shildon's works as of any other:

> "Thus meditating, she was conducted into the smith's department. Here, about 140 forges and 400 men were at work. Any one of these forges would have been a respectable "smiddy" in a country village. They stood as close to each other as space would allow, so close that their showers of sparks intermingled, and kept the whole shed more or less in the condition of a chronic eruption of fireworks. To Bob's young mind it conveyed the idea of a perpetual keeping of the Queen's birthday. To his mother it was suggestive of singed garments and sudden loss of sight. The poor woman was much distressed in this department at first, but when she found, after five minutes or so, that her garments were unscathed and her sight still unimpaired she became reconciled to it.
>
> In this place of busy Vulcans – each of whom was the beau-ideal of "the village blacksmith" all the smaller work of the railway was done. As a specimen of this work, Will Garvey drew Mrs Marrot's attention to the fact that two Vulcans were engaged in twisting red-hot iron bolts an inch and a half thick into the form of hooks with as much apparent ease as if they had been hair-pins. These, he said, were hooks for couplings, the hooks by which railway carriages were attached together, and on the strength and unyielding rigidity of which the lives of hundreds of travellers might depend.
>
> The bending of them was accomplished by means of a powerful lever. It would be an endless business to detail all that was done in this workshop. Every piece of comparatively small iron-work used in the construction of railway engines, carriages, vans and trucks, from a door-hinge to a coupling chain, was forged in that smithy."

A little further on in the tour the group reach the truck and van department where the relevance of the work seen in the blacksmith's department becomes apparent.

> "Bob, whose mind was sharp as a needle, saw a good many pieces of mechanism, which formerly he had only seen in a transition state, now applied to their ultimate uses. The chiselled, sawn and drilled planks seen in the first department

were here being fitted and bolted together in the form of trucks, while the uses of many strange pieces of iron, which had puzzled him in the blacksmith's department, became obvious when fitted to their appropriate woodwork."

Though a principal purpose of the works was to create new wagons to enter service on the North Eastern Railway, much of the work at New Shildon was also to repair existing broken ones in order to extend their service life. It would seem a never-ending occupation. Whilst it is possible that George Allan and Thomas Bulch may have worked side by side in the blacksmith's shop of the railway works, we don't know that for certain. We do know that both were, for that brief time at least, employed in the Blacksmith's Department. We can be sure that throughout this and their involvement in the brass bands, they would have been very aware of each other whether as friends, workmates or competitive rivals.

As already explained, Shildon was once the site of two railway works sites, the Shildon Works itself and the earlier Soho Works where some of Hackworth's pioneering engineering and repairs for the Stockton and Darlington Railway had occurred. These were both in addition to a Locomotive Department where steam locomotives were stabled in a roundhouse for day to day operation. The smaller Soho Works was designated to be closed during 1883 just after George joined the company. The Shildon Works conversely was constantly expanding. Once also renowned for locomotive production, Shildon was now exclusively engaged in the fabrication and repair of the less glamorous but extremely important wagons used by the NER. If George hadn't already known it, he would soon discover that there were many different types of wagon in demand: coal and coke wagons of varying capacity, goods wagons, trolley wagons, timber wagons, speciality wagons for cattle, fish, fruit, glass, railway sleepers, boilers, tanks and salt, each requiring different components to be produced by himself and the others in his department, and his apprenticeship would require him to learn what was required in the production of those parts to an expected standard.

1883

The year 1883 saw the birth of George's youngest brother Edwin. Hannah Allan was forty-three years old when Edwin was born. He would be the last of the children that George's parents were to have together.

On 24 August 1883, the New Shildon Temperance Band, buoyed by success the previous year, took part in another contest at Tow Law as part of the Tow Law Floral, Horticultural and Poultry Society annual show. This contest had a more local feel than the Shildon Show contest, with the Temperance band competing against the Blackhill Band, Tanfield Lea, and Tow Law Model Band. Courtesy of the Consett Guardian seven days later we hear that the day brought brilliant weather and drew a record crowd to the event, and that the contest for best stove and greenhouse plants was marred somewhat by the collapse of the table supporting those plants in which most were damaged. The Temperance Band played well, coming second to the Blackhill Teetotal Band.

A few days later on the 8 of September, Tom's band took to the platform again along with the Blackhill Band, Tanfield Lea and four others in yet another contest at Pelton Fell. This time an unnamed set of quadrilles and a march were the test pieces and those other two bands were placed first and second respectively. New Shildon Temperance finished somewhere among the other seven bands that took part though, again, the exact scoring or placing is not recorded.

Tom and the band seem to have an understanding from their successes that the prize money from taking part in contests could be a key means of keeping their band funded and equipped. Though as the above story shows, the band were not guaranteed to win a prize at every contest they entered, and there would be travelling expenses incurred every time they took part. The Temperance Band made another two documented appearance in August of 1883. They competed once again at the Shildon Show where they were unplaced in the contest for bands from the county, and they joined in to provide music at a Friendly and Trades Societies Demonstration Gala in the Woodside Grounds in the nearby major market town of Darlington, along with a number of other bands including one from Cockerton on the western outskirts of that town.

From the reports of the band's activities during Tom's tenure as bandmaster, one thing we are able to learn is that their concert repertoire was beginning to include more and more of Tom's own compositions and arrangements. For example the Northern Echo of 29th Sept 1883 sets out a programme of music the band were due to play the following day in Stanhope Green Park, Darlington which included the march "The Typhoon," Bulch's arrangement entitled "Reminiscences of Weber" based upon pieces by that composer, his own solo polka "Tritone" and his arrangement of Waldtenfel's "Homages aux Dames." Thomas's style of conducting, common to a number of conductors of his era, also gave him the opportunity to play solo cornet with the band, something you don't tend to see with modern brass bands today where the conductor is exclusively responsible for orchestrating and managing the togetherness and dynamics of what is being performed.

How many of these self-composed pieces were published at that time is uncertain at the time of writing, but as we know "Typhoon" had been published it seems likely that some of the others may have also available in printed form by that time. The name, T. E. Bulch, had commenced its spread into the consciousness of the the brass banding communities. Pieces that were not yet published could still have been played by his own band using his handwritten music manuscripts. We can suppose even that he would 'road-test' new pieces to determine how well they sounded before submitting them to his publisher. Perhaps, then, that Sunday afternoon concert in Darlington could have seen the debut for one or more of the pieces mentioned.

Parting

At this point the relevance of our description of the emigration of the Malthouse family to Australia becomes evident. We have ascertained that of the four Malthouse brothers, John appears to have been a close friend to Tom Bulch, however most of the evidence for that is yet to be presented to you in this story.

Tom's grandson, Eric, tells us that after John's emigration he maintained correspondence with Tom by letter, which of course would have been the only option to most common people at the time. The Royal Mail despatched fortnightly mail steamers in both directions. Incredibly, Australia was linked to the rest of the world by submarine telegraphy cables as early as 1872, enabling brief but important messages to be passed between the continents, though this was not a means for mass communication.

That process of ordinary individuals at opposite ends of the globe communicating this way is really quite remarkable when you think about it in comparison to the capabilities we have today. At the time I write this I can send an e-mail anywhere in the world in next to no time at all. From the moment I hit "send" it can be passed from server to server at lightning speed and the longest part of any delay would be the time it took you, as recipient, to check your inbox. In 1883, a letter might take upwards of sixty days to be received. Exchanges would require a great deal of patience. The mail ships also carried detailed correspondence from journalists concerning news of events in the world. When the Malthouse family arrived in Adelaide years earlier the newspapers were buzzing with news from The Cape which had also arrived on that same ship. As that city was the first port of call on the continent, news was generally relayed on from there overland by one means or another.

The letters John sent to Tom no longer exist so their precise content is not known. Considering how most conversations by letter flow we can hypothesise, though, that John might have included news about how he and his family were getting on; a little about how Australia differed to the North-east of England, observations of strange things he might have seen, well wishes to be conveyed to friends of family left behind and perhaps something about having become involved in an Australian band. Somewhere in these messages John, according to Eric, made a proposition to Tom to the effect that he too should travel to Australia and that he would do well there. John, whether knowing his own limitations as a bandmaster or simply missing his friend, offered Thomas his bandmaster's position in the Kingston and Allendale Brass Band. Eric also suggests, from learning passed down within the family, that there may have been something about the suggestion to move to Australia that Tom may also have felt offered better prospects for his health. We don't know that Tom had any underlying health issues or ailments particularly but it's certainly possible that a shift between the climates might have been perceived to have been beneficial to certain conditions.

Whatever it was that John Malthouse included in those letters to Tom Bulch, it was enough to convince him that his future would be best served by taking a passage to Victoria. Furthermore, he was not going to travel alone. Whether they had been inspired by Tom's decision, or persuaded to accompany him, three of his fellow New Shildon Temperance bandmates also decided that their future, too, lay over the oceans. These three were Samuel Lewins, James Scarff and Joseph Garbutt.

Sam Lewins was born at New Shildon on 30 December 1861, meaning that, though he was a year older, he and Thomas Edward Bulch shared their birthday. By the time of the 1881 census, he was living with his widowed mother at a house on Simpson Street. He had originally been a trombonist, but under Thomas Bulch's direction as bandmaster, he switched to playing euphonium. According to details on the ship's manifest, he worked alongside Tom and George in the blacksmiths department at the NER Shildon Works, so would have had that working relationship with both young composers. It's worth noting that point, for in later years when he too became a bandmaster in Australia it was Sam Lewins that was to be the most likely of the emigres to play the George Allan compositions that could be bought there.

James Scarff had been born a little later than these two, in 1863, making him the youngest of the four emigrants. He joined what became the Shildon Temperance Youth Band in 1874, at age eleven, and became a cornet player like Tom. By the time he emigrated his family were living at 5 East Street, Shildon and he was employed as a flour miller. His father worked at a brickworks in Shildon.

Joseph Garbutt, the oldest of the group, having been born on the 20 January 1856, was the son of David, a railway engine driver and his wife and Elizabeth. Their family had once lived in Main Street in Old Shildon but had moved down the hill to busy Station Street in New Shildon by the 1880s. Joseph, as well as being a bandsman, worked as a railway fireman and may have shared a footplate with his father. He had married Mary Jane Peverley on the 4th of December 1883, only months before the journey, yet on the ship's manifest, he is shown to be travelling alone. Whether the couple could not both afford to travel at the same time, or whether Mary Jane needed further persuasion, we must simply guess. It may have been also connected with the fact that she was expecting a child at the time Joseph travelled, and may have wanted to have the child in England. She was certainly pregnant when the couple had married in December as their first child was born on 23 May 1884 at The Commercial Inn, Strand Street, New Shildon. Mary Jane definitely stayed behind for some significant time as is evidenced by her having recorded as having attended someone else's wedding in Bishop Auckland district during 1885; but she did eventually make the crossing to Australia to join her husband before 1888 after which the couple expanded their family and set up home first in New South Wales and then Western Australia.

How the four afforded to travel is unclear but we know for certain that the four young men began their journey on the 22 March 1884 as the event is once again conveniently reported by one of the regional newspapers; and from that it is also made quite clear that the four were among the 'darlings' of the town. The Daily Gazette for Middlesbrough of Monday, 24 March 1884 looked back two days to the date of their departure; though in the spirit of some poor quality journalism it misrepresented Sam Lewins's name as 'Lowes', and Scarff's name as 'Scott', so I have corrected in the following quote to avoid confusion:

> "Departure of Shildon Residents for Sydney. – Between two and three thousand persons assembled at the Shildon Station on Saturday night to bid farewell to James Scarff, Samuel Lewins, Thomas Bulch and Joseph Garbutt, all lately employed at the Shildon shops, and who have started for Sydney intending to make their homes in the colonies. They were all members of the Shildon Temperance Society, and much respected in their native place."

Once again I feel a need to explain that the term 'shops' is used as an abbreviated form of 'workshops', as opposed to retail premises. It's also interesting that Sydney had been given as their destination as we know that they were in fact bound for Melbourne. Whether the inaccuracies cast some doubt on other aspects of the report such as the claims of two to three thousand persons being present, you may speculate for yourself.

When you visit Shildon Station now, or even look at a photograph of it at the time, it would be hard to imagine between two and three thousand people being safely present; and equally hard to imagine such a number of persons bothering to see a neighbour off on the journey of a lifetime. Though of course, there would have been an understanding that this would probably be the last time that they would see these four native born lads. The group travelled, probably with very limited possessions but which included their musical instruments, by rail from Shildon to Darlington and from there onwards to London. There they had a couple of days to wait and prepare for the voyage. They were scheduled to set sail on board the Greenock Steamship Company's ship "Gulf of Venice," a 2,923-ton iron steam screw brigantine that had been built the previous year in the shipyards at West Hartlepool by the shipbuilders W Gray and Co. A notice in the Western Daily Press of 25 March 1884 gives us a clue as to the terms under which the boys were sailing and what their costs might be:

"STEAM TO AUSTRALIA. THAMES AND MERSEY LINE STEAMER GULF OF VENICE will Embark Passengers at Gravesend, Eleven o'clock a.m. on THURSDAY 27th March, and at Plymouth, 10 o'clock a.m. on SATURDAY 29th March. Has a few Berths Disengaged. Accommodation unusually lofty, very liberal dietary. Fares from 12 Guineas. Passage about 45 days. Apply to J GAVIN, BIRT & CO, No 27 Leadenhall Street, London, E.C."

The Western Morning News on 31 March gives us a little more information regarding the occupants of the vessel on that journey following its departure from Plymouth as its only other British port of call where it stocked up on coal to power the engines throughout the voyage. The ship had a crew of sixty-five, had taken on board 345 passengers at the dock in Gravesend on the south bank of the River Thames in London and had subsequently taken on a further forty-six steerage passengers during its brief stay in Plymouth. In addition a general cargo of coal, bricks and logwood. Each of the lads registered on the ship's passenger manifest, giving their occupation as well as name. Tom registered his occupation as 'fitter', which suggests that not long before leaving New Shildon he may have changed jobs at the railway works to one where instead of fabricating components in the blacksmith's department, he would instead have been fitting those parts and other components as part of the overall assembly of wagons.

Even so, that was a life he had now left behind. Tom, Sam, James and Joseph travelled as unassisted emigrants. Decades earlier the migration of British workers had been incentivised by successive Governments, keen to populate the new territories with loyal British subjects to ensure a long lasting control over the region. Such schemes had ended for the territory of Victoria in around 1871 so unless the four had been 'sponsored' to travel they were responsible for paying their own way. Less wealthy passengers travelled in 'steerage', a term for decks lower in the body of the ship, while the wealthier ones occupied cabins on upper decks. Information recorded about a cabin or steerage passenger was usually very brief. Females, children, servants and steerage passengers were frequently left off passenger lists. Some passengers were only listed under their surname, or the initials of their first name, or as part of a family group, for example, Mr Smith & family.

Of the voyage itself, Eric Tomkins in his family history recounts that Tom later spoke to family members of his coming to Australia aboard that vessel and that the journey itself had not been pleasant. Newspaper reports confirm that the journey was not straightforward: the ship was hampered by heavy seas and during the fifty-eight day voyage, the ship lost first one, and then another, of the blades from a propeller, reducing its speed and efficiency. Consequently the ship's rate of travel was reduced from twelve knots to just nine and it was necessary to consume more coal than usual to achieve the distance. Despite the unpleasant conditions Tom, James, Sam and Joseph between them had the means to brighten the situation for their fellow passengers, and the crew, by practising their music together on board the ship. Tom would certainly have brought sets of band music with him, particularly his own works which would have been important to him. There would probably have been pieces of dance music in the quartet's repertoire, quadrilles, schottisches, waltzes or polkas. Though many people played an instrument in those days before television and radio, it's probable that a small ensemble like this, used to playing music together, would have been a rare treat.

Eventually, the ship did make port, Adelaide first, and then Melbourne before moving on around the coast to Sydney. When the four travelling companions from New Shildon arrived at

Melbourne, Australia on 21 May 1884 we are told it was none other than John Malthouse that came to greet them.

Above: the SS Gulf of Venice, aboard which Tom Bulch and his friends from New Shildon made their passage from London to Australia.

Creswick and Ballarat

John travelled with the four young bandsmen to the area in Victoria where the Malthouses had established their home. This was in the area of Creswick, some 18km north of the city of Ballarat. Creswick had been founded in 1842, initially as a sheep station, but had exploded into a small town during the 1850s Victorian gold rush during which its population had temporarily boomed to around 25,000 before falling again. Two years previous to their arrival it had been the site of Australia's worst mining disaster in which twenty-two men had drowned.

Tom needed work quickly, and though gold mining was still active in the area, the life of a miner held no appeal for him. With his background as a blacksmith and fitter Tom, along with James Scarff, took a job at the Phoenix Foundry in Ballarat. Both might have felt they recognised the name of this place as, by coincidence, there had also been an iron foundry in Old Shildon that went by the same name. Though long gone it is remembered even today through the naming of two streets,

Foundry Street and Phoenix Place, that sit adjacent to the former foundry site at the north-eastern edge of Old Shildon. The foundry in Ballarat was sited on Armstrong Street, where Central Square now stands, and had commenced as a one-man operation in the 1850s set up by a Lancashire born engineer and blacksmith, George Threlfall, and had grown to become a partnership that emerged as one of the major industrial operators in Ballarat. They constructed, repaired and re-sold static steam engines, boilers, stamp heads, quartz crushing machinery and pumping machinery principally to support the gold mining industry. By the time James and Tom arrived they had progressed into civil engineering projects, and a line of manufacture that both Thomas Bulch and James Scarff would have been eminently familiar with: locomotive building. Photographs of operations within the Phoenix Foundry reveal an environment very similar in appearance to the North Eastern Railway works at Shildon: the two men would have felt quite at home there.

Both Thomas and James joined the Ironworker's Assistants Union, and James, in particular, seems to have settled in at the foundry. Neither Sam Lewins, nor Joseph Garbutt, followed the others into the foundry to the best of our knowledge. We'll return to them in a few moments. The foundry also had its own Phoenix Foundry Brass Band which looks to have been set up in the year before Tom and James arrived. Tom may have had a brief involvement in this band, but it was James who was to make a commitment to it. A retrospective of his life published in the Herald Newspaper of Melbourne on 15 October 1921 tells us that as well as assisting Tom as principal cornet player in the Allandale and Kingston Brass Band:

> "Mr Scarff's fine cornet playing attracted the attention of Mr J B Gray, the conductor of the Phoenix Foundry Band, Ballarat, who invited him to accept the position of principal cornet to his band. Mr Scarff remained with the band for five years, and he also served for six years with the 3rd Infantry Battalion, under Mr Gray's conductorship."

The latter band also had a relevance to Tom's early Australian experiences. He was asked, in parallel to being master of the Allendale and Kingston Brass Band, to also serve as the bandmaster of the 3rd Battalion Militia Band: this during a period when J B Gray was not fulfilling that role. The 3rd

Battalion Militia in Ballarat had evolved from a volunteer regiment to a part-paid militia regiment during November of 1883, not long before Tom had arrived in Ballarat. Enlisting into the militia as bandmaster would thus ensure some additional income. Though it was configured to be a military band rather than a brass band it was nonetheless a task to which Tom felt he was equal.

Tom was already being inspired by his new surroundings, and, clever enough to know that by creating pieces of music that had titles with some relevance to the player or listener he might create an emotional connection that might help to make them popular. He set about producing his first Australian works. Either shortly after his arrival in Australia, or possibly before, Tom added a new march to his catalogue of compositions, which he entitled "Ballarat." Whilst a logical conclusion to draw would be that that he experienced the city of Ballarat before composing that march, there is evidence that may contradict that. The march was published in England, once again again by T. A. Haigh of Hull who had published the "The Typhoon." Perhaps having had the significance of Ballarat explained to him in letters from John Malthouse, Tom may have seen an opportunity to make his name quickly in Ballarat by arriving with a prepared musical tribute. It could even have been that Thomas anticipated that the fee he would receive for the publishing of Ballarat might help assure his passage there. Whether the piece was composed before or after his arrival there, it was certainly an appropriate first Australian subject for him as it would be in and around the city of Ballarat that he really started to raise his profile and make his name.

Things got off to a good start quickly, as Tom created an impression with the public, officials and press alike through his work ethic, skill as a musician and ability as instructor to bandsmen. The very first mention of Thomas in the Australian press appears in the Ballarat Star of the 14th of November 1884 which explained how Tom had conducted the Allendale & Kingston Brass Band as they "discoursed sweet music" at the 24th Exhibition of the Smeaton Agricultural Society. The same issue of the Star advises citizens that among the attractions at the Charity Sunday event at the city's Eastern Oval there would be a programme performed by the 3rd Militia Band under Tom's conductorship. Many Australian cities had adopted the oval as the shape of grounds reserved specifically for sports, probably with continuing the homeland tradition of cricket in mind, though these grounds were also used and adapted for the new entirely Australian flavour of football which traces its roots back to the late 1850s. When not hosting sports these oval recreation areas were perfect for large public gatherings and concerts. Just a few days later, on Monday, 24 November 1884 the Ballarat Star offers another more descriptive report:

> "The people in Sturt Street on Saturday evening received a musical treat of no mean order. The Allendale and Kingston Brass Band, under the able leadership of Mr T E Bulch, performed in the rotunda, to the delight of many hundreds of persons, who testified their approval by loud clapping of hands.
> Mr Bulch, who is bandmaster to the Ballarat Militia, is a musician of a high order of merit, and like nearly all German artists, he possesses a wonderful command over the instrument on which he performs. It is no matter for surprise then, that his Allendale and Kingston Band are so perfect, and it is little wonder that a number of musical critics should on Saturday night applaud them."

Such glowing praise and ringing endorsement could surely not possibly have been more pleasing to Tom had he written it himself. After outlining the programme performed that evening, which included three pieces of Bulch's own composition, the article continues:

> "The march 'Ballarat' is to be performed at the Band Competitions at Christmas-time. Mr T A Morrison, the Mayor of the City, at the conclusion of the performance, invited Mr Bulch and his musicians to refreshments at Lester's hotel. The Mayor proposed the health of 'The Bandmaster and Band'. In doing so he said that he was delighted with the musical treat which the boys from Allendale and Creswick had given that night at the rotunda, and he felt sure that every person in the large crowd that gathered around the band-stand was also highly pleased with the performance. Mr Morrish replied on behalf of the bandmaster and band, and said that the efficiency of the musicianship was due to Mr Bulch's ability as an instructor."

The article further continues with the promise that with the permission of the City Council the band would, during the summer, give a number of Saturday night performances in

Ballarat, and a number of sacred performances in the Botanical Gardens on Sundays. One point worthy of note in this report is the misconception of Tom being a 'German artist'. It appears as though the journalist has misperceived the origin of his surname as being German. It's certainly an unusual one and does have a Teutonic ring to it, though we can see from censuses in the decades preceding Tom's birth that it may have been an evolved surname. When Tom's own father was born and christened in North Yorkshire in 1835 the family name was recorded on all documents as Bulshey. There are other families using that, or Bulchey, in Yorkshire and Northumberland, though it may have been a derivation of an older or foreign name. The family were known as Bulshey as late as the 1851 census when they had relocated to Bondgate in Darlington and Tom's then fifteen year old father was apprenticed to a tailor. Then, as we saw earlier, within ten years he had married, switched occupation, relocated to Shildon and decided to shorten it to Bulch. This comparatively rare choice of surname has made it somewhat easier to trace and re-assemble his son Tom's own story from records and newspapers.

For a few generations at least, without knowing its older origin, Thomas's lineage was as British as 'fish and chips', and probably more British than that of the reigning monarch of the day; but whatever the truth behind the origins of the Bulch surname there was something about the look and feel of the name that caused this particular journalist to assume German lineage. For now such myth might serve Tom well, bringing the implication of the skill of a German musician to which the writer alluded, and a certain exotic appeal. A significant number of Victorian composers resorted to using exotic European sounding pen names to help boost sales of their music, having found that their own commonplace British name often had the opposite effect. In later life, though, this perpetuated misunderstanding would cast a shadow over Tom's success.

New Shildon

Half a world away, in New Shildon, in the late summer of 1884 the Bulch household on Adelaide Street experienced a brief ray of sunshine quickly interrupted by a cloud of sadness. Tom's mother, Margaret had fallen pregnant during 1883 and in July of 1884 gave birth to a daughter, whom she and her husband named Emily. The baby was not blessed with good fortune and did not survive beyond her first 6 weeks. The sister Thomas Edward Bulch never knew, was buried at All Saints Church in New Shildon on 28 August.

Daily life at the North Eastern Railway works continued for George Allan, as yet still living with his parents. The family continued to be involved with the day to day running of All Saints Church and its parish. An example of this is a case where George's father John Allan is mentioned in the Northern Echo of 8 October 1884 co-running a 'gentlemen's stall' at a bazaar at the National School in New Shildon to raise money for church repairs at All Saints. The money was needed for repairs to the church organ and to contribute money towards a day school and mission room at the nearby village of Brusselton. According to a history of this church compiled in 1968, a copy of which is held by the Durham County Library, 1884 was also a stormy year during which the church roof and spire were significantly damaged. It's possible the fundraising mentioned was connected to this damage.

Later that year, as New Shildon was perhaps winding down in anticipation of Christmas and New Year celebrations, we hear some news in the Daily Gazette for Middlesbrough of 22 December:

> "The Bishop Auckland Free And Easies – On Saturday night the above Free and Easy was packed to the door. The New Shildon Temperance Band, accompanied by some friends, gave the programme. The entertainment concluded with a sketch, "Don't spoil the piece." Prizes were given, Mr G Allan first, Miss M Bulch second."

This reveals a few possibilities regarding acquaintance, though explains nothing explicitly. The 'free and easy' night was an evening of entertainment wherein amateur singers did 'turns,' usually to piano accompaniment, and a forerunner of sorts to the Music Hall scene. Another use of the term that fits neatly in the context of this particular article is one relating to an event almost like a talent contest where prizes would be offered, though the performances on the whole would be rendered by the artists unpaid. Sometimes, depending upon the prize offered, these events might attract singers from some distance. We know that the Bulch family as a whole were enthused musicians, even though only the boys were permitted to join the brass band. We know equally that George Allan sang as he spent time as a choirboy at All Saints church. It's a treat to see his name alongside that of a member of the Bulch family, whom we can safely presume to be Tom's younger sister Margaret Bulch.

Tom's older sister Mary Jane, as we explained earlier, was married by 1884 and would be Mrs Summerbell. Tom's even younger sister Minnie would only have been about seven years old so not old enough to attend. Though George was a member of the Saxhorn Band it's more than likely that he still had friends and former bandmates in the Temperance Band. You could imagine the proceedings to be quite jovial, and drenched in festive goodwill, though naturally only within the permissible boundaries of the spirit of temperance.

Ballarat

In Ballarat, Tom Bulch had elected to join the ranks of the Ballarat Musical Union; a collaboration of musicians who had been preparing for a spectacular Christmas concert since the summer of that year. The Ballarat Star describes the build up over several instalments commencing on 20 August:

> "The Ballarat Musical Union is evidently determined to lose no time in catering for the musical taste of the public, arrangements having been made for the production of Haydn's "Creation" on Christmas night, for which the Alfred Hall has been engaged. The society now numbers 120 performing members, of which 50 are male voices; while the orchestra, under, the leadership of Herr Braun, is receiving numerous additions, and already comprises many of the leading musicians of Ballarat. Mr Fred Herbert has accepted the position of honorary pianist. Notwithstanding the unpropitious state of the weather on Monday night, there was a full rehearsal, over a hundred members being present; and the choruses were very successfully gone through with the band accompaniment."

On Christmas Eve the Ballarat Star relayed a rallying call to the Ballarat Musical Union membership for a final rehearsal:

> "The members of the Ballarat Musical Union are requested to attend a full rehearsal at the Alfred Hall this evening, to commence at half-past 7. Miss Bessie Pitts, who will arrive by the mid-day train to-day from Melbourne, and Signor Modini

will be present. As this will be the final rehearsal all the members are particularly requested to attend."

Then on Christmas Day itself the concert took place and was reported on 27 December. The performers comprised of one-hundred-and-eighty lady and gentlemen amateurs, aided by an orchestra of twenty-six performers among whom Thomas Bulch was listed as a cornet player. The orchestral and choral performance, conducted by Mr W S Matthews was enjoyed by an audience of around two-thousand. The report concluded that *"all who had the pleasure of listening to the oratorio on Christmas Night augur well of the union's future."*

The following day, Boxing Day, was doubtless unusual for Tom it being his first Christmas enjoyed in the bright warmth of the Australian summer as opposed to the dank gloom of British winter. He and others connected to his Kingston and Allendale Brass Band, had organised a band contest to take place on that date. Though this has, on occasion, been reported as the first to ever have taken place in the territory of Victoria that isn't true. There had been brass band contests taking place there in the eighteen-sixties and seventies, if not before. The contest was held at the Creswick Oval in the Creswick Botanical Gardens, as a consequence of there having been no equivalent recreation ground in the Kingston and Allendale area. Details had been announced in advance in the Ballarat Star of Tuesday, 21 October 1884, where it was explained that the competing bands would play Tom's quick march "Ballarat," which the newspaper claimed had been composed especially for the occasion. That may well have been true, but it was not the first occasion at which the people of Ballarat had the opportunity to hear it played, as Tom had conducted the band playing that very march during a concert on Sturt Street on the 22nd of November; a month before the contest. As was the tradition back at home in England, the band contest was held in conjunction with athletic sports events. The organisers, among whom Thomas was undoubtedly key, had mustered prizes of £20, £10 and £5 for the three top placed bands. Alas however, as it had been organised at comparatively short notice and coincided with the festive celebrations, only two of the bands invited took part. The first of these was the Daylesford Borough Band, with twenty-eight members, and their opponents were the Egerton Brass Band with its twelve personnel. The contest coincided with other events in nearby Ballarat which had drawn greater crowds. Despite these factors the event was reported as a success. In hosting the athletic events the band had teamed up with the Allendale Fire Brigade and a number of prominent citizens of the area, and after these events, the attention of those present became focused on the musical centrepiece of the contest. As the bands played, Tom Bulch, the young contest adjudicator in his first such engagement in Australia, listened to the bands from inside a small tent a few yards of the bandstand so that he might hear but not see the bands. A reporter in the Allendale, Smeaton and Kingston Telegraph said of Tom's "Ballarat" march:

> "The piece is a somewhat heavy one, each prominent player being afforded an opportunity for exercising his ability. At the conclusion of the piece the public gave a hearty cheer."

There was a brief moment of chaos as part way through the Daylesford Band's rendering of the test piece a strong wind passed through the recreation ground causing a number of the band members to lose their sheet music and places in the piece. They recovered quickly. Having heard both bands Tom announced a winner and, despite their difficulties in the windy conditions, that winner proved to be the Daylesford Band. He also paid tribute to the 'pluck' of the band from Egerton for competing with their larger and more experienced opponents. Among the extra prizes Tom had available to issue was a sterling silver mouthpiece reportedly offered by F Besson & Company of London, which was to be given to the best cornet player on the day. Tom adjudged that this should be awarded to Mr Scorer, the solo cornet player from the Daylesford Band. This was a matter of some small controversy and discussion as Mr Scorer had performed without his Daylesford Band uniform, leading some to believe that he wasn't genuinely a member of that band. If Tom hadn't realised it before, he was in the process of learning what most other band contest adjudicators of his day had learned perhaps since the beginnings of band contesting, which is that a decision, however well founded it was thought to be, was often followed by controversy and differences of opinion. The concerns on this occasion were swiftly quashed as Scorer was well known to many present and had clear associations to the band. Even if he had not been, the provided rules of that contest had made allowance for one 'professional' player or conductor with each band. The declaration of the winners was followed by a demonstration of gentlemanly conduct, with the victors giving a rousing three-cheers to their bested opponents, who returned the tribute. Afterward, the bandsmen and officials retired to a dining booth for celebratory toasts and speeches. Mr Jacobs of the Egerton Band proposed the health of the Daylesford Band while Mr Geo. Page of the latter responded with statements of credit to Egerton. He went on to compliment the efforts of the Allendale and Kingston Band in initiating band contests in the colony. Mr John Gascoigne of Allendale and Kingston prophetically stated that he looked forward to the time when Victorian brass band contests would prove as attractive as they had in the mother country.

For Tom Bulch, too, this was a victory of sorts. He could now, at such a young age, rightly claim to have fulfilled that trusted role of band contest adjudicator, generally reserved only for those known to have the deepest knowledge of how such music should be performed and what separated a great performance from a mediocre one. It's true that only two bands had competed, and his involvement owed much to his confidence in claiming the right to carry out that role and having been involved in the organisation of the event; but nonetheless it was a very important step forward, and one he could reflect upon. How cruel, then, for a cloud of tragedy to cast its shadow over the moment.

New Shildon

On that same day, Boxing Day, 26 December 1884, Tom's grandfather, Francis Dinsdale, bandmaster of the New Shildon Saxhorn Band and perhaps the 'godfather' of band music in that town having founded a musical dynasty there, died at his home at 6 St John's Road, New Shildon.

The former railway signalman, at age of seventy-one, had succumbed to the effects of chronic bronchitis. His death certificate indicates that his son-in-law, Thomas Bulch senior, was present at the end. There may have been other family members too, given the size of the family and the closeness of the community at that time. How quick or slow the decline had been, and whether he was still active in running the Saxhorn band or not is not explained anywhere, but the loss of such a personality in the town, after his having so positively influenced and encouraged the lives and opportunities of so many within his community, must surely have been sorely felt.

Francis's death was registered on 27 December by Dr Robert Smeddle, and registrar Joseph Jopling. At the opposite end of the earth Tom Bulch, possibly thinking ahead to his twenty-third birthday on the 30th and reflecting on 1884 as a momentous year in his own life; looking forward to the start of another new year and whatever it may bring, was entirely unaware of the passing of the grandfather that had played such a part in setting him on this path. If the family wrote to notify him, it would take over two months for him to hear the news.

Another family development at the beginning of 1885 was that another member of the Bulch family had decided that their future lay in Australia. This was Tom Buch's uncle, Christopher Bulch, who had decided to relocate with his wife, Ann, and three daughters to New South Wales. Leaving behind his job as an Engine Fitter at the Darlington Railway Works, Christopher and his family took passage on the SS Aberdeen which left Gravesend on the 24th February. They arrived in Sydney on the 13th April and registered as unassisted immigrants. Though there is no evidence of this new branch of the Bulch family interacting with Tom after this date, we do know that Christopher was instrumental in founding a Mechanics Institute and School of Arts in Keiraville where he settled and became a respected local figure. He died in April 1908.

Ballarat

In Victoria, Tom Bulch had been working on other new musical compositions with which to entertain the people of Ballarat. A report printed on 11 March 1885 in the Ballarat Star reports an early airing of some new music:

> "The Kingston and Allendale Brass Band (Mr T. E. Bulch, bandmaster) are to play the following programme on the balcony of the Unicorn Hotel this evening, commencing at half-past 7 o'clock. Contest March, "Ballarat," T. E. Bulch; valse, "Boccacio," Suppé; anthem (sacred), "Vital Spark," Harwood; tonguing polka, "Mon Ami," T. E. Bulch; selection, "Notre Chère Alsace," Klug; caledonians, "Bobbie Burns," T. H. Wright; contest march, "Jumbo," T. E. Bulch; National Anthem."

Whilst Bulch's march "Jumbo" had been previously reported as played back in November of the previous year, this is the first printed report of the playing of "Mon Ami," a solo polka that would be played by bands in Australia and Britain until well into the early Twentieth Century. That there are reports of it being played in England, Ireland and Scotland suggests that at this time Tom was still sending new compositions back to Thomas Haigh in Hull to be published much as he had done with his very first Australian pieces such as "Ballarat." Haigh was certainly exporting his Amateur Brass (and Military) Band Journal to be distributed in Australia.

Until the very end of the eighteen eighties the only reports we see of bands playing Bulch music are of pieces published by Haigh, so perhaps Tom thought his existing relationship with Haigh could be the answer to the question of how to spread his fame as a composer in Australia. By far the most references to his compositions being played during the second-half of this decade however, are of bands conducted by Tom himself. It seems it took a few years for him to achieve renown as a composer of fine band music.

There are signs that there must have been some correspondence between Tom, in Ballarat and other members of the Bulch family back in New Shildon. One key clue to this lies in the planning of his brother Frank's subsequent emigration to Victoria. Perhaps this had always been something the brothers had in mind. Perhaps they had reached an agreement that through being unable to afford two fares at once Tom would go first and Frank would follow. An alternative possibility is that perhaps after Thomas arrived in Victoria and saw the prospects that the territory offered, he made the suggestion that his older brother join him. We can only speculate. Whatever the case a second emigration looks to have been co-ordinated between Britain and Australia, and appropriate arrangements made. By February 1855, just over a month after the death of the brothers' grandfather, plans were at an advanced stage and the community of New Shildon were rallying to help make it happen. A newspaper story in the Northern Echo of 28 February 1885 reads:

"The New Shildon Temperance Band, and others, gave a concert in Bishop Auckland Temperance Hall last evening, for the benefit of Mr F Bulch, who is going to Australia."

One can't help but wonder whether George Allan was among the 'others' contributing to this concert. Frank had married on 7 June 1884, not long after Thomas's arrival in Australia. He was a year older than Thomas and, unlike his brother, had chosen the life of a coal miner.

One of the principal reasons New Shildon had been established as the point of origin of the locomotive-drawn stretch of the Stockton and Darlington Railway was it's proximity to a series of very productive of coal mines in the South West Durham coalfield. Coal was originally brought there from collieries further inland such as at Etherley and Witton Park, but coal was later discovered in the land around Shildon, and pits sunk at which many local men were subsequently employed. Coppy Crooks, Eldon, the Black Boy and Adelaide Collieries were all on land surrounding Shildon, however given that Frank and Isabella had lived at 6 Vaughan Street prior to emigration it is highly likely that he was employed at the Shildon Lodge Colliery immediately opposite those houses. Though productivity fluctuated depending upon the seam being worked there was, broadly speaking, no shortage of mining employment.

Frank's wife Isabella, née Dixon, had been born in Haughall, Durham, but came to Shildon when her parents had moved there in search of work. Frank and Isabella used their scant savings, and the money raised for them, to procure passage to Australia on the SS Lusitania. Not of course the ill-fated White Star passenger liner that was torpedoed by the Germans during World War One. This earlier, less famous, 'Lusitania' was built in 1871 and transferred to the Orient Line, in 1877, from the Pacific Steam Navigation Company for which it had been built.

The Lusitania, a Royal Mail steam ship weighing 3,877 gross tons, was just under 380 feet in length, had one funnel and, like many ships of her era and class, three masts rigged for sail. Like the 'Gulf of Venice' that had transported Tom Bulch she travelled at a speed of around twelve knots, which equates to roughly just under fourteen land miles per hour: not fast by modern standards, and it's clear that a journey of this distance took a long time. This ship could accommodate 84 first class, 100 second class and 270 third class passengers.

On 4 March 1885, Frank and Isabella boarded the ship at the designated embarkation point; the loading berth at Royal Albert Dock, Gravesend. A further British port of call was

Plymouth on 10 March. Then followed a voyage via Naples and then the Suez which it left on 20 March heading for Adelaide and Melbourne after which she would proceed to Sydney. It must have seemed an extraordinary adventure for the couple to see such places as they passed on their way.

On the 8 April, while his brother Francis and sister-in-law Isabelle were at sea, twenty-three year old Thomas Edward Bulch was married. His bride was Eliza Ann Paterson, daughter of John Southey Paterson, then mine manager of the Davies's Junction Gold Mine and resident of Glendonald in the district of Creswick. It does strike as slightly strange that Tom did not wait until his brother Frank had arrived in order to solemnise and celebrate so momentous an occasion, though this could be explained by the fact that at the time of the wedding Eliza, two years his junior, was heavily pregnant. To have the marriage happen any later would risk the couple having their first child out of wedlock, which in the Victorian era would have been an act that carried significant social stigma. Eliza's father was a man of some social standing and may have been influential in ensuring that the wedding took place before the infant was born. Whatever the circumstances around arrangement and timing of the wedding, and whether he was personally satisfied with the match, the marriage certificate later showed that John Paterson had provided his written consent for the wedding prior to it taking place.

Young Tom had arrived toward the end of May 1884, so assuming that he was the father of Eliza's child, as opposed to someone who had agreed to marry her to spare her reputation, then the couple must have been introduced at some point within Tom's first two or three months in Australia. It must have been something of a whirlwind romance. Perhaps Eliza had her feet swept from under her by Tom's dashing appearance as this young Englishman in band uniform who could not only produce sweet melodies from his cornet but also hold an entire military or brass band under his sway to great effect. The attraction doubtless flowed in both directions but Tom Bulch very probably cut an interesting figure at this time. The wedding ceremony was conducted by the local Presbyterian minister, Charles Robinson, possibly in accordance with John's Scottish roots and values, and took place at his house at Glendonald. Though that sounds unusual, to have a wedding at home rather than in a church or chapel, it was perhaps more common than we imagine at that time. At the conclusion of the ceremony, Tom, who had given his own profession as Musician, and that of his father, interestingly as 'Clerk', signed the certificate, as did his new wife. The act was then witnessed by Tom's closest friend John Malthouse, and Eliza's sister, Mary Elizabeth Paterson. Tom now had a new family on Australian soil, as well as his family back in Shildon, and a father-in-law whose expectations he would have to live up to in looking after Eliza.

The SS Lusitania, bearing Frank and Isabelle, arrived in Adelaide on the morning of the 16 April 1885. From there she sailed on to Hobson's Bay, Melbourne where she arrived on the 18th and Tom and Frank were reunited. One interesting aside is that on completion of that particular voyage, an unusual destiny awaited the ship. It was almost immediately commissioned and converted as an Armed Merchant Cruiser for six months in 1885 during an incident in history known as the 'Russian Scare', wherein the Southern Australian territories feared they would come under attack from Russian warships as a consequence of hostilities between Britain and Russia over Afghanistan. The Sydney Morning Herald of 23 May 1885 describes the occasion of the Lusitania being taken out for trials in her new converted form as a 'man-of-war' and firing practice in which *"she had acquitted herself as an armed cruiser."* As events transpired, the fears proved unfounded and after the brief period of service the SS Lusitania was returned to her owners and subsequently re-engined in 1886.

On arrival in Ballarat, Frank, as Thomas had before him, took a job initially at the city's Phoenix Foundry, and documentary evidence exists of his time as a worker there. He would not, however, remain there for very long. As with his younger brother, Frank had come to Australia to create the best life he could, and needed an occupation in which he could leverage what expertise he possessed from his beginnings in England. Frank, through the family connection between his brother Tom and John Paterson, secured a job that better suited his mining background than work at the forge. The former coal miner became a gold miner, perhaps hoping that if his new employer took him under his wing he too might graduate to management. In addition, having previously been alongside his brother as a member of the New Shildon Temperance Band, Frank also joined the ranks of Thomas's 3rd Militia Band as well as the Phoenix Foundry Brass Band. This creates a possibility worth speculation that, though there is no documented evidence to support it being fact, perhaps Thomas did this also.

One early, brief, mention of Frank Bulch in Australia was published in the Ballarat Star of 30 July 1885 explaining that he was among the most recent donors to the Ex-Captain Muir Relief Fund, having paid in one shilling. Muir had once been Captain of the Ballarat City Fire Brigade, until his retirement from that post in 1874. Despite this retirement he continued to be involved in fire-fighting and when, in May 1879 an extensive fire broke out in Melbourne, he travelled with the Ballarat City Brigade down to Melbourne where he was involved in the dramatic rescue of the Christie family. Afterward he remained an influential figure and attended the Fire Brigades Conferences. By April of 1885, however, he was being afflicted by an illness prompting the creation of this fund to support him by June. Muir survived this unnamed illness passing away many years later in 1907.

On 29 May 1885, Thomas and Eliza's first child was born at Dana Street in Ballarat; a daughter whom the young couple called Ethel. Baby Ethel thus became the first native born Australian member of the Bulch family. The second native born Bulch emerged at the same address a mere five days later.

Frank Bulch's wife Isabella had become pregnant prior to embarking on the voyage to Australia and on the 3 June 1885 a daughter, whom they named Olive May Bulch, was born as a new cousin for Ethel. The two births were so close that Eliza Paterson's sister Mary, when registering the births, was able to register both at the same time. These were happy, if chaotic days indeed for the Bulch brothers founding their new dynasty in a new world. The two girls having been born just those few days apart it's possible that the families imagined their lives mapped out as close friends, possibly celebrating their birthdays together. The sense of an expanding family may have been of comfort to Tom, having previously left the rest of his large family back in England. Tom and Frank, in return, were bound to have been missed by relatives back in Shildon who may have felt they might never see the two brothers again.

Having decided that working at Ballarat's Phoenix Foundry was not what he was cut out for, Tom commenced planning a venture that would enable him to fully transition to making a living from music. His idea involved a business partnership with John Malthouse, his close friend and fellow ex-New Shildonian.

Whether the venture was planned after Tom arrived in Victoria, perhaps through spotting a gap in the market, or whether it was conceived by the two before he left Britain is unclear. What the two had in mind, though, was a significant undertaking for a young man who only two years before had been a mere railway blacksmith the North-East of England. Over a hundred and thirty-five years later, Tom's grandson, Eric Tomkins who remembers his grandfather's later years and would often discuss the events of his life with his aunts, Tom's daughters, speculated that one key enabler of what happened next may have been Tom's new relationship with his father-in-law. John Paterson, through his rise to becoming a mine manager and a life of careful choices, was a man of some means, property, reputation and social standing. Eric explained to me that he knew from what aunts had told him that John had helped set his own sons up in farming with gifts of land and property. It is not unthinkable that in order for Tom to keep his new wife, John's daughter, in the manner to which she deserved, John might have invested in his son-in-law's business.

When John Paterson had emigrated, from Scotland with his brother, he went to Inglewood and the goldfields area in the North of Victoria. Eric's own family research led him to understand that John had some mining success there before coming south to settle in Creswick for a while. A seemingly driven and confident man, he had been investing in the local gold mines as well as managing some of the larger mines. Eric advised me that by the time John Paterson died in 1899 he had become wealthy and had set up a trust to manage his wife's Sarah's affairs. From the outset Eliza Bulch had an interest in Tom's music store business and in later years, when Thomas was away, Eliza would play a part in running the store. How John Malthouse financed his part in the business, if at all, is unclear. However it was enabled, Tom Bulch and John Malthouse elevated themselves to the status of traders and businessmen. Malthouse, of course, had experience of the world of retail, as his mother had previously run a shop on Alma Road in New Shildon prior to emigration. Their joint knowledge of music combined with Malthouse's family background could well have been what gave them grounds for an investable business case. On Saturday, 24 October 1885, an announcement was printed in the Ballarat Star for all in that locality to see:

"Music, Music, Music – Messrs BULCH and MALTHOUSE have great pleasure in announcing to the public at Ballarat and surrounding districts that they have opened a MUSIC WAREHOUSE in Bridge Street opposite the market. PIANOS, ORGANS and HARMONIUMS, and every description of Musical Instruments kept in stock. Sheet Music, Music Books, Tutors, &c. Note the address - BULCH AND MALTHOUSE, Music Warehouse, Bridge Street, Ballarat."

The announcement was repeated as an advertisement in subsequent issues of the paper, to ensure that as many prospective customers as possible were aware of Tom and John as the newest merchants in the bustling city of Ballarat. These two were not the first to open a music store in Ballarat. In fact the city was already quite well served. The main retail area of Ballarat, Sturt Street, had several such shops in the years preceding the opening of Bulch and Malthouse. There was a Mr A T Turner who had been open since at least 1866 and Mr J E Tepper at number 119. By the mid-1870s Mr J Harrison had a pianoforte and music warehouse at number 137 and Mr J Summerscales at number 6 on the same street which by 1877 claimed to be the largest music store in the colony and which gradually extended to Bridge Street. There was also Sutton and Co. at number 39, Ewins, a piano seller at number 3 and Birtchnell's elsewhere on that same street. Even in a quickly growing city and in times where most families aspired to own a piano or some other instrument that could be played at home, competition for customers would be fierce, and another music warehouse in the city would hardly have been popular with the established store owners. Thomas and John's perceived advantage might perhaps have been their involvement, and connections, with the community of musicians through the brass bands and involvement with the Ballarat Musical Union.

Despite this challenging and competitive situation, Tom was now a businessman in control of his own destiny and further along the road to fulfilling his personal ambitions. His life was becoming very much a model picture of Victorian aspiration and success through self-development. When this news inevitably found its way back to Shildon via the mail ship you would imagine that his parents would have been very proud of their enterprising and determined son.

You may be feeling by now that this has become all about Tom Bulch, and wondering what happened to the young George Allan. However, as Thomas was born over a year before George and had to take a journey to fulfil his destiny there is more to say of that at this point. Be assured that we will catch up again with George shortly.

The year 1886 started well enough for Tom in Ballarat, now master and conductor of multiple bands, brass and military, and independent businessman. The Ballarat Star, detailed as ever in documenting daily life in the city, keeps us informed of events. On 27 February 1886, it reports:

> "The Militia Band played a number of selections last evening in the Sturt street rotunda. A large crowd of persons assembled to listen to the music rendered by the band, under Mr Bulch's leadership, and an excellent treat was afforded."

In April, Tom became involved in a venture that might allow him to reinvigorate a legacy that he had left behind in New Shildon through the formation of a new temperance brass band in Ballarat comprising only musicians that had taken the temperance pledge and abstained from drinking alcohol. Perhaps, as his grandfather had learned before him, and his uncle Edward Dinsdale had determined back in his former homeland, Tom was finding that even in Australia a better standard of musical performance could be elicited from bandsmen that were not tempted by the 'demon drink'. This episode in his life was brought to our attention through the writings of Australian brass historian Jack Greaves, but greater detail endures in the local press of the time. The Ballarat Star of 6 April 1886 documents something of the initiating moment:

> "A preliminary meeting was held last night to consider the advisability of forming a Temperance Brass Band. The chairman, in opening the meeting, remarked that a city like Ballarat should have such a band, as there were plenty of young men in Ballarat that would make good musicians, and would gladly join, and he was happy to see that the first step had been taken. Offers were received from several old players desirous of joining the band, and from a Ballarat firm offering to supply instruments on very easy terms, so as to be within the reach of any juniors. There was also an offer from one of the leading bandmasters, who has for the last several years successfully conducted the Shildon Temperance Brass Band in the recent

contests in England. It was resolved to call a general meeting at the Prince's room, Alfred Hall, next Monday night, at 8 o'clock, of all persons desirous of forming such a band, to appoint officers and a committee. The aid of all Blue Ribbon and temperance societies is earnestly solicited."

So we see here that Tom had thrown his hat into the ring from the outset, and it's possible the meeting had been instigated by his suggestions. Most bands begin in this way, with the formation of an essential committee rather than the formation of the band itself. A later article on the 13th mentions the newly formed committee planning to advertise for an instructor, and this they duly did in the same issue of the Star, but it was Tom whose application was successful. The notion of a Temperance Band in Ballarat was not a new idea. At least one similar project had started in the late 1860s, decades before Tom's arrival in Australia, but it had not endured. Might this iteration, with a proven bandmaster committed to the temperance cause prove more successful? While that committee went about assembling the resources they needed, we hear more news on 5 May 1886, of an event involving Thomas's first Australian band:

"The Allendale and Kingston Brass Band will (weather permitting) play the following programme to-night near the Post Office, Allendale, at 8 o'clock. Conductor, Mr T. E. Bulch: — Grand contest march, "Chef d'Oeuvre," by T. E. Bulch; waltzes (contest), "Mountain and Glen," by H. Round; grand selection (operatic), "Gems from Weber," by T. E. Bulch; solo tonguing polka, "Mon Ami," by T. E. Bulch. Interval. Grand contest march, "Typhoon," by T. E. Bulch; grand fantasia (descriptive), "Joan of Arc," by H. Round; quadrilles (contest), " Frost and Sun," by Frost and Son; waltzes, "Boccacio," by von Suppe; National Anthem."

This is the first reported performance of Tom's first arrangement of pieces by Weber, "Gems from Weber." a new attempt to arrange the work of another composer. As we don't believe Tom had yet found an Australian publisher by this time, and we have not found evidence of this piece being published by T A Haigh, it is possible once again that the band were playing it from Tom's own handwritten manuscript rather than printed music. The piece was played exclusively by Tom's own bands until the early 1890s. Then, later that month, on the 25th we hear that:

> "The Militia Band performed the following programme at the International Fancy Fair. Grand march, "Glorie et Patrie" (Bogarde); valses, "Clarine" Karl Kaps; grand selection (on Irish airs), "Pride of Ireland" (H. Round); tonguing polka, "Mon Ami " (T. E. Bulch); lancers, " United Kingdom" (Wright); valses from the opera "Boccaccio "(von Suppe); march, "Happy Moments " (T. E. Bulch)."

Again, there is an early mention of another new Australian composed piece; "Happy Moments." As well as Tom already displaying his pride and confidence in being able to include his own works in the programmes, he is also showing that he was able to adapt his compositions to suit the instrumentation of a military band. This was quite common for composers of his era, and was a tactic George Allan too would also employ, having an understanding of the role of instruments beyond only those traditionally used by brass bands would serve him well. Tom had the Ballarat Temperance Brass Band up and running by 11 June where, along with the Blue Ribbon Choir, they entertained at a Blue Ribbon Union Tea Meeting and Musical Entertainment at the Alfred Hall. Tea was served at six thirty pm though tickets were available for the concert only, which of course was punctuated by speakers denouncing the demon drink and all who partook of it. In the meantime, donations toward the band's upkeep continued to roll in, with notable donors receiving printed recognition in the Ballarat Star.

Despite the title of that most recent march, 1886 was a year of few 'happy moments' for the Bulch family, and many moments of sadness. The first in the a chain of tragic events concerned Frank Bulch. On 22 July, Frank was working as usual under John Paterson at the Davies's Junction Mine when a terrible accident befell him. The Ballarat Star of the 23rd gives a detailed account of the catastrophic event:

> "FATAL ACCIDENT AT THE DAVIES' JUNCTION MINE. Our local correspondent yesterday writes: "A fatal accident happened at the Davies' Junction Company's shaft at noon today. Two men, respectively named William Bray and Frank Bulch, were working in a drive which was only two sets and a half from the main drive. The manager, about three quarters

of an hour previous to the unfortunate accident, gave instructions for the drive to be stopped, on account of it being very poor, and the men were preparing to abandon it when, by some means, the timbers have slipped, and both men were thrown down in the drive. Bulch was killed almost instantaneously, but Bray lived a short time after the accident. Bray cried out for the men to lift the timber and dirt off his back, but before he could be released life was extinct. The ground was very firm, and only about 18 inches or 2 feet of stuff fell with the timber on the men. A miner named Thomas Reardon, hearing the noise of the fall, rushed to the mouth of the drive and found Bray lying with his face downwards the timber and dirt only covering him to about the middle of the back. Bulch was married and leaves a wife and one child. He is a brother of Mr T E Bulch, the esteemed leader of the Kingston and Allendale brass band. Bray who is advanced in years, has a brother in Clunes, and he is reported to be a nephew of Billy Bray, the famous Cornish preacher."

As with other mining accidents of the day, the tragic incident was widely reported across the continent, including this brief report in the territory of Tasmania by the Launceston Examiner on Friday, 23 July:

"Wm. Bray and Frank Bulch were smothered shortly after noon to-day in a wash-dirt drive at the Davies's Junction Company Mine in Creswick. The ground is reported to have been very heavy. The bodies have not yet been recovered. Bray is the nephew of Billy Bray, the famous preacher, and Bulch is a brother of Mr T E Bulch, the well known Ballarat bandmaster."

Though that Tasmanian account adds little to our understanding of the accident, it does contain one interesting insinuation, which is that while you might expect the most local of newspapers to have pointed out Frank Bulch's relationship to a local bandmaster, it is a minor matter of added interest at this point that Tom's celebrity was reported in Tasmania. Setting that aside, though, consider the impact of this event on Tom Bulch. Frank was his older brother, and one of only two close blood relations on the Australian continent, Tom's baby daughter being the other. To add to this agony Tom must surely have been mindful of his own part in his brother's decision to make his life there, and without the connection to Tom's father-in law Frank might never have been working at the Davies' Junction Mine that fateful day. Thoughts like these must have been torturous and hard for a still quite young Tom Bulch to bear. To darken the situation further, Tom's grandson Eric explained to us that as Francis Bulch's principal relative, the task of arranging his brother's funeral fell to the young bandmaster. The Ballarat Star of 26 July explains the funerary proceedings:

> "Funeral at Creswick. The funerals of the late William Bray and Francis Bulch, the two men who were accidentally killed on Thursday while working in a wash-dirt drive at Davies's Junction Company's mine, took place (writes our correspondent) at the Creswick Cemetery on Saturday when, as two hearses were seen on the Clunes road in one procession, a large number of people were reminded of the time when 21 of the unfortunate miners who lost their lives in the Australian disaster in December, 1882, were borne along that road to the same burying ground. Young Bulch who was laid in the silent grave on the 25th anniversary of the date of his birthday, was a member of the band of the 3rd Battalion Militia, and about 100 rank and file of the B Company of that Battalion under Captain King, attended to pay a last tribute of respect to their deceased comrade. The hearse containing his corpse was preceded by a firing party of 12 men, who, after the solemnities at the grave, fired three volleys, and members of the Militia Band walked beside the hearse in the procession. The deceased, while residing in Ballarat, was connected with the Phoenix Brass Band, and at the time of his death he was a member of the Kingston and Allendale Brass Band, the members of both of which attended the funeral and played "The Dead March in Saul" with muffled drums. The burial service of the Church of England was conducted at the grave by Revs J Glover and J Harnson. Bray, who was 62 years of age, was buried in the Wesleyan ground, the Service being read by the Rev T Angwin. The proceedings were of a very impressive character. Both men were, of course, connected with the Miners' Association, and a large number of miners walked in the procession. The usual levy will be made on the whole of the members of the association for the relatives of the deceased men. The Militiamen and Phoenix Band arrived at North Creswick by train at 4 pm, and returned to Ballarat by the evening train, leaving Creswick at 6:20. The works at the mine, suspended on Thursday, were resumed on Sunday (last) night."

When Tom's grandfather had died it was he that had to wait in ignorance while news sluggishly arrived by the Royal Mail Steamer from England. This time Tom was the Bulch to bear the weight of being the only one of his family to know that Frank had perished until news arrived in Britain, unable to share that grief with his parents or brothers and sisters. Whether the news was communicated back to Shildon in a letter to his family by Tom, or by Frank's wife Isabella, or most likely by both, eventually the news did arrive and was subsequently duly reported in the Darlington published newspaper, the Northern Echo on 1 September:

> "A SHILDON MAN KILLED IN AUSTRALIA – Letters have been received at Shildon from Australia announcing the death of Francis Bulch, a native of New Shildon, and formerly a member of the Shildon Temperance Brass Band. It appears that Bulch was working at the gold mines near Ballarat, and was smothered along with his mate (Wm. Bray), by a fall of earth, on the 22nd of July. Deceased was almost 25 years of age."

Throughout this, Tom's wife Eliza had again been heavily pregnant, and the couple's roller-coaster year took an upturn on 2 August when at their home on Bridge Street in Ballarat their second child was born. The child was another girl and they named her Adelina Maud Bulch. This happy moment for the family was brief as tragedy had visited the Bulch home once again just a few days later. In the second week of August, Tom and Eliza's daughter, Ethel became ill. A doctor visited the family on the 9th to examine the fourteen-month-old infant but, despite whatever treatment he had been able to administer or prescribe, the condition worsened. On 10 August 1886, Ethel Bulch, the first native Australian member of the Bulch family, after a week of illness died from a combination of bronchitis and "suffocation of the bowels." The task of registering baby Ethel's death was taken by her grandfather, John Paterson, who was at this same time defending himself in a case alleging his negligence in his not having tested a steam boiler that collapsed at the Davies' Junction Mine. His defence was that he was waiting for the delivery of a new steam pressure gauge to enable the test as the one they had was not fit for the purpose. Meanwhile, Tom and Eliza as parents made arrangements for yet another family funeral. Eliza was buried, following a Church of England service, two days later at the cemetery in Creswick. As a result of this turmoil and tragedy it was not until the tenth of September that Eliza registered the birth of her second daughter Adelina.

On 25 September we learn of an appearance of the Ballarat Temperance Band the previous day, and that Tom was continuing with his duties with it in spite of any grief he would have been carrying:

> "The Ballarat Temperance Brass Band, under the leadership of Mr T. E. Bulch, discoursed the programme as advertised by us yesterday, in front of Messrs I. and J. Roff's tailoring establishment last evening. Crowds of people were present, who showed their appreciation by frequent rounds of applause. The band regretted having to finish the programme about 9 p.m. rather abruptly on account of the serious illness of the youngest son of Mrs E. Ingram, of the Royal Standard hotel. The band adjourned to Mr McIntyre's, Bridge street, where a repast was laid to the order of Mr Roff. After the repast, Mr Roff thanked the band for their services, which was responded to by Mr Roberts. The band sang "For he's a jolly good fellow," and then dispersed." The Ballarat Temperance Band played a number of other engagements in the city towards the end of the year including one on the 1st October on Sturt Street, "immediately opposite Messrs Horsley Bothers."

Another item in the Star on the 30th explains something of the make-up of the band:

> "The band, which numbers some 25 members, consists of pledged abstainers, every intending member having to sign the pledge before being admitted a member of the band."

On the first of October, the Temperance Band gathered at the centre of Sturt Street, opposite the store owned by Messrs Horsley Brothers, to render a programme of music including the quick march "Melbourne" by Percy Pogson, a contemporary of Bulch.

The very next day, the 2nd of October, yet another tragedy was to befall the Bulch family, this time back at home in New Shildon. Thomas's mother, Margaret, the daughter of Francis Dinsdale, died at the family home, 40 Adelaide Street. According to the death certificate, the cause of her death was an obstruction of the bowels. Tom's brother, Jerry Bulch, is recorded as having been present at her passing, but it is highly likely that many of her children, as well as her husband, would have been present at what must have been a terribly distressing and uncomfortable demise. In current times, where state-provided healthcare is available in Britain, it's hard to imagine now how helpless a family must have felt in witnessing the demise and loss of a loved one so potentially unnecessarily. In Victorian Britain it was a hard, and usually inescapable, fact of life.

Above: All Saints Church, New Shildon, opened in 1868 to become the parish church for both the Bulch and Allan Family.

Margaret Bulch was buried on the hill rising east of the town, in the churchyard at All Saints Church, on 5 October. Yet again it would be weeks before this heartbreaking news would reach Thomas and he would again have to suffer the anguish of losing another member of his family and possibly felt regret at his not having been there.

On the 11th of October, Mr W Noble, the popular founder of the Gospel Temperance Mission in London, visited Ballarat to appear at a temperance meeting at the Alfred Hall at which the Ballarat Temperance Band, under Tom Bulch, gave anthems from the balcony and accompanied the choir. The meeting was mostly to give a platform to the speaker, of course, who after the local speakers was received with enthusiastic applause, and by the end twenty-one more followers signed the temperance pledge and donned the symbolic 'blue ribbon'. The meeting was repeated the following night.

The end of October saw Thomas return to band contesting, this time with the 3rd Battalion Militia band. Jack Greaves tells us in his account of Thomas's career, that to celebrate the eighth anniversary of the Creswick Miners Association on the 27th, a public holiday was declared and a large sports meeting held during which a band contest took place. Bulch's 3rd Battalion Band was one of four who competed and was awarded the first prize. Prout's Band of Ballarat and two bands from Daylesford were the other entrants. The announcement of the result was greeted with much applause, for both Bulch and the band itself were held in high esteem in the district. The prize was placed in the window of Bulch and Malthouse's Music Warehouse for all to see. We learn on 18 November, yet again in the Ballarat Star, that the Temperance Band were working on preparations to host a contest of their own:

> "We have received from Mr S. Jamieson, secretary of the Ballarat Temperance Brass Band, a programme of the brass band contest to be held in Ballarat on New Year's Day, in connection with the above band and the Ballarat Cricket Club. It is the intention of the band to hold such contests annually, believing that they will give a fresh impetus to brass bands in Ballarat and district, as the prizes will be of sufficient value to secure numerous entries and induce young men to devote more time to that useful and. intellectual study, viz, music. It may be added that the first prize amounts to £30 16s, the second to £20 10s, and the third to £12 12s."

The prize money, for a contest at the time, does appear to be quite a significant incentive. A cricket match was arranged, to take place at the Eastern Oval, with a Ballarat team lining up against a South Australia side. To support the prize for the band contest, donations were taken, and C E Jones agreed to organise a fundraising lecture. On 4 December, it was announced that the contest would be extended to include a category for drum and fife bands, and the range of prizes extended accordingly to accommodate this. The Temperance band continued to fulfil a number of mainly charitable engagements throughout the year including a demonstration of the Young Men's Christian Association on 3 December with an address by the Bishop of Ballarat.

The idea of the Temperance Band's New Year's Day Band Contest wasn't proving to everyone's satisfaction and this letter signed by a "bandsman" appeared in the press on the eighth of December:

> "SIR, —I notice in your advertising columns that a band competition is to take place on New Year's Day. I would respectfully suggest to the committee of the Temperance Band the advisability of holding the event on some more suitable date. On New Year's Day thousands of our townspeople take a trip to Lal Lal or some other place of attraction, in fact there are a number of bandsmen who, to my knowledge, have: made arrangements already to go picnicking, shooting, and such like, and have actually engaged their traps and paid deposits on same. It is very questionable if a sufficient number of bandsmen will be in Ballarat that day to compete. For these reasons, the event, if held on New Year's Day will in all likelihood be a failure. Were the committee to select a Friday half holiday there would not only be a full attendance of competitors, but I venture to predict there would be a largo muster of the public, who would gladly avail themselves of the pleasure of listening to the contest. Hoping the hint will be taken."

From midnight into the earliest hours of Christmas Day, Tom and the Temperance Band made a tour of the streets of Ballarat playing carols. A further appearance of the band on Boxing Day was expected to be cancelled owing to absences of sufficient band members through other commitments, though members did convene to play carols again throughout the town and city.

On New Year's Day, the much-awaited band contest was due. The press advised that six fife and drum bands with members numbering over two-hundred in total would participate, playing pieces of their own choice. The fife and drum bands did compete, but there were no brass bands participating that day – it seems those who agreed with the writer of the above letter had their way, and a compromise had been reached. After this, the Ballarat Temperance Band, so industrious in the closing stages of 1886, loses momentum suddenly. There is a report on 22 January of a Half Holiday Union Excursion at the Lal Lal racecourse at which the band were present and "Discoursed good music throughout the afternoon." Then the Temperance Band mysteriously vanishes, though this might be explained in part by what happened next in the life of Tom Bulch

Bulch's Model Band

On New Year's Eve of 1886, the day after Tom celebrated his twenty fourth birthday, the 3rd Militia Band were scheduled to present a program of military music in the battalion orderly room. Tom was not happy with physical arrangements for the concert and confronted the 3rd Battalion's Commanding Officer. A raised platform that was usually erected for the bandsmen to perform upon on such occasions had not been set up and consequently Tom refused to allow the band to play. This seems to have been the culmination of issues between Tom and the Militia and he resigned from the post of bandmaster. He may have had it in mind to do so anyway and been awaiting an opportunity, or it may have been that the Militia had been dissatisfied with his diversion of time to the Ballarat Temperance Band which one might expect to become the new focus of his attention. Instead, though, Tom took the radical step of creating a brand new band, inaugurated on 10 January 1887. It would be one for which he would exert much more direct control. Echoing the pattern that Thomas had seen back in England through bands such as Leeds Model Band and Milburn's Model Band, this new band was named Bulch's Model Band.

By integrating his own name into the name of the band Thomas was arguably 'nailing his flag to the mast' and stamping his authority on proceedings. Though the band would have a full committee as usual, he would dictate how the band was managed, and through the inclusion of his name his own reputation was staked on the outcome. He'd have had to be confident that he would make this new band work. It wasn't a unique idea though. Nearby Prout's Ballarat Band was also named after its bandmaster. Perhaps Tom had enviously seen something of the control that Samuel Prout had over his band, which was reputedly the oldest private band in Australia, and felt that if he emulated this he could create the truly great brass band that he aspired to lead.

Brass historian Jack Greaves tells us that a significant contingent of the 3rd Militia Band resigned in support of their former bandmaster, and we see that they joined his model band.

It's highly probable that members of his Temperance Band also joined him in the new band, and we know for certain that Shildonian men such as the Malthouse brothers and James Scarffe transferred their loyalty to the new project. Sam Lewins was not among them, as he had left Ballarat for the city of Bathurst in 1885, though we shall see more of him later.

By forming his own band, Tom would have to find funding for uniforms, instruments, travel and all the sundries required to keep a band operational. One advantage he had was that through his own music store and suppliers he would be able to acquire instruments for players that did not have their own, and decide his own terms, possibly even supplying them to his own bandsmen at close to the price it cost him to acquire them. No time was wasted and the band was 'contest ready' by the time of the United Fire Brigades Jubilee Tournament on Friday, 25 February at the Friendly Societies fields in Melbourne. That contest was, as so often the case at that time, something of a sideshow to the physical contests between the fire brigades across the region, but nevertheless attracted some very good bands. It was a tremendous outcome for Tom when Bulch's Model Brass Band came second ahead of St Joseph's and was beaten only by a band from Launceston. Their prize was a silver plated cornet donated by Sutton's music store whose chain of music shops was headquartered in Melbourne.

Tom was always keen to have his Model Band take part in, or be one of the organising forces behind, initiatives that had some kind of benevolent purpose. In many ways, Tom would have found Australia very different to the country of his birth; the climate, the wildlife and the appearance of towns and cities. In other ways, however, there were distinct similarities. Just as in the county of Durham, the Australian colonies like Victoria and New South Wales depended greatly on mining economically. Consequently they also occasionally suffered similar tragedies that profoundly affected communities. In March of 1887 there was a terrible explosion of gas at a colliery in Bulli on the eastern coast of New South Wales. It was one of the worst industrial disasters in that region's mining history, killing eighty-one men and boys, leaving fifty women without husbands and 150 children fatherless. Though the incident occurred hundreds of kilometres away from Ballarat it was widely reported in the Australian press. Within a month Tom and the Model Band had mobilised in aid of the families. The Ballarat Star reports:

"A moonlight concert was given by Bulch's Model Brass Band in the Eastern Oval last night in aid of the Bulli Explosion Relief Fund. Prior to the concert a grand torch light procession was held, and this formed a most attractive feature of the proceedings. It was headed by the Soldiers Hill Fife and Drum Band, after whom came the Ballarat Fire Brigade, the Ballarat East Fife and Drum Band, the Soldiers Hill Fire Brigade, Bulch's Brass Band, and the Ballarat City Fire Brigade, in the order named. There was an excellent muster of firemen and bandsmen, and the procession assumed huge proportions as it marched up and down Sturt street and thence to the Eastern Oval. A raised platform was there provided, and on this Bulch's Band took their stand and went through the following programme.

Overture, "Knight Templar,' H Round,
March, "To Arms," Newton,
Valses (contest), "Homage aux Dames," Waldteufel,
Contest selection, "Gems from Weber," T E Bulch,
Contest march, "The Typhoon," T E Bulch,
Anthem "Daughter of Zion," T Clark,
Valses, "Mountain and Glen," H Round,
Trombone solo, "Death of Nelson," Braham,
"Dead march in Saul," Handel
"God save the Queen".

The band played in first-class style, proving the thoroughness of the instruction they receive, and their performance evidently pleased the large audience that had assembled There were between 2000 and 3000 persons present. There was £19 taken at the gates. The band expect to be able to hand over £40 to the fund."

As well as being the year that Tom founded his Model Band, 1887 was also a significant year for Queen Victoria who had been on the throne for fifty years and as such was about to celebrate her Golden Jubilee on 20 June. Tom saw an opportunity in this occasion to create a patriotic tribute and put it on the market. So far as we can tell Tom did not have any publishing or distribution arrangements for his band music at this time and there are no newspaper reports or programmes showing Australian bands playing any of his band pieces beyond those previously published by T A Haigh back in England. Tom was a multi-instrumentalist though, and just as adept at writing down pieces for other instruments. To commemorate the Jubilee he composed both band and piano variants of a work he called "The Jubilee March," and working with F W Niven's printing company in Ballarat he had the piano music printed so that it could be sold to the public via the shop he ran with John Malthouse. Thus Bulch and Malthouse became music publishers. An attractive front cover sheet was produced with the title of the piece in ornate lettering and a beautiful detailed sketch of the view across the Thames to Windsor Castle, partly wreathed by oak leaves. Tom hoped the patriotic mood surrounding the day might result in sufficient sales of the music to make this new branch to his venture worthwhile. The rear cover featured a bold advertisement for the shop and makes mention that Bulch and Malthouse were also the sole agents in Victoria for the Manchester Brass and Military Band Journal. The Ballarat Star reviewed the newly published march in its issue of the 6th of June:

> "We have received from Mr Thomas E. Bulch, leader of the Model Band, a copy of "The Jubilee March," composed by himself in honour of Her Majesty's Jubilee. Particulars regarding the production are advertised. The march is a skilfully written composition, bearing no traces of amateur workmanship, and as arranged for the pianoforte is easy of performance. We can confidently recommend it to pianoforte players as a "new piece" of more than ordinary merit, and deserving of wide popularity." Queen Victoria came to the throne on 20th June 1837 so this piece was to celebrate 50 years of her reign."

Another piece in the Argus of Melbourne on 18 Jun 1887 reads:

> "From Messrs Bulch & Malthouse, the publishers, Ballarat, we have received copies of "The Jubilee March," composed Thomas E Bulch for band, and arranged in this form for pianoforte – a well marked measure in the key of C."

Given that territory was named after the monarch, there was indeed much patriotic fervour on 20 June with celebrations all over Victoria to mark that Golden Jubilee of Queen Victoria. Tom determined that his Model Band would play their part. On the day itself, set up on the balcony of Messrs Bean, Son and Co. in

Ballarat, the band played a suitably patriotic set commencing with the full band arrangement of the "Jubilee March," followed by other pieces; "Patriotic" and "England's Queen" by J Frost and 'Victoria Regia' by George Webb. Tom's hard work, and many hours put in with his bandsmen, was not going unnoticed. The Ballarat Star of 19 July 1887 offers an insight into how the, still relatively new, band was beginning to be perceived:

> "Bulch's Model Band, of which Ballarat residents have reason to feel proud, have already distinguished themselves in musical contests, but during the approaching spring and summer weather they will, we hear, excel their best performances in the past. As a bandmaster Mr Bulch has displayed considerable ability, and as an organiser he is said to have few equals in this district. Twice, and sometimes three times a week, he has his men at practice, and among the selections rehearsed are new and choice pieces, as played by the leading operatic and military bands of Europe. When the fine weather sets in the public will frequently have an opportunity of hearing the Model Band in open air, and these recitals, together with those of other local bands of note, should be looked forward to with interest by lovers of good music. The performers under Mr Bulch are constant in their practice, mainly with the view of winning further musical laurels in Victoria and elsewhere."

Then, on 16 August 1887, the same newspaper includes an overt appeal for financial support for Bulch's Model Band to assist towards the cost of travel to an upcoming contest in Adelaide.

> "We understand that Bulch's Model Brass Band intend journeying to Adelaide in order to compete at a band contest to be held in connection with the Jubilee Exhibition in that city in October. The members of the band, which carried off second honours at a recent competition, have been practising assiduously for some time, and are determined, if possible, to better the position they then gained. The band numbers about 30 members, and, as the expense of such a trip would so great, it has been suggested by an admirer of the band that it would be a graceful act on the part of the public to bear at least a portion of the burden. The members of the band have, since their organisation, been prominent in assisting charitable efforts, and have also treated the public to several first-class programmes of music gratis. As the honour of the city would, from a musical point of view, be at stake, no doubt the suggestion will be well

responded to, and we presume the band would accept assistance that would be thus spontaneously offered."

New Shildon

It would be easy to wonder what, if anything, had been happening to young George Allan in all the time that Thomas Bulch was undertaking this change from humble blacksmith's apprentice to a celebrated figure of Ballarat and self-made businessman.

Being fair to George the long working day of a blacksmith's striker at the North Eastern Railway works would have left him precious little time for composition and self-promotion, were those objectives even in his nature. Being the younger of the two by fifteen months would, in these early stages, also have meant that he would always be slightly behind Tom in building his musical profile. The Shildon Works was expanding by 1885 and the Blacksmiths department to where George attended daily, moved to a huge new building commissioned by the North Eastern Railway on expenditure of several thousand pounds and constructed by Messrs W and R Blackett of Bishop Auckland. There was more good news for New Shildon as the NER had also decided to close its carriage workshops at Hopetown in nearby Darlington, meaning many of the Darlington workers engaged in the production and repair of wagons at that site were expected to transfer to Shildon Works. The company were demonstrating their faith in the Shildon operation, and this brought added security for its people.

The death of Francis Dinsdale left the New Shildon Saxhorn Band leaderless. Someone new had to grasp the baton or the band might have to fold. For his fellow bandsmen, George Allan looked to be the answer. We can't be absolutely certain that George Allan was the first replacement, but there are no documented reports of any other person also having been bandmaster of the Saxhorn Band in this period. It's difficult to interpret from the evidence available whether assurance of the continuity of the band was smoothly managed after the death of Francis Dinsdale. Nor, for that matter, do we really understand how easy or difficult it was for their rivals, the Temperance Band, to recover from losing their own bandmaster along with a contingent of their principal players. We do know of course that both bands did continue, though neither are recorded anywhere as having entered a band contest during the remainder of the eighteen-eighties, suggesting that this brief period may not have been the easiest of times for either band.

New Shildon Temperance Band did also continue to be active, one documented example being that on 2 August 1887 the band played a selection of music to celebrate the return to Shildon of the Rev H. Spurrier from his seven-week honeymoon in the Highlands of Scotland. He and his new wife were greeted by around five thousand parishioners with fifty girls dressed in white to meet them at the church gates.

By becoming the bandmaster of the Saxhorn Band, George had secured himself a small additional income, improving his circumstances slightly. There were also developments in matters more personal. During the early 1880s George commenced courting Elizabeth Willoughby. Elizabeth had been born in 1860 in a colliery house on Arthur Street, Billy Row near Crook, to William Willoughby and his wife Hannah. This made Elizabeth a little older than George. William was occupied as a coke-burner and living at the village of Auckland Park, between New Shildon and Bishop Auckland, by the time George and Elizabeth met. As with the Bulch and Allan families, the Willoughby family had been a large household of thirteen people, though by 1871 most of the children had grown up and moved out leaving only the parents with three daughters: Elizabeth, Ellen and Emma. As the 1880s began, Elizabeth, like many young working class women in generally poorer communities found employment as a domestic servant. Her employer was the Reverend George Leighton BA, the Church of England Curate of St Cuthbert's Church at High Etherley. It would have been a residential post and involved carrying out domestic chores for the Curate and his wife Sarah. There were two other residents, Mary and Frances Kendall who were related to the Curate's wife. In such a role Elizabeth would have had little time or opportunity to meet any potential husband. This post probably came to a natural conclusion in or around November 1881 when the curate and his family left Etherley to accept a post at the probably more prestigious, Church of St Mary at Morchard Bishop near Exeter. Elizabeth subsequently returned to live with her parents.

How and when George Allan happened upon, and fell in love, with his sweetheart Elizabeth is a story lost in time. It could have been at an engagement of the Saxhorn Band, or it may have been a chance meeting in Shildon, or Bishop Auckland, or at another social event. We can only imagine the circumstances.

Above: St Anne's Church, next to the Town Hall at Bishop Auckland, where George Allan married his sweetheart, Elizabeth Willoughby in 1887

The couple arranged a wedding to take place on Tuesday, 16 August 1887. We might have expected that this would be at All Saints Church in New Shildon, given it was the church with which the Allan family had the closest connections. Instead, though, the chosen venue was St Anne's Church, located on the busy marketplace at Bishop Auckland. This might have been the preference of Elizabeth or her family. St Anne's may well have been the church they attended, though, living at Auckland Park, they would have had other choices nearby. We know very little of the wedding ceremony itself, and whether many or all of either family attended, or whether any of the people from Shildon, bandmates or workmates, made the short journey to Bishop Auckland. The marriage certificate does record, however, that the ceremony was witnessed by William Addison Birkbeck, and Elizabeth's sister Emma Willoughby. These two may have already been sweethearts themselves at that point, but if not, something certainly emerged between them as three years later they too were married. George and Elizabeth's wedding was declared in a modest announcement in the Northern Echo on Thursday the 19th of August:

> "Allan-Willoughby – At St Anne's Church, Bishop Auckland. George Allan of New Shildon, and Elizabeth Willoughby, of Auckland Park."

After the wedding, George moved in with his in-laws at Auckland Park for a while as the couple prepared their own arrangements for the future. Employment records show that he was still employed at the Shildon Works during this time so living there would have added a couple of miles to his walk to work each day unless he managed to hitch a lift on one of the coal trains following the Black Boy Colliery line through the Prince of Wales railway tunnel into New Shildon. In any case he'd have had a little more time to plan how, on his modest blacksmith's striker's wage and with the fee he received as bandmaster, he might be able to move with his wife back to Shildon. During this period George also ended his membership of the Mechanics Institute for a while. It's possible that being absent from New Shildon in the evenings he would not have been able to benefit from its facilities and also that he needed to save every penny to set up a new home. Around this time George also managed to secure an additional income, for in 1886 we see the first reported instance of a George Allan composition being played. On 29 April 1886, on the Mansion Lawn at Felixtowe, the Harwich and Dovercourt Excelsior Band included a galop called "Checkmate" in their programme. Within months this was also being played by bands in Dunster, Greenock, Ipswich, Stoke and Slaithwaite. George Allan had joined Tom Bulch among the ranks of published brass composers.

It's possible that "Checkmate" might not have been his first published work. Trying to trace and recreate a comprehensive catalogue that includes all of George and Tom's compositions has proved extremely difficult. No complete and reliable list exists and we rely on building evidence from old programmes, newspaper reports, advertisements by publishers in the brass press of the day and examination of band libraries and private collections. The more evidence with respect to a piece, the more certain we can be, with the ideal proof being that we have seen it for ourselves. I've been able to verify almost all the pieces we mention in this work, though in some cases the understanding that a piece of music was by one of these two composers remains tentative until we find conclusive proof. Where this is the case I shall express this clearly.

One particularly interesting tentative case worth mentioning from the early days is a march called "The Cyclone" which is reported as having been performed by bands including the Crooke Brass Band, Northfleet Temperance Prize Band and the Black Dyke Band over the years. The first report we have seen was a performance by the Band of the Sunderland Constabulary in Mowbray Park on 6 September 1887. What makes this particular title interesting is that we've also see a report of a Tom Bulch march called "Cyclone" reportedly having been performed by the 3rd Glamorgan Rifle Volunteers Band during 1888. The year suggests that if Tom did create a march using this title, then it would have been created and published before he left Britain.

Why would two composers, so well acquainted, create two marches with almost identical titles? Given Tom's first published march was "The Typhoon" it might be reasonable to assume that he could have chosen "Cyclone" as another wind related title, and yet there are more newspaper references to "The Cyclone" being attributed to George Allan. Excepting the possibility of an error, it may have been that at one point the two decided to see which might create the better march of same title or that they could be two outcomes of some other co-operative or collaborative effort.

It's not unusual for two composers to coincidentally choose the same title for completely different compositions. Taking George Allan's best known two marches, "Knight Templar" and "The Wizard" as examples, the former title was also used by Harry Round and the latter by William Rimmer. Throughout their careers Tom and George would use the same title at least five times, though for compositions created years apart. The "Cyclone" incident is most interesting simply due to its timing, being at a time when both New Shildon born composers were most likely to have known of each other's activity and had opportunity to interact.

Other verified composition titles attributed to Allan appear around this time, all of which were published by Thomas Haigh of Hull in his band journals. They include a schottische entitled

"Dew Drop" and marches called "Silver King," "The Storm Fiend" and "Won From The Waves." The latter, by coincidence or otherwise, shares its title with a boy's adventure novel available in the 1880s that George may have known, written by Victorian author William H G Kingston who died in 1880.
Whatever fees George received from his publisher for these works would have been of help to him in preparing to find a new home to share with his new wife. Elizabeth was certainly on his mind. In one particularly romantic gesture, George used his wife's surname as the title for a polka he composed. Thomas Haigh published the polka, "Willoughby," in the Amateur Brass (& Military) Band Journal and advertised it in the Brass Band News of September 1888.

Ballarat

In Australia, Tom and his friend John Malthouse found an opportunity during 1887 to move their Bulch and Malthouse Music Warehouse to a new and more prestigious location at 16 Sturt Street, quite close to the office of the Ballarat Star newspaper. At the same time Tom was continuing preparations to take his Model Band to Adelaide for an important opportunity to prove themselves at the high profile band contest being organised to take place at the new Jubilee Exhibition Grounds and Building that had been opened on the day of Victoria's Jubilee. The team of family members and friends surrounding the Model Band stepped up their appeal to the people of Ballarat to fund the trip. The approximately 380 mile distance to the capital of South Australia's territorial capital required that both transport and accommodation would need to be covered. The Ballarat Star included a bold and frank appeal on 2 September:

> "Bulch's Model Brass Band, the premier musicians of the colony, made a special appeal to the citizens of Ballarat for assistance towards defraying their expenses in proceeding to Adelaide to join at the International Jubilee Exhibition in a band competition on the 1st of October. The competition is open to all brass and military bands in Australia, and prizes amounting to £90 are to be given. As Ballarat has reason to feel proud of Bulch's Model Band, the residents of the district will doubtless make another display of that generosity for which they

are well known. All letters are to be addressed to Mr S. Jamieson, hon. secretary, Grant street, Ballarat East."

The Ballarat Star continues making the case on the 10 September 1887:

"Ballarat, which has always been to the front, is to be represented in Adelaide at the Intercolonial Band Competition to be held in the Exhibition Building on 1st October by Bulch's Model Brass Band, who carried off second prize at the Intercolonial Band Competition held in Melbourne, and who are the present premiers of Victoria. The band is at present practising five nights weekly under the conductorship of Mr Bulch, and should be amongst the prize-takers. A benefit is to be tendered to the band on Monday next, commencing with a torchlight procession. The proceeds are in aid of defraying the expenses of the band to Adelaide."

With such determination, the band succeeded in raising the funding they required and all twenty-five members departed for Adelaide on schedule. Brass historian Jack Greaves in his account of what happened at the contest, which took place on October the first, explains that the running of the contest was imperfect and there were several aspects of its organisation that left much to be desired. Six bands competed, most with fewer than twenty players. At their turns to play, Bulch's Model Band gave rendition of two of Tom's own pieces; "The Typhoon" and his arrangement "Gems of Weber." At the conclusion they were placed second on points behind the Eastern Suburban Volunteer Band of nineteen performers. Whilst the bands played out in the open air in the Exhibition Grounds, the panel of three judges assigning points for the performances, were positioned within the new Jubilee Exhibition Building. In a letter of protest later written by Tom to the organisers, this located them "at an elevation of at least sixty feet above the bands and distant by one-hundred yards." He claimed, justifiably so from Jack Greaves's perspective, that from this position they couldn't possibly have heard the finer points of the music being played. Tom's protest, and those from two other competing bands were dismissed, and not everyone agreed with them. The Wallaroo Times of Wednesday, 5 Oct 1887, naturally championing one of their their own local band, presents an additional perspective on why the result was felt dissatisfactory:

"The Band Contest. —The great Band Contest at the Exhibition, in which the Peninsula were represented by Bartley's Military Band, came off on Saturday last. Lovers of music in this district were all anxious to see our men at the top, but in this they were disappointed. However, when it is considered that there were six bands competing, including one from Victoria, and that our band was the smallest in point of number, there is no reason for complaint, seeing that they obtained third prize.

Of course musicians are not proverbially the most easily satisfied, and therefore it is no matter for surprise that protests have been entered against the awards, and that one bandmaster has vehemently condemned the Judges through the Press.

However, our men have not taken any part in this but have rested content with the decision whatever their opinions may be. The grounds of the protests are (1) that the Eastern Suburban Volunteer Band played one professional, and (2) that those who were not members were allowed to play. It seems the band was entered as the Eastern Suburban Volunteer Band. Some time since, some members of the band were dismissed for not turning out on the occasion of an important parade, but although, not members of the Band, their services were retained for Saturday's contest."

The same publication goes on to say elsewhere in a summarisation of the day's news:

"The Ballarat bandmaster does not take his 'gruel' kindly."

Tom, confident in his own ability and that of his Model Band had felt slighted by the judges decision. Nonetheless, Bulch's Model Brass Band had come a worthy second and returned to Ballarat with their prize. Within days they were back on the city's streets playing a selection of music that included more new Bulch compositions. We read on 4 October 1887:

"ROTUNDA CONCERT. Bulch's Model Band from Ballarat, which obtained second prize in the brass band contest, gave a concert at the Rotunda on Monday evening. There was a large attendance. An attractive programme was presented, including the two contest pieces, the first, "Gems from Weber' arranged by the bandmaster (Mr. T. E. Bulch), and the other, a march, 'The Typhoon,' also by the bandmaster. Each of the items was well received and applause throughout was liberally bestowed. The following numbers were also given :— Overture, 'Knight

Templar' (H. Round); strand march, 'The Giant' (T. E. Bulch); trombone solo, 'Death of Nelson' (Braham): polka (tonguing), ' The Gumsucker' (T. E. Bulch) ; quartet, 'An Evening Prayer' (H. Round) ; valses, 'Mountain and Glen' (H. Round)."

Tom and his business partner John Malthouse had been looking for ways to expand their business and decided on opening a second branch. By the December of 1887 a new Bulch and Malthouse Music Warehouse opened on the High Street in Maryborough with John Malthouse having relocated to fulfil the post of manager. Tom, and wife Eliza, continued to run the Sturt Street branch. This increased business footprint, raised their profile and opened up new revenue possibilities away from Ballarat. Advertisements for the business, such as this one from the Avoca Mail that year, began to include both addresses:

"Pianos, Organs, Music. – Messrs Bulch & Malthouse want the public to know that they have in stock Pianos by the most noted makers, also the Estey Organs, which are unapproachable in every essential quality. Can be had on easy terms, or lowest prices for cash. Concertinas from 5s' each, accordions from 10s, violins from 10s. A large and splendid stock to select from. Sheet and book music in great variety. Note the Address —BULCH & MALTHOUSE, Music Warehouses, HIGH STREET. – MARYBOROUGH, and 16 Sturt Street, Ballarat."

Later that year on the twenty-first of December, with Christmas, Tom's birthday and New Year's Eve approaching, the Launceston Star and Sydney Daily Telegraph both reveal Tom's next goal for the Model Band. This was a return to fundraising mode to enable attendance at another prestigious contest:

"The band contest to be held in Sydney in January next promises to be a great success, and will undoubtedly be one of the most interesting features of the celebration week. Entries for competition close on the 20th inst., but already a number of bands have entered, among them being the Garrison Band, Hobart; St. Joseph's Band, Launceston ; South Australia Militia Band; Eastern Suburban Volunteer Band, Adelaide; Albury Town Band; Mudgee Town Band, and and the Band of the N.S.W. Naval Brigade. Other bands have notified their intention of entering, including the City Band, Launceston, and Bulch's Model Band, Ballarat, both said to be very good bands. The promoters of the contest are doing everything they possibly can to perfect arrangements and make the 'gathering of the bands' worthy of the week celebrations."

Having also been without a publishing deal for his band music in Australia, Tom progressed the Bulch and Malthouse business to the next level. Those familiar with brass music will have noticed that the pieces mentioned a few paragraphs previously as being played by Bulch's band, entitled "Knight Templar," "An Evening Prayer" and "Mountain and Glen," which were works by the composer Henry Round. Tom would have received these by purchasing Wright and Round's Liverpool Brass and Military Band Journal. Though this journal, started in 1881, was printed and published in Britain, it and many of the other brass journals of the day were distributed throughout parts of the British Empire where an appropriate market appetite existed.

There's not a great deal known about the beginnings of Wright and Round as music publishers. Henry Round was a band teacher who, prior to the company's formation, hand-wrote and lithographed parts he had composed and arranged, in order to meet demand. Co-founder Thomas Hargrave Wright, initially very active in the business, retired well before his passing in 1914 aged seventy-nine. Based in Liverpool, these two also published the Brass Band News, a popular paper with a very wide distribution and convenient channel to predominantly advertise their own music as well as acting as a source of valuable advertising revenue from others. They were considered the leading publishers of brass band music in the last quarter of the 19th century, catering for bands at all levels.

With a barely rivalled market position, distribution network, value of their proposition and the strength of sales, Wright and Round achieved a strong and reliable uptake by subscribing bands. The bands performed the pieces that caught their bandmaster's eye and which they enjoyed from the journal, and ignored the ones that didn't. It became gradually clear that a composer might stand more chance of seeing their piece performed through its appearance in a journal than through attempting to sell the pieces to bands individually themselves.

There were some advantages to this. For example that compositions by composers back in Britain were able to be played and heard in places across the Empire that their creators, in most cases, would never visit themselves, nor ever have found customers in their own right. George Allan for example probably never would have been aware that bands and audiences in far flung places such as Charters Towers in Queensland, or Windsor in New South Wales, were enjoying his music while he was on his way to the Shildon Works for a shift in the blacksmith's department.

From Tom's perspective, however, the question on his mind as with many other Australian musicians, was with only mainly British journals in circulation, where was all the Australian band music? How could such music be progressed without depending, as he once had, on publishers like T A Haigh back in Hull. Like Robert De Lacy before him Tom, from his next actions, clearly believed a new Australian produced brass band journal could be the perfect way to ensure loyal repeat purchase of his own compositions. In 1887 he decided to take a leap of faith and commence publishing his own, and to emphasise its native purpose he called it the Australasian Brass and Military Band Journal. To do this he must have been surely confident that he would be able to compose, or else arrange from the works of others, all the pieces that would be needed to ensure production with the necessary frequency. Band journals were usually published monthly. It would feature his own work almost exclusively. Despite reducing dependence other composers, the production of each issue, the acquiring of subscribers and the management of active subscriptions would still require a great deal of organisation, effort and coordination. As always Tom's starting point was the Ballarat Star who printed of 24 October 1887:

> "It will be interesting to the musical public of Ballarat to know that at a recent competition, at which the leading brass bands in England took part, and which was won by the Honley Brass Band, the test piece which was played by all the competing bands was the contest march "Chef d'Oeuvre," by Mr T. E. Bulch, of Ballarat, which reflects considerable credit upon that gentleman's abilities as a composer, and which has been classed by the publisher (T. A. Haigh, of Hull) as a masterpiece. Mr Bulch, instead of forwarding his productions to England for publication, has arranged with a Ballarat firm to print all the music here, and he is now editing a journal which is styled "The Australasian Brass and Military Band Journal," which has already found its way into the adjoining colonies as

well as having a large Victorian circulation. We wish Mr Bulch every success in his new venture."

Indeed the Honley Band did compete in a march contest as part of an overall brass band contest at the annual Shildon Show in August 1886 at which, though it is not named in reports, they could well have played "Chef D'Oeuvre," in which case Thomas would almost certainly have heard about it by post from his family or former bandmates. Initially, and in a surprisingly bold and possibly expensive move, Bulch and Malthouse advertised their journal in Britain as well as Australia. An advertisement for the Australasian Brass and Military Band Journal appeared in Wright and Round's Brass Band News towards the end of 1887 seeking subscribers in Britain. An annual subscription would be required to be paid in advance and would cost twenty-four shillings for the brass band edition, twenty-eight shillings for the military band edition and extra parts could be obtained for an added annual rate of one shilling and sixpence. Postage to the United Kingdom was extra at four shillings. The subscribers list for the year ahead included new works by Tom; "The Elephant," "The Gumsucker," "Soldier's Pride," "Good Shot" and "The Giant" among arranged works by others which included an arrangement of "Fair Maid of Perth" by Glaswegian violin composer and arranger Carl Volti.

It was an open fact that the journal as a whole was the work of Tom Bulch himself, though as we say above he drew inspiration from the work of others producing full brass band arrangements. That, particularly in Australia, began an unfortunate process whereby among banding communities the name of Tom Bulch gradually became confused with those of the original composers who were sometimes presumed to be pseudonyms. Unintentionally muddying the water further, Tom would progress later to using pseudonyms making it difficult to know which names are and aren't Tom Bulch. Perhaps having considered the marketability of the Australasian Band Journal, or else having received suggestions, the title of the journal later evolved to become the Intercolonial Brass Band Journal.

Adoption of the new journal may not have happened as quickly as Tom wanted, but gradually a number of Australian bands, if not the British ones, adopted it alongside their regular British favourites. Looking slightly ahead for example an issue of the Wagga Wagga Express, of January 1892, reports minutes from a meeting of the Wagga Town Band which included a resolution that the band will continue to subscribe to Wright and Round's Liverpool brass journal, but also Bulch's Intercolonial Brass Band Journal.

In the last years of the eighteen-eighties and the early eighteen-nineties we see that the newspaper and programme inclusions of Tom Bulch compositions evolve from describing performances only by whatever band he was conducting at the time to a description of an extending reach initially within Victoria and then out into Southern Australia, Queensland and New South Wales.

New Shildon

The dawn of eighteen-eighty-eight brought another wedding celebration for the the Allan family in New Shildon. This time, on the 17 January, George's older brother William was marrying his sweetheart Mary Ann Metcalf and, unlike George and Elizabeth, the couple chose the family's nearby All Saints Church.
George's father, John James Allan, signed the register as a witness. Perhaps William had been a little closer to his father than George, as he had initially followed his father into tailoring but later seemed to be one of those people unable to settle in one job and able to turn his hand to most things. During his lifetime he spent time, after tailoring, as a plumber, and electrician at the railway works and, when the great British favourite dish of fish and chips became popular a fish frier.

The following month George's uncle, Ralph, died. Ralph had arrived in New Shildon at about the same time as George's father. A shoemaker, he established a life and family of his own in the town, but after he passed away, his widow moved west, away from the clatter and industrial smuts of Shildon to the far quieter agricultural market town of Crook.

Despite temporarily living with in-laws, away from New Shildon and his closest relations, George managed to keep-up the New Shildon Saxhorn Band. Though they and the New Shildon Temperance Band don't seem to have been actively seeking contests, there were engagements to be had. The Daily Gazette for Middlesbrough reported that while the local Tory clubs were 'holding high holiday' at Windlestone Park, on 25 August 1888, the New Shildon Saxhorn Band was assisting in the celebration of the first anniversary of the Shildon Liberal Club:

> "The proceedings, which were jointly under the auspices of the Liberal Club and Shildon Branch of the National League, began with a procession through the streets. The sturdy Liberals and Nationalists of the place assembled at the Liberal Club and, headed by the New Shildon Saxhorn Band, paraded the principal streets of both Shildons. The demonstration was followed by a public tea, at which over 1,000 people partook of the good things provided."

A meeting was later convened at which the then Tory government of the time was condemned in the strongest terms. The Prime Minister of the day was the Marquess of Salisbury, who had been elected in 1886, and there would not be another general election until 1892. The 1884 Representation of the People Act had extended the right to vote to men that held or rented property or land that exceeded ten pounds in value. This still excluded forty percent of men, and all women, from having a say in who governed the country. In addition, during most of the Victorian era, the two parties sparring for political control of the nation were barely separable in terms of policy or regard for the type of working man as might be found in New Shildon. Nonetheless, prospective Members of Parliament still required votes, particularly after the 1884 Act, so parties established clubs and held rallying events, at which there would always be room for stirring music.

On that particular point it's worth noting a contrast between the life of George Allan and the life of Thomas Edward Bulch which is that, excepting the occasional contest test piece, we have very little information about what music the New Shildon Saxhorn Band played. There is a distinct difference throughout the Victorian era in the way newspapers reported events involving the brass bands. In parts of Britain we are lucky if the reporter adds that a band entertained at a particular occasion and it's rare that we are treated to an understanding of what was, or would be, played. It tends to vary from newspaper to newspaper, with some reporters occasionally listing the programme for the reader's benefit. In almost all cases where the New Shildon Saxhorn Band entertained, the reporters completely neglected to describe what was played as if such detail were of no import whatsoever.

There are cases where we are given the programme, particularly if it seems the reporter is interested in the music, but most often where the concert is being advertised in advance by the band or park authority. Of course to advertise a programme for an upcoming concert would require expenditure of money, which the industrial bands of the north found scarce enough to begin with. This has left us with no information as to whether, or with what frequency, George included his own compositions in programmes of music played by the Saxhorn Band. We get no understanding of which of his pieces he, or his band, particularly favoured, or which of them endured in the composer's preferences. In all of the research I have done towards this work I have not once seen any newspaper reference to a George Allan composition having been played by the New Shildon Saxhorn Band and I find that profoundly sad. In part I suspect this has contributed to some of the difference between how Tom Bulch and George Allan are regarded right up to the present.

Right from the beginning of Tom Bulch's career in music he seems to have recognised the importance of this. During his time as bandmaster of the New Shildon Temperance Band, the Allendale and Kingston Band, 3rd Militia and now Bulch's Model Brass Band we have seen, in both Britain and Australia, detail of the programme played, or to be played, included in the reports of events, and we have far more information regarding how he included his own work. It's rare that we have to rely upon finding this in paid advertisements, and it is as if Tom had courted the journalists and ensured that they were provided with the list of programme items to include in the report. We can be certain, from the detail in some of the pieces written during his time in Australia that he was also prepared to feed tit-bits of band news to the papers or else, as we shall see, if he wanted to be heard, ensure this by writing open letters through the press. It feels as though we can conclude from this that whilst George appears to have seen little value in anything other than daily work, family life and the act of creating and performing music itself, Tom in contrast gained an early appreciation that in order for his ambitions to be realised it was essential to engage in a little self-publicity. No doubt operating a business located only a few doors down from the Ballarat Star office offered a convenient advantage in this respect.

Ballarat

In Ballarat there was a busy year ahead for Tom and the men of Bulch's Model Brass Band. On 14th January 1888, the Ballarat Star tells of the band running through pieces at a concert ahead of the contest in Sydney which they had been preparing for:

> "The promenade concert given in the Eastern Oval last night by Bulch's Model Band was well attended, and the music was much enjoyed. A long and varied programme was gone through, and among the pieces played were those which are to be produced at the Centennial Demonstration to be held in Sydney shortly. Prior to the concert the fire brigades, Ballarat City, Soldiers Hill, and Ballarat East Fife and Drum Bands, and the Railway and Soldiers Hill Brass Bands joined in torchlight procession to the grounds. A platform stage was here erected for the band, and gas jets opposite the stand and ladies' reserve gave the Oval a brilliant appearance. On the conclusion of each number Mr Bulch and his musicians were loudly applauded. A charge of 6d was made for admission to the grounds, and the amount taken at the gates was £15, and this, together with the proceeds of the sale of tickets outside, will after paying expenses give a profit of about £20. The band will leave for Sydney shortly."

On the 23rd, the Star expands upon on the band's plans:

> "Bulch's Model Band, who have entered for the Sydney Centennial competitions, leave Ballarat by the 7.10 p.m. train this evening for Melbourne, en-route to New South Wales. The contests will commence on Wednesday. At 6.30 this evening the Model Band will muster in front of the Star office, and will next march up Sturt street and along Lydiard street to the Western railway station. To-night the band will remain in Melbourne, starting for Sydney by express at 6.40 on Tuesday, arriving at their destination early on Wednesday morning. A representative of the band left Ballarat for Sydney on Saturday, for the purpose of securing accommodation for the musicians in the capital of the sister colony. The following members of the band have entered for solo competitions: — Cornets — J. Carah, R. Malthouse; euphoniums — A. Ferguson, V. Lorimer. Appended are the names of the Model bandsmen who are to represent Ballarat at the competitions:— T. Malthouse, soprano cornet, E flat; J. Scott, solo, do, B flat; J. Curah, do; R. Malthouse, do; A. Briant, repiano, do; P. Reiffel, 2nd cornet, do; J. Clark, do; F. Hoare, 3rd, do; J. Collier, do: J. Malthouse, solo tenor, E flat; J.

Shepherd, 1st do; W. Holt, 2nd do; S. Jamieson, 1st horn, do; H. Lockett, 2nd do; H. Knipe, 3rd do; J. Thom, 1st baritone, B flat; C. Grove, 2nd do; T. Haymes, 1st tenor trombone, b flat; A. Hutson, 2nd do; A. Ferguson, solo euphonium, do; J. Tolliday, bass, do; V. Lorimer, bombardon, E flat; E. Jewell, do; P. McNamara, do; W. Middleton, side drum; R. Butland, bass drum; Geo. Bree, drum major; T. E. Bulch, bandmaster. It is probable the results of the contests will not be known until the end of the week."

Whilst the list of the bandsmen, with it's abbreviations of 'ditto', makes a challenging read it has some importance in that it tells you more of the ongoing importance of Tom's relationship to the Malthouse brothers whose intervention brought him to Australia. Tom's probably closest friend John, otherwise living at Maryborough to run the second branch of the partnership's music stores, remains a tenor horn player in the band. Thomas Malthouse features on soprano cornet, whilst his brother Robert is among the solo cornet players. Of the four, only George Malthouse, usually among the bass section, is missing. The story of George Malthouse, whom as you may recall was separated from his brothers for a time as a lad, is a particularly sad one which we'll return to before this account concludes.

The Grand Centennial Band Contest took place at the Carrington Grounds in Sydney. On this occasion Bulch's Model Band, as at Adelaide, took second prize. They were beaten only by the 4th Regiment Band from the city of Newcastle in New South Wales which was conducted by William Barkel. According to the Ballarat based band historian Robert Pattie, that band was considered to be one of the finest bands in Australia at that time and held an imposing record of contest success. The Eastern Suburban Band, victors from the Jubilee Exhibition contest at Adelaide finished fourth this time, 17 points behind Bulch's Model Band, and fifteen fewer than Launceston City, Tasmania, in third. Tom might have been forgiven for relishing that change in the Eastern Suburban Band's fortunes, though for the winning band on this occasion he had only respect. Later, in around 1894, he would compose the march "Newcastle" as a tribute to their bandmaster, William Barkel, whom he clearly held in high esteem.

Thomas's own stock in banding circles was increasing sufficiently so that on occasion others made clear they wanted their past associations with him known. In the Illawara Mercury of Wollongong on 4 February 1888 he was 'name-dropped' by H Collings, a fellow former Shildon bandsman making a new life for himself in the colony:

> "Mr Bulch, leader of Bulch's Model Band, which gained second prize at the contest in Sydney, was first comet player in a band at Childern *(sic)*, England, when Mr H. Collings, now a resident of Wollongong, was conductor."

We've been unable to find any reference to a Mr H. Collings conducting either of the New Shildon bands in the period when Tom Bulch was active in New Shildon though it may still have been the case. As we saw with Robert De Lacy, conductors were occasionally brought in especially for contests.

Tom often used appearances of the band as an opportunity to raise funds to keep the band operating and defray contest expenses, as well as ensuring the small regular fee he took for his own services as bandmaster. But he also saw an important duty of the band as being present at events that would benefit other worthy causes. In December 1887 the Model Band was one of five bands marching with the Ballarat fire brigades as part of the procession to the Eastern Oval for the fourth annual charity service of the Old Colonists Association of Ballarat. Now, in March of 1888, following their good result at Sydney, the band gave their support to another benefit event.

> "HUMFFRAY BENEFIT CONCERN AND WELSH PIC-NIC. A grand Pic-nic of Welshmen and friends in the Botanical Gardens is announced for Friday, 2nd March. In the evening the above concert will be held in the Academy of Music, the use of which has been kindly granted by .Sir W. J. Clarice, ... A good programme has been framed. Mr Philip Jones is musical director, and all available local vocal and instrumental talent will assist. The promoters now claim public support on this occasion on behalf of an old resident, a former Parliamentary representative, and one of the Pioneers of Ballarat. It is hoped that this will be a bona fide benefit, not one in name only. The indefatigable secretary, Mr. J. Williams, and his aides are working hard to secure success. Bulch's band and the popular Welsh harpist, Mr Llewellyn Thomas, will perform. Tickets are to be had at the booksellers and music shops, Sutton's and Harrison's."

The event was afterwards reviewed thus:

"For the first time for several years St. David's Day has been allowed to pass without the holding of the usual Welsh national festival. The memory of the annual Eisteddfod was, however, revived last evening, the occasion being a benefit concert tendered to Mr J. B. Humffray by some of our most popular amateur vocalists, assisted by the Barak Dramatic Company, the whole being under the direction of Mr Phillip Jones. Many of the items in the programme were selected from the national melodies dear to the Cymru, giving to the entertainment a sufficiently Welsh character to render it an acceptable substitute for the usual Eisteddfod celebration. Each of the two parts of a well-selected programme was opened with a performance by Bulch's Model Band, given with the precision, perfect balance of tone, and excellent effect for which the band has earned for itself a high reputation."

Wednesday, 7 March 1888 saw the first annual meeting of Bulch's Band, which as an act of transparency was reported through the press. The details therein reveal interesting aspects of the running of the band including the degree of Tom's own influence over how things were run and a summary explaining the financial workings of the band, which in its first year involved a substantial amount of money for that time:

"BULCH'S MODEL BAND. The first annual meeting of the band was held in the bandroom, Sturt street, Wednesday evening, Mr Bulch, bandmaster in the chair. Correspondence. — From the Ballarat City Fire Brigade, asking the band if they would in future act as the brigade band. — Request granted. A new set of rules drawn up by the committee were considered, and, after slight alterations, were adopted. The secretary read the balance-sheet for the past year. The band was formed on 10th January, 1887, and were thus nearly 14 months from their formation, but owing to the band attending the Sydney Band competition held on 26th January they were unable to hold their meeting at the proper time. The receipts for the year amounted to £405 and expenditure to £440 6s 3d, leaving a debit balance of £35 6s 3d. The following: items are included in the expenditure:—Uniforms, £79 6s; instruments, £66 17s; bandmaster and music, £47 12s. The band has won three second prizes during the year, amounting to £110 5s, viz., second in Melbourne, 26th February, 1887; second in Adelaide, 1st October, 1887; and second in Sydney, 26th January, 1888. They have also received £75 5s from paid engagements. The band has also assisted in the cause of charity, having on several occasions given their services gratis, and in April last gave a promenade concert on the Eastern Oval in aid of the sufferers by the late Bulli disaster, the net proceeds handed to the fund amounting to £41 10s 6d. The committee begged to congratulate the members upon the success of the band in the past and hoped they would excel their previous performances in the future; the total strength of the band at present was 28 members, and it is intended to increase that number to 35, as it is intended to hold a contest on a larger scale than any yet held about Christmas 1888, either in Melbourne or Sydney, when the New Zealand bands will be present. The winners of the first and second prizes in the Sydney contest were pure brass bands, i.e., had no reed instruments, and both were supplied with a complete set of instruments from the same maker, viz., F. Besson and Cos., of London. The following offices were balloted for, and duly elected:—President, Mr John Robson, J.P.; vice-presidents, Hons. D. Ham and H Gore, M's. L.C., Messrs A. Kortlang, and U. T. Hager; bandmaster, Mr T. E. Bulch (re-elected); assistant bandmaster, Mr J. Scott; secretary and band sergeant, Mr S. Jamieson (re-elected); treasurer, Mr G. Bree; corporal, Mr J. Thom; committee. Messrs J. Carah, T. Malthouse, J. Thom, C. Grove, J. Tolliday, J. Scott, E. Jewell, R. Butland. Messrs J. Coliver and Butland were elected librarians for the ending quarter. The following were elected patrons of the band: Hon. Phillip Russell, M.L.C., Hon. Colonel Smith, M.L.A., J. Russell, M.L.A., E. Murphy, M.L.A., C. E. Jones, M.L.A., Messrs W. Bentley, and I. Jonas. The offer of a new bandroom by Mr Abrahams, tobacconist, Sturt street, was accepted, and a special vote of thanks was passed to him for the generous offer. It was decided to hold a sale of gifts in about three months, proceeds to be devoted to the reduction of the debt and purchase of new instruments. A strong committee was formed to carry out the scheme. Votes of thanks to the retiring officers for their past services, and to the chairman, and the meeting closed."

From this report, you get a sense that Tom wanted to prove that his band could be the best not only in the town, or colony, but possibly the continent. The Australian band scene was growing and Tom was desperate to keep up with it.

On 2 April, Bulch's Model Brass Band headed yet another procession to the Ballarat Eastern Oval. This time the aim of the parade was to draw attention to the Ballarat Public Library Sports. It was relatively quiet on account of fine weather the previous day having tempted people away from the city to the suburbs. Then on 12 October 1888, according to the Ballarat Star, we see one of those marvellous moments where threads that were woven in New Shildon early in the story re-converge ever so briefly in a way that reveals a tiny glimpse into obscure relationship between Tom and George. Bulch's Model Brass Band had been engaged to perform a concert on the balcony of the North Grant Hotel that day. Tom had, as always, prepared a programme for the band to play, and would have rehearsed the pieces in the bandroom beforehand. What makes this particular programme slightly more interesting to us is that Tom selected a march entitled "Forward" by his old bandmate and near neighbour George Allan. This piece had been published by T A Haigh in the Amateur Brass and Military Band journal in 1887, suggesting that either Thomas was still acquiring this as an import from Britain, or alternatively that George or some other Shildonian had sent it to him. This rare incident suggests that, if nothing else, Tom was certainly aware of George's early progress towards being a published composer, and that he felt this piece worthy of being played by the Model Band on this occasion.

On 11th November 1888, Thomas's wife Eliza gave birth to a boy at the family home on Albert Street, Ballarat. The couple decided to name him after his father, thus he became Thomas Edward Bulch Jr.

New Shildon

As the weather began to cool in Australia, back in County Durham spring was turning to summer. Living away from New Shildon may have meant that George had a longer journey to his workplace, but that the house at Auckland Park was less crowded than his former family home also seems to have afforded him the space and opportunity to compose, and we see that by the end of that year he had created at least seventeen confirmed pieces for Thomas Haigh's journal since the latter started publishing his work. It's probable there were more than this. Though these included a couple of hymns and some dance music, the majority were quicksteps, or marches. He also created two contest marches designed to demonstrate the ability of all sections of the band. These he entitled "Defiance" and "The Dragon." Another piece of note created that year was a march entitled "Jupiter" which is interesting because years later he would create a contest march bearing the exact same title which shared little if any musical phrasing with the 1888 version. The New Shildon Saxhorn Band seem to have had a quiet year though.

Only a few days after the birth of Tom's son, George was similarly blessed when, at the Willoughby family home, William Street, Auckland Park, Elizabeth Allan gave birth to a daughter, whom the couple subsequently named Lillie. The young couple had Lillie baptised at the local, but now long since demolished, St Phillip's Church in Auckland Park on 5 December 1888.

1889 seems a far quieter year for George Allan, possibly on account of his newly acquired status as a father. One notable fact about this year is that during this year he made his return to New Shildon, bringing his wife and baby Lillie with him. The Allans had obtained a home at an address that those many bandsmen familiar with original copies of his marches "Knight Templar" and "The Wizard" might find familiar. So far as we are able to tell, The Allans were the first family ever to be resident at the newly built number 2 Pears Terrace. This house was only a very short distance from Chapel Street, where George was born, and Adelaide Street and Redworth Road where he had grown up. It was conveniently sited just over a railway footbridge from the Mechanics Institute on Station Street, a cluster of shops and importantly only a short walk from the railway wagon works where George was employed. At that time the house was also on the very eastern edge of New Shildon facing further along the railway track that ran by the end of the street. Thus the hiss, puff and whistle of locomotives and the rumble and clack of new and repaired wagons being led out to the world would be part of the daily background soundscape for the Allan family. 2 Pears Terrace was to remain the family home for the rest of the couple's married life.

From their front window, George and Elizabeth would have had a view of a countryside landscape that over time would include a view of Shildon Colliery pit, nicknamed Dabble Duck on account of the constantly wet land. This old pit, dating back to at least the early 1870s, had a fluctuating number of miners, but seems to have been a relatively small one until the mid-twentieth century. It was in the ownership of Messrs. George Pears and partners which without any doubt, given the fact that the houses overlooked his property, accounts for how the street came to be named Pears Terrace.

Above: No 2, Pears Terrace, New Shildon where George Allan lived with his wife and family from 1889 until his retirement in 1925.

George's composing activity seems to have slowed at this point, but not to a halt, with quadrille "Florence," a schottische "The Sunbeam" and a quickstep "Tidal Wave" all being published this year, as well as a march named after the nearby Roman town of Binchester. Though we see fewer verified compositions being published for a while we do notice a reinvigoration of the New Shildon Saxhorn Band. The Northern Echo tells us how on 11 May 1889 the band provided music at a mass meeting of miners at the ball alley in Old Shildon. It was, the journalist claimed, the largest that had been held in the Auckland district. The lodges of New Shildon, Adelaide, Auckland Park and St Helen's Collieries were represented, and street processions with handsome lodge banners took place "amid the éclat" given by performances of the New Shildon Saxhorn Band. The Newcastle Journal picked up on the same story and gave more detail of its objectives which were to foster greater unison between the men of the attending collieries in their campaigning to limit the working day to ten hours. That reference to a "ball alley" looks to relate to a walled court in which the now somewhat lost sport of "fives" would have been played. This was a game with a number or formats but usually played with hands, or occasionally bats. Nowadays it is usually associated with public schools, but it appears to have temporarily been something of a Victorian craze. A quick delve into contemporary reports reveals that a number of such a facilities were present in the area during the latter part of the nineteenth century, including one at Spennymoor and one at Canney Hill just above nearby Bishop Auckland.

There is a suggestion, reported elsewhere, that the New Shildon Saxhorn Band may have competed at a band contest featuring six bands at the Auckland Cricket and Football Club Gala, though other conflicting reports noted that it was a Coundon band, so perhaps a journalistic error. In any case whichever band was unplaced in the top three. Otherwise, both Shildon brass bands were absent from the notable contests of the area in this year. Even the band contest at the Shildon Horticultural Show on 11th August, described by the Northern Echo as "in its way the leviathan of the North" saw neither of the town's two bands enter.

July of 1889 did see the New Shildon Saxhorn host a sports event, most likely as a fundraiser to raise money to keep the band going. Geographically, though an important town, New Shildon was much smaller, and of far lower standing than the city of Ballarat. Consequently George and his bandsmen found their fundraising potential greatly curtailed in comparison to that of Bulch's Model Brass Band. This sporting event would be quite typical of the kind of event they relied upon. It took place on Saturday, 27 July, having had to be twice postponed on account of poor weather. The band had organised, and encouraged competitors for, a variety of featured races, games and also included a football competition. Four football clubs took part and victory was ultimately experienced by the Shildon football club, for which they carried off a cup valued at one-pound two-shillings and sixpence. According to the reports the committee considered the attendance to have been encouraging and they were satisfied with the results.

Ballarat

In Ballarat, the year was to be another significant one for Thomas Bulch. A new year commenced amidst the summer heat with the Model Band once again in pursuit of contest success. The Ballarat Star of New Year's Eve 1888 reported that the members of Bulch's Model Band were to meet that very afternoon at the Western Railway Station, to proceed to Maryborough by the 3.30pm train to take part in the band contest being held in the new Town Hall there at seven o'clock. Maryborough was, of course, host to Bulch and Malthouse's second branch of their Music Warehouse business, and where John Malthouse, solo tenor horn player in Tom's band, was resident. The Ballarat Star on New Year's Day 1889 provided a breakdown of the outcome.

> "BAND CONTEST AT MARYBOROUGH. Our local correspondent last night wired: "The band contest in connection with the Highland Society's demonstration, to be held at the Prince's Park to-morrow, took place in the Town Hall to-night. The first prize was, £30, and a silver-mounted baton; second prize, £5. The bands competing were Bulch's Model Band (Ballarat), and Bowenvale and Avoca bands. The programme consisted of a selection, march, and waltz, for each of which the judges allowed a maximum of 15 points, or a total of 45 points. The results were as follows:— Bulch's Band, 43 points, 1; Bowenvale Band, 35 points, 2; Avoca Band, 12 points, 3."

Though it was less prestigious in terms of the number and calibre of competing bands, this was a very decisive result of which Thomas must have been proud. His Model Band were adjudged to have been only two points short of a perfect score of forty-five. The Argus of Melbourne explained that the band had, according to the judges, lost one point on account of expression and another one for harmony in the march piece. On 14 March, Tom's band were back to the business of entertaining the people of Ballarat:

> "The moonlight concert given on the Eastern Oval last night by Bulch's Model Band was well attended. Prior to the opening of the entertainment a number of rockets were sent skyward, while at intervals in the performance crackers, Catherine wheels, and squibs were exploded. As usual Bulch's band played their

programme in excellent style, and the audience were not slow in showing their appreciation of the ability displayed by the musicians. The pavilion was brilliantly illuminated with coloured lights, and the whole appearance of the grounds was very pleasing. The takings at the gates amounted to £12."

It sounds like quite a spectacular event, a little ingenious, and far from the impression one might have of a stiff and 'proper' Victorian occasion. Less than a fortnight after this fantastic concert took place an unexpected disaster was to be visited upon the Bulch and Malthouse business. This incident was widely reported, but as always, and on this occasion no doubt helped by their office only being based a few doors away, it is the Ballarat Star that contained the most detailed account:

"A conflagration that might have proved a most disastrous one broke out last night shortly before 5 o'clock in the block of wooden buildings in Sturt street, situated between Lyons and Raglan streets. The fire was first noticed by a young man named W. Mortimer, an employe at Messrs Harry Davies and Co's establishment, who was passing at the time, and caught sight of a glare through the window of Mr T E Bulch's music warehouse. He at once gave the alarm at the City Fire Brigade station, which fortunately happens to be not more than about 100 yards from the scene of the fire. The brigadiers turned out smartly, and at once went to work on the burning buildings. The doors were broken open, and a stream of water put on in the interior. Another hose was taken on to the roof, but the pressure proved to be so weak that for a while there was only a trickle from the branch. This occurred at a most critical period of the fire, and had there been any wind blowing the whole block of buildings must have been consumed. The water came at last, however, and by dint of judicious work the firemen succeeded in confining the flames to three of the shops. The Ballarat Brigade were quickly on the scene, and also had a stream of water playing on the flames. Two of the shops burnt belonged to Mrs Reardon, one of them being untenanted, while the other shop was occupied by Mr T. E Bulch, music seller. The third shop was owned and occupied by Mrs Saunders, a dealer in millinery, haberdashery &c. These shops were completely gutted, and the whole of their contents destroyed. The adjoining shops were those occupied by Mr Thompson, jeweller, and Mr Jolly, bookseller, and those were almost untouched by the flames. A crowd of several thousand persons assembled in Sturt street during the fire. A number of youths endeavoured at one period to burst in the door of Mr Thompson's jewellery establishment, but were prevented by Sergeant Charles. We understand that the building owned by Mrs Saunders was insured in the Liverpool, London, and Globe Company for £150, but the stock was uninsured. Mrs Reardon's property was not covered by insurance. Mr Bulch, who is at present absent from Ballarat, had an insurance of £450 over his stock. It is not known whether the fire originated in Mr Bulch's shop or in the unoccupied premises next door. The brigadiers of both West and East deserve the greatest credit for their efforts, which resulted in the saving of perhaps thousands of pounds worth of property. It may be mentioned, as a peculiar circumstance, the unoccupied shop was but recently tenanted by Mr Thompson, who removed two doors nearer Lyons street, and thus just escaped the fire."

It is difficult to express just how devastating an impact this fire would have on Tom's business aspirations. It's true that, as the report states, his stock was covered by an insurance policy. We must remember though, as Eric Tomkins points out in his family history of T E Bulch, as a composer many of his manuscripts and private papers would have been destroyed in the fire. Getting back on his feet would not be so simple as to re-stock the store from suppliers. What had caused the fire that day? Was it mishap, or mischief? Tom was elsewhere at the time, so presumably the business was being managed by Eliza in his absence. There is no indication in the news reports of any mischief or vindictiveness. Fires are a common hazard, particularly with timber buildings. The minutes from the monthly meeting of the Ballarat Fire Brigade from the following month show that there were ten other fires they had to contend with that month and a small number of false alarms. One cannot help but wonder whether there may have been more to the situation than a simple accidental fire.

Of course Bulch and Malthouse were a partnership, so John Malthouse would also feel the impact of this catastrophe. Tom's grandson, Eric, tells us that after the Sturt Street fire Tom managed to obtain some space in a sports store over the street from the burned-out shop, and was able to continue selling what wares he still had. That new instance of the business was in his own name only. Bulch and Malthouse, for whatever reason, were no longer a partnership. Something about the fire incident appears to have caused a falling out between these two old banding comrades. Whether John Malthouse considered Tom to be in any way responsible, perhaps through his absence at the time of the fire, or whether John felt that Thomas asked for support to an extent he was unprepared to meet, we'll probably never know. Tom's insurance policy paid out, as this letter in the Ballarat Star of 18 April 1889 confirms:

> "Fire, Fire, Fire. To the Editor of the Star. Sir, I have much pleasure in notifying the PROMPT SETTLEMENT of my CLAIM in full against the NEW ZEALAND INSURANCE COMPANY for loss sustained by me at the fire in Sturt Street, MESSRS BROKENSHIRE and COLTMAN, the local agents having settled with me this day. T E Bulch. 17th April 1889."

Interestingly it seems the emphasis of the letter serves more as an advertisement for the Insurance Company than it does a public notice on Thomas's behalf. From July, though, his concession area in W Owen's Sports Depot on Bridge Street was back to offering concertinas, accordions, violins, flutes and piccolos, and he was once again advertising in the Ballarat Star. We shall probably never understand the extent of the falling out between the two, however events in the following year suggest that the argument was not, perhaps, terminal for their friendship.

New Shildon

Easter of 1890 saw Thomas Edward Bulch make a return to the contesting scene at New Shildon, in spirit if not physically. On 16 April 1890 the Ballarat Star reports:

> "At the New Shildon Band Contest, which took place in England on Easter Monday, the test piece was a march "Chef D'Oeuvre," composed by Mr. T E Bulch of Ballarat."

What's remarkable is that the news article was printed not long after Easter so the word must have travelled fast, perhaps by telegram, else Tom must have known well in advance. It's unlikely that anyone other than Tom would have provided the Star with this snippet of information. Tom was probably quite pleased that his status as a composer still held relevance in the town of his birth, though one can't help but wonder what significance this might hold to his fellow citizens of Ballarat.

Regarding what we know of that particular contest, the

Northern Echo of 9 April, 1890, tells us that it was indeed held on the Easter Monday, 7th at a field near Shildon Lodge Colliery. It was hosted by Tom's former band, the New Shildon Temperance Brass Band. The article states that the principal test piece was "Nil Desperandum" by Harry Round, though as often was the case there was an additional quickstep contest for which the test piece, despite not being named by the Echo, most probably was "Chef D'Oeuvre."

The bands competing that day were; Whitworth, Spennymoor Temperance, Anfield Plain, Hartlepool North Eastern Railway Band, Hartlepool Operatic, Cockerton Band and Stockton Model Band. Whitworth came out on top to take the main prize, and the Spennymoor Temperance Band picked up the prize for the quickstep. Neither of the Shildon bands competed; not unusual as the Temperance Band were the organisers, yet there was a programme of dance music given by George Allan and his New Shildon Saxhorn Band later. This is slightly odd given that the Temperance Band were hosts, but may indicate that there was camaraderie between the two bands. Perhaps having the Saxhorn Band play afforded the gentlemen from the Temperance Band the opportunity to relax and enjoy the occasion.

Not so unusual was that there was some controversy attached to the contest in that the Hartlepool Operatic Band were disqualified at some point in the proceedings. Rumours were circulated that the Hartlepool North Eastern Railway Servants Band may have raised objections about their local rivals, but in a letter to the editor of the Hartlepool Northern Daily Mail published on the 9th of April, the secretary of the NER Servants Band publicly and strenuously denied the accusation.

Having examined the evidence that remains of the lives of Tom Bulch and George Allan, one of the most noticeable differences between the two was their respective approaches and attitudes to press coverage. To Tom, a strong profile in the brass band or local press what something he recognised as an absolute necessity in order to help him achieve his goals and aspirations. He clearly had an appreciation that people needed to be aware of who you were and what you achieved, step by step, to become a recognised figure. He was immodest in a most professional way. Though things didn't always work out for him as well as he clearly hoped, we have also seen, through the language used to describe his work and deeds, that he was generally successful in nurturing appreciation and respect. George, who felt bound to his traditional manual occupation in order to provide for his wife and family, was far more prone to avoid the limelight. Perhaps he felt it unnecessary, or that attaining a lofty reputation for his composing achievements could make it harder to fit in with his family and workmates in a rough and broadly ungenteel working community. His granddaughter described him as a quiet man, suggesting he preferred a low profile. It is possible that this comparatively low profile in the general and music press, was not of his own choosing, and more a reflection on the attitude of journalists of the north-east of England to the cultural contribution of the brass band movement. From what I have seen, their Australian counterparts throughout this period seemed to demonstrate greater enthusiasm for describing the developing cultural aspects of their society. The unfortunate effect is that more is said overall of Tom, than of George, and this makes it harder to explore the latter in equivalent depth.

There is, however, one incident in that takes place in 1890 that does reveal a little more of the human nature of George Allan beyond his musical capability. It relates to a brush with the justice system. On 15 August 1890 the Durham County Advertiser reported on a court case involving the, then twenty-six year old, George:

"James Jameson brought an action against George Allan, both of Shildon, for the value of a gable end or dwelling house, valued at £14 18s. Mr Leyburn appeared for the plaintiff, who is a railway inspector and who owns property. It was alleged that the defendant lives in his own property, adjoining some property owned by plaintiff, and there was some land adjoining this property. Defendant commenced to build on this property and in doing so commenced to make holes into the gable end of the plaintiff's property, which was the matter in dispute. Defendant has asked if there would be any objections to him building on this property, and received an answer that there would be no objections providing that he committed no injury, but on its being built it was discovered that defendant had drove into the gable end. James Francis Adamson, a builder and licensed valuer, living at Shildon, proved to the erection of the gable end spoken to by plaintiff. His Honour gave judgement for £9, and asked the defendant how he could pay it, and he replied that he could not pay it as he was only a Blacksmith's Striker, and had but 19s per week. It was mentioned that the defendant was the teacher of a band, and on being asked what he received for his services as a band teacher he replied that he had 2s 6d per night, but that, he said, went for refreshments. His Honour: Then instead of having refreshments , you had better pay the amount into court until the debt is paid. – An order was then made that he pay 10s per month until the whole amount is paid, with costs."

The Northern Echo of 13 August 1890 presents a slightly different angle on the court case:

"House building at Shildon. Joint ownership of a gable wall. Yesterday, at Auckland County Court, James Jamison, railway inspector, sued George Allan for £14 18s, for use and support of a gable wall at Shildon. The case was that the defendant had built a house whose joists rested on plaintiff's gable wall, extending also to the garden, which defendant, on his side, had painted. Thomas Reed, the builder was called. He said he built the house and sold it to Jamison. Witness had bargained with plaintiff for use of gable wall on his own behalf, but finding the walls below standard measurement of the Local Board bye-laws, he could not be a party to a wrong act and he did not pay. (Loud laughter.) He admitted asking plaintiff's permission to use the gable, and had promised to see plaintiff paid. Defendant now swore that his agreement with Reed was for a complete house. The Judge found for £9. – Messrs J & R D Proud (par Mr Labron) were for plaintiff; Mr J T Proud defended."

These accounts tell us a few things about George. The nineteen shillings a week he earned as a blacksmith's striker in 1890 would equate to earnings of around ninety nine pounds in 2018; not a great deal of money. That said, his additional earnings as a bandmaster would be a welcome and regular boost, and we now know what he could earn per evening teaching the band, though not how many evenings he spent doing it. Unsurprisingly George made no mention of his other earnings from his music publisher, which is just a little unfortunate for us. We know also from this report that he was able to employ humour when placed in a tight spot, and there is the additional insinuation that unlike Tom, George was not an adherent of the temperance pledge. In saying that we interpret 'refreshments' as those being provided by the ale house and that his two shillings and sixpence weren't spent on cups of tea. His likely enjoyment of a tipple is perhaps why George remained with Francis Dinsdale and the Saxhorn Band when the New Shildon bandsmen broke into two camps. We also understand from the report that George's house was his own, and not rented.

Later, at the end of August, we hear news that the Saxhorn Band were once again entertaining the Liberals of Shildon. The Northern Echo reports of 1 September, 1890, speaks of a:

> "Great Meeting at Shildon. Speeches by Mr A E Pease and Mr Paulton M.P. The anniversary of the Shildon and District Liberal Club took place on Saturday. The Shildon Saxhorn Band, bandmaster George Allan, played spirited selections through the town, and a public tea, largely attended, was held in the P. M. Schoolroom, followed by a meeting which filled the capacious building."

We can never be sure of George's own political leaning, but it may not have been coincidence that the Saxhorn Band seem to have been regularly engaged for these rallies, and might even have some connection to possible sponsorship by the railway company. Arthur Pease was the son of Joseph Pease, the Darlington based investor in the old Stockton and Darlington Railway whose family had been influential in bringing industrial prosperity to the Shildons. Joseph had once been MP for what was then the Mid Durham parliamentary constituency. The support of a Pease for James Mellor Paulton, at this time MP for Bishop Auckland constituency, would have been influential in assuring the backing of many of the railwaymen that may have been eligible to vote. George, as a property owner, may well have been one of them.

Ballarat

In January 1890, Bulch's Model Band acquired a significant and prestigious patron:

> "The secretary of Bulch's Model Brass Band has received the following communication from his Excellency the Governor:— "Government House, Melbourne, 27 January, 1890 — Sir, l am directed by his Excellency the Earl of Hopetoun to request you to he good enough to inform the members of Bulch's Model Brass Band that he has much pleasure in according his

patronage to the band. — I am, yours faithfully, E. W. Wallington, Private Secretary. S. Jamieson, Hon. Sec."

In March they also secured the patronage of the City of Ballarat Fire Brigade. On 7 March, Bulch's Band were party to another grand spectacle at the Eastern Oval:

"FRIDAY EVENING. HERR SCHOOT, CHAMPION DRUMMER OF THE WORLD, Who performs on 20 Drums, Descriptive of the SIEGE of PARIS. For ONE NIGHT only. Bulch's Model Band will play a first-class programme."

The drummed piece was to be a simulation of Prussia's 1870 siege on the French capital as part of the Franco-Prussian war which involved a significant bombardment of the city. Herr Schoot would also perform his drummed "grand imitation of a railway train" and the band's programme would include Tom's "Queen of Beauty," "Battle of Eureka," and "Opossum Hunt" as well as "Bonnie Jeannie Gray" by one Godfrey Parker whom we shall return to in a moment. On the 28th of March we receive an update, via the Ballarat Star on how the Model Band were progressing:

"The annual meeting of the band was held last night; Mr Mitchell in the chair. Correspondence from secretary Eight Hours'Anniversary, asking the services of the band in the procession; request granted. The secretary reported the total number of members to be 25, and that it was intended to increase this number; also that the band were compelled to call for tenders for a new set of uniforms, which had been accepted, and which would cost the members about £70. It was unanimously resolved to have a bazaar and art union, in aid of the uniforms, about the 24th May, and that donations and articles be solicited from the public. A strong committee was formed to carry out the arrangements. The band has secured the patronage of his Excellency the Governor, the Earl of Hopetoun, in consideration of their previous performances. It was reported that the band was the premier band of Victoria; that they had attended the United Fire Brigades Demonstration at Sandhurst on 12th March, accompany the City Fire Brigade. The following officers were balloted for and duly elected for the ensuing year:— President, Mr John Robson, re-elected; vice-presidents, Messrs J Kirton, M.L.A., T Curnow, Captain Leggo (re-elected), J Roff, Mayor Little, J Dunn, M.L.A.; bandmaster,

T E Bulch; assistant bandmaster, Mr V Lorimer; secretary, Mr S Jamieson, re-elected; treasurer, Mr W Apps; sergeant, Mr J Thom; corporal, Mr T Malthouse; drum-major, Mr G Bree; committee, Messrs M Spear, J Hodge, J J Dixon, G Malthouse, J Murphy, P McNamara. A vote of thanks to the chairman closed the proceedings."

In this we see that brothers Thomas and George Malthouse continued to support Tom in the running of the band, though there is no mention here of Tom's erstwhile close friend John. The Eight Hours procession mentioned took place on 21 April, on which occasion the band appeared in full parade uniform.

There were numerous other bands in attendance too, accompanying the various unions and groups of workers in procession with their banners in a colourful celebratory display. The Eight Hours movement was a global one, and longstanding at that. Their objective was to see the introduction of an eight hour working day, with eight hours of recreation time and eight hours rest for every worker. The movement in Australia achieved its first success in 1856 when the Stonemasons Society was the first to win these terms; though it took much longer for some other segments of workers to see the reduced hours implemented. A demonstration march was an annual feature on the workers calendar until the beginning of the 1950s.

The Model Band was engaged for a far sadder purpose on 4 May when it led the funeral procession of Ballarat fireman Arthur Reece, an Engine Officer who had passed away at the tender age of thirty one.

Later that month, on Friday 23 May, the band were again engaged, this time to provide music during a planting of trees in the Victoria Park. This was a project that had been progressed by Mayor Little who was at that time the vice-president of the band. Mayor Little had issued fifteen hundred invitations to citizens to plant trees on the three hundred acres reserved for the purpose, and of those one thousand two hundred and fifty were accepted. Throughout the planting, Bulch's Model Band performed a programme of music. As well as many individual trees being planted on behalf of the numerous respective ratepayers of the city, there were also groups of different varieties planted on behalf of specific organisations active in the city at that time. It was an excellent demonstration of people working together to support and execute a common purpose, and became known thereafter as Arbour Day. In all, over three thousand trees were planted that day making Victoria Park a marvellous spectacle, and many of them still stand and can be admired today. The last was planted by quarter past twelve, whereupon the band ended proceedings by playing the British National Anthem.

During May, Tom, Eliza and one of their children, took a trip to Tasmania. They boarded the SS Flinders from Melbourne on the 26th bound for Launceston. They were joined on that voyage by John Malthouse, the first sign we have seen that the falling out over the Sturt Street music warehouse fire had not entirely ended the friendship between the two old Shildonians. Their stay in Tasmania was brief, with the party returning to Melbourne on the 29th. We believe that this was Tom's first visit to the territory of Tasmania though we have found no clues to indicate any business purpose of trip.

Interest in Bulch's Model Band at this time was at a peak and their engagements were numerous. We single out but a few examples here. The month of August saw them engaged on a torchlight procession event held to benefit a Mr Dunstan of Ballarat. This was followed not long afterward by another to benefit the Soldiers Hill Fire Brigade's ground fund. September saw the band give a concert performance from the band rotunda on Sturt Street, November brought appearances at the Ballarat Horticultural Society Spring Show and the Ballarat Holy Ghost College Sports at the Ballarat Oval.

On 30 November, Eliza Bulch gave birth to a daughter at the family home, which by then was on Armstrong Street, a street of single storey houses leading north away from the busy centre of Ballarat. Again, Eliza herself registered the birth, though it took her until 9 January the following year to find the time to do so. The Bulch household was becoming a busy place.

December reveals more evidence that any falling out between Tom and John Malthouse had been set aside. The Mount Alexander Mail of 10 December 1890 informs us that:

> "The brass band contest to be held at Maryborough next week promises to be a great success, some of the best bands in the colony having entered the contest. Mr T E Bulch, of Ballarat, will act as judge."

John had engaged his old friend to act as adjudicator at a contest held under the auspices of Malthouse's Model Band of Maryborough. This explains in part why John was no longer involved in the running of Bulch's Model Band in Ballarat. It's interesting that he too had chosen to follow the "model band" nomenclature. The Bendigo Advertiser on 18 December 1890 described the proceedings thus:

> "The town was in full holiday attire yesterday. In the morning a special train conveyed some three hundred passengers to Ballarat. Later in the day an excursion party numbering about five hundred arrived in Maryborough and were hospitably entertained by Mayor Field. A band contest also took place in Princes Park. The Eaglehawk, Donald, Bowenvale and Thompson's Castlemaine Foundry bands taking part. There was a large gathering in the park and after a very close contest, the judge, Mr Bulch of Ballarat, awarded Bowenvale first prize, Castlemaine second and Eaglehawk third. Mr Malthouse, of Ballarat, took first prize for a cornet solo."

Above: John Malthouse, who had been Tom's best-man and business partner, pictured in later years with his daughters.

The prize-winning "Mr Malthouse" referred to was John's brother Robert Malthouse, who had for a time left Ballarat but, as we can see, kept up his cornet playing.

Following a day to celebrate his twenty-eighth birthday Tom and the Model Band concluded their busy year by playing a selection of music on New Year's Eve on Sturt Street from eleven o'clock at night until the city bellringers rang in the New Year at midnight fuelling anticipation in all present of what the year ahead might offer.

During 1890, a new composer began to make himself known to pianists and bandsmen across Australia; Godfrey Parker. The first published brass march we have discovered by this person was "Bonnie Jeannie Gray," though it was closely followed in 1891 by a march called "Craigielee" which we'll come back to shortly. What's important to us is that these pieces were first performed in Australia by Bulch's Model Brass Band. There is a very good reason for this which is that Mr Godfrey Parker wasn't a person in his own right at all, but a composing pseudonym for Thomas Edward Bulch. Why Tom chose this year to do this is elusive. His grandson Eric Tomkins's explanation, passed down through his parents generation, was that Tom was worried that he composed so many pieces that people would tire of seeing his name. This might be particularly pertinent when set in the context of Tom publishing a band journal. As we already revealed, most, if not all of the musical content of that journal was Tom's own work, so you can understand if buyers perhaps fed back that they might prefer to see pieces from a variety of composers as they might expect with other journals available in that period. Additionally, as he was also selling piano music through his own music shop he may have perceived a desire from customers to see new names on the shelves. Producing his own musical compositions under a variety of names was an easy, if illusory, way to meet that expectation.

Tom wasn't alone in this. Many of the leading and widely published brass composers of the era, including Tom's contemporaries William Rimmer and James Ord-Hume, did likewise. There were a variety of reasons. Some, like Glaswegian violinist and string composer Archibald Milligan found that music put on sale under a more exotic surname, in his case "Carl Volti," performed better; and having discovered this tended to produce all of their music under that pseudonym thereafter.

In the years that followed, Tom appears to have adopted differing musical personalities and preferences to suit his composer pseudonyms, yet throughout continued to additionally compose and promote music under his own name.   An interesting question is the one as to why Tom chose to use the name Godfrey Parker?.   It's certainly no more exotic than Thomas Edward Bulch, and holds little aura of mystique.   A partial theory on my mind is that the forename, 'Godfrey' might well have been reminiscent of the well known and regarded British composer, conductor, regimental military bandmaster and adjudicator Charles Godfrey junior who had judged Tom's New Shildon Temperance Band and awarded them second prize back in England.   Godfrey's music was popular so maybe Tom thought that buyers seeing the name might make a subconscious connection. It's mere speculation and might have no relationship to the truth.

Tom was equally adept as an arranger as he was a composer. We see evidence of him arranging piano and violin pieces by other composers for full brass and military band. What points to Tom Bulch as the arranger in these cases is that like Tom's own work they are reported in Australia first and are played by Bulch's Model Band before appearing in the repertoire of other bands. The evidence is added to significantly when we see reports of band programmes in the press where Tom's name is cited, interchangeably on multiple occasions, with the name of the original composer. Unfortunately, over time, and probably for very good reasons, some of these names have again become incorrectly mistaken as being pseudonyms of Thomas Edward Bulch.   There is much readily available evidence to support our understanding of the true and separate identities of this cluster of mainly British composers whose pieces Tom arranged for brass band; this possibly without those original composers ever knowing it.

We already mentioned Carl Volti, actually a pseudonym for Archibald Milligan, an eccentric Glaswegian violinist and champion of traditional Scottish music, who achieved great renown during and before Tom's boyhood years.   Milligan's "Highland Wreath" albums of traditional pieces for violin were widely sold and it's possible that Tom may have owned some before travelling to Australia. His arrangement of "The Fair Maid of Perth" understandably translated easily into an Australian context. Others whose selected works we believe were subject to a Bulch arrangement include Charles Le Thierre, a pseudonym for a London based brilliant piccolo player and former military bandsman named Thomas Wilby Tomkins who became a drunkard and ended his days destitute in the workhouses; and Theo Bonheur, a pseudonym for Arthur Charles Rawlings, a prolific London based piano composer and son of a blind piano tuner. Both were published widely enough for Tom Bulch to have been exposed to their work even before he came to Australia, and it's quite likely that he even sold their piano arrangements from his music shop. In later years Tom's own piano compositions would be compiled in books of sheet music alongside these composers, a factor which has perhaps simply added to the confusion over identities.

Tom was though, as we shall see later, quite open about his use of pseudonyms when composing. Certainly open enough for us to be able to use admissions in the press to validate our understanding of some of the principal names he used. Godfrey Parker is very definitely Tom Bulch, as were Eugene Lacosta, Pat Cooney and Henry Laski. We believe that Parker was the first. A further clue, explained to us by Eric Tomkins, to both Parker and Laski being alternative facades for Tom Bulch himself is that some of the waltzes he created for piano were given names based upon wordplay involving the names of members of Bulch's own family. For example the piece "Adelina" by Parker was a dedication to Thomas's daughter Adeline Bulch, and Laski's "Myrine" a combination of Myrtle May's name and Adeline's. Anther example of combined names used to produce a title is "Noralla" composed under Tom's own name.

New Shildon

1891 was a census year in the United Kingdom, and so produces another snapshot of people's whereabouts in New Shildon. George Allan, his wife Elizabeth, and their daughter Lillie, were now well and truly set up in their little house at Pears Terrace. They had been joined by a new arrival. George and Elizabeth appear to have spent quite a chaotic Christmas at the end of 1890; Elizabeth being heavily pregnant and ready to give birth. On 27 December 1890, a daughter was born and the couple named her Beatrice. On 29 January, the family converged upon the nearby All Saints Church for a Christening ceremony.

The stability and occasional tranquility of having a home of his own, for his family, gave George greater opportunity to be productive with his music, and he had seen a significant number of pieces released through his publisher, Haigh, in the previous year. These included the quadrille "Florence," schottische "The Sunbeam," and a number of marches including "No Retreat," "The Mechanic," "The Willow," "The Royal Archer" and "The Knight." 1891 would prove to be as productive a year with more marches being dominant among his published works that year. These included "Granville," "The Fawn," "The Old Adjutant" and "The Sax Horn" which seems to be either a tribute to the instrument family that inspired his band, or else a theme for the band itself.

Nearby, at 65 Adelaide Street, George's parents John and Hannah continued to keep house, though the home had become somewhat less congested now that many of their sons and daughters were grown up and setting up homes of their own. Only George's brothers, James, Ralph and Edwin remained with their parents, along with their sister Ada. James was by now old enough to work as a labourer, but the rest were still at school.

On the opposite side of that same street, and a few doors down, at number 40, Thomas Bulch senior, now a widower, kept the house going through his wage as timekeeper at the Shildon Works. His daughter Margaret stayed with him as housekeeper now that his wife was no longer alive to fulfil that role. Tom's brother Christopher, by then eighteen years of age, was living there too, though now he too was employed at the railway works as an engine fitter. Though Shildon works stopped producing locomotive engines over a decade previously, engines were still key to the operations at the site and still required maintenance. Younger children Ada and Frederick also lived there and continued their schooling. Jerry Bulch, Tom's brother, had by this time married and left the family home to live at 6 Auckland Terrace with his wife Emily (née Thompson) and daughter Minnie. This was Emily's mother's home. As a widow she would otherwise have lived alone, though she had a job as a draper's assistant.

One family name that was by then absent from Adelaide Street is that of Dinsdale. The remaining sons and daughters of

Francis Dinsdale had all moved elsewhere for work or family reasons.

The year 1891 sounds to have been a quiet one for the bandsmen of New Shildon, with few reports of significant events and none at all of their participation in any band contests. The year had begun with a particularly hard winter, but even once that had passed, the town's bands receive barely a mention.

The organisers of the annual Shildon Horticultural Show decided not to hold a band contest that year, and instead engaged the Band of the Queen's Own Cameron Highlanders as well as the Whitworth Brass Band to simply provide straightforward concert performances. It feels as though the instruments of the respective sets of New Shildon bandsmen had been shelved and losing their shine. The Daily Gazette for Middlesbrough from 4 July 1891 does give a report upon the annual Durham Miners Gala, describing the procession of all the miners union lodges through the city with their respective banners and bands. It reads:

> "Then came Auckland Park, and this lodge once more took premier honours for its turn out. It was accompanied by the Shildon Band and behind the banner walked something like two thousand workmen, with an appreciable sprinkling of the fair sex."

There is ambiguity as to which of the Shildon bands was marching on this day. It could have been the Temperance Band, though with George's family connections at Auckland Park through his in-laws it could just as well have been the Saxhorn Band.

A notion had occurred to the enterprising Tom Bulch as to how, now that he was publisher of his own music, he might reoccupy the void that had been created when his music stopped being published and printed in Britain. If he were to send several copies of his newer sheet music back home, members of his family might act as his agents in Britain. Around 1891, Thomas had composed the march "Second To None," which beneath its title shows his own Australian address, as well as that of his agent in England. The details are, however, a little perplexing. They read "T Bulch, Gurney Street, Darlington."

According to the understanding passed down through the Bulch family, Tom's father, Thomas senior, had acted as his agent, though we know that in this period his father remained resident in New Shildon. However, the census of 1891 reveals that Thomas's younger brother, John Bulch, whilst working as a steam engine fitter at the Darlington locomotive works, was lodging at number 5 Gurney Street with a family named Taylor. A scan of other properties on that street reveals no other Bulch family members. This presents an element of mystery. Why would the music state the name "T Bulch" as agent and not "J Bulch"? Also, why an address at which the twenty-year-old John is merely boarding when the family has a permanent home in New Shildon? A possible but still relatively unconvincing explanation is that it was being used as a correspondence address and that any mail was being passed to Thomas senior only a short distance away by rail. But why do that? There is something about this arrangement that does not seem quite right.

Whatever the case, we know that for a short time at least someone in Tom's family was helping him to maintain a British market for the music that he produced and printed in Australia. The endeavour appears to have been largely unsuccessful as although we have discovered over sixty instances of the march "Second to None" having been played by various bands, none of those were in the United Kingdom. Held back perhaps by inexperience, sheer weight of competition or lack of the time required to act effectively as distribution agents, Tom's family were ineffective in facilitating sale of his music in Britain.

Ballarat

Despite this, out in Australia 1891 appears to have been a busy and successful year for Tom. On 26 January, Bulch's Model Band provided music at the Australian Natives Association 'Foundation Day' event to mark the date on which the first ship landed at Sydney Cape to found a colony there. Tom, however, was not present with his band. He had been personally engaged to go to Bathurst in New South Wales to judge a band contest. Tom's good friend and former New Shildonian, Sam Lewins, had founded a brass band there and, as part of that city's Anniversary Day celebrations, had organised a Grand Brass Band Contest on the city's Show Grounds. Sam being one of the principal organisers of the event was doubtless a factor in securing Tom's involvement.

The organising committee had secured prizes worth one-hundred pounds in value which comprised cash sums as well as a Besson Desideratum prototype cornet, E flat tenor horn and a conductor's baton. The test pieces were a grand selection from Weber, arranged by Tom himself, 'Kyrie & Gloria' from Mozart's Twelfth March, and a new contest march composition also created by Tom himself appropriately named "Bathurst." This march, which we first see reported as being played in preparation for their part in this contest by the 3rd Australian Infantry Regiment Band on the 12th of that month at the Alfred Square Pavilion in Parramatta, would prove to be a popular and enduring march in Australia.

Those familiar with brass band contesting in England sometimes look at Bulch's contest marches and wonder where the musical complexity, that is a usual feature of a British contest march, lies. Some of the answer can be found in the differences between the format of a British band contest and its Australian counterpart at that time. In the Australian format the bands were required to physically march whilst playing with the standard of marching being marked as well as the playing of the piece. On this particular occasion, Tom himself awarded the points for the quality of the playing of "Bathurst," and one Warrant Officer Toovey issued the marks for discipline, regularity and general quality of the marching. The following full account was printed in the Bathurst Free Press and Mining Journal;

> "The members of the District Band deserve the highest praise for their efforts in organising a day's amusement and pleasure for the people such as never before was experienced in Bathurst. The Secretary Mr. Appleby, worked with untiring zeal, and he was ably assisted by the committee who stood by their principal throughout. The committee undertook a great responsibility by incurring the risk of upwards £200 to be spent in prizes, &c. It is gratifying that the public have proved that they can appreciate an effort of this kind made for the advancement of the town. The bands arrived on Saturday, and most of them gave a proof of their skill on wind instruments by marching through the principal streets. Yesterday morning crowds assembled at an early hour near the Royal Hotel to witness the start for the Show Ground where the contest was to take place. The bands marched off at intervals of a few moments after each other and were loudly applauded as they passed through the line of appreciative onlookers. Arrived at the ground the men took up their positions on a raised platform and the competition

commenced. The committee had acted with great wisdom in securing the services of Mr. Bulch, of Ballarat, as judge. Mr. Bulch has made this class of music his special study for many years, and has composed and arranged pieces which are played by every band in the colony. He was not acquainted with (any) one of the bands, and to show the appreciation in which his selection was held, members of each of the competing bands complimented Messrs. Appleby and Lewins on their choice, and said they would be perfectly satisfied with the decision whatever it was. Thus assured, the committee felt, at the commencement of the contest that they were going to have a pleasant and enjoyable affair, but subsequent events proved that though some of the bandsmen might be good on the instruments, they were bad losers. Entries were received from the following bands :— Wagga Town Band, Wollongong Town Band, Lithgow Independent Band, Lithgow Imperial Band, Newtown Band, 3rd Regiment, V. I. Band, Merewether Brass Band, Naval Artillery V. Band. These put in an appearance with the exception of the Wagga Wagga and the Naval Artillery. The different bands drew for positions and played in the following order : — 3rd Regiment, Newtown, Lithgow Imperial, Lithgow Independent, Wollongong, and Merewether (Newcastle). A special room had been erected for the judge at a convenient position to the stand. The room was closed in so the judge had no opportunity of seeing the different bands nor of knowing in what order they were competing. The first piece was a selection arranged by Mr. Bulch from Weber's operas Der Frieschutz, Oberon, and Euranthyie. This being accomplished the quick march 'Bathurst' composed by the judge, was played, the marching being judged by Warrant-officer Toovey. The next part was the rendering of the 'Bathurst' march and 'Kyrie and Gloria' from Mozart's Twelfth March, by the six bands. The performance of these pieces was greatly appreciated, and the public loudly applauded. The judge had a difficult task before him in making his awards, and asserts that never before has he known of a number of bands playing so well as these. In Victoria there are three which are equal to the six which took part, but he gives the palm to New South Wales for quality and excellence of execution. Green's Band, from Lithgow, has only been under command for ten months, and yet their performances are spoken highly of. Those competent to judge consider that some of contestants have, in practice, paid too much attention to the more difficult movements, while the simpler passages were detached. The Wollongong had, however, not overlooked the simpler movements, and accordingly carried off the laurels, the Merewether Band coming in for second place. For the third position the 3rd Regiment and Newtown had scored an equal number of marks, and each was called back, the former gaining in the second attempt, secured the prize. The decision of the judge was received with cheers, and evidently met with the approval of the crowd as well as the performers, as no word of dissent was uttered by the latter. About 6 o'clock the vast concourse of people (upwards of 2000) made their way homewards."

Where the article had referred to 'bad losers,' this reference was to a continuation of the article that recounted the events of a separate Cornet Contest that took place on the evening following the band contest.

On 1 February, Bulch's Model Band teamed up with the Sebastopol Band to provide music at a grand church parade for the Manchester Unity Independent Order of Oddfellows as part of their benefit event for the local orphan asylum. Just over a week later, on the 9th, the band mustered at their usual meeting point at the fire station to join a parade paying last respects to the recently deceased Mayor Hickman. On the 19th and 20th of March the band were engaged to play music at the Ballarat Horticultural Society's Autumn Show. To add a little spice to the occasion, Tom and the band issued a challenge contest invitation to the St Joseph's Band, one of the best bands in the neighbouring territory of Tasmania who were at that time visiting Victoria, with a suggestion that this take place on the 19th. Alas, we shall never know which band would have come out on top, as the Ballarat Star of that date explains:

"Regarding the challenge given by Bulch's Band to St. Joseph's Band, no contest has yet been arranged. Representatives, of Bulch's Band were last night in attendance at the Buck's Head hotel awaiting Mr Harrison, of St Joseph's Band, but the Tasmanian leader sent word that he was unable to be present. It is, therefore, thought that the competition will not take place. Tomorrow evening, at the Exhibition, St Joseph's Band will compete against the Militia Band. A well-known Melbourne bandmaster has been appointed judge."

Bulch's Model Band did, however, fulfil the request to provide selections of music at the show and thereby fulfil their engagement. Later that month the band also provided several selections of music, over multiple nights between 30 March and 2 April, as part of the Australian Juvenile Industrial Exhibition.

In April, another band contest was held as part of the Easter Monday Fire Brigade Demonstration in Benalla. The committee gave a cash prize of thirty pounds, to which valuable trophies were added by Sutton Bros, of Melbourne, and T Bulch. Three bands competed, with Albury Band taking the prize and Benalla Band finishing as runner up. Then, on 17 April the band, once again, mustered at the Fire Brigade Station to entertain at the Ballarat City Fire Brigade Anniversary Picnic, while the evening of 28 April brought the band's annual meeting. The attendance was boosted in numbers despite challenging times:

> "The annual meeting of the Bulch's Model Band was held at the City Fire Brigade on Friday evening last, Mr M. Spear occupied the chair. The secretary reported the band to be in a sound financial position, and free of debt, they having just purchased a Besson 5 valve euphonium, at a cost of £17 17s. The band now numbers 30 performers, and whilst old members are lost by removals from the district, new members are constantly joining. The election of officers for the ensuing year then took place, the following being duly elected:— President, J. N. Dunn, M.L.A.; vice-presidents, J. Kirton, M.L.A., E. Murphy, M.L.A., Mayor Shoppee, Captain Leggo, Mayor Gale, and T. Curnow; bandmaster, Mr T. E. Bulch; drum-major, Mr Geo. Bree; band-sergeant, Mr J. Thom; corporal, Mr T. Malthouse; secretary, Mr S. Jamieson; treasurer, Mr W. Apps; committee, Messrs J. Hodge, M. Spear, M. Williams, W. McNamara. Mr E. Ashley was proposed and duly elected a member of the band."

The same day saw announcements in the press that the band would not only play a programme of music outside the Mechanic's Institute the following Friday, but also unite with Sebastopol Band, Prout's Band and the Militia Band for a benefit concert for a fellow bandsman who had been very ill for some time. On Sunday, 17 May those bands came together on the Eastern Oval for a Sacred Instrumental Programme with admission at the gates costing a silver coin donation towards the benefit fund. On Friday, 22 May Bulch's Model Band played the "Dead March" at the funeral procession of Captain Charles Leggo, who as you may have recognised from the report of the band's annual meeting had, until his death, served as the band's vice-president. He had also held other posts of office in the city with Wendouree Rowing Club and the City Fire Brigade. His family owned the Leggo and Sons brewery in the city. On 15 June 1891 the ever reliable Ballarat Star tells us that:

> "Mr J. W. Kirton, M.L.A., will address his constituents in the Academy of Music to-night. He will deal with the leading events of the last session, and also with the matters now occupying public attention. Accommodation will be provided for ladies in the dress circle. Bulch's Band has kindly volunteered to play selections prior to the opening of the meeting. The mayor of the city will preside."

The eagle-eyed will have again spotted from the reports of minutes that Kirton was a vice-president of the Model Band, but those not familiar with the administration of the territory of Victoria may not know that the initials MLA stand for Member of the Legislative Assembly, the lower house of the Victorian parliament. Tom, it seems, was quite adept at securing the support and involvement of influential people to assure the success of his band; and it sounds so far that they were indeed a success; and very much in demand. This perhaps makes what happens next all the more surprising. On Wednesday the 1 July 1891 the Ballarat Star reported that Tom proposed to move to Melbourne:

> "The many friends of Mr T. E. Bulch, musician and composer, will regret to hear of his proposed removal to Melbourne, he having entered into an engagement with Messrs Sutton Bros., music warehousemen of Elizabeth Street. Mr Bulch was in business in Ballarat for five years. He was at one time bandmaster of the Allendale Brass Band, and afterwards bandmaster of the 3rd Regiment, and for the past five years has fulfilled the same position in the Model Band, having trained many of the players. His services as a judge at band contests were frequently sought, his later engagements in this capacity being at Maryborough, and at Bathurst, New South Wales. He is the editor and publisher of the "Australian Brass and Military Band Journal." Under the able leadership of Mr Bulch the Model Band have distinguished themselves in various parts of the colony and also in Adelaide and other places. Before Mr Bulch leaves for Melbourne the members of the band will entertain him at a farewell social, at which he will be presented with a valuable testimonial."

Though Tom had left the post, it appears that even later in the year in October the band officials were keen to give appreciation for his contribution as the Ballarat Star of Friday, 2 October 1891 attests:

> "Tonight the president of Bulch's Model Band, Mayor Dunn, will present the late Bandmaster Mr T. E Bulch with a handsomely framed group of photographs of the members and officers of the band. The presentation will be made at the Ballarat East Town Hall, at 9 o'clock, in the presence of the officers and members and the bandmasters of the other local bands."

As it transpired, Tom was not able to attend the presentation, though the report of the gathering contains an excellent summarisation of his achievements, and reason for his standing, in Ballarat.

> "The members of Bulch's Model Band assembled at the Ballarat East Town Hall last evening, at the invitation of the mayor of the town, Mr J. N. Dunn, president of the band, to present a very handsome large sized picture containing photos of 36 past and present members of the band to Mr T. E. Bulch, who has so efficiently acted as their band master for the past five years. The picture is 5 feet x 3 feet 6 inches. The band, which was originally started with the object of playing at the Fire Brigades' Demonstrations, has been singularly successful under the leadership of Mr Bulch. During the first year of its inception the band succeeded in carrying off the second prize at the Melbourne Fire Brigades'Demonstration, valued at £23, and since that time has been awarded the following prizes, viz, Adelaide Exhibition, second prize, valued at £27 10s; Sydney Centennial Band Competition, second, valued at £60; and the first prize at Maryborough, valued at £23. A number of bandmasters from other local bands attended to show their respect to Mr Bulch. An apology was received from Mayor Shoppee. It was intended to perform, in the Town Hall gardens, the contest pieces to be placed at Maryborough, but owing to the unfavourable weather the arrangement had to be abandoned. The band, however, under the leadership of Mr Malthouse, played several pieces in the Town Hall. Afterwards, the mayor explained that a telegram had been received from Mr Bulch, stating that, owing to illness, he was unable to be present, much to his disappointment, and that Mr G. King would accept the presentation on his behalf. The mayor then,

on behalf of the band, in a humorous speech, made the presentation, and eulogised Mr Bulch, its founder, and spoke of the successes which the band had achieved. Mr Geo. King, on behalf of Mr Bulch, tendered his sincere thanks for the handsome presentation, which would be treasured by Mr Bulch and his wife and family. He hoped the same enthusiasm would be extended to the new bandmaster. Mr Murphy, M.L.A., and ex Mayor Gale and Cr. Peady were present. The mayor invited the band to partake of refreshments provided in the council chambers. The toasts of the bands represented were drunk, and responded to by Mr Gray, of the Militia Band, and Mr Front, of the Sebastopol Band. Several selections were given, and a very enjoyable evening spent."

Thomas Edward Bulch, the hard working, talented lad from the railway town of New Shildon in County Durham had truly been taken to the hearts of the people of Ballarat; and particularly its banding community. In musical terms he had made an enormous contribution to placing Ballarat firmly on the map. The bandsmen there were reluctant to lose his services entirely and elected to retain his services in some capacity as an occasional instructor to the band. How poetic, though, that his successor as bandmaster of Bulch's Model Band should be John Malthouse; the man who persuaded Tom to come to Australia and had handed over the baton of his own Kingston and Allendale Brass Band when Tom consequently arrived.

There are a couple of T E Bulch compositions of note that are particularly worth highlighting here. The eighth of May 1891 was the day on which the city of Sandhurst in the territory of Victoria officially changed its name to Bendigo. This new name was a corruption of the biblical middle name of the English boxing champion William Abednigo Thompson who ran the southern area of the city. Tom later created the march "Bendigo." The piece is described in an issue of the Lyons' Special List of Brass & Military Band Music of the day as:

"A fine march in 2-4 time with syncopated solos for basses, euphoniums, trombones &c. This march is respectfully dedicated to Mr. Jas. Northcott, Sandhurst, the oldest bandmaster in the colony. – 1s 6d."

Northcott's band became Northcott's Bendigo Brass Band following the renaming of the city. The other composition of note connected to 1891 is not attributed to Tom Bulch, but to

Robert Malthouse the Shildonian cornet player of Bulch's Model Brass Band. It is a piece called "Whitworth." Though not in Tom's name, it bears all the hallmarks of a Bulch composition. We saw previously the report that the Whitworth Band, hailing from the colliery village of the same name situated only a few miles away from the town where both Thomas Bulch and Robert Malthouse grew up, had competed and won at the march contest at Shildon during 1890 at which Thomas's march "Chef D'Oeuvre" was test piece. Robert Malthouse was not a prolific composer, this may have been the only work in his name, and as it was published in Buch's own brass band journal, it is suspected that Thomas Bulch most probably had a significant hand in its creation.

Other Paths

I'd explained earlier in this narrative that we would come back to Samuel Lewins. Though his, Tom's and George's threads will continue to interweave it's worth a moment to give an outline of his life after Ballarat. In 1885 Sam moved to Bathurst where he took work as a blacksmith for the local railway company. As there was no brass band in Bathurst at the time, and seeing the potential for one, he formed the Bathurst Railway Band, which later became the Bathurst District Band and became his life's passion for the next fifty years. In the document that commemorated his fiftieth year in charge of the band it states:

> "In addition to his ability as a bandmaster and band-trainer, he has been a good business man having induced the members of the organisation and its different committees to maintain a first class band for 50 years. This has never been in debt, and has at all times been able to expend money for contests, and general upkeep, which undoubtedly was due to his leadership.
>
> His life with the band has not been all "beer and skittles." He has been an indefatigable worker, and a man who always surmounted the greatest difficulties which no one but an enthusiast would dare face. He has started bands, got them into a state of efficiency, and then has come a rift in the lute, followed by disorganisation necessitating a commencement all over again. Yet the genial and energetic Sam has come up smiling every time, and at present beats a telling time to as fine a band as anyone could wish to hear, members of which, with the citizens of Bathurst, are very proud. It is due to these wonderful

and sterling qualities exercised over a period of 50 years that the public of Bathurst, both past and present, have come to treat him with such admiration and respect, and to such extent that there is probably no man in the district more loved and respected.

He is one of the fathers of bands and band contesting in Australia. The history shows his connections in this respect: the name of Lewins has come to be associated with band music in Bathurst until today it is almost a tradition. Generations of bandsmen have seen Mr. Lewins, bandmaster of the Bathurst District Band, conducting the fine combination of players, and hundreds of young players have passed through his hands, securing the benefit of his fine tuition. Mr Lewins did not forget his own family, and incidentally it might be mentioned that with sons, sons-in-law, and nephews, he could start another band today of 14 or 15 good players.

The Bathurst public has recognised in many ways his great worth as a bandsman and citizen, and on several occasions he has been the guest of the citizens at complimentary concerts, and smoke socials, and presented with handsome gifts in recognition of his successes in contests, and for his great work with the band and for Bathurst in general. Few local musicians are deserving of the same amount of gratitude from the citizens as is Mr Lewins, whose unostentatious, but consistent efforts in the cause of music and charity have provoked the spontaneous expression of esteem which has endeared him to all. In conclusion we tender him our best thanks, and sincere appreciation for all the good work and services he has performed for this band during the 50 wonderful years. We sincerely hope that he will be spared for many more years life of pleasure with his old love, the Bathurst District Band."

The gifts presented to Sam by the Mayor of Bathurst included a silver reading lamp and fountain pen towards which contributions were made by his bandsmen. There was also a token of appreciation from the Methodist choir. As an additional tribute to Samuel a set of commemorative bronze gates were erected in Machattie Park, a performance location favoured by the band after its opening in 1890 and where a rotunda was also built for the band. These gates were later removed from the original site and replaced elsewhere but can still be seen today. Samuel had married Elizabeth Jane Catley, a year or so after his arrival in Bathurst. Together they had six daughters and four sons. After several years service as a blacksmith, a trade he had in common with his old bandmate George Allan, he later worked as a fitter in the Bathurst railway workshops. Throughout all this time, his home in Bathurst sported a sign over the front door that read "Shildon," something which has remained there to present times; a small reminder of his roots to all who passed by.

Above: George and Tom's former New Shildon Juvenile bandmate, Samuel Lewins set up a life, and band, in Bathurst, New South Wales.

The band would regularly play in the Bathurst courthouse gardens, and Samuel frequently ensured that their given programmes of music often included pieces by his old childhood friends Thomas Bulch and George Allan. We will mention one or two occasions of this later. Sam led his band to win the

Australian Championship three times before he retired from the band in 1935 after fifty-three years at the helm. He passed away on 23 May 1940 aged seventy-eight, while his wife survived him by six years living to be eighty-one. They were buried together in Bathurst Cemetery.

Later, in the 1950s, Brilliant Street, nestled in the area that housed the city's railway workers, was renamed Lewins Street in his honour. Not a bad tribute for a humble lad from the North-East of England.

The other young bandsman of note who travelled to Australia with Tom and Sam was, as you probably recall, James Scarffe. As we saw, James worked for a time with Tom at Ballarat's Phoenix Foundry. Whilst at the Phoenix Foundry he was an active trade unionist and is reported as having been involved on the part of the workers of the Ironworker's Assistants Association in a dispute over wages in 1889. James was among the union representatives at a conference at the Ballarat City Hall on Friday, 5 April 1889 that resulted in a lockout and shutdown of the foundry on the 15th, throwing out five-hundred workers over and above the 130 striking ironworkers' assistants. This created tension between the ironworkers assistants and their fellow workers who were opposed to the strike but losing wages on account of it. That was, of course, what the foundry owners were counting on; discord that would bring the workers back cap in hand without changing any terms. The strike extended to two other nearby foundries; the Union Foundry and Cowley's Foundry with pickets standing vigil at all three. Married men with dependent families were keen to return to work blaming the stand-off over wages and conditions on the younger single men with less to lose from a prolonged closure. Eventually, having lost enough money themselves, the foundries did attempt to re-commence operations while the strike continued, though many of the other unions for the other trades at the plant, including the iron-moulders and boilermakers ordered their members to stand by the ironworker's assistants. The company attempted to counter by bringing in other labour, however it was clear that many of the alternative workers were not up to the job. Eventually new terms were offered to the workers who accepted at a conference and the strike was brought to a close on 8 May 1889.

As for James Scarff, he, like Sam Lewins, carried on his music throughout his life and also saw appreciatory retrospective articles summarising his achievements written in the press; such as this from the Herald newspaper of Melbourne on 15 October 1921:

> AN INTERESTING CAREER. Mr James Scarff of the Malvern Tramway Champion Band is distinctly a link with the past, and the story of his band life makes interesting reading to present-day bandsmen.
>
> James Scarff was born at Shildon, Durhamshire, England, on October 31, 1863. When 11 years of age he became a member of the New Shildon Temperance Band, playing tenor horn, subsequently transferring to the B-flat cornet. His musical companions were S Lewins, who later became the solo euphonium player, and T E Bulch who shared the position of principal cornet with Mr Scarff, and later succeeded his uncle – Mr Edward Dinsdale – as bandmaster. The band competed at a number of contests with a fair measure of success.
>
> Early in 1884, Mr Scarff and his companions, who were all of a similar age, decided to leave for Australia, and they arrived here in May of the same year. The adventurous trio settled in the Allandale district, Mr Bulch being appointed bandmaster of the Allandale and Kingston Brass Band, Mr Scarff ably assisting him as principal cornet. After a brief stay with the band, Mr Lewins proceeded to new South Wales, where he formed the Bathurst District Band in November 1885, and has since acted continuously as its conductor. Mr Scarff's fine cornet playing attracted the attention of Mr J B Gray, the conductor of the Phoenix Foundry Band, Ballarat, who invited him to accept the position of principal cornet to his band. Mr Scarff remained with the band for five years, and he also served for six years with the 3rd Infantry Battalion, under Mr Gray's conductorship.
>
> Mr Bulch made his headquarters in Ballarat, where he formed Bulch's Model Brass Band – a very fine combination. Mr Scarff became associated with this band, which later became known as the City of Ballarat Brass Band. Upon Mr Bulch's departure from the district, Mr Scarff was appointed to the conductorship, and this position he held for the next 17 years.
>
> In 1915, Mr Scarff enlisted in the Australian Imperial Force and he was appointed to the conductorship of the Ballarat Camp Band, with the rank of band-sergeant. Subsequently, he had

charge of, and was a playing member of, various other military bands, being demobilised in December 1918. Early in the following year he joined the Malvern Tramway Band, of which organisation he is the official collector, and where his services and advice are greatly valued.

Mr Scarff has also been successful in the writing of band scores and selections. The leading bands of Australia and New Zealand entrust their most important work to him. Mr Scarff also held the conductorship of the Ararat Citizens band for more than two years. he was also bandmaster of the Nazareth House Band for two and a half years and the Learmouth Brass Band for two years.

As a member of the Ballarat Leidertafel, he was associated with the production of many important musical works. He was also the principal cornetist with Her Majesty's Theatre (Ballarat) and Mr George Herbert's Orchestras.

Once again, this is an outline of significant achievement and another illustration of the noble aspects of the brass band movement. If you consider for a moment that Tom Bulch, John Malthouse, Sam Lewins and James Scarff were all tutored by Francis Dinsdale and his son Edward; not forgetting that George Allan also emerged from this stable. Then consider how many bandsmen these five bandmasters then went on to mentor, guide and tutor over the remainder of their own lifetimes. Then how many of those bandsmen they taught possibly also went on to pay forward their learning. In this way you can see that so many brass bandsmen today can trace a line of musical inheritance back to New Shildon, and to Francis Dinsdale and beyond to musical forebears of whom we know nothing.

Melbourne

Still feeling the financial effects of the fire that destroyed his music warehouse business in Ballarat, Tom Bulch decamped his whole family, with all their possessions, to Melbourne so that he could start his new job for Suttons Music. As an already proven and prolific composer of music for bands, piano and even violin, and with an established record for producing high quality work, Tom's employment was a worthy acquisition by the company. He had already sold a few of his Australian era pieces early in the decade to Suttons, or Lyons, as two of the established

Australian music houses at that time. Lyons Music had already received, for example, the marches "Craigielee" and "El Ave" as well as galop "Opossum Hunt" and schottische "Jolly Sailors." They would publish other works by Tom throughout the 1890s.

As well as composing, the other great skill that would have made Tom attractive to Suttons was his ability to arrange the music created by others particularly for alternative instrumentation. We highlighted already that this had, over time, created confusion over the pseudonyms associated with him, but it also meant that he would often go uncredited for work that he undertook. His grandson Eric recalls conversations between Tom's son and his own father Charles Tomkins concerning how Tom was often requested to tidy-up someone else's composition without receiving any credit for it. This makes it difficult to form a true appreciation of the scale of his output.

Following his relocation to Melbourne, Tom did two things. First he quickly established a new 'operatic' brass band which, as with his Ballarat band, he ensured included his name. Thus, on 14 October 1891 another brass band contest took place at Maryborough at which there were two bands with Bulch in their name competing. Bulch's Model Brass Band of Ballarat, consisting of thirty players, and the twenty bandsman of Bulch's Operatic band of Melbourne. The second thing Tom did in Melbourne in 1891, was to re-establish his own music store, so he was not working exclusively for Suttons. This new shop was on Chapel Street in the district of Prahran where he was running his new band. The small retail property was rented from landlord William H Drew, and required an additional annual City Rate tax of two pounds, ten shillings and eight pence to be paid.

The contest was held in the grounds of the Prince's Park, and other competitors included the Donald Band, Creswick Jubilee Band, Collins Street Melbourne Baptist Church Band and Bowenvale Band. There were also four entries for euphonium, and three for cornet solo side competitions. At the conclusion of the main band contest, despite only recently having been formed it was Tom's Operatic Band that carried off the laurels having scored 58 points; ten points ahead of Bulch's Model Band making them runners up. The Collins Street Baptist Band earned 46 points to come third.

On 25 November, Tom provided his musical services for a concert at the Town Hall in Melbourne that featured the North Melbourne Military Band. On this occasion he was present as pianist rather than bandmaster as the programme included a number of songs with piano accompaniment.

By the beginning of 1892 Bulch's Operatic Brass Band had made a slight adjustment to its name, adding the name of the district of Melbourne in which they were centred to become Bulch's Prahran Operatic Brass Band. They began their banding year immediately on New Year's Day by rendering a selection of music at the Friendly Societies Gardens at an event held under the auspices of the Grand United Order of Free Gardeners. Ever confident in the quality of his own music, the programme that day featured five of Tom's own compositions. On the 5th of March, the band, billed as Bulch's Champion Amateur Operatic Band on account of the contest win at Maryborough, performed a number of pieces of music at a 'monster demonstration' of the unemployed at Studley Park, north of the Prahran district, at which a collection was held. In advertising for the occasion the band was described as the 'coming band of Australia'.

Despite such prediction of greatness there are relatively few reports of appearances of the band during 1892. This may have been due to Melbourne having numerous other established bands and the difficulty in gaining engagements ahead of them, or it may simply have been that in a city larger than Ballarat it was, perhaps, harder to hit the news. In contrast, Bulch's Model Brass Band, now under the baton of Tom's former New Shildon bandmate James Scarff, continued very clearly to be very much in demand, with many reports of their appearances featured in the press.

New Shildon

In New Shildon, 1892 also seems to have been a quiet year for George Allan and the New Shildon Saxhorn Band, with no publicly reported appearances of that band appearing in concert or contest. There may have been good reasons for this connected to one of the darkest, and most disruptive, events in the industrial history of County Durham, the 'Great Strike' of 1892.

In that year the coal owners of the various pits and collieries making up the Durham coalfield, driven by what they believed to be economic necessity, proposed a significant reduction in the wages of coal miners in their employ. The Durham Miners Association saw this as the moment to play their strongest hand.

The Association had formed when the miners of the various collieries and pits across the county had agreed that strength in protecting their rights would be found through unity, and the perceived injustice of this particular wage cut was deemed sufficiently appropriate a moment as to trigger a demonstration. They had made similar stands, in 1879 for example, and now it was time to put up arguably their biggest fight yet. The nation needed Durham county's coal. In the year previous, this coalfield had contributed thirty million tons toward the 185 million tons produced nationally. The Miners Association was confident that any refusal to back down on the part of the mine owners would cost them dearly. The coal owners, however, refused to relent on their intention to cut wages. It seemed as though large scale industrial action was going to be inevitable. In light of this, preparations were made. On the Friday previous to the planned date of action, ponies and equipment began to be withdrawn from the mines in readiness. Despite discussions taking place between representatives, the deadlock between the miners and their masters remained unbroken.

The ensuing strike, when it commenced on 14 March 1892, was to prove the largest undertaken by coal miners throughout the heyday of coal mining in the North East of England, though to call it a strike solely on the basis of the withdrawal of labour would be something of an oversimplification. It was more of a 'stand-off' in which the coal owners also ensured that the workforce was locked-out from any mines, pits and collieries whose workers were affiliated to the Durham Miners Association until such time as they agreed to submit to the owners will and accept the reduced pay. Rather than ensuring the swift agreement and return to work of protesting miners, discontent spread to the collieries that were not at that time affiliated to the Association. On 18 March, around ten-thousand miners from other collieries in the county also demonstrated their support by joining the strike. The coal they brought to the surface would not be the means to break the resolve of their colleagues. Soon, almost all of the 92,588 miners of Durham joined the strike.

Unlike in later cases in living memory where there was a unity between the mining communities across different geographical regions, the Durham coal miners in 1892 made their stand alone. Coal continued to be mined across the rest of the nation's coalfields.

By this point, you'll be wondering how any of this would affect George Allan in New Shildon given that he wasn't a coal miner. It is often overlooked that the impact of such a strike extended beyond the miners and their families to other parts of the community. The effect was particularly felt across the network of other workforces that either existed to support that industry, or which depended upon it. The North Eastern Railway company, George's employers, fell firmly into both those categories and were expected from the outset of the strike to bear significant losses. Almost all the coal extracted across the county was transported by rail, requiring North Eastern Railway employees, locomotives, wagons and sidings to distribute it. Even the locomotives themselves required coal to function. The clattering forge and blacksmith's workshop at the Shildon Works, where George fulfilled his long shifts, also required coal as fuel. Trimmers, teamers, shunters and batterymen were 'thrown idle' by the dispute. The management at the New Shildon works, having calculated how they could continue to operate with reduced access to necessary fuel, announced that the working week there would be cut from six days to only four. Naturally the workforce would only be paid for the days they worked. These wagon builders were, in a sense, fortunate. Those railway workers involved in the transport of coal were laid-off until the situation was resolved.

Impacts of the mining dispute reached out like tentacles to touch other major employers in the North-East of England. Steelmaking and ironworking were also dependent upon a steady and reliable supply of coal and its derivative, coke. By 21 March, only eleven of the forty furnaces of neighbouring Cleveland were operable, with the rest in danger of shut down. Ironstone miners producing raw materials for the furnaces were also laid off. Quarries producing limestone for blast furnaces ground to a halt as demand dried up. Owners of coke ovens made the difficult decision to shut them down, risking damage to the fabric of the ovens as they cooled. On the river Tyne, by the end of March, two-hundred steamships stood idle for want of fuel, or for want of cargo.

The miner's federation agreed with the Coal Porter's Union that they should not handle foreign coal lest that undermine the position of the Durham Miners. In homes across the region a domestic effect was felt, as newspapers of the time explain, because the water for many coal producing villages not connected to the mains water network was delivered by colliery enginemen. Consequently such places experienced water shortages.

The protracted stalemate between owners and workers caused many to re-evaluate their personal circumstances. This deeply felt industrial situation was particular to County Durham. Many wondered how long it would last. In those days there was no welfare state upon which to lean for support. In an era of subsistence wages and comparatively mean existences, a mass break in employment lasting only a few weeks would bring hunger and potentially drive desperate acts. It was widely known throughout the county that there was work elsewhere in the country. Newspapers reported that many unmarried young men left the towns and villages of Durham in droves to seek paid work in Wales or other areas unaffected by the strike. The Northern Echo at the end of March gave their assessment of the state of the county:

> "Never since the great strike of '79 – yet even then – have the colliery villages been so quiet as at the present time. The pulley wheels at the pits are rarely seen to move; the locomotive engines that were only a few weeks ago kept constantly on the move hauling in and out of the sidings full and empty wagons are at a standstill; and the long stretches of coke ovens that used to illuminate the scene by their lurid fires have ceased to burn. So far as I can learn not a man belonging to the four associations (Miners, Enginemen, Mechanics and Cokemakers) is working and now that the men have been paid off, the only persons seen about the pits are a few officials and the village constable."

Many men and families, of course, remained where they were, especially those for whom relocating was not such a straightforward undertaking, such as families with elderly relatives to care for or larger families. For such folk, generally already conditioned to a tough life, day to day existence became harder than usual and the effects could only be partly relieved by the strength and support of close knit communities coming together. Even farmers felt the pinch. At the market at Bishop Auckland, just a few miles away from New Shildon, much of the produce on sale, such as butter and eggs, went unsold as families lacked money to buy such goods. Soup kitchens were operated by community organisations and friendly societies to feed those most in need.

As well as the increased personal hardship, the impact to George Allan, and the other bandmasters across the county, was that many band members left the area, or else were unable to keep up practice. We'll see evidence later that this continued to be a challenging factor throughout the remainder of the eighteen nineties. Nonetheless we also know that George Allan and his New Shildon Saxhorn Band supported their brethren and neighbours in their struggle. We see at least one piece of evidence of their support for the miners relating to their attendance and contribution at a rally on The Batts, a strip of land adjacent to the River Wear at Bishop Auckland, on 27 May 1892. George and the New Shildon Saxhorn Band were, on this occasion, joined by the New Shildon Temperance Band and others from Bishop Auckland, Howle, Whitworth and Newfield. Each band led a cohort of the striking miners on their march to the rally and then, at the conclusion of the speeches given to put fire in the bellies of the men, the bands reinforced that effect by playing rousing marches. Perhaps it was the significance and effect of such music at these occasions that underpinned George's own love of march music over other band music formats. The bold and impressive music could speak to the souls of the working men assembled, much as it did in military situations, elevating their spirit, telling them to stand firm, that they were strong, that as long as they stayed together they would prevail. Many of the men would carry the spectacle, those march tunes, and the key messages of the speakers, away in their minds for the days ahead.

Reports of the demonstrations by miners in the regional newspapers were accompanied by letters from correspondents declaring neutrality in the matter and yet speaking out against the Miners Federation and subversively seeking to turn communities against, and weaken the resolve of, the miners maintaining the strike. The dispute was eventually settled through the intervention and mediation of an unlikely source. Brooke Foss Westcott had been elevated within the Church of England to become Bishop of Durham in 1890. The Birmingham born former teacher, theologian and writer, the son of a botanist, had a reclusive reputation, but also that of a Christian socialist and took particular interest in the mining communities of Durham. His intervention consisted of a series of conciliatory discussions concluding in a congress at Auckland Castle on 1 June 1892 at which the representatives of the miners were persuaded to agree to break the deadlock by accepting an only slightly lesser reduction in wages than the one the coal-masters had originally proposed. Pay would consequently be reduced by ten percent rather than fifteen, and the men would be allowed to return to work. The dispute had run for eleven weeks and three days in total, though there would be an economic aftershock that continued to make working life in the county difficult for some time ahead.

In many ways the Durham Miners Association could be seen on this occasion, and based upon this outcome, to have failed to protect the needs of its members as well as had been hoped; and the price paid by the population of the county had been the endurance of much hardship. Yet it was still a crucial demonstration of the persuasive power and importance of a united workforce as stakeholders and a key step in the progress of the labour movement. The incident had also brought much financial discomfort to the coal owners who, though unlikely to have faced starvation, lost much revenue.

By the end of summer some semblance of social normality had resumed. The annual Shildon Show went ahead and, once again, a brass band contest was included in the entertainment. George and the New Shildon Saxhorn Band did not take part, though the New Shildon Temperance Band used this event as an opportunity to return to contesting. Earlier in the year, they had advertised their intention to hold a brass band contest on Easter Monday, but there is no record of that contest taking place. Having been scheduled to occur in what became the peak of the miners strike, it may have been impractical, inappropriate or impossible for an Easter contest to go ahead. We should remember too that many bands in those days were funded by industries related to, or in some way dependent upon, coal. Access to facilities or funding may have been part of sanctions mid-strike, though we have no documentary evidence to support that supposition.

The adjudicator of the Shildon Show Band Contest, Joseph Owen Shepherd of Liverpool, determined that the New Shildon Temperance Band's rendering of Harry Round's test-piece arrangement of works by Mozart was the least proficient of the six bands that had entered. Nonetheless, and unlike the Saxhorn Band, they were back in contesting action. Though they didn't know it on that day it was to be the beginning of a golden period for Tom Bulch's former band.

What we know of George Allan's New Shildon Saxhorn Band in 1892 is that, despite probable depleted numbers, they were active and still entertaining in the community. The 1890s was the decade that saw the eruption of a great bicycle craze in Britain. Though bicycles were not a particularly new invention, the craze had been triggered by the invention of the 'safety cycle'; a bicycle with a chain drive and gearing, an innovation that suddenly made cycling much more exciting and comfortable. It also moved the notion of bicycle racing to a whole new level. Neighbouring Old Shildon was fortunate enough to have its own cycling ground, established in 1887 by a new Cycling Club, on land adjacent to Dean Street which nowadays serves as the home-ground of Shildon Association Football Club. On the Saturday, 13 August 1892 the club held its sixth Annual Cycling Festival. This featured a number of races for the cycling enthusiast including a one mile novice handicap, one mile race for more experienced cyclists, a one-hundred yards flat race and a two-mile race. Of course no Victorian event was complete without music to lift the occasion, so George and the New Shildon Saxhorn Band were engaged in that capacity for the afternoon and, in spite of some inclement weather at first, one local newspaper confirms they did so ably.

Though less prolific during 1892, George did find time to keep up, and occasionally concentrate on, his composing work despite living at the edge of a town that was anything but peaceful. Pears Terrace sat on the western boundary of a colliery adjacent to a railway line leading to and from the works and was very much within earshot of the heavy hammers of the works forge. Over and above this, by the end of 1892 the vicinity around Pears Terrace was still in development. The local unitary council development board had been seeking to improve the surrounding streets so as to meet a particular standard that they could be adopted by that authority for ongoing maintenance. The Northern Echo of 16 November tells of a meeting of the Shildon Local Board:

> "The Surveyor reported that Fryer Street was now completed in a satisfactory manner and that he had served notices on the owners in Back Alma Road West, Pears Terrace and end of East

Street, with a view to these streets being put into a proper state and afterwards being taken over by the Board."

On 5 December, the same newspaper reported that:

"Shildon and East Thickley Local Board. – The local board invite tenders for the levelling and Macadamising channelling &c. of (1) Back Alma Road West, and (2) Street behind Pears Terrace and end of East Street. Plans &c. may be seen and full particulars obtained on application to the Surveyor, Wm A Mason, Local Board Offices, Shildon."

Then the Northern Echo of 21 December 1892 tells of a further related meeting of the Shildon Local Board.

"Tenders had been received for the making of Pears Terrace and the end of East Street, New Shildon – that of Mr John Moore for £142 15s 4d being accepted."

There are a small number of Allan compositions that appear for the first time in 1892 including the galop "Runaway" and the lancers format dance composition "Social." Before the year ended George also restarted his membership of the New Shildon Mechanics Institute. His membership throughout his adult life was largely uninterrupted but there do seem to have been periods where, perhaps through economic necessity it was allowed to lapse. Finally,1892 also brought a family celebration for the Allans as it was the year that George's younger brother James married Elizabeth Jane Donkin after which the couple moved into their own home at number 14 Scott Street, not far at all from Pears Terrace.

Melbourne

Having spent a while settling in to his new life in Melbourne, Tom Bulch may have been feeling that his new job as a musical editor, coupled with his role as bandmaster of the Prahran Operatic Brass Band, was not yet enough to keep him either fully occupied, or else sufficiently well paid. Before long he had taken on even more responsibility. It is during this year that Tom was offered, and accepted, the post of bandmaster to the Melbourne G.P.O. Military Band.

Naturally having accepted this role he also wanted to make his mark on the band by adding a number of his own compositions to their repertoire. That the military band format included additional woodwind instrumentation did not daunt him in the slightest. Having already been a military bandmaster with the 3rd Militia he knew how those instruments fitted into the soundscape and was already very capable when it came to creating parts for them. How Tom Bulch came to be invited to be bandmaster of the Post Office's military band is untold, but we do know that he was conveniently located to do so. The impressive General Post Office building, where both organisation and band were headquartered, was situated where the city's Bourke Street meets Elizabeth Street. The impressive design of that building had been the outcome of a competition held in 1858, with separate designers being responsible for the exterior and the interior. It took almost seven years to build, and was further extended in 1887, just a few years before Tom's arrival in Melbourne.

Above: Tom Bulch (far right) with his Melbourne GPO Military Band.

What was most convenient for Tom was that the GPO building was diagonally opposite his second place of work, Sutton's Music Warehouse, on that same junction between Bourke Street and Elizabeth Street. Tom's grandson, Eric, told me that the band would play for the benefit of those gathered and passers-by from the steps outside the building every Friday night, which at the time was a late shopping night. He also recalls from family stories passed down by his mother, aunts and uncles that Tom would watch the postmen set off from the Post Office each morning on their bicycles, and watch them returning again when their delivery rounds were completed. By the October of 1892, Tom had the Melbourne GPO Military band satisfactorily under his baton and the first known report of his conducting them was proclaimed in the Melbourne Herald of Tuesday, 25 October:

> "The G.P.O. Military Band will play a grand programme of instrumental music under Bandmaster Bulch, in the new Victoria Pavilion, Esplanade (Beach) South Melbourne, tomorrow (Wednesday) evening, at 8 o'clock."

Taking on the new responsibility had not caused him to abandon his Operatic Brass Band project. A further report from the same newspaper, a month later on 25 November, shows that on occasion he might might even be presented with the the opportunity to have both his bands play at the same engagement.

> "The General Post Office Military Band and Bulch's Operatic Band will give an open-air performance in the new Victoria Pavilion, on the South Melbourne Esplanade at 8 o'clock this evening."

Elsewhere, the press continued to include many stories of appearances and achievements of Bulch's Model Brass Band, of which, of course, he was now no longer in control. This may have been bitter-sweet for Tom, it being the band he created so successfully, and which bore his name but was an incomplete project.

This early point in the eighteen-nineties, though, is where we really begin to see Tom's profile as a composer rise in Australia. Our analysis of around three thousand band programme reports shows that prior to this point almost, but not quite, all of the mentions of his pieces being played involved one of his own bands, and that from this point onward we begin to see an increasing number of bands across Victoria and new South Wales including his music in their performances. The territorial creep of his reputation gradually extended to Southern Australia and Queensland by the middle of the decade, not to forget Tasmania where the St Joseph's Band were among the first to adopt his music. The earliest bands championing his work included Northcott's Bendigo Brass Band, for whom Tom specifically created that march "Bendigo", Sam Lewins's Bathurst District Band, quite unsurprisingly given Tom and Sam's shared origins and the Wagga Town Band in New South Wales. These were followed shortly thereafter by bands in Camperdown, Lismore, Yarraville, Avoca, Gawler, Dandenong, Gawler, Adelaide and Eaglehawk to name but a few. It seems that it took a few more years before the reach of Tom's music extended into Western Australia.

The nom-de-plume of Godfrey Parker also continued to grow in reputation, whilst that of another of Tom's alternative personas made a debut appearance. Tom appears to have adopted Henry Laski as a composing pseudonym during 1892.

Why did Tom choose the name Henry Laski? It's quite an unusual name yet there's no obvious word-play within it. We might have found one possible connected clue in the newspapers of Melbourne in 1892 which is that, though the name is indeed a rare one, there was indeed a Henry Laski resident in that city, and for a brief moment in June of that year readers of the Melbourne newspapers knew his name. The Age reported on 15 June regarding dairyman Henry Laski of Mahoney Street who had been caught diluting his milk by adding 15 percent water, and was consequently fined four pounds with added costs of two pounds and and two shillings. Might it just be possible that Tom, seeking inspiration as to how he might dilute the prominence of his own name for new pieces of music, happened across that story and chose Henry's as his own additional name? It is purely a guess but with such a rare name it does seem to be a tantalising coincidence.

As the Intercolonial Brass Band Journal grew in terms of subscribers and distribution we begin to see instances where almost the entire programme being played by a band on particular occasions might be Tom's work, either under his own name or that of Parker or Laski. For example, when the South Egerton Band played a programme of music outside the Post Office in Egerton, Victoria, on 16 December 1892, they elected to play Bulch's "Bathurst," "Phonograph" and "Good Shot" with Godfrey Parker's "Adelina," "Gollity" and "The Grasp of an English Hand" and also Henry Laski's "My Polly," concluding as always with the National Anthem. They and their audience might have seen this as a nice mix of pieces by leading composers of the day, whereas in truth it was all the creative work of one man.

As 1893 arrived it promised to be another key year for Tom Bulch. On 3 March his Prahran Operatic Band contributed a programme for a varied concert at the impressive Royal Exhibition Hall in Melbourne held in association with the Fitzroy Football Club. This programme included an overture composed by Henry Round entitled "Knight Templar," which is interesting in that if you were to mention that title to any bandsman in Britain today it would be George Allan's world-famous march of the same name that they would recall rather than Round's overture.

By early March, Tom, driven either by need for more money or else surplus spare time, had added another band to the portfolio under his wing. The Mercury and Weekly Courier newspaper of 9 March 1893 proclaims:

"BRASS BAND FOR COLLINGWOOD. A MEETING was held at Campbell's Engineer's Arms Hotel, Johnston Street, Collingwood, on Wednesday last for the purpose of forming a brass band in Collingwood; Mr Bostock was in the chair. An apology was received from Mr Keele, his absence being caused through visiting Geelong on fire board business. It was carried unanimously that the band be called The Collingwood Operatic Band, and under the conductorship of Mr T. E. Bulch. The election of office-bearers was as follows:- President, Cr. Keele; vice presidents, Crs. Beazley, Wilkins, and Kreitmayer; committee, Messrs. Swan, Walker, Woolcock, and S. Gibson, (Foy and Gibson); treasurer, Mr Bostock; trustees, Messrs. Morrish and Prout."

The district of Collingwood wasn't far from Prahran, being situated northeast of that district and close to the centre of Melbourne. Thomas had the band, presumably made up of experienced players and perhaps even bolstered by members of his Prahran Band, in shape and ready to perform in no time at all. The same newspaper less than two weeks later on 23 March advises of their impressive progress:

"The newly formed brass band of Collingwood, played their first programme of music before a large assembly of the public at Studley Park, on Sunday last, under the able conductorship of Mr T. E. Bulch. About twenty members took part in the performance, which was well received and highly appreciated by all present."

Tom was determined to achieve a full complement of players and advertised locally for additional bandsmen.

> "TO BANDSMEN. – Wanted, PLAYERS for all Instruments for the Collingwood Operatic Brass Band; also. Beginners that will be taught thoroughly. Practice on Monday evenings at Birmingham Arras Hotel, Smith Street, Collingwood. Bandmaster, T. E. BULCH."

With Tom's name on the header featured at the top of much of the popular music now being played by Australian bands and appearing in the press, his was becoming one of the most recognisable banding names in Australia. Would proclaiming that he was now the bandmaster of Collingwood be enough to ensure significant interest?

In the meantime, it appears that Tom either left the service of Suttons Music Warehouse to strike out again on his own, or else came to some arrangement with them. Assisted by his wife Eliza, Tom opened a new music store at number 73 Bourke Street East, Melbourne. He quickly arranged for advertisements to appear in the press declaring that they were "the cheapest house in the city for violins, accordions, brass and orchestral band instruments." Readers were also informed that the latest issue of his Intercolonial Band Journal was in stock on the 1st April. It seems Tom used the job offered to him by Suttons, in the larger city of Melbourne, as the ideal springboard to enable him to relaunch his own shop in its larger commercial centre. Working for himself once more enabled Tom to carry on composing to keep the pages of his own band journal full. This in what time remained in between being bandmaster and running the store. You would reasonably expect that this ought to be enough to keep even the most capable musician occupied to the point of proving almost unsustainable. Soon, though, the ever ambitious and driven Tom Bulch would attempt to take on even more business. Before that would happen, however, it was on the domestic front that both he and Eliza found themselves a little busier.

At the newest Bulch family home, Beaconsfield Villa, Peel Street, in the Windsor District of Prahran, Melbourne, on 11 March, twenty-eight-year-old Eliza Ann Bulch gave birth to another daughter. The couple named her Alice Bertha Bulch.

With running bands, a store, a brass journal, as well as composing reams of music for brass band, military band and piano, it's reasonable to suspect that Tom would have little time free to assist Eliza in the raising of another infant, nor Eliza time to aid in the running of the store. The Bulch household must have felt busy and chaotic.

On 4 April 1893, a number of newspapers in New Zealand reported that for their next annual contest, the committee of the Brass Band Association of New Zealand had agreed that rather than use a contest composition by Charles Godfrey, they would select one test piece from Wright and Round's catalogue and adopt one supplied by Tom Bulch.

Some significance in this decision lies in the fact that Charles Godfrey junior had, of course, been judge at Tom's first reported contest with the New Shildon Temperance Band in Newcastle. To have become a perceived to equal this much respected authority on the banding movement would have been food for thought for him. An additionally pertinent dimension to the decision lies in the fact that in making this decision the Association had taken into account correspondence from a number of providers of music from Australasia and England, which included a letter from the mentor that had worked with his grandfather's New Shildon Saxhorn Band, Robert De Lacy, publisher of the London Brass Band Journal. The committee subsequently wrote to Tom, and to Wright and Round, requesting their submissions of test pieces. At a meeting of the same association that took place on 26 June, the representative of Wellington Garrison Band suggested to the contest committee that they write to Tom to request that he act as a judge at the forthcoming contest. This suggestion was declined. A few days later, on 5 July, the Secretary of that same band wrote to Wellington's Evening Post newspaper outlining the reasons for this recommendation being that as Tom Bulch had been entrusted to provide a test piece there would be no better-placed bandmaster to be able to interpret how the test piece should be played. The public airing of the debate continued a week later in the New Zealand Mail with another anonymous writer arguing in favour of Tom's engagement:

"NEW ZEALAND BANDS ASSOCIATION. TO THE EDITOR. Sir,—The above association has thought fit to reject the suggestion of the local Garrison Band anent the appointment of Mr T. E. Bulch, the Victorian bandmaster, as adjudicator at the next band contest to be held in this Colony. Considering that a more able judge than Mr Bulch cannot be found in the Australasian Colonies having gleaned his experience in the North of England, where crack bands exist — and that the gentleman named is entrusted with the arrangement of the test selection, we think his rejection unwise on the part of the Bands Association. As the secretary of the local band says, 'Mr Bulch would be highly competent to judge his own arrangement,' and, having a full score, would more readily detect mistakes or omissions by the various ' mouthpieces,' when they occurred. Mr Bulch, it is said, has a wide knowledge of military band instrumentation, and has achieved great praise for his spirited quick-steps, the minor parts of which bandsmen speak of as interesting, artistically arranged, and full, while the test pieces arranged by him, although not written for virtuosi, are, nevertheless, brimful of awkward readings — such as broken time and chromatic runs, &c, calling forth all the musical talent of the executants for the creditable rendering of the whole. Mr Bulch, it is further stated, conducts all contests on the system adopted in the Old Country, and never judges—not even a quick step— without a fully written score to guide him in his judgment. His notes are comprehensive and instructive, his decisions never questioned, and bands can ever rely that the best band will win.—I am, &c,"

The test piece that Tom created for the contest was "Roberto II Diavolo," an arrangement based upon the work of the same name by Meyerbeer. It was described by yet another correspondent in the press as being "calculated to test the powers of the performers to the utmost," while another writing for the Otago Daily Times observed that it:

"...will be found a much severer test than the other test selection provided by Mr H. Round from Verdi's works. The piece abounds, with difficulties that the best of the bands will have to work hard and well to overcome. Solos are provided for most instruments, but the only one of particular note is that allotted to the cornet. There is a fine duo cadenza for cornet and euphonium; and the basses have plenty of good work. As a matter of fact, we do not think that, with "Verdi" also to work up, the bands—or the majority of them at any rate —have sufficient time to properly prepare Mr Bulch's fine selection. It may be noted as a remarkable omission that the arranger has not appended the metronome marks, and, unless conductors are tolerably familiar with the opera, there is likely to be a wide divergence of opinion displayed as to the tempos."

Despite the letters of recommendation in the press, Tom didn't receive his invitation from the New Zealand Bands Association, and the contest went ahead in November with one Mr G A Martin of Wanganui occupying the adjudicator's tent. The Invercargill Garrison Band emerged as the finest of the bands rendering the test pieces on the day. This episode does, though, give a clear illustration of the degree of esteem in which Tom had begun to be held across the Australian and New Zealand brass band movement, and the extent to which he had built up the reach of his reputation by this point in his life.

On 2 May 1893, Tom's Melbourne GPO Military Band submitted a programme of music as part of a "concert and dramatic entertainment" contribution to a fundraiser for the Telegraph Clerical Cricket Club at the Hibernian Hall, Swanston Street. The Melbourne Punch covered the event in brief. In the build up to July, Tom, already stretched by his various duties, had somehow taken on even more responsibility. He partnered with two associates, David H Hannah and a French-Australian bandmaster by the name of C Foret, to start an additional venture; a regular newspaper for musicians to be published monthly, commencing in July, which the group entitled The Intercolonial Orchestral and Brass Band News. It was an ambitious move and a venture into territory Tom had no experience of. He may have observed, however, how Wright and Round's similar but well established paper, the Brass Band News, and other such papers published in Britain were used as a platform for promotion and sales of band music. Perhaps this was part of the reason he agreed to, or sought, this partnership. This new Australian banding newspaper claimed to be the first of its kind on that continent. A much later account of Tom's contribution to Australian banding written in 1916 describes the venture with an honest appraisal of the shortcomings of Tom's involvement:

"Bulch published music, but he did more: he began the publication of a band paper, and it was in this connection that he displayed an amount of confidence in his journalistic ability, that had no-support in facts. Whatever merit he had as a writer of music it was soon plain that he had little as a compiler or dispenser of news. Luckily he did not embark on his newspaper publishing enterprise on his own. He had partners, David Hannah and C Foret. Hannah knew just about as much about newspapers as Bulch did. But Foret, who was a compositor, had the practical part of the business, and was the bulwark of the new firm. "The Intercolonial Brass Band News" was the imposing title of the new venture. I have said that neither Bulch nor Hannah were cut out for newspaper work. Yet both men did much towards successfully launching the paper: Bulch because of his reputation among bandsmen, and Hannah because of his ability to push sales. Hannah was for years associated with Fitzgerald's Circus, playing solo cornet in conjunction with Von der Mehden. With the circus, he travelled from end to end of Australia and through New Zealand and Tasmania as well. And wherever Dave went the merits of the "Intercolonial Brass Band News" were heralded. But the infant publication, though vigorous, required more nursing than either Bulch or Hannah were prepared to give it. The result was that these two "got out" leaving the venture in the hands of Foret (pronounced for-a), a volatile little Frenchman, who was brave enough to take up the load alone. The paper first came out as the "Intercolonial Orchestral and Brass Band News," not as the "Intercolonial Brass Band News" which was a later name given to it by Mons. Foret."

By taking this account in now we are reading ahead a little in our story, but it's worth understanding how bold a venture this was, and that Tom was prepared to take this kind of risk to further his ambitions. Having an influential interest in such a publication offered him the perfect vehicle in which to enrich not only the banding community of Australia, but also his own reputation, which as the retrospective above explains was already sufficient to ensure some measure of success in launching the paper. Tom, never one to miss an opportunity to mark an event with a special composition, created and published a contest march entitled "Intercolonial Brass Band News" or "IBBN" for short. The Traralgon Record of 8 August 1893 reviews the second issue of the paper and offers a product description:

"Musical.– We have received the second number of the "International Orchestral and Brass Band News," and though this, which is, by the way, the only musical paper printed in Australia, was first issued in July last, it has been greatly improved in the meantime. This paper is to be published on the first of each month. Its size is about that of the "Australasian," and consists of eight pages of reading matter. Its principal object appears to be to keep a record of the doings of the various bands in this and the other colonies, and the journal will, therefore, be found of great service to bandsmen, especially as with each issue is given a solo with variations suitable for any brass instrument. The paper also contains much matter of interest to any who study the art of music, and we therefore wish the proprietors every success in their venture. Mr D. H. Hannah with Messrs. Foret and Bulch, are the proprietors of the journal, and any of Mr Hannah's friends in this district can obtain all information from him by writing to his address, Frankston."

As the year drew to a close Thomas entered his GPO Military Band into a band contest that was set to take place on New Year's Day at a Carnival Sports event. For the contest to go ahead a minimum of five bands were required to enter. By the time of the deadline for applications only four had entered. The organisers, still hopeful, extended the deadline to the 20th of December. In the meantime, the future of that contest hung in the balance.

New Shildon

1893 was also a very interesting one for for George Allan. A new monthly publication was founded for British bandsmen that would go on to feature a great number of George's compositions during the remainder of the latter part of the nineteenth century.

The Cornet was a venture started by Fred Richardson of Sibsey, Boston, Lincolnshire. According to his obituary written in 1932, Fred had started his life in very humble circumstances, having been employed in the coal trade, and worked his way up to being a self-determining business entrepreneur and publisher. He was reportedly always interested in band music, but prior to becoming a publisher of music and banding news Fred, and his brother Robert, used to run prize competitions which they advertised in newspapers of the day. This kind of competition, requiring people to pay to enter, may well have been how the pair gained sufficient money to break into the world of business. One example of the brothers' competitions was printed in the Thetford and Watton Times and Weekly People's Journal of 17 May 1890 which trumpets:

"Prize competition (No. 4) – £5, £3, £2, £1, 10s, 10s, 10s, 10s, to those counting most correctly the letter 'T' in verses only, of first four chapters of GENESIS (old edition). Fee 1s, P.O. or 13 stamps and stamped envelope. Closes June 4th, result June 11th. Ties divide and £2 extra will be given for the first correct. F Richardson, Sibsey, Boston."

Fred and Robert were, here, taking a calculated risk that with each competition more entries would be received than necessary to cover the cost of the prizes. It's a classic technique still being echoed in the ad-breaks of reality TV shows in the early twenty-first century. The idea is to make the competition a challenge so simple that it is easy to enter, and offer a prize that makes an investment of a single shilling seem worthwhile. Just about every house in Britain possessed a Bible in 1893 and counting instances of the letter 't' in the named chapters was easy enough to be fun but would not take long.

Fred Richardson was also interested in motor cars, and his business ventures would earn him enough to be able to access them. The invention of the internal combustion engine and its subsequent improvement throughout the 1870s and 1880s created communities of enthusiasts across the country. Fred, being one such, soon found himself elected as the first secretary and treasurer of the South Lincolnshire Automobile Club. Of his personality we are told that he was "greatly esteemed" by the people of Sibsey, who were acquainted with his genial disposition. Whether Fred Richardson was a musician or had any experience of the brass banding community beyond appreciating the music not transparent; but, as Tom had seen the similar opportunity in Australia, Fred saw this opportunity and grabbed it with both hands. According to brass historian and academic Roy Newsome, the Cornet followed an approach and format similar to that used by Wright and Round for their publications. Through a combination of Fred's imitation of this winning formula, and his business sense and confidence, he ensured that The Cornet became a very successful rival publication.

As Tom Bulch had discovered already, to make your publications popular with the brass community it helped to invest some of your revenues into the contribution of prizes to high profile brass contests so Fred provided prizes such as medals to be awarded to the best soloists at contests.

George Allan, by 1893, was still not yet at the peak of his musical creativity; but we do see him that year bringing the New Shildon Saxhorn Band back into the band contesting circuit and enjoying some success. They arrived with instruments and uniform on Saturday 9 September at Belmont near Durham. The adjudicator was Joseph Gaggs, a renowned brass conductor and band contest judge of the day who four years previous had been engaged in a similar capacity by the New Shildon Temperance Band for their April contest, and the test piece on the day was "Sweet Harmonies," composed that year by George's contemporary James Ord Hume. The Jarrow Express reports the results six days later:

"A band contest, in connection with the Pelton Fell Prize Band, was held on Saturday, for which 20 bands entered, and of these 18 competed. The first prize in a quickstep competition was carried off by New Shildon; 2, Murton Colliery; 3, Hebburn Colliery; 4, West Pelton. Test piece conductor George Raine, 1st and special prize for best euphonium solo, New Shildon, George Allan, 2; Hebburn Colliery, 3; West Pelton, Thomas Wood, 4."

This was an excellent result. The New Shildon Saxhorn Band under George Allan had taken first prize in the march contest, generally considered to be a lesser aspect of the contest to the "test piece" in which they had taken second prize. If it's correct that there were eighteen bands competing then, for a band seemingly absent from contesting for a significant period, this was quite an achievement. George's efforts to improve the New Shildon Saxhorn Band appear to have garnered some appreciation from the members and officials of the band. On Saturday, 2 December the bandsman gathered together and, as the Durham County Advertiser reported six days later, paid tribute to their bandmaster:

"The Members of the New Shildon Saxhorn Band met on Saturday at the Black Bull Inn to present a silver mounted baton, with a suitable inscription, to Mr George Allan, their bandmaster. The baton was supplied by Hogget and Sons, Darlington. In the absence of Dr R W Smeddle, who was detained through his professional duties, the presentation was made by Mr James Robinson, the oldest member of the band. – Mr Allan responded in suitable terms."

The Black Bull Inn, demolished some decades ago, stood at the corner where Adelaide Street meets Byerley Road close to the site of the former railway works entrance. Being of substantial size, it appears to have served as a rehearsal venue as well as general meeting place for the Saxhorn Band.

Above: The Black Bull Inn, once at the corner of Adelaide Street, New Shildon, where George was presented with a baton by his band in 1893.

You may think that a good contest result such as this would have re-elevated George's Saxhorn Band to being the town's premier band again. However, the New Shildon Temperance Band had also been hard at work throughout 1893 to maintain their supremacy. They too returned to the brass contesting scene in 1893, and they did so with a renewed passion. They also made one simple change that seems to have allowed them to maintain their edge. Whether through financial support from subscribers, donors or patronage of the industries of the town, the Temperance Band hired in the services of an specialist external conductor with a proven track record for contest success. Quite why they elected to engage a conductor from out of town isn't explained anywhere, but it wasn't uncommon for bands to do so if aiming to join the ranks of the 'crack bands' of the day. The increasing affordability of rail travel also made it viable for such influential band conductors to traverse the still relatively compact northern region of Britain that they might work with a number of bands in parallel.

The Temperance Band's chosen conductor was William Holdsworth. Like Robert De Lacy decades earlier, Holdsworth was a professional conductor who would accept work with the right band for the right fee, wherever that may be across the North of England. His conducting career commenced in around 1887, and by the time he was engaged by the New Shildon Temperance he had already tasted considerable success with the Brighouse and Rastrick Temperance Band, Wyke Old Band, and the West Hartlepool Operatic Band. He conducted the latter to several prestigious contest placings in the years 1890 to 1893. His engagement would be a statement of the Temperance Band's ambition, and might even have drawn more talented players to the band.

There was a concession to be made in such an arrangement, which was that the New Shildon Temperance Band would never hold exclusivity over his services. Like any professional conductor, Holdsworth would follow the money and take on as much work as might ensure a good living. This proved no deterrent to the Temperance Band members and committee who commenced a relationship with Holdsworth that would last right through to the turn of the century. It would elevate them to a success from beneath the shadow of which the older Saxhorn Band, with their limited means, would never truly emerge.

Holdsworth had been born in Cleckheaton, lying almost equidistantly between Leeds, Bradford and Huddersfield, on 18 June 1861. His father was employed as a wire drawer. Whatever childhood and education he received was brief and humble. Before he was nine years old, like many children of his generation, he was working as a brickyard labourer alongside his older brother. Having grown up around Wyke in Yorkshire it was most probably as a juvenile member of the Wyke Old Band that he learned how the instrumentation and dynamics of brass music worked. We can see no evidence of his having received a formal education. Yet by 1891, when he was twenty-nine years of age, we can see that in that year's census that he declares himself as being a 'Professor of Music,' and owner of his own home at 3 Carr Row, Wyke. This represents quite a transformation in status. He and his wife Ruth raised a large family and eventually relocated to base themselves in Armley near Leeds.

Holdsworth, like Tom Bulch, had a reputation for being able to both play the cornet and conduct the band simultaneously. In a conducting career spanning twenty-seven years, up until 1914, he is known to have conducted at least sixty-six brass bands at contests, all situated across Yorkshire, Northumberland and County Durham. During the eight years that he was working with New Shildon Temperance he also conducted thirty-three other bands at some point or another. Many of these bands enjoyed much contest success under his baton. In 1893, though, it was New Shildon Temperance getting off to a flying start; coming first place in May at Castle Eden; again in July at West Hartlepool; and yet again in August at Witton Park. Additionally, the band were placed second at contests in Blackhill and Greatham, and picked up a third place prize at the Frosterley contest. Driven most likely by economic necessity, Holdsworth occasionally crowed as his successes were published in the likes of the Brass Band News. There could be no doubt that he possessed the capability and qualities unlock the best performance from a good group of bandsmen.

This would undoubtedly create difficulty for George and his Saxhorn Band. Surely if a bandsman in the town was of a certain degree of talent and prepared to sign up to the Temperance pledge, then it would be hard to resist the urge to exchange the uniform of the Saxhorn Band for that of the Temperance Band should the opportunity of a vacant seat arise. Furthermore, surely the Temperance cause would be delighted to see another townsman reject the evils of alcoholic drink.

1893 ended, and 1894 began bringing a further blessing for George Allan when, on Sunday, 18 February at the family home on Pears Terrace, his wife Elizabeth gave birth to a son. The pair named him William Willoughby Allan, using his mother's maiden name as a middle name. From later documented evidence it seems that that throughout his life many would know him as "Willoughby," but also as Bill. He was christened at New Shildon's All Saints Church on 22 March 1894; and the event was reported in the April issue of that church's parish magazine. George, by then, seems to have started putting some of the blacksmithing skills, learned in the workplace, to private use, perhaps seeking private clients for small jobs. We have seen a reference book from that year entitled "History, Topography, and

Directory of the County Palatine of Durham, comprising A General Survey of the County and a History of the City and Diocese of Durham" published by Francis Whelan & Company in which George appears. This was the second edition of a monumental volume that contains some history, a review of the county town by town, village by village, but which also serves as a directory of significant persons, principally businessmen and tradesmen. The compilation of information in this book would have been an enormous undertaking, presumably in the hope that it would prove an indispensable reference and that many copies would be sold. George's entry in the directory of notable New Shildon residents lists him as "Allan, George, (j) blacksmith, Pears Terrace."

Of the total population of New Shildon, which in that year was something exceeding 1,760 persons, only 198 residents are named and listed in the directory, most of whom are offering some kind of goods or services. That he is listed presents an impression that George may have been trying to supplement his income through a little moonlighting; perhaps making small pieces of ironwork for neighbours. Whether he possessed the facilities to do this at home is questionable. The yard of his Pears Terrace home is very small and doesn't look like it could have hosted even a small private forge. It's perhaps possible that he might, with or without permission, have used the facilities at the railway works for this purpose. It's a little interesting that George, by then a published composer and prize winning bandmaster, chose to be listed as a blacksmith. Was that an indication of how he predominantly saw himself; as a skilled and time-served manual worker first and foremost, with his musical skills serving merely as a hobby? Or was it simply that the opportunity to take private blacksmithing commissions outside working hours was a more important and lucrative opportunity for him at this time?

George was not the only Allan family member listed. The directory also named his father James as still plying his trade as a tailor and resident at Adelaide Street. George's act of listing himself as a blacksmith might have been an indication of him attempting to make ends meet, though this is by no means definite. We do know that also during this year he once again allowed his membership at the Mechanics Institute to lapse, though his wife had continued membership from 1894 through to 1897.

Despite the Saxhorn Band having been firmly in the shadow cast by the Temperance Band during the previous year, George evidently had them working hard throughout 1894, and they seem to have made plenty of appearances. While the Temperance Band had their cash prize-haul from their contest successes to add to whatever subscription or sponsorship they received, the Saxhorn Band had to conduct their own fundraising to maintain their uniform, instruments and pay for travel and band room hire etc. The Darlington & Stockton Times reported on Saturday, 31 March 1894 that:

"Two sacred concerts were given in the Co-operative Hall, under the auspices of the New Shildon Saxhorn Band, collections being taken for the purpose of purchasing new instruments for the band."

April saw the band continuing the long-standing tradition of contributing to events held by the friendly societies. The Darlington & Stockton Times mentions on 28th:

"Church Parade – On Sunday Evening the members of the New Shildon branch of the "Independent Order of Oddfellows" (Kingston Union) met at the Lodge Room, Black Bull Inn, and paraded the principal streets, accompanied by the Shildon Saxhorn Band, prior to attending divine services at St John's Church where an eloquent sermon was preached to a large congregation by the Rev. Horatio Spurrier, M.A., vicar."

Clearly, there were people, groups and societies still willing to engage the services of the town's older band. The July issue of the New Shildon All Saints Church parish magazine tells how on 23 June 1894, George and the New Shildon Saxhorn Band were engaged by the church to provide music for a ceremony to lay the foundation stone for a 'mission room'. A procession had been planned for the day, with the Saxhorn Band at its head and a line of scholars and teachers following on behind. The procession left All Saints School, which had been built by the church of the same name, at two-thirty in the afternoon playing the hymn "Brightly Gleams Our Banner".

Midway through 1894 Wright & Round's Brass Band News began to receive correspondence from a writer contributing under the pseudonym of 'Ravenswood' offering insight into the workings of brass bands in the Shildon district. Among these the writer includes the occasional snippet about the New Shildon Saxhorn Band. The first features in the July 1894 issue of the paper, and explains how the band played 'for the Auckland Park P. M.' on 17th July and then at the Bicycle Sports Club, now Shildon's football ground on the 30th of that same month. In between these two engagements, on 21 July to be precise, the annual Durham Miner's Gala occurred. This annual working miners' pageant of the Durham coalfield and the music is brought remained a highlight of George's personal annual calendar. Thanks to the Darlington and Stockton Times we know that this time the Saxhorn Band marched ahead of the miners and banners from New Shildon and Shildon Lodge Collieries during the procession into the city of Durham.

The Gala represented a very serious political statement as a demonstration of the combined collective power of the miners of Durham's coalfield, whom we should not forget had been bested by the coal owners in the bitter dispute two years previous. Yet for a lover of brass music such as George was, it was also an unprecedented opportunity to hear almost all the other bands from across the county, and the music the they had chosen to play each year. It's possible that from time to time he might even have had the pleasure of hearing one of these bands play a march of his own making. Perhaps the powerful emotions that this occasion stirs as the bands pass through the narrow streets lined with onlookers, as they do even today despite the demise of the coal industry being decades behind us, was in some way influential in George's musical development as a march specialist. Once all the respective communities of miners had arrived at the racecourse, the speeches were made. The men would crowd around the speakers' platform to try to hear what their representatives and advocates had to say about the year past and the year ahead. That year rousing speeches were offered by MPs C Fenwick, J Havelock Wilson, John Burns and L A Atherley-Jones, as well as Isadore Isaacs of the solicitors that represented the Durham Miners Association. Burns used his speech as an opportunity to give his views on reducing the daily working hours of the coal miners to eight hours, to allow for equal measures of rest and recreation. After the speeches came the time for revelry before the assembly dispersed back to their home settlements.

If George was again, as we are told, inspired by the Gala to compose another march then there are a number of candidate pieces that were published by Haigh and other music publishers that year, including "The Ovation," "Bertha," "Raleigh," "Sailing Homeward," "Skidby" and a contest march "Windlestone" titled after the country estate of the landowning Eden family which stood barely a couple of miles from New Shildon. Another march appearing in this year which was unlikely to have been inspired by the Durham Miners' Gala is the piece "The Hunwick Rover" which was most likely named for a player from the Hunwick Rovers football team that were a frequent opponents of the teams from the Shildons. The compositions that would make George's name an enduring one in the minds of brass musicians were yet to come. As the summer wore on, the engagements kept coming. The Darlington & Stockton Times of 11 April reports upon the Heighington Flower and Agricultural Show stating:

> "A fine musical programme was supplied by the Shildon Saxhorn Band, and at the close dancing and sports were indulged in."

'Ravenswood', in his 1894 reports for the Brass Band News, states that he had expected the Saxhorn Band to attend a contest taking place at Darlington, but that the band had not appeared. He had anticipated that they would have been among the prizes had they taken part and admonishes the bandmaster by adding "Come George, rouse them up a bit, it will never do to miss chances like these." Later that month, though, we see the Darlington & Stockton Times include a report of the Shildon Flower Show that presents differing attitudes to the Temperance and Saxhorn bands:

> "The town prize band, under the efficient conductorship of Mr Harry Gibbon, gave a grand afternoon concert in their recreation ground on the Spoil Banks. In spite of the rather inclement weather a large company of delighted listeners were present. The collection in aid of the new instrument and tuition funds, realised the handsome sum of £3 10s. The Saxhorn band also gave a selection of music on the band-stand in the show field, and were fairly patronised."

The 'prize band' of course refers to the Temperance Band, of whom Harry Gibbon was day to day bandmaster and conductor when they were not playing at contests. Though in the view of the writer of that article the Temperance Band had the power to 'delight' they somewhat sniffily thought it was 'fair' of people to at least give the Saxhorn Band an audience. Ravenswood adds further insight into the emerging gap between the Saxhorn and Temperance bands when he writes the following in the Brass Band News:

> "The New Shildon Saxhorn have not done much lately. I hear they are practicing for the Pelton contest, and I should like very well to see them in the prize list. But what is all this nonsense I hear, George, about the Sunday concerts? Surely there is room for both bands to play: it looks very much like as if you did not like to see your neighbours get on so well. Away with such petty jealousy and strive to do ye likewise."

The Saxhorn Band did, as Ravenswood predicted, take part in at least one band contest during 1894, which was on 25 August at Pelton Fell. Darlington & Stockton Times and Ripon & Richmond Chronicle on 1st September 1894 proclaims:

> "Success of Local Bands" "On Saturday at Pelton Fell, under Mr Allan's able baton, the town Saxhorn Band took fourth place in the band contest, the test piece being "Flowers of Beauty," arranged by Mr J Ord Hume."

The Pelton Fell contest at the Recreation Ground there was judged by the noted composer James Ord-Hume himself, and ten bands took part. In the same report it mentions how the town's 'Prize Band', again the Temperance Band, took two second place prizes at Tow Law that week. An interesting quirk of this event is that it creates yet another connection between George Allan and Thomas Bulch in that both composers had their bands judged by James Ord-Hume, albeit on entirely separate continents. Ord Hume would, as we shall later hear, make a journey to Australia and judge at a prestigious contest that Thomas Bulch had a hand in establishing.

Membership of the New Shildon Saxhorn Band wasn't just about the music and discipline. There was occasionally time for fun and games, usually with a fundraising objective. In September the Darlington & Stockton Times relates one such occasion:

"Saxhorn Band – Under the auspices of this band, on Saturday afternoon, a football competition was held in a field near to Shildon Lodge Colliery, kindly lent for the occasion by Mrs S E McNaughton. Owing to scarcity of time, the competition was not finished, and the two Dinsdale and Shildon teams left in the competition will compete for premier honours on a future date at present unsettled. In the quoit handicap, the two prizes were divided between Bell, Wright, Matthews and Teesdale. The first prize in the throwing ball at wicket competition was won by Teesdale, and the second prize by R Foster. The proceeds were in aid of the new instrument fund, but owing to the small attendance present, only realised a small sum."

As the year drew to a close we see one further update from Ravenswood in Wright & Round's paper, which tells us that the Saxhorn band were at the Witton Park quickstep contest on 25 October but were not in the prizes. He also tells us that they were having another fundraiser, a Christmas prize draw and wished them every success with that venture.

Melbourne

Regarding Tom Bulch, it seems that 1894 saw him busy as ever. He had ended 1893 with a contest, not for bands this time but for composers, the objective being to submit the best piece of marching music for brass or military band, and on this occasion Tom was organiser rather than competitor. The Launceston Examiner reported on the Tasmanian bandmaster Charles Trussell having been honoured as a winner in that contest. Trussell was a contemporary of Bulch, having been born in London two years before the latter and arriving in Australia three years after. He settled initially in Maryborough before moving on to Tasmania. The motivation for Tom's composition contest is unclear, though it could have been an attempt to seek new materials to include in his brass band journal. For example, if Tom saw any merit in any of the submitted pieces, even if they had not won the contest, he may have approached the creator offering to publish it.

There were also indications that Bulch had in mind to initiate a grand new band contest which would involve bands from across the Australias territories and New Zealand which would, if it could be realised, take place in Melbourne. An article in the Southern Cross newspaper ponders on the idea:

"The idea of an Intercolonial, Band Contest to be held in Melbourne, promulgated by Mr T. E. Bulch, music-publisher of that city, is being pretty fully discussed both here and in Australia. On the other side it is meeting with very much favour. In New Zealand some hold the opinion that it would be absurd even to think of a New Zealand band competing with such crack Australian bands as Sydney Permanent Artillery, Newcastle 4th Regiment, and others. But there is no doubt that if a representative band could be formed, in some such way as cricket and other teams are (and there is ample material to form such a band with) there is every reason to suppose N.Z. would carry off the palm: —and the prize money. We hope to hear of Mr Bulch's efforts being carried to a successful issue."

It appears though as though the Australasian continent was not yet ready for this venture; it did not take place in 1894. Tom, meanwhile, was still otherwise active with his Operatic Band. On one evening in January they provided a programme of six selections at a concert at the Carlton Tennis Club. The Melbourne GPO Military Band also continued to benefit from his leadership, performing at a picnic of the Post and Telegraph Department at Mornington, whereupon:

"...the Post Office Band under the conductorship of Mr Bulch discoursed some inspiriting music".

It was around this point that Tom created the march "Postman's Parade" for the GPO band. This seems to have proved popular with bands in the latter half of that year and continued to be commonly played for many years. Tom, not one to miss an opportunity to satisfy his market, also created a version of "Postman's Parade" for piano which was reviewed thus in a newspaper of the day:

"Speaking of music, I have received the 'Postman's Parade,' composed by Mr T Bulch. It is dedicated to Mr John Springhalt, Superintendent of the Mail Branch G.P.O., Melbourne, and who is a well-known resident of Prahran. The Parade is written in two fourth time, the key being B flat. It is easy, tuneful, and graceful, throughout, and is likely to be a popular march for others besides Postmen. An excellent lithophotograph of Mr Springhall embellishes the initial page."

Band programmes across Australia were now beginning to bulge with the compositions by Bulch or one his pseudonyms, or those whose work he had arranged for different music formats. In Ballarat, his name continued to thrive through its association with the Model Band he once instructed; still undertaking countless engagements under the leadership of fellow former New Shildonian, James Scarffe. Tom's collaborative venture of running a brass band newspaper also continued apace. The Australian Town & Country Journal of 23 June 1894 includes a review of The Intercolonial Orchestral and Brass Band News:

> "Vol. 1, No. 2. This journal is intended to contain a mass of news respecting the progress of brass band and orchestral music in the colonies, and, judging from the number before us, it seems well adapted to accomplish that object. A supplement contains half a dozen original pieces of dance music arranged as solos for the cornet, but playable on other treble instruments. These compositions are by Messrs. T. E. Bulch, Harris, Godfrey Parker, and C. Trussell, all of whom are well-known musicians. The letterpress in the number before us is interesting, and the journal promises to be an advantage to music and musicians throughout the southern hemisphere."

You can imagine that all of this activity, in parallel to running his music store on Bourke Street would be a great deal of work and certainly difficult to sustain. Yet Tom's drive and personal ambition clearly continued to motivate him. He was also not shy in publicly coming forward with his views on musical matters. A choir contest taking place at the Queen's Festival in Melbourne in 1894 prompted him to put pen to paper to create a letter to the Editor of The Age newspaper of Melbourne:

> "I was surprised when I read Dr Torrance's letter in your issue today re the above competition. He states it is unreasonable to expect a judge, to point out the defects of the various competitors, or to state any reasons for giving any particular choir the first prize. He also states it is impossible to specify them to the satisfaction of the competitors. I say it is not impossible to capable judges, to turn in a report which could be easily understood, and it is their duty to do so. I have taken part in a great many competitions, both vocal and instrumental, in England and the colonies, and the judges in every case furnished a fully detailed report. I have always understood that

competitions were intended for educational purposes, but if we are to accept Dr Torrance's theory then there is nothing educational about them. In conclusion, I wish it to be understood that I am not questioning the judges' decision, but merely pointing out a judge's duty. — Yours &c., T E BULCH. 73 Bourke-street, 26th June."

The letter has a direct, no-nonsense timbre and the air of a man stamping his authority on a matter. Naturally, the correspondence prompted a lengthy reply from Dr Torrence, dissecting Thomas's critique, and ending:

"Let each choir come with a determination to do its best, not to be the best, and I think "education" will follow. Apologising for the length of this letter, which I trust may not bring down more vials of musical wrath upon my head, — Yours, &c., G W TORRANCE. Balaclava, 2nd July."

On Friday 24 August, Bulch's Operatic Band performed a short programme at the Unified Friendly Societies Hall, Queensbury Street, Melbourne, as part of a Grand Vocal and Athletic Entertainment which was held for the benefit of a certain Mr P Matthews. That same month, Tom published his patriotic overture "Austral" which was soon adopted enthusiastically by bands, among them the St Joseph's Band of Launceston, Tasmania, who played it at a number of engagements that summer.

Tom was also commissioned to provide a quickstep to the New Zealand Band Contest Committee as a test piece for a quickstep contest scheduled to take place on 13 October. Quick to see an opportunity to promote their businesses he arranged with his partner from the Orchestral and Brass Band News, Foret, to award a four-guinea gold medal to the band that accrued the most points in the playing of both his own, and Wright and Round's test pieces at the contest. Additionally, free copies of their paper would be presented to each of the winning bandsmen in the quickstep contest. He also promised to provide two guineas worth of band music, from his own stock, to the band that won the march contest. Tom ended up submitting not one, but two test pieces, a selection, "Reminiscences of Weber," based upon extracts of operas composed by Carl Maria von Weber, and a new march entitled "Dunedin Navals." The latter was created in tribute to the

Dunedin Naval Band of that city; a curious choice given that the same band would compete in the contest.

One New Zealand brass critic, writing under the pseudonym "Quaver," observed that the print quality of "Reminiscences of Weber" was not up to scratch and that some parts were unreadable in places. He anticipated that the piece being provided by Wright and Round would have their characteristic high print quality. Their test piece that did eventually arrive and turned out to be "Schubert" by Henry Round. The contest resulted in some controversy, with Timaru Garrison, Invercargill Garrison and Dunedin Engineer's bands all being accused of fielding players that they appeared to have brought in to strengthen the bands' abilities specifically for the contest.

On 28 November, Tom conducted the GPO Military Band at a special musical evening of the Australian Natives Association's Prahran Branch at that district's Town Hall. The event featured a number of the city and district's musical societies and was initiated with the objective of raising money to provide literature for the blind. Next came a trip to Tasmania. Tom set out for the neighbouring island territory aboard the SS Yolla, arriving on 11 December, which of course would be the height of the summer in Australia, not as bitter a time to be at sea as the British reader might perceive. We are given no documented explanation for the trip, but it was a relatively brief visit as he was back to conduct his GPO Military Band on the South Melbourne Esplanade, near the promenade pier, on Weds 19th December.

New Shildon

The year 1895 appeared to be a quieter year for George Allan in New Shildon. There is not a great deal of evidence to suggest that the Saxhorn Band band had been set back in any way; perhaps it was simply the case that engagements went unreported. One report from the Northern Echo tells of the 9th Annual Sports of the Shildon Amateur Cycling Club which had just been held and had proved to be as popular and successful as its predecessors. The article adds that:

> "the new Shildon Saxhorn Band, under the leadership of Mr G Allan, played popular selections and added greatly to the enjoyment of the afternoon."

One of the officials issuing prizes that day was Dr Smeddle, who had presented George with the commemorative baton purchased by the men of the Saxhorn Band two years earlier. George seems to have steadily maintained his composing activity and we see a number of pieces published and others emerge as being performed that we have not seen in previous years. These include the marches "Waltham," "Greystock," "Aronia" and "Blytheville" as well as waltz "Morning Breezes," and the overtures "Cavalier" and "Romola".

When considering the titles of George Allan's compositions there appears a randomness that differs to Bulch's approach in entitling his works, which make his inspirations for choosing them a little obscure. Tom's titles are often derived from significant events, such as "The Battle of Eureka" where the prospectors of the Australian goldfields came under siege during their dispute with the governor's authorities at the Eureka Stockade in 1854, a tale he would have heard much about on his arrival in Creswick. He also chose valiant and militaristic sentiments, military units, places he had visited, bands that he had connections to or places of contests that he had some involvement in. He even named a piece after the Intercolonial Brass Band News, a publication he had a business interest in.

So far as we know, though it sounds like a location, there has never been a town or village called "Blytheville" in the United Kingdom. All the signs indicate that by this point in his life George was not especially well travelled, and would have struggled to do so by his own financial means. Though there is a Blytheville in Arkansas, in the United States, founded in 1879, it would have been of little particular relevance when George Allan was composing in the mid-1890s.

However, there is something in the title "Blytheville" that may offer us a clue as to a possible cause of inspiration for some titles of George's pieces. Britain at the end of the Victorian era was famed globally for its reputation as a maritime nation. Parts of the North of England, as well as Scotland, were particularly famed for shipbuilding. Now, it just happens that there was an iron screw steamer called Blytheville which was launched by William Gray and Company of West Hartlepool on 28 July 1877, two years before before the founding of the American city of the same name. This ship was initially owned by a Mr B Brewis of Darlington, close to New Shildon, and was given its name by the owner's daughter. A coincidence? Perhaps, but when you consider that Allan's list of titles also includes "Elmville" and see that the William Gray company launched another screw steamer Elmville from the same works in 1889, though this time for a different Sunderland based owner, you see the potential of a pattern forming.

If we follow that thread we discover that a good many of George's composition titles correspond to names of ships. Sometimes they are shared with more than one vessel, right up to some of his later and greatest marches that include "Knight Templar," "Battle Abbey," "Senator" and "The Wizard," at which we will arrive later in the story. Looking again at "Blytheville" we can see, in the July 1895 issue of Wright and Round's Brass Band News, that the composition was featured in an issue of J Greenwood and Son's Northern Brass and Military Band Journal. In the advertisement, it was described as "A first class march. Good show for everyone. Sure to please." The piece was still being advertised as available as part of this journal in January of 1896.

Greenwood and Son's Journal was based at 42 Somerset Street in South Shields on the north-east coast of England. The first reported reference we have found to "Blytheville" being played by a band was when it appeared in a programme offered by Dennison's Band on 13 April 1895, at Marine Park, also in South Shields. George's repertoire of compositions does include one other title using the suffix "-ville" which is the later march "Shawville." This one has connections contrary to the maritime engineering theory, in that around the time it was created a street of houses had been built in New Shildon, which had been named Shawville Terrace. These houses still stand today, though they are now considered, and numbered as, part of the town's Redworth Road.

Whilst we cannot say without any doubt that there was something about marine engineering that George found inspiring ,there are still some convincing arguments in favour of the theory. Shildon is close enough to the ports of the North-East coast for George to have seen all these names on ships, were he to wander around those ports. He may not have been especially well travelled, through constraints relating to his occupation and income, and may not have been for example to "Battle Abbey" in Hastings, or "Nevada" in the United States; however the ships with these names may well have come to him. He was a blacksmith engaged in heavy engineering and manufacturing in an era when great technological advances were being made in naval engineering. He may well have had access to books and periodicals, through his membership of the Mechanics Institute, that featured articles on these ships. Perhaps there was a different reason for finding inspiration in the names of ships; one more romantic in that these vessels travelled the globe, as George's old bandmate Tom had done, in an age when George perhaps realised that he would not. Equally possible is that there is nothing at all in this theory and that George simply picked words he saw that he liked the sound of driven by necessity to at the very least give titles to his musical pieces, whether significant or not.

Melbourne

As for Tom, well, he had his own nautical encounters. On 30 January 1895 a pleasure boat called the SS Hygeia left the railway pier at Port Melbourne for a moonlight excursion down the Port Philip Bay. Entertaining the passengers on board, through their performances of selections and dance music, were Tom Bulch and his GPO Military Band. Tickets were made available for a shilling and sixpence each with proceeds going to the excursion's organisers, the St George's Christian Doctrine Society of Carlton. The first day of February then brought the same band on the South Melbourne Esplanade before yet another appearance on Wednesday, 14th where they gave "a number of excellent musical selections" in McGregor's band rotunda, Beaconsfield Parade.

Saturday, 23 February brought, once again, the annual picnic of the Post Office and Telegraph Department at Portsea, for which, of course, the GPO Military Band was the natural choice for musical entertainment, and who did not disappoint in their delivery of promenade and dance music. The band returned to the Esplanade on 13 March. and on 5 April, the military band gave their final performance of that summer's season once again at the rotunda on Beaconsfield Parade.

With those engagements duly fulfilled, Tom was able to concentrate on furthering his reputation as a contest adjudicator. A contest was due to be held in Queensland as part of the Bundaberg Agricultural and Pastoral Society annual exhibition on the 17th and 18th of July. Prizes totalling £100 in value were offered and by early May it was announced that Tom, the "Professor of Music and publisher of the Intercolonial Brass and Military Band Journal," had been engaged to judge. It wasn't practical to travel to Bundaberg by land, so Tom once again boarded a ship from Melbourne. This was the Maranoa which, on 11 July, set out for Brisbane arriving on the 14th. From here he was able to travel onwards to the city of Bundaberg. The Gympie Times and Mary River Mining Gazette of 23 July 1895 gives a narrative of the contest, republished from the Bundaberg Star, and tells of Tom's subsequent activities there. The reporter's account of his speech particularly reinforces what we know to be Tom's typical regard for Temperance values and professional standards.

> "The Bundaberg Band Contest. The Band Contest was continued throughout Thursday, and excited great interest. The result in popular parlance was foreknown, and all felt assured that Gympie was to bear away the blue ribbon. The judge's decision proved that the vox populi was again correct for he placed the bands as follows: —Oddfellows (Gympie) .. 140 points; Town Band (Gympie) .. 140 points; Town Band (Bundaberg) .. 125 points; Advance (Maryborough) .. 105 points; Federal (Lismore, N.S.W.) .. 90 points. These were out of a possible maximum of 200 points. The two tieing bands played off a selection again, and the Oddfellows won by a few points. The Gympie Town played in this event, under great disadvantages, as rain was falling heavily at the time injuring their music sheets, and the noise of the sideshows on another occasion compelled them to stop. The win was a popular one, the visitors being heartily cheered. In giving his decision Mr Bulch congratulated the Society on the contest. All the bands were a credit to the towns, and compared very favourably with bands in Victoria. There was really very little difference between the competing bands. The cornet and bombardon playing was excellent. He said the men altogether were the finest lot of bandsmen he had ever come in contact with. Not one was drunk, not one used bad language. He had come here to judge, and he had given honest decisions to the best of his ability. (Applause.) He highly complimented the Lismore band on their pluck in coming so far to compete. (Cheers were given for the Lismore band.) He thanked the people of Bundaberg for the uniform kindness be had received at their hands."

On his return journey Thomas had to travel via Gympie where he made a brief stop.

"Mr Bulch, the adjudicator, arrived on Gympie by the mail-tram on Saturday, en route for Melbourne, and breaking his journey here the members of both local bands at once decided to entertain him at a smoke concert. They mustered in good strength in the Exchange Room after the evening call; a number of friends of the bands were also present. Mr J. L. Mathews, in the unavoidable absence of Mr Smyth, presided, and in a neat speech proposed Mr Bulch's health. He congratulated the Gympie bands on their success at Bundaberg, and said it was all the more gratifying from the fact that their guest's decision confirmed the judgment given by Mr Charlsworth at Gympie about which so much fuss had been made. Mr Bulch, in reply, remarked that he had been treated most hospitably, both at Bundaberg and Gympie, and his trip had been a most enjoyable one; Gympie had two good bands, and there was no doubt they had conducted themselves like gentlemen right through the contest. He could assure the assemblage it took him all his time to decide between them. He came to the conclusion each day to give them the same number of points, and that the fairest thing to do was to require them to ' play off,' and in 'playing off' there, was no doubt that the band which received the first prize played best; they played better than they had done previously, whilst their rivals did not play quite so well as they had done before. He hoped that if they had another competition on Gympie they would not allow hurdy-gurdies and such distracting noises as were allowed at Bundaberg whilst the music competitions were on. His remarks on the playing would be sent to Bundaberg in the course of a fortnight, and might probably be of value to them on some points. Songs and recitations followed, and a merry two hours' jollification was brought to a close by the honouring of the toast of the chairman, which was proposed by Mr W M Jones (bandmaster of the Gympie Town Band), and supported by Mr J Snell (bandmaster of the Oddfellows' Band)."

Tom returned to Melbourne on the ship Eurimbla, which departed on 30 July and arrived on 1 August. As his overall absence had been quite a long one at around twenty days duration, the GPO Military Band had continued to fulfil engagements under the baton of deputised conductor Mr D Rose. Ever true to his word, Tom despatched a full and frank report of his rationale behind the scoring of the Bundaberg contest to its organisers, and this was duly published in the press for all to see. It was very detailed account and offers praise and criticism in unmistakably clear terms, highlighting moments of poor tuning, poor adherence to the spirit of the music at times and perceived probable poor instrument quality. He lavished praise where he felt it due and, in an echo of his speech at Gympie, concluded with a statement of protest at the organisers having allowed bagpipe playing, hurdy-gurdy and bass drums from the side shows to be played during the contest.

The beginning of September saw Tom named as a 'Professor of Music' engaged alongside E Rawlins and Mr W Thornthwaite to form the panel of three judges at a band contest arranged between the City and Garrison Bands of Tasmania. His co-judge, Rawlins, came with a letter of recommendation from the renowned British bandmaster, Charles Godfrey, with whom of course Tom was familiar from his brief contesting career in England. As events transpired however, Tom, perhaps beginning to struggle to sustain meeting so many demands on his person, was unable to make travel arrangements that would see him arrive in Tasmania in time for the contest, and he was substituted on the day by Mr W Tenyson-Bates of Hobart, Tasmania.

A second chance to adjudicate in Tasmania arose later that year when the organisers of the Australasian Axemens Association planned their annual Axeman's Carnival to be held in November. It was recommended to the event committee that they 'cable' Mr Bulch to invite him to adjudicate. By 'cable', they meant sending a telegram. Though considered an archaic and primitive means to communicate now, this technology enabled the late Victorian world to engage in relatively rapid contact over long distances. It was particularly useful in connecting separate landmasses by deploying cables across the ocean beds. New Zealand, for example, had been connected to Australia by cable since 1876, though it was often unreliable as strong tides caused scouring of the protective surface surrounding the cable, requiring it to be relaid periodically. That particular cable had just been relaid, in 1895, though a second cable had also been deployed across the Tasman Sea between Sydney and Wellington in 1890. Despite this speedy means of conveying messages being available, the committee reported in the Launceston Examiner of 29th October that no reply had been received from Mr Bulch. The Chairman resolved to write to a friend in Melbourne immediately and have that friend contact

Tom to enquire whether he would accept the engagement. As a backup plan the secretary of the committee was advised to write to several other professional musicians on the same subject. By 2 November however the matter was resolved and an announcement made:

> "Regarding the Band Contest the services of Mr T E Bulch, of Victoria, have bees secured as judge, for the sum of £15. The appointment should give satisfaction to the whole of the bands entered for the contest, as Mr. Bulch is eminently qualified for the position."

Tom Bulch sailed to Launceston, Tasmania, aboard the Pateena on 21 November. As on his trip to Bundaberg earlier in the year, he travelled alone. Presumably, his wife Eliza took care of both family and Melbourne based business affairs in her husband's absence. The ship made port at Launceston on the 22nd where Tom was entertained at a sacred concert by the Launceston Garrison band before setting out overland for Ulverstone on the coast to the north-west. The Launceston Examiner gives an account of the first day of the Axemen's Carnival contest:

> "The first night's contest of the country band competition was held this evening in Crawford's store. The building was well filled. The weather was fine, and visitors from all parts were present. The excursion train was well patronised. Eight bands had entered; Scottsdale, Stanley, and Porter's did not compete, the latter out of respect to the memory of the late bandmaster, Mr J F. Porter. The arrangements for the contest were carried out by Mr C Findley, Mr Bulch acting as judge in the enclosed compartment. Each band was loudly applauded, and the following programme was gone through - Ulverstone Band (P. D. McLaren, conductor), "Evening thought,"; Lefroy (J. Tevelein) "Lurline"; Zeehan (J. Caddie), "Masaniella"; Wynyard (F. Harper), "Wales"; Devonport (J. Henkel), "Austral." Selections were played afterwards by each band, but not for competition."

A second day of competing followed, and on account of their rendition of "Ever True" the following evening Tom adjudged the Zeehan band to be winners, with the band from Ulverstone as the runners up. The decision was popular and received with much applause from the spectators and supporters of the bands present. Thomas arrived back in Melbourne, disembarking from the Pateena, on 3 December.

On 20 December, just a few days before Christmas, and only ten days before Tom's own birthday, the family welcomed another new arrival when Eliza brought son John Southey Paterson Bulch into the world at their home at 244 Madeleine Street, Melbourne. The child was named in honour of his maternal grandfather. Tom would not have long to enjoy the comfort of home, and time with his wife and recently extended family. After a Christmas celebration, but before his thirty-third birthday, he and business partner, Monsieur Foret, boarded the Arawatta bound for Sydney en-route to Wollongong, just south of the New South Wales capital, to take his place in the judging tent once again.

A Jolly Swagman

In examining the events of 1895, we have arrived at a point in Tom Bulch's life where something happened for which he is perhaps best known, but which is often misunderstood. Though what happens centres upon 1895 it is a happening that perhaps has its roots in Tom's youth.

We know from earlier in his story that Tom was not only adept with brass and military band instruments but as a young lad also learned to play piano and violin. In learning and practicing this day by day he would have been exposed to some of the traditional music for those instruments as well as newer pieces composed or arranged by musicians some of whom would become his peers and contemporaries. He'd have acquired a wealth of musical knowledge, and familiarity with some of the most popular pieces of the era. This in turn would give him inspiration to draw upon. With the brass band scene being relatively new when Tom was first composing, he, and his contemporaries would from time to time set about arranging versions of traditional tunes for the full array of brass band instruments. One such piece to undergo transformation by the pen of Tom Bulch was the traditional Scottish song "Thou Bonny Woods of Craigielea" for which words had originally been written by Robert Tannahill of Paisley in Scotland which were then set to a tune by James Barr. That first, and original, version was created prior to Tannahill's death in 1810 so had been around for many decades, and become reasonably popular with generations of musicians and lovers of traditional tunes.

How, specifically, it came to Tom's attention is not entirely clear, but a theory with very significant probability is that the link was created through the published work of Carl Volti. We know that Tom had already arranged "Fair Maid of Perth," credited to Volti. It is a name that has long been connected with Tom Bulch, and often misunderstood as being a pseudonym of the latter. On close inspection though, we know them to be two distinctly different physical individuals and we do know something of the real Carl Volti.

The name Carl Volti sounds so much like a name that a fan of wordplay like Thomas Bulch would have chosen. It gives the exotic illusion of originating on the European mainland rather like Henry Laski, which sounds at once perhaps both Polish and French. Of course the word 'volti' does have a musical meaning; it is an instruction to turn the page of music, often used with the term 'subito' meaning quickly. We revealed already that the name Carl Volti was indeed a pseudonym; but not Tom's. Carl Volti was born Archibald Milligan in Glasgow on the 29th January 1848, which makes him a decade and a half older than Bulch. One documented source tells us that his father, and several uncles on his mother's side, were fiddlers. One of them being George Hood who was at that time one of the best known in Scotland. Young Archie was greatly influenced by his uncle's visits to the Milligan house. His first instrument, reportedly, was the tin whistle, with the effect that he and his friends started a whistle band, with Archie being the leader and teacher. Having felt to have exhausted the possibilities of the tin whistle, Archie's father, James, had his old fiddle fixed up for the youngster and upon it the first piece he learned was "The High Road To Linton." Already we see similarities between Milligan and Bulch. Both learned violin as youngsters. Both too, though revealed in a different context and execution, were it seems keen 'whistlers', and both also taught piano.

Volti/Milligan was a music teacher, and seemingly one with a curious sense of humour or mischief. In the Glasgow Evening Citizen of Friday, 21 August 1868, both Archibald Milligan and Carl Volti are advertising their teaching services in the same column of the newspaper, the respective adverts being barely an inch apart. Milligan advertises as teaching piano, harmonium and violin at his address in Eglinton Street, While Volti requests that his prospective students enrol at 1 Renfield Street for violin and piano lessons. The addresses given aren't too far apart, but interestingly they are on opposite sides of the River Clyde which bisects the city. The logic behind this second address is possibly explained by an advert from the previous year, promoting sale of a a Volti composition:

> "The Citizen Galop. By Carl Volti. John B. Galbraith, 1 Renfield Street. This "sparkling galop" is increasing in popularity every day."

It appears therefore that the 1 Renfield Street was the address of his publisher. The publishing of "The Citizen Galop" was a milestone for both Archibald Milligan and Carl Volti in that you could say it was connected to the 'birth' of Carl Volti. An interview with Milligan in the Falkirk Herald of 17 November 1909 reveals a great deal about Volti's origins, and confirms indisputably that Milligan and Volti were one and the same.

> "Despite the wealth of melody that Scotland can call her own, there have been times (says writer in the "Weekly Welcome") when it seemed as if our grand old airs were to be superseded by modern inventions, and allowed to be forgotten altogether. To-day there is little evidence of such a national calamity. We have again awakened the value of this heritage of song that our forefathers have bequeathed to us, and to no-one are we more indebted for reawakening the lore of Scottish music than Carl Volti.
>
> His life-work has really been to foster a love for Scottish music, and his success can be well gauged by the popularity of his "Highland Wreaths" —a series of Scottish selections that is known to every amateur orchestra in the country, and which is called upon to provide items for the programme at every church social and Saturday evening concert from John o' Groat's to Galloway.
>
> From his pen have come practically the only Scottish selections suitable for amateur bands, and it is often matter of comment amongst fiddlers that it should have been left to a foreigner to perform such a valuable service to Scottish music.
>
> Despite his cognomen, however, the gentleman in question is Glasgow boy born and bred, and has spent the last fifty years of

his life teaching music within a few minutes walk from the Jamaica Bridge.

My, real name is Milligan," remarked Carl Volti in the course of a crack I had with him the other day in connection with his work on behalf of Scottish music, but I was forced to change it to get the public interested my musical publications. It is rather amusing how I came call myself Volti. The first composition published, "The Undine Polka," bore my own name, "A. Milligan," but it was not a success. A music seller in the city suggested that the commonplace name of the composer was responsible for that, and advised me to publish under a nom-de-plume.

I thought the idea a good one, and started to manufacture a name on the spot. Noticing a copy Carl Czerny s 101 exercises for the piano standing on a desk, I asked him what he thought of Carl for a start. 'Capital!' he said. 'But what next?' 'I don't know; let's try the musical dictionary.' I picked up a copy that was lying on the counter, and went over the half of it without finding anything to please me. Impatiently turning to the last page the word 'Volti' caught my eye. 'What you think of Volti?' I cried. 'Just the very thing. Carl Volti will be a splendid name.'

It was decided to use it for my next composition, 'The, Citizen Galop,' and whether the name did it or not, this piece turned out a big success, and could be found in almost every house that had a piano."

Under the persona of Volti, Milligan seems to have been quite active on the musical performance circuit as a number of newspaper articles attest. This is a little unusual in the sense that many composers, rather like Tom Bulch, adopted one or more pseudonyms as a background persona; names that only existed on the published sheet music. Archibald Milligan took a different approach by bringing Carl Volti very much to the fore, adopting this alter-ego not just as a nom-de-plume, but also as a stage name. An example appears in the Greenock Telegraph and Clyde Shipping Gazette on 25 November 1879 writing of a concert in the Freeland School, Bridge-of-Weir:

"The instrumental pieces were performed by Carl Volti, of Glasgow, and a select party of his advanced violin pupils, consisting of several violinists and one violoncello."

Volti compositions were quite extensively published, particularly by the Glasgow based publisher James S Kerr. Though available individually they also often featured in compilation books, of which Kerr published at least nine; "Kerr's Collection of Merry Melodies for the Piano", "Kerr's First/Second/Third/Fourth Collections of Merry Melodies," "Kerr's Caledonian Collection," "Kerr's Collection of Reels and Strathspeys," "Kerr's Violin Instructor and Irish Folk-Song Album," "Kerr's Thistle Collection," "Kerr's Modern Dance Album." More than thirty five pieces attributed to Volti are included in only the first of those volumes. This understanding of Carl Volti being Milligan's creation is reconfirmed after his death by the probate records from 1919 which communicate the following:

> "MILLIGAN, Archibald, (Carl Volti), 20 Abbotsford Place, Glasgow. Died 5th January 1919 at Glasgow, testate. Confirmation granted at Glasgow, 12th March, to Sarah Juliet Sommerville or Milligan, 20 Abbotsford Place, aforesaid, his widow, Executrix nominated in will or deed, dated 24th March 1893 and recorded in Court Books of Commissariot of Lanark 6 March 1919. Value of estate £1479, 16s 9d."

What's notable there is that his musical pseudonym is officially documented on a public record. The Volti name was a huge part of part of Milligan's life and identity. So, how has it become the case that many people have misunderstood Bulch and Volti to be one and the same? One clue may lie in a document that I located on the National Library of Australia's 'Trove' site; an item entitled "Kerr's collection of latest dance music. Book VIII." As with most of Carl Volti's music this collection was published by Kerr of Glasgow; in this case during 1920, the year after Volti's death. A quick glance through the contents of the book, shows it to appear like a 'who's who' of names associated with the Thomas Edward Bulch story. T E Bulch himself, Henry Laski, and yet another name we know to have been a Thomas Bulch pseudonym; Godfrey Parker.

The following are the pieces of music included:

1. "My Polly": waltz on Rose Smith's popular song / composed by Henry Laski ; arranged by Alfred C. Wood

2. "Adelina": schottische / composed by Godfrey Parker ; arranged by Alfred C. Wood
3. "Ever True": waltz / composed by D. Miller Wilson ; arranged by Alfred C. Wood
4. "The Village Festival": march / Carl Volti
5. "The Cap and Bells": polka / Rose Smith ; arr. by A.C. Wood
6. "Clarice": mazurka / composed by Godfrey Parker ; arranged by Alfred C. Wood
7. "Myrine": valse / Henry Laski ; arr. by Alfred C. Wood
8. "Tit Bits": quadrille / C. d'Esteve ; arr. by Alfred C. Wood
9. "Les Militaires": valse / composed by Rose Smith ; arranged by Alfred C. Wood
10. "Barn Dance": / by Carl Volti
11. "The Blue Bell Polka": / arranged by Alfred C. Wood ; composed by F. Stanley
12. "Dreams of The Past": valse / arranged by Carl Volti ; composed by Charles Le Thiere
13. "The Melbourne": march / Carl Volti
14. "The Australian Lily": valse / arranged by Carl Volti ; composed by Leonard Gautier
15. "The Cyclist's Polka": / arranged by Alfred C. Wood ; composed by D.M. Wilson
16. "Nina": valse / Alberto Zelman
17. "Thelma": waltz / composed by Franz Garna ; arranged by Alfred C. Wood
18. "Flight from Pompeii": galop / E. de Beaupuis
19. "Orynthia": gavotte / Carl Volti
20. "Minuet (à l'antique)": / E. de Beaupuis
21. "Assembly": grand march / Carl Volti
22. "The Postman's Parade": quick march / T. E. Bulch
23. "Les Fleurs d'Australie": valse / arranged by Tom Howard ; composed by Henry Laski
24. "Irresistible": gavotte / E. de Beaupuis
25. "Verona": valse / Alexander Law
26. "Sweet Dreams": valse / composed by Rose Smith
27. "Happy Thoughts": schottische / T. E. Bulch
28. "Jolly Hop": polka / Jules Renardi.

Readers with some familiarity with Tom Bulch will also have spotted another name with whom his is often confused and entangled; that of Charles Le Thiere. However, as I explained earlier we know that Le Thiere, was Thomas Wilby Tomkins, the troubled ex-Grenadier Guards military bandsman born in Islington who ended his days in terrible poverty. Our understanding of the connection between T E Bulch and Carl

Volti and Le Thiere was not that Tom personally claimed these pseudonyms, but that he arranged a number of pieces by these composers for brass or military band. We know of course that Bulch was a talented and diligent editor and arranger and employed by music publishers in Australia in that capacity.

Tom's grandson, Eric, explained to us that his uncle, Thomas's son, was occasionally incredulous as to how Tom did not receive credit for many of his arrangements where his name did not appear on the printed music. It's probable that in arranging pieces for full band and applying the additional scope and polyphony he might have introduced touches that were personal to his own composition style, thus perhaps making some of the pieces feel more reminiscent of his own work while carrying the melodies provided by the original composer.

However the confusion arose, we do know that among the pieces of traditional Scottish music that Carl Volti rendered for piano and violin was a piece called the "Craigielea Polka." This was based upon the melody from Tannahill and Barr's "Thou Bonny Woods of Craigielea." Our hypothesis is that this was a piece that Tom Bulch would have had ample opportunity to be acquainted with as a pianist and violinist. Thus we progress our hypothesis by stating theoretically that it had a significant probability of having been the inspiration for a piano march called "The Craigielee March" which was published under the name Godfrey Parker in 1891. We know that Godfrey Parker was definitely a name used by Tom Bulch. Not wanting to miss an opportunity to maximise income from a good march, Tom also issued it as a brass band arrangement.

A question you might have now is why he changed the spelling from Craigielea to Craigielee? On that we can only guess. However, it is worth observing that on Lewisham Road in the Windsor district of Melbourne, which leads south from Prahran where Thomas Bulch had settled for a time, there was a house named Craigielee. This was home in the 1880s to a family called Howden. There was another, too, just a few streets away in Bendigo Street, Prahran. Perhaps one of these had caught Tom's eye one day and reminded him of the tune. I must stress this is pure speculation, but it's an interesting coincidence.

Looking at the Australian newspapers we can also see references to the original song by Tannahill and Barr which were contemporary to Tom and which use the same spelling. Perhaps there is a possible connection in that too. The first mention in any newspaper that I have found of the march "Craigielee" by Godfrey Parker is in the Ballarat Star of 17th September 1891, where it was performed by the Sebastopol Brass Band under their bandmaster Mr S N Prout. This is no surprise given that Bulch was a Ballarat resident at the time, and selling his music in that city. The programme also featured Tom's "Jolly Sailors" and "Opossum Hunt," plus the march "Whitworth" written as Robert Malthouse. Also on the programme was the overture "Fair Maid of Perth."

Returning to 1895, it was a year by which Bulch/Parker's "Craigielee" would have been owned by a good many brass bands across Australia, and possibly even considered a little out of date. It was also a year in which the tune would be up-cycled once more, as it had been by Tom in 1891; and it was thanks to his version that this occurred. The Warrnambool Brass Band still occasionally included Tom's "Craigielee" in their repertoire, and were sometimes engaged to provide entertainment at the horse racing meetings at the racecourse in Warrnambool. On one fateful occasion a lady called Christina MacPherson happened to be there to hear it. She writes down what happened next in a letter, penned many years later to a Dr Wood.

> "Dear Sir, In reading your impressions about music in Australia I was interested to note that you had mentioned the song "Waltzing Matilda" and through it might interest you to hear how 'Banjo' Paterson came to write it. He was on a visit to Winton, North Queensland, and I was staying with my brothers about 80 miles from Winton. We went into Winton for a week or two and one day I played (from ear) a tune which I had heard played by a band at the races in Warrnambool, a country town in the Western District of Victoria. Mr Paterson asked what it was. I could not tell him, and he then said he thought he could write some lines to it. He then and there wrote the first verse. We tried it and thought it went well, so he then wrote the other verses. I might add that in a short time everyone in the district was singing it.
>
> There are always numbers of men travelling about the country, some riding and some on foot and they are usually given rations at the various stations that they come to, but in Queensland the distances are so great that they help themselves without asking. On this occasion my brother and Mr Paterson were out riding and they came to a waterhole (or billabong) and found the skin of a newly killed sheep, all that was left by a swagman, and he

made note of this incident. After Mr Paterson returned to Sydney he wrote and asked me to send him the tune. I am no musician but did my best, and later on he told me he had sent it to a musical friend of his who thought it would make a good bush song. It was included in the Student's Song Book, and was frequently sung at the Community Singing. I hope I have not bored you about this. Yours sincerely. Miss C R MacPherson. PS I presume that you know that "Waltzing Matilda" means "carrying a swag" and "jumbuck" is the natives' name for a sheep."

Christina was the daughter of the owner of the Dagworth sheep station at Winton, which was where one Andrew Barton "Banjo" Paterson had stayed during a visit to that locality. The piece of music Christina MacPherson had heard the band play was Godfrey Parker's "Craigielee." Its melody is so unmistakably similar to Waltzing Matilda as to make it immediately recognisable. In this way, Thomas Edward Bulch had quite unknowingly, and quite indirectly, contributed something to the bush song that was to eventually become considered practically an unofficial Australian national anthem. The song has become ingrained in the folklore of Australia, even deemed significant enough to see the opening of a dedicated museum and culture centre in Winton, Queensland, to tell its story. The original centre was destroyed by a fire in 2015 but has since been rebuilt.

The Shildon people who know a little of Tom Bulch will say to you when asked, "Oh, he's the man who wrote Waltzing Matilda." Of course, Tom can no more claim that honour than could James Barr, Robert Tannahill, or Carl Volti. The song is clearly the work of 'Banjo' Paterson. Yet Tom was surely a catalyst; a link in the chain of events. Had he not arranged the march, Christina MacPherson might not have heard it at Warrnambool or subsequently played it to Banjo Paterson inspiring him to find the words to fit. Given that he had made note of the event of the sheepskin and billabong it's probable that a song would have emerged eventually. It's very likely, though, that it would have sounded quite different and so successful a reception as it received would not be guaranteed. Though not quite the creator of Waltzing Matilda, there is more that Tom should be remembered for, given his influence on shaping band music in Australia. Next he would extend his reach of influence to New Zealand.

New Zealand

The Christmas 1895 issue of The Bulletin features adverts for both "Intercolonial Band News" and "Bulch's Band Journal" declaring them as available from 128 Russell Street, Melbourne. A subscription to the Band News cost four shillings per year and the Journal one pound and six shillings for military band and one pound and one shilling for the brass band version. This was strictly payable in advance. The advertisement also mentions Bulch's music being in stock, with price lists available on application. All correspondence regarding these publications was requested to be sent to Mr C Foret at the given address. Sample parts of Bulch's latest music were explained to be published in every issue of the Intercolonial Band News.

Back in England, readers of the January 1896 edition of Wright and Round's Brass Band News received an update on Tom's progress via an article derived from the Intercolonial Brass Band News. In a broad update about the improving state of band contests in Australia it stated that, "Mr T E Bulch, the well known composer, is frequently judging." Would George perhaps have encountered this snippet if browsing that issue of the paper?

Meanwhile, Tom was preparing for another contest. The Wollongong band contest commenced on New Year's Day 1896 and ran till Thursday, 3 January. A detailed account describing proceedings was published in the Newcastle Morning Herald and Miner's Advocate:

> "WOLLONGONG BAND CONTEST. The greatest interest was taken by the residents of Wollongong and the district in the band contest which was commenced there on New Year's Day and finished on Thursday. The attendance numbered fully 3000, and although the following day was not a holiday, there were considerably over 1500 persons present. The judge (Mr T. E. Bulch) was located in a closed tent some distance away from the competitors, so that he could not possibly see any of the bands. His notes were made as each band played, and then placed in locked boxes which were not opened till the conclusion of the programme. The proceedings were inaugurated by a procession, which was formed in the following order :-Parramatta Model, Barkel's Model, 4th Regiment, Gympie, Canterbury Engineers, Newtown, Wollongong, Naval

Artillery, and Bathurst. The bands were despatched. at intervals, and after playing at the intersection of Crown and Corrimal streets were dismissed. The 4th Regiment played the "Cyclone," and Barkel's model "Chef d'Oeuvre" on the march. On arrival at the ground lots were drawn to decide which band was to play first, and fortune favoured the 4th Regiment. The selection was, "William Tell," which was played admirably. Then came the Gympie Band with "Il Lombardi"; Naval Artillery, "Verdi"; Bathurst District, "Les Hugenots"; Newtown, "Roberto il Diavolo"; Wollongong, "Honoria"; Parramatta, "Verdi," and Barkel's Model with "Ernani." The above pieces were the selections made by the bands themselves. The second day the test piece, "Anna Bolena," was played by all the bands, and the result of the contest was as follows: 4th Regiment, 165 points; Newton, 148 points; Bathurst, 125 points; Gympie, 124 points; Parramatta, 124 points; Barkel's Model, 123; Naval Artillery, 108; and Wollongong, 105. The 4th Regiment were thus easy winners. For the selection "William Tell" they scored 95 points, and 70 for the test selection. They therefore won the first prize of £60, and the conductor (Mr Barkel) a gold medal. The second prize of £380 goes to Newtown, and the third of £10 to the Bathurst Band. The Gympie and Parramatta bands each scored 124 points, and the fourth prize of £5 was divided. The 4th Regiment were also successful in carrying off the first prize of a brass drum and a year's subscription to the "Band Directory of Band News" for a waltz or set of quadrilles scoring 45 points, whilst Barkel's took second place with 38 points."

"The march contest -was won by Wollongong, 101 points, Bathurst 100 points, Naval Artillery 98 points, Newtown 98 points, 4th Regiment 97 points, Gympie 92 points, Barkel's Model 92 points, and Parramatta 91points."

"At the conclusion of the contest, a meeting of band representatives was held, when it was decided to hold an intercolonial band contest in Sydney. Mr J Palmer, of Sydney, was appointed secretary, and Mr T Mellor treasurer. The following district secretaries were appointed: Mr W Armstrong, Sydney; Mr Bonnet, Northern District; Mr P Kennedy, South Coast; Mr Williams, Western District; Messrs. Short and Piper, Queensland; Messrs Foret and Bulch, Victoria; South and West Australia, Tasmania, and New Zealand."

So it seemed that the conference of bandmasters at Wollongong brought Tom a step closer to his grand dream of an Intercolonial band contest, pitching the best bands of each of the Australasian colonies against one another for the ultimate honour. Such a contest would surely require a significant prize, and could be very lucrative for its organisers. Furthermore we see that Tom and his business partner, Foret, had taken the responsibility for arranging participation from the regions not represented otherwise by the committee. Did he not yet have enough to try to achieve? Perhaps his stake in the project and its success was too high for him not to push for its success. After the conclusion of the band and vocal contests in Wollongong, the Mayor of Wollongong heaped praise on Bulch and Foret for the way they had conducted the contest:

> "It was needless for him to speak in terms of praise of Mr Bulch, that gentleman's acknowledged musical ability, his spirit of fair play, his many manly attributes of character, made him a judge in whom bandsmen had implicit faith, and his decision on this occasion had given satisfaction."

The sixth day of January saw Bulch and Foret leave Wollongong by train, probably with some confidence that their plan was now in motion and had a team behind it. Then on 7 January, they boarded the Aramac, bound for Melbourne. There is an item of correspondence that was subsequently published in the Cumberland Free Press in which Tom communicates words of encouragement to George O'Shea, bandmaster of the Parramatta Model Band. It gives away something of his character:

> "Dear Sirs,— In reply to yours of the 8th inst, I am surprised to hear that anyone should think your band not eligible to compete against such bands as the 4th Regiment, Newtown, and Bathurst. Had your band played a better selection for the open test I have not the slightest doubt you would have been placed in a better position. Your band gave the best interpretation of 'Anna Bolena,' but was deficient in quality of tone to the 4th Regiment. I can only confirm my remarks at Wollongong, viz., that you will make a name for both yourself and the band in the near future. In conclusion, I would advise your band to stick to practice and show your friends at the next contest that you have a perfect right to be classed as one of the best bands in Australia. With kind regards."

Of course, after each contest Tom continued to issue each band with a written critique of how well he considered their performance to meet the required standard, many of these would be published in the press, but I include only one from that contest here as an example so that the reader can see the tone and content typically issued:

> "CONTEST SELECTION, "ANNA BOLENA" No. 6. — Larghetto: very fair opening but basses not in tune, in bars 27 to 30 sustained notes out of tune. Moderato: tempo too quick, but played fairly well. Poco Piu Mosso: very good, but rall. overdone. Larghetto: cornet very good, but one of the basses getting wrong notes in bars 26 and 27, soprano flat in bars 52 to 56. Moderato: crescendo not attended to, but band plays nice and smart. Larghetto: cornet gets nice tone but plays amateurish, crescendo very good, cornet poor in cadenza and missed top C. Alio: tempo too quick and band plays with poor tone and style, wrong notes observed in bars 51 and 52. Larghetto: euphonium plays with poor style and accompaniment, could be much better, cornet plays with poor style and tone, evidently nervous. Alio Vivace: very smart, but not without a few faults in intonation. Piu Mosso: a shade too quick for this band and tone very brassy. This band hasn't the quality of tone of some of the previous bands, not so good as Nos. 1, 3 and 4, but better performance than No. 2 (Barkell's Model) and 5 (Bathurst). Points 55."

Though I doubt any band or bandsman likes to receive criticism, these notes clearly offered each bandmaster hints as to what to look out for in order to develop their band.

Despite placing so much attention on adjudicating and progressing his concept of a grand Australian band contest, Tom still found time to compose. After all, he still had to make a regular income. Brass band compositions and arrangements continued to be released, and a new piano composition, the "Parthia Schottische," was published by Paling and Company that year. It was described by one reviewer as a brisk and danceable piece, whilst another breaks down the piece for the prospective buyer:

> "[it] consists of a short introduction, followed by the schottische, which introduces four distinct and tuneful melodies, all In schottische rhythm, so well marked as to make it a welcome addition to dance music. It is well and simply constructed throughout, and is also arranged for full military and brass bands. The title page is attractive and the printing excellent."

More news on Tom's progress also reached England when his status as an international celebrity of the brass band world was employed in an advertisement in the Brass Band News to help sell Silvani and Smith's brand of cornet.

> "TESTIMONIAL from T E Bulch, Solo Cornet and Bandmaster of Champion Band of Australia, Winners of the £100 Prize, Melbourne, Nov. 19th 1895:- The cornet of your make brought out by me to Australia I used for solo work for a long time. It was really a GRAND INSTRUMENT. In a weak moment I was induced to part with it for £11 11s 0d. A fortnight back I offered a big price for it, but OWNER WOULD NOT SELL. I have found no make to suit me like the SILVANI & SMITH. Note! The instrument is now 10 years old, this is the finest tribute to the value and wear of the Silvani and Smith make."

This advert ran in the newspaper for a few months. It is likely that Tom received a fee for his endorsement. There was more good news. Impressed by his conduct and judging the previous year, the United Australasian Axemen's Association reached out to him again requesting him to fulfil the same position at the same band contest which was going to be held in conjunction with the Axemen's Carnival on 7 November.

In April, Tom was also declared by the Brass Bands Association of New Zealand to be one of the shortlisted judges for a band contest to be held in that country. There had been suggestions he should be engaged in previous years, though on those occasions others had been preferred ahead of him. If successful on this occasion, he would be required to travel to New Zealand for the first time in his life. This would necessitate his spending more time away from his business in Melbourne than he had done thus far. The short list also included a New Zealander, Mr G A Martin, and a fellow Victorian, Mr A Grieve, both of whom had been the judges at this contest in previous years. Tom awaited news from the selecting panel. In the meantime the June 1896 monthly issue of The Bulletin included another review of The Parthia:

> "From W H Paling I have received the "Parthia Schottische" by Thos E Bulch. The "Parthia" is a lively, grig-like musical trifle, none the worse for being evidently inspired by 'Her Golden Hair Was Hanging Down Her Back'."

By the beginning of August, the announcement was finally made that Tom had been chosen for the New Zealand band contest which had been scheduled to be held in Dunedin towards the end of October. Tom was praised and heralded for his work as a composer, proprietor of a band journal, and for his association with some 'good bands in England'. An additional announcement explained that he would provide the quickstep test piece for the contest. He set to work to create a new march, 'The Moa,' in honour of the enormous flightless bird of that name that was once native to New Zealand but by then sadly extinct.

Though a new opportunity was now open to Tom, not everything seems to have been going so well at the Melbourne Post Office, where an inquiry had been triggered based upon the accusations of one Mr Hamilton, a Member of the Legislative Assembly, concerning costs within the service's electrical engineering department. The inquiry took several months due to a number of adjournments and was eventually concluded in the summer, and its conclusion seems to have created a residual atmosphere of bitterness and resentment. The Post Office management came up with a proposal to improve spirits as the Herald of Melbourne reports on 6 August:

> "There is at last to be harmony in the Post Office. From out of long months of mutual recrimination, hate, jealousy, and intolerance comes a desire for a better state of things, and the agency whereby this is to be effected is, strangely enough, a brass band. The initial step has just been taken by electing Lord Brassey, Mr J G Duffy, and Mr Jas. Smibert patrons, Mr SprInghill president, and some twenty-one gentlemen more or less distinguished in the service vice-presidents. These are only a few of the officers, the others are legion. Neither the Premier; nor. Mr B T Vale has been asked to take an instrument, but we notice with satisfaction that a Mr Best has been fitted with the exalted position of Band Sergeant. The instrument fund is to be raised by means of entertainments and subscriptions, so that the instruments will be the property of the band, and not of the members individually. Mr T Bulch is to be bandmaster, but it has yet to be decided who is to call the tune. Let us hope, however, that the Post Office Band will have its music sweeten the atmosphere of the department and soothe the savage breasts of some of those gentlemen whose mutual distrust has been so much in evidence lately."

The change in policy concerning this new band, from individual ownership of instruments to their being the property of the band itself, would be a measure that Tom would have recognised, and may even have suggested, as important to ensuring the continuity of the band. Rather than having to find a new member who owned the right instrument every time someone left, the band simply retrieved the instrument and allocated it to a new bandsman. In this way the band and bandmaster was also able to choose, and thus control, the type and quality of instrument used, which would also be advantageous to the overall sound. Once again, though, by agreeing to take charge of the General Post Office Brass Band it appears that Tom was taking on even more responsibility, and one has to wonder how he felt he might be able to do full justice to all the roles he now needed to fulfil.

Having made plans to have his business affairs covered at home, Tom, on 10 October boarded the ship Talune at Melbourne, which was heading to Dunedin, New Zealand. This was a longer voyage by sea than the ones he had made to reach Tasmania. Furthermore the story passed down through the family is that after Tom's original journey to Australia, he not once thereafter enjoyed the process of travelling by sea. Mercifully for him, Dunedin is one of the cities at the western extremity of New Zealand, though on the edge of the country furthest away from Australia. The Talune arrived at Port Chalmers, situated in Otago Harbour some miles east of Dunedin on the morning of 17 October. This contest committee had taken advantage of a midweek half holiday to stage the quickstep contest on the afternoon of Wednesday, 21 October at the Caledonian Ground there. As had become customary, to build anticipation and interest the contest was preceded by a public parade to the hosting showground. The competing bands assembled as a massed band at the city's Octagon at one o'clock in the afternoon to play Bulch's contest composition from the previous year "Dunedin Navals." The quickstep contest would be followed, in the evening, by a solo contest held at the Garrison Hall. Fourteen advance entries had been received from bands wanting to take part in the band contest. On the first day, however, the Oamaru Navals Band and the band from Christchurch did not arrive. We are told that all the bands were represented in the grand parade, though not all at full strength and, though hundreds marched along with the parade, the expected volume of sound created by the massed band did not quite live up to expectation.

Following arrival at the contest ground, a draw took place to determine the order in which bands would perform, and Tom, not of course permitted to know which band was playing when, was sent to be concealed in a tent. As had become the custom in Australia and New Zealand the bands would be judged not only on performance standard but also the quality of their marching and drill. Each band knew in advance that they had to march once around the circle before the assembled crowd then one hundred yards up to the centre of the ground. This last manoeuvre was to be conducted in exactly 120 paces. As if the bands did not have enough to concentrate upon that day, the occasion was somewhat spoiled by rain. A correspondent in the Evening Star described Tom's quickstep "The Moa," thus:

> "We have said that the quickstep used, and composed by Mr Bulch, was suitable from a bandsman's point of view and lively to listen to. It is written in E flat 6/8 time. There is a good bold opening in unison; after that a silent bar, then the opening passage repeated in a different key; answering passages from cornets, trombones and euphoniums are succeeded by a rather trying passage for cornets; then comes the bass solo with accompaniments in triplets for the remainder of the band and short chromatic phrases; this is followed by a pretty trio with crescendo on the sixth bar from the end dying away to piano immediately. The trio will probably be accounted the best part of the march, which as a whole suited the purpose very well, though some of the players might have preferred a heavier test than it provides."

It was the Dunedin Naval Band that carried off the quickstep first prize that day, followed by the Invercargill Garrison and Kaikorai bands respectively. In the evening the solo contests were held for trombones and E flat bombardon. The trombone solo contest finished with a tie on points, so was resolved through a 'play-off' between the three best players on the following morning. This took place ahead of the further solo contests for B flat bombardon, tenor horn, E flat soprano cornet and baritone horn. A correspondent in the Oamaru Mail hinted that Thomas's judgement was not entirely, in their opinion at least, unquestionable:

> "So far Mr Bulch (the judge) has reversed every decision given by Mr Grieve at Timaru last year. A most remarkable instance was that Davie, of Kaikorai, the champion horn player for years, was left out of the prize winners this morning. Some uneasiness is felt of this as to what may happen in the grand contest, but the most competent judges approve of Mr Bulch's decisions so far, and profess great confidence in them."

Also on the second day the first of the test selections, "I Puritani," which had been arranged by J A Kappey based upon airs from Bellini's opera, was performed by each competing band. At the end of this session no outcome or advantage was declared, as the honours were to be bestowed based upon the playing of both of the two test pieces. The second would be played the following evening after the solo contests for B flat cornet and soprano horn. In the meantime any possible outcomes were left to be discussed and speculated upon by spectators, possibly in the hope of building anticipation.

From six-thirty in the evening on the final day of the contest each band, in turn, played their renditions of the second test piece, "Tannhauser;" a process which lasted until eleven-thirty. At the half-way point, there was a brief intermission which was reported by the Otago Daily Times.

> "The 10 minutes intermission, which was granted after half the bands had played, was welcomed by those who were not so nervous about losing their seats as to not embrace the opportunity of getting "a mouthful of fresh air," as the supervisor put it, and the judge was apparently relieved at the chance to escape for a brief interval from his cage. Mr Bulch had not returned to his post when the first band to play after the interval filed onto the stage and took up their positions at the music stands, but the supervisor directed them to retire again, and when they had left the stage he conducted the judge back to his place. To the great amusement of the "house" who were not slow to take notice of the fact, some liquid refreshment was handed to the judge, so that he for one was not content with fresh air only."

Given Tom's Temperance movement sympathies it's quite likely that the liquid refreshment was non-alcoholic. The winners, falling only eight points short of a maximum score of two hundred, were the Oamaru Garrison Band, a full twenty-two points clear of the runners up, Wellington Garrison. Afterward, Tom addressed the gathered crowd to express that he had given a decision to the best of his abilities. This was received with applause.

On the Saturday following the contest Tom dined with the Oamaru Garrison band, giving an address which was reported in the Evening Star:

> "Mr Bulch, who hails from Yorkshire, the great centre of amateur band in England, stated that he had not heard such playing as the Oamaru Garrison Band's since he left home."

One has to question whether this embellishing claim to be from Yorkshire is Tom's construction, that of the reporter or of others present. New Shildon, where Thomas was born and spent his early life, is not a Yorkshire town. We know from reports that as a young man he made occasional forays into the northernmost reaches of Yorkshire, and that he saw a good number of top bands from Yorkshire when they came north to compete for prizes. It would also be fair to say that he had Yorkshire family lineage though this does not quite constitute hailing from that part of the world.

Later, we start to get a sense of some disquiet about arrangements for the contest. A small article in the Lake Wakatip Mail of 30 October tells us of a claim that Tom had been fined five pounds by the organising committee for not submitting a full musical score of one of the test pieces to the committee to be used in future. The Otago Daily Times of the same date elaborates, stating that it was an open secret that during the proceedings the relationship between Tom and the organisers had become strained. It appears the organisers had stipulated that the score for the test piece should be scripted and handed over, on the night of the finale, as Mr Grieve had done the previous year. When the time came however Thomas intimated that he had not written it, deeming it unnecessary. He was then invited to a meeting of the committee on the Wednesday which he had not attended claiming afterwards that the invitation had not arrived in time. The committee again requested submission of the score and resolved to fine Thomas five pounds from his overall fee of fifty pounds. There also seemed to be plenty of press commentators that were happy to take to the pages of the various newspapers across New Zealand to offer their own critique of the bands, and the marks awarded by the judge. It seems now that everyone desired a say on the outcome of the contest, and nobody was to be above critical scrutiny.

Another inclusion amongst the press coverage following the 1896 New Zealand contest was an endorsement that appeared in a few papers wherein Tom professed his approval of Besson Instruments. Doubtless in making his debut in New Zealand he had espied an opportunity to lever some advantage or payment based upon his reputation. Though presented as a letter, this is clearly an advertisement and reads:

> "In reply to yours of the 24th inst. asking my opinion regarding Besson Instruments, I beg to state that in my experience (which extends over 22 years) I approve of BESSON INSTRUMENTS as being UNDOUBTEDLY THE BEST. I might state that I have won a great many prizes both at home and in the colonies, and have used nothing but Besson Instruments and must compliment you for being the sole agent on the South Island for so celebrated a firm of brass instrument makers. Yours truly, T E Bulch."

We have already seen that Tom had previously endorsed other manufacturers. Clearly, in endeavouring to make his living from his music and reputation he must have felt all means to be fair game.

There is, a further incidental point regarding this contest. It is one of those lovely moments of coincidence that we see occasionally throughout the detail of this tale end-to-end, which is that two days after Thomas Bulch left, the Dunedin Engineers Band held a concert at St Clair. That concert included both of the test pieces from the Dunedin contest as well as Tom's new quickstep "The Moa"; but what makes this moment so interesting to us is that their opening piece at that concert was the march "Binchester" by George Allan, written in the late 1880s and named after the Roman fort and settlement, not far from Shildon, that archeologists had begun to excavate in earnest that same decade.

With his engagement in New Zealand concluded, Tom was not yet able to head back to Melbourne, for his next contest engagement was nearing, and this required him to return to Tasmania. He was travelling with two conductor's batons which were to be presented to the bandmasters of the first and second placed bands at the Axemen's band contest which on this occasion was to be held in Latrobe. The Daily Telegraph of Launceston printed a written description of the opening day:

> "LATROBE BAND CONTEST — The band contest, in connection with the U.A.A.A, Limited, was opened last night, the Latrobe, Ulverstone, and Devonport Bands competing. Mr Bulch, of Victoria, acted as judge. Prior to entering the convincing ground the three bands paraded the streets to the strains of the "Wairoa" march, played by two of the number, the local bandsmen bringing up the rear in silence owing to the absence of its bass players, who put in an appearance hall half an hour later. On arrival in the show grounds the bands drew for places, resulting in Devonport taking the stand first, Ulverstone second, and Latrobe third, the judge being incarcerated in a tent close by. The waltzes played respectively by the bands in the order named were "My Polly," "Myrine," and "Love's Messenger." The result of the contest will not, of course, be known till after the march test on Monday, but the public have already given their decision as to first place, the second and third being looked upon as problematical. The Latrobe and Ulverstone bands, which were each excellent combinations two or three years since, have gone back very much, whilst Devonport exhibits a steady advancement. The first two waltzes played last night, printed under the nom de plume of "Laski," were, strange to say, both compositions of Mr Bulch, the judge. The night was very cold, and the attendance consequently small, there being less than £5 taken at the gates."

That the reporter observes that "Myrine" and "My Polly" were both Tom's own compositions is interesting. One wonders whether bands chose to play Tom's own pieces in order to curry favour from the judge, or perhaps whether they did not know these to be Tom's pieces. It is striking how often Tom was required to judge bands playing his own music, though of course when it came to judging how well it was played nobody should quite know how a piece ought to sound better than its creator. The fact is also possibly a symptom of how deeply into the DNA of the Australian banding scene Tom's influence had penetrated. This ambitious lad from a humble family of agricultural labourers and railwaymen in the North-East of England now held many bandsmen across a whole continent in his thrall.

Once the Tasmanian bands had played their test pieces, on the night of Monday, 8 November, Tom handed his decision and summary of points totals to the contest officials in a sealed envelope. These were then declared with due ceremony to all in attendance. The winners by a clear seven points were the band from Ulverstone. The band from Devonport were placed second followed by Latrobe in third. A few days later, the Tasmanian brass band commentator "Moderato" pronounced his approval in the Launceston Daily Telegraph:

> "I was very glad to see the committee had the good judgment to select such an eminent authority on band competitions as Mr T E Bulch as judge, his reputation both as conductor and composer being known so well throughout Australia."

Tom was then able to return home to tend to family and business affairs for a while, as well as to reconnect with the bands under his control. This had been his longest period of absence from home since his arrival in Australia, and surely this would have brought difficulty for his wife, who had been left to tend to his business affairs at home whilst caring for their children. On 30 December 1896, the day of Tom's birthday, another band contest in New Zealand used a Thomas Bulch composed grand quickstep as a test piece, that being named "The Attack" which though we don't know for certain was possibly composed by him specifically for that contest.

New Shildon

Across the globe, 1896 was to prove a pivotal year for George Allan. The music papers of the day would regularly feature a profile article describing a musician deemed worthy of highlighting, and, perhaps through his growing acquaintance with the Lincolnshire music publisher Fred Richardson of Boston, George was featured in a Portrait Gallery article within the pages of The Cornet of 14 November 1896.

This article, penned by a commentator using the pseudonym 'Thornleyite', is headed by a portrait photograph of the then thirty-two year-old George. It is one of only two images we have seen of him during all of our research. He bears a sober and serious expression on a face framed by dark hair that is even then beginning to thin from the front revealing a high forehead. His dark thick eyebrows are matched by an equally dark horseshoe moustache and what seems a small beard of a type that would nowadays be referred to as a 'soul patch.' He wears a dark jacket in a popular style of the day with a tie around the neck of a white wingtip, or Gladstone, type shirt collar.

Above : Photograph of George Allan as he was presented in the Nov 1896 issue of The Cornet, the earliest image we have seen of him

The article reads as follows:

> "Mr Geo. Allan, BANDMASTER, NEW SHILDON. Mr Geo. Allan was born at New Shildon, on March 21st 1864 and is now 32 years of age. At the age of 9 years he was thoroughly taught

the Sol-Fa System under a good master, and very shortly after took 1st baritone in a local brass band. He afterwards joined as solo tenor in the New Shildon Juvenile Band. At this time he was also a member of the church choir and I believe it was the question "What can you learn in a brass band as to theory etc.?" which this choirmaster asked him, that led Mr Allan to try what he could do in that line, and with the aid of the works of Marx, Stainer, Clementis and others, combined with hard study, he brought himself before the brass world as a composer of some for the very best music for brass bands."

"Mr Allan is also solo cornet and conductor of the New Shildon Saxhorn Band, and during the last two years has had the band at seven contests with the following result: 1 first, 2 seconds, 2 fourths and 3rd for quickstep, and this in spite of losing men through slackness of work and otherwise."

"As a teacher he is hard working, steady, and courteous. he is just the right man in the right place, and I would like to see him come out as a judge for brass band and quartette contests, for he is a thoroughly capable man for the work, and a man that can and would give fair and accurate decisions."

The writer's wishes would prove prophetic, or at least to be the kind of endorsement that a bandmaster might require in order to undergo that transformation to be invited into the fold of contest adjudicators in the North East of England. There were, after all, many existing adjudicators across the region with a known track record. It would take a leap of faith for contest organisers to place their trust in this relatively young unproven fellow. The process of band contesting in England was somewhat more mature than its Australian counterpart, though figures such as Thomas Bulch had been working hard to remedy that. Contests in mid-nineteenth century England had been quite different occasions to those a bandsman might encounter today. They had a reputation, even among bandsmen, for being badly organised undisciplined affairs and an excuse for over-indulging in alcoholic drinks and bawdy behaviour. You'll remember in earlier chapters how Francis Dinsdale had been reported as losing control of his New Shildon bandsmen on occasion through the effect of drink, and how the Temperance movement sought to bring professionalism to banding by shunning alcohol. There were also allegations, and doubtless definite cases, of corruption. Even the grander concerts involving the so-called 'crack' bands of the day were not above criticism. With little formal hierarchy of governance and a lack of clearly defined and accepted rules on proceedings, there was still much to be desired. Rivalries developed between bands that often fermented into dislike and forms of civil action between organisations. Contest judges could expect, on occasion, rough treatment and abuse from those that might dispute the validity of their decision. They might also be physically jostled or assaulted for their efforts should they produce a decision that offended one party or another. The contests could be passionate affairs with neighbouring towns playing out age old rivalries through their brass bands.

By the time George looked likely to enter the fray, things were to an extent improving. The formation of brass band associations led to the establishment of agreed principles and sets of rules. Though these did not always clear up the disputes, they at least offered a framework for those trying to enforce them. Early mentions of brass band associations occur in Scotland with the Glasgow and District Brass Band Association and the Bon-Accord Brass Band Association in the 1860s and 1870s, though in the year George had been suggested in this article to be a worthy candidate for adjudicator, an association had not yet been formed to cover the North-East of England.

There are no reports of George occupying the judge's tent during 1896 though, it would simply be a matter of time. He still had some way to go to catch up with his old bandmate Tom Bulch. The Cornet article reveals a further similarity between the two, though in pointing out that George was both solo-cornet player and conductor. We know that Tom would also take on both roles with his bands. One wonders whether this was based upon the example set by their mentors; Francis or Edward Dinsdale? We can only presume that they observed the habit somewhere in their development. It was not uncommon practice, yet would seem quite out of place today.

It was not a prolific year for George in terms of published compositions, though it was the year in which the contest march "Lefebvre" was introduced. Unlike George himself, his music continued to travel, and just as George might occasionally see updates in the papers on Tom's achievements, Tom would occasionally happen upon instances of George's music being played. The march "Lefebvre" would be one such piece, when

Tom would hear it being played, and judge the performance, at a band contest in 1898. Another march played this year was entitled "Aronia," seemingly named after a berry producing shrub introduced to Europe from America.

The following year, 1897, also seemed a quiet one for George. We have not identified any compositions that were explicitly published in this year, though there are several that appear for the first time in newspaper reports of band programmes. These include the march "Boscombe" which would be played many times by the Newcastle City Band in New South Wales as well as by bands around the United Kingdom.

The hoped for invitations to act as a band contest adjudicator do not appear to have materialised in great quantity. According to the academic and brass historian Roy Newsome there had been a feeling around this time that the brass band movement had peaked, and perhaps that there were too many contests, with just about any fair or festival predictably featuring one. Was the novelty wearing a little thin, or had the unruliness become tiresome?

A general social change was brewing in England, particularly through the growing influence of the Trade Union movements as well as the beginning of what was to become a steady decline in participation in organised religion. There were new interests and sporting activities emerging, to which people were drawn. Many musical societies had ties to the more social aspect of the various churches. Additionally, beginnings of music recording technology were starting to encroach into the home and social environment. In some ways we are led to believe that the brass band movement had begun its gradual drift away from the mass popularity of its peak years and closer towards the position of being a specialist interest and the preserve of a dedicated minority. 1897 brought something of a slight resurgence though, perhaps as it was the year of Queen Victoria's Diamond Jubilee and her people loved a royal celebration.

The New Shildon Temperance Band, were still the darlings of the town, and had a flurry of contest successes the previous year picking up the first place at the Witton Park contest and a pair of second prizes at Middlesborough and Houghton le Spring respectively. However, for the Diamond Jubilee celebrations it was to George and New Shildon Saxhorn Band that the organising committee turned. The Daily Gazette for

Middlesbrough on Saturday, 12 June announced details of the coming celebration in Shildon:

> "Notwithstanding the fact that the Shildon District Urban Council were somewhat late in starting to arrange for the celebration of the Queen's Diamond Jubilee, the Committee recently appointed have now got the arrangements well in hand. It is practically settled that the programme on the 22nd inst. will include a great procession headed by the New Shildon Saxhorn Band, from the market place, through the principal streets of both the Shildons, to a field opposite the railway station where tea will be served to all the children of the town under 15 years of age. The aged people will also be supplied with a substantial tea."

In addition to the civic celebration and as part of a series of 'National Thanksgiving" services for the reign of Queen Victoria, another grand procession took place on 20 June through Shildon from the Market Place along Church Street to St John's Church in Old Shildon. This procession too was headed by George and the New Shildon Saxhorn Band at the head of urban councillors and members of the town's friendly societies. Later, in the evening, a further service was held at All Saints Church which had become the regular place of worship for the Allan and Bulch families.

August once again brought the famous annual Shildon Show which, of course, included a band contest as part of its programme. The Saxhorn Band had been absent from this contest for a few years now, yet in 1897, perhaps due the Temperance Band being absent that year, they entered the contest ensuring that the hosting town was represented. The show took place on the 21st and the adjudicator engaged was Mr J Walker. The organising committee, inspired by the patriotic mood surrounding the Queen's Diamond Jubilee the previous month, selected James Ord-Hume's "Victoria Regina" to be the test piece. A strong field of ten relatively local bands took part hoping to win their share of an overall prize fund totalling twenty-five pounds. The band that came first in the field would win ten pounds, a trifling amount at today's value but one which carried significant spending power in 1897. The judge's decision was that the Eston Miner's Old Band's performance was the finest that day, followed by Thornaby Ironworks, Middlesborough Erimus, Cockerton and Spennymoor Temperance. The New

Shildon Saxhorn Band, along with the Darlington Temperance and Brandon Colliery were unplaced. This would have disappointed George whose band had been doing much better earlier in the decade. A reporter in the Northern Echo lamented later that week that:

> "Some regret was felt that the Saxhorn Band did not find a place in the prize list last Saturday. The members have been increasing in their efforts of late in practice, but unfortunately they were not considered up to their competitors."

The Saxhorn Band had been going for forty years by this point, and that they were not doing better would surely have been a frustration for George, who possibly also felt that part of his own reputation locally was inextricably tied to how the band performed. The article in The Cornet in 1896 had explained the difficulty he had experienced in keeping a full complement of musicians in the band. We've also seen how the band had fallen into the shadow of the Temperance Band to whom we have theorised that many good players may have defected in light of their comparative success. It would not be unreasonable for George to wonder and doubt on the future of the band.

Melbourne

Life for most of us can be a 'roller-coaster ride' of numerous high points and low points. We have heard how, in terms of musical success at least, George Allan's life back in New Shildon was experiencing a dip. The fortunes of Tom Bulch, half a world away in Melbourne that year, were proving not a great deal better. His next adjudicating engagement which we see evidence of was at the Australian Natives Gala at Rutherglen held on the 26th of January. This was the second such annual event to be held by the Rutherglen branch of the A.N.A. and promised to raise funds for district charities through a spectacle of athletics events and both foot and cycle races. The newspapers communicated that the organising committee felt that they had been fortunate to secure the services of so 'honourable and fair' a judge for the event, which itself was described as greatly and beneficially "cementing the bonds of brotherhood amongst the younger generation who have no recollections of the motherland, and must, therefore, look to this vast Southern Continent as their native soil and home." This was very much in line with the principles of the Australian Natives Association, an organisation founded along the lines of a friendly society in 1871, which only men born in Australia were permitted to join and one which sought a new patriotism specific to Australia as well as lobbying power with a view to ensuring the dominance of white colonists families and rejection of non-white immigration. It's an organisation to which Tom, born back in the British 'motherland,' would not have been admitted.

The Southland Times of 27 February 1897 includes an excerpt from a letter penned by Tom Bulch:

> "Mr Bulch, writing on the subject of the New Zealand bands, says: — "In my opinion, we could not get 12 bands in the whole of the colonies to compare with those that played at Dunedin. There are certainly faults to be found in them, as indeed with any band in the world almost, and one of the worst of these is in intonation, particularly in slow movements. A movement of semibreves and minims takes playing — although very few bandsmen think so. There is also room for improvement in collective performances. The individual playing was very good. On the whole, I find bandmasters too apt to exaggerate all expression marks; in piano passages, time and tone must be studied, and several of the bands suffered in intonation through trying to play these passages too pianissimo. Another fault was in the fortes, which in most cases were overdone, the result being that the band got a very coarse tone. These are faults that lie mainly with the bandmaster, who should remedy them. Undoubtedly, the Oamaru Garrison, Wellington Garrison, Kaikorai, and Invercargill Garrison Bands are a credit to New Zealand — the last-named band being the finest I have had the pleasure of listening to on the march. Had the contest been held in the open air there can be no doubt that they must have scored much better; and I might say that I think the Association, if they can see their way clear, should hold their future contests in the open air. It is a better test for the bands, and more satisfactory to the judge, as he can then detect every weakness in the playing. Mr Bulch refers to 'the splendid discipline prevailing amongst the men,' and expresses the opinion that 'New Zealand may well be proud of her brass bands.'"

In April we see reference to a performance by the Advance Band of Maryborough of Tom's selection "Lurline" which is credited to 'Herr Bulch', a reminder to us that his nationality continued to be misinterpreted as German. Misunderstanding of this type possibly amused Tom and would only later come to have dark consequences. That particular selection also had significance as it was chosen to be the test piece for the West Coast Band Contest in New Zealand. This choice had been made based upon Tom's recommendation to the organising committee by letter. The committee declared that any bands registering to compete would need to hand in any copies of "Lurline" that they had, to prevent them from practising it before the other bands had a copy of the music. When the official copies they had ordered arrived the bands would each receive theirs. The committee also replied to Tom's letter ordering ten full band sets of the selection plus an additional full score copy.

Tom's old Model Band in Ballarat, still bearing his name, continued to be popular in that locality and to fulfil many public engagements. His music, including those very first pieces he had composed in England, continued to be popular with bands across the continent, and his production of new pieces was as prolific as ever. Publishers continued to advertise his work widely; yet behind the scenes Tom was by this point struggling to keep his own music business in Melbourne viable. In May of 1897, Tom, then based at Elgin Street in the Carlton district of Melbourne, experienced the humiliation of being publicly declared insolvent. Both the Age and the Argus of Melbourne published the same brief story on Saturday, 29 May 1897:

"NEW INSOLVENTS – Thomas Edward Bulch, Elgin Street, Carlton, musician. Causes of insolvency: Pressure of creditors and falling off in business. Liabilities, £349 4s. 9d; assets £69 19s 2d.; deficiency £279 5s. 7d. Mr Cohen, assignee."

The Age of Melbourne then followed this up on 8 June:

"GENERAL MEETINGS IN INSOLVENCY – General meetings of creditors were held and closed before the Chief Clerk in Insolvency yesterday in the estates of Thomas Edward Bulch of Carlton, musician; Richard Herbert Webb of Prahran, no occupation; Donald McIvor of Footscray, sawyer; John Edward Thomas of Melbourne, clerk."

This was a major setback to the public reputation of the ambitious and hard-working Tom, with a wife and growing young family to feed, clothe and take care of. One can imagine the tensions the situation would have created at home between

Tom and Eliza. It's not clear how the situation arose, but you can see from what we have learned about the amount of work that Tom took on that doing everything well could easily have become unsustainable though it could equally have been the consequence of a few bad financial choices. To raise funds for Tom's creditors, an instruction was raised to J Lyons and Co to sell off as much as possible of Tom's stock of music. Adding to the public humiliation, the following announcement was posted in The Age:

> "Tuesday 29th June at 11 o'clock. At the Hall of Commerce A, B and C Queen Street. To Musicians, bandmasters, music dealers and others. In the insolvent estate of T E Bulch, Musician of Carlton, J Lyons and Co have received instructions from S H Cohen Esq., assignee in the above estate, to sell a large quantity of complete sets of band, piano, dance, sacred and secular music, by leading composers, without reserve."

Tom's stock would be auctioned for whatever could be raised. Bearing in mind that this would include much of his own work the sale would make it difficult for him to earn a living, or raise money to start again. Palings of Sydney advertised to bandsmen that they could provide everything needed for the competition including a large quantity of band music by Bulch and Smith; so it was possible that Tom could still be receiving income through sales of his compositions elsewhere.

There was hope for the family in that he was still able to make some money as a bandmaster and through occasional engagements as a contest judge. In November of 1897, he was announced as having been chosen to be judge for a Band Contest, billed as Intercolonial, that was scheduled to take place in Bendigo on New Year's Day 1898. On the day of the contest the weather was reportedly fine with a refreshing breeze as a large crowd gathered on the Show Ground in the northern district of Bendigo for its annual Athletic Club Sports meeting, which also included the Intercolonial Band Contest. The grandstand, according to the reporter, presented a very gay appearance, being packed with ladies in holiday attire to watch the cycling and foot racing. Around the ground publicans had erected booths serving refreshment to satisfy the thirstiest of the gathered throng. The intercolonial nature of the contest was merely represented by the fact that the Hobart Garrison band from Tasmania was present. The remaining bands were all from the colony of Victoria. These were the bands from Hopetoun, Northcott's Bendigo City Band, Eaglehawk, St Arnaud and Code's Melbourne Band. Following the established tradition the bands marched in procession to the Show Grounds, having started out at Charing Cross. They were judged on their appearance and marching, with the Hobart Garrison Band putting their military discipline to best effect and picking up far more points for marching. Bands had points deducted for their bandsmen being untidy, wearing dirty boots, neglecting to shave, having a greasy uniform or a dirty instrument. The contest was structured so that each band had to give their best rendition of a selection, a set of waltzes or quadrilles and a march. Enclosed in the adjudicator's tent Tom was doubtless unsurprised to hear, once again, many of his own works; "Les Fleurs D'Australie," "The Moa," "Roberto II Diavolo" and "Myrine." He later commented that he could not help but smile when the respective secretaries had submitted the pieces for him to familiarise himself, as he recognised many as his own. He may have been more surprised to discover that one band had chosen to play a piece by the other composer born in his hometown. The Hopetoun Band had chosen to play George Allan's march "Lefebvre." Tom awarded highest points in the march contest to Northcott's and Code's bands jointly. It was the Code's Melbourne band, however, that excelled in the waltz and selection to finish as the outright victors to claim the top prize of £100. Northcott's and Eaglehawk came second and third respectively. Though we don't know what Thomas Bulch thought of Allan's "Lefebvre" as a piece of music, we do have his published judges notes that help us understand how he felt about how it was rendered that day:

> "No. 6 Band (Hopetoun).— March, "Lefebvre" (Geo. Allan). Good opening, but coarse tone at times, cornet made slight slips and very indistinct on semiquavers, soprano very good, band not too well in tune. This is the making of a very fine band, but require better instruments to produce that fine massive tone so essential. Points, 16."

The remainder of 1898, though, appears to have been quiet for Tom. Band programmes across the land were regularly containing his compositions, such as the waltz "Nada" and selection "Sydney by Night" which had recently been published, but there is little news to be found of his personal engagements.

The insolvency probably shook up his life to the extent that it was necessary to restructure his activities though he was, as we shall see, far from finished.

Otherwise, in Melbourne in 1898, as in Britain, there was a change afoot and one which would lead to reshaping the way Australia would view its place in the world. For some years the idea had been circulating that Australia should become a sovereign nation rather than a colony of the United Kingdom. On March 16 1898 political representatives of the five Australian colonies met in Melbourne to adopt a constitution that they hoped would lead to that formal and official change in their status. Australia was, almost inevitably, coming of age and seeking the right to self determination, and we'll return to this later.

New Shildon

While 1898 may have been a quiet year for Tom Bulch, it was quite the opposite for George Allan. Though 'Thornleyite' proposed in The Cornet in 1896 that George might make a fine contest judge, we see little evidence of demand materialising for him during 1897. In 1898 he took a leap of faith and invested a little money to advertise his services in The Cornet.

> "George Allan, the well-known composer, is open for engagements as a CONTEST ADJUDICATOR – For terms apply:- Pears Terrace, New Shildon."

The wording would be George's own, but that he chose to state that he was well-known gives us a tiny insight into the degree of confidence he may have had into the truth of that statement. The evidence backs up his claim. He had at least twelve years as a published composer and adoption of his music had begun to reach what seems to be a peak. We do need to bear in mind that unlike Tom who was his own master and able to afford himself some flexibility by, for example, having his wife take care of the music store while he travelled, George was in the employ of the North Eastern Railway Company and had to be available at the works during all his working hours. For George to judge a contest it would need to be at a time when he was available. This limited his travelling range. Engagements would need to be within a few hours by road or rail and on suitable days. For contests in the North-East of England this perhaps wasn't so much of a problem as most bandsmen across the region were subject to similar constraints. Most contests would take place on holidays or at weekends; though Saturdays were generally a working day for many. George could not expect to go to Ireland or Wales as Tom had gone to New Zealand and Tasmania. Nonetheless, successful inclusion into the lists of trusted judges, even locally, would give George an opportunity to supplement his income.

By August, with the British summer well underway, these opportunities were beginning to emerge. With his name known as a composer, enquiries became engagements that in turn became chances to secure a reputation for having the ability to judge with authority, fairness and integrity. What's interesting is that George hadn't up to this point been tremendously successful at contests as a conductor, and it could have been a reasonable supposition that bandsmen locally might have asked on that basis whether he knew enough about performing to make a good judgement. It was his composing reputation that seems to have been the decisive factor. The New Shildon Saxhorn Band's first reported appearance that August was at the local Sunday School festival where the band led a procession of banners and children through the streets of Shildon. Then came the first of his reported adjudicating engagements. This was a contest at East Hetton, between the cities of Durham and Sunderland, and of which we know little, other than to say that following each band's rendering of the test piece, which was James Ord-Hume's "Scotland," George awarded the first prize to the Willington Silver Band. In the accompanying march contest the winning band was the Birtley League of the Cross with runners up being Quarrington Hill. It was the first time a band contest had been included in that particular show. "Liberal prizes" were offered according to the Durham County Advertiser on Friday, 12 August. In truth, and in comparison to some of the values we had seen reported at other shows, they were rather modest at £5, £3 and £1. The papers also misreported George's home town as being Stockton.

Appropriately, and interestingly, it was his own townspeople who were next to secure his services. These were people who knew him best of all, and knew that though the Saxhorn Band's trophy cabinet was bare of treasures, they had faith that he would give a just and worthy decision. The occasion was the thirtieth Annual Shildon Show on the Vicarage Field on 20 August. As a well run and reputable show, the organising committee had ensured that the prize money of £25 overall was one worth competing for. Once again the test piece was "Scotland,' selected from the repertoire of the highly regarded James Ord-Hume who had on at least one previous occasion been the judge at Shildon. The Durham County Advertiser reported six days later, giving us the only available information on how this contest unfolded:

> "A brass band contest confined to bands not having won a certain amount of prize money brought no less than eleven competitors. The awards of the judge (Mr George Allan) were:- 1, Eston Miners; 2, South Derwent; 3, Birtley League of the Cross; 4, Cleveland Steel Works; 5 Sunderland Temperance; 0, New Shildon Temperance; 0, Willington Silver; 0, Spennymoor Temperance; 0, Jarrow Borough; 0 West Hartlepool Borough; 0, Hartlepool Recreation."

This matter of fact reporting style was often adopted by the press writing about brass band contests in the North of England, an outcome listed with little background as if announcing the results of the fancy poultry or rabbit contests at the show. But nonetheless we are able to learn pertinent facts. For example, that at his first contest as a judge in his home town George had to give his assessment on the performance of the band that for almost two decades had been rival to his own, most probably being conducted by William Holdsworth, though it is not confirmed. We'd doubt that George would have deliberately scored them outside the prize placings, as he would not have been able to see the bands as they performed, but the Temperance band would be disappointed. One can't help but wonder if there were rumblings of discontent locally over the outcome.

On 3 September George made his way to Thornley for their Colliery Brass Band Sports and Band Contest. This time the test piece was "Zampa" by Ferdinand Herold. Just as at Shildon the previous month the Eston Miner's Band triumphed in both selection and march. They were followed by Hebburn Colliery Band in both categories. Then, on 10 September, he travelled the relatively short distance to Witton Park to officiate at their contest. This time six bands competed for prizes totalling eleven pounds in value. On this occasion the bands were allowed to choose their test piece rather than render one selected for them. The test piece winners, having also travelled furthest to be there, were the Felling Temperance Band followed by Willington and Spennymoor Temperance. In the march contest, there was a tie between the bands from Oakenshaw and Spennymoor.

If you were to venture out today to visit some of the settlements that sent their bands to these Victorian era contests it would be easy to think that the contests were of little significance. Following the closure of the heavy industries that caused each village to spring into being, most are much depleted. Yet these were vital and independent communities usually in the shadow of combinations of a pit head, cokeworks, brick or pipe works, steel or iron works or other busy industrial sites. It's true that the prize money was much less than that offered at the contests Tom Bulch was officiating in the same decade. In terms of prestige the contests didn't garner the same kind of coverage in regional newspapers as the Australian writers offered on their contests. It's also true that the contests George was engaged for didn't feature the 'crack bands' of the day; such as the Yorkshire and Lancashire bands whose names have become legendary. But to dismiss them as insignificant would be doing them a disservice. The places were more populous than in the present day and to the bandsmen of the proud communities taking part results mattered no less than to the bandsmen of the crack bands in grander contests. It's quite possible though that they received such scant attention in the press simply because there were so many contests. Every town or village event appears to have had a band contest associated with it. Cynics might suggest, perhaps not unreasonably, that it was the best way to ensure that there would be music to accompany the event.

At around that same time attempts were being made to bring some kind of greater order and structure through the formation of a Northern Counties Amateur Brass Band Association. This body, not to be confused with the current Northern Counties Brass Band Association in Scotland, held its first contest in Jarrow in June of 1898, while the Cleveland and South Durham Brass Band League also held its first contest at the Victoria Football Ground in Stockton on Saturday 23rd July. Though those formal bodies would evolve, a gradual change in the nature of the banding community was underway and 'order' was coming. So too were further contest engagements for George Allan. The winter that began at the end of 1898 became the spring of 1899 and with it a new contest season. On 22 May, George began with a trip to Howden-le-Wear where no fewer than ten bands from across the North-East region gathered to compete for prizes of £8, £4 and £3. These were the Spennymoor Temperance, Willington, Heworth, Auckland Park Temperance, Birtley Temperance, Hunwick, Oakenshaw Colliery, Peases West and Eston Miners Old bands in addition to the local hosting band Howden-Le-Wear Temperance. Yet again it was the apparently in-form Eston Miners Old Band to whom George awarded the top prize for both test piece and march contests.

Coincidentally, George's next contest destination was Eston, near the booming industrial town of Middlesbrough. This contest, on 29 July 1899, required the bands to play a challenging test piece as usual, and also a waltz of their own choice. There were five bands competing, though not the Eston band themselves. This time George awarded the first prize to the Cleveland Steel Works Band. The second prize of five pounds was won by Charlton Band of Hope and the two pounds third prize was split between Willington Silver and Middlesbrough Erimus. Cleveland Steel Works also claimed a prize for the best march played on the day.

Just one week later, on 5 August 1899, it was off to Kelloe Colliery, East Hetton as part of the thirteenth annual show of the East Hetton Horticultural Society. The show comprised of the usual array of exhibited flowers, fruit, vegetables, rabbits, pigeons, poultry and industrial work and some children's competitions and sports. The entries for the associated band contest were few, with Hartlepool Recreation Band, Thornley, Oakenshaw and Quarrington hill being the four taking part. As it was 'show season,' and with most shows including a band contest, the bands could take their pick of several taking place most weekends. This time they were competing for a seven pound first prize, with further prizes of two pounds and one pound. George's decision was for the Hartlepool Recreation Band for their rendition of the test piece, the set of waltzes "Sunny Spain" by Mr J Fitzgerald. He then awarded Thornley Colliery Band a further one pound prize for their quickstep march. In an additional category for best solo on a brass instrument, he gave the decision in favour of a Mr W Fairpley of Birtley.

Throughout 1899 George continued to maintain his membership of the New Shildon Mechanics Institute, while his younger brother Ralph also took out a subscription. He seems to have been only marginally less active than usual as a composer as the end of the nineteenth century appeared on the horizon. The only piece we've been able to confirm as being published in 1899 was a polka entitled "Randolph" which was published by T A Haigh, though others first appear in press reports around this time, including an overture, entitled "Gabriani," which was to become very popular and widely played, and a fantasia entitled "The Village Feast." Both were published by F Richardson in his Cornet brass band journal and later acquired by Wright and Round in a takeover of that business. There were marches too, such as "The Delegate." George's decision to further his adjudicating career seems to have been at the expense of time spent with the Saxhorn Band, as there were no reports of them making a public appearance or entering any contests during that last year of the century.

Melbourne and Ballarat

In a seemingly rare reversal of fortunes, and perhaps due to his still being hampered by the after effects of his second insolvency, Tom Bulch also appears to have had a subdued year. On St Valentine's Day, 14 February 1899 he was announced in the press as being in contention for selection by the committee organising a band contest to be held in Armidale. His shortlisted rivals for the engagement were a Mr G O'Shea of Renshaw and a Mr Charlesworth of Sydney. A comment in the Armidale Courier relating to the selection dilemma read that:

> "With such talent as applicants for the position doubtless the very best procurable man will be availed of by the committee; a fact in itself which should assure the success of the contest."

This serves as a reminder that Tom frequently faced competition for such appointments. Evidence suggests that rather than always being invited, prospective judges for the Australian contests were often requested to submit a tender stating their proposed fee and services. The committee would then weigh up which was the best offer. Naturally a good reputation was key to even reaching the shortlist.

One month later it was explained that it had been agreed for Tom to be retained by that organising committee, and committee member Mr S J Kearney was to liaise with him on the selection of one of his compositions as a suitable test piece. In the event though, it was clear by the end of April that the contest had not attracted the volume of entries that the committee had anticipated. A decison was made to cancel the contest. The committee consequently agreed a settlement fee, paying Tom £5 for breaking their agreement with him.

Sunday 19 March brought a Grand Musical Carnival held on the South Melbourne Beach in aid of the St Vincents Hospital Fund. A principal feature of this was a concert performance by Bulch's Operatic Band which had been volunteered to the charitable cause by Tom himself. An advertisement in The Record the day prior promised that the band would appear under his own personal conductorship.

If the press coverage is to be believed, while he was less in the limelight for a while, Tom continued to compose and be published throughout the year. New pieces included the waltz "Elsinore" and the march "Federation" under the pen name Henry Laski. Under his own name he also produced two marches, "Lyndhurst" and "Forward," which through curious coincidence share their names with two earlier compositions by George Allan. There would be several times this would happen during the lifetimes of the two men. Others that make their first appearances around this time include quicksteps "The Druid," "Flora Bell" and "Far Fa The Gloamin." A selection, "Gems of America" would also prove to be popular going forward. We also see that Bulch's Band Journal continued to be advertised as being available through outlets such as Palings in Sydney and Brisbane. Tom was as good as back on his feet, though he had learned how precarious his financial situation was. His grandson Eric has told us in correspondence that times hereafter were often financially difficult for Tom and Eliza. Where 1899 left very little residual news of Tom to tell us of how he contended with the challenges of looking after his family, 1900 was to be far more interesting though much of it has already passed before we receive our first news.

On 5 September, the press carried announcements of an exciting new brass music spectacle being planned to take place in Ballarat, the city in which Tom had first settled following his arrival in Australia. This was to be a Great Intercolonial Band Contest which would be part of the city's already established South Street Competitions which promised to be the biggest ever attempted in the city. South Street is an area of Ballarat that runs parallel to, and south of, the main thoroughfare of Sturt Street. Since 1879 when a Young Men's General Debating Society was founded in that locality, there had been a Royal South Street Society. In 1891 that society founded a Grand Annual Eisteddfod of Australasia, which extended over ten days of contests that subsequently evolved and prevailed to be one of the premium cultural events in the Australian calendar to this day. Part of the plan for expansion in 1900 was the addition of a band contest for the first time, and the plan was the closest thing so far to Tom's dream of an Intercolonial contest that would pit the best bands of each territory against each other. It was practically a dream come true. The City Oval had been reserved as a suitable venue. Bands would be expected to play the contest selection piece there on Friday, 5 October and a march or quickstep contest on the following day. There would be additional supplementary solo contests for individual musicians playing cornet and euphonium. These more subtle performances required an indoor setting so the Alfred Hall was booked on the evenings. This particular contest was to be truly 'intercolonial'. By the time particulars had been announced the entries received had naturally mainly been from the territory of Victoria; Hopetoun Band, Eaglehawk, the Lord Nelson Band of St Arnaud, Geelong, Prout's the 3rd Battalion Band and Bulch's Model Band. There was, however, representation from Tasmania in the form of the Launceston Garrison 2nd Battalion Band; and New South Wales was represented by the Bathurst District Band. Not one, but three judges were engaged to provide a decision on aspects of the brass band performances, Lieutenant Riley, Mr Ernest Wood and, of course, making his return to Ballarat, Tom Bulch. To the best of our knowledge this would be the first, and only, time Tom would judge the band that bore his own name, presenting a situation that could be perceived to be somewhat awkward.

The prize money on offer for this prestigious contest was certainly ambitious; £260 being offered in total across the categories. The winners of the main and most challenging part of the competition, the selection, would leave with £150. For the quickstep the top prize was a still very impressive £35. When compared with the typical prizes of less than £10 on offer in most North East of England contests in that period, this prize money was a very attractive incentive for bands from territories many miles distant from Victoria to travel to Ballarat, assuming they were confident enough of standing a chance of claiming a prize. To contribute towards ensuring a good crowd, cheap excursion trains were scheduled by railway companies to help bands and spectators get to Ballarat. Following a pattern we have seen established for Australian band contests, the competing bands were instructed to assemble on the Friday morning for a grand parade to the show ground. The rendezvous in this case was the junction of Sturt Street and Bridge Street, at nine o'clock in the morning sharp. This, conveniently for press reporters, placed the start location just opposite the office of the Ballarat Star. The ritual was repeated on the Saturday, the second day of competing, though a noon scheduling meant everyone benefitted from a later start that day. Though there were covered stands at the Central Oval, the greater majority of those attending, including the bands, would be out in the open air as the contest was being staged outdoors. Consequently, success was dependent upon good weather, and both days were indeed blessed in this respect. The press reports made clear that the way the band contest was run represented a distinct departure from previous years, but the new format proved justified and a huge success. This raises the question as to how much influence Tom might have had over the way the contest was run. There is much about the description of the contest that we recognise from previous descriptions of contests Tom was involved in, yet much of the detail is absent so it's difficult to determine the extent of Tom's involvement.

The rules for this contest were prescriptive in terms of expectations of the bands. Reed instruments, used generally by military bands only, were permitted, but interestingly drums and cymbals were prohibited. Each band was to comprise of a minimum of 16 and maximum of 24 bandsmen. In the test selection contest, each band could choose to play either two selections or one selection and an overture.

With specific regard to the story we are telling, the South Street Contest of 1900 was doubly interesting in that it presented the opportunity for something of a reunion of those former bandsmen from New Shildon that had come to Australia in 1884. Of course Tom himself was present. As the Bathurst District Band had made the journey, so too was their bandmaster Sam Lewins. The trio was completed by Bulch's Model Band conductor and cornetist James Scarff. The occasion was sweetened further by the presence of fellow cornetist Robert Malthouse and his younger brother George Malthouse still playing B flat bass in the band that Tom had founded. All of these were, of course, childhood bandmates in New Shildon. It's also probable that Thomas Malthouse, then recently made cornet player and master of the Smeaton Brass Band, was present. This particular Malthouse brother, though, had been quite seriously injured in an accident in July 1899, the effects of which might explain his absence from participation. It would be wonderful to think that these men might have found some opportunity to be together as the weekend progressed. Imagine just a few minutes in the chaos of this grand occasion, to come together to reflect upon how far they had each come, geographically and musically.

To briefly explore Thomas Malthouse's misadventure, he had been employed as a carpenter at the Hepburn Estate Extended Mine at Smeaton and had, with the mine manager, Mr Renfrey descended to the depth of one-thousand feet to inspect old workings. Whilst they were carrying out the inspection there was a fire damp explosion caused by the candle Thomas was using to carry out the inspection, and consequently both were badly burned. Thomas Malthouse suffered serious burns to the head, face, mouth and eyes, the front of his body and his arm, and it was expected that he would lose his sight as a consequence. Renfrey, though burned, was largely unscathed in the long term. According to a small piece in the Ovens and Murray Advertiser reporting on how his brother Robert heard the news, it seems there had become something of an attraction to disaster among the Malthouse brothers, it reads:

> "Mr Malthouse [meaning Robert] had a narrow escape from death some time ago at Rutherglen, and since then his three brothers have sustained accidents of a more or less serious nature."

On Robert Malthouse's reference, there is a story in the Ballarat Star of 1885 wherein his wrist was lacerated by 'the bursting of a gun' but this may not be the incident referred to.

Thomas Malthouse claimed for £1500 damages against the Hepburn Estate on the grounds that he said he had been ordered, by the manager into the mine with a lit candle instead of a safety lamp, and that under the applicable mining regulations it had been the manager's duty to either test the air before sending the miner in, or issue such a safety lamp. He had attempted to return to work after the accident but had found that his injuries prevented him from carrying out long shifts of duty. The company defended against the accusations with the argument that the mining regulations only applied where the mine was being worked and as this section being inspected was in disuse they were not obliged to follow such regulations. They claimed that Thomas had been negligent of his own accord. The judge found in favour of Malthouse but only awarded £300 and ten shillings damages plus costs. Thomas had been left after the accident with heart problems and a growth on his arm where the skin had been burned. Despite this, when recovered from the initial effects of the accident, he continued to act as bandmaster for the Smeaton Brass Band, and did so into the early years of the twentieth century.

On the march to the City Oval, a number of the bands chose to play a Bulch march. Bulch's Model Band appropriately played "The Typhoon," Bulch's first published march. The Eaglehawk Band chose "Postman's Parade" and Hopetoun "On the Warpath." Most likely unknowing of the connection the Lord Nelson St Arnaud Band completed the New Shildonian reunion, in spirit at least, with a rendition of George Allan's "The Delegate." The bands were staggered so that they could be clearly heard as they passed the cheering crowds lining the way without the sound of the next marching band spoiling their tone. The attendance, helped by the fair weather, was reportedly a record for attendance at any outdoor event held in Ballarat. It would be a good weekend for fans of Tom's music. In the selection contest at least two bands elected to play his "Reminiscences of Weber." In the quickstep contest the Lord Nelson Band played "Postman's Parade" and the Bathurst District Band played "Bathurst," the march Tom had composed especially for the contest in that city and which they had long since adopted. Bulch's Model Band again played Tom's debut march "The Typhoon".

When the judges had submitted and totalled their scores Prout's Band finished top of the pile for the quickstep contest, having a five-point lead over the Bathurst and Geelong bands who would engage again in a play-off the following day to determine who took the second place prize. Bulch's Model Band, disappointingly, were ranked second from last. After the quickstep play-off, Sam Lewins conducted a massed band to offer more music before his Bathurst Band played a further selection, "Songs of England" after which the crowd dispersed; many heading for the solo contests at the Alfred Hall.

Robert Malthouse entered the cornet solo contest and was the first player to give his rendition of the test piece "My Old Kentucky Home." As he played through the piece, reports of the contest tell us that he made a number of slips and, realising that he would not be able to win, he retired without completing the piece. The winner was Mr Graham of Prout's Band, a decision that came with some controversy as reporters thought it to have been an 'uneven' performance.

On the second day the bands mustered outside Suttons Music Store to see the draw to ascertain that day's order of play. Then they assembled outside the Ballarat East Town Hall, forming up to once again march to the Oval. The points sheet from the first day of competing had been deposited in secrecy in a ballot box which was displayed in full view of all present at the centre of the green so that nobody would be able to read it until the final results were to be calculated. The attendance was lower than the previous day, with about 4,000 spectators assembled to hear the bands. For their second selection, both Bulch's Model Band and Prout's chose to play Tom's "Reminiscences of Weber," which some other bands had also chosen to play the previous day. The Lord Nelson Band played his arrangement of a Verdi piece, but the other bands chose works by other composers. Amid much excitement, the point totals for each band were contributed by all the judges and totalled before the eagerly awaited results were publicly announced. The declaration that the Lord Nelson Band of St Arnaud had triumphed was greeted with loud cheers from both public and assembled bandsmen. Sam Lewins and the Bathurst District Band were placed second, with Prout's, providing some local pride in finishing third. It may perhaps have been the foot of the table of results that provided the biggest shock of the day. Bulch's Model Brass Band, the band Tom had founded in that city, had been placed at the bottom of the pile having scored seventy-five points fewer than the winning band. This outcome would have come as a major blow to the band, and Tom's old friends Robert Malthouse and James Scarff. As the bandsmen from Bulch's Model Band reflected on the result, a play-off took place between the Bathurst and Geelong bands to see who would take second place in the previous day's partially inconclusive quickstep contest. The Bathurst District Band was deemed to have played better this time and were awarded the second prize, to much applause.

Then on the evening Thomas Bulch, Ernest Wood and T Riley judged the euphonium solo contest, declaring Mr Lorimer of Bendigo winner, after which a banquet and smoke night was given for the competing bandsmen by the Ballarat Battalion in their Orderly Room. This was presided over by the Battalion's commanding officer, Colonel Williams and the Mayors of the Town and City. The dignitaries thanked the organisers and bands for their part in the success of the event and its effect on the city of Ballarat. The behaviour of the bandsmen, often a bone of contention during the Victorian era remember, had this time reflected great credit upon them. The efforts of Tom and others towards professionalising, and instilling discipline within, the attitude of bandsmen appears to have paid off. Sam Lewins gave a speech, speaking up in praise about the organisation of the contest. He claimed that his band had never been treated better than they had in Ballarat, and vowed to return at a future date. Records don't confirm whether Tom and the other judges attended the banquet or bore witness to the toast that was proposed to them. It is quite possible that he may have offered apologies as his next judging engagement required him to travel for a band contest being held at Dimboola, some distance to the west of Ballarat, on 9 October.

The outcome of the contest for Bulch's Model Band quite probably introduced some strain to the relationship between Tom Bulch and his former charges, though we should not forget that the scoring was provided by a panel and not Tom alone. We have no reason to think that Tom would offer any favour to his old band simply on the strength of past connections, and we must remember that the judges awarding points for music rather than appearance and marching, would not know which band played when. In the judging notes from the quickstep contest, however, there had been much criticism of Bulch's Model Band's band's appearance and performance. They had lost points for dirty boots, the front line not being properly dressed, marching out of line, not wheeling properly. Having a sense of his regard for standards we can suspect that Tom too felt some shame that the band that still bore his name had slipped from its former state of prestige.

Away from Ballarat, at the Dimboola Agricultural and Pastoral Society's show, four bands competed, each playing a march, selection and a waltz. This was a more local affair, with bands from Warracknabeal, Nhill, Natimuk and Horsham. Tom, being the only judge this time, found in favour of the Nhill band, who consequently claimed the nine-pounds first prize.

Anyone who felt that it might be a long time before they saw Tom Bulch in Ballarat again following the South Street Competitions may have been surprised when, on 13 November, the Sportsman of Melbourne announced that he had been reappointed as the bandmaster of the Ballarat Militia Regiment. This being, of course, the post he had resigned years previously after falling out over the arrangements for the New Year's Day concert. We can only assume that an opportunity may have been presented to him during his time in Ballarat preparing for and officiating the contest. Tom's return to the city created the curious anomaly that there was already a band in Ballarat bearing his name, and yet he was going to be leading an entirely different one. He had almost come full circle. In the period between that announcement and the 24th of that same month, the committee governing Tom's old band made a decision that Bulch's Model Brass Band would adopt a new name, severing the last tie with their former bandmaster and mentor. Turning over to a new chapter in their history they became the Ballarat City Band. Whether this was triggered by a souring relationship between the band and Tom, or whether it was driven by his return to take charge of the Ballarat Militia Band, is not clear. It may even have been expected and planned for some time based on feelings that Tom's influence was long since diminished. Whatever finally caused the transformation, the band, still going strong today, will always be the band that was formed by Tom Bulch, the ambitious young railway blacksmith from Shildon in County Durham.

The Ballarat City Band made its first appearance under that title on 24 November, offering a performance as a prelude to a lecture on "The Paris Exhibition" at Her Majesty's Theatre in Ballarat. They played a number of selections in front of the theatre between seven-thirty and eight o'clock pm. The press occasionally forgot about the name change and, doubtless through habit rather than malice, reported upon the band giving the name as Bulch's Band.

On 15 November, Thomas guested as conductor at a concert given by the Prahran City Band at the City Hall in that district of Melbourne. Then, within no time at all, and despite still being a resident of Melbourne, he was once again an active bandmaster in Ballarat. On Friday, 7 December, at the Annual Sports of the Ballarat College on the Eastern Oval, and under reportedly pleasant skies, Thomas Bulch conducted the 3rd Battalion Militia Band through "some excellent selections of music." The very next day, a cricket match was held between sides from Ballarat, and Melbourne. This took place on the Wendouree Asylum ground. A report described that:

> "The enjoyable nature of the proceedings was considerably added to, by the presence of the 3rd Battalion Band (by the kind permission of Colonel Williams) who played a number of selections, under the conduct of Bandmaster Bulch, in a highly meritorious manner."

We don't know whether Thomas made a permanent move back to Ballarat straight away, or when he closed the music shop he had restarted in Melbourne, but he certainly seemed to be receiving deliveries at Ballarat. An announcement in the Ballarat Star of 11 December advised that, among other goods, there were items at Ballarat West railway station that awaiting his collection. The announcement was repeated in the Star on the fourteenth. On 16 September, a thanksgiving service was held at the Cathedral Church to honour soldiers returned to Ballarat from duty elsewhere. As part of their own duty, the 3rd Battalion Militia Band were in attendance. The Ballarat Star reported:

> "The music for the service included "Te Deum" and the National Anthem, both of which were accompanied by the Battalion Band under Bandmaster Bulch. Kipling's "Recessional" was also sung."

By 27 December, just before his birthday, Thomas made clear it that he was expecting a prolonged stay in Ballarat, through his advertising other services in the Star.

"Mr Bulch, bandmaster to the 3rd battalion, is prepared to receive pupils for all brass instruments. As Mr Bulch is well known as an instructor, he should be well patronised by intending bandsmen."

New Shildon

Back in County Durham, George, like Thomas, continued to juggle his bandmaster duties with those of contest judge. The first contest the Saxhorn Band took part in that year did not require a full complement of bandsmen. On 2 April 1900, the Daily Gazette for Middlesbrough reported that:

"Under the auspices of the Whitworth Prize Brass Band a quartet contest for brass band instrumentalists was held in the Town Hall, Spennymoor, on Saturday. The attendance was large. The competing bands were: Spennymoor, Birtley, Wingate, Rise Carr, Willington, Shildon, Milburn's Model (Middlesbrough), Browney Colliery, Rise Carr (No. 2) and Shildon Saxhorn. The judge, Mr Thomas Snowdon, Spennymoor, gave his awards as follows:- 1, Milburn's Model; 2, Wingate; 3, Rise Carr; 4, Birtley; 5, Spennymoor Temperance."

In May the full band was called upon to provide music at a celebration that perhaps first requires a little context.

In October 1899, after tensions had arisen relating to Britain's increasing influence in southern Africa, a war broke out between the British Empire and two Boer states, the Transvaal Republic and the Orange Free State. The Boers, named after a Dutch and Afrikaans word meaning "farmers," had been an influential presence in the southern African territories since the time the Dutch East India Company controlled that part of the continent, prior to the incorporation of the southernmost Cape Colony into the British Empire in 1806. This conflict became the Second Boer War. Initially, the British Empire's forces had been unprepared, and the well equipped and trained Boers quickly gained an upper hand, winning battles at Colenso, Magersfontein and Stormberg. The general in command of the Empire's forces in that region, General Redvers Buller, was consequently replaced by Lord Kitchener and Lord Roberts, and the number of troops significantly ramped up. As was often the case Britain, being a comparatively small nation stretching resources across a far reaching empire, could not rely solely on troops from the British Isles. They brought in supporting forces up to a number of around 153,000 colonial troops. These comprised of Australians, New Zealanders, Canadians, Indians, Natalese and Ceylonese troops, as well as around one hundred thousand black South African auxiliaries and a few African allies to support the 347,000 soldiers that had been transported from the home nations. The Boers had only around 63,000 troops, auxiliaries and foreign volunteers to rely on in their sieges of Mahikeng, Kimberley and Ladysmith. Consequently, by the time the British Empire had gathered its forces the odds had overwhelmingly flipped back in its favour; but not before the Boers had inflicted very heavy initial casualties on the British.

The British Empire stormed Orange Free State and the Transvaal. Gradually they wrested control of the territories from the Boers, many of whom were captured and assigned to grim concentration camps; a term most associated with their employment by the Nazis during the Second World War. The British proved just as keen to use them in this particular conflict, and they were not exclusively for adult male soldiers. Over 26,000 women and children died in the squalid conditions of British concentration camps during this war. As we mentioned, the town of Mahikeng, then referred to as Mafeking, had been besieged early in the war in a stand off that endured up to the end of April. The British garrison there was commanded by Robert Baden Powell, who would become a much loved national hero as a consequence of these events. He is perhaps best known and remembered as the founder of the Scouting movement. The battle for control of Mafeking dragged on for 217 miserable days as the Boers did not prioritise the capture of the town. They simply cut off its supply and transport routes and thereafter shelled it sporadically. The greater number of the Boer troops were deployed to higher priority zones elsewhere. As a consequence of this decision not to end the siege decisively the British contingent at Mafeking held out through a combination of cunning, intelligence and weight of numbers numbers.

On 12 May, the Boers sent 240 soldiers in to attack, but the besieged forces were alerted and managed to repel the attack killing or capturing many of the Boers involved. Then, on 17 May, a column of 2,000 British Empire troops, including Robert Baden-Powell's brother Baden, arrived effectively and decisively ending the siege. The Relief of Mafeking was of little strategic significance in the war, which would drag on largely in guerrilla form for another two years until the Treaty of Vereeniging was signed on 31 May 1902. Despite this, the Relief of Mafeking caused a jubilant reaction in Britain when news of it arrived, having been staged by telegraph. The nation broke out in celebrations as word spread across its length and breadth.

In the North-East of England the news arrived on Friday, 18 May. Bonfires were lit, shops ordered to close, gaily coloured bunting hastily hung across the streets, flags and tricolour ribbons displayed. The festivities became boisterous in some places such as Witton Park, not far from the Shildons, where a twenty-four year old Mrs Appleby was accidentally shot by a miner who had been a little too careless with his loaded revolver. In the Shildons the celebration was said to have rivalled that of the Queen's Jubilee of 1887. This being a railway town, when the news was first received late in the day, it was greeted by the whistles of the locomotives and the cheers of the drivers and their stokers. On the Saturday a parade commenced from Hildyard Terrace, with Police Inspector Lowes at the head, followed by a replica wooden cannon and many schoolchildren. Overhead the red white and blue bunting decorated the streets. This parade, as was customary, took in the principal streets of both Old and New Shildon before terminating at the Market Place to receive addresses from dignitaries. On the evening the parade was repeated; this time with both the New Shildon Temperance Band and George Allan's New Shildon Saxhorn Band filling the air with patriotic and uplifting march tunes.

There are suggestions around this time though, that all was not entirely well with George's relationship with the New Shildon Saxhorn Band. Perhaps the band were finding the other demands on George's time, his composing, judging and perhaps his family, detrimental to their collective interest. Whatever the reason behind it, we see in the Daily Gazette for Middlesborough on the 21st of May the following advertisement:

"Resident Bandmaster Wanted for New Shildon Saxhorn Band; Cornet player; miner. Apply F Quinn, Secretary, Shildon, Darlington."

Had George tendered his resignation? Had the band placed the advertisement of their own accord? It's largely a mystery.

Perhaps between them, they had agreed to advertise to see what options arose that might allow George time to concentrate on the other aspects of his life. We don't know if the advertisement was met with any applications. The evidence suggests that, though the advert had been placed for three days in a row, George did not relinquish the post.

On Friday, 8 June 1900, with memories of Mafeking already fading, the Durham County Advertiser tells of George's next known engagement:

> "Willington – On Saturday afternoon a band contest, promoted by Willington Silver Band Committee, took place in a field kindly granted for the occasion by Mr W F Longstaff, Low Willington. Eight bands competed. The following are the awards by Mr G Allan, Shildon, who officiated as Judge. Selection:- First Prize Sunderland Temperance, also cornet, euphonium and soprano medals; 2nd, Birtley Temperance; 3rd Spennymoor Temperance and trombone medal; 4th, Sunderland East End. Quickstep divided between Sunderland Temperance and Birtley Temperance. The test piece was 'Norma' by Mr W Rimmer."

William Rimmer was a contemporary of Allan and at times they shared common publishers; the first being T A Haigh. Rather like Tom Bulch, Rimmer was a more prolific composer, being published by multiple publishers and earning his living from his music. It's never really clear to us throughout George's story why he never chose to take that step to elevate his musical endeavours to that next level and leave behind his job at the wagon works. Whether it was a question of opportunity, competition, confidence, self-belief, or whether he simply enjoyed his job, his conclusion seems to have been that his place was there in the dust, heat and clamour of the blacksmith's department of the North Eastern Railway works.

There were a great many brass band contests during this period. Some argued that there were too many. If George Allan had chosen to make a go of it he possibly could have. We should remember, though, that when Tom Bulch took the first step into professional musicianship in Australia, his father-in-law had supported him in opening a music shop which, in turn, helped him support his wife and his family. Perhaps for George, the absence of such a catalyst meant such a leap of faith was too great a risk to consider.

Then, on Saturday, 14 July 1900, George Allan made a journey to South Yorkshire to adjudicate at a contest organised by the Dodworth Brass Band. This was held in the grounds of Grove House, the home of Mr H A Allport, a Justice of the Peace. It took place on a sunny day, which helped attract a reportedly large attendance. The eight competing bands were offered a choice of three test pieces for the selection contest. These were Rimmer's "Norma" again, "Oberon" by Harry Round and "Songs of England." The first two were the more popular choices. After listening through all eight performances George awarded the first prize of ten pounds in the selection to the Hinchcliffe Mill Band. Cleckheaton were placed second for a prize of six pounds and Holme third for three pounds. Interestingly those three bands were all conducted by one man; Angus Holden. George found Cleckheaton to be the best performers in the march contest. Overall, twenty-four pounds in prize money was given out that day. After the results had been announced, George declared that all of the bands, who were unknown to him prior to the contest, had played very well indeed and he claimed he had great difficulty in coming to a conclusion, especially in the quickstep contest.

On Saturday, 1 September 1900, another fine and suitable day, George found himself sitting in the adjudicator's tent at the Brandon Society's annual exhibition near the city of Durham. This was reportedly the first time a band contest had been included at this particular exhibition. According to the press there was, once again, a very large attendance on the day, with exhibits being displayed throughout five marquees sited on a field adjacent to the colliery village. The location commanded a fine and extensive view of the surrounding countryside, enabling those attending to observe the farmers and their labourers harvesting across the landscape. The show comprised of the usual amateur sports and an array of floral, poultry, rabbits, pigeons, painting, industrial project and vegetable displays. Side-shows had also been set up as added attractions for visitors. Seven bands entered the contest, which proved attractive to those in attendance. The scores awarded by George on that day concluded that the Seaham Harbour Bottleworks Brass Band were the finest at rendering the test piece. In the quickstep contest, the points were tied between the Sunderland Temperance and Seaham Harbour Bottleworks bands. George declared that, rather than declaring a further play-off for first place, the prize money should instead be split between the two bands. This received the audible approval of the 'music critics' in the audience. Afterwards, in the evening, the tents were lit up creating an atmosphere that caused the younger visitors to linger far longer than was traditionally customary.

On Saturday, 10 November George was reported as being back in charge of his band at a re-opening of the LIberal Club in Shildon. The building had been closed for a series of extensive renovations and refurbishments. A re-opening ceremony was conducted by the recently re-elected Mr J M Paulton, the Liberal Member of Parliament who had held the seat for Bishop Auckland since the seat was formed in 1885. The 1900 United Kingdom general election had been fought largely on the basis of support for the Boer War, and had been a resounding Conservative victory. Much of the North East of England, however, remained a Liberal stronghold. Paulton's opponent in that election, William Hustler Hopkins, on the strength of Tory association with the national sentiments regarding the Boer campaign, had come closer to unseating Paulton than any Conservative opponent yet. The victory was seen as particularly important for Paulton's Liberal supporters. Whether George was politically part of that group is obscure, though the Saxhorn Band were often engaged, it would seem, by the Liberals, and never to our knowledge by the Conservatives. The refurbishment of the Liberal Club had entailed an expansion of the Reading Room and repositioning of a staircase to enable better access to the Billiard Room. There was also a dedication of the reading room to a Mr J Jamieson, a prominent Shildon supporter of the LIberal political cause. Prior to the arrival of the esteemed MP, the New Shildon Saxhorn Band paraded the streets of the town playing music, before marching to the railway station to await the arrival of the three-thirty afternoon train upon which Paulton, not a resident of the area, was due to arrive. Following his disembarkation from the train, he was driven slowly up to the Liberal Club in a procession headed by the George and the band playing, presumably among other things, an arrangement of Handel's "See the Conquering Hero Comes" from Judas Maccabaeus. When the parade reached the Liberal Club, by this time packed to the rafters with supporters, speeches were given and the new reading room officially unlocked.

November also saw the publishing of a number of ticket draw results in the press in relation to the band, suggesting that the New Shildon Saxhorn Band was attempting to fundraise for instruments, music or uniforms through employing draws or raffles at this time.

1901 commenced with a shock over the death of Britain's beloved monarch, and Empress, Queen Victoria. Hers had been such a long reign that most of her subjects had known of no other monarch. She had spent Christmas at Osborne House on the Isle of Wight, and there, at the age of 81, lame through rheumatism, partly blinded by cataracts in her eyes, she weakened and eventually passed away on 22 January. The whole nation, and far reaches of the British Empire, fell into mourning. A funeral, long planned and designed by the Queen herself, was conducted on the 2nd February at St George's Chapel, Windsor Castle. This was followed by her interment alongside Prince Albert in Frogmore Mausoleum at Windsor Great Park. Victoria's heir apparent was her son Edward VII, who immediately inherited the titles. However his coronation was scheduled for 26 June the following year. This gave an inspired George Allan plenty of time to create, and have published, a patriotic overture to celebrate the new king and for there to be plenty of time for it to remain topical.

The first reference in the press we see relating to the playing of "King Edward" was in the Dundee Courier of 8 May 1901 where it was declared as being part of a programme to be given by the Cupar Town Band the following evening in the Hood Park.

The census of 1901 gives us an opportunity to ascertain the whereabouts of the Allan family that year. George and Elizabeth continued to reside at 2 Pears Terrace with their daughters, Lillie and Beatrice and son William. George's gave his occupation as Blacksmith this time, though we know from the rail works wages books, held at the national Archives in Kew, that he was still a Blacksmith's Striker or assistant to the Blacksmith. We can never be sure why George never took the leap to becoming a blacksmith. Perhaps it simply suited him to be the second man. In any case, he appears to have been consistent in his work and doesn't feature in the 'fines' books we have seen. The rail workers could be fined for any breach of the works regulations, slacking off, arriving late or leaving early. Outside of the workplace, George and his brother Ralph continued their membership of the Mechanics Institute, possibly retiring there occasionally to relax, read the books, newspapers or periodicals, or attend an interesting lecture. The Institute also had games facilities so the members could enjoy billiards for example in their leisure time. Ralph, then aged eighteen, was still resident at 65 Adelaide Street with father, John, and mother Hannah. Also there was brother Edwin, then aged twenty-two. John, at this time, was in his mid-sixties but still plying his trade as a tailor and draper. That he is listed in the census as an employer implies that it was his own business. Nearby at number 68 Adelaide Street was another son John Robert, now a joiner and wagon builder at the works, where he might have seen his brother George daily.

We know of only one judging engagement for George in 1901 which was the Brandon Band Contest held on Saturday, 31 August. The particular band contest had been advertised in the press for weeks beforehand as one of the attractions of the eighth Brandon Colliery Flower Show and Sports. Those advertisements had included instructions for interested bands to contact the show secretary to acquire a copy of the rules. Nine bands submitted an entry, those being; Hebburn Colliery, Sunderland Temperance, Seaham Harbour, Willington Silver, Spennymoor Temperance, Thornley Colliery, Hetton Colliery, Hamsteels and Brandon Colliery. In the test piece contest, where on this occasion the bands could select their own from a given list, offering the listener some variety, the Sunderland Temperance band were unable to repeat their success at the previous year's event. This time George awarded more points in favour of the Hebburn Colliery Band, pushing the band from Sunderland to second place. Seaham Harbour, the previous year's runners up, came third. As tradition now dictated there was also a separate march contest. In this the Hebburn Colliery again triumphed over their rivals from Sunderland.

George continued to compose and to be published throughout 1901. A number of his musical creations including "King Edward," previously mentioned, were selected for, and published in, a new and seemingly short-lived brass band journal. This was the Standard Band Journal, which appears to have been an experiment by the owners of the Boston Standard newspaper. This is implied by the fact that the journal declares itself as being produced by the Standard Publishing Company of Boston, Lincolnshire. In this it shares some geographic commonality with Fred Richardson's Cornet Brass Band Journal, and one wonders whether it was perhaps a joint venture involving Richardson. Others from George's works included in the journal were marches "Niobe" and "On Parade" and the fantasia "The New Century" which we have seen a few times as being played in the same programme as "King Edward." These latter two pieces have eventually been included into the Wright and Round archive catalogue of compositions which can still be bought today, suggesting that at some point the rights were sold to Wright and Round. That Fred Richardson also sold the rights to his Cornet Journal pieces to the same company supports the hypothesis that the Standard Journal had some connection to him.

Above: Solo cornet part from George's march "Niobe," as published in the short lived "Standard" Band Journal in 1901

Ballarat

1901 begins with a little confusion with regard to interpreting the engagements that Tom Bulch and his band were involved in. This is due to the factor that we mentioned earlier, whereby Tom had returned to Ballarat. There are stories in the press early in that year mentioning Bulch's Brass Band which could mean the 3rd Battalion Militia Band to which he had returned to be in charge, or the City of Ballarat Band which up until the previous year had been Bulch's Model Brass Band. One example we have seen advises that Bulch's Brass Band appeared on 7 February at the Rokewood, Pitfield and Berringa branch of the AMA's sports meeting.

Tom did receive a contest adjudication engagement for which he did not have to travel very far at all. This was the band contest at the 1901 Ballarat Exhibition. The competing bands once again included his former charges, the City of Ballarat Brass Band as well as Code's Melbourne Brass Band, Geelong Town, Lord Nelson Miner's Band (of St Arnaud), Prout's Ballarat Brass Band and the St Augustine's Orphanage Band. Knowing of his ability to create a suitable test piece, the organising committee had requested that Tom do so, and consequently he had specially arranged a selection from "Jessonda" by the German classical composer Louis Spohr.

The contest took place on Friday, 22 February at Ballarat's Eastern Oval, with tickets costing 1s for general entry with premium spots in the grandstand and reserve costing an extra 6d. As tradition now dictated the bands assembled at ten-thirty in the morning away from the showground for a public parade to the Oval. Lieutenant Colonel Williams of the 3rd Battalion acted as the general co-ordinator officiating over the event. Following a draw to determine their order, from eleven-thirty onwards the bands commenced playing in turn, each giving their best rendition of "Jessonda." Tom listened from the screened confines of the judging tent. Concerning the test piece arrangement from the first day, one press reporter declared that:

> "Those who have been fortunate enough to hear it pronounce it to be a most classical and refined selection."

A break then ensued before the bands fell in again at three o'clock in the afternoon for inspection and to commence the military drill contest. Each band would play a quickstep march in turn while the judges marked their musical accuracy, appearance and marching discipline. The points awarded for the first day's test pieces were sealed in an envelope to be kept safe and revealed only after the second round of performances on the the next day. The Saint Augustine's Orphanage Band had particularly attracted much public support on account of their youth, and reportedly played very well. Bulch's former band, now the City of Ballarat, were said by at least one commentator to have played well but that they did not pay particular attention to their timekeeping.

A cornet solo contest then took place on the Friday evening after the band contests, with competitors playing a piece entitled "Sabrina" that had again been composed especially by Tom for the event. Mr L Osborne of Melbourne beat W Graham of Ballarat to that prize by three points, with seven other competitors finishing behind the pair.

Saturday dawned bringing with it the second daily parade to the contest ground. It was unsurprising to hear some bands again choose Bulch pieces to march to. The Ballarat City band stuck with their tradition of playing their former bandmaster and founder's first march "The Typhoon"; as did Geelong Town. Prout's chose two of Tom's pieces; "Constellation" and "Newcastle." This day saw the bands play their second test piece, which was the one they chose themselves from a list offered by the organising committee. Once Tom was again concealed within the judging tent for the sitting it was the St Arnaud's Band that played first, giving a selection of Rossini pieces. Next was Ballarat City with Tom's own selection of works by Weber. St Augustine's played Harry Round's "Linda di Chamouni" and Prout's chose the Weber selection again. Code's played a selection from "Faust" by Berlioz and Geelong offered Harry Round's "Tannhauser". The prizes on offer that weekend stood at £150 for first place, £70 for the second, £30 for third and £20 for fourth place. When you compare these with the prizes offered back at the town and village contests that George Allan was adjudicating these were grand prizes indeed demonstrating the gulf in perceived prestige. Furthermore there were extra cash prizes of £30, £20, £10 and £5 awarded for the military drill. These were claimed by Prout's, Geelong, Lord Nelson and Ballarat City, in that order. When the points were totalled from both days of test selections, Code's band of Melbourne had emerged clear winners, followed by Lord Nelson, Prout's and Geelong. We gather that at the announcement Code's band "completely lost its discipline and broke out in every manifestation of delight" at the result. This is perhaps understandable with a prize of £150 at stake. At half-past-five in the afternoon, the bands came together for a grand finale parade. An evening euphonium solo contest followed at which Tom awarded the prize to Mr J Ogilvie from Code's band. His conduct and judgement throughout were again stated in the press as having been well received.

As the year slipped on into April and towards the southern winter season a letter appeared in the Ballarat Star on the 29th:

> "A COMMENDABLE SUGGESTION. (To the Editor.) yours, etc., A HELPER. Sir,—I see by yesterday's "Star" that Mr Adam Scott has kindly sent you the sum of one guinea for the purpose of starting a fund for providing firewood, etc., for those in need during the coming winter. I think it is a good idea of his — one which I think will meet with the approval of nearly everybody. Further, I would suggest that a Sunday programme of music, supplied by our brass bands, should take place, say next Sunday week, at the Eastern Oval, weather permitting, and a collection taken up at the gates, which I am sure would realise a good sum, considering it is for so worthy an object. Let it be on the same lines as one previously given by our bands in aid of the soldier's statue fund. Starting from the City Fire Brigade, march to the Oval via Sturt and Bridge streets. I would like to see Mr Bulch, bandmaster of the Militia Band, take the matter up and confer with the other bandmasters on the subject, who l am sure, would only be too willing to help. Also the firemen of the Ballarat City and Sebastopol Brigades might take part in the march. Hoping Mr Bulch will get going at once, yours etc. A HELPER."

This looks to have been a crafty move on the part of the writer. The bands were well known for their support of charitable causes and for producing good results in that respect. Having been suggested so publicly it might reflect badly on the organisations named if they did not take up such a charitable challenge. Interesting too that the writer named Tom directly, a suggestion that he considered him to be a positive influencer where charitable endeavours were concerned.

Around the same time Tom and the 3rd Battalion Militia Band had a sad duty to fulfil. They were called upon to attend the unveiling of a plaque at Beaufort which had been installed to honour the memory of a fallen comrade. Major G A Eddy had been one of the first Australians from Victoria State to fall in the Boer War and had begun his military career with the 3rd Battalion Militia. After the unveiling ceremony, the band gave a 'well selected' programme of music.

On 13 May, a day before news of the Relief of Mafeking would filter through to the Australian public as it had back in New Shildon, the 3rd Battalion Militia were given a very special engagement to fulfil concerning a rare royal visit to Melbourne and Ballarat. The Duke of York, brother of Edward VII and now heir apparent to the British throne, had made a voyage to Australia with his wife for a royal tour. Prince George had visited Ballarat twenty years earlier as a youth, and been welcomed enthusiastically. This return visit would prove no different. On the day the Prince was due to arrive at Ballarat, citizens flocked to the railway station and thickly lined Lydiard Street and Victoria Square. Flags and bunting adorned every building in an expression of patriotism and imperial pride, though such sentiments may not have been universally felt.

The route the royal couple would follow had been published in the ever efficient Ballarat Star enabling the public to find the best spots to view the entourage. Tom Bulch, the 3rd Battalion Militia Band and B Company of the 3rd Battalion were on point as a guard of honour at the railway station, with a company of one-hundred men from the Mounted Rifles, to greet the arrival of the special train. The station had been specially and unusually dressed and furnished lavishly for the occasion. The Prince and his wife were accompanied by the then Prime Minister of Australia, Edmund Barton, the Attorney General and Victoria State Premier. Following a formal greeting session with the City Mayor and Town Councillors, which took place inside the station, the Duke and Duchess exited the building as Tom conducted the 3rd Militia Band through the National Anthem. The couple then began their tour. They travelled to the Soldier's Statue, a publicly funded memorial to the soldiers of the locality who fell in South Africa. The Duke and Duchess ceremonially laid a foundation stone then travelled to the Town Hall Gardens to plant trees, again in ceremonial manner. They were then presented with a silver casket containing specimens of gold from the North Woah Hawp Mine before proceeding via City Hall, where they were serenaded by the Ballarat City Band with 1,200 school children en route to Alexandra Square. With the City of Ballarat band also performing, James Scarff became the second Shildon born bandmaster that day to conduct their band for the royal couple. Next, with the peal of the City Hall bells beginning to fade, the couple received addresses at Alexandra Square, formally naming it, before journeying on to the South Star Mine to receive a presentation and gift from the Chairman of Directors there. Concluding a packed itinerary they returned to the railway station via Sturt Street where they stopped to view the Women's Ward at the hospital that was dedicated to Queen Victoria in her Diamond Jubilee year.   The couple then departed by the four o'clock train. A grand banquet of the civic dignitaries followed, after which a celebratory firework display was given.

The seasons began to cool by June, during which, on Friday, the 21st of the month, a social reunion of former comrades from the 3rd Battalion Militia was held at the Trades Hall, Ballarat.   Tom was the natural choice to provide a programme of music along with a Miss Anderson who provided vocals.   Thirty two couples partook of twenty dances played. Then there followed an evening banquet over which Tom presided.   Toasts were duly raised to "the King," "the officers," "the band" and "the ladies." Tom had, at about this time, been working on a new selection arrangement "Gems of Meyerbeer," based upon the operatic works of German composer Giacomo Meyerbeer, which was to be used as a test piece at the next South Street Competitions.

On 27 June Tom attended, and contributed a number of instrumental and vocal renditions to a farewell at the Orderly Room for the 3rd Battalion Militia's former bandmaster Mr Gray, whom you may remember had also run the Phoenix Foundry Band for some years.   Gray had secured a post at a large foundry in Brisbane so was leaving Victoria. On Wednesday, 17 July he attended yet another function at the City Rowing Club for another well-liked citizen leaving Ballarat.   Mr Charles Tulloch, this time, who was being transferred from the Ballarat Branch of the Commercial Bank to one at Footscray. Tom sang some of the songs rendered and provided piano accompaniment throughout.

The 29th of August brought the return of popular figures to Ballarat, with Tom and the 3rd Battalion Band engaged to welcome the Mayor of Ballarat and his wife back to the city. A social function comprising over 1,200 persons was hosted at the Alfred Hall which had been suitably decorated to present a warm welcome back for the couple.   The band played Tom's "The Commanding Officer's Parade," "The Empire," his new selection "Gems of Meyerbeer," a waltz "Elsinore" composed under his alter ego Henry Laski, and an his arrangement of Glaswegian

293

violinist Carl Volti's "Fair Maid of Perth." Then followed an interval, after which musical duties were picked up by Harry West's Orchestra. Dancing continued until the early hours of the morning.

By early September, anticipation was building for the Ballarat Musical Festival and South Street Competitions, which again would include a major band contest. For this, extremely generous prizes totalling two-hundred pounds were announced. Consequently a large contingent of the best bands deemed the contest worthy of the cost of travelling. The final list of entrants comprised of; the Newtown Band (New South Wales), Newcastle Band (New South Wales), Albury Band (New South Wales), Gawler Band (South Australia), South Australian Railways Band (Adelaide), Hobart City Band (Tasmania), Queenstown Band (Tasmania), and from Victoria, Northcott's Band, Hopetoun Band, Geelong Town Band, Code's Band from Melbourne, Lord Nelson Band from St Arnaud, 3rd Battalion Militia Band, Prout's Brass Band, Ballarat City Band, Soldier's Hill Band, St Augustine's Band from Geelong and the Eaglehawk Band. It was abundantly clear that this was going to be a very serious contest. Unlike the previous year, however, Thomas Edward Bulch would not be judging but competing. During the contest the bands would play two selections, one fixed and one 'own choice'. Bands would then mass to play a new march Tom had created especially for the occasion. Before the contest took place, though, there were other duties to perform.

On Sunday, 15 September the 3rd Battalion Militia band took part in a funeral procession for Mr Walter S Douglass, a member of K Company of the Mounted Rifles. Accompanied by a firing party, the procession was led by Thomas and the Militia band playing, as they had many times before, the "Dead March" from Saul. The way was lined with spectators. On Saturday the 28th Tom and the Militia band were in attendance at the unveiling of a memorial to Sergeant Charlie Vaughan of Learmouth, another prominent local casualty of the Second Boer War. The Ballarat Star, in describing the unveiling, waxed lyrical on the validity of Australia's part in the conflict:

> "It was to such men as Sergeant Vaughan, who did so much for their country and civilisation, that the people owed a great deal. South Africa had proved the dumping ground for Australia's sons, who were now known throughout the world for the splendid work they had performed. It was thought by many

that there was no need to send men from Australia to fight in South Africa, but those who had watched events must acknowledge that there was great need. When that petition was sent calling upon Great Britain to settle the grievances of the Outlanders, it was the duty of Great Britain to respond to the call. The British nation must protect her subjects wherever they might be. When those in responsible power in these states called on eligible men to come forward their action was adversely criticised, but it was necessary that we should show the mother country and the world at large that we would recognise our responsibilities as British subjects."

On Wednesday 9 October, Tom entered the judge's tent once more. This was at the Agricultural Show that took place at Dimboola in the west of the Territory of Victoria. Unlike the grand contests such as the one coming up in the city of Ballarat, this affair sounded more akin to the type of contest George Allan found himself judging back in Britain. Four bands competed; Dimboola, Nhill, Warracknabeal and Natimuk. Each played a selection of music for the pleasure of those in attendance. The Warracknabeal Band won by a single point with Nhill second, Natimuk third and Dimbool propping up the field.

Also that month W Paxton & Co, music publishers of Melbourne and London were advertising, among their many new publications that they offered for sale, a book entitled Bulch's Cornet Tutor. What is interesting about this, other than that it reveals to us that Tom was as happy to create music tutorials for beginners as he was to produce test selections to try Australia's finest bandsmen, is that Paxton published music created by composers often confused as being Tom Bulch pseudonyms; one example being Theo Bonheur, the pseudonym used by Arthur Charles Rawlings. This may have contributed to some of the confusion surrounding these pseudonyms. It's also interesting to consider that Tom Bulch's influence as a music tutor was extended through such books, beyond all of the pupils that he had taught directly over the years, and into many homes. Many cornet players would have started playing cornet by following Tom's method.

Saturday 19th October, brought an official inspection of the 3rd Battalion Militia by Major-General Downes at Ballarat's Russell Square. Tom and the Militia band provided music for the formal march past of the inspected troops. Then, at last, on Thursday, 24 October, the much anticipated first day of the second South Street Competition Grand Interstate Band Contest arrived. Having adjudicated the previous year, this was to be Tom's first opportunity to experience the competition from a participant's perspective. Though oddly he had also contributed the test piece for the selection contest; "Gems of Meyerbeer." This presented a peculiar situation. How would the bandmaster fare in conducting his own band through his own composition? Though some might have felt that his familiarity with the piece gave him an unfair advantage, it also surely placed more pressure on him to have the band play it perfectly.

The grandstand at the Eastern Oval in Ballarat was once again reportedly 'well patronised' and the lawn 'thronged'. An estimated 2,000 spectators watched the first day unfold. Of the eighteen bands that had registered to compete two, Bendigo and Hobart City, had failed to arrive at all. Nonetheless, the remaining bands presented an extremely strong and seriously competitive field. With the exception of the Locomotive Band of the South Australian Railways, who ironically had been held up owing to a delayed train, the other fifteen bands massed on Sturt Street opposite the office of the Ballarat Star and together as one played the piece "Will o The Wisp" under conductor John Robson. They then, in turn, commenced the march to the Eastern Oval at five-minute intervals. Tom and his 3rd Battalion Militia band were the last of the fifteen to set off.

The judge, concealed inside the hessian tent at the Oval this time was one Lieutenant Herd. A number of perceived 'improvements' were mentioned by reporters writing about this 1901 event, one of which was that the refreshment 'booths' were under the control of the Woman's Christian Temperance Union, most likely assuring the event's organising committee that no alcoholic drinks would be offered for sale to the public during the contest. Anyone hoping for a jolly nip or a hearty ale would be sorely disappointed. Prizes in the main contest this year were £200 for the best band, £75 for second place, £40 for third with a fourth prize of £20.

In a change of format it was decided that rather than have all the bands perform a test piece on day one, the entries would be broken into three groups that would each render different combinations of the test piece, own choice selection and quickstep march across the three days. This somewhat more complicated programme meant that each of the three days of the contest had equal significance, greater variation to watch, and could have been made in the hope that it might improve upon the previous year's dwindling attendances on days two and three. Tom and the 3rd Battalion Militia Band were drawn to be in the group that would play their own choice selection and quickstep on the second day two and the Meyerbeer test piece on day three.

As each day at the Oval came to a close, the points awarded by the judge were once again locked away to avoid being leaked to bands or the press and to maintain suspense whilst denying any psychological advantage to bands that had scored well that day. The points would be totalled and sorted, and the winner revealed, at the end of the third day only. After the test selections on day one, some variety was offered during a brief interval in the form of a callisthenics display by eight boys of the St Augustine's Orphanage, which was followed by the first round of the quickstep march contest, again featuring only the first band group. The day's proceedings were closed by a massing of bandsmen present to play "Will o' The Wisp" again under conductor Robson.

Day two of the contest brought Tom's first opportunity to show what his band could do through the performance their own choice test selection, for which he had chosen his own arrangement of the works of Lohengrin. The draw had resulted in Tom first having to stand by and hear James Scarff and the Ballarat City Brass Band play his "Gems of Meyerbeer." Tom would almost certainly wish to better that band's performance, particularly with this being his own musical arrangement. According to the writer from the Ballarat Star, the Ballarat City Band's playing of the piece seemed to go well:

> "Bandmaster Scarff had his forces well in hand, and his indications were clearly and crisply taken up, the attack being admirable throughout. Tempo was a trifle slower than that adopted by most of the other bands, and if there was any error in the reading of the piece it was that there was a little too much soft music."

On the afternoon Tom's 3rd Battalion Militia Band produced their quickstep march piece, for which he had chosen his own "The Commanding Officer's Parade"; which was described as:

> "a composition marked with well-marked lines and in every way adapted for the purpose for which it was written. The band

turned out in first-class order, uniforms and instruments being clean and well cared for. The men marched in excellent lines with intervals well marked, but they finished the 100 yards slightly under contract time. Their wheeling and counter-marching were done with splendid precision, the lines being splendidly maintained."

Being, by their very nature, a military band, this section of the contest was the 3rd Militia's chance to really shine, and they had largely taken it well. On the evening, Tom and his band were to offer their performance of the own choice test piece they had selected. It was reported thus:

"The first movement, after the opening gave the cornets an excellent, opportunity for a display, of which they fully availed themselves. This was followed by a full band movement, which in turn was succeeded by a pretty effect, in which the horns and euphonium showed to advantage. An excellent euphonium solo played with good delicacy of feeling showed what that instrument is capable of in the treatment of soft music, and another horn and euphonium duet was rendered with considerable taste. This was followed by a piano passage, in which the trombone was used very effectively. Taken as a whole, the band gave an excellent rendering of the piece, though they have been heard to better advantage in it. The music was capitally balanced, and light and shade were used with considerable judgment. Though the band discoursed plenty of soft music, there was an absence of the pianissimo playing by some and the balance of tone was well maintained."

Throughout the weekend Tom had plenty of opportunities to hear some of his own compositions played. In the quickstep contest on day two the Albury Band played his "Newcastle" and Eaglehawk his "Constellation." The following day St Arnaud played "Chef D'Oeuvre" and under Scarff the Ballarat City played again the band's legacy favourite "The Typhoon." These latter two marches created during Tom's days back in England showed that they could stand the test of time and compare to many pieces that had been composed since. With many of the other compositions at the contest being of English or European origin, there could be no doubt in Thomas's mind of his position at that time as one of Australia's premier composers of brass band music. On day three, the 3rd Battalion Militia were the second band to play the Meyerbeer test piece with presumed pressure on him to conduct the band well and for them to render it faithfully. The Ballarat Star's account of their performance was as follows.

> "The Third Battalion, under bandmaster T E Bulch, opened very effectively, save that the euphonium soloist was a little "off colour." The cornet solo was much better taken, and the full score music was given with a roundness and evenness of tone that were quite refreshing. The staccato passage was rendered very crisply, and in the various changes that followed a considerable amount of musical expression, the accents being very clearly marked. In one or two parts the band adopted a somewhat different rhythm from that chosen by other bands and as the conductor is the composer it is reasonable to suppose that he carried out his own intentions. Taken altogether, an admirable balance of tone was maintained; the modulations were artistic, and the rendering generally was a very acceptable one."

Despite this review, Tom's efforts and those of his band, were not enough to secure a prize place at the conclusion of the contest. The winners of the selection category, and the prestigious two-hundred pound prize, were the Newcastle City band of New South Wales. Second place was taken by Code's of Melbourne, followed by St Arnaud and Newtown of New South Wales. The 3rd Battalion Militia Band came twelfth and the City of Ballarat second from last. This would have been a blow to the morale of both. There was limited redemption for Tom's band in the Quickstep contest where they were placed third, having scored the joint top marks for their marching and highly for their musical performance. For this they were awarded fifteen pounds. James Scarff's Ballarat City Band improved in this contest too, coming ninth.

The South Street Competitions, of which this was but one part alongside all the other various artistic, musical and literary competitions, had again been a huge spectacle. It concluded with a grand military tattoo that saw an estimated 15,000 people gather at the Oval to celebrate and enjoy the finale. This show featured a display by the Scottish Regiment as well as the 3rd Battalion supported musically by Tom and the band. The main spectacle of this tattoo was a simulated ambush by Boers on a small camp of British soldiers, reprisals for which consisted of a retaliatory attack on a Boer homestead with bombs and fireworks concluding with the capture of the Boer guerrillas and the house being razed to the ground. The band then massed once more to play the National Anthem.

With normality restored to the streets of Ballarat, Thursday, 21 November saw the Militia Band occupy the Rotunda opposite the office of the Ballarat Star to render a number of selections:

> "in a manner which was highly creditable to Bandmaster Bulch, and a source of enjoyment to the large number of listeners."

Then on Saturday, 30 November, the Evening Journal of Adelaide reported as it looked forward to the Australian Natives Association Carnival and Sports in the city, which was scheduled to tale place on 27 January 1902. This event, as well as a new 'cask rolling' contest, also naturally included a brass band contest. The adjudicator for the latter was announced as being Tom Bulch. On 24th December the Evening Post of New Zealand also announced that Tom had been shortlisted as a possible judge for the band contest to be held there in 1902 under the auspices of the North Island Brass Bands Association. It went on to explain that the conclusion would be declared on 4 January. Bandmasters of the bands making up this New Zealand bands association would be balloted to enable the decision.

New Shildon

In 1902, the first of that year's band contests we know George Allan to have been involved in took place on Whit Monday, that being 19 May. This contest was at the village of Howden-le-Wear near the market town of Crook, in County Durham. George had arrived, not to judge, but to compete. He had with him a full complement of his New Shildon Saxhorn Band. Prize money of twenty-four pounds and ten shillings had been put up by the contest's organisers, and that had proved sufficient to attract twelve bands from across the region. The Spennymoor and Sunderland Temperance Bands were there, as were Hebburn Colliery, Charlton's Star of Hope Band, Willington, Cornsay Institute, Butterknowle, Auckland Park, Consett Ironworks, Albert Hill and Hamsteel's. Though these bands had converged upon the village, one person notably not present was the noted contest judge and one-time conductor of the Shaw, Rochdale

Old and Glodwick Bands, Mr Albert Whipp. Two telegrams had arrived from him advising the contest organisers that Whipp had missed his train at two changes en route from Lancashire. This situation had the makings of a catastrophe for the committee. Twelve bands on site, and an anticipating audience, but no judge. What good fortune that one of the conductors present also had a reputation as an experienced contest adjudicator. Step forward Mr George Allan.

Arrangements were agreed, and the New Shildon Saxhorn Band forfeited their opportunity to take part in the contest so that it might go ahead. The Shildon bandsmen were probably quite disappointed in this outcome, having set aside their day and doubtless borne the expense of travel from Shildon. The Howden-le-Wear contest required each of the competing bands to make their best attempt at one from a choice of three selections. These were "Euryanthe," "Songs of Other Days" or "Songs of Shakespeare." Only the Sunderland Temperance chose the latter of the three pieces. The other bands had chosen and rehearsed one of the first two. Having, by due procedure, listened to each band's performance, George awarded the first prize of ten pounds to the band from Hebburn Colliery, with Charlton's and Willington taking joint second place and Cornsay and Spennymoor fourth and fifth respectively. In addition, he had prizes to award to the best euphonium player, which went to the player from Charlton's Star of Hope. The prize for best horn went to Hebburn Colliery, best trombone player Sunderland Temperance and best cornet to a player from Cornsay. It hadn't turned out to be the day that George had anticipated when he boarded the train at New Shildon station that morning, but he had saved the day by standing in, as the best man on the spot, to ensure that the contest could go ahead satisfactorily.

Incidentally, Mr Whipp did get his opportunity to judge at the Howden-le-Wear band contest. He was engaged for the subsequent years; 1903, 1904 and 1905. It would have been nice to think the organisers might have considered George again, but that organising committee stuck to their original conviction that Albert Whipp was the best man for the job. Though George had experience and an increasing reputation as a composer, Whipp's record as a contest-winning conductor in his own right was better. Perhaps that was the decisive factor, or the added influence of his regular advertisements appearing in Wright and Round's Brass Band News.

Despite this, George had a busy year in 1902. His next engagement was 17 May, for a small band contest a short journey away by train, in the market town of Barnard Castle in Teesdale. Only four bands were taking part in this contest, part of a series by the Teesside Brass Band League. The five contests in that series were held with the objective of winning a silver cup which, if won two years in succession or three times non-serially, would become the property of a band. This contest being on a Saturday, a large crowd had gathered in the grounds of the town's castle ruin, after which the place was named, to see each of the bands perform a march and then a set of waltzes. After George had listened intently to each performance, noting down the points earned by the bands, he awarded the first prize for the march category to the band from the village of Butterknowle followed by St Helen's and Barnard Castle in second and third respectively. In the performing of waltzes, Middleton-in-Teesdale was the victorious band.

Next, on Saturday, 17 June, George made another short trip to Middlestone Moor near Spennymoor. Here he had been requested to adjudicate at another contest organised by the Middlestone Moor Literary Institute. This was held, along with an accompanying sporting event, on a field conveniently sited adjacent to the Institute building. The weather on this occasion proved 'inauspicious for a sporting event' and consequently, the attendance was poor despite the forty-five pounds offered in prizes across all events. Of this fifteen pounds had been set aside for the band contest, attracting six bands. As usual, there was a pre-determined test piece, which was William Rimmer's coronation themed selection "Sons of Brittania." The event also included a quickstep contest. After declaring the final points scored, George consequently awarded the selection first prize of eight pounds to the Cornsay band and their conductor Benjamin Gordon. This band had a particularly good day as they were also triumphant in the quickstep contest. Furthermore George also awarded their euphonium player a silver medal for being best. Willington came second in the test piece, and the third prize was divided between Spennymoor Temperance and Darlington Temperance.

The summer of 1902 brought with it changes in George's day to day working life. For many years he had spent his days in the Blacksmiths Department at the Shildon Works alongside a master blacksmith acting as his striker, wielding the larger hammer and acting on the instructions of the former. According to the wages books from the works, his role changed on 5 July to that of wagon painter. We cannot know for certain whether this change was his own choice, or imposed upon him by the management at the works. At the time he'd have been thirty-eight years of age, so would surely still have had the strength needed to continue as a striker. We do know however, that as a consequence, his pay dropped slightly to a rate of four shillings and fourpence. It would be nice to think that as George had been doing well as a composer of brass band music and occasional contest judge, perhaps with enough money from those activities supplementing his wage so as to make this a viable choice for him. It's more likely, though, that this career change was related to a large scale reorganisation of the North Eastern Railway's workforce that was announced in the May of 1902. The company had three major works sites conducting building and repairs of company rolling stock. These were located at Darlington, York and, of course, Shildon. On 8 May, it was announced in the regional press that the engineering work was to be reorganised so that it would take place at only two sites. Building and maintenance work in Darlington was to cease, and fabrication buildings there were to be converted to locomotive running sheds of a size sufficient to house a hundred locomotive engines. The Darlington site, however, had a sizeable and skilled manufacturing workforce, and to lose this resource would have been a highly undesirable outcome. Consequently the North Eastern Railway also planned the transition so that all engineering workers from Darlington that had been involved in the building and repair of carriages would be transferred to the York works. Likewise, those that had been engaged in the repair and building of wagons would relocate to New Shildon. This would substantially increase the workforce at Shildon, and result in the redesignation of some of the workers already there to new roles. The specific influx of workers from the Darlington Blacksmith's department was what most likely saw George reallocated to the painting department.

If George had hoped that his overture for the nation's new monarch would be timely, in light of the forthcoming Coronation celebration, he was to be a little disappointed. The Coronation of King Edward was originally scheduled to take place on 26th

June. Community committees across the land frantically planned the royal celebration of a lifetime for that day, but on 24 June, the heir apparent was diagnosed with appendicitis and the ceremony confirming his ascension postponed. Plans were put on hold as the nation eagerly waited to see what would happen next. In the meantime, George had another contest to attend. This time he was heading east to Eston, then a village just south of the industrial port town of Middlesborough. This contest took place on Saturday, 2 August. Little published detail is available to describe the proceedings, but we know that only three bands competed that day. A band of employees from Cleveland Steel Works, the Charlton's Star of Hope Band and the band from Cockerton near Darlington. The first of these three emerged as winners, with both of the the other two tied for second place.

Two weeks after King Edward VII was declared ill with appendicitis, he was described in the press as sitting up in bed again smoking a cigar, and declared to be medically out of danger. The long-awaited Coronation was re-scheduled for 9 August 1902 and those celebration committees, across both nation and empire, dusted off their plans. It would be nice to be able to state how many copies of George's "King Edward" overture had been sold through the Standard Brass Band Journal in the period since it was published, but that is a statistic that eludes us. Of course, George wasn't the only composer to create a celebratory coronation composition. It is quite possible that, having never known another monarch in his lifetime, he truly intended it to be a tribute to the new king. Had naming the overture for the monarch been merely a marketing ploy to boost interest in buying the piece it may not have been the greatest approach. Interest in the piece seems to have been quite short lived, probably due to it being very much 'of the moment'. There are reports of bands playing it throughout 1902. In June the Birstwith Brass Band played "King Edward" at the Sunday School Festival and Anniversary event that took place at Shaw Mills, and the Band of the Ashburton Company 5th Volunteer Battalion, Devonshire Regiment performed it at a cottage garden show at Broadhempston. Later in the year it was reported as having been given airings at Horton, Axminster, and Cockermouth. We'd imagine too, that George himself would have ensured that it was heard in the Shildons, where a grand celebration was held with temporary triumphal arches being erected at the end of a number of the principal streets dedicated to the new King and his wife Alexandra. A number of photographs from that day still exist showing the streets decorated appropriately. though we've not seen any accounts of how else the day was celebrated.

Above: Main Street in Shildon decorated to celebrate the coronation of King Edward VII - was George's "King Edward" performed that day?

At the beginning of September, the annual Brandon Colliery Exhibition was held once again on the fields adjacent to the colliery. On the occasion the weather was perfect and under blue skies thousands were reported to have flocked to the "rich, unique and most extensive exhibition." The reporter from the Durham County Advertiser went on to say that:

> "...attractions were of a varied character, for in addition to the usual display of flowers, fruits and vegetables, there was a band contest in which the best bands not only locally, but from a considerable distance, were engaged. A rich feast of music was thus provided, and which it is needless to say, was duly appreciated by the many hundreds of people gathered around the bandstand."

Ten bands competed that day and, once again, it was George Allan concealed in a judging enclosure who would decide which was best in both selection and march categories. In the former, once the points scored by each band had been totalled and sorted, it was the band from Cleveland that finished top of the pile to take the main prize. They were followed by Cockerton and Willington in that order. In the march contest the Cleveland band again triumphed, with Cockerton Band once more placed second.

Any reported appearances of the New Shildon Saxhorn Band are few and far between by this time. They may have been involved in those Coronation day celebrations but nothing has been found to prove this. In light of the advertisement we saw in 1900 containing their appeal for a new bandmaster, and given the time George must have been spending composing and judging at contests, the band may have been losing momentum. There is one engagement that is recorded, which took place in October of 1902 and begins with a sad occurrence at Eldon Colliery. A boy had been killed in an accident in the pit. Tradition was held in those days that when there had been a death the pit was not worked for the remainder of that day. On this occasion, the management had broken that custom, possibly on account of the accident taking place late in the afternoon. This deeply upset the mineworkers, and the next day not a man turned in for work in protest. Naturally, the management disputed the workers right to do this and issued a court summons covering all four-hundred men. The summons was returnable at Bishop Auckland Petty Sessions on the morning of 30 October. With no choice but to attend, the miners wanted to make a show of it, and arranged a march for that day as a demonstration of their solidarity in the matter. They engaged George Allan and the New Shildon Saxhorn Band to lead the way. On the day of the court appearance, the band and pitmen assembled in Shildon and marched in procession all the way to Bishop Auckland, a distance of about three miles. They arrived at Bishop Auckland at about half past ten in the morning where the streets were lined with thousands of people; some in support, others simply curious. When the procession reached the principal trading strip of Newgate Street the band began to play the "Dead March" from Saul. A number of pit lads now led the procession wearing white cloaks, bringing a sense of sombre theatre to the occasion. The band was followed by the column of mining men dressed mainly in black. Their Miner's Association Lodge banner was paraded, draped partially with black cloth and ribbon as was the custom whenever there had been a fatality at a mine. The vicinity of the courthouse was crowded throughout the hearing. The miners were represented by Mr E Shortt, barrister-at-law, his fee most likely having been funded by the Durham Miner's Association. The judge agreed that rather than try each of the 400 men individually, to try the first and apply the same ruling to all the defendants. The Bench, typically and predictably being men of similar class and stature, found in favour of the mine management and owners and fined each man five shillings plus legal costs. Though not miners, George and his bandsmen stood alongside them that day and would have shared their collective hurt and disappointment at the outcome.

Ballarat

Returning to Australia, we mentioned earlier that a ballot of bandmasters was being held to determine who would judge at the New Zealand North Island band contest, and that the results were to be announced in early January of 1902. Tom Bulch lost by two votes to the Wellington-based judge J. Otto Schwartz, who had attained the support and votes of seven of the association's bandmasters. Despite this, Tom too was in for a busy year.

On 25 January 1902 the Australian Natives Association Band Contest and Sports Carnival commenced in Adelaide, South Australia. The arrangements were announced to the public, via the press, from as early as the 4th in a bid to ensure that as many people knew to set aside those days to attend the grand contest. The bands, the announcements read, would assemble at Victoria Square on the first of the two-days of the event, for a march to the city's Jubilee Oval, the chosen location for the contest. Starting on a Saturday, the contest would be punctuated by a free Sunday, continuing instead on the Monday. A grand finale had been planned for the event, in which the competing bands would mass together as one to play Tom's "Hopetoun" march. The contest had been planned along similar lines to the Ballarat contest held at the end of the previous year, with bands playing the test selection and own choice pieces on alternate days, so as to give variance to maintain interest from the public over the full duration of the contest. Tom had also been engaged to judge. The secretary of the organising committee declared this fact in the Adelaide press as a strength of this particular contest, partly in response to criticisms of arrangements for previous contests there.

On Thursday, 16 January, a parade of the 3rd Battalion took place in Ballarat, after which the men of battalion retired to the Buck's Head Hotel to present a framed group of photographs of the band to Drum Major Thornton, as a mark of gratitude for his services during the South Street Competitions and throughout his sixteen years service with the band. To conclude the evening songs were sung by a number of members of the company, each accompanied by Tom Bulch at the piano.

On the day before the ANA Adelaide band contest, Tom arrived in Adelaide, disembarking there from the express train from Melbourne. A former resident of Adelaide Street in New Shildon, the town that once stabled Timothy Hackworth's early Stockton and Darlington Railway locomotive, 'Adelaide,' he had arrived once again at this far better known namesake. His expected arrival was of such import to the band contest arrangements that the timing was announced in advance by the local press.

On the next day, proceedings began at two o'clock in the afternoon in the Victoria Hall with a contest concentrating on trombone solos and cornet solos. Of the fifteen cornet players that entered, only ten appeared to give their performance. Similarly, of the ten trombone players registered as entrants, only five actually took part. The test piece for the cornet solo was Balfe's "When Other Lips," while the trombonists were tested with "The Artist". The full band contest took place in the evening from eight o'clock in the evening, with the afternoon having been reserved for a series of associated sporting events including bicycle and foot racing. Concerned over the condition of the lighting at the venue, the committee had organised for the placement of three acetylene lamps to ensure that the fading evening light would not spoil the spectacle. They had also placed an extra one-thousand seats in front of the bandstand in anticipation of an exceptionally large crowd. At the appointed time the bands, as planned and declared in the press so many days earlier, gathered at the base of the statue of Queen Victoria at Victoria Square. They then, following the ANA Corps, marched one by one at three-minute intervals to the Jubilee Exhibition Gardens. Six bands had entered, but only five were represented. Rigg's Gawler Band, The Adelaide Military Band,

Moonta Mines Model Band, Port Adelaide City Band and the Central Mission Band. The Advertiser of Adelaide offered a description of the scene:

> "The streets were lined with people, who gave the bandsmen a hearty reception as they marched past playing a martial air, and the Exhibition Gardens and terraces were crowded in anticipation of the novel and interesting competition. The pavilion in the centre of the gardens had been enlarged for the accommodation of the bandsmen, and on the east side at a distance of about 25 yards was placed a small tent, from which the judge listened to the music without being able to see the players. Notices were prominently placed requesting those present to remain quiet during the playing of the various selections and also asking them not to mention the name of the band performing in the hearing of the judge."

Riggs's Gawler Band were the first to perform and, having the right to choose to play any composition they desired for this stage of the contest, chose a selection by Verdi. The Military Band, second to appear, also chose Verdi; a selection from "Il Trovatore" to be precise. The Central Mission Band played third with selections from "Attila." The Port Adelaide City Band next, with a selection from Wagner's "Tannhauser" followed finally by the Moonta Mines Model Band airing yet another Verdi selection. After that formal part of the competition had closed, and while Tom was privately summarising the points scored, each band contributed a march to fill the anticipatory pause. There had been an expectation on the part of the organisers that Tom would then conclude the first day by writing up the points scored so far on a blackboard for all to see, however he was not happy to do so, preferring to keep the scores secret so as not to break the tension and carry the sense of anticipation over to the following day. The organisers remained resolute, however, and, after something of a scene on account of the points totals having been already locked away, Tom retrieved them and they were announced. At that stage, with the mandatory test piece still to be played, Rigg's Gawler Band was ahead, which was, according to one journalist present, a popular decision.

As explained before, Tom's Sunday was free of any judging responsibilities and we know little of how it was spent. Then Monday afternoon arrived, bringing with it contests for Euphonium solo and brass quartettes, after which the bands met once again at the Queen's statue on Victoria Square for a second parade to the Exhibition Gardens at the Oval. This time the bands would be expected to play their best rendition of the official contest test piece, an overture entitled "Dramatique" based upon the work of Alberto Zelman. As you might expect by now, it had been arranged especially for the contest by Tom himself. A commentator in the Adelaide Evening Journal declared "Dramatique" to be:

> "…a melodious and agreeable piece of music which while of no great intrinsic value is evidently a severe and thorough test of the capabilities of a modern wind band and the powers of its principal soloists. Indeed so difficult is this composition that even its interpretation by the prizewinners, meritorious as it was, came a good way short of perfection."

After all attempts at the test pieces had been offered, and during the build-up to the announcement of the winners, the bands combined as advertised to play Bulch's "Hopetoun" march, which was named after the small town in Victoria territory that lay almost equidistantly between Adelaide and Melbourne. The contest result, based upon the totals of points Tom awarded to each of the bands respective of the merits of their playing, proved popular with the audience that day as they concurred that Rigg's Gawler Band deserved to come top of the group again. Over the two selection rounds their combined points made them clear overall winners of the fifty pounds top prize. The South Australian Military Band achieved second place, Central Mission Band third, Port Adelaide fourth and Moonta Mines narrowly bottom of the pile. Finally, the proceedings were closed traditionally, with 120 of the bandsmen playing the National Anthem under the baton of G H Williams, bandmaster of the Moonta Mines Band. On Tom's own performance and conduct as judge of the contest, the Advertiser declared its satisfaction:

> "In no single instance has Mr Bulch failed to give entire satisfaction in allotting the first prizes, and in only two cases was there any question with regard to his second awards, which is a very good average."

Afterwards, both the Express and Telegraph, and the Advertiser, printed a brief interview with Tom about the proceedings, which is a rare opportunity to hear his outlook on band contests 'in his own voice', albeit via the pen of a reporter:

"A CHAT WITH MR BULCH. Mr T E Bulch, the well-known regimental bandmaster and composer of Ballarat, who acted as judge in connection with the band contest promoted by the metropolitan committee of the Australian Natives' Association, left Adelaide for Ballarat on Tuesday afternoon. Speaking to a representative of 'The Advertiser' before his departure, Mr. Bulch said: 'Of course I have yet to send in my official report to the committee, but I may say that the contest on the whole was a very good one, and it was certainly carried through in a manner which reflected the greatest credit upon all concerned. The management of the contest is all the more praiseworthy because the affair was somewhat in the nature of an experiment, but I feel sure it will only be the forerunner of many such successful competitions.'

Do you think these contests do good? 'I am sure of it,' was Mr Bulch's reply, 'and it is owing to the competitions held in Ballarat and Melbourne that many excellent bands which previously were very weak and unsatisfactory have been brought forward. With regard to your local organisations, I think Riggs's Gawler Band has improved quite 100 per cent since it entered the lists in Ballarat. The Military Band is also very good, but I look upon the Central Mission as the coming band in South Australia.'

And what about the playing of the test-piece? 'Well,' replied Mr Bulch, 'I fancy some of the bands thought they had a soft thing' in Zelman's overture 'Dramatique,' but they were greatly mistaken, as it was specially written as a catch piece. None of the bands were really up to the mark although if the Military Band had had its full complement of reed instruments it would have been better. The interpretation of the test piece given by this band was the best of the lot, the tempo was good and the general effect excellent, but the Gawler Band instruments were more in tune, and their actual playing was better than that of their immediate rivals. The matter of interpretation and tempo, of course, rests with the bandmasters. With regard to the playing of the Central Mission Band in the test piece, it must be said that the bass was rather coarse and vulgar, and the bandmaster was very much to blame at one point in the last movement, where he substituted 6-8 for 2-4 time. I was very sorry to see the Loco, and Police Bands stand out of the competition, as the efforts made by the metropolitan committee were deserving of better entries and support.'

'With reference to the solo work,' added Mr Bulch, in answer to a question, 'the cornet and trombone solos were very good, the former particularly so, but only two or three of the euphonium solos passed muster. The brass quartets were also excellent. Of course,' said Mr. Bulch in conclusion, 'the position of a judge is a very unpleasant one, and he cannot give universal satisfaction, but I have been acting in that capacity in all the States – Victoria, New South Wales, Queensland, Tasmania, and now South Australia, as well as in New Zealand-and so I take little notice of adverse criticism, being conscious that my judgments are thoroughly impartial, and as strictly fair and correct as my capacity admits.'"

It's interesting to reflect that even by 1902, over fifty years into the era of the brass band movement, the ideal format for brass band contests was still a matter of debate; and how Tom and to an extent George played a part in that evolution, though the former in Australia was clearly much more influential. After the contest, as he usually would, Tom collated his final narrative and comments on the performances of each band and submitted them to the competition committee. They were subsequently published in a number of the Adelaide newspapers, from 17 February onwards, for all to read.

Through the Ballarat Star of 13 March 1902, we see relatively rare evidence of Tom composing for a slightly different musical format. We know that Thomas played the violin, though much of his published output is focused on brass or the piano. A notice in this newspaper declared that he had created an arrangement for string band entitled "Star of the Season: Dolly Grey" specifically for the Ballarat drapery and clothing company, James Tyler and Co. They had, that month, arranged a show to exhibit the new goods for the Australian autumn and winter season. The collection included material, millinery, hats, furs and jackets. To brighten up the launch event Tyler's had engaged McNamara's String Band to play at their arcade, and this special commissioned arrangement was one of the many pieces played.

Throughout early 1902, probably much to the annoyance of the band, and bandmaster James Scarff, the Ballarat Star still on occasion referred to the Ballarat City Band as being Bulch's Model Band. Perhaps, on account of it having been such for so long, members of the public would too, and it may have proven a matter of habit. There may even have been those who felt the renaming to be a mistake. Whatever the case, that particular band was finding it harder than it should have been to stamp its new identity on the city.

Above: James Scarff, former New Shildon youth band colleague of Tom and George who had travelled to Australia with Tom in 1884 and later became bandmaster of Tom's band in Ballarat.

In April, on the 17th, Tom and the 3rd Battalion Band had the unfortunate duty of attending another funeral, this time for Mr James Parkinson, who had been a member of A Company of the Battalion. He had met with an unfortunate, and fatal, accident the Monday before. As was customary, the band played the "Dead March" on the solemn parade to the cemetery where addresses were given before a firing party fired three volleys over the grave.

In May 1902, the last of the Boers holding out against the British Empire forces surrendered leading to the Treaty of Vereeniging being signed on the 31st of the month. As part of the treaty the British offered what were felt to be relatively generous peace terms to the Boers. The South African Republic and Orange Free State were now no longer independent republics and instead officially became part of the Union of South Africa. When news of this reached Ballarat the President of the Ballarat Exhibition Commissioners gave 'an entertainment' at the Exhibition Buildings in honour of the declaration of peace. Tom Bulch was one of a number of named invitees, along with the commanding officer of the 3rd Battalion Militia. A number of toasts were proposed throughout the proceedings, including those raised to "The British Empire and her Dependencies," "The 3rd Battalion," which had of course seen the sacrifice of a number of sons of Ballarat to this particular war, and "the Chairman" of the Exhibition Committee for his part in organising the tribute. Across the city, various societies separately contributed to the peace celebrations among streets draped once again with patriotic bunting.

Despite this continuation of his hard-earned relative high social standing, ongoing strong sales of his compositions, and the pay he received as bandmaster of the 3rd Battalion Militia, Tom's family finances continued to see costs outweigh his personal means. On the 24 June, the Ballarat Star once again published a small piece that would have caused Tom some significant embarrassment:

> "A case of some interest engaged the attention of the magistrates at the City Court yesterday morning. It was an application under the Fraudulent Debtors' Act, in which Mr J. Carthew was the judgment creditor, and Mr Thomas Bulch the judgment debtor. The latter was proceeded against in order to ascertain whether he had not been in a position to satisfy an order of the court, made some time ago, for £11 13s, only £2 of which had been paid, leaving £9 13s still due. Eventually, after the chairman had expressed the opinion that there had been no extravagance on the part of the judgment debtor, an

order was made for the payment of the amount by easy instalments."

A further article in the same issue adds to the potential embarassment of the situation by revealing significant detail of Thomas's earnings at the time, something few people would really relish being made public at any point in their lifetime. To be reading this as part of a study into the lifetime of a man over a hundred years later offers a very useful perspective into the day to day difficulties Thomas might face in this period. The article reads:

"A BUTCHER'S BILL. Proceedings under the Fraudulent Debtors' Act were taken against Thos. Bulch. An order was made by the court some time ago against him for £11 10s in favour of Mr J Carthew, butcher. Mr C Hamilton appeared for the judgment creditor. The judgment debtor stated that the order had been made in his absence from Ballarat. From November 1901 to January 1902, he was receiving £2 a week from the militia, and since the 1st February he was only getting 25s. He also received either £10 or £12 from the South Street competitions, but that was before November — before the order was made. He did not keep any books, and would not swear when he had received it. Since November 1901 he had not instructed any pupils at all; in fact, he very seldom did any teaching. In January he received £17 at Adelaide for judging in a band contest there. Mr Hamilton—Will you swear that it was not more than £17. Witness— No, I won't; but I am almost sure that was how much I got. Have you had any money from any other source? No. I have many and many a time done things for charity, but I never got anything for that. Witness was allowed time to go and find when he received the money from South Street. On returning he said he had found that he was paid before November. He had to pay all his expenses when he went to Adelaide, his train fare, his hotel expenses, etc. The latter amounted to £3 3s a week, for when engaged in these matters — in acting as a judge — he could not live in a sixpenny hash shop. Regarding the debt, he admitted it, but then there were a lot of lawyers' expenses. He was quite willing to pay the money. All the furniture was in possession of his wife at the present time. Mr Hamilton pressed to have the judgment debtor ordered to pay a small sum per week. Mr Shoppee failed to see that he had been guilty of any extravagance. For a man to keep a wife and five children on the amount he had, it would not allow of any saving. It was decided to make an order, starting a month hence, to pay 10s a month for the first six months, and after that 5s a week."

Can you imagine being the subject of such a brutal public assessment of your personal finances in your local press, and how that might have made you feel when you next set foot outside of your home? This would have been devastating to Tom's reputation and resulted in the levelling of all kinds of accusations and criticism in public or, more likely, behind closed doors. From a biographer's perspective though, such detail is a regrettable blessing. There are a number of particularly interesting aspects over and above the detailed breakdown of Thomas's income during this period. For example, that his wife Eliza is the possessor of the furniture; a sensible measure in that by separating the ownership and isolating them from Thomas's liabilities, these home comforts have been protected. Another is the involvement of Mr Shoppee who we know from much earlier newspaper reports to have been an official with a supporting interest in Bulch's Model Band, so perhaps was disposed to offer Tom some sympathy. A third interesting aspect of this legislative interview is the sense that we get from Tom that as a respectable contest judge he had to maintain an image and standard by choosing the kind of accommodation those people that engaged you would expect you to use, as opposed to the 'sixpenny hash shop'.

We get something of a sense that Tom was still finding it something of a struggle to break free of his humble origins as a former railway engineer, born of a modest family in a small industrial town. Despite the helping hands and goodwill he had encountered along his life to this point, the hard work, long hours and endless self promotion was still no substitute for a comfortable start in life when it came to finding your place among the ranks of a perceived respectable society. We begin to get an understanding, perhaps, of why Tom was always looking to take on that one additional responsibility that always seemed to stretch his personal resources, time and availability, just an inch too far to make it work out. It's all the more heartbreaking to have seen how over the decades up to this point Tom had never left any evidence or impression of being a ruthless and selfish man. A proud one perhaps, but he had always been quick to throw his lot in with whatever charitable endeavour was current, and to look backward to help those that had experienced misfortune or hardship. Even by seeking to improve their musicianship it seems to me that Tom simply wanted those pupils and bandsmen to tread the path of aspiration which he himself had discovered, or had shown to him, decades earlier.

On 26 June, we see mention of yet another new band associated with Tom in Ballarat; an Operatic Band. Was this a case of him taking on yet more work again in order to make the instalment payments on his outstanding debt. Another possibility, though less likely, is that he had invited his former Operatic band from Prahran into Ballarat to perform. Whatever the case, we're advised that this band offered a programme of music at eight o'clock in the evening on that date from the balcony of the Commonwealth Hotel on Post Office Place in Ballarat. Around a month later, we see a notice in the Ballarat Star that Tom was taking another band under his experienced wing:

> "The Railway Band, which has been in recess for some time, will meet again this week to resume practice. At the meeting, the appointment of Mr T. Bulch, as bandmaster, will be confirmed, and it is intended that the band will appear more often in public than it has previously done."

One does have to wonder how one person could have the energy to accommodate all this work without jeopardising any one of these projects by being spread too sparsely. Additionally, he continued composing music, resulting in new pieces for brass band emerging throughout this period. These included a patriotic selection, quite possibly inspired by the end of the Boer War, entitled "The Empire" which was quickly picked up by, among others, the Maclean Brass Band and his ever faithful friend Sam Lewin's Bathurst District Brass Band who included the composition in their programme for a concert to celebrate the Coronation of King Edward VII.

Despite just having revived the Ballarat Railway Band, or perhaps because of it, given that he said himself that contests were the best way to improve a band, Tom had them work hard to test their mettle at a band contest. He entered them for the next upcoming band contest in Ballarat, where they would be pitched against the abilities of the Queenstown (Tasmania) Band, Hobart Garrison, Launceston City, Code's Melbourne Brass, Geelong Town, Geelong Orphanage, Hopetoun, Ballarat City,

Lord Nelson, Soldier's Hill, Prout's, Benalla, Newcastle City, Loco Band, Gawler, Boulder City and Invercargill bands. This was as stellar a field of Australian bands as you could have hoped to experience at that time, and to do well at such a contest would be a serious mountain to climb in the short time that Thomas had been in charge of this hitherto dormant band. It would definitely require some hard work.

Before that Ballarat contest took place, however, Tom had another one to attend and judge. The eighth day of October 1902 saw the commencement of the Benalla Band Contest, some way north-east of Ballarat, as part of the annual Benalla Show. We're informed by the press that the band contest, along with the 'hunter's trials,' were the two eye-catching aspects of the show even though only three of the four bands that had originally entered turned up to take part. The missing band that day was the Albury Town Band, a name that would soon take on a new relevance in this story. This contest at this show sounds much more like the type of band contest that George Allan had found himself being engaged to adjudicate over in Britain. Certainly not as prestigious as the grand band contests Tom had been called to in the principal cities. Of the three competing bands, the Benalla Mechanics Band, Wangaratta and Border United Corowa Band, the latter chose to play Thomas's own "Chef D'Ouevre" in the march contest. This may have worked against them, given that he knew the piece inside out. In his adjudicating notes, he criticised the playing of the bass horn section in the opening bars, noting that they made the same mistake on each of the three occasions throughout the playing of the piece where these musical phrases appeared. After both march and selection were taken into account, the Benalla Band came out as having been best in Tom's opinion, capturing the first prize of thirty pounds. When Tom's judging notes were later published in the local press it would seem that the Wangaratta Band particularly were hit hard by his criticisms, and a letter quickly appeared in the Benalla Standard of 17 October 1902:

> "The Late Band Contest. — A correspondent, signing himself 'Tempo,' thus writes to the ' Wangaratta Chronicle' in reference to Mr Bulch's remarks on the late band contest: — 'To those of us who take an interest in our band, and who thought the bandsmen were making fair, if not rapid, progress (first under the teaching of Mr Webber, and, more recently and up to the present, under Mr Lupp), the biting and crushingly adverse

criticism of the judge at the above contest (Mr. Bulch, of Ballarat) comes as a severe disappointment. If after such a long tuition on the newest and best of instruments found by our public, added to the steady drain on our public for maintenance, the sum total of progress amounts (even in a measure) to such a summing up by the judge as 'out of tune', 'out of time', 'not properly understood', 'tamely played', 'amateurish', 'scramble to finish', etc., is it not time the band committee met with a determination to discover and sit down hard on any cause or causes that tend to retard the advancement of our band?"

A few days later, another correspondent wrote to the same newspaper in defence of the besieged Wangaratta band, implying that Thomas's critique of the band had more to do with a personal rebuff at some point prior to the contest:

"THE LATE BAND CONTEST. In reply to the letter signed 'Tempo'' commenting upon the performance of the Wangaratta band at the recent contest, 'Enthusiast' contributes the following to the last issue of 'The Chronicle.' Noticing a letter by 'Tempo' in your Wednesday's issue, I think it is only fair to Mr Lupp and his bandsmen to offer an explanation. Being a musical enthusiast and supporter of the band, I visited Benalla and heard the various bands play, and the general opinion among those present was that there were very few points between the three bands; in fact, the rendering of the march by the Wangaratta band made them favourites for that piece. The judge's remarks are very misleading and would lead one to believe that the performance of the Wangaratta band was bad and out of tune throughout. This is as absurd as it is annoying. The general performance was almost void of errors, and the tone of the band was considered even better than the winning band. The leading cornet of the latter band was so much out of tune that he had to change his instrument during the performance of the selection. Such remarks as 'tame', 'out of tune', 'amateurish', etc., are not exactly mistakes or blunders, and therefore can be referred to without fear of challenge. Any thoughtful person will immediately notice that the judge's remarks are not in a friendly strain, and are not given with the idea of instruction, as they should be; and I unhesitatingly say that they display some spitefulness. To give reasons for this would be rather personal, but I understand Mr Bulch s application for the position of bandmaster to the Wangaratta band was rejected in favour of Mr Lupp. The remarks on the performance of the march by Wangaratta band ran thus: 'Nice, clean, crisp style of playing'. It seems incredible to me that these good points should vanish so suddenly in the performance of the selection, where I presume the band would be able to show with better advantage. It may be news to your readers that the judge was well aware of what pieces the bands intended playing. I have procured a copy of the Wangaratta selection, and find on comparing same with judge's remarks that several movements have not been referred to. I have called on the bandmaster and asked him for information re this. He informs me, smilingly, that they were well-played movements. It is strange that these movements should not have been dealt with by the judge, and this gives room for further thought. In conclusion, I must add that notwithstanding the adverse remarks of the judge I am of the opinion that our band is better than ever, and should like to see the members try their luck at Sydney contest in December next. In reference to the above statement concerning the exchange of cornets, Mr Pleloung explains that it was not due, as stated, to the cornet being out of tune, but owing to the valves of the instrument sticking. He handed the instrument to one of the bandsmen, and after a few bars, it having been made alright, he took it again and finished playing with that instrument, which goes to show that it was not out of tune."

From these letters we get a sense of the emotions roused by the judge's remarks at a band contest, and the politics that prevail in the brass band movement arguably even to this day. The implication in revealing that Thomas knew which pieces each band was to play in advance, was a suggestion that he would then know which band was playing and be less than impartial as a consequence. Of course, to judge how well a band play a piece the judge would have to be familiar with it, and would customarily have a full band score before them as the piece is played. When a judge such as Tom committed his comments to public scrutiny then what could often follow might be, as we have seen, a critique by interested parties every bit as strong as that applied to the playing of the music by the bands themselves, and the insinuations of letters like this had the potential to wound a judge's reputation every bit as much as a poor review for a band. You can equally see how it might be beneficial for an outspoken contest adjudicator to have a thick skin. The incident continued to spark further correspondence, though this time in support of Tom and his capability and integrity as a contest adjudicator. I've included it here not just in the interest of balance, but because it reveals a little more about the process of contest judging and give some contemporary explanation on the nature of the judge's report:

> "TO THE EDITOR. Sir.— In your last issue, you give publicity to a letter by 'Enthusiast', from the Wangaratta Chronicle, dealing with the Judge's decision in the above contest. As steward for the band contest, there are several statements contained that I must, in fairness to the local band, the judge and the society, under whose auspices the contest was held, endeavour to refute. I take objection, first, to the statement that "the judge was well aware what pieces the bands intended playing." Certainly, the full scores for the four selections and the four marches were forwarded to the judge some days before the contest, but he did not know the selection or march that any individual band played. As steward, I met Mr Bulch at the station, took him to my own home, to his hotel and into the tent provided for his use, before any of the bands commenced their performance, and before the draw took place for places. He was quite unaware that only three bands were competing until the third march had been played, so much so that when I called for the No. 1 band for the selection he rang for the fourth march to be played first, showing to any fair-minded individual conclusively that 'Enthusiast's' statement is utterly without foundation. Again, 'Enthusiast' thinks it strange that movements well played should not have been dealt with by the judge. He is apparently ignorant of the method adopted by most competent judges for deciding a contest. The judge commences with, in this case, 100 points, which, if the band attain, means perfection. All that is necessary, therefore, is that any movement played 'tame', 'out of tune', 'amateurish' etc. – which notwithstanding 'Enthusiast's' opinion, are blunders, and must detract from the general performance — must mean less than perfection, and render it necessary to deduct a certain number of points. But the 'etc.' covers a very large portion of the ground, and I am not surprised at 'Enthusiast' condensing it so nicely. It does not read so well to say that the euphonium, trombone, and cornet do not read the copy correctly; that the movements are not played as marked, and the men have no chance to play their parts; that their tempo is too quick, so much so it can only be described as 'evidently playing to catch an early train.' For these and other mistakes in their selection, 'Verdi,' the Wangaratta lost 40 points. I do not intend to say that 'Enthusiast's' opinion with regard to the band is wrong. They may be better now than ever they were before; but, if so, well, they must have been bad. I pass over the uncalled-for remarks which he calls 'rather personal', with regard to the judge,

contenting myself by observing that Mr Bulch is too well known a musician for any such remark to be taken seriously by the public generally, and that after hearing the Wangaratta band play here, no doubt he is congratulating himself on not having received the appointment 'Enthusiast' mentions. He cannot understand a band playing a simple march 'Washington Grays" in a nice, clear, crisp style, and the same remarks not being applicable in a difficult selection. I might say, for his instruction, that it is a parallel case with a person singing a simple, easy song well within his compass, which he might be able to do creditably, and attempting something beyond his scope and compass which proves an utter failure. 'Enthusiast' says the leading cornet was so much out of tune that it had to be changed during the performance of the selection. This I deny, being in a position to see all that happened, the valves of the instrument stuck during the performance of the march, and the performer handed it to one of the bandsmen, and after a few bars it was made right and used to finish the march. So far as being out of tune, the judge's remarks are, 'cornet fine', 'cornet a little off at times', 'cornet splendid'. In conclusion, I might say the gentleman who knows so little and says so much might have given us the benefit of his name, and the chances are he might obtain the position of judge at our next competition; but perhaps he could not better have described himself in a word, for Webster says an enthusiast is one whose imagination is heated, and the 'Enthusiast' in question must be red hot. Trusting you will find space for this in your next issue — I am, yours, etc., THOS. W. WARREN, Band Contest Steward."

Setting aside that, as band contest steward, you might expect Mr Warren to wish to defray any suggestions that the contest was held on anything other than a fair basis, it would doubtless have been of comfort to Tom to see someone fighting his corner and defending his reputation so skilfully and authoritatively.

From events taking place in October, we learn more about the Ballarat Railway Band and Tom's involvement. It had been reinvigorated not as a brass band, but as a military band, rather like the 3rd Battalion Band. In the Australian contests, military and brass bands were usually able to compete alongside each other, and Tom was perfectly comfortable composing for, or tutoring, either band format. On 17 October, Tom set up the Ballarat Railway Military Band on the Rotunda on Barkly Street East in front of the Town Hall where from eight o'clock in the evening onwards they gave the public a programme that heavily featured favourites from Tom's own repertoire. These included "The Commanding Officer's Parade," "Elsinore," "Sandhurst" and "Royal Irish," as well as the still relatively new selection "The Empire." These Friday evening concerts became something of a regular engagement for the band, offering much welcome entertainment as well as raising their public profile and giving them valuable performance experience.

In October, the South Street Competitions were once again in full sway, with a wide variety of musical, literary and artistic skills being on display. The adjudicator for the band contest this time was the highly respected professional bandmaster, judge and composer James Ord Hume, a contemporary of both Tom Bulch and George Allan. Ord Hume had been born in Edinburgh in 1864 and had had become a celebrated name on the British brass band circuit. He had been bandmaster of many bands including the 3rd Durham Light Infantry and the Aldershot and Farnham Institute Brass Band, been a successful prize-winning band conductor-for-hire and would throughout his lifetime compose and arrange a huge quantity of band music. He had ascended to judging band contests only a couple of years before George Allan, though his experience, reputation and availability as a music professional ensured him opportunities far beyond the reach of an amateur like George. Having said that, during James Ord Hume's early years of adjudicating band contests George Allan may have encountered him at local contests of the type he himself may have judged, such as at Willington (1894), Barnard Castle and Hunwick (both 1895) and Spennymoor (1898 and 1899). Like Bulch and Allan, James Ord Hume was also a cornet player, and was every bit as eminent as Thomas Bulch at this time but enjoyed the extra celebrated quality of being a visitor from the mother country.

In the build-up to the South Street Band Contest the correspondent 'Musicus' in the Adelaide Register, providing some gossip of the proceedings, mentioned that while Prout's Band had been practising their military marching at the Ballarat Eastern Oval, Thomas Bulch's Ballarat Railways Band had been espied at the Railway Sheds "putting in some solid work at their contest piece." The line up of the Railway Band for this contest saw Thomas teaming up once again with two of the Malthouse brothers who had been part of his Model Band in his earliest days in Ballarat, and of course shared his town of birth. Youngest brother George Malthouse had the B flat bass, whilst former cornet player Robert Malthouse now played the euphonium in the Railway Band. Something we also see here for the first time is that Thomas's eldest son, Thomas Edward Bulch Jr., who would have been about fourteen years of age, was to play 3rd cornet.

On Thursday, 30 October, with the contest commencing, the bands in time honoured fashion, massed in the Prince of Wales Square opposite the Ballarat Star office, and collectively played a piece entitled "The Emperor" before following the traditional parade route to the Eastern Oval. Each band was preceded by a boy holding a placard to tell the onlookers which band they were watching. For the first day of the contest, the Railway Band was drawn third to play their version of the test piece, Harry Round's arrangement of "Mercandante." According to a commentator:

> "The band opened well, though the tone was rather hard and not broad enough. In the first cornet solo, the player was out of tune, and one or two slips were noticeable. The volume of sound was good, though wanting in feeling. The euphonium solo was only moderate and there was a lacking of time in the performance. They finished better but the band wants a lot more practice."

That evening they played their own choice test piece, they:

> "Essayed the splendid "Lohengrin" overture, but can hardly be said to have been successful. The selection is an ambitious one for a young band to take in hand and while in some parts they were fairly successful, in others they were eminently the reverse, and again they failed to realise the conception of the author, who produced what is one of the most classical of all classics. There are opportunities in the piece for some of the finest effects that a band is capable of producing, and without being too severe, it might be said at once that they were not produced."

On the next day of the contest the band played their own choice selection, an arrangement of the works of Rossini, which was far better received, with comments including "a very well rendered selection in both tone and precision," and "the timbre of this band is good and the soloists are very good indeed." Later that day their rendering of the march "The Commanding Officer's Parade" was more scornful. "This band is the most untuneful yet." "Very much out of tune indeed, a very poor attempt."

At the conclusion of the contest, James Ord-Hume was evidently impressed with the overall spectacle and particularly that the Australian format of march contest required to bands to physically and precisely march while playing. Assuming that his comments were not a form of flattery, he said via a reporter for the Ballarat Star:

> "I thoroughly endorse the idea of this quickstep contest, as I am of opinion that brass bands, when marching, should always be spirited, and also neat and uniform in the ranks. The music should always be of a bright and military nature, and, indeed the band should always prove, by its marching in public, its standard of excellence. A good marching band should prove a "cue" to the programme that has to follow. This is the very best competition I have ever judged, during my experience throughout the whole of the United Kingdom, and I sincerely believe that no other competition exists in which such uniformity is so excellent in quick march competition; also I note the very excellent drill to which each band is subject. Truly, Ballarat is an example to us all in the matter of educational competitions, both to bandsmen and audience. Win or loss we have all learned something, and I sincerely hope that England will copy a little at a time from this great event at Ballarat in vast and far-off Australia."

Assuming the praise to be sincere, and we have no reason to doubt it to be so, then Tom Bulch must surely be regarded as a key influence on how band contesting in Ballarat was conducted, the quality of which had drawn praise from his highly regarded peer. Alas, though his recently revived Ballarat Railway Band didn't earn a prize in either selections or quickstep. They came ninth in the latter and in the selections contest were spared the last place only by James Scarff and the Ballarat City Band. We can be almost sure that, with his personal reputation at stake, Tom would not have been at all happy about that outcome.

In early November, Tom made his way to Maryborough to judge brass solo contests at the annual musical and elocutionary competitions of the Maryborough branch of the Australian Natives Association. One might wonder whether he spent time with, or was even perhaps engaged, as a result of his long-standing friendship with, John Malthouse who was resident there. The contests judged were for cornet solo, euphonium, tenor horn and trombone, and concluded on the sixth day of the month after which Tom was bound for Melbourne.

On 8 November, Tom occupied the judge's tent at a band contest in Northcote Park, Melbourne. Five bands had entered, but one, the St Augustine's Orphanage Band, was prevented from taking part on account of its not having first joined the Victorian Band Association, headquartered in Ballarat. A proposed resolution, of having the band join the association there and then, was thwarted by the objection of one of the other competing bands. That consequently left only four bands to perform the test pieces; "Les Fleurs D'Australie" by Bulch himself, the march "Independentia" by R Hall and James Ord-Hume's arrangement of "Gems from Sullivan's Operas." The Prahran City Band emerged victorious, with Northcote's taking second prize and Stender's South Melbourne awarded the third and final available prize. On 15 November, the Ballarat Railway Band performed a selection of pieces from the Rotunda in front of the Ballarat East Town Hall. Though the press declared it thoroughly enjoyable it was an occasion of little other note. The band was also announced as engaged for the Windermere Australian Natives Association Sports Gathering that was scheduled to take place on New Year's Day at Burrumbeet Park Racecourse. The Ballarat Star of 23 December 1902 reveals something of Thomas's mindset following the recent poor performances at the South Street Contest. It says:

> "The Ballarat Railway Brass Band is making rapid progress under the leadership of Mr T E Bulch. During the recent excursion to Bendigo, the band played a programme of music, and the performance elicited highly favourable comment. The band has entered for the South Street Competition, and assiduous practice is now being indulged in. In addition to the big competition, an entry has also been made for several other events."

It looks as though Tom was very keen to have his band re-enter the ring at the South Street Contests and show he wasn't finished yet as either bandmaster or conductor. The band ended their year at the annual races of the Springdallah and Linton Relief Fund Racing Club which took place on 29 December and at which they reportedly performed to the satisfaction of all present.

New Shildon

The winter months at the beginning of 1903 were, in terms of reports of activity, typically quiet for George Allan, but by the spring, in their seasonal way, adjudicating engagements began to blossom again. In the monthly press for the brass band community it had become long common for regional correspondents to contribute a column explaining what was happening in their locality. In practice many of these correspondents waxed and waned and the boundaries of their respective reporting territories moved to include or exclude bands. Occasionally over the decades New Shildon found its way into these reports.

The April and May issues of Wright and Round's Brass Band News for 1903 we start to see a new commentator operating under the pen name "Harmonious," commentating on the Mid Durham District. His contributions generally included a tit-bit of news here and there on George's New Shildon Saxhorn Band. Harmonious, whose true identity remained anonymous as was the practice, only contributed during 1903 and for whatever reason ceased to contribute early the following year. Nonetheless his scratchings give us a tiny extra insight into the goings on concerning the New Shildon Saxhorn Band during that period. In April his report reads, "Shildon Saxhorn are quiet at present. Join the association Mr Allan," while in May he attempts to provoke the band even further:

> "Shildon Saxhorn are you working on the quiet? as I expect to see you turn up at Howden. I hope we haven't to wait so long this year before there is a judge to put in the tent at Howden as the appointed judge did not turn up in time for starting the contest last year."

There is an implication here that whoever Harmonious was, he might well have been at the Howden-le-Wear contest when George was elevated, at the last-minute, to the position of contest judge so that there might indeed be a contest. It's possible, even, that George and Harmonious were acquainted. The writer's prodding to encourage George to sign his band up to the 'association' suggests that at this time the New Shildon Saxhorn were outside that circle, which may have been down to preference of either George, his band members, or both.

On Saturday, 23 May, George fulfilled the role of judge at a band contest at Hebburn Colliery. This event was promoted by the Hebburn Colliery Prize Silver Band as part of the Hebburn Athletic Sports which took place during the afternoon in a field near Hebburn Railway Station. That would have been convenient for George who most probably travelled there by train. Eight bands had entered the contest but, as we have now seen so many times, one had dropped out meaning that only seven competed. The contest had been limited to bands that were members of the Durham and Northumberland Association. Having heard all the music, George awarded the first prize for the march contest to Murton Colliery, which came with a modest cash prize of a pound, but which also saw the band receive the Deuchar Challenge Cup. Second prize in the march was divided between Spencer's Steel Works and Felling Colliery. The test piece was the selection 'Le Domino Noir' by Daniel Amber for which George awarded the more impressive cash prize of ten pounds to the Cockerton Prize Band. Second and third prizes of five pounds and three pounds were divided between Spencer's Steel Works and Backworth Institute. Murton were placed fourth and Felling fifth. There was also an individual prize to be awarded to the best euphonium player on the day. George awarded this to the euphonium player from the Cockerton band. The Hebburn Colliery contest was covered by the local press, with the Shields Daily Gazette including their write-up the following Monday. The Jarrow Express also reported on the occasion but in a journalistic blunder misrepresented George's hometown as 'Shields' rather than Shildon. The reporter probably misheard, or misread, and made an assumption that George had travelled south from either North Shields or South Shields, either side of the mouth if the river Tyne; a reminder perhaps that we cannot always entirely trust what we read in journalistic interpretations and to check out facts where possible.

On Saturday, 4 July it was off to the Poultry Show and Band Contest at Hetton-le-Hole, north east of the city of Durham. This was another town connected to Shildon by rail, being served by a station on the North Eastern Railway's Durham Elvet and Murton Branch Line, making it easy once again for George, an employee of that same company, to travel there. This contest, hosted by the Hetton-le-Hole Livestock and Sports Society took place in the Hetton Hall grounds, not far from the railway station, roughly where the Eppleton Colliery Football Club ground, which replaced the hall, now stands. As was usually the case, the show in its broader context, covered prize exhibitions of all classes of poultry, pigeons and rabbits generally kept by the working man. The accompanying band contest was, for some reason, restricted so that only bands that had not won a prize exceeding seven pounds during 1902 were eligible to enter. This kind of restriction had become common at band contests during this era and was possibly introduced to assure bands that might enter that they would stand a chance of winning something through the knowledge that 'crack' bands which had previously proved themselves were excluded. It's an interesting principle, though from the perspective of a potential onlooker it might imply that they were to be denied some top-notch performances. Having heard and noted in detail each of the five participating bands' rendering of both test selection, "Scottish Memories" and the own choice quickstep pieces, George decided on merit that the top prize for the test piece should go to the band from Felling Colliery. The band from Spennymoor came second, Jarrow third and though the band from Willington only came fourth they did win a one pound prize for the best rendering of a march. A total of fourteen pounds in prize money was awarded that day, with the top prize for the selection test piece category being seven pounds.

By coincidence, the home-town of the winning band was George's next destination as a contest judge. On 11 July George travelled to Felling, again well connected to Shildon by rail and served by a North Eastern Railway company station, for a contest being held under the auspices of the Felling Colliery Band. Their contest committee had raised sixteen pounds in prize money, and there was also a cup on offer. Six interested bands entered, representing Blyth, Willington, South Shields, Hebburn, Jarrow and Spennymoor. As usual, there was a selection test piece, this time being chosen by the bands from a list, as well as a march contest for a typically comparatively minor prize. Of the selections listed that the bands might choose to play, four of the bands chose "Le Domino Noir," while Willington Silver and the Blyth and District Band elected to play Charles Godfrey's arrangement of "Don Sebastiano." When George summarised the points he had awarded, and the bands were ordered accordingly by placings, the results were announced. On this occasion, the Hebburn Temperance Band, under their conductor George Hawkins, came forth to claim their eight pounds top prize as well as the cup.

One interesting point of note is that on this day the Hebburn Temperance Band competed at two contests; the other being at the village of Philadelphia near Hetton-le-Hole where the adjudicator, a Mr J Brier, of Bradford, awarded them second place. When I was researching this I initially assumed that there had been a mistake in the reporting, but I've been able to confirm that the band did indeed compete at both events. Both locations were again well connected by rail, though I do find it odd, and almost discourteous, that a band might leave one contest before its conclusion to put in an appearance at a nearby town. The results of both contests are both published in the August 1903 edition of Brass Band News.

That same edition of Brass Band News also contains another attempt by Harmonious to provoke George and his band:

> "Shildon Saxhorn are contenting themselves with giving sacred concerts. Come, Mr Allan, are you not going to have a try at a contest before the season is over? You have a few contests near home for August; try your luck. Shildon Temperance also giving concerts. I expect you will soon have a good band out of your young players, and I wish you success with your plated instruments. Glad to hear you have cleared the debt off."

One wonders whether the suggestion that George try his luck at a contest might be as much of a 'challenge' as a suggestion, given that he was at this time more active as a judge of bands than a high-achieving bandmaster in his own right. It does raise an interesting question, though, as to why George was not putting the band in for more contests. As an experienced judge he was clearly not averse to band contesting in principle. There are a number of possibilities that we could speculate upon. It may have been that the band members as a whole were not interested in contesting, or that it was not financially or logistically viable for them. It may just as equally have been George's decision, perhaps fearing that poor results for his band in local contests might prejudice his chances of being hired as a judge, or even that participation in contests with his band might be perceived as a conflict of interest that might compromise the perception of his impartiality or integrity as a judge. The possibilities behind his avoidance of contests, or joining the band association, are manifold.

On 25 July 1903, George headed eastward, following the North Eastern Railway's Normanby Branch, to Eston once again to be the contest adjudicator at the contest there. This time the contest featured five bands; Charlton's Star of Hope, Skelton Old, the band of the Dorman Long iron and steelworks, South Bank Old and the Middlesborough Trades Band. As usual the contest consisted of playing a challenging test selection, on this occasion which, as at Hetton-le-Hole earlier in the year, was William Rimmer's "Scottish Memories," followed by a separate march contest. When George's marking of each band's attempt was concluded, the Charlton's Star of Hope band tied with Skelton Old Band for first place. South Band were placed third. Charlton's band also took the prize for the best march performance.

Then. on Saturday 22 August, George took a trip to Willington's Annual Flower Show which, naturally and typically, included another band contest. This show was later described by a reporter as being of "fur and feather in full coat and plumage, and produce at the highest state of maturity." The weather that day was reportedly clear and bright and, with the town being well placed centrally in the district by both road and rail, the event drew a reportedly enormous crowd from the surrounding coal mining towns and villages. One particular special excursion train depositing its travellers onto the streets of Willington had come in from South Shields on the coast, which would itself have been an attraction on as fine an August day. Though the main shopping street in Willington was described as a "scene of bustle and crush" all day, it was the show ground to which the crowds flocked. The large marquee for horticultural exhibits, central to the event, was filled with the sweet fragrance of the exhibited flowers and plants. Elsewhere there were industrial and mechanical displays, which included model making and taxidermy, as well as a display of entries of fine art, poultry and livestock. Once again that year the test piece for the selection was Rimmer's "Scottish Memories," and the band contest drew a strong field of twelve bands to which it was George's task to listen carefully and provide scores so that winners might be identified for both selection and march. He determined that the first prize was deserved most by the Hetton Colliery Band who also picked up soprano and euphonium medals. The band from Felling came second, also earning a medal for best trombone performance. South Moor were placed third and also received a medal for best cornet performance of the day.

On Saturday the 29 August 1903, Charles Vane-Tempest-Stewart the 6th Marquess of Londonderry, in his capacity as the President of the Board of Education, paid a visit to what was by this time simply being referred to in the press as Shildon; neither Old nor New but singular and implicitly combined. The purpose of his visit was to formally open new extensions to the National Schools there. The rapid expansion in coal mining activity in the area had seen an increase in the population of the town and there had been concerns that the schools were struggling to accommodate the additional children. The town's National Schools, run by the Church of England, and at that time under the direction of the Reverend Canon Horatio Spurrier, had been enlarged. This expansion was a significant achievement for a church school as Shildon's populace was comprised of all denominations, yet there was reportedly enough in the way Spurrier ran the schools that met the approval of even the 'nonconformists'. Lord Londonderry arrived, from the family seat at Wynyard, by motor car, to be presented with a golden key by Canon Spurrier, with which to unlock the latest new building. As well as many interested members of the public, a fellow peer Lord Barnard and an authority of the church, the Bishop of Richmond, were present. Once all had taken their places inside the new schoolroom, a meeting with speeches ensued. Londonderry waxed lyrical about last having visited Shildon thirty years previous as the Conservative parliamentary candidate for South Durham, and on his pleasure in the fact that no child had ever been withdrawn from religious instruction at the school. In true Conservative spirit he expressed his pleasure in the fact that by taking funding from private industries locally, without mentioning probable additional fundraising by the church itself, such Voluntary Schools were saving the nation money. At the end of the speeches, Lord Barnard reminded those present how fortunate and honoured the people were to have had Lord Londonderry visit the town, after which three cheers were proposed for Canon Spurrier before everyone retired to enjoy sporting events between the children. Present at the ceremony were George Allan and his New Shildon Saxhorn Band, who played selections of music at intervals. Though not participating in band contests they continued to be active in their community.

This understanding is emphasised in the September 1903 issue of the Brass Band News, wherein the taunting Harmonious reports:

> "Shildon Saxhorn have also been engaged in several places, but never had a try at a contest this year. I hope you are not fainthearted, as I hear performances on the contest field which I think you could beat."

The 12th of September 1903 brought with it the seventh Annual Langley Park Show, under the auspices of the Langley Park Floral, Industrial and Livestock Society. This was yet another of the region's agricultural and horticultural shows to now feature, amongst its other attractions, an almost obligatory band contest. As well as the usual exhibitions of flowers, vegetables, dogs, industrial items, poultry, pigeons, rabbits and cats there were a handful of entertainments engaged especially to provide a little added glamour to the event. These included:

> "Trumpeter C Daly (late of the 9th Lancers) trumpeter to Lord Roberts on the great march from Cabul to Candahar in the Afghan war; the Weimars, in their humorous speciality "Sloper on the Wire" introducing their eccentric musical entertainment; Prof. Grey, novelty pedestal act; Bob Padley, contortionist, acrobat and staircase performer; and the Torros, trick and comedy cyclists, introducing the unicycle, skating on wheels etc."

In all, a total of 2,025 entries were attracted to participate across all the competitions taking place on the showground that day. For the band contest, a prize pot of twenty pounds had encouraged twelve bands to enter in advance, though only eleven of these took part on the day. George Allan had been employed as adjudicator. The weather on this particular day had not been kind to the event's organisers. Several heavy showers of rain arrived during the afternoon which rendered the show field in a "very miry state, and in a more or less degree affecting the gate." Despite this the show still drew a large attendance, with those present reportedly expressing a view that it may have been the best of the Langley Park shows to date. The band contest, as standard, included both a selection and march contest, with prizes on offer for both. This time though, the selections played were of the bands' own choosing, creating the benefit of offering the audience a little variation in what they heard. From George's perspective, this kind of contest might be considered trickier to judge than when every participating band is playing the same piece. After his usual careful consideration of each performance, the first prize was awarded to the West Pelton Band followed by South Moor and Guisbrough Priory in that order. Unusually three bands tied on points for fourth place, those being Browney Colliery, Hetton Colliery and Sacriston. In the march contest, the victors were the band from New Brancepeth, which would offer them some cheer as they had only achieved second from last in the selection contest.

The morning of 23 September brought a sad occasion that would have been of significance to both George and, if he knew about it, Tom Bulch. In his sixtieth year, the music publisher Thomas Albert Haigh had passed away. Haigh had, of course, been the man who placed faith in Tom's first march composition and published it in his popular Amateur Brass and Military Band Journal, giving him the credibility at so young an age that had helped propel him on his journey to celebrated status in Australia. Haigh didn't only publish his brass band journal, though. Other publications included Haigh's String Band Journal, which in 1889 had featured a string arrangement of George Allan's schottische composition "The Sunbeam" and Haigh's Fife and Drum Band Journal which had occasionally included arrangements of Allan's work in that format, one example being the march "The Mechanic" in 1890. Haigh had been George's principal publisher throughout his amateur musical career, so he would surely have felt the loss profoundly. We read of Haigh's start in life earlier in this account, but we'll briefly return here to setting out in brief the second half of his life. Like Robert De Lacy he is reputed to have been a teacher of bands in various parts of the country before settling in Hull in 1877 to start his printing and bookseller's business, also as we know publishing music for brass bands. In the 1880s, Haigh had embarked upon a journey into Freemasonry, being initiated into the Alexandra Lodge on 17 June 1885 and being 'passed' on 15 July, then 'raised' on 19 August that same year. He received his certificates on 5th October and continued on a path that would see him become Worshipful Master of that Lodge as well as a member of the Lodge Mark Master Masons No 182, and Alexandra Royal Arch Chapter, No. 1,511. He had also been a member of the Hull Musical Union, having joined that institution when it was first established.

By 1891 the Haighs had moved from 1 Cranbourne Villas to the grander Belgrave House, 3 Anlaby Road, Hull with his wife Ellen's widowed mother. By 1901 the couple had opened their Music Warehouse at 32 Albert Avenue not far from Anlaby Road. The couple did not have any children but regularly advertised to employ youngsters in the Hull area to work at the family shop and print works, delivering errands or writing addresses on the envelopes for delivery by post. Haigh advertised his business in "White's Directory of Hull" of 1882, and both the 1893 and 1899 editions of "Kelly's Directory of Hull and its Neighbourhood". Though Thomas Haigh had now passed away, the business in Hull appears to have continued after his death, whether by his wife and other employees, or perhaps having been sold. The business continued to advertise for staff until as late as 1907. As for the "Amateur Brass (and Military) Band Journal" though, we don't know whether its publication ceased immediately as a consequence of Haigh's death, but we have observed that the journals were no longer advertised in publications such as Brass Band News. Many of the journals operated a subscription model where bands would be encouraged to re-subscribe annually, but publishers would advertise to attract new business. Whatever exactly happened, we have not seen any George Allan pieces published by it after Thomas Haigh's death.

With Haigh's journal being one of George's main outlets for his compositions, the death of the publisher would have forced him to re-think his strategy over how and where his work might be published. In October's Brass Band News, Harmonious tip-off the readership that there had been:

"No news from Shildon, but I saw a few Shildon players playing for other bands at Langley Park. I would rather have seen you with your own bands at the contest."

The ever improving mobility brought about by an ever expanding rail, automotive and public transport system in the now Edwardian era appears to have brought about the phenomenon we see quite commonly today whereby if players are not satisfied with the ability and aspiration of their local band, they will play for others within travelling distance. In the same update regarding the small handful of bands from the Mid-Durham area he offers another explanation as to why a good few of the bands in that area were struggling.

> "I am sorry to hear in our district of very bad attendances at the band practices. Some excuse themselves through the bad weather which we have had lately in the north. The biggest evil is the bandsman who goes off his head through football, who sometimes misses practice week after week. What a band should do is to understand whether they have a band or a football team, as bands are better off without such men who have to run off to every football match within a radius of twenty to thirty miles. Weed them out, you are better off without them, as it is very disappointing for two-thirds of a band to meet for practice to find the other third gone off to the match. These men are in general the grumblers at the contests when not in the prizes. If you have any heart at all in your band, don't neglect it for the least trifling thing that crosses your path."

There may definitely have been some truth to this in the noticeable decline in activity of the New Shildon brass bands. Shildon's football club, still going today, was established in 1890, and eventually moved to the site of the cycling track at Dean Street in the Old Shildon area. In 1907 they would join the North Eastern League and then eventually the Northern League which was founded in 1889. League football in the North-East of England quickly became a huge sensation with rival towns taking to the pitch for local honours week in, week out in front of large enthusiastic crowds. Was George struggling to keep his band active and together for this reason, or was the other point made by Harmonious an equally important factor? Maybe his better players, if they had the means to travel, had started to play with bands elsewhere that they deemed to offer them better money or prospects of success and recognition? This, if true, would surely be reflective, in part, of a gradual transition in emphasis from community pride and cohesion to one of personal performance and esteem. The effects of this completed transition are still felt today in the North East of England, and doubtless beyond, where players deemed good enough will travel several times a week between counties to play with a top band, while the local bands that taught, mentored and developed them struggle with short numbers comprised of youth and senior players or else fold for want of capable musicians.

In what spare time he had remaining, George, and his brother Ralph, continued their memberships of the Mechanics Institute which sat just over the railway footbridge from George's house. This would be Ralph's last year of membership, though we are not sure why. It's possible that he had become dispirited with the Institute as around this time the building was reportedly no longer suited for the purpose and starting to show signs of structural issues. The Institute's committee were already looking to the North Eastern Railway Company, the employer of most members, regarding some remedial action.

Ballarat

Around ten and a half thousand miles away in Ballarat, Thomas Bulch's first reported engagement of 1903 was as part of a bazaar to raise funds for the Sebastopol Fire Brigade in Ballarat. This took place on Wednesday, 11 February. Tom, and his Ballarat Railway Band, paraded the streets of that borough prior to offering a programme of music outside the Town Hall to encourage attendance at the event. To enable their participation, the Railway Band members had been transported to the event at no charge, at the order of Mr Gummow, the manager of the Tramway Company.

At around that same date in February 1903, Tom resigned his post as bandmaster of the 3rd Battalion Infantry Band. No explanation is reported for this, but we do know that he was replaced by Private Arthur Francis Prout of the 3rd Battalion Infantry Band. Arthur was the youngest son of Samuel Prout, the bandmaster of Prout's Ballarat Brass Band which, as Ballarat based brass band historian Robert Pattie tells us in his history of that band, was one of the earliest bands in Ballarat as well as possibly being one of the oldest civilian bands in Australia and also the first private band in the colony of Victoria.

On Sunday, 2 March Prout's Ballarat Band, the Ballarat City Brass Band and the Ballarat Railway Band teamed up to present a concert at the Eastern Oval with an objective of raising funds to keep Prout's band going. Tom's Railway band played along the parade way to the Eastern Oval whilst Prout's band, with their renditions of "True as Steel," "Herald," and "Silver Trumpet" and James Scarff's Ballarat City Band playing "Mercandante" and "William Tell" were the entertainments given at the site. A 'satisfactory sum' was collected, but it was also a great display of the collaborative spirit and camaraderie among the bands of Ballarat at this time, that they would combine in such a way to support one of the bands.

At the beginning of May, the Glen Innes Examiner and General Advertiser reports that Tom was once again in contention as prospective judge for a band contest that year at Lismore:

> "A movement is now on foot with the view of getting a brass band contest in Lismore at the end of this year, under the patronage of the Caledonian Society, with minimum aggregate prizes of £300. The first prize will run as high as £150. The scheme is not a dream or a castle -in-the-air, it is all but decided. It is not a question of money (the money will be found right enough when required), but a question of minor details. The judgeship will be offered either to Mr Bulch, or Mr Bates, who are the two fairest brass band judges in Australia. Lismore people want to have the decision of the contest above suspicion so that they should make it an annual affair. In fact, the local brass band is willing to debar itself from the contest, should any objection be found by any of the competing bands."

This, being cited as one of the two fairest judges in the country, is another example of the high regard within the brass community for Tom's perceived integrity in respect the brass contesting process.

In the summer of 1903, Sutton's Proprietary Limited Issued two new musical pieces for piano by Tom, a waltz named "Florina" created under his pseudonym Henry Laski, and a song under his own name entitled "Home Visions." They were reviewed together by the Punch of Melbourne on 30 July. In this particular review, the writer seemed to be unaware that the composers were one and the same. On Florina he wrote that "this waltz is very tuneful, and will become very popular, being easy to play." Of "Home Visions" the writer called it "an exquisite little item, full of melody, and has a beautiful sentiment." On 29 July, "Home Visions" was played at an entertainment held for the benefit of the St Patrick's branch of the League of the Cross at the St Patrick's Hall in Ballarat, with the reporter from the Ballarat Star pointing out proudly that it had been written by a "Ballarat old boy, Mr T E Bulch." The Advocate newspaper of Melbourne explains that on that occasion it had been sung by a Miss Alice Myers, but adds that its writer is "formerly of Ballarat," though so far as we know Tom was still resident there at that time. On 8th of August, Suttons were advertising "Home Visions," in the Age newspaper of Melbourne, as being available from their Melbourne, Ballarat and Bendigo stores. They describe it as "charmingly pretty" explaining that it can be acquired for the price of two shillings, with a further penny to be paid to have it delivered by post.

Notes published in the press on 23 September, after a meeting of the Victorian Band Association, tell us that Tom's name was one of four suggested by that association to the Ararat Athletic Club as being a suitable choice for contest judge for a second class band contest they intended to hold on New Year's Day. The said Athletic Club had been applying for the patronage of the Victorian Band Association for their event. This was also duly granted at the meeting.

Having resigned from the 3rd Battalion Band, Tom must have felt that he had space in his weekly routine to take on another responsibility for, on 10 October 1903, the Ballarat Star reveals that Tom had recently also become bandmaster of the Soldier's Hill Brass Band. Soldier's Hill is a district to the north of Ballarat and its band, on that date, played a programme of music on a square sited between Ascot Street and Windermere Street.

Our next news of Tom also relates to the Soldiers Hill Band whom he conducted on the balcony of the Robin Hood Hotel from eight o'clock on 5 December. This is also the last reported news of him in 1903. The mooted band contest at the Caledonian Society's show in Lismore, for which Tom had been recommended, did not go ahead. The society did hold their event on Boxing Day, but the only music involved in this gathering of Australians with Scots heritage was a performance of Highland pipers.

The year, on reflection, appears to have been one of modest opportunity for Tom and his family, and perhaps not an easy one. In my exchanges with his grandson Eric Tomkins, discussing Tom's fortunes and highlighting those moments in the press where he was reported as being in financial difficulties, Eric told me that he had heard from his parents generation that Tom was often short of money. This, I suppose, is still something that those who seek a living from music will often tell you. With very rare exception occasional hardship seems to be part of the lot of those who devote their lives to bringing music into our lives. Even those most celebrated will be able to relate stories of such moments of hardship. There are times when Tom seems to have been doing well, and times when things went less smoothly, with fortunes changing according to circumstances. The newspapers of 1903 were still filled with many many accounts of his music being played by bands across Australia and New Zealand, but that doesn't mean that Tom was benefitting from sales of the pieces, particularly those that in times of hardship he had relinquished, or sold the rights to, in order to settle with creditors.

Of course, many of the mentions of Tom Bulch's pieces being played by bands would also be those that were written, and probably also bought, many years previously. Old favourites like "Chef D'Oeuvre" for example, of which we see at least six mentions as having been played by bands that year, were created before he had even arrived in Australia and published by the recently deceased Thomas Haigh. To continue to make a living from sales of band and piano music Tom would have to keep that creativity flowing and stay abreast of the needs of players and trends in music. Whether for that reason or not, 1904 would indeed be a productive year.

On Friday, 22 January, a Water Carnival, with the aim of benefitting a number of charities, was held on Lake Wendouree, the body of water by which Ballarat is sited. The carnival involved many boats of various types, from pleasure boats to canoes, taking to the lake in full decoration, with accompanying land and water based sports events occurring throughout the day. In the evening there was an organised display of illuminated boats on the lake, and a torchlit procession with the city's bands and fire brigades taking part. Children from the city's orphanage gave a display of maypole dancing and callisthenics. The fire brigade created a 'fire-snake' on the lake, which was a series of floating fires towed by a leading boat. The grounds by the waterside were illuminated by fairy lights and Chinese lanterns. A grand finale had been intended to be a grand firework display by the Phoenix Fireworks Company. Alas, as the evening had progressed rain had set in forcing that particular feature to be abandoned, and the event instead concluded with the burning of a ship constructed especially for that purpose. Despite the terrible weather, the boat burning illuminated the landscape splendidly. Throughout this evening display, Tom Bulch and the Soldier's Hill Brass Band had offered a programme of suitable music. It appears that at some point word must have reached the band that a rumour was circulating that, despite this being a charitable endeavour, the band had been paid for their services. Consequently, Tom and the secretary of the band wrote to the editor of the Ballarat Star to allay any suspicions that the band had been paid for their involvement in the charity fundraiser. The letter, published next day, reads:

> "AN EXPLANATION. To the Editor of "The Star." Sir, - Owing to a misunderstanding as to the Soldiers Hill band playing at the Water Carnival last night, we desire to state that Mr Murphy, of the Wheatsheaf hotel, did not engage the band, but that our services were strictly voluntary, and offered with the idea that we were giving our assistance to the movement by playing on that side of the lake. – Yours, etc., T. E. BULCH, Bandmaster. A. TREGONNING, Hon Sec."

At eight o'clock on 30 January, the Soldier's Hill Brass Band were again seen entertaining the people of the area from the balcony of the Robin Hood Hotel. The band appear to have tried to commit to these Saturday evening performances, which may have been intended to earn the band small but regular amounts. On Saturday 6th February, an article in the Ballarat Star declares that as well as making an appearance in the square between Raglan and Lyons streets that evening they were also appealing for donations from the public to help them fund a journey to Geelong in March to compete there. The announcement points out that attending band contests, particularly those away from Ballarat, was an expensive objective. This might account for why neither the Ballarat Railways Band, nor the Soldier's Hill Band, were involved in contests the previous year. Tom, though, as we have seen in his own words, was a great believer in the positive influence of contests in making a band focus on, and improve, its quality of playing. It is probable that, having taken on these bands, he would have been looking out for an appropriate contest. One at a suitable level to test their skill and mettle, and see if they could progress toward the standard he would expect of them. To achieve some success at contest might not only boost the band's pride and self-esteem, but might also do something to boost Tom's reputation as an improver of bands.

On Sunday, 31 January, the Soldier's Hill Band, under Tom's baton, played selections of music in front of the Trades Hall ahead of a meeting held there by the Ballarat Labour League. The Labour Movement in Australia had a long tradition, but at this point was undergoing something of a revival. The speaker at the event was a Mr Tunnicliffe, who gave a speech on "Social Ideals," tracing the evolution of such up to the utopian and scientific stage, and claiming that modern socialism had a definite scientific basis. Whether Tom or his bandsmen had any party affiliation, or stayed to watch the speech, is something we don't really know.

1904 reveals a little more information on the early life of Tom's eldest son, Thomas Edward junior. So far, barring a few mentions of Thomas junior appearing as a young bandsman and cornet player in his father's band, there has been little to learn. On wife, Eliza, and how the other children fared or spent their time, we have even less to draw upon. On Thomas junior, however, we see in a report of a cricket match that took place on 13 February 1904, evidence of his being a keen young sportsman. This first report we have seen tells of his role as bowler for the St Luke's junior cricket team in their victory over the team of St Peter's Choirboys. St Luke's won by an innings and fifty-two runs, with young Thomas Edward taking eight wickets for ten overs. St Luke's, so far as we are able to determine, was a small Anglican church on Bond Street in the Mount pleasant district of Ballarat, just south of Soldier's Hill. That Thomas junior was playing for their Cricket team implies that the family as a whole had may have had some connections to this little church at the time. This possibility is made all the more likely by the fact that at this time Tom and Eliza and their children were living at number 81 Bond Street, as evidenced by the Australian electoral roll for 1903.

At the meeting of the Victorian Band Association held on the evening of Thursday, 18 February, those present received correspondence that Tom had been appointed a judge for the Stawell Band Contest to take place later that year. One can only assume that the Association, as a governing body, had to be notified to ensure that arrangements met with their approval if the contest were to, perhaps, be held under their auspices and by their rules.

In the Age of Melbourne on 27 February 1904, an advertisement appears for "Sutton's Brass Band Journal (with Reeds)" which states that it is being edited by T E Bulch. This suggests that Tom had re-entered the employment of Sutton's, which had a Ballarat branch as well as locations in Melbourne, Geelong and Bendigo. We suppose that Tom's insolvency had seen him relinquish, or possibly sell, his Bulch's brass journal which could have led to his appointment as the editor of Sutton's journal. The issue of that journal that had been made available that month was mainly comprised of Thomas's own compositions, and though it had just been published, not all of the pieces were new compositions. For example his march "The Commanding Officer's Parade" had been around since at least 1901. The issue also included his arrangement of Flotow's "Indra" and his solo tonguing polka "The Tripod." The issue also contained pieces under Bulch pseudonyms, such as Henry Laski's "Bright Eyed Nancy" and Godfrey Parker's "Trixie" and "Breathe Not Of Parting." There are also a couple of pieces that could well be by Bulch pseudonyms but which are somewhat insensitively titled by today's standards; "The Coon's Patrol" by Pat Cooney, and "King of the Coons" by Arthur Kingsbury. Looking at the combination of names used in conjunction with the titles of the compositions there is more than a hint that these might well be made up names. We have no hard proof to connect them to Tom Bulch with any certainty.

Published at the same time we see adverts for Sutton's Musical Magazine, which included piano renditions of some of the same pieces by Tom. "The Coon's Patrol" is described as "a melody that sets you on the go as soon as you have heard it"; and "King of the Coons," "when once heard you cannot help whistling it.." "The Commanding Officer's Parade" also makes an appearance alongside some old Godfrey Parker, Eugene Lacosta and Henry Laski pieces from previous years, republished, or else being re-rendered by Tom from their full band format. The Henry Laski waltz, "Nada," for example has first been found being played by bands as early as 1898, and "Adeline," written as Godfrey Parker and bearing the name of Tom's daughter, was first played by bands in 1892.

Tom's engagement to the post of bandmaster of the Soldier's Hill Brass Band was only formally announced in the Ballarat Star towards the end of March 1904, so he could have been in an 'acting' or trial capacity in that role before then. The band may equally simply have been late in announcing the appointment. At the same time the band announced that, as we have seen, they would support the Labour League's Sunday meetings, and take any fine weather engagements for which donations might be received. The committee running the band also declared that the band would commence rehearsing for the next South Street Band Contest.

In April 1904, Suttons began advertising another new publication; Sutton's Cornet Tutor, which was of course created by Tom Bulch. This book was touted as "the easiest to learn from, the simplest to understand," and proclaimed itself to be equally applicable for tenor horn, baritone, trombone and euphonium. It was made available at a price of one shilling and sixpence, with a surcharge of two pence if the buyer wanted it sent to them by post.

On the evening of Tuesday, 26 April, the Soldier's Hill Brass Band assembled outside the Australian Natives Association Hall to render selections of music ahead of a benefit concert in aid of the Soldier's Hill Cricket Club. The band played for the attending audience as they arrived, a useful indicator for anyone in the area who didn't know that there was something interesting taking place at the hall that night. The programme of the event included a section of ballads, of which one was "Adeline," being sung by Mr Naylor, accompanied by the song's composer, Tom, at the piano.

During the year Tom had also been working upon another piano piece of a less sentimental nature. This was something more akin to his descriptive fantasia, "The Young Recruit," created around ten years earlier though still very popular with bands at this time. This time, Tom's inspiration was an event that happened in that very year.

In the late nineteenth century, Japan had been undergoing a transformation into a modernised industrial state, with a desire to be recognised as being equal in stature to the dominant Western powers of the day. In 1894 they had waged a territorial war with neighbouring Korea. The Koreans were supported in that conflict by Chinese forces, which the Japanese had forced into a rout. This, and a significant victory on the part of the Japanese navy, enabled them to not only occupy Korea, but also the Liaodong Peninsula, a province of China. China and Japan signed the Treaty of Shimonoseki, which formally ceded the Peninsula to the Japanese. This was to be a short-lived occupation. In the subsequent period, Russia, Germany and France intervened to force the Japanese, who were not yet confident that they could defeat those powers' combined forces, to withdraw from the Liaodong Peninsula. In 1897 the Russians constructed a fortress at Port Arthur, on that peninsula, to act as a base for their Pacific Fleet. This action was undertaken by Russia as an opportunity to counter the British leased occupation of Weihaiwei, the coastal port in China's Shandong province. To the Japanese, however, it was perceived more as a move directed against their position in the region.

In December of 1897 a Russian Fleet appeared in the vicinity of Port Arthur and the following year the Chinese formally leased the land there, and its surrounding waters, to Russia. Having fortified Port Arthur, the Russian engineers then, in 1899, proceeded to connect it by rail to Harbin and the South Manchurian Railroad. At the same time, they began to encroach upon Korea acquiring mining and forestry concessions by the Yalu and Tumen rivers. By 1903 the Russians, having stationed 100,000 troops there, had strengthened their position in Manchuria. In the meantime, Japan had signed the Anglo-Japanese Alliance of 1902, in effect also making Australia and all the other parts of the British Empire allies of Japan. The basis of the alliance was that if any other nation intervened to assist Russia in any conflict then Britain would enter the conflict on the side of Japan. This lessened the probability of Russia receiving assistance from Germany or France. Diplomatic negotiations were opened and an agreement for Russia to withdraw her troops from Manchuria was agreed in principle. This was expected to have happened by the 8th of April 1903; though Russia took no action to withdraw the forces. Diplomatic talks between the powers continued, without satisfactory resolution, until January of 1904.

On 8 February, 1904, Japan, having lost patience and faith in diplomacy, and with their terms not having been met, declared war on Russia. Three hours before the Russians received the declaration, the Japanese fleet attacked the Russian Far East Fleet at Port Arthur, leaving the Russian Tsar incredulous. Their next objective was the neutralisation of the Russian Fleet at Port Arthur. The same evening they declared war, they launched a torpedo boat attack on the fleet in port, damaging the heaviest ships of the Russian fleet. The attack was still, however, indecisive. The Japanese then tried to blockade the port by sinking ships filled with concrete in the mouth of the port, but the waters were too deep for this to be effective. The Russians then tried to break a small number of ships out of the port, but these were damaged by Japanese mines, resulting in one ship, the Petropavlovsk, being sunk. The Russian navy learned from this encounter and were soon deploying mines of their own.

Below: Covering artwork for the piano issue of Tom Bulch's naval fantasia "Bombardment of Port Arthur"

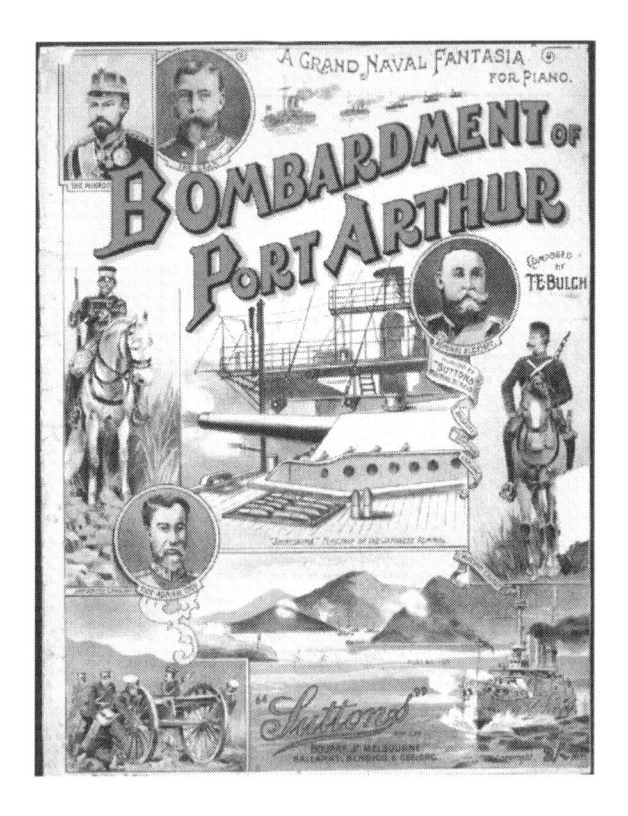

In April 1904 a siege of Port Arthur commenced. The opening of this assault was the inspiration for Thomas Bulch's piano descriptive composition, "The Bombardment of Port Arthur," which was presumably imagined based upon newspaper reports and accounts of the battles. The Japanese made many subsequent attempts to capture strategic hilltops surrounding Port Arthur by making frontal assaults by land forces, at the cost of many men. It was only later that year in December 1904 that they were able to capture a hilltop that enabled them to shell the fleet down in the waters below leading to a victory. The musical movements of Thomas's fantasia, start with "Night at sea outside of Port Arthur" followed by "Choir of rugged sailors on the warships singing the Russian National Anthem" which leads to the "Japanese preparing for action" and "General Togo giving the orders to bombard." The next movement is the bombardment itself, simulating the sound of the guns. There then comes a sixth larghetto movement with the "Japanese singing their National Anthem in honour of their victory," and the "general rejoicing on board the Japanese fleet." This piece of music was beautifully illustrated in full colour on the front with portraits of The Mikado, The Czar, Vice Admiral Togo and Admiral Alexieff as well as scenes of the action in order to aid the buyer's imagination. The piece was reviewed in the Ballarat Star on 25 April 1904 in which the correspondent wrote:

> "Something very much up to date is "The Bombardment of Port Arthur," a realistic piece of descriptive music setting for the piano composed by Mr T E Bulch and published by Suttons. It is a very stirring bit of writing, and no better indication of it being exactly what is wanted can be given that the report of the publishers that quite a large demand was made for it immediately it was put on sale."

The Soldier's Hill Band continued to attract engagements, including an appearance at Mr E Beacham's Hotel on Grant Street on the evening of Saturday, 7 May. Then on Monday, 13 of June 1904 it was Thomas Edward junior's turn to take the stage, as part of a brass quartette making a contribution to the programme of music at the Federal Hall on Sturt Street. This was for an event arranged by the Newington branch of the Australian Natives Association.

On 29 June, another article from the Ballarat Star tells us more of the younger Thomas Edward's sporting nature, albeit not in a manner that might earn a lad a good reputation in the neighbourhood.

> "STREET FOOTBALL. Three lads, named respectively Thomas Bulch, George Heed, and John Shackles, were charged with playing football in the Haymarket. The evidence of Constable Carey was to the effect that the lads took possession of the place on market day, and caused considerable restiveness amongst the horses. Senior-constable Stallard stated that there

had been several complaints regarding the practice of footballing in the streets, but on the lads promising not to offend again, they were discharged."

While it seems relatively trivial an offence, it's possible to imagine the horses being unsettled by the game, and we can be thankful of it being reported as it gives us more insight into how, and where, Tom's son liked to spend his free time.

On the 16 July 1904 we hear in the Age newspaper of Melbourne that despite his recent appointment to the bandmaster's position of Soldier's Hill Brass Band, Tom had been one of sixteen applicants for the bandmaster's post of a new brass band being formed at Sale, which is around 100 kilometres east of Melbourne. Tom had been successful in his application and was announced in the press as being the new bandmaster. The Gippsland Times tells us that he was appointed with a salary of one pound and ten shillings per week, and mentions that his son is also a cornet player, perhaps in assumption that his son would also be joining the newly formed band. In that same paper of 18 July, the Secretary of the band, Mr A Allan, invites applications from people wanting to join the band, and points out that Thomas Bulch would be arriving on Saturday the 23 July. Of what specifically tempted, or caused, Tom to leave Ballarat for a second time we can't be certain. Perhaps the prospect of earning an improved regular weekly salary was a possibility, though we do know that Suttons did not have a branch in Sale at that point so it's not clear whether Thomas's relationship with them had broken or whether he would expect to continue to work for them more remotely.

The Daily Telegraph of Launceston, on 23 July 1904, reveals yet another of Tom Bulch's pseudonyms, though this time lesser known and one that we have only seen used once. The article explains how the St Joseph's Band had been rehearsing the test piece for the next South Street Contest in Ballarat for which a test piece was "Lucretia Borgia" which it attributes to Paul Vallianare and appends the comment "(otherwise, T E Bulch)" adding that "this selection is full of beautiful solos and duets, and, as usual with the old Italian masters, is melodious in the extreme."

"Lucrezia Borgia" is an opera by Gaetano Donizetti which premiered in Milan in 1833, and revised twice during 1840. Tom's work would be to extract a selection of the principal themes combining them into a condensed arrangement for brass band. Given that Tom had arranged other such operatic works under his own name it's not clear why he would choose to do it this time under another new pseudonym. The only possible reason I can see is that with it already having been announced that the Soldiers Hill Brass Band were to compete in the South Street Competitions, contributing a test piece under a pseudonym would possibly avoid claims of unfair advantage from other bandmasters. That said, if the newspapers were able to disclose that Vallianare was Tom Bulch, it was clearly a badly kept secret.

On Friday, 5 August 1904, the Sale branch of the Australian Natives Association held an Anniversary Smoke Night at the town'e Old Mechanic's Institute. This was a gentlemen's evening of speeches and toasts, at which around 80 of the noted members of the district were present. The principal theme of the evening was the unity and harmony of the Australian peoples of all territories as a single nation, making the point that, despite the international flavours of the colonisation of the land, the country should remain loyal to the British Empire by which it was founded. During the proceedings, and at the end, instrumental selections were rendered with recitations. The music for these was provided by a compact six-piece orchestra which included both Tom and Thomas junior on cornets. Such reports suggest a closeness between Tom and his son, bonding through matters musical.

By 23 October, a full band arrangement of "The Bombardment of Port Arthur" had become available, and one of the first bands reported to play it was the Hannan's Federal Brass Band of Western Australia who included it in their instrumental concert set at the Carrington Grounds, Kalgoorlie that evening. At that event, it was announced that it was the first time that the new piece had been played in Australia.

Tom then returned to Ballarat to take the baton with the Soldier's Hill Brass Band, as planned on the opening day of the grand brass band contest at the South Street Competitions on Thursday, 27 October. Lining up as part of his band once more were old friends and fellow Shildonians Robert and George Malthouse, two of the four brothers who had been instrumental in tempting Tom to Australia in the first place. The weather for the event, held as always at the Eastern Oval, was described by the Ballarat Star as "royal" which we assume to be positive. A draw took place at Sutton's store, at eleven-fifteen in the morning, to determine the day's order in which the bands would play. The Soldiers Hill Band's rendering of Tom's test piece arrangement from "Lucretia Borgia" was described by a spectator, rather than the judge, as follows:

> "This was the first band to appear. It opened with a fair volume of sound, but somewhat blatant. The allegro movement was taken with a fair amount of precision and animation. In the largo movement, the opening euphonium solo was fairly taken, but in the cornet solo following there were one or two slips. The accompaniment was supplied with subdued volume by the basses. The lower G was only fairly taken by the cornet. The change to allegro vivace was well marked, and in the largo following a euphonium solo was taken in fair tone and with nice flowing rhythm, but intonation was not quite certain at one point, and, at the close, there was a suspicion of blurring. The moderato was well taken and with very fair volume and not bad balance. In the tenor solo, which was very fairly taken, there were one or two trips on notes, but the tone was good; intonation in the cornet duet towards the close was not all that could be desired. The allegro vivace was not badly taken, but the band lacked balance, and tone might have been improved. The andante formed an excellent change, in which, once again, the cornet figured largely and satisfactorily. The vivace movement succeeding might have been taken with a little more fire, and the conclusion was only moderately effective."

There were twelve further bands competing, each of which took their turn throughout the day at either the test piece or their own choice selection. Then followed the first part of the Quickstep contest, in which Tom's band would not be playing till the following day. At the beginning and end of the day, and also at an appearance by Lord Northcote, the Governor General of Australia and his wife, the attending bands massed to play the contest's official march "South Street" which, though written under the pen name Hall King, is understood to be another of Tom's making. The remaining pieces for each band would be played at contest's continuation on the second day. On that day, the Soldier's Hill Brass Band played their interpretation of Tom's "Gems of Verdi." An observer for the Ballarat Star wrote:

"SOLDIERS HILL BAND "Gems of Verdi," by T E Bulch, was the band's own choice. As the band was conducted by the arranger, it is reasonable to suppose that his wishes in the rendering of the music were carried out. In the opening largo movement there were several sharp contrasts, which were well noted. The volume of music was good, and the balance was very fair, but the tone was rough. After an allegro, another largo was given with piano effects very well rendered, the cornet being heard to good purpose in this and the succeeding passage. In the following movement, chiefly piano, the attack was anything but certain, and the solo instruments were not always distinguishable. The balance was not maintained and there was a raggedness about the music that did not give pleasure. A well played cornet solo was not well accompanied, the rippling accompaniment on the baritone and euphonium being too soft to be effective. The finish was only moderately effective, and the balance was never properly maintained."

Tom's band also had to execute their march for the quickstep contest on the second day. The reporter from the Star said of the Soldiers Hill Band:

"This organisation chose "Gibraltar" as the tune to which it marched. Tempo was a trifle on the quick side, as the journey was negotiated in 57 sec. The lines on the first trip were not too well maintained, but the band subsequently improved, and after the turn and wheel came down with good precision to well marked music, though the tone might have been improved. The counter-marching was well managed, lines being still well kept, and the performance was one which reflected credit upon the band."

The official judge though, Lieutenant-Colonel Wallack, was less impressed and when points had been awarded for appearance in the inspection, drill and standard of musical performance, the Soldier's Hill Band were placed eleventh from thirteen. In the more important part of the contest, across the two test pieces, the Soldier's Hill Brass Band had been placed by judge W G Bentley twelfth from thirteen bands, a result of which Thomas would not have been proud. Though he would certainly have hoped and expected to do better, he had only had a relatively short time to shape and prepare the band. It's interesting to consider whether these short tenures, in contrast to the comparatively long term influence he had on the once successful Bulch's Model Band years earlier, had begun to detrimentally impact Thomas's reputation as a bandmaster, or even a contest judge.

The contest outcome wasn't the only way in which things weren't going so well. The Gippsland Times of 27 October 1904 announced that Thomas Bulch had already resigned from his post as the bandmaster of the Sale Brass Band. Something very clearly had gone wrong there. We can only speculate that either the number of, or calibre of, band members recruited had not been as expected. Perhaps there had been a falling out over other arrangements.

Tom's career seems to have been in a state of uncertainty and flux, not knowing where his future lay. We see the Bulch family spend some time just over the border into New South Wales at Howlong, near Albury, where on 28 October it was reported that one of Tom's sons had again been in a spot of misfortune:

> "A serious mishap occurred to a lad, the son of Mr Bulch. He was playing with another boy, and whilst so engaged fell and sustained a fracture of the collar bone. the patient's injuries were attended to by Dr Kearney."

We're given no clues as to why, or for what duration, the Bulches spent time at Howlong. Yet Tom doesn't seem to have quite given up on the notion of running a band in Sale. An advertisement appeared in the Gippsland Times on 24 November 1904 as follows:

> "Bulch's Brass Band, Sale. All desirous of joining above band are requested to register their names at shop next door to Bennett' Jeweller, those having instruments naming same. T E Bulch, bandmaster."

This suggests that Tom's problem with Sale was less around whether he thought it might work and more, perhaps, about how it was being brought about. He may have felt that if he could do things his own way then perhaps Sale had the right potential to match the opportunity, and good results might ensue. An editorial piece in the same newspaper reinforces the point, also giving a few additional clues as to what was going on in Thomas's life at that time:

"An attempt is to be made to establish another band in Sale, and in our advertising columns, Mr T E Bulch, bandmaster, invites all desirous of joining Bulch's Brass Band to register their names at the shop next to Mr A W Bennett's. Mr Bulch has been engaged to prepare the Geelong Town Band for contests at Ballarat at the end of January, and will enter on his duties in about a fortnight's time."

It sounds very much as though Tom would have had a considerable amount of travelling to do over this handful of weeks as Ballarat, Howlong, Sale and Geelong were all significant distances from each other. Geelong was on the coast across the bay west of Melbourne, whereas Sale was quite a distance to the East. It would be true to say that although transport around Australia would have improved since his arrival in the country some twenty years earlier it would still have been time-consuming and expensive. For that latter reason it's also unlikely that Eliza and the children would have travelled with him each time, though the family do seem to have stayed for a while at least in Sale. We hear more of Thomas's preparations for the Ballarat contest in the Geelong Advertiser of Friday, 9 December:

"Arrangements have been completed by the Town Band for the running of a special train to the Ballarat B grade band contest on Boxing Day at reduced fares that should ensure good booking. The band is shaping well on the contest pieces, and Mr T E Bulch, who has been appointed conductor for the contest will take the members in hand on Thursday next. He will give the band nine days hard practice before the contest."

It's not clear whether in doing this Tom was attempting to set himself up as a specialist contest conductor in the mould of those like William Holdsworth who had, some years after Tom's departure form England, conducted the New Shildon Temperance Band, among many others, only at contests. Holdsworth in the early years of the twentieth century would advertise, in the Brass Band News, his achievements in terms of the quantity of contest wins with the various bands that he conducted; he became very much a contest specialist. If that were to be the case, though, Tom's own track record since the turn of the century could have made selling the idea difficult. It's speculation though, and perhaps it was simply that the Geelong

Town Band had found themselves without a conductor, and thus requested his help.

Whatever the reason, the venture was in vain. On 12 December 1904, the Ballarat Star announced that the Boxing Day second class band contest in Ballarat had been abandoned by the Victorian Band Association officially as a result of a decision made at their meeting on Friday 9th December. Some of the Association's members felt that though the Association was formed to supervise and structure the contests, it was not their job to put contests on themselves and seek funding etc for the prizes. The preference of those members was that the running of contests should be left to the South Street Society who were better equipped and set up to manage such events. At the same time, though, it was noted that the South Street Society made no provision for second class bands. It is also understood from a later report also that a number of the bands due to compete on Boxing Day had begun to pull out of the contest, leaving its viability open to question. There were disagreements on many factors of the contest including the venue and, ultimately, the will to run the event ran out. Naturally, the competing bands weren't happy at all. Consider for example that the Geelong Town Band, having made arrangements with the rail company to run a special excursion train, would need to break those arrangements. There was speculation that the Band Association's very existence was in threat as a result of the debacle, with a number of bands threatening to withdraw their membership.

From there Tom and his family appear to have spent a quiet few months in Sale working out his next move. The notion of a brass band in Sale itself didn't gather sufficient traction. By mid-May 1905, it seems that he had decided that his family's future lay in an opportunity elsewhere, namely Albury, just across the border into New South Wales. The Border Morning Mail and Riverina Times explained what had happened in this article of 17 May 1905:

"ALBURY TOWN BAND. NEW BANDMASTER APPOINTED. Mr W J Lester, secretary of the Albury Town Band, has informed us that Mr T E Bulch, of Sale (Victoria), has been appointed bandmaster in place of Captain Drury, resigned. Mr Bulch had a conversation with Mr Harold D Griffith, a member of the committee of management, at Sale some weeks back and recognised in Mr Griffith a playing member of the Albury Town Band which he had once conducted at the Druids' Contest in Melbourne. Mr Griffith mentioned that the Albury Band required a conductor and from this conversation the appointment arose. Mr Bulch will receive the same remuneration as the ex-conductor, £180 per annum, and an agreement will probably be entered into on the new conductor's arrival early next week. Mr Bulch in an accomplished cornet player and will be accompanied by his son, who plays a soprano cornet. Amongst the new bandmaster's qualifications is his ability both compose and arrange band music. The range of his compositions may be indicated by mentioning the marches 'Typhoon,' 'Battle of Eureka,' 'Antipodes' and 'South Street.' He is also known as having arranged Weber's 'Grand Reminisces.' Mr Bulch, like Mr Pogson, a former Albury bandmaster and Mr Barkel (Newcastle Band) comes from Yorkshire, whereof hail many accomplished band musicians. Mr Bulch has also had experience as a judge at band contests throughout New Zealand and many of the States of the Commonwealth and is the author of several contest pieces. It might be of interest to mention that the Albury Band at the Druids' Contest, under the leadership of Mr Bulch, secured fifth place out of eight competitors; only 4 points separated them from the winners, who tied with 89 points. The new conductor will, it is expected, take over the band early next week."

We'll return to Tom Bulch's time in Albury, but first we must observe George Allan's experiences of 1904.

New Shildon

The year began with an update once again from 'Harmonious' in the year's first issue of Wright and Round's Brass Band News. For whatever reason this was the correspondent's last round up of happenings in the Mid-Durham area, and nobody else picked up the task. It's part of the beginning of a general a decline in regional update contributions right across the Durham area, almost as if its importance declined for a time. Of George and his band 'Harmonious' writes:

> "Shildon Saxhorn have had a grand concert, and it was a great success both musically and financially. I expect you will be making some of the bands take a back seat when you are out again."

I've not been able to discover anything else about this concert, but presumably, it would have taken place in December of 1903 and either been, in part at least, a fundraiser for the band or else some charitable purpose. The band may well have needed some additional funding this year, for a decision had been made to take part in the Wear Valley Band League, a series of contests along with the Peases West Band from Crook, the Willington Silver Band, Frosterley, Wolsingham Steelworks Band and Stanhope Saxhorn Band. As with most league systems, the idea was that each of the competing towns would hold its own contest throughout the contesting season, to which each of the league member bands would endeavour attendance to compete. There were prizes for each contest and then a trophy awarded to the band that performed best throughout the whole season. Even though the distances between these competing towns and villages were relatively modest, in an era where wages for working-class men were meagre and little leisure time was afforded them, it was still quite a commitment for a band without industrial sponsorship to make. Another thing we can't be certain of is why the band chose to enter the league, though as we have seen, the taunts from 'Harmonious' throughout 1903 may have played their part. George would later advertise in the Brass Band News so may well have been a reader. If not George, then possibly one or two of his bandsmen. There may well, of course, have been other influencing factors.

Another small piece of news in this year was that on the 7 January, Mr J Greenwood of South Shields, who had published some of George's compositions in his Northern Brass Band and Military Journal, passed away after a short illness. Though Greenwood had not published many of George's pieces, and this particular journal was one of the minor ones of its day, it would have struck George particularly following the prior death of Thomas Haigh. He still had Fred Richardson's "Cornet" band journal as an outlet, but he may well have been beginning to consider a new approach.

On Saturday, 4 June 1904 George conducted his Shildon Saxhorn band at the Wear Valley Band League contest at Lister's Field, Crook, where the band came fourth from six. The adjudicator that day was James Brier, and the test piece "Beatrice di Tenda" by Vincenzo Cellini published by Wright and Round. Peases West, Willington and Frosterley were the three placed bands, in that order. There was also a separate march contest which was won by the Willington band. In the July issue of Wright and Round's Brass Band News Mr Brier's judging comments were published. The New Shildon Saxhorn Band were selected to be second to play, following the Wolsingham Steelworks Band, and Mr Brier noted the following of their performance, though of course he would not have known at the time that it was the New Shildon Saxhorn Band:

> "No. 2 (Shildon Saxhorn; Conductor Geo. Allan) – Allegro marcato – Fairly good opening but rather a scramble at bar 4, tone not the best, bar 12 again not together, group of semiquavers for 2nd cornet not nicely played. Andante-bass not satisfactory, good cornet, but spoilt next bar by others joining him, soprano no means safe, much out of tune at bar 9, tutti rather rough tone, soprano fairly good in imitation; repiano at letter D fairly good. Andante mosso – nice cornet, all going fairly well, soprano fair at bar 6, but do not overblow, you are getting a little sharp: at bar 10 all going nicely again, 4 bars before letter F band a little rough, cornet nice again, good euphonium; at letter G all very nice. Allegro-baritone good, repiano fairly good, not quite in tune; euphonium a little unsteady at letter H; euphonium cadenza good. Allegro moderato- nice euphonium and accompaniments nicely played, cornet and euphonium play well together. Piu mosso – fairly good, but finishes rather loosely by the soprano. Andante sostenuto – repiano too course and spoils balance; at letter K horns and baritone not in tune; cadenza fairly good, repiano too loud again, soprano in minims coarse 6 bars before letter L, soprano fails at last bar. Allegro mostoso – fairly good, but soprano enters rather badly, cornet makes slight slip; letter M cornet repiano and soprano do not go well together, band good on ff. Piu mosso – soprano rather rough, and not a good finish by band. 80 points (4th prize)"

The purpose of the judge's narrative, as we have had explained to us in the context of Tom Bulch's judging comments, is to explain the reasons why points were deducted from the maximum attainable. In the judge's general remarks a little more is revealed about the kind of day upon which the contest took place:

> "One very noticeable feature of to-day's contest was the out of tune playing. I have, however, no doubt that the blazing hot sun had something to do with it. I cannot think that some of the

bands are in the habit of playing out of tune to the extent that they did on Saturday. When the sun is as hot as it was on this occasion it is best to keep the instruments in their cases until just before they are going to be used."

The Brass Band News of September 1904 describes how George and the New Shildon Saxhorn band got on at the same Wear Valley Band League's Frosterley Contest, held in Rogerley Park on the 13 August. It proved a popular event with the attendance being, up to that point, a record for any contest held by the association; this in spite of the weather threatening rain all day. Mr J H White, a composer and adjudicator from Manchester, was the occupant of the judge's tent. The other entrants were, of course, the other five bands from that league; the Willington Silver Band, Frosterley Band, Stanhope Saxhorn Band, Wolsingham Steelworks Band and the Peases West Silver Band. The judge's comments on the performance by the New Shildon Saxhorn Band, who played their rendering of the test selection "Anna Bolena" third were as follows:

"(Shildon Saxhorn; conductor Geo. Allan). Allo vivace – Unison not precise, plu bars very fair; letter A, cornets and horns, etc., are good; letter B, not in tune; soprano at letter C is good, cornet and euphonium very well together, basses have good tone, ff. very good indeed. Larghetto – Cornet entrance rather too stiff, accompaniments not precise; soprano at letter F is out of tune, cornet very fair, arpeggios moderate, trombones very fair, euphonium at bar 14 moderate, rall. And morceau too forced; cadenza moderately rendered. Allegro – Triplets very fair; horns etc. very much out of tune, band from bar 12 very fair; letter H to end only moderately rendered; piu mosso too wild; cadenza very fair. Larghetto – Accompaniments not together, flugel has a fair tone and style, basses at bar 9 not together, euphonium moderate, soprano with responses is too forced; interlude at bars 25 to 29 is very loose. Quartette – From bar 30 soprano has good tone, but forces his notes; the under parts are not well balanced, and the accompaniments are too loud. Allegro, Entrance for trombones good, cornet and euphonium not in tune, soprano and horns very fair; letter M moderately played; a good finish is made. This band has the makings of a good soprano player, if he will only strive to keep his tone under control. (4th Prize)."

The band from Wolsingham Steelworks emerged as winners of that particular contest followed by Frosterley and Peases West, the latter of whom also carried off the prize for the best march.

On Saturday, 4 September the New Shildon Saxhorn Band hosted their stage of the Wear Valley Band League contests, and all six of the league's bands took part. The event was to be a huge success for the Willington Silver Band as they took first prize for both march and test piece as well as picking up medals for both best soprano and best trombone.

The Durham County Advertiser, of 16th September, reports that on the 10th of that month George was himself the judge again at a Brass Band Contest held as part of the Langley Park Floral, Industrial and Live Stock Society's eighth annual exhibition on the preceding weekend. Six bands entered the contest, which was conducted under the rules of the Durham and Northumberland Brass Band Association. The test pieces were "La Favorita" and "Songs of Schubert." Special encouragement was given for the best solo baritone and best solo cornet. As often happened the newspaper misprinted George's surname as 'Allen', but clearly stated New Shildon as his home town. The event was blessed with "beautiful weather and a great crowd of people" to explore the five giant marquees erected to exhibit the creatures and produce from across the region. There is no record however of which of the bands George Allan adjudged to have been best on the day.

On 15 October, the six bands of the Wear Valley League convened at Stanhope for that band's contest. The adjudicator on this occasion was Mr George Wadsworth who did not enjoy the Shildon Saxhorn Band's rendering of either test piece or march to be sufficiently good to see them placed in the top four on points. The form band of the year, the Peases West Band won the top prize for the test piece, and the hosting band from Stanhope were best in the march contest. Of what occurred at the Willington and Wolsingham contests that year, there is nothing published that we have been able to find. We do, however, know the outcome of the Wear Valley Association's contest season. In the November 1904 issue of Brass Band News, the New Shildon Band are included in updates on the Bishop Auckland District as submitted by correspondent The Rover. Peases West were reported to have won the Wear Valley Band League Cup that season, but were reminded that they had to win it three times in a row to keep it, and also to remember to invite the other bandmasters from the league, which would have included George, to the presentation ceremony. Of the Shildon Saxhorn Band The Rover states encouragingly:

> "Shildon have a fairly good band if the style of playing was a little smarter. The tone of band is very good. I hope to see you stick in and let us see you give the league bands a surprise next season. You can do it!"

Far from being the beginning of a fresh attempt at winning the Wear Valley Band League, however, the beginning of the year 1905 seems to have brought about the mysterious disappearance of the New Shildon Saxhorn Band. When the bands that made up the Wear Valley Band League for the year 1905 were announced, the Shildon band was not one of them. There is no explanation published anywhere specifically for this. We can speculate that one of a number of things may have happened. Perhaps, with all the new distractions that the turn of the century had introduced for the working classes, interest in brass banding in the town of Shildon had declined to the extent that the task of filling all the seats across two full bands was no longer viable.

In his centenary retrospective of the British Bandsman newspaper, a social history of brass bands, the writer, Alf Hailstone, points out that the year 1905 was a year of economic depression in Britain and that this was a contributing factor in the demise of a number of bands. This had put pressure on the band contesting scene as bands scrabbled over what contest prize money was available. Allegations of corruption abounded in the band contest scene, whilst the erstwhile typical fee of three pounds and ten shillings for a contest adjudicator dropped to typically just fifteen shillings. Publications like the British Bandsman looked out upon a banding community struggling to deal with desperate times, sufficiently so for the editor to write "Keep together lads. Trade is slack at the moment but who knows what a prayer and good fellowship might bring." Not enough to keep the New Shildon Saxhorn Band vital it appeared.

There are so many possibilities as to why the band didn't continue; the truth behind the reason will forever elude us leaving us only fuel for speculation. Perhaps any remaining interested members of the Saxhorn Band joined forces with remaining members of the New Shildon Temperance Band to keep that going, though that formerly high-achieving band's last known contest appearance under this name was also in 1905, taking place on 12 June. Maybe the Saxhorn band had become frustrated with the lack of success in the band league, or had struggled to stay financially viable enough to buy new instruments or maintain old ones. Perhaps the bandsmen had become frustrated with George and his separate interest in judging band contests plus composing his own music; after all, he would have had precious little time outside of work in which to do all this as well as look after a wife and family. Perhaps it was George that had become frustrated and disenchanted with the week by week demands of staffing, tutoring and equipping a band. Regardless of the precise reason, most organisations follow a cycle in which they are formed, wax and wane and eventually disband. It seems that in 1905, it was the New Shildon Saxhorn Band's turn to reach the end of that cycle. During this difficult period evidence suggests that the brass band community in Shildon as a whole slipped into something of a slumber. The legacy started decades earlier by Francis Dinsdale appeared to be in grave danger of disappearing altogether.

It seems however that dimming embers of the banding movement in the Shildons were not fully extinguished, but rather smouldered and smoked away in the hearth for some years. We know that the Shildon Temperance Band managed to stay functional, making rare reported appearances such as when on Thursday, 22 June 1911 the nation celebrated the coronation of King George V, and the band would take part in a parade through the town. We also know that in the early twentieth-century we see a handful of reports concerning a Shildon Wesleyan Band, which it has been suggested by local historians may have been an evolutionary development of the Saxhorn band. There is nothing I have yet seen documented anywhere that proves this theory, nor have I seen anything that connects it to George Allan, though it's quite possible that a re-framed band and its master could have parted

The Temperance Band, still part of the legacy of Francis Dinsdale, and upon which Tom Bulch was an early influence, certainly did continue. If we imagine ourselves in 1905, peering into the future very briefly we will see an advertisement in the

Darlington and Stockton Times of 12 August 1911 proclaims that the Heighington Show will feature the 'Shildon Band' which suggests that in the minds of the organisers at least there was only one worth mentioning, the implication being that is was unnecessary to be specific as to which for that reason. We would also see the Temperance Band standing in for the band of the Band of the Grenadier Guards at the 1911 Shildon Show, after the former cancelled their appearance. The band was, on this occasion, conducted by Harry Gibbon, despite his ill health causing him to have resigned as director of the Shildon Choral Society earlier that year. We'd see Gibbon keeping that band going throughout the war of 1914-1918 during which it finally drops the 'Temperance' label to become the New Shildon Silver Band, a name it retains up until 1937 after which it is to become sponsored by the London and North Eastern Railway, or LNER, Brass Band right through until the 1970s.

So though there was something of a lull, the lineage of the bands founded by the Dinsdale family would continue, and what was once the Temperance Band would return to contesting at which it would once again succeed. However, we must return, now, to 1905 for all of which we write here takes place in the future. Yet, so far as we have been able to see, none of the town's banding ventures from here onward appear to have had any direct influential involvement from George Allan. As an Anglican, and with no documented evidence to suggest it, we feel it's unlikely that he had any hand in the running of the Wesleyan Band, though it's possible that some of his bandsmen may have found seats there. Though George was no longer a bandmaster, his greatest achievements, arguably, and those for which he is best remembered today, were yet to be attained. We'll continue his story after a further trip to the far side of the globe.

Albury

When we last left the Australian thread of this story, in mid-May, Tom Bulch had joined the Albury Town Band as their new bandmaster. This new appointment was, perhaps surprisingly, broadly reported across the region, with notices appearing in the Sydney Morning Herald, The Age in Melbourne, the Wodonga and Toowong Sentinel, Wagga Wagga Express, Gippsland Times, Sydney Mail and New South Wales Advertiser, Australian

Town and Country Journal, and Yackandandah Times. It felt as though someone, possibly Thomas himself, wanted the world to know that he wasn't quite done yet. He arrived in Albury on 24 May, with the events surrounding his arrival captured by a reporter from the Border Morning Mail and Riverina Times.

> "Mr T E Bulch, the newly appointed bandmaster to the Albury Town Band arrived last evening by the express. He was met at the train by members of the committee of management and bandsmen. On reaching the Albion Hotel an informal welcome was tendered to Mr Bulch by the president, committee and bandsmen. There were present, Messrs Blake (chair), Harold D Griffith, Laughton, Ashby, Louhes, Carter, Walling, Schneider, Burton, Doughty, Oddie and McCulloch. The president in a few words of welcome proposed the toast of the bandmaster and trusted that their relations would be harmonious. The committee wished the band to be in keeping with the importance of the town and were extremely anxious for its success. Mr Ashby supported 'the foregoing remarks. Mr Bulch replied, and in the course of his remarks deprecated the fact that bandsmen were on the committee of management. This he had found previously to be subversive of proper control. The committeemen referred to were personal friends of his, but this did not alter the principle. Mr Bulch concluded by hinting that he would do his best to make the band worthy of the town."

Straight away we can see that expectations in Albury were high, and equally that Tom was quite prepared to assert himself from the very outset by levelling a critique at the band over the way it was run. No gentle approach to making changes over time. Tom set straight to work.

At the beginning of June, he was also announced as one of eleven judging candidates long listed for the upcoming band contest at Gympie in Queensland. All of the listed prospective judges would receive a letter requesting their terms for engagement, and each, assuming they were interested in the engagement would duly respond to the committee by letter to be considered at a future meeting. When Tom received his request for terms, the matter was very soon reported in the Albury Banner. It would have provided him with a ripe opportunity to remind citizens of Albury, should they have had any doubts, how well he was regarded within the banding fraternity.

On Sunday 18 June, Tom gave his new band their first public airing since taking control. On a 'perfect' afternoon in the Albury Botanic Gardens he put the band through their paces performing a programme of music that, as you might expect, included several of his own compositions. The attendance on the day was strong and a sum of eight pounds was raised in gate fees. The band also announced that it would give a concert in aid of the Albury Benevolent Society, and additionally visit the Newtown Orphanage to give a concert there.

On the morning of 15 July 1905, readers of the Albany Advertiser in Western Australia were informed, while perusing their daily paper, that Tom Bulch was composing a new march as part of the preparations for the forthcoming Albany Band Contest and Eisteddfod. Tom clearly wasn't inclined to rest his talent for composition whilst bringing his new latest band up to speed.

On the evening of that same day, in Albury, passers-by were able to enjoy a performance by the Albury Town Band, staged on a balcony opposite Messrs W S Norman and Co's premises. Tom again ensured that the programme highlighted a number of his pieces of the moment. Listeners could enjoy his march "Light Artillery"; his arrangement of Verdi's works; his march "Flying Squadron," penned under the pseudonym Eugene Lacosta and thought to be a reference to a competitive yachting team; his quadrille "Melodique" and the galop "Carbine." The band announced just after that weekend that they were requesting quotes from companies to provide the band's new uniforms, which were described as being of navy blue serge, with black braid and navy trousers with a wide red stripe. The uniform would be completed with a navy cap featuring a turned down peak and broad band of black braid.

Returning briefly to the matter of the Gympie band contest, the Gympie Times of 3rd August advises that, of the eleven nominations for contest adjudicator received, those from Messrs Barkell, Bulch and Wade had been shortlisted. Tom had requested a fee of thirty-five pounds to cover all his expenses. This was a significantly higher sum than many of the other candidates, but clearly, and in spite of this, Tom's reputation had been sufficient for him still to be among the final three. Mr Barkell of Newcastle, to whom Tom had dedicated his march "Newcastle," had requested twenty-six pounds. Mr Wade of Bathurst asked for forty-five guineas. Eventually, from the shortlist the committee settled upon the tender from Mr Wade, and Tom was denied his thirty-five pound fee. Another interesting point of note was that one of the other 'also-rans' for the engagement had been fellow ex-Shildonian Sam Lewins, the bandmaster of Bathurst District Band, who had requested fifteen pounds plus hotel expenses. Thus, we see Sam also striving to be involved in the contest circuit.

On Wednesday, 23 August 1905, Albury celebrated Arbor Day. A number of trees had been supplied by the Government for planting, and a large crowd of people assembled on grounds near the Albury Train Station to take part or watch. With the town's Mayor unavoidably absent, Alderman Brink presided and planted the first tree. Tom and the Albury Town Band provided entertainment at an afternoon tea, held for all involved immediately after the planting.

Tom and the Albury Town Band were present over the three days of the Albury Show, running from the 12th to 14th September, providing selections of music for the entertainment of attendees at various times throughout the event. The band were, for the first time, proudly resplendent in their new band uniforms. Then on Sunday, 15 October the band joined the Albury Citizens Band and the Albury Choral Society at the Albury District Hospital Annual Demonstration. This event, taking place on the Albury Showground, was to raise funds for the hospital. It turned out to be a perfect day for such entertainment too, being both warm and bright. A reported attendance of around 1,500 people were present for the musical spectacle and accompanying sports. The men wore their Sunday-best, and ladies donned their finest millinery.   A vocal ensemble, comprising of more than 150 vocalists, stood on the tiered grandstand during their performance, while the Choral Society, Citizens Band and of course the Albury Town Band took turns to render fine pieces of music and song. These included a Tom Bulch arrangement of Wagner's works. After the conclusion, and once collections from the various Albury churches had been taken into account, it was estimated that about seventy pounds had been raised for the hospital.

On 29 October, the Albury Town Band made good upon their promise to entertain at the Newtown Orphanage. Than, on November 8th and 9th a monster Floral Fete, Carnival and Sports took place in Albury. This spectacle included cricket, cycling, quoits, a motor car exhibition, racing of various sorts including a "Gretna Green Race" with dressed up brides and grooms, a "cigar race" and log chopping. The evenings were given to torchlight processions, the first of which accompanied by the rival Albury Citizens Band, and the second by Tom and his Albury Town Band. These evening parades were followed by masked parades and fairy dances by artificial light, the ascent of a mammoth fire balloon, and fireworks. Wherever there was a spectacle like this throughout his lifetime and in his locality, it feels as though Tom Bulch was never going to be far away. Both of the Albury bands gave selections at intervals throughout.

As Christmas approached, though Tom was no longer present in Ballarat the bands there made sure he was not forgotten by playing his works; particularly when Prout's Ballarat Brass Band gave a rendering of a specially arranged selection of carols by Bulch at their concert on Christmas Eve at the Eastern Oval in Ballarat.

In Albury, on Christmas Night, Tom conducted his own band through a sacred open-air concert on the Sports Ground at Albury. The concert also included a vocal segment. Then, on New Year's Day, rounding off the year, we see a hint of a side to Thomas's life that we've not seen before in any of the other places he'd lived. At the Jindera Races which took place very near Albury, we see that in the Handicap Hack Race, for a prize of two pounds over seven furlongs, the second placed horse "Gambil" has an owner named Bulch. This is almost certainly connected to Tom and his family. We oughtn't to be too surprised that Tom might have fleetingly taken an interest in racing; after all, there are some clues in the titles of some of his pieces such as "Final Flutter." This is, however, the first indication that he may have been directly involved in horse ownership. In equestrianism, the term 'hack' is used to indicate either riding a horse for light exercise or else exhibition or show horses where the quality and manners of the horse were important.

New Shildon

With no band to tutor and mentor, it would seem, 1905 comes across as very quiet musically for George Allan. We see nothing written of him having conducted at contests or concerts, and few references to his officiating at contests. However, it does appear that the period from 1904 onward is pivotal, and that he had made a decision that will take him upon a path towards arguably his greatest achievements.

In examining this, we should bear in mind that, unlike Tom, who had chosen to give over as much of his working life to music as was possible, George, while clearly gifted, remained an amateur musician. To him, music was a hobby, and a passion he pursued outside of his working hours. With a physically demanding job, long working day and a family to raise, his involvement in music, though occasionally fruitful, would always be overshadowed by other responsibilities. Time away from the paint shop at the North Eastern Railway wagon works was precious, requiring careful choices as to how it was best spent. How much ought he to spare for musical pursuits?

Faced with no longer having to be in charge of the brass band he inherited from his mentor, he appears to have decided that his greatest strength lay simply in composing, and that he wanted to concentrate most of his efforts in that direction. Furthermore, he evidently decided that from now on he would publish the music he created himself.

To some extent, this second decision may well have been prompted by other changes that meant that he was no longer connected to a network of people that in the past had taken care of the publishing. We've seen already that publishers Thomas Haigh and J Greenwood had passed away. In addition, Fred Richardson of Sibsey, near Boston, who had also published George's works in his "Cornet" band journal, had increasingly suffered ill health and been forced to retire, selling his business to Wright and Round. It doesn't appear as though George contributed many works directly to Wright and Round, though there are some later examples such as "The Belle of Bohemia." It could be that most of those pieces, some of which are still available through the Wright and Round archive catalogue, would be those to which the rights were acquired upon purchase of Richardson's "Cornet" business. The dates of such pieces, including "King Edward" and "The New Century" support this view. Wright and Round, most probably, did not require George's services directly. They already turned out band music in tremendous volume, principally through the pen of Henry Round, though he too was to pass away in 1905. Some writers on the subject have suggested that Round's demise resulted in that company becoming somewhat less pioneering in their output.

If George were to continue to provide music to the bands he would need to find a new outlet, and we believe this is why he chose to chance his arm at self-publishing. The venture seems to have begun with the publishing of the march "Battle Abbey" in 1904. This appears to be the first of a collection of pieces to have been printed under George's adopted banner of the "Popular Brass Band Journal." Each of the new pieces under this journal title displayed his home, and publishing, address, 2 Pears Terrace, New Shildon.

The Popular Brass Band Journal was less of a band 'journal' in the traditional sense in that it was not generated on a guaranteed monthly or quarterly basis and we have seen no evidence anywhere of George setting up and maintaining a list of regular subscribers paying in advance for a full season. George published, and sold, each piece individually. To bands buying the music, however, having a proper journal title at the head of each part certainly made it look the part, being similar in presentation to the music produced by the far bigger companies with which he was trying to compete. It also helped him to establish an identity in that every piece was immediately identifiable as being his work.

There is one other possibility which, though pure speculation, I do want to set out here. There is absolutely no evidence to support this hypothesis, yet perhaps George, who would surely have been aware through his residential proximity to the remaining members of the Bulch's family, or the reports of such in the British brass press, of Tom Bulch's setting up journals in Australia, saw his chance to finally follow suit. It's possible even that his inspiration might otherwise have been former Shildon bandmaster Robert De Lacy's London Journal. Though George would not have known De Lacy, his old mentor could well have told him tales of those days of the Saxhorn Band. I fear that connecting these events is little more than a romantic notion of a lifelong spirit of competition and inspiration, yet it is a possibility worth pondering.

As regards the printing of George's music, the earliest of his self-published pieces were lithographic prints. It would have been necessary to require that somebody, most likely not George, carefully transcribed his handwritten manuscript, etching it onto to sheets made from a lead and tin alloy. This required a set of specialist etching tools designed for the specific purpose. These tools included a five-clawed tool that

would be used with a straight edge to etch the parallel lines of the music stave
, punches to represent the clefs and notes and gouging tools to add expression lines and letters around the musical notation. This process required great attention to detail and a very particular skill set. Any mistake made in transcribing the music to the printing plates would result in every musician playing that part incorrectly, so the publisher would want to ensure that they could trust the printer. Though corrections could be made at the print works if proof-reading of any of the parts revealed a mistake, once the music has been printed in quantity it was too late. George promoted his works for sale by taking out small personal advertisements in the music press of the day. It's probable that he also touted his work to his own network of contacts across County Durham.

We mentioned that we believe "Battle Abbey" was the first to be self-published, and we think it was composed and printed in 1904. The first band that we have seen reported as playing it was the Luton Red Cross Band on 27 August 1904, who performed it to a crowd at Luton Town Football Club. However it was not until the February 1905 issue of Wright and Round's Brass Band News that we see the following small advertisement that ran issue by issue until July.

> "SOMETHING GOOD! Bands wanting good CONTEST MARCHES send for "Battle Abbey," winner of many contests in 1904; also my two new marches for 1905 contests. "La Maestro," a splendid thing for good bands, sure to win, and "Bravura," just the march for 2nd class contests, very effective and will suit any and every band. Price 1/3 nett per march. Extras 1d. each – Postal Orders to GEO ALLAN, Music Publisher, New Shildon, Co Durham."

As his Popular Brass Band Journal was not a subscription journal, George would need to work harder to, first of all, let people know when his new works were available and then establish a reputation for good music to make bands want to keep buying the next one. The commencement of his self-publishing venture marks the beginning of a 'golden era' in his career as a composer. It would be a period during which he created the enduring contest marches that would earn him the specialist nickname, in banding circles, of "The March King," though, depending upon preference, there were other contemporary claimants to that title. Up until this point many who would have perhaps known both George and Tom, may have felt George's contribution to the global brass music repertoire to be comparatively far less significant, though the time had now come for George to shine.

To a researcher, the kind of small advertisement George placed in 1905 is a truly wonderful thing as within its wording it carries something of the personality of its creator. As with the interviews that expose the words that Tom Bulch chose to describe the importance of good quality band contests, these are the words that George Allan chose to sell his music. This is the closest thing we can see to an expression of the creator's intent. It's implicit that George isn't just trying to churn out any old marches here; he is looking to carefully create contest winners, marches that show his skill, as composer at least, in bringing out the best in a band. Though aiming for contest winners, we can see through his description of "Bravura" that he's not only trying to provide for the best bands, but aiming to offer something to bands at different levels. This we see also in Tom Bulch's approach to composition. To make some money from selling music to bands you need to appeal to as many as you can across a broad market.

On George's declaration of "Battle Abbey" having been winning at many contests in 1904, it's a claim that is difficult to qualify. March contests were considered something of a sideshow to the main event of the test-pieces and consequently it's rare that whenever the winning band in a march contest is declared in the press that the march is named. The earliest reference we have seen to "Battle Abbey" being played at a march contest was found on the excellent website brassbandresults.co.uk, telling of the 17 July 1915, when the Calfaria Brass Band in Wales played it at the Penygroes March Contest in Llanelli, Carmarthenshire. Alas, it was not a winning march on that occasion.

On Saturday 4 February 1905, George was once again applying his contest judging wisdom and experience. This time it was for a slightly different format of contest to those we have seen him involved in. The Yorkshire Post and Leeds Intelligencer provides more of an explanation:

> "The Stockton Druids Silver Band held a quartet and solo contest in the Borough Hall, Stockton, on Saturday. Mr George

Allan, of Shildon, was the judge. For the solo contest 23 entries were received, and of these 20 competitors took part. Result:- 1, A Howarth, Brotton, who played a selected piece; 2, A. Mann, a cornet player, whose piece was "Carnival Di Venice." In the quartet contest it was expected eight bands would have taken part, but one of these, Hebburn Temperance No 3, was compelled to leave in order to catch their train. Seven bands competed, the result being:- 1, Milburn's Model; 2, South Bank Silver Prize Quartet; and 3, Guisborough Priory No. 1."

On 2 September 1905, an open brass band contest took place at Middleton-in-Teesdale as part of the 39th annual show of the Middleton-in-Teesdale Agricultural Society. George Allan once again spent much of the day in the adjudicator's tent. The show was reported to have included a particularly fine set of classes of shorthorn cattle drawing comment from Lord Barnard, in attendance in his capacity as president of the society. The band contest looked to have been a popular draw, with twelve entering, but as so often happened, for some reason two of the bands had to withdraw leaving only ten to compete. For this particular contest, the bands were given the opportunity to choose their own test piece rather than play a set composition. Other than Middleton-in-Teesdale, the home band that day, the other participating bands were largely from the towns and villages of the South-Durham area, though entries were attracted from as far away as the North-East coast through the Hartlepool Borough Band and Redcar Steelworks. When the points George had awarded were revealed, it was one of George's fellow conductors from the 1904 Wear Valley Band League, J B Wright and his Willington Silver Band, that were rewarded for being the best band on the day. The band from West Auckland came second and the prizes for third and fourth were split evenly between Auckland Park and Hartlepool Borough. The Willington Silver Band had also excelled in the march contest, beating Auckland Park into second place. They also won the only two supplementary medals that were available at that contest; for best soprano player and best conductor.

Later that same month, on Saturday, 16 September, we learn through the Leeds Mercury that George was engaged as the judge for a brass band contest at Dodworth, near Barnsley. This may well have been the furthest south that he would ever travel for a band contest, and it certainly gave him the opportunity to hear some bands that he would have been unfamiliar with. The Dodworth Old Brass Band who promoted the contest were not competing, but other entries came from ten other places including Mexborough and Rotherham. As regards the outcome, the paper tells us that:

> "The Dodworth Brass Band also promoted a contest which was held in the grounds adjoining The Grove, lent my Mr H A Allport JP. Mr George Allan, New Shildon, Durham, was the judge, his awards being as under:- Selection – 1, Holme; 2, Thurlstone; 3, Parkgate; 4, Dannemora. Quickstep – 1, Holme; 2, Dannemora. The medal for trombone solo was also won by Holme."

The test piece was "Le Pre aux Clercs" by Ferdinand Herold arranged by Charles Godfrey Jnr. Naturally, a march contest also formed part of the overall event, in which the bands from Holme and Dannemora came first and second. One can't help but wonder whether George used these opportunities to network and promote his own compositions and journal.

As we move into 1906, we see a reminder that getting your message out to the buying public regarding the availability of the music that you have created, and trying to do so on a working man's tight budget, wasn't always a straightforward matter. George limited his advertising to the 'personal adverts' columns of the banding press. These were small discreet adverts that tended to appear towards the rear of the papers. Remembering that one of the main purposes of Wright and Round's Brass Band News, as just one example, was to extol the virtues of buying from their own catalogue of music, it was unlikely that an independent seller would be offered a prominent spot without paying a premium for being in competition with the major publisher. We see also at the beginning of this year that even having submitted an advertisement you weren't necessarily guaranteed it would appear as and when you intended. The January 1906 issue of Brass Band News, for example, included the following brief notice.

> "We offer our apologies to Mr GEO. ALLAN, of New Shildon, for leaving out his advertisement last month. It came at the last moment and got mislaid. Very sorry."

It was most likely a genuine mistake, but one which may have cost George a small sum in potential sales. If George submitted any payment with that request to advertise, he wasn't to see any value from it until the April issue of the same paper, where the following advertisement appears.

> "Contesting Bands should get the following Marches:- "La Maestro," "Battle Abbey," "Bravura," "The Gale" and "Senator." Five well known Good Things, money-getters, not pot boilers. Price 1s 3d each set. Extras 1d. Bandmasters send stamp for specimens, – Geo Allan, Publisher, New Shildon."

The same advertisement continues to appear in May, June and July as well as August. We do know that at least one contesting band purchased "Senator" that year and set to work to include it in the band's repertoire. It was played in a band contest on 8 June 1906, Whit Friday, at Bottom Mossley by the Slaithwaite Band, and it remains one of the pieces that George composed which is still popular today in concerts or entertainment contests.

Spring of 1906 brought bad news to the Allan family. George's sister Ada had been living away from New Shildon and working as a housekeeper for an elderly gentleman, James Buck, a yeast dealer of Spring Gardens, Brompton on Swale in North Yorkshire. On 4 March, at the age of only thirty-one she died. Dr Shelps, declared the cause of death as 'pulmonary consumption causing heart failure'. These days we'd know this former term as tuberculosis. The Allans must have been expecting her death as according to the certificate her father John James Allan was present with her when she passed away, and it was he who reported the death to the registrar. Ada's body was brought back to New Shildon where a funeral was held on 8 March 1906. On the 1901 census Ada is shown as James Buck's niece, however the relationship is quite obscure. What we do know is that James had been married to Eleanor Mary Buck who had been a visitor at the Allans home when the 1861 census was taken. It's also possible that Ada's older sister Mary Eleanor Allan may well have been named after her. Eleanor Mary Buck, originally born with the surname Stainsby, had lived with James, who was a carter by trade, in the Monkwearmouth area of the coastal port and shipbuilding town of Sunderland. She herself had died in 1897. It appears then that Ada's erstwhile occupation of taking care of James was some kind of family arrangement.

On Saturday, 2 June 1906 George was engaged for a band contest that was probably as far north as he had ever travelled on such duties. His destination was Bo'ness, more correctly known as Borrowstounness, a Scottish industrial river port town on the south bank of the River Forth a few miles west of Edinburgh. Conveniently for George, Bo'ness was well served by rail, though the journey would have required him to change from the North Eastern Railway Company to the North British Railway Company at either Berwick or Carlisle, depending upon which route he preferred or which was more affordable. This was the sixteenth such contest held at Bo'ness by the Kinniel Reed Band, who had offered a total of £66 in prize money across the two classes of band competing on the day. The prize money, as well as the reputation of the contest, had attracted ten bands to compete in the first class, and eight in the second class. Compared to other contests George had been involved with prior to that date, he would have a long day ahead of him. As with his trip to Dodworth the previous year, this contest gave George an opportunity to hear bands he most likely would not have heard before. The bands in the second class category, that would be playing their own choice test pieces, represented such towns as Falkirk, Kinnaird, Townhill and Laurieston. The ten bands in the first class category included those same four places as well as Kelty, Dykehead, Musselburgh, Kirkaldy and Bo'ness itself.

This contest is one of the rare occasions where George's comments on the bands were preserved through having been published in the Fife Free Press and Kirkaldy Guardian on 9th June. They are detailed and, as with the adjudicator's notes produced by Tom Bulch that we showed previously, are technical in terms of their use of musical terminology and critique of the performance. They also, however, include a little of George's character, so we'll include here his comments on the first placed band, as well as those on one of the other competing bands from the first class contest. The test piece's musical score, the document that tells the conductor what all parts of the band should be playing at any moment throughout, is in this case divided into sections labelled with letters of the alphabet. Hence why you'll see phrases such as "nicely in tune solo bars at S" and "cornet not certain at T." For the newspaper reader, without the musical score in front of them, this would mean very little, though an overall impression of the performance can be gained. For the band's conductor, hoping for a critique of where they did well, or went awry, they would be able to refer to their own copy of the score and know exactly which phrases the contest judge was referring to. Similarly, a non-musician will notice much Italian being used. This isn't simply the adjudicator trying to appear clever. Whilst many a reader would find these phrases meaningless, they are universal to conductors worldwide almost in the same way as to how the use of Latin is universal in botany. Band conductors across Britain, be they miners, engineers, technicians, clerical workers or indeed a blacksmith's striker recently having become a wagon painter, like George, would know the meaning of these musical phrases from the musical education passed down to them by their tutors and predecessors. The top band at the Bo'ness contest, was the brass band from Polton Mills, of whom George commented on their selection of "Beethoven" as follows:

> "Opens sostenuto ma con troppo; a good toned band; continues well up to letter C; letter D fugue fine. Soprano also good; very fine at F; a splendid movement. A very difficult selection going all right, cadenza very nice, good syncopation, grand unisons at N; fine music in here, splendid.   Trombone slight slip on cadenza. Solo Larghetto – fine trombone, also arpeggios and the expression of the band is fine; continues on without much fault; S to T very good. Trombone and cornet duo very nice indeed; U horn and flugel fine, also band accompaniments excellent; recitative by cornet just right. Fine bass in andante, grave next movement and the whole band is like an organ; good on soprano, and band responds smartly. Cornet fine solo also; band out of tune just before finish; right on to adagio cantabile. Euphonium very fine indeed; finest baritone today, shows off in this movement; well done euphonium. March – nice body of tone, excellent. All, con brio splendid. A fine selection, best today, and exceedingly well played."

The band from Laurieston finished among the unplaced bands with their rendering of a Rossini selection, earning the following commentary:

> "Opens very nice indeed; effect spoiled just before entering next movement; too harsh top cornets. Allegro marzeale very fair. Poco Pio Mosso rather slow.   Lento – trombone very nice; cadenza too detached. Andante – solo for cornet nice style, and band fair; Andante good expression; E to F perhaps overdone;

duo cadenza wrong move on trombone, otherwise good. Euphonium plays this nice; just before letter I band not together. Euphonium cadenza – very fair; could be improved; too much alike in each phrase. Andante solo – gets tame between J and K; nice last few bars. Allegro mod. – good tone, and cornet nice; fine up to cadenza, which was fair. Andante grazioso – nice expression and good tone. Soprano splendid. Grazioso – uncertain entry. Euphonium nice on to cornet solo, towards end off tune; Fanfare after U splendid up to V, then not together; 2nd time right, good finish."

After George's points deductions for errors or poor playing had been calculated, the top five bands in the first class contest were, in descending order, Polton Mills, Musselburgh, Kirkaldy Trades, Bo'ness and Townhill. In the second class contest Townhill Band triumphed, followed by Laurieston West and Kinnaird. Further prizes were awarded to R Campbell of the Kirkaldy Trades band for the best performance on a baritone horn that day, James Graham of the Musselburgh band for excelling on cornet, and George Smith of Polton Mills for best euphonium. It had been a long day for George, for the bandsmen and for the audience. This had not gone unnoticed by one particular commentator in the same newspaper writing under the pseudonym 'Saxhorn' who appears to have some connection with the Kirkaldy Trades band, and levelled criticism at the contest organisers thus:

"The Trades had a long wait before they performed, and mounted the contest stand after nine o'clock had struck. The band had but finished when out popped the judge from his wigwam and briefly addressed his very much tired and worn out audience in the following strain - "That he did not know if his awards would give general satisfaction." On the face of it those contest committees who this season have taken to running on lines that combine the first and second section bands taking part, cannot be too strongly condemned. The great length of time that the judge has got to sit and listen to a mixture of good, bad, and indifferent music is quite enough to give him a fit of the blues. It is only next to a miracle should he not lose his head. Besides the long wait on before the last drawn bands perform tends to upset the bandsmen, to say nothing of the hurry-scurry that many of the bands have to experience to catch their home going train. Such faulty arrangement on the part of committees in running band contests, who, for a prize money draw, prolong the contest into a late hour, hold out no inducement for first section bands to compete. Band contests in the open-air should be finished not later in the evening than 7:30."

This was one expressed opinion, and we could never be sure whether it is a view with which George might agree, but it seems a rational criticism. We can't know what George's travel arrangements were for that weekend, though it is highly doubtful that he would have been allowed by his employer to travel the day before. It's probable therefore that he had a very early start at Shildon station to get to Bo'ness in time. One would like to think that with the contest ending so late in the day, he would have been able to stay the night before making his own way back.

It seems that, as long as there have been band contests, there has been controversy, strong opinion and varying views on how they should be run. In Australia, Tom Bulch had been active in trying to help the brass band scene formulate an approach. In Britain, George Allan, regardless of his views, would as a man merely seen as a gifted amateur, have had little influence in this respect.

The third of August 1906 brought with it the 107th annual show of the long-running Barnard Castle Agricultural Society, which naturally incorporated a band contest. George was the organising committee's choice to occupy the adjudicator's tent. Nearby the gathered throng, under fine blue skies, admired the sheep, horses and cattle registered for the various livestock prize categories. These included a number belonging to the local peer and landowner, Lord Barnard, who as well as presenting prizes along with the Marquess of Zetland, would receive several himself. The bands taking part in that particular contest were ones that George knew relatively well. They represented Hunwick, Evenwood, Willington Silver, West Auckland, along with Barnard Castle as the home town band for the day. In George's trusted opinion, the Willington Silver Band, one-time fellow competitors of George's own Saxhorn Band in the Wear Valley Band League, had played the best rendition of the test piece "Beauty's Bower" earning themselves the eight pounds first prize money. They also pipped the band from West Auckland to the first prize in the separate march contest.

Closer to home, there was bad news for George regarding the New Shildon Mechanic's Institute, of which as we know, he was a regular frequenter and long standing member. The Institute's hall, on Station Street, as well as having been outgrown by that organisation, had developed structural faults, cracks having been observed in the walls of the hall. The Institute's Centenary Book, written in 1933, explains that at a meeting on 2 April 1906, a decision was made to close the hall completely. The committee requested that, the then President, Mr R Pick, should look to exert his influence with the North Eastern Railway company for support, particularly in light of the revenue lost by having to close the hall and denying its availability to regular users.

Albury

Returning to Australia, on 8 January 1906, the committee of the Albury Town Band met at the town's Council Chambers to discuss the year ahead. Tom Bulch was present, by invitation. After discussing the usual formalities around operation of the band, the committee asked Tom whether he considered that the band in his charge was capable of competition success at the forthcoming Geelong band contest, running from the 22nd to the 24th of February. With the travel and accommodation expense that would be incurred by sending a whole band to Geelong, this was not a trivial question on the part of the committee.

> "Mr Bulch replied, that he considered the band a high-class organisation capable of holding its own in any company, and its chances of competing successfully at Geelong was as bright as that of any band of which he knew. It would, he felt sure, do credit to its supporters and to the town of Albury if the opportunity was afforded."

On the strength of Tom's testimony as to his faith in his bandsmen, the committee approved the decision to enter the band into the contest and immediately set about the matter of organising fundraising measures to meet the cost of contest expenses. They agreed that a concert on the Albury Sports Ground was the way to get the ball rolling. Tom, who was already involved in the contest remotely, having arranged "Verdi's Works" as the pre-determined test piece for the concert, would create a programme of special band selections for the fundraising concert. One would be the band's own choice test piece for the same contest, his arrangement of "Weber's Works."

Tom's confidence had once again placed his personal reputation on the line, and he would have known that he would have to work hard with the bandsmen to achieve an outcome to satisfy the committee. He had already started rehearsing the band in separate sections to make sure that each section of the band knew its parts in the test piece before bringing the whole band together. The fundraising campaign carried on throughout January, culminating in a bazaar, arranged to provide a new uniform for the band members, not for the Geelong contest but another arranged for Easter.

On Saturday, 3 February, the band gave a programme of music from the balcony of Ebbesen's Town Hall Hotel, in Albury, which included a number of Tom's own pieces. These included "Sambo's Birthday," "Dainty Daisy," "Little Dark Eyes" and his earliest published composition from his New Shildon days, "The Typhoon." Then the next day, the band spent the entire day practising their marching discipline followed by the test selections on the Albury Show Ground.

On the 6th and 7th of February, the band were involved in a charitable event for an entirely different cause. This was a gymkhana to benefit the building fund of the local Catholic Church. The Albury Town Band started the event by leading a procession along the way from the Albury Post Office to the Show Ground, before leading a further grand procession around the show ring, to the reported delight of onlookers. One of Tom's daughters took part in that procession, dressed up as one of a number of penguins drawing a carriage of mermaids. What followed was a Grand Medieval Tournament featuring various combat scenes also accompanied by music from the Town Band. This was followed by a 'musical ride' with mounted ladies and gentlemen in uniform attire executing a number of tricky manoeuvers to the music from the band. Other entertainments, in addition to the various sideshows, included an 'all nations' football match, a 'ladies' race featuring men in costume, a concert and a 'First Aid Race'. The revelries continued until well after eleven o'clock at night.

The 14th of February brought the promised fundraising concert on the Sports Ground at Albury. This time, the band teamed up with a small number of singers to deliver a programme that included not only the test selections from the forthcoming contest, but also a programme of songs. On the previous day, the committee of the band had met and in doing so had agreed to commit the band to two further appearances. The first would take place at the Mechanics Institute for the concert of the Choral Society, and the second in the local gardens at Geelong on Sunday 25th February, the day after the Interstate Band Contest at Geelong. This latter concert was subject to necessary permission being provided by the Mayor of Geelong.

The band set out on its journey to Geelong, travelling first by land to Melbourne, and then across Port Philip Bay aboard the SS Courier, arriving in Geelong on the afternoon of Thursday, 22 February. Here they were met at the wharf by the president and secretary of the Competitions Committee, as well as the St Augustine's and Daylesford Brass Bands who musically accompanied the Albury band to their quarters at the town's Orient and Queen's Head Hotels. In the evening, the Mayor of Geelong addressed all of the competing bands in the Market Square before sending them off on their march to the park. The Albury Town Band were the second marching band in the procession.

At the park, the rush to enter the contesting ground was too much for the small gates to handle, and some men took to leaping over the fence to avoid the crush. Some 2,000 paying members of the public were reported as attending that first sitting of the contest, with many more content to listen for free from outside the park fence. The judge, Mr John Robson, who shared commonality with Tom in that he too was a former bandmaster of the Ballarat 3rd Battalion Militia, entered his judging tent, accompanied by his shorthand writer for the occasion. They were also accompanied by a representative of the Victorian Bands Association, to ensure fair play. This additional official proved to be none other than Tom's fellow former Shildonian, the Ballarat bandmaster, James Scarff.

The first task for the bands was to play the standard test piece, Tom's own arrangement of "Verdi's Works." The Albury Town Band were drawn last to mount the rotunda to play. The solo cornet player that evening was Tom's son, Thomas Edward Bulch junior, who seemingly had become a fine cornet player in his own right. A press commentator stated that the Albury Band's rendering of the selection was "brighter and more agreeable to the audience, though the performance was not free from fault." The contest continued in like manner for the next two days, with the own choice test piece being the next session and the finale being the quickstep contest. In organising and arranging the Geelong Contest it it had previously been agreed that on the final day, after entrants had played but before any results were announced, the bands would mass under Tom Bulch's baton to play accompanying music for a bioscopic display using Messrs Johnson and Gibson's new Electric Bioscope. Following this accompanied visual display, the results of the contest were announced. This time Tom's hard work in preparing the band had paid off, as the judge felt that the Albury Town Band had done well in rendering both the test piece, and their own choice selection on the second night. Well enough to earn second place, only four points behind the winners. Sadly that difference in points represented a substantial difference in prize money. The winning band collected one-hundred pounds as their reward; Albury collected only twenty. In the quickstep contest the band had done less well, coming fourth, though the selection contest was the more prestigious achievement. Tom would surely, if slightly regretfully, have been content with in attaining such a good result while competing against the likes of the Geelong Artillery, Geelong Town bands as well as selection test winners Daylesford. He may have taken extra satisfaction that the latter had been placed below Albury in the quickstep. The result was certainly good enough to satisfy the commentator from the Border Morning Mail, a newspaper local to Albury, who said as much in their edition issued on 26th February. The Albury Banner also congratulated the band on the "manner in which they acquitted themselves."

New Shildon

Far away on the other side of the world, an important moment arrived for Tom's father. Thomas Bulch senior had either decided, or been compelled, to retire from his post as the timekeeper at the New Shildon's North Eastern Railway works at New Shildon as of the end of February. His employers demonstrated a modest appreciation of his services as explained by this brief notice in the Northern Echo from 2 March 1906:

"Mr Thomas Bulch, late timekeeper at Shildon Wagon Works, was yesterday presented with a purse of money on his retirement from that position after close upon 52 years of service under the North-Eastern Railway Company."

Above: A photograph believed to show Thomas Bulch senior (centre wearing bowler hat) in a group photograph with colleagues outside the Shildon Railway Works canteen.

One could imagine the journalist responsible congratulating himself at the idea of a 'late timekeeper' when writing this. It would have been a quite significant decision for a worker like Thomas to decide to retire in 1906. There was no state pension provision to be had in the United Kingdom until 1908, when a payment of five shillings a week was introduced, but only for men aged seventy or over. This at a time when the average life expectancy of a man was only forty-seven years, though we should be mindful that this age is somewhat skewed down-over by the high rate of infant mortality at that time. Another news article however, this time in the Auckland Chronicle being more local, hence more detailed, adds more insight into his standing in the community at that time.

> "A number of the oldest standards at Shildon Wagon Works have recently retired on their pensions and thus have been severed links with the early days of the works in the time of the Stockton and Darlington Railway. One of the best known, not only at Shildon but over a wide district, is Mr Thomas Bulch, timekeeper, who has close upon 52 years service in. Mr Bulch has not always been a timekeeper, for he was a fireman for four years when on 29 August 1861 he had a serious accident which occasioned a remarkable amount of sympathy in the district.
>
> Mr Bulch was at that time firing engine no. 149, driver Robert Aaron. The line from Darlington to Windermere had just been completed and a tradesmen's excursion has been run from Darlington to give people the opportunity of viewing the newly opened out country. Engine no. 149 was sent to bring it back. They were coming away down but when crossing a bridge it gave way, and the engine and several carriages came off the line. Bulch was imprisoned by the engine, and to add to his sufferings the lead plug gave way and the sludge cock was open, and as Bulch lay there, unable to stir, steam and boiling water were escaping onto his limbs. He was dreadfully scalded, and although he was not expected to live, he got better and started to work as timekeeper after being off seven months. His mate, although not so seriously scalded as was his fireman, injured his ankle and, blood poisoning setting in, he died very shortly after.
>
> Mr Bulch, as may be imagined, has seen many changes at Shildon Works, in fact, they are practically new works altogether with the additions and all the latest improvements. He is a well-known figure and held in high respect."

Thomas Bulch senior's post-retirement support network took two forms. Firstly there were his own offspring, many of whom, unlike Tom and his older brother Frank who had emigrated, remained in the locality of Shildon. Jeremiah Bulch, better known locally as Jerry, was a prominent citizen of Shildon and had become a reputable businessman and trader there as well as being one of the regular organisers of the annual Shildon Show. Also, Thomas senior had, on 22 November 1892, at All Saints Church, taken a second wife. The second Mrs Thomas Bulch, as with the first who had passed away six years previously, was named Margaret. She had been born with the surname Brass, and was a widow with a family of her own when she married Thomas. She and her late husband Cuthbert Harrison had previously lived, with their children Fred, Mary Jane, Margaret and Alice only a few doors away from the Bulch family on Adelaide Street. By 1901, the Bulch family home had become the residence of a merged family of Bulches and Harrisons. The household consisted of Thomas and Margaret; Thomas's son Fred, now a steam engine fitter; step-son Fred Harrison, classified on the census as an 'imbecile' so probably suffering from some sort of mental disability though he had previously worked in the wagon painting department at the works; and step-daughter Mary Jane Harrison. There would probably have been plenty of people around Thomas that he could depend upon, enabling him to retire.

Albury

On Sunday, 18 March the Albury Band gave a sacred concert in the Botanic Gardens, collecting voluntary donations totalling four pounds, two shillings and sixpence at the gates toward the running costs of the band. The programme of music included the test piece from the Geelong contest among other Bulch compositions and arrangements such as "The Young Recruit" and a recent creation "Baby Elephant." Friday the 29th brought a performance on the balcony of Miss Moore's Railway Hotel, Wodonga; while Sunday 1st April took the band to Rutherglen to play at a benefit convert for resident Arthur Warren as part of an initiative organised by the Rutherglen Town Band. A further fundraising sacred concert followed on 8th April where they aired three contest numbers they would be playing at the Albury Musical Competitions at Easter. By this point, the band were well practised and in fine form, being tipped in the press as contenders to win the upcoming Albury contest.

The Albury Musical Competitions were the jewel in the crown of the Albury Musical and Literary Festival which ran until Easter Monday, 16th April. This particular contest saw the Albury Town Band pitted against the Wagga Citizens Band, local rivals Albury Citizens Band, and bands from Corrowa and Wangaratta. The appointed judge was Henri Stael of Sydney. Once again Tom's eldest son featured as solo cornet player for the band. Albury Town were drawn to play first, and began with their rendition first of the own choice test piece, Tom's own arrangement of "Weber's Works," followed by a waltz "Homage to the Ladies." After the test selections the bands took turns to play their chosen quickstep whilst on the march. In that contest the band had chosen to play Tom's own march "King Pin." Then, at the end, the bands massed under the baton of the judge, Henri Stael to play "Federation," another piece Tom created under the pseudonym of Eugene Lacosta, followed by "Waggon Hill." Then the large crowd hushed to absolute silence in anticipation of the announcement of the winners. Albury Town Band won the B Grade Championship contest by a margin of four points over their nearest rivals the Wangaratta Band, and in doing so collected a considerable cash prize of £75. This was added to moments later by the five pound prize the band had won for coming second in the quickstep, bested only by the other local band on the day, the Albury Citizens Band. Both of Albury's bands received a hearty cheer from the predominantly local audience. Finally, Tom had been able to demonstrate that, with the right band before him, he was still a successful bandmaster at this level.

Above: Tom Bulch (centre wearing top hat) with his Albury Town Band at the Albury Band Contest in 1906

We learned from those Albury and Geelong contests that Thomas Edward junior had also begun to make his mark as a fine solo cornet player. Tom's other children were reaching an age where they could become involved in things too. On

Tuesday, 18 April, Thomas's youngest daughter, Alice, took part in a children's competition, in front of an audience of friends and relatives, at the Albury Mechanics Institute. She was part of a team of convent schoolchildren competing in an 'Action Song' contest for teams of children under fourteen years old. One of the Bulch boys was a keen footballer playing for a team called the Hopetouns and then the Briton Juniors team.

Braced by their contest successes, and doubtless fatigued by the intensity of it all, the Albury Town Band took a well-deserved break from rehearsing. The end of the hiatus was announced in a notice printed in the Border Morning Mail and Riverina Times on Tuesday, 8 May, which read:

> "ALBURY TOWN BAND Resumes PRACTICE TONIGHT. All members are requested to attend. Important! – T BULCH, bandmaster; W J Lester, Hon. Sec."

That rehearsal was followed on Friday, 11 May by the committee of the Albury Town Band treating their bandsmen to an evening meal at the Albion Hotel on Dean Street, in recognition of their successes that season. Fifty persons attended, including the bandsmen. After the meal, the chairman proposed a toast to Tom Bulch, before making a presentation to him. This was greeted with cheers. The chairman said that:

> "Mr Bulch, on the 24th of the present month will have been twelve months in charge and all would agree that during that period he had simply worked wonders in the Albury Town Band. (hear hear) He had gone into his work sincerely, and whole-heartedly and had accomplished much more in the time than the committee had anticipated."

In an unconscious echo of the retirement gift presented to his father months earlier in Shildon, the chairman of the Albury band handed Tom a purse of sovereign coins as a token of appreciation. Following further speeches in his praise, Tom gave the assembly his response, complimenting the hard work that had been invested by the bandsmen towards their achievements. He then set out his desire for a next challenge; that the band should travel to Sydney to compete, and win, at a Grade A contest there. This suggestion was well-received. He declared that there was nothing the Albury Town Band could not do, as long as they stuck together and attended practice regularly. This latter point was perhaps made as a hint that attendances at practice were not all they could be. Tom went on to declare that, with the possible exception of his Model Band in Ballarat, there had never been a band in his life "in which there were associated a better or more genuine set of good fellows than those which constituted the Albury Town Band." Further toasts followed after which Tom took to the piano, to accompany singers as well as a cornet solo from Bandsman Richardson, before the evening reached its musical conclusion.

Later that same month, the Albury Town Band provided music at a Smoke Social at the Oddfellows Hall, held for the great and the good of Albury and the surrounding district. A meal opened the evening, followed by toasts and speeches, leading to a programme of instrumental music. Then on Saturday, 26 May 1906, the band entertained at a postponed Empire Day demonstration in which an estimated 1,100 local children took part. This was followed on the 28th by an Empire Banquet after which the Albury Town Band played a series of patriotic airs.

On Thursday, 5 June, Lord Northcote, still the Governor-General of the Commonwealth, paid an official visit to Albury, being received in true patriotic style. A display of flags and other patriotic decoration had been installed throughout the town. Northcote had arrived at the Albury railway station at ten o'clock in the morning, where around 5,000 citizens were present to greet him. Naturally the Albury Town Band were present to play the National Anthem as he emerged from his railway carriage onto the platform. A general tour of Albury followed, taking in the various schools and public features of note, before a luncheon at the Mechanics Hall. Lord and Lady Northcote were then conducted to inspect the local hospital, watch a football demonstration and visit the local orphanage. Later, further entertainment was hosted in their honour at the Mechanics Institute.

On 28 June 1906, news of Tom's recent achievements reached New Shildon in the form of a news article published in the Auckland Chronicle. If George Allan didn't read it himself, it's likely that friends, family or neighbours would have passed on the key message therein. The article read:

> "Those who know Mr T E Bulch will remember him as being a member of the New Shildon Temperance Band and one of the

chief musicians of the town. Since his emigration to Australia his interest in musical matters has not decreased but rather the opposite, and now another success has come to him. The "Sydney Mail" says that the most important item in the festival was the competition for the B grade band championship of New South Wales. This brought into the field five of the best bands in the border district of the two states, including the Albury Town Band, conductor T E Bulch. All these bands paraded in brilliant and tastefully designed uniforms of military type. The result of the band contest was not made until a late hour but the declaration of the Albury Town Band as winners of the principal event was the signal for a scene of wildest enthusiasm. The many friends of Mr Bulch will hear with pleasure of his success."

This article was almost certainly included in this local newspaper through the intervention of someone local to Shildon; possibly a family member, or a former colleague in the Temperance Band. Tom Bulch had been absent from Shildon for twenty-two years by that point, and excepting the possibility that copies of the Sydney Mail had become available in County Durham, there is a strong implication that Tom had continued to correspond with at least one friend or family member back in his town of birth. A further implication is that of how proud Tom must have been to win a contest, and how important it was, to him, to share that news back in England.

Back in Australia, at a meeting of the Town Band committee on 10 July 1906, Thomas sealed a deal with the committee to allow the band to travel to either a contest in Sydney or Ballarat to test their abilities against a better class of band. A good outcome at either of those contests would put his, and the band's, reputation where he would perhaps expect it to be. The band, and its extended community of helpers, re-entered fundraising mode so as to ensure they had the means to cover the anticipated costs. To begin with they gave a Sunday performance, once again, at the Botanic Gardens on 15 July, a winter month in Australia. Then, on 18 July, the band tried out something new. They organised what was expected to be the first of a series of social evenings at the Mechanics' Institute at which the card came 'Euchre' would feature. This was a trick-taking card game, invented in the 1860s, played by two pairs of players. One hundred and fifty people attended, with the card games being played from eight-thirty in the evening through until ten at night. Thomas's son seems to have done well and ended up among the prize winners collecting a tobacco pouch as his reward. Afterwards, a supper was served, before Tom took to the piano to play dance music, keeping that up until one o'clock in the morning. A profit of about twenty pounds was raised towards the band's travel costs.

Three days later, on the 21 July 1906, something happened thousands of miles away that would bring sadness to the whole Bulch family. Less than five months into what had proven to be an all too brief retirement, the patriarch of the family, Thomas Bulch senior, passed away at seventy years of age. He had taken an "apoplectic fit" at the family home, 48 Adelaide Street, which had left him in a coma from which he did not recover. According to the death certificate, his son Fred was with him at the time of his passing. The death was certified by Shildon's works doctor, Dr Robert Smeddle. Again we turn to the Auckland Chronicle, of 25 July, for more information:

> "One of the oldest stalwarts in New Shildon, Mr Thomas Edward Bulch of Adelaide Street, passed away on Saturday morning as the result of a stroke suffered a week or two ago."

The article then repeats much of what was said earlier in the year about his railway accident, but goes on to add a little more detail.

> "Of a quiet, inoffensive, nature he made many friends, for whom it was also a pleasure to listen to him giving his reminiscences of his early days. When a young man he was known to be a good singer, and his services were in great request. In conversation with Mr C Hogwood, retired engine driver, that gentleman said that so far as he knew he is the only one alive who helped to release Mr Bulch and drive him home again. Mr Hogwood was working in the shops at that time and when news of the accident reached Shildon, Mr Bouch at once sent an engine and van to bring the injured men home. Mr Hogwood remarked that it was a strange sight to see the engine down the battery and some of the carriages in the field. Strange to say the third mate, Richard Hill, was uninjured. He is now dead."

An account of the funeral at All Saint's Church followed, explaining that it took place on the Tuesday afternoon and that Thomas was laid to rest in a coffin of Oak, with his wife and her offspring present, as well as a great many members of the Bulch family. As always it would take some time for this news to reach Australia, so Tom would remain unaware, and would, of course, have been unable to be present as family and friends gathered at New Shildon's church on 24 July 1906 to say their last farewells before he was buried. If the sadness and grief at his death were not tragedy enough for Thomas's sons and daughters, there was another shock in store. It emerged after his death that two years earlier, on 18 June 1904, Thomas senior had written a new will that left the entirety of his estate to his second wife Margaret, explicitly stating that if she did not outlive him everything was to be left to her two daughters Mary Jane and Alice. For whatever reason, all of his own direct descendants, the children of his first wife, had been disinherited. We know, from word passed down through the family to Thomas Edward's grandson, Eric Tomkins, that the Bulch family did not take this lightly and contested the will. As is so often the case, however, the challenge was an unsuccessful one, and the will of 1904 was upheld. One can imagine the bitterness that may well have arisen in New Shildon over that outcome. The family would surely have resented that Margaret Harrison, who had taken their mother's place at their father's side, had now succeeded in inheriting everything he possessed; his legacy of one-hundred-and-thirty-eight pounds and four shillings, and the family home of 48 Adelaide Street where she would continue to live after his death.

All of this was taking place far away from Albury, and Thomas most probably only followed events through correspondence from his brothers and sisters. In the meantime, still unaware of his bereavement, Thomas awaited the decision of the committee of the Albury Town Band on which contest the band would attend. That committee met on 28 July and, based upon responses from both Ballarat and Sydney contest organising committees, the Albury Band committee decided that Ballarat would be the band's destination. They caveated that decision with a condition that they would endeavour to pay only the railway fares of the bandsmen, and that if the bandsmen and bandmaster agreed to that condition, that the band should enter both A and B grade contests. The total expenditure in railway fares was expected to amount to somewhere between fifty and sixty pounds. The test selections for the Ballarat contest were communicated as being "La Reine De Saba" for the A Grade competition and Rossini's "Semiramide" for the B Grade. When the bandsmen learned of this decision many objected on the grounds that their own personal finances would not extend to cover the accommodation and living expenses costs that the Ballarat contest would incur. Some made the point that, as bandsmen, they gave their services for the entertainment of the town without charge all year around. They submitted a counter-proposal that the band committee should at least agree to provide a portion, or half, of their additional expenses for accommodation and food etc. Tom himself also objected to the notion of entering the A Grade contest as well as B Grade, now believing the latter to be the more realistic target. This would mean, however, that at best they could only win fifty pounds. This would not be enough to cover the cost of the rail fares. The whole venture hung in the balance while the committee contemplated this proposed compromise, which would surely see the band's finances depleted even in the event of a win. A meeting was scheduled for Monday 6th August to make a decision.

As the bandsmen awaited the committee's decision, Tom took them, on Sunday, 6 August, to the Newtown Orphanage at Albury. Here they rendered a programme of music as part of the celebrations for Orphanage Month. Members of the public gathered to hear the music, as well as a group of sixty orphans who sat in a circle around the band watching. Father Griffin, in charge of the orphanage, made a speech at the end of the concert, making special mention to thank the band for their periodic visits to cheer up the orphans. After this a collection was made, with the orphanage as beneficiary, realising a sum of twenty-five pounds, five shillings and sixpence. The Sisters of Mercy gave tours of the institution, during which many people reportedly also commented on what a fine job Tom had made of raising the Albury Band to such a "first-class standard".

The Albury Town Band had an active ladies committee, in which it seems that Eliza Ann Bulch, Tom's wife, was actively involved. In those days, unlike the present, the ladies were generally excluded from all matters relating to the making of music, so the committee busied itself supporting their men-folk through the business of securing the financial wellbeing of the band. This ladies committee had been behind organising the euchre party mentioned earlier, and at the beginning of August were making preparations for another fundraising social at the

Mechanics Institute. They were divided as to whether it should simply be a dance, or organised along similar lines to the euchre party recently held. The matter was deferred to a meeting of the main committee, which was also due to decide on the bandsmen's recent demands. When this meeting came around, on Monday the 6th of the month, it was decided that the attendance was too limited to finalise the decision, so the meeting was again re-scheduled for Friday, 10 August, further delaying resolution of the issue.

Alas, the proceedings and the decision of that later meeting were not published in the press; though the Albury Band did not compete at Ballarat that year, so our only reasonable conclusion must be that the demand of the bandsmen was rejected and that the bandsmen themselves felt the alternative to be unaffordable. Nonetheless, the fundraising social organised by the ladies committee did still go ahead on 15 August and was, once again, a success, with ticket buyers enjoying dances until one o'clock in the morning.

On Sunday, 26 August, the Albury Town Band assembled, along with the children of St Matthew's Sunday School, to march in procession to St Matthew's Church, Albury. As they marched, the band played and the children sang an arrangement of "Onward Christian Soldiers" specially created for the occasion by Tom Bulch. A special church anniversary service followed, during which the band accompanied the hymns using arrangements that Tom had again specially prepared. The band also played during the offertory, and then led a procession from the church, up Dean Street to the old Telegraph corner playing Tom's recently composed march "ABCDEF." They then gave a programme of music at the Botanic Gardens, again primarily comprised of Tom's own compositions. A collection was held to boost the band's funds. It was reported afterward that they had a heavy week of rehearsal ahead of them, with a Show Week coming up.

As part of his having settled in Albury, Tom and Eliza set up yet another music shop. Under the name of Bulch and Co, they took premises in Wittmer's Buildings on Townsend Street, Albury selling:

> "Pianos, organs, brass instruments, music and everything pertaining to the musical profession. All business under the

personal supervision of T E Bulch (Bandmaster of the Albury Town Band and Walla Band)"

This latter band were based in Walla Walla, a small town some thirty or more kilometres north of Albury. It seems that once again Tom's earnings as both bandmaster and composer were still not enough to support his family. Rather than seek employment by another, and despite his previous experiences, he still preferred the option of running a music shop and taking a second band under his wing. Consequently his resources were once again spread thinner. He commenced advertising the music shop in the local press during September 1906, though it may have been opened before that time.

Sunday, 23 September saw the band give yet another open-air concert at the Botanic Gardens, realising another small but welcome sum towards the band's running costs. They also gave a programme of music at the Germanton Show, a seemingly particularly equine affair, around the same time. Then, 3 October saw the band at the Public Schools Demonstration at Albury, offering a programme of music as the children presented their gymnastic and dancing displays on the Albury Show Ground where eleven maypoles had been erected. Whilst it may seem odd to English readers to hear of maypoles erected in September, this was of course approaching spring in Australia.

That same day a report of a meeting at the Albury Hotel might reveal a little with regard to Tom's political leanings at this time. It was held to support the candidacy of Sir William Lyne as the sitting member for The Hume. Lyne had been the 13th Premier of New South Wales from 1899 to 1901, as a member of the Protectionist party who advocated protective tariffs on trade to allow Australian industry to grow and provide employment. Lyne had also, in 1901, had the opportunity to become the first Prime Minister of Australia, but had failed to form a government. At this meeting, Tom pledged to be part of a central committee of electors in Albury that would forward Lyne's interests. The following year Lyne would accompany then Prime Minister Alfred Deakin to a colonial conference to try to persuade Britain to dispense with its policy of free trade. Tom Bulch may well have been personally acquainted with Sir William Lyne as we learn that on Saturday, 29 September, Lyne was present at the annual picnic of the Walla Walla Brass Band, of which Tom was bandmaster, and definitely conductor that day. The picnic, with free refreshments served beneath a large marquee, was blessed by good weather and well attended. It included a grand fundraising concert for the band, featuring a variety of local singers, opened by Lyne himself who departed shortly thereafter.

On 17 October the Walla Walla Band gave a concert as part of the Mission Festival at Walla Church, after which Tom took them to play a concert at the Gerogery Cricket Ground as part of Hospital Saturday on 20 October 1906. Once again, the band provided background music for a series of races run by competitors of all ages. Throughout the proceedings visitors deposited donations in a 'hospital box' kept on prominent display. Teams of ladies also gathered at various points around the district with collection boxes. This overall effort led to over £170 being raised for the Albury District Hospital.

On the evening of 6 November, Tom received a belated award at a presentation event held as part of an Oberon Quartette Party at the Albury Mechanic's Institute. A local worthy, Doctor Woods, was present to distribute the gold medals to the prize winners from the Albury Musical and Literary Festival that had been held in April. Woods, on presenting the award to Thomas, as representative of the whole band, confessed that he had an interest in another band in the area, but expressed his admiration for the performance given by the Albury Town Band and commented on how Tom had lifted them from a position of mediocrity to one of superiority. He declared that it had become a band "of which every resident of the town was justly proud."

Tom must have spent much time travelling, most likely by rail, between Albury and Walla Walla throughout in order to tutor both bands. On 10 November, he was putting the Walla Walla Band through their paces again, at a concert in aid of the Doctor's Residence Association. This accompanied a sports event that included, among its other contests, a novel slow bicycle race.

The fifteenth of November saw Tom return to the Albury Town Band again, to offer the first of a series of summer concerts on the Albury Sports Ground, preceded by a parade, once again from the old Telegraph office. The programme included his new selection arrangement of the works by Meyerbeer. This had been created for the Albury Town Band to perform at the band's return visit to the forthcoming band contest at Geelong which would again take place in the coming

February. There was a charge of sixpence per ticket, with funds raised going to support the band's Geelong contest expenses.

On the evening of Friday, 7 December, the Albury Town Band presented a further programme of music on the Albury Sports Ground. Again the goal was to raise funds, and despite being without their two Eb bass players and a trombonist they gave another airing of Tom's "Bombardment of Port Arthur" which a newspaper report around that time proclaimed had by then gained such favour in Japan as to be adopted as one of their principal army tunes. The piece was given, according to the correspondent from the Border Mail and Riverina Times, "to fine effect, the various stages of the movement being vividly portrayed." The band revealed to their audience, during that evening, a plan to hold a grand demonstration on New Year's Eve in aid of their Geelong competition fund.

When New Year's Eve arrived the band did indeed assemble on the sports ground as promised, along with members of the Albury Choral Society. A large crowd had gathered in the brightly illuminated grounds to enjoy the spectacle as part of seeing in the New Year. In addition to the various renditions by both choir and band, Tom himself, having just celebrated his forty-fourth birthday the day before, offered a cornet solo as part of the programme.

New Shildon

1907 brought more darkness to the Allan family, though it seemed to have begun ordinarily enough. With the summer contesting season some way off George Allan had been investing free time into composing music and working on a new piece entitled 'The Gale' for publication.

His first brass contest engagement came on 29 June, at Shotton Colliery, east of Durham and towards the coast. Evidence points to this being the first time a brass band contest had been held in this particular mining community, and the press definitely stated it as being the first to be organised by the Shotton Colliery Brass Band. A prize pot of fifteen pounds still managed to attract a field of nine competing bands to perform the test pieces which, according to different accounts, was entitled either "Prairie Queen" or "Prairie Flowers," with another test piece title given as "Winter Roses." As usual, the contest was being held as part of another wider event, the Shotton Colliery Band's first Annual

Sports, with races and other sporting events taking place throughout the day. An 'ambulance competition' saw a tied outcome between teams from Hetton, Murton and Wingate, while local lad, J Kent, of Shotton Colliery won the schoolboy race.

Having heard all the bands playing the test pieces before emerging from his adjudicator's tent, George awarded the first prize of eight pounds to the band from Hetton Town, along with their conductor, Mr J Bennett. The Willington Silver Band maintained their reputation by coming a respectable second for four pounds in prize money, with the Sunderland East End Band and Sunderland Temperance Band coming third and fourth respectively. Bands from Birtley, Hartlepool, Seaham, Wingate and Sunderland Borough were the 'also-rans' on the day. In the march contest George again found Hetton Town to be the best of the bunch.

The July 1907 issue of Wright and Round's Brass Band News contained George's latest small advertisement, introducing the banding community to his latest work. Unlike his advertisements the previous year that had run for several months, this was a one-off and gives the impression that George had posted it just to remind people that he was there. Perhaps something had been going on in his life during this time that made it harder to get on with the business of composing and publishing music, or else the cost of advertising was generally prohibitive. This particular advert read:

> "CONTEST MARCHES – These still lead the way!! "Senator," "La Maestro," "Battle Abbey," "Bravura" and "The Gale." Another ready shortly. – GEO. ALLAN, Publisher, New Shildon."

George's parents, John and Hannah, continued to live at 65 Adelaide Street in New Shildon, with their two youngest sons Ralph and Edwin. Ralph had carried on the family trade of tailoring, working with his father. Very nearby, at 68 Adelaide Street, one of George's other brothers, John Robert Allan, had set up home with his wife Jane Ann, née Ross, and by 1907 they had brought three sons into the world; George William, John James and Robert Ross Allan. Like his older brother George and most of their neighbours, John Robert was in the employment of the North Eastern Railway at the railway works, as a joiner and wagon builder.

On Sunday, 21 July 1907 something happened that would shock the Allan family terribly. On that particular evening John Allan, and his wife Hannah, were downstairs in their small terraced home when, at around ten o'clock, they heard their son Ralph come into the house, take off his coat, and go straight upstairs to his bedroom. According to a report later in the Auckland Chronicle he had been at his brother's house for supper. We don't know which brother, so there are several possibilities there. Hannah had also been preparing supper, so she had called up from the bottom of the stairs to Ralph for him to come down. No reply was forthcoming. Sensing something was amiss, the couple went upstairs and entered the bedroom. There they found Ralph on his knees with a deep gash in his throat. He had cut his own throat. Immediately the couple called out for someone to summon a doctor, but in minutes Ralph's life had ebbed quickly away and by the time the doctor arrived there was nothing to be done. Ralph Allan, tailor of New Shildon had, at twenty eight years of age, succeeding in taking his own life.

The next morning, an inquest was quickly arranged and overseen by a Mr Proud. Evidence was presented that Ralph had been suffering from "delusions" that he had been "suffering from a complaint." Though a doctor had told him he was "quite mistaken" he still "cherished the delusion." The inquest also heard that Ralph had been in a mentally depressed state for some time prior to the incident, and "fancied that people were talking about him." On the morning of the day prior to taking his own life, he had been seen to draw his hand across his throat in demonstration saying "I cannot stand it any longer, I must do it." Further evidence had been submitted by Police Constable Oliver and a Miss Graydon. The inquest jury returned a verdict of suicide whilst of unsound mind. The causes that lay behind Ralph's mental state are unclear. Whether there were events in his life that had led to his depression, or whether the problems were of a more medical nature, then there would most likely have been little support, treatment or sympathy, for a man suffering depression symptoms. Whatever had caused Ralph's disturbance, he was certainly not alone during this period. In the year 1905, just two years previously, male suicides in England and Wales had peaked at their highest recorded rate of 30.3

suicides per 100,000 men. This rate has only been matched once in the years since. Suicide was almost a national phenomenon. If the accounts reported in the press are true then it seems clear that, whatever the reasons for his troubled dissatisfaction with existence, Ralph was determined to find a peace that he felt he could not find in life. For the family he left behind, this tragedy would surely have affected them profoundly. To his parents, the terrible memory of what they had seen could be recalled every time they entered that room, bringing with it the lingering question as to whether they could have done anything to prevent their son's death. For George, and his remaining brothers and sisters, there would surely be a sense of grief and loss, for a brother, and one-time bandmate from the New Shildon Saxhorn Band whose time on this earth ended tragically and too soon.

The Allan family gathered at All Saints Church on 24 July for a service and burial, their last farewell to Ralph. Attitudes to suicide had softened somewhat by the early twentieth century, after the 1880 Burial Act came into effect permitting a burial on consecrated ground with ritual, though it was still then considered a crime, and a sin, to attempt to take one's own life. Following a law that was established in the mid-13th century, it had been practice up until 1822 for the Crown to take all of the possessions of any man that had committed suicide. Though this was no longer the case, there would still have been a stigma in connection with the Allan family regarding Ralph's tragic demise.

Only a few weeks later, George, still probably reeling from the shock of his brother's death, was called to adjudication duties yet again. His destination was Grangetown east of the industrial port town of Middlesbrough and again easily reached by train through having a station on the Darlington to Saltburn route. This contest had been arranged by the Cleveland Steelworks Band, principally made up of employees of the massive works, in the shadow of which the small Grangetown had been built. The settlement consisted of little more than nine streets with a market square, church, chapel, a hotel and a literary institute. The old town, and its original works, has now been all but eradicated, though another huge steelworks was later erected nearby and some of the land where the streets of Grangetown once stood have been replaced with modern housing. The Steelworks band had managed to collect fifteen pounds to offer as prize money for the test piece contest, an arrangement of Verdi's "Il Trovatore" that had been published and made available by Wright and Round. They had also raised a small prize for the march contest. Five bands entered, and the contest had been limited to admit only bands that had won no more than ten pounds in prize money since 1905. George's adjudication notes from the contest were published in the September issue of Brass Band News for all to read. The band from Dorman and Long's Redcar works had points deducted for tuning and timing issues that saw them finish outside the top three, while Guisborough Priory gave "a very good finish to a very fine performance; good tune and intonation." There were still few issues in their performance, though and they were placed third. The band from South Bank merely offered "a nice performance." which saw them share the fourth prize with Dorman and Long. The Skinningrove Band was the one that shone on the day, with their cornet player's work being at times "very artistic, just right" and overall rendition being "capital." Their performance earned them the top prize of eight pounds and a cup; while Middlesbrough Borough Band, of whom George said "a very good rendering indeed; band well in tune generally." took second prize. The Guisborough Priory Band made a better showing in the march contest to take that small first prize, followed by Middlesborough Borough band in second.

Later that month, on 24 August, George caught another North Eastern Railway train to Bridlington on the Yorkshire coast for yet another band contest. This particular contest would be held in the grounds of the People's Palace near Bridlington Quay, which had opened, just over ten years prior, in 1896. Unlike many of the contests George had attended that were principally organised by a band, this one had been organised by the two managers of the People's Palace, J W and W H Delmar. It was an 'own choice' contest for both quickstep and selection, resulting in a little more variety for the listener and for this, as one reporter pointed, out "the pleasure of the audience was all the greater." Prize money of twenty-five pounds surprisingly attracted only four bands on the day. Others had initially applied to enter, but when the event arrived neither the Scarborough Borough Prize Band, nor the Wilson Line Prize band, turned up. The reporter covering the contest for the Hull Daily Mail attributed their absence to these two bands fearing they would have been unable to beat the Barton Cycle Works Band, who appear to have had a solid reputation around that time. Interestingly for George, they were being conducted by a conductor with an excellent reputation for winning prizes, and with whom he would have been familiar on account of his having had previous involvement with the New Shildon Temperance Band. Barton Cycle Works Band's conductor was none other than William Holdsworth. In the quickstep, bringing an interesting twist to the contest, Holdsworth and the Barton Band had decided to play George's own contest march "Senator," and clearly impressed in doing so, as George saw fit, without knowing which band it was, to award them the first prize. The Hull Waterloo Prize Silver Band came second for their playing of William Rimmer's "Ravenswood." In the more prestigious selection test, the first prize was awarded again to the Barton Cycle Works Band for their playing of Owen's arrangement of "Faust." It appears that there was certainly something to the Hull Daily Mail reporter's assertion regarding the formidability of that band. Their euphonium player was also rewarded individually with a medal donated to the contest by London based instrument manufacturers Besson. The Hull Sons of Temperance Band, making their first ever contest appearance having been formed but nine months earlier, came second having played a selection from "Poliuto" by Donizetti. The Hull Waterloo band finished in third place for their run through of Harry Round's arrangement of "Tannhauser." In summing up after the contest, a reporter noted that George had said the first placed band had:

> "...stood out prominently in both contests, but that for the second place in the selection contest the competition had been close, there being little difference between the bands. The second prize in the selection had been awarded mainly on account of the tune."

This contest represents the first case we have seen of George judging a band playing one of his own marches. This, of course, was an experience familiar to Tom Bulch, who was often commissioned particularly to create music for his contests. It may well have happened to George before this though, as we have previously mentioned, the British newspapers and band press made very little of the march contests, so we rarely learn what pieces were played. If we imagine ourselves in George's shoes for a moment, he could have forgiven himself for briefly taking satisfaction in the fact that Holdsworth, being an accomplished specialist contest conductor and occasionally boastfully in the Brass Band News about his contest achievements, considered "Senator" right for his bands to play at contest.

As we move on into 1908, as usual, recorded evidence of happenings in George's life are scarce through the cold dark winter months. Then the evidence begins to re-emerge in spring, as though from hibernation. The first thing we find is that once again, ahead of the band contesting season, he is promoting his work in the brass press:

> "CHAMPION CONTEST MARCHES. – "Senator" (the topper), "La Maestro," "Battle Abbey" (2nd edition), "The Gale" and "Bravura." All worth playing: no wasters. Price 1/3 per set. Publisher Geo. Allan, New Shildon."

George ran this advertisement every month right through to August, probably the last issue likely to sell anything for that year's contest season. You get a feeling from this that he knows he's on to something with "Senator." We have no idea what feedback he was getting from the bands that had bought it, but as we have seen, he had seen at least one very top quality band perform it at a contest and been impressed. It can't be denied that there is something special about this march that has caused it's playing appeal to endure right through to the present day. It has a lasting audible appeal, and there is evidently a joy in the playing of it, that transcends its age. Not long after we began our small group to uncover and explore the stories of George Allan and Tom Bulch, I was contacted by a representative of a high school marching band in California. This young man was quite desperate to obtain a copy of "Senator" for their school band to play. These kinds of bands are very different to anything George might have seen in his lifetime, having an instrumental array more akin to a military band, yet this did not deter their admiration of the piece, nor put them off arranging it to suit their band's format.

To pursue this side story a little further, these school marching bands also engage in contests, though as with the Australian bands the music is played on the march in full legacy military style uniform, and with the discipline of the march being almost as important as the music. Two further aspects separate this kind of band from the brass bands of Britain and Australia. Firstly, each band is accompanied by a carefully choreographed display team bearing items like shields and, what I can only describe as, fluffy rifles that are twirled and thrown high in the air, all combining to create quite a spectacle. The second differentiating factor is that the music is all played by the band from memory, which makes the whole thing all the more impressive. As I'm sure I mentioned before the British contest march is created to be played by a seated and static band, allowing room for more concentration and complexity in its dynamics. A good British brass band could play these on the march, though it would be most unusual to see a march of this complexity played that way from memory on these shores.

Spring brought another bereavement in the Allan family. Hannah, George's aunt and wife of his uncle, Ralph, passed away. Ralph himself, a shoemaker in life, had passed away over a decade and a half earlier at their home on Magdala Terrace in Shildon, after which Hannah had moved away to Crook with her stonemason sons. She later moved with eldest son to Bishop Auckland where she had seen out her final days.

30 May 1908 brought George's first contest adjudication engagement of that year, of which we are aware. This time he'd taken a train from Shildon to Brotton-in-Cleveland near the North-east coast between Saltburn and Staithes. This contest was the second to be organised by the Cleveland Brass Band Association and was slightly different in that there were two sections of graded abilities competing. For the more advanced bands in the first section, the test piece was "Truth in Marchera" which was played that day in turn by Charlton's Brass Band, Guisborough Priory Band, Grange Town, Skelton Old and Skinningrove Miner's Bands. There was so fine a difference in the standard of playing by Guisborough Priory and Skelton Old bands that when George checked the points scored there was a tie for first place. The issue was resolved by having those top two placed bands split the combined first and second place prize money. The Skinningrove Miners' Band came third. For the second section, there was a smaller field of only four bands to offer their best rendition of "Songs of Wallace." It was the Brotton Temperance Band, one of the two hosting bands, that emerged triumphant. Their near neighbours and fellow hosts, Brotton Old Band, came second, with North Skelton third and Lingdale in fourth place. The Whitby Gazette, published six

days later, gave a brief report mentioning only that the contest was well attended and that the bands played well.

In June we see evidence of another development. That month's issue of Brass Band News included a solo cornet sample from a waltz composed by George Allan entitled "Queen of Society" which had been published by Wright and Round as part of their Liverpool Brass Band (& Military) Journal. Thus it appears that while George was concentrating his efforts in part upon his own published line of contest marches, he also still seems to have been selling some compositions to Wright and Round for a while. It would have been interesting to quiz George to understand his strategy and to understand why he self-published the pieces that would later be considered to be his best. Perhaps Wright and Round felt his contest marches to be too difficult for the mass market. Perhaps George didn't feel that Wright and Round offered enough to justify his selling them his best work.

June brought uncertainty tor George and his fellow workers at the Shildon railway works. At the beginning of the month an announcement was made at the carriage works in York, by the North Eastern Railway management, that owing to a scarcity of work they intended to lay off men in batches over a number of weeks until several hundred had been dismissed. As you'd expect this caused a nervous tension among the workers there. Three thousand men were employed at the York carriage works, none of whom, in this era before the Welfare State, would relish the prospect of unemployment. The particular concern for Shildon was that the North Eastern Railway's statement indicated that there were similar plans there too. The sense of gloom in New Shildon was worsened by further news, in July of 1908, that the "Dabble Duck" colliery, which George's house on Pears Terrace overlooked, was set to close having been deemed unprofitable by its owners. These owners had been trying to negotiate with the North Eastern Railway to mine beneath surrounding land owned by the rail company where it was understood that much more coal could be had. That negotiation had proved fruitless, and the decision was made to lay-off the two hundred men working there and close the mine, after having operated it for forty years. Residents and businesses of New Shildon feared the negative economic effect of these two announcements predicting a downturn in trade in the town.

Saturday, 5 September saw George travel to Tursdale for a slightly different format of band contest. This one was held in conjunction with the Tursdale Colliery Annual Show. Nine bands came together on the show field to offer, not the usual intricate test selection, but a march each, followed by a set of waltzes. Some of the bands that day, George was familiar with as one-time fellow members of the Wear Valley Band League. These included the Peases West and the Willington Silver Bands. The latter of these two carried home the prizes for march and for waltzes that day. Peases West and Chester-le-Street were the other two placed bands in both categories.

In November another of George's one-off advertisements was printed in the Brass Band News:

"The "Popular" Christmas Number – Now Ready. No samples; they are unnecessary as the music is guaranteed good. Send 1/3 for a set (20 brass) Extras 2d. – GEO ALLAN, Published, New Shildon."

This was the first of a number of almost annual Christmas arrangements George would publish, where he brought together hymns and carols. So far, in our research we've not found a copy of one to examine or hear, and it's not made clear what pieces were arranged for that particular Christmas Number. Not offering samples was a bold move, but might also have helped to keep down costs.

The beginning of December brought more tension between wagon builders and the North Eastern Railway company over the rates paid for piece-work. This resulted in the wagon builders standing idle from the first week of the month. If wagons weren't being built, they also weren't being painted. George and his family faced a bleak Christmas and New Year, relying on any savings they had plus any income from George's composing work. The stand off between the railway company and their Shildon staff ran right through until Tuesday, 12 January 1909. The men of Shildon works had consequently gone seven weeks without pay before managers and workers negotiated a settlement and agreed that work would recommence the following Monday. The settlement resulted in a new piece-work rate of twenty-four shillings and sixpence, as well as the instatement at Shildon of new facilities equivalent to those that had previously been installed at the York works.

Albury

Rewinding the clock slightly, to catch up with events in Australia, New Year's Day of 1907 saw Tom's Albury Town Band join forces with the visiting St Augustine's Orphanage Band who had travelled up from Geelong. This band, with an average bandsman's age of fourteen years, along with its bandmaster, the young Percy Jones, aged only twenty-one, had been engaged to give a concert at the Sports Ground in Albury. As part of the wider programme, the Albury band rendered Tom's contest selection "Meyerbeer's Works" from the previous year. One can't help but wonder whether watching the young cornetist, Percy Jones, conducting the boys band, reminded Tom of himself at that age. He too had been considered an accomplished musician early in his career. The visit by the Orphanage Band appears to have given Tom an idea, for within a few days, on 14 January to be exact, a notice was placed in the Border Morning Mail and Riverina Times as follows:

> "Mr T E Bulch, conductor of the Albury Town Band, notifies that he is about to start a brass band for boys with musical leanings and have the effect of turning out players capable of taking their part in any brass band."

A follow up in the same newspaper on 14 January reads:

> "NOTICE TO PARENTS. I am about to start a boys brass band on the lines similar to those of St Augustine's Brass Band. Parents are invited to communicate with the undersigned care of Bulch & Co, or at his private residence. T E Bulch"

Later that month a new tension emerged between the committee of the Albury Town Band and their bandmaster. A report in the Morning Mail of a band meeting on 21 January contained an indication that Thomas was not happy with the attendances of bandsmen at practice.

> "If we are to do any good at Geelong the members must attend practices regularly. If they do not I'm not going to Geelong: we'll simply make fools of ourselves."

Tom also pointed out that he could not generate lucrative engagements whilst the bandsmen were being so lax. Toward the end of the meeting, Tom wanted to raise the matter of the Geelong Contest further, but was stopped by the committee as they excluded the press and public. It was afterwards rumoured, according to the Morning Mail reporter, that "Mr Bulch, owing to long-standing friction with the committee had tendered or was about to tender his resignation." The reporter blamed the rumour on the committee's exclusion of the public, which he pointed out was contrary to their constitution. Such rumours were probably not helped by another rumour published in the very same issue of that newspaper that Tom was about to fulfil a vacancy to become bandmaster of the Albury Citizens Band. Were he to do this, he would surely provoke the anger of the Town Band committee. The situation must have prompted a few conversations behind closed doors, as the Border Morning Mail followed up with a report on 23 January explaining that the Town Band committee did not want to lose Tom's services, and had therefore agreed to increase his remuneration by ten shillings per week to three pounds in total. In return, the newspaper speculated that Mr Bulch would forego the opportunity to apply to run the Citizens Band.

An additional condition of the pay rise, further reported on 15 January, had been that Tom should also disengage from his post as the bandmaster of the Walla Walla Town Band. The band committee wanted to ensure that the Albury Town Band had his undivided attention. Tom agreed to these conditions, and fundraising concerts, to defray some of the costs of travelling to Geelong, were hastily pencilled into the band's calendar. The Morning Mail also tells us something of how the Albury Town Band's ladies committee would also support the fundraising. Groups of the wives, daughters and girlfriends were apportioned part of the town in which to canvass support for a fund-raising garden social and concert at "Loma Loma," Mr Roxburgh's residence. Tom's daughter, Adeline, for example, was paired with another canvassing the north-west section of town. Now that his children were older, Tom's band business had become much more of a family concern. That concert went ahead as planned on 27 January, and the Town Band were joined in the performance by the Albury Choral Society. A dip in temperatures toward this tail-end of the Australian summer season had caused some of the patrons to stay away, though it was afterwards deemed to have been a success. A refreshment marquee had been laid on for convenience and, no doubt, to bring in a little more money for the cause. Again, Tom's daughters were instrumental in its running alongside other ladies associated with the band. This is one of the few reported occasions on which it is apparent that though the playing of music was something exclusively for the boys and men, much of it would not have taken place were it not for the frequently unacknowledged resourcefulness and organisation of the ladies.

Around about this time Tom's Bulch & Co. publishing business released a new waltz for piano, with an additional brass band arrangement. This piece was entitled "Darling Dolly," and was written under his pseudonymous alter-ego, Henry Laski. Tom's use of pseudonyms is interesting, as it seems that quite often the identity of the true creator was really a very badly kept secret. For example, the Border Morning Mail, doubtless relaying information provided by Tom himself, wrote a review in which the truth is revealed quite freely.

> "DARLING DOLLY" A NEW WALTZ. We have received from the composer "Henry Laski" (Mr. T E Bulch, conductor of the Albury Town Band), an advance copy of a new set of waltzes, entitled "Darling Dolly." The music is melodious, tuneful, and catchy, and sets the feet a-tapping right away. There is that swing and rhythm inseparable from any waltz which becomes a favourite in the dancing world. Some waltzes it is abominable to dance to, but "Darling Dolly' is decidedly not of this class. The music runs to the words "Good-bye Darling Dolly. I will think of you. When the ship is sailing. O'er the ocean blue. Promise me, my darling. You'll be true to Jack. And my wife I'll make you. When the ship comes back."
>
> "Darling Dolly" is copyright and is sold, by the publishers, Bulch & Co. Albury at 2/- nett for piano and 3/ nett for-brass band. There should be a rush for copies as the set should be added to every piano player's library of dance music, if not for the purpose of encouraging a local composer, then because of the tunefulness and merit of the music."

On 8 March 1907, an advertisement appeared in the Albury Banner and Wodonga Express that at the Walla Walla Annual Sports being held on 1 April, the Walla Walla Brass Band would appear under the baton of "Professor T E Bulch." Would this notice go unnoticed by the Albury Town Band committee, who had expressed that they expected him to cease his engagements with that band? A few days later, on the 12th, the local press announced a line up of bands that had entered the District Championship Brass Band Contest, which was to take place in Albury over the Easter Festival. The Albury Town Band would test their mettle against the Albury Citizens Band, Wangaratta Town Band and the Wagga Citizens Band. Having done so well the previous year, much was expected of Tom's band, not least of which was that they to maintain their status as the districts premier band. In the build up to the contest, the Town Band took to practising every evening in the open air, to the rear of their practice room on Smollett Street. According to the Border Morning Mail, these sessions attracted a "large number of pleased listeners." The same newspaper, on 28 March, goes on to say how:

> "The music has at times more the effect of a first-class orchestra – especially in the subdued movements – than what is ninety-nine times out of a hundred obtained from brass bands. Mr Bulch is to be highly congratulated upon his work of the past few weeks, and the bandsmen themselves must not be forgotten."

The article went on to speculate that the prizes offered in this 1907 contest ought to be already won if these rehearsals were anything to go by. The reporter clearly knew something about music for, as predicted, when the Band Contest was concluded on 2 April, the Albury Town Band did indeed emerge as clear winners. Having played their version of the test piece, Rossini's "La Cenerentola," and their own choice piece, Tom's own "Meyerbeer's Works," the band finished seventeen points ahead of their nearest rivals, the Wangaratta band. For their hard work they were rewarded with the considerable prize money of fifty-five pounds. Of "Meyerbeer's Works," a reporter related that:

> "The solo cornet was particularly worthy of note and the faults in the whole band were very few. It was a pleasure to listen to the excellent music and the bandmaster is to be complimented upon his good conception of choice. The selection was a beautiful one and was handled by a master."

Tom would particularly have really enjoyed the remark about his son's solo cornet work. After the contest, the Albury Town Band posed alongside the Wagga Citizens Band for a photograph that would be published in the Leader illustrated newspaper of Melbourne on 20 April. Through their performance in the march contest, the band added to their winnings such that their total prize money that day was seventy-two pounds, in addition to which Tom himself earned a gold medal. His reputation in Albury continued to ride the crest of a wave. His achievement also did not go unnoticed further afield. A report of a band meeting in Yackandandah, captured in the Yackandandah Times of 11 April 1907, reveals how that band had sent a scout to Albury to try to tempt Tom to come to work with them. The scout, one Mr McKintyre, reported back to the meeting that Tom would not be drawn away from Albury as the committee there had, as we revealed earlier, recently raised his salary to keep him solely at their disposal.

At the end of April, a further meeting of the Albury Town Band committee saw that body agree that Tom had earned an honorarium of five pounds and five shillings on account of the hard work he put in towards winning the Albury contest. The committee also indicated being in favour of sending the band to both the Ballarat South Street Contest and the Geelong contests.

Something we take quite for granted in modern times is recorded music, almost as if it has been ever-present. It's hard, for some, to imagine that back in the 1900s it was still a relatively new phenomenon. On 9 April 1907, in another story in the Border Morning Mail, Mr J B Thomson of the "Leading Book Store" in Albury was telling a reporter how he has just returned from Melbourne where he had been buying gramophone stock from the newest selections offered by the Edison and Stirling companies. Among the records he acquired were two or three that featured compositions by Tom Bulch. Presumably, in highlighting this Mr Thomson was hoping to create a few extra sales. The information does beg the question though, of what Tom would make of such recordings. Would he consider them to be a technological marvel he could revel in, given that his music could be preserved so indelibly? Would he find them, perhaps, difficult to listen to, possibly being analytically critical of how the recording bands had played it, or because by its very nature it lacked the full dynamic range it would have had if being played live before him?

A dinner was held at the Albion Hotel on 9 May, for the bandsmen of the Albury Town Band. Fifty persons were present, including a handful of civic dignitaries. At points, both the Mayor and Mr W H Ashby proposed toasts to Tom, as bandmaster. Tom, according to the Border Morning Mail, responded that what the band had achieved so far was "as yet nothing," and was still in its infancy. He was not as elated as many might expect over the victory, for he considered it to have been an easy one. It was not only, in his opinion, what was done in the band room that made a band. He also expressed an opinion that the position of bandmaster was not an enviable one, as the public had eyes upon him and whatever he did. He asked the band members present not to become "swollen-headed" at their recent success.

The next day, Tom demonstrated his personal musical versatility again by providing the accompaniment to singing at a celebration of Alderman Conrad ten Brink, which was held at the Albury Mechanics Hall. Alderman ten Brink had served the town and district for many years, and was about to leave on a 'health tour' that would last several months. The great and the good of Albury, as well as a few from neighbouring towns, converged at the hall to see him off. Speeches of good will were made and, as was often the case, the evening ended with songs sung around the piano.

By the end of May, the Border Morning Mail advised its readers that according to the report of the committee at the Annual General Meeting of the Albury Town Band, the junior band which Tom had initiated at the beginning of the year, "continues to be a source of attraction to the lads of the town who, under Mr Bulch's tuition, are receiving a first-class musical education." Tom, later in the same meeting, suggested that something be done to retain the boys he was training so that he was not educating lads to join other brass bands. He suggested setting up a "second-eleven" to shadow the main Town Band.

Tom's sons appear to have spent much of 1906 playing football for teams in the Albury area, an interest that they had previously participated in whilst in Ballarat. There are reports of their names as part of the squads in a good number of football matches that year. A report in the Border Morning Mail of 6 June tells how, in one match against the Imperials team:

> "On the bounce the Borders forwarded and Bulch scored a sixer, which was followed with a small point"

Then later:

> "Borders, by nice marks and clever handball attacked the Imps territory and Bulch scored a goal."

Readers in Britain might find the mention of a 'sixer' perplexing. It is of course a reference to the scoring system in Australian Rules Football, that nation having had their own format of the game of football since at least the mid nineteenth century.

In early July, Tom was releasing more new published music. The Albury Banner, on the 5th of that month, was happy to oblige him with a review in which, if he had once again hoped to maintain the secret identity behind his pen names, he could have been somewhat disappointed.

> "New Music, Mr T. E. Bulch, the enthusiastic conductor of the Albury Town Band, is a prolific, as well as a successful, composer of popular music. Indeed, the identity of Mr Bulch has almost been lost in the multiplicity of his pen names. Most people have difficulty in making one name known in the artistic world, but Mr Bulch is an enviable exception to this rule. We have before us, for instance, five recent compositions from Mr Bulch's pen. 'Beauty 'Waltz' and 'Maid of the Mist' are two waltzes by 'Henry Laski,' in his characteristic style. The themes are melodious, and 'catch,' with swing and general 'go' sustained throughout. Three descriptive fantasias— 'The Life of a Fireman,' 'Life of a Chorister,' and 'Life of a Blacksmith'— by 'S Redler' are very effective. The melodies are adroitly varied, to suit the characters of the different pieces. These compositions should prove of unusual interest to students of the pianoforte."

On 17 July, the band hosted a Plain and Fancy Dress Ball at the Albury Mechanics Institute. Once again Tom's daughters had played their part in its organising, along with other ladies associated with the band. They also took part. Adeline attended in fancy dress as the 'Daughter of the Regiment', whilst Alice joined a group of her friends dressed in Irish attire. Son, Thomas junior, featured in the band again by playing solo cornet.

411

A supper, as usual, was provided by the ladies committee. At a later meeting, the ladies were congratulated on having generated a profit of thirty two pounds and ninepence for the band. When the men of Albury Town Band attended their contests later that year, the ladies could be assured that it was in no small part due to their efforts. On 25 August, the band were fundraising for another cause. They all travelled to the Newtown Orphanage, and there played a programme of music for residents and visitors which, according to the Border Morning Mail the following day, "each and all seemed to justly appreciate." The concert drew a large attendance, and a collection raised forty-two pounds for the orphanage. A reporter from the Albury Banner noted that the band had further improved markedly since a decision had been made to take the band to the Ballarat band contest.

In September Tom fell ill. We're not sure what the specific ailment was, but it was short-lived, so likely to have been a cold or bug. The Border Morning Mail explained that a concert planned to tale place in the Botanical Gardens on the 22nd was cancelled for that reason, but on the 27th the public was advised that the following concert, due to take place on Sunday, 29 September would go ahead.

For the thirteenth of October, Tom had planned a combined concert in which the Albury Town Band would join up with the band from Rutherglen to give a fundraising concert in order to top up the remaining money needed to provide the band with transport to, and accommodation at, Ballarat. Given that Tom had been instrumental in founding and shaping the prestigious Ballarat band contest, a successful return to Ballarat and good outcome in the contest, would surely be very important to him. This particularly after his unimpressive contest results there with the 3rd Militia Band and the Ballarat Railways Band in more recent years.

The collection from the concert with the Rutherglen band brought in an extra fourteen pounds. Mr Collings of the Rutherglen Band expressed his pleasure at being able to help the Albury Band and wished Tom and his band the best of luck at Ballarat. Despite the looming contest appearance, there was time remaining for just one more fundraising push. The band squeezed in a last concert at the Albury Mechanics Institute on 18 Oct 1907. On this occasion the band showed off their prowess by playing Bulch's "Beauties of Meyerbeer" and the test selection "The Mountain Sylph." The Morning Mail the next day expressed that the weather for the concert had been 'oppressive', which had in turn led to a limited attendance; though the general mood had been improved by the contribution of songs added to the concert by well-known singers from the town.

On Monday the twenty-first, as had been planned for some weeks, the Town Band band left Albury, bound for Ballarat. They were accompanied by the Mayor of Albury, Alfred Waugh, and the President of the band, Mr Blake. Thomas reserved a few moments, before departure, to advise a reporter from the Albury Banner that he was confident that the town's bandsmen "would give a good account of themselves." Arriving at Ballarat the bands settled in to prepare for the contests. According to the Ballarat Star the bands were invited, on the morning of the 23rd October, to meet the Mayor of Ballarat East, Councillor Pearce. All the bands did so that morning, with each being scheduled a meeting at 30-minute intervals. The Albury Town Band's appointment was at half-past eleven, along with the band of the Australian Light Horse from Sydney. Later, at eight o'clock in the evening, the visiting bandsmen were invited to attend the annual conference of bands in the hall of the Manchester Union of Oddfellows. The Grand Champion Band Contest would kick-off the following morning at nine o'clock at the City Oval. Therefore, despite the temptations and entertainments the city offered, the Albury bandsmen were expected to keep clear heads in readiness. The conference discussed, at length, the system of judging and other rules relating to band contests. One particular matter on that agenda was the requirement of residency. In order to qualify to play for the band each bandsman representing an area should be resident there.

Today, in Britain, as in top-flight team sports, a bandsman playing for a band can reside, and travel from, anywhere and still represent a particular band. Consequently we see the best players, motivated by both prestige and monetary reward, often switching bands and regularly travelling great distances to play for the best bands. Back in 1907, the Band Association in Australia had expected that a bandsman should have been resident in a town he represents for at least two months. At this conference this qualifying period was extended to six-months.

The 1907 Ballarat South Street Band Competition, as part of the overall South Street festival, was a huge success for the city of

Ballarat. It raised over a thousand pounds through gate revenues and drew many visitors to the city. The weather was reportedly spectacular, and all kinds of side displays were laid on for visitors, including a military reenactment.

For Tom and the Albury Town Band, however, the contest did not prove to be the great success that they, and the supporters families and officials back in Albury had hoped for. As Tom had predicted, the contest proved a much sterner challenge than the local contest earlier that year. Having said that, what they achieved was still far better than Tom had managed in the B Grade with the Soldiers Hill Band, or with the Ballarat Railways Band prior to that. In the test piece and own choice selection contest they were placed fourth from nine bands, behind Broken Hill, Zeehan and Port Pirie. It had been a close affair though, with only six points separating them from the top placed band. In the quickstep contest they were placed fifth, with Prout's Ballarat Brass Band taking the honours. Tom would probably have noted at the end of that contest that his former band, once operating as Bulch's Model Brass Band but now the Ballarat City Band, had been placed fourth amongst the A grade bands for both the test pieces and quickstep competitions.

Though brass banding at that time was still very much the exclusive preserve of men, doubtless to the despair of ranks upon ranks of excellent bandswomen that demonstrate equal capability today, it was clear that Tom wanted all his children to have an understanding and practical experience in music. We learn from the Albury Banner, issued on the 1st November 1907, that Tom's daughter Alice had sat her 'Preparatory' musical examination in St Matthew's Hall at the Convent of Mercy in Albury on Friday, 25 October, and had been successful in passing. The examinations were governed and administered by Trinity College, London. The article noted that Alice was a pupil of Mr P L Grey. The news was relayed by newspapers as far away as Sydney.

A few weeks later, on 3 December 1907, the Bulch family name appeared in the Albury press for a different reason. Tom's son, and two of his friends, had been caught by the local police and were being publicly shamed for another relatively minor, yet costly, transgression. The Border Morning Mail of that date, one of three local papers that ran the story, explains:

"Cycling on Footpaths. At the Albury Police Court yesterday Arthur Kelly, Thomas Bulch junr. and John Breit junr. were each fined 5/ with 6/ in costs, in default 14 days imprisonment for riding their cycles on the footpaths in Kiewa, David and Dean Streets respectively. The fines were paid."

At the beginning of February 1908, the town of Albury was bristling with excitement at the prospect of a planned visit by one of Australia's brightest celebrities of the day. This was Dame Nellie Melba, more properly known as Helen Porter Mitchell, but who had derived this stage name as a shortened form of her home city of Melbourne. Nellie Melba was one of Australia's true stars, based upon her operatic performances, and a huge sensation wherever she went. She was a year older than Tom, and throughout a remarkable career that spanned from 1887, right through to her death in 1931, she was considered as quite possibly the most famous Australian alive. Her reputation soared, not only because she was considered a terrific operatic soprano singer, but also through her record of showing great generosity and encouragement to the younger artists following in her footsteps. She was well loved throughout Australia, but also worldwide, on account of her travels to Britain, Europe, Russia and America. A visit by Nellie Melba was cause for celebration in any Australian town. Even today, well over a hundred years later, Australians know her face through its having been long featured on the Australian one-hundred dollar note. Many of us that will not have heard her sing would still be familiar with a Peach Melba, or Melba Toast, which were just two of four recipes first created in her honour by the French chef Auguste Escoffier.

Melba had been booked for a concert in Albury scheduled for Thursday, 6 February. The newspaper reports estimated that around two-thousand people gathered at the railway station just to witness her arrival. Thinking ahead, the Albury stationmaster had erected a barrier on the station platform to prevent the excited crowd from pressing forward and crushing the opera singer. This foresight proved it's value when the singer arrived and stepped down from the observation car at the rear of the Sydney Express for then the "crowd surged like waves of the sea." At the station entrance, Tom Bulch awaited with the Albury Town Band to "welcome the prima donna with musical honours." The band played while she waited to get into the car that was ready to whisk her away to the Globe Hotel. It took a few minutes to get Nellie to the car for as she left the station it had become obscured by the crowd, with some members of the throng clambering onto it so as to get a better view of her arrival.

Once at the Globe Hotel, Melba would spend the night relaxing ahead of the concert at the Albury Mechanics Institute the following evening. Part of the reason for her booking in Albury was to inaugurate the new stage that had been built at the Institute. Whether Tom attended the concert is something we don't know, though it's hard to imagine that a music aficionado such as he, with a penchant for arranging operatic works for brass bands, would have let such an opportunity pass him by. He may also have felt it a great honour for the band to be part of the welcoming celebrations for such a distinguished singer.

In early March 1908, Tom appears to have taken yet another brass band under his wing. This time it was the Jindera Brass Band, based in the small town of that name that lies on the road between Albury and Walla Walla. The Albury Banner and Wodonga Express of 6 March tells us how that band had been practising, under his guidance, ahead of a concert to benefit the Jindera Bush Fire Brigade. The concert was scheduled to take place on 18 March, and had been postponed from the previous year. When it happened, it was deemed by the press reporter that covered it to have been a huge success. The band, under Tom's baton, was said to be "at its best," the hall full, band and singers loudly applauded after each piece in the programme. Not everyone, however, was pleased. On 25 March, while Tom had been spending time putting the Jindera Brass Band through their paces in preparation for the benefit concert, the committee of the Albury Town Band met and consequently decided to dispense with Tom's services as bandmaster. In his place, as a temporary measure, they appointed another member of the band. The outcome of that meeting was then published in the Border Mail and Riverina Times, on Friday, 27 March, in a report in which the journalist also questioned the wisdom of the decision:

> "It seems a pity, after the undeniably valuable work the late conductor has put in, that the band should lose the services of Mr Bulch, whom we feel certain that committee will have much

difficulty in suitably replacing. The frequent successes of the band in competitions are in the main due to his skill and painstaking instruction. He is also a composer of no mean order, and even the famous Besses of the Barn Band do not scorn to include his compositions and arrangements in their repertoire."

The news circulated quickly, accompanied by fresh rumours, particularly with there being another significant brass band in the town of Albury. The secretary of that band was quick to attempt to pour water on them three days later via the pages of the same newspaper.

"CORRESPONDENCE. THE CITIZENS MILITARY BAND (To the Editor.) Sir,—We wish to contradict a rumour that is current re Mr T E Bulch and the Citizens' Band. In fairness to Mr Bulch we wish to state that there is no communication whatever in the rumour that Mr Bulch is to take over the conductorship of the Citizen's Band, as there has not been any arrangement of any kind before or since when Mr Bulch severed his connection with the Town Band, nor has Mr Bulch ever approached the Citizens Band on the subject. Any negotiations that may occur with Mr Bulch and the Citizens Band will be given publicity. Thanking you for your valuable attention – Yours. HARRIS and WITTMER, Hon. Secs. A.C.M.B Albury, March 28"

This letter suggests that the severance in the relationship between the Town Band and its master had been at Tom's instigation, however, the committee made plain, via several newspapers, that it was their decision to terminate the agreement. The public dialogue, via the press, did not end there. A further letter was published having been written by a person under the pen name of Annual Subscriber:

"Sir, - I hear Mr Bulch has been given no reason as to why his services were dispensed with by the Committee of the Town Band, beyond the bare words "on account of the condition of the band." Also, that Mr Bulch's first intimation of his dismissal was a paragraph in a certain paper, and that the letter of the president dispensing with his services did not reach him till after he had read the news in the public press. This method of dealing with Mr Bulch is so like that adopted with the previous bandmaster (Mr Drury) that I want to know if all the actions of the Town Band Committee are on a par with the way in which they treat their bandmasters. I want to ask the band committee a few questions, and if it does not answer then I hope Mr Bulch will satisfy my curiosity. They are - (1) Is it a fact that Mr Bulch, within the last few weeks, removed his business of a music-seller and phonograph dealer to Dean Street, in the block between Olive and Kiowa Streets? (2) Is it a fact that an annual collection of subscriptions for the Town Band was made in September last, and that the next annual subscription was made early this month – an interval of only six or seven months intervening? (3) If, had Mr Bulch been dismissed before taking up this latter annual collection, said collection would not have been less than half, hence the bandmaster was not got rid of till the public subscriptions were safely in hand? (4) If the reason why a band contest was not included in the Musical and Literary Festival programme for the coming Easter was because some of that committee, who are also members of the Town Band Committee knew that they would not have Mr Bulch to win the prize for them this time, and so could not bother about what was the greatest feature of their previous competitions? (5) If the matter of commission on band instruments (which is always a perquisite of the bandmaster) had anything to do with rendering Mr Bulch distasteful to some members of the committee? I could ask a lot more questions but will take breath until I get answers to the above. – Yours etc."

There was definitely an element of controversy in what had taken place. The Albury Town Band committee chose not to respond publicly and to-and-fro regarding the matter, in the newspapers, ended there. Within days, a new bandmaster named Cunningham was instated. Tom's newspaper advertisements for his music store confirmed that he had indeed moved his business to new premises at Dean Street, and within days it was also clear that he did take appointments as bandmaster to both the Albury Citizens Band and the Jindera Brass Band. Had he not, it could be supposed his only alternative would be to find another band elsewhere.

Tom set straight to work with the Citizens Band, organising a benefit concert to take place on the afternoon of Sunday, 12 April. This had the objective of raising money to enable the Newtown Orphanage to a have a telephone installed. Neighbours of the orphanage had provided the necessary telephone poles, so all that remained to be funded were the cables and insulators. This , as the Border Morning Mail and Riverina Times put it, would be the first time the band would appear publicly under "one of the most capable conductors in Australia." As always, the concert was a hit with a large crowd that had gathered to hear the band play their programme of music. Naturally the concert programme included several of Tom's's own compositions. Doing so would not be as egotistical as it might sound, given that a great many Australian bands at the time would include one or two Bulch pieces. It's probable that the Citizens Band had been playing his works for years, and had probably bought some of his more recent pieces from his shop. For this concert the notable inclusions were "Gigantique," the waltz "Flowers of Australia" and "Torchlight Parade." A reporter for the Border Mail highlighted that "it was remarked generally that already there has been a decided improvement in this playing of the band since Mr Bulch took charge."

Though Tom was no longer engaged to the Albury Town Band, his advertisements in the Albury Banner took some time to reflect this change. This was, barring the possibility that he had left them that way to annoy the Town Band committee, perhaps owing to the fact that he had paid up front to run the advertisement for a pre-set period of time.

On 15 May, Tom attended a public smoke social that had been arranged in honour of one Dr Irmer. This had been organised by the German nationals of Albury and took place at the Albury Hotel. With over one-hundred people present, it was referred to as one of the most successful functions of its kind ever held in Albury. Toasts were proposed to the honoured guest, to the King, and to the Kaiser. After those, Dr Irmer gave an eloquent speech during which he:

> "…referred at some length, and in especially impressive terms to the happy relations now existing between Germany and England, and pointed out that this was only natural in view of the blood relationship existing between the Royal families of the two nations. If that continued there would be no fear of war as the two powers could defy the world."

Looking back at this speech now it would seem remarkably naive, as when trouble did indeed flare up in Europe just ten years later creating a terrible global conflict, the insecurities between these royal cousins, and their other first cousin the Tsar of Russia, would be part of the the cause. After the speeches, some of the company present gave renditions of songs, accompanied on piano by Tom Bulch. The evening terminated at eleven o'clock at night after renditions of "Auld Lang Syne," "Der Wacht am Rhein" and "God Save the King." Surely not one person present would have perceived the approach of those metaphorical dark clouds gathering on the distant horizon, fuelled by the very thing they had believed would hold them together.

On 22 May, the Citizens Band relocated briefly to Jindera for a concert and dance at which Tom acted as Master of Ceremonies. Then two days later on Empire Day, so chosen as having been the birthday of the late Queen Victoria, Tom led the Citizens Band and units from the local military forces in procession from the drill hall to St Matthew's church for a special service. The Town Band was also in attendance.

Reports of Tom's activities through the Australian winter months are few, suggesting that his time was probably quietly invested in his shop, his composing work and in rehearsing the Citizens and Jindera bands for the spring months. The band did, however, offer another concert at the Newtown Orphanage in the first week of September. On 18 September, the Bulch family celebrated a wedding. Tom's eldest son and namesake married Miss Ivy Veronica Cozens, daughter of Mr R B H Cozens of Albury. Curiously it was described as a "quiet" wedding in the Albury Banner, with the marriage service being taken by Reverend Canon Bevan at St Matthews Church. Whether there was a particular reason for the wedding to be quiet, other than perhaps shyness of the couple, we'll never truly know.

On Monday, 12 October, the committee of the Albury Citizens Band held their annual meeting at the Albury Town Hall, with Tom in attendance. The report of the year's progress commented on how the band had successfully secured his services as bandmaster, how the band had made good progress under his leadership and that expectations were that they could rise to a high standard of efficiency. They had thirty-one players in the band, and average attendance at practice was twenty-four. The band's finances were also deemed satisfactory. Then on Sunday, 28 October, the band took part in the last local military church parade of the season at St David's Presbyterian Church.

The Australian spring brought news of Tom and Eliza's daughter, Alice. Musical examinations had been conducted on 23 October by Mr Schilsky of the Trinity College of Music,

London. Among the successful students listed in an article in the Albury Banner was Miss Alice Bulch; a student of Mr P L Gray who had attained a Junior Pass. Tom's daughter was continuing her own journey through the world of music.

The Citizens Band started November with a Sunday afternoon concert on the first day of the month at Bowna. This was intended to raise more money for band funds. Later that month, on the 13th, we see Tom once again short of personal funds. He had appeared in the local Small Debts Court with respect to a claim by John Carew and Son for five pounds and twelve shillings for goods sold and delivered. The court predictably found in favour of the plaintiff, with court costs adding to Tom's debt. It appears that history was, once again, repeating.

The 19th of November was the second day of the Albury Racing Club's Spring Meeting and, despite the weather being perfect for the occasion, only a moderate crowd had gathered to watch the Hurdle Race, Trial Stakes, Spring Handicap, High Weight Handicap and Farewell Handicap. Nevertheless, Tom and the Albury Citizens Band were on site to provide "spirited" music for those present to enjoy between the races. The remainder of the year passed by with relatively little of significance happening other than Tom's forty-sixth birthday on the 30 December.

The beginning of 1909 was almost as quiet in terms of evidence of activities of Tom or the Citizens band. One of the reasons for this may have been revealed by the Border Morning Mail of 4th March. The article tells that, at a meeting of members of the Albury Citizens Band, Tom had complained of the poor attendance of bandsmen at practice. We saw previously that on average seven of the bandsmen would be absent from each practice. Tom tendered his resignation there and then. The band had failed to meet his exacting expectations, and its bandsmen had failed to demonstrate the commitment and passion to attain the quality he expected. The band members discussed the matter, before accepting Tom's resignation and resolving to seek a successor at a future meeting. With both the Albury Town, and Albury Citizens, bands alienated, and only the Jindera band to supplement his income from the music store, Tom's future in Albury would surely be in doubt. It seems, however, as if the previous report in the Border Morning Mail, did not reflect the situation as Tom saw it, for only two days later, a letter was published providing his personal perspective.

> "To The Editor. Sir,- having read a paragraph in your issue of Thursday last, re Citizens Band Meeting, I might state that I did not tender my resignation as bandmaster, neither do I intend doing so. It is no doubt a fact that my complaint of irregular attendances of members is quite true, as I hold a copy of the roll call. It has been said to my own knowledge that the said paragraph was a mild way of getting rid of my services so as not to injure me in any future application I might make for a similar position. Neither band in Albury, nor any other in Australia, can accuse me of sending in my credentials to secure a position as bandmaster. Holding now a unique position as Hon. Sec. and Bandmaster, as I do, you would not expect me to write my own death warrant. Yours etc. T E Bulch. Hon Sec. and Bandmaster, Citizens Band, March 5."

Whatever had actually happened, it certainly seems as though Tom's relationship with the band, or otherwise the newspaper, was ailing.

Toward the end of the month, Tom again provided piano accompaniment for a social evening hosted by the Albury's German community. This time it was in honour of Dr Muller, who was leaving Albury for a trip to Germany. As at previous event, both King and the Kaiser were toasted before songs were joyously sung.

In May, at a meeting of the Albury Town Band the secretary sang the praises of their new bandmaster, Mr Cunningham, stating that the band had progressed as well under him than it could have under Mr Bulch or any other bandmaster. Might this have been put on record specifically to injure Tom's pride, or that of critics who had opposed dispensing with his services?

The winter months continue to offer scant news of events relating to Tom's life, and they are punctuated only by the occasional appearances at social evenings, where he would round each night off accompanying singers at the piano. In July this was at the annual social of the military forces of the local Battery at the Drill Hall. In October, it was the twenty-fourth annual meeting of the Albury Deutscher Verein, once again the German community. While the newspapers were sprinkled liberally with reports of bands across the continent playing his compositions as frequently as if they were part of the flowing lifeblood of Australia itself, Tom's own star appeared to be fading. He continued to receive support locally, however, and the debate in the correspondence column of the Border Morning Mail was reinvigorated at the beginning of October when the Albury Town Band lost its most recent bandmaster. A writer, using the pen name Artemus, kicked off the discussion:

> "Sir, - Being an admirer of music I took the opportunity of visiting the Sports Ground to hear the Bathurst Band, who were on their way to Ballarat to compete at the South Street competitions, and having heard them play I was thoroughly convinced that the Albury Town Band (who competed two years previously) were much better representatives than they at least as far as N.S.W. was concerned. Now as the Town Band is without a bandmaster, I for one would like to see Mr Bulch reinstated, as we all know he has value as a musician. I feel quite sure that this would be of desire to the general public of Albury, and they are the people who support the band. Hoping that some other pen than mine will take this matter up. Yours etc."

Hot on the heels of that letter, a further one appeared the next day in the same column; this time from Silent Worker.

> "Sir, — I feel pleased that someone has voiced the opinion of the public re Mr Bulch's ability as a bandmaster. Having been a bandsman under Mr Bulch I can safely say that the majority of bandsmen are of the same opinion. The band never was up to the same standard before or since Mr Bulch was conductor, which was then a credit to the town. If Mr Bulch is given full power to control the band as his musical ability warrants, and not to be hampered by non-musical committeemen who have no knowledge of running a band, the public, more especially the bandsmen, I feel sure, will not regret it. I hope my brother bandsman will give it serious consideration.—Yours etc."

These appeals, doubtless not helped by the general tone of criticism targeted at the committee, fell on deaf ears. Tom was not reinstated. The rift had widened to a breadth that could no longer be bridged. Sadly, matters concerning the Albury Citizens' Band were even worse. As the year drew to a close, an agreement was reached that attendance had dwindled to the point that the band was no longer viable. Arrangements were made to formally disband, and also to dispose of the band's assets. On 30 November, the Albury Citizens Band advertised that they were selling fourteen instruments, a drum and all of their sheet music, inviting tenders to purchase the lot. Prior to the sale, the instruments were put on display at the band secretary, Mr L V Harris's, cycle shop. A tender was subsequently received from a Mr York, of Melbourne, who offered thirty-five pounds. This surpassed the pledges by rival bidders, and at a meeting on the 6th of December, it was agreed that Mr York's tender would be accepted. The proceeds from the sale were distributed among worthy causes in the area by the band's former President, John Wilkinson. Albury District Hospital, Newtown Orphanage and the Albury Benevolent Society were among the beneficiaries.

The Albury Town Band remained without a bandmaster well into January of 1910. Arrangements were eventually made to appoint a Mr Percy Pogson, who was at that time in the employ of a band in America. Pogson would not be able to get to Albury until Easter at the earliest. Concerned that the band would deteriorate in the meantime, a correspondent named Subscriber voiced their opinion in the Border Morning Mail. They concluded their letter by saying:

> "The band must have a bandmaster – and one now. I notice it was suggested recently that Mr T E Bulch, who did much in bringing the band to the high position I referred to, should be reappointed. Perhaps because Mr Bulch did not favour reed instruments in the band, for which the band recently went to some expense in procuring, it might not have had consideration. I do not write this with any favour towards Mr Bulch, but simply say that, if the band is to have a bandmaster, that one should be appointed, and which should not be a difficult matter. Yours etc."

One wonders whether this letter reveals something of the truth regarding the original falling out between Tom and the Albury Town Band Committee. Was it connected to an intention to start including reed instruments? It would be odd if that would cause a problem, as he had composed for this combination and had worked with military-style band format. For example the Melbourne GPO Band and the 3rd Battalion Militia. Almost immediately Tom responded via the same channel:

"CORRESPONDENCE – THE TOWN BAND CONDUCTOR. (To The Editor.) Sir. – Noticing a letter in to-day's issue re above band, I would suggest that the committee appoint permanently Mr W J Lester as bandmaster. He is as good a man as I am for the position, in fact he told me so, and that is sufficient proof for anyone musically inclined. It is not generally known that some fifteen months prior to my dismissal from the band (and the only dismissal in thirty years as a bandmaster both in England and in the Colonies), that the appointment was offered to Mr Percy Jones, bandmaster of the St. Augustine's Band, Geelong, at a salary of £4 per week. In conclusion, I cannot understand why the public allows about two men on the committee to run the whole show as they like. – Yours etc. T E Bulch."

This particular letter was first brought to my attention by Tom's grandson Eric, who added, "By the tone of the letter I feel the hurt of my grandfather after all his efforts to raise the standard of the band."

On 15 December 1909, there was a happy distraction for Tom and Eliza Bulch when they became grandparents for the first time. Daughter-in-law Ivy May had become pregnant earlier that year and on the day in question now brought baby Thelma Evelyn Bulch into the world. This little girl became the first of a new second generation of native born Australian members of the Bulch family. Despite this moment of happiness, it seemed certain the Albury chapter of Thomas Edward Bulch's story had reached its final page. He must have spent his birthday at the end of December wondering what he might do next, and where.

New Shildon

The cold winter months between the end of 1908 and 1909 brought no cheer to the Allan family. Not only had the dispute at the railway engineering works brought financial hardship but, on 30 January 1909, the family patriarch, John James Allan, died from heart failure whilst at a property on nearby St John's Road. He had continued to work as a tailor and draper right up to his death. George's younger brother Edwin, who at that time was resident at Pearl Street on the outskirts of Old Shildon, was the family member that took the sad duty to report his father's passing. John was then buried three days later in the churchyard at All Saints Church, with family and friends in attendance. He left behind an estate valued at £771 19s and 10d, mainly to his wife Hannah, but George was also named as a beneficiary.

The death of her husband would have been a terrible blow to Hannah, who now found herself living alone and without a regular income in what was once a bustling family home. It would have been much comfort, though, to have all the remaining family members living nearby. George's house at Pears Terrace was only a few hundred yards away from Adelaide Street, and he and his wife would be able to visit easily, as would her grandchildren Lillie, Beatrice and William. Another son, John, also lived nearby with his family. His brother, James, only a few doors further away. Nonetheless, it's possible to imagine Hannah occasionally found herself lonely in her home filled with family memories and the dark haunting recollection of her son Ralph's suicide.

As spring approached, it was clear that George had been working hard through the winter months, finding some source of significant inspiration. The April issue of the Brass Band News contained another of his discrete little advertisements toward the back page, which announced the publication of what was to prove to be one of his best brass band contest marches. In fact, this would arguably be one of the greatest brass band marches of his era, if not of all time.

> "'The Wizard,' Grand New Contest march for 1909. One of the finest marches ever published for contesting and programmes. Sure to win. Price 1/3. – Allan, Publisher, New Shildon."

It's worth considering here that even George himself knew he was on to something with this march. To make this claim in his advertisement was not simply sales pitch and bravado. At the time it was published, this piece of music was a real departure from the standard fare on offer. It's difficult to play well unless you have a really capable band at your disposal. That in itself raises a particularly interesting question. Given that George was now no longer engaged to any of the brass bands in Shildon, how on earth did he know how well this, or any other of his compositions, would turn out? Was it simply that he had an incredible ability to visualise the music? Was he perhaps working with another brass band, further afield, in some unrecorded partnership? If the answer is the latter, it would have to be a band of no mean ability. It has been suggested to us that, at some point, he worked with the Leasingthorne Colliery Band, though not as bandmaster. We have no evidence to prove that he did. However he was doing it, George Allan, the talented amateur composer, had, in creating "The Wizard," taken the art of brass band contest marches to a whole new level. On account of his limited means to promote it, sales and performances of the march would have gathered momentum very slowly at first. The first reported instance we have seen of it being played was by the Lincoln Malleable Ironworks Prize Band on the 20 May as part of a free concert put on by the Corporation at the Arboretum. Hathern Old Prize Band, also played it on the Round Bank at Hathern in Leicestershire, on 10 July 1909, the same month in which we saw it first advertised. For a while it also became a favourite of the Sowerby Bridge Band who first played it on 27 May in the People's Park at Halifax. From there, however, the fame of "The Wizard" gradually snowballed to the extent that even today it is one of a handful of pieces that the very best brass bands in the world turn to when aiming to win at a march contest. Incredibly it still has a freshness and vibrance that transcends time and can stir audiences and bandsmen today as much it would have whenever it was first played.

On Saturday 10 July 1909 an annual charities carnival, in aid of the Newcastle Infirmary and local Nursing Association as well as local Nurse Wood, was held at Bishop Auckland. This was only a train stop away from Shildon and within easy walking distance for many. The event reportedly attracted many thousands of visitors to the market town. A key feature of the charities carnival was a procession that featured decorated horses, decorated gentleman and lady cyclists, assorted tableaux depicting scenes, pit ponies and individuals and groups in comic costume. As the parade set off, the heavens opened in the true spirit of the British summertime, and rain poured down until the procession had almost reached its terminus. From that point in the day, though, the weather cleared up considerably and events continued in the Bishop's Park, the splendid grounds of Auckland Castle, home for centuries to the Bishops of

Durham. Among those other features that took place in the Blshop's Park that day, was a band contest. The appointed judge, to decide which was best from the four bands that had entered, was George Allan. The bands that day were the Houghton-le-Spring and District Silver Band, St Helen's and West Auckland Band, the Auckland Park Brass Band and and Brandon Colliery Silver Band. The test piece that day was "Garland of Roses" which had been composed by John A Greenwood, a protégé of George's contemporary, William Rimmer. The Brandon band pulled out all the stops to win both the test selection and quickstep prizes. Houghton-le-Spring came second, with St Helen's and West Auckland Band third. Auckland Park's soprano horn player picked up a medal for their part in the test piece. The outcome was slightly marred by the other three bands having some issue with the Brandon Colliery Silver Band, resulting in them lodging a complaint and disputing the validity of their entry. The reason was not published, alas; nor was the outcome.

In July, George took a trip to the village of Penshaw, once again well connected to the North Eastern Railway network, being situated on its Newcastle, Leamside and Ferryhill line. This was, of course, to judge another band contest, though very little is known about it except that the own-choice test selection category was won by Murton Colliery Band, with the South Moor Band coming second.   That result was reversed in the accompanying march contest.

Then, in August, George has placed another of his adverts in the personal ads section of Brass Band News. This one read:

> "These Marches are winning all over. "The Wizard" (new), "General," "Senator," "La Maestro," and other grand 'uns. Treats! Only 1/3 per set. - Geo Allan, Publisher, New Shildon."

We learn something new about George in September of 1909. On Saturday the 4th, he attended the Coxhoe Flower Show in an entirely different capacity to anything we have hereto become familiar with. That day he was neither band conductor nor adjudicator, but conductor of the Old Shildon Male Voice Choir. The Old Shildon choir had existed for probably as long as George had been involved in music, and as we have seen that as a former choirboy, and a young man with a fine enough voice to win a prize at a local Free and Easy competition, he may have participated in it. But it had for decades been the task of Henry Gibbon to conduct it. On this particular occasion, for whatever reason, George Allan took his place. Under his baton the choir provided a concert of sacred music. It is probable that Gibbon and Allan were acquainted through the choir or work as well as having been bandmasters of rival bands for several years, and that George may have been asked to step in for an occasion where Gibbon had been unable to fulfil the duties.

As we head into 1910 George's involvement with music seems to quieten a little. There are no reports of him having adjudicated at contests during that year. There is a sense that the banding community had changed since the beginning of the Twentieth Century. Through the influence of key figures such as John Henry Iles, the contesting structure became more formal and introspective in its quest for ultimacy in determining which are each region's, and the nation's, finest bands. This contesting structure of regional competitions, national finals, leagues and associations seems to have placed its trust more upon a narrowing pool of trusted professional adjudicators.

Some writers covering the history of the brass band movement have expressed that in the late Victorian era it was thought by many influencers of the brass movement that there were too many contests; inconsistent in quality and format. Many welcomed the new standards and rules, and of course the prestige that the improved contests brought. From 1910 onward we start to witness a reduction in the 'village band contests' held in conjunction with the local agricultural or horticultural shows, and see fewer but better organised key annual contests. Opportunities for amateur adjudicators like George Allan, however capable, seem to have diminished markedly.

The pinnacle of achievement for bands, was to achieve success at the National Band Festival, initiated by John Henry Iles and Sir Arthur Sullivan in 1900, which by 1910, in an echo of Enderby Jackson's Grand Band Contests of the early 1860s, was preparing for its eleventh event at the Crystal Palace in London. The ultimate prize at this contest was the National Challenge Trophy, which came with a one-thousand guinea prize and, in the five years prior to 1910 had been won by bands conducted by George's contemporary, William Rimmer. One could forgive George for looking on, enviously or admiringly, at the achievements of those that had started out as he had, but who had been afforded the luxury or opportunity to become professionals in their field. The calibre of brass band contest marches George Allan had begun to produce since the turn of the Twentieth Century stand tall alongside those of his more illustrious brethren; yet there would be no room at the top table for this 'gifted amateur' and simple blacksmith turned wagon painter from New Shildon. There had, however, been an element of choice in the path George followed through his life. Tom Bulch had proven that. Had George harboured a strong enough desire to do so, he could have attempted to follow a professional path with his music. It would have been hard, but not impossible.

Tom had certainly been helped by the fact that, when he had arrived in Australia, the banding community was less developed than in Britain, and surely recognised that as a factor in his favour. To have attempted to follow the same path in Britain would almost certainly have proved far more challenging. Whether a life-choice imposed upon George, or one he willingly embraced. He settled into his pattern of being a part-time writer and publisher of music for brass bands; fitting it around raising his family, and progressing it in whatever scraps of time that remained available to him at the beginning and end of each working day. After the New Shildon Saxhorn Band had been wound-up there is no evidence of him having acting as conductor or bandmaster of any brass bands local to Shildon. This consequent reduction in available news makes it harder for us to determine how George spent much of his time throughout these years. One thing we have been able to tell, though, is that the spate of misfortunes upon the Allan family continued into 1910.

On 18 August 1910, George was present to witness as another of his younger brothers passed on from this life. This time it was the turn of James Allan, who at the time had been living close to their mother on Adelaide Street. James and his wife Elizabeth Jane, née Donkin, had lived at number 42, with their three children Walter Donkin Allan, William Edward Allan and Alice Mowbray Allan. The family had also taken in Elizabeth's mother Jane Donkin, née Mowbray, but she too had already passed away by 1910. James had been a labourer for the railway company for most of his working life, but at the time of his death his occupation was declared as 'hawker'. His death was caused, according to the certifying doctor, Robert W Smeddle, by phthisis pulmonalis, which is the archaic medical term for tuberculosis; the disease that affects the lungs and causes a gradual wasting away of the body. As this was an airborne transmitted disease, George, James's wife Elizabeth, his children, and any other family members were taking a risk by tending to their stricken relative. Yet, with hospitalisation and modern medical options not being available, this would have been the only possibility. Prior to the 1950s, and the gradual introduction of vaccinations for some of the life-threatening infections that are rarely encountered today, the majority of men aged fifty-five or below in the UK died from an infectious disease rather than injury or natural causes. Among these, tuberculosis was the most prevalent. Before 1915, it was the leading cause of death for men under seventy-five; the majority of deaths after that age being put down to senility.

Thus, watching helplessly, and bringing what little comfort they could, would have been a common experience for British families in industrial areas. The slow gradual concession of a person to tuberculosis was a truly horrifying, pitiful and hopeless demise to witness. The medical certificate states that George was present at the time of James's death. He could have been deeply affected by the experience. James was only forty years old when he exited this world, leaving his wife and family behind to figure out for themselves how to get by without a husband and father. The death was certified on 20 August. The service for James's funeral was conducted at All Saints Church, by William Byers. After his death, Elizabeth kept the house on and scraped a living as a fish seller.

Whether for family reasons such as this, or for any other, George does not seem to have advertised any new compositions for sale during 1910. It's almost as if his attentions were diverted by other matters, some of which we will consider when we look at 1911.

Geelong

The events that took place in Albury during 1909 had left Tom Bulch in limbo. He was still resident in the town, and still had a music shop business there, but surely could not be happy, or possibly financially solvent, without a band in his charge. Across the continent, bands were still playing his music. His was still a name to be reckoned with within the Australian banding community. The organisers of the South Street Competitions in Ballarat had even selected another of his marches, "Pile Arms," to be performed when all the bands at massed under a single conductor at the conclusion of the contest. Yet, for a brief time Tom's career seemed directionless.

In July 1910, as part of an article in the Mount Alexander Mail, the Thompson's Foundry Band in celebrating twenty-five years of their history cited Tom as one of the best bandmasters from the state of Victoria to have ever conducted their band. If Tom had read that he may well now be contemplating what such a bandmaster might be without a band to lead. As fortune would have it however, an opportunity to resolve this predicament seems to have emerged in the coastal town of Geelong, on the western edge of Port Phillip Bay a few miles from Melbourne.

We don't know precisely when Tom moved his family and business interests to Geelong, but the first hint that he had done can be witnessed in an article in the Geelong Advertiser on 17 Sept 1910. This promotes a forthcoming King's Clock Concert to complement a film, "Incidents in the Life of the Late King Edward." For this, the Geelong Town Brass Band had agreed to occupy the orchestra and provide pieces by Mr T E Bulch that included "Gems of Meyerbeer." To be clear, this article is not explicit that Tom was definitely present and involved, yet there is something implicit in the wording 'provided by' that suggests he may have become connected to, or started a relationship with, the band. The situation is very quickly clarified by a follow-up article appearing in the Geelong Advertiser on 24 September:

> "GEELONG TOWN BAND. The vast improvement in the playing of this band has been frequently commented upon. Under the baton of Mr T E Bulch the bandsmen are confident of giving a good account of themselves at Ballarat next month on the occasion of the annual band contests. This band through no fault of its own, has had many ups and downs, and it is pleasing to see it, at last, reaping the reward for its pluck and perseverance. The band will render the grand selection for the Ballarat contest, "Memories of Meyerbeer" at the Kings Clock Concert on Thursday next."

Thus it is revealed that the Geelong Town Band had indeed become the latest brass band to secure Tom's services. As always, he wasted no time in showing off his talents as the new bandmaster in town, and also as a musician in his own right.

At a musical and dramatic entertainment at St Mary's Hall, Geelong, on 24 September 1910, Tom teamed up with drummer, Mr G F Twentyman, to provide bugle and piano effects to a drum solo piece explained as being a "Descriptive Battle March." Interestingly, he was described, in a newspaper write-up in the Geelong Advertiser, as being "of Ballarat," despite his having been resident for some time in Albury.

On the evening of the Kings Clock Concert, which was being held in aid of the King's Clock Fund, His Majesty's Theatre in Geelong was packed. The Geelong Orchestral society rendered ballet music from Rosa Munde, followed by a concert of various songs from the assembled cast of characters of the Geelong Operatic Entertainers. Then the Town Band offered their rendition of the Meyerbeer arrangement. A commentator in the press wrote:

"The band has made striking progress, and its performance last night under the baton of Mr T E Bulch was appreciatively applauded."

More songs followed, as well as a pantomime ballet by Miss Parker's pupils; comprising a dozen tots in striking costumes. Then a silent movie was screened, accompanied by music from the Geelong Orchestral Society, after which the National Anthem completed the night.

On Monday, 17 October, the band gave another concert, at the Geelong Mechanics Hall, to top up funds they had raised to cover their expenses for the Ballarat South Street Competitions. They were aided, this time, by members of the Operatic Society. There is a suggestion in this that the various musical societies of Geelong were adept at cooperating to put on a richer show. Miss Parker's pupils, again, gave their popular pantomime ballet. Chamberlain's Orchestra also contributed, and the owners of Sculthorpe's Bioscope, which was used to project, first a comedic moving picture about tightrope walking, then another about a clergyman trying to uplift an abandoned woman.

Since its inauguration, the South Street Competitions in Ballarat had become a huge and even more prestigious event. Its band contest had also grown. In 1910 a record number of brass bands entered. Ten bands signed up for the Class A section and seventeen for classes B and C combined. The Ballarat Star hailed it as the greatest band competition ever held in the southern hemisphere; a justifiably correct claim. It must have thrilled Tom to see, after having been influential in the development of band contests in Victoria since his earliest days on the continent. The conclusion of the South Street Competitions, overall, coincided with the final day of its band contest, creating something of a grand finale on Saturday, 22 October. Tom's former protégés, now the Ballarat City Brass Band, had elevated themselves to competing in the A Grade contest. In this, they were placed fourth for the test piece, and third for their quickstep. Tom's latest charges, the Geelong Town Band, finished up twelfth from fourteen in the B grade test piece, but fared better in the quickstep where they came fourth. Geelong Town Band were also represented in the C Grade contest, where they were placed fifth from eight in the test piece, but came top of their field in the quickstep contest.

There is little to discover of Tom's other movements throughout 1910, though the Geelong Advertiser does reveal that on Saturday, 16 December 1910 some solo competitions were arranged to encourage players in connection with the Independent Order of Rechabites Band. Tom was engaged to act as adjudicator. As we move into 1911, Tom appears to have settled down in Geelong and, with his first few band contest results with that band under his belt, he had reestablished his name as a key figure in the community. This would not be, however, as bandmaster of the Geelong Town Band. He rounded off 1910 by celebrating his birthday on 30 December, followed by a Municipal Concert in Geelong's Johnstone Park on New Year's Eve. Commencing at ten o'clock at night, the concert involved the band playing a mixture of his own pieces, including "Sandhurst" and "Canterbury Engineers," and pieces by others. These were all played before a backdrop of projected silent films. The concert also featured a local singer Bert Johnston, who sang a number of songs, among which was Tom's piece "Adeline," which we are told by a writer from the Geelong Advertiser "was particularly enjoyed." The grand conclusion of that concert was the bringing in of the New Year, with whatever it held in store for everyone.

Within days of that concert, the Geelong Town Band had been rebranded by its committee, to become the Geelong City Band, which was explained in the press as being "by virtue of

Geelong's improved status municipally." Then, on 26 January 1911, an article in the Punch, published in Melbourne, explains that a well-known local figure was returning to Geelong, in a move that would see the end of Tom's tenure of the Geelong City band:

> "Percy Jones, the orphan boy who created the almost unrivalled large brass band of St Augustine's Orphanage, Geelong, has just completed three years study in Europe, and will return to take charge of the Geelong Town Band. He has heard all the finest bands in Germany, France and England. His own performances have been received with general favour."

Tom was of course acquainted with Percy Jones, who had taken his St Augustine's Orphanage band to Albury and inspired Tom to attempt to set up a boys' band of his own. Following his return to the city, Jones would become a music teacher at Geelong Grammar School and Geelong College, and later become the father of Percy Jones Jr, who himself became a monumental figure in the development of Australian church music and music education. His achievements with the St Augustine's band were highly rated and more recent than Tom's own moments of glory in Ballarat. It appears that Tom's reputation had been trumped and, seeing a greater opportunity for success and honours, the band had ousted him. It's quite possible that this had always been their intention, and that Tom's appointment had been deliberately temporary. It may equally have been sprung upon him. In any case, Tom would retain control and conductorship of the Geelong City Band until early April, whereupon the celebrated Percy Jones picked up the reins. The rebranded Geelong City Band gave another, well attended, concert in Johnstone Park the Saturday following New Year. This time the guest singer was James Moore of Melbourne who exhibited his vocal prowess. Tom again added some of his own pieces in the programme, including his descriptive military fantasia, "The Young Recruit." Once again, silent bioscope pictures were projected to enhance the spectacle. Such concerts appear to have become a regular Saturday night entertainment through the warm summer months, with a variety of other singers joining with the band in turn; local performers such as Frank Peachey and K H Collins.

On 23 February 1911, a small report appears in the Geelong Advertiser, opening a tiny window on one episode in the life of Tom Bulch upon which one may only speculate. It read:

"LOST – Cheque, drawn in favour of T E Bulch; payment stopped. Return "Advertiser" office."

Tom also continued to find personal musical engagements away from his band. The Geelong Mechanics Institute often held citizens concerts and variety programmes around this time, and Tom's ability and versatility at the pianoforte would usually see him involved as an accompanist. On one occasion, taking place on Wednesday, 13 September, a number of leading Melbourne artists used his services, including Banveen the "human cello" who entertained "on his many instruments, including the banveenophone, dulcimer, guitars, banjos, fairy chimes, mandolins etc." As had become customary, a number of silent films were also shown including, on this occasion, "Jim Bridges," "Indian Bride" and "Girl Detective." The short format of such movies meant that several could be shown, and as they lacked any audio content it was usual for atmospheric accompanying music to be provided by a pianist. This required someone skilful enough to be able to watch the film and improvise to emphasise the dramatic effect of whatever scene was being shown. It could require musical expression of high drama, edge of the seat tension, happiness and joy, comedic tumbling or deep pathos. If you've ever watched a silent movie at home you'll know that, following the advent of film with sound, studios later added pre-recorded piano accompaniment to many of the older silent films, so you've probably never had to watch one entirely without audio. If you had, you'd appreciate just what these accompanists added to the experience and enjoyment of those films. His grandson, Eric, tells us that Tom was one of those persons in Australia, around that time, with a reputation for being able to think 'on the fly' and provide the right music for the right moment. This was exactly what he was doing on this occasion at the Geelong Mechanics Institute. It enabled a new, and small but regular, additional income for him.

You might have noticed that these occasions, though involving the showing of moving pictures, weren't taking place in cinemas. The moving picture industry was, even by 1911, still relatively young. The first screening of a film in Australia is thought to have been in 1896, the year after the Lumiere Brothers showed the first silent film in Paris. Such films were not made natively in Australia until 1906, when one was shot telling "The Story of The Kelly Gang." This was also the year that Mr T J West erected the first Australian purpose-built hall for showing films. In the early days of cinema, many parts of Australia relied upon a visit from a travelling exhibitor bringing all the equipment necessary to show a moving picture. Otherwise, films shown by local projectionists were shown in a range of adapted venues; often rented halls or tents.

Only ten Australian made silent films were produced in 1910. In a spurt of growth these were followed by a further fifty-one during 1911. Though though these numbers seem quite small, the fact was that Australia was one of the more productive countries at this time. With so little content in circulation it took a while for cinema buildings to be required. However, by 1911 developers were sensing the future and climbing aboard the bandwagon. In Melbourne, just over the bay from Geelong, there were twenty-five permanent cinemas by then, each serving the city's various urban localities. Geelong itself now had the Geelong Picture Theatre, which is mentioned in a number of newspaper articles throughout the year. Yet it was still common for other suitable non-cinema buildings, such as the Mechanics Institute, to be booked for screenings. The series of Citizens Concerts in Geelong continued to attract a strong following. At another example taking place in September 1911, Tom again displayed his improvisation skills and versatility accompanying the movies "Hero Track Walker," a railway drama; "His Honour Saved," a military drama and "Two Brothers," a western ranch drama. Another event later that same month, held in conjunction with the Corio Bay Anglers Club, involved a special interest film on the subject of "Trout Breeding" that had been brought from Sydney for the occasion. Some light relief was provided afterward in the form of a comedy entitled "The Two Fishermen." Overall this probably made a refreshing change from the steadily emerging stream of wild west films and railway adventures.

On Thursday, 28 September, another Citizens Concert at the Institute featured a silent picture, "The Spanish Gypsy," and also the singer, Mr Cuthbertson, who introducing a song entitled "Black Watch." This had been arranged by Tom, with special drum effects being provided by Mr Twentyman, with whom we saw Tom collaborate musically before. The band, on this occasion, was not the Geelong City Band but the Geelong Artillery Band. Tom was not conducting, of course. His place was at the piano. Advertisements for subsequent events at the venue consistently feature the combination of this band and pianist.

By October, Tom, doubtless driven by a need to get back to working with a band, had become involved in a movement to start a new brass band. The story was picked up on the 17th of that month by the Geelong Advertiser:

> "BAND FOR GEELONG WEST – An enthusiastic gathering of bandsmen was held at Geelong West last night to discuss the formation of a brass band in the borough. It was mentioned that several leading residents had promised to support the movement and after a long discussion on the scope of the organisation it was decided to form the band. Mr T E Bulch, late of Ballarat, who was present by invitation, was appointed bandmaster. It was decided to convene a meeting of citizens at an early date to launch the movement."

By November, we see in newspaper advertisements that Tom had also started to fulfil duties as the improvising pianist for moving pictures at His Majesty's Theatre in Geelong. As more pictures were being made or imported, their showing became an increasingly regular event. Venues started to schedule multiple evenings for different films throughout the week. Whilst Tom's name was still scattered widely throughout the pages of the nation's newspapers on account of brass and military bands playing his lifetime's work in band music, personal mentions of his appearances were now more frequently shown in connection to his accompanying those flickering images on the big screen. Despite this, he was not yet ready to leave behind the world of brass banding. On Wednesday, 8 November, twenty-five musicians, including both men and boys, met at the Geelong West Fire Brigade building to form the new Geelong West Borough Brass Band. Officials were appointed, before Tom was confirmed as the newly instated bandmaster. The band's first secretary, Mr Kinkaid, urged those in attendance to "pull together and attend practices regularly." The band were encouraged to strive to do well in competitions, particularly in Ballarat. Tom, himself, declined the opportunity to give a lengthy speech, stating only that he would reserve his talk for band practices. That band inauguration meeting was followed, on Monday the 13th, by a further meeting at the Geelong West Town Hall, convened by Mayor Dickins. Immediately before it took place, the fledgeling band assembled outside, on Pilkington Street, to play a handful of selections.

Within the meeting, the Mayor proposed not only to have a band for the borough, but also a park in which they might perform. He expressed his preference that the Council buy the land required for it. He supported his view that this facility was a priority by explaining that, at that time, citizens seeking somewhere to spend their evenings were required to stray outside the borough to find such a facility. He saw founding the new band as the forerunner to many other social improvements. A summary of the meeting printed in the Geelong Advertiser includes some detail of the proposed financial arrangements:

> "Mr Bulch had taken up the band on liberal terms: each of the bandsmen paid 6d per week into a band fund from which he would be recouped for his services. It would not be their fault if next year they were not at the top in Ballarat (laughter)."

The new band started out with significant debts of one-hundred pounds for instruments acquired from the Independent Order of Rechabites Band, but had been supplied with uniforms to the value of eighty pounds and sheet music to the value of fifty pounds. The Mayor felt that the establishment of a good working committee would soon see the one-hundred pound debt paid off. Councillor H J D'Helin proposed that the band be named the West Geelong Municipal Band and pledged to pay off a tenth of the band's debt himself; a gesture that was received with much applause. He also quickly gathered a collection from those present, to the value of six pounds, and found himself as one of three Councillors assigned to the band committee. Before a final vote of thanks by the Mayor, the band title was amended slightly to become the West Geelong Municipal Brass Band. The first band practice took place on Monday, 27 November, at the band's adopted centre of operations, and site of their first meeting. This was the Geelong West Fire Brigade Hall. In seemingly no time at all, they were fulfilling their first public engagement, under Tom's baton, by rendering selections of music between ladies swimming races at a carnival of the Ladies Western Club, held at the Gentlemen's Baths in Geelong.

As the year drew to a close, bringing Tom's forty-ninth birthday, and then New Year's Eve, the Geelong West Council summed their year's achievements. In doing so they announced that they had purchased, from Mr J W Reid, a plot of land at the intersection of Upper Autumn and Pilkington streets. This was to become the promised public park for West Geelong. It appeared that the people of West Geelong had much to look forward to.

Back in the town of his birth, 1911 had been another census year, and in the details captured we see that none of Tom's blood relatives remained at what was once the Bulch family home of 48 Adelaide Street, New Shildon. The house was by then only occupied by Tom's step-mother, Margaret, and her own daughter from her first marriage, Mary Jane Harrison. The pair, as frequently happened, had taken in a lodger; William Brass, a road mender working for the Shildon Urban Council. It appears that all of the dispossessed Bulch family offspring are all now grown-up, and dispersed from New Shildon. Tom's brother, John, had moved several times to arrive by this year at West Cornforth, working as a colliery fitter with a family of his own. Younger brother Jerry, who became one of the key figures in the organisation of the Shildon Horticultural Show, was by 1911 resident at 68 Church Street, Old Shildon, with his wife Emily May and daughter Minnie. He had become established as a coal salesman. Elizabeth, Tom's sister moved to Bishop Auckland, having married Frederick William Holt, a coke worker. The couple took in their brother Frederick as a lodger. Another brother, Christopher Bulch, and sister Ada, had embarked upon their own adventures, emigrating to America.

New Shildon

One person who was most definitely still living on Adelaide Street, at number 68, was George Allan's mother Hannah. She was now seventy-three years of age. Her own children had either moved on with families of their own or, as we have seen, died. Pears Terrace, where George and Elizabeth lived with two of their children, Beatrice and William, was only a minute's walk away from Adelaide Street, and it's highly likely that George and his mother would be regular visitors to each other. The couple's other daughter, Lillie, then aged twenty-two, had moved a couple of miles away to take care of to Elizabeth's mother,

Hannah Willoughby, at her home at Vyner Street in the village of Close House. The 1911 census lists Hannah as being a widow of private means.

George continued his day to day duties, painting new and repaired wagons at the North Eastern Railway wagon works. His son, Bill, being of working age, had commenced employment as a house painter for a local builder.

In terms of musical composition we don't see George adding anything new to his self-published portfolio during 1911, though he did place a small advert in The Cornet of April 1911 that a number of his existing compositions are still available for purchase. These included "Battle Abbey," which is now issued as a third edition and of which he had only a few copies remaining; "The General," which he describes as "a treat"; "Senator," he declares as "always winning"; "The Wizard," of which he says "this is splendid, grand effects"; and two easier contest marches "Bravura" and "The Gale." There is a suggestion that sales of his music have been steady, allowing a little added financial stability for the family.

Broadly speaking the brass bands across the mining communities of the North East of England were struggling to get together enough bandsmen to practice. This was in part as a consequence of the 1908 Coal Mines Regulation Act, also referred to as the Eight Hours Act, which had resulted in a reduced working day for mineworkers and consequently seen the introduction of a three or four shift rotation pattern. These shifts made it difficult for them all to be available at the same time to rehearse. With no band in his charge this wasn't of direct concern to George, though he would still rely upon a thriving band community to purchase his music.

He might have been more directly concerned about the ongoing absence of the Mechanics Institute, the former building of which still stood just over the railway footbridge on Station Street. It had now been closed for some years, and though the organisation continued to muddle through, as a continued member he would have been among those campaigning for a new building. At a prizegiving speech on Wednesday, 8 February, Alderman J W Pearse was goaded by an attendee, Mr J D Rider over promises of a "beautiful Mechanics Institute" that had been long promised to replace the present building. A little later that year, the North Eastern Railway company gave their go-ahead for construction to begin on a new, company funded,

Railway Institute building to be erected at a new site belonging to the company on the town's Redworth Road. This was literally just around the corner from George's home on Pears Terrace, and almost as convenient as Institute's the former location. As things transpired, the hope that this might be built quickly were dashed as other events came to the fore. The Institute at Shildon may have been the first such institute in the world to be associated with the railways; but 1911 brought another, less desirable, first. This was to be the year in which the first National Railway Strike occurred. It was the first railway related industrial dispute to draw in rail workers from companies right across Britain.

This strike had been preceded by a series of localised disputes between railway workers and their employers, generally over pay and conditions. Industrial action on the North Eastern Railway had taken place during July 1910, and was centred on Newcastle. This spat had been triggered by perceived injustice in the transference of a shunter for disciplinary reasons. The consequence was that signalmen, porters, drivers, guards and other grades of workers from Gateshead and the surrounding district did not show up for work on 19 July. This strike action spread throughout the North Eastern Railway area, with Shildon and Darlington railway workers quickly joining those withdrawing their labour in support of their colleague. The stand-off was ended when the company management promised to investigate the grievances of workers, though discontent was still rife. A movement re-emerged among the rail union membership to campaign for an eight-hour working day for railwaymen. A separate movement among the same trade unionists aimed to eliminate workers that would not become part of the unions, as these men weakened their unified position. A withdrawal of labour was threatened unless the company desisted from employing such non-union staff.

In February 1911 tensions were further stoked by the dismissal of six NER company employed fish porters at Hull. The Shildon workers resolved to hold a vote, on Sunday, 5 February, to decide whether to join a strike in support of their Hull branch colleagues. Strike action was averted when the company agreed that the case of the fish porters would be heard at the next meeting of the Conciliatory Board. A further strike, centred on Shildon itself, was narrowly averted in May 1911. This particular tension had been stoked up after a closure of rail facilities at Tebay and Wear Valley Junction as a consequence of which a number of the locomotive drivers and firemen from those sites had been transferred to Shildon. After a number of the drivers consequently retired, being older than the firemen, it was found that there were too many firemen and as not all the resulting driver vacancies had been filled there was not enough work for the excess firemen. The strike was averted through the intervention and suggestions of one George Tully, a driver and former chairman of Shildon Urban Council who suggested ways to run more trains staffed by the Shildon men.

In yet another example of the localised disputes leading up to the national strike, an article in the Hartlepool Northern Daily Mail of Tuesday, 11 July 1911 explains that the North Eastern Railway had been engaged in a dispute with the General Railway Workers Union, and finally reached an agreement over improved pay for the various professions at works across the region. These included Shildon, and the detail revealed that wagon painters like George would consequently receive a basic pay rate of twenty-one shillings per week. That was three shillings per week less than the basic pay rate for an apprentice blacksmith, which is what George had started out as, and quite a lot less than the basic rate for a qualified blacksmith. Additional money per-man would be gained for 'piece work'. In terms of estimated equivalent value, this basic weekly wage of twenty-one shillings in 1911 would compare to earning just over ninety eight pounds a week in 2020. The railway workers unions were keen to provide a demonstration of their unity and strength nationally. They were particularly discontented by the formation of, and activities conducted by, conciliation boards that had been set up to negotiate between railway workers and the companies. The companies themselves, of course preferred this to having to deal with the unions, as the outcomes were usually weighted in their favour. Unofficial industrial action across the workforce commenced over July and August of 1911 eventually triggering a convention of officials from the four principal rail unions in Liverpool, with a view to coordinating national action. One outcome was that the unions jointly issued an ultimatum to the railway companies demanding that they accept direct negotiation with their representatives or face a national strike.

In a bid to avert the strike, the Liberal Prime Minister, Herbert Asquith, advised the rail companies that he would deploy police and troops to keep the trains running. Winston

Churchill, who flip-flopped between the Conservative and Liberal parties throughout is time in politics, was at this time a Liberal MP and the Home Secretary in Asquith's cabinet. He moved to suspend the Army Regulation, which would otherwise have meant that the rail companies themselves would have had to request military deployment for their protection. This change enabled the government to order troops out to thirty-two towns in England and Wales, of which New Shildon was one. Sensing the defiance of the rail companies, the unions resolved to commit to national industrial action, which commenced over Friday the eighteenth and Saturday the nineteenth of August 1911. The latter of these two dates had been the scheduled as the day of the annual Shildon Show, which was of course disrupted by the consequent inability of visitors and exhibitors alike to reach the town by rail.

Above: The Inniskilling Rifles temporarily posted to Shildon's station, works, signal box and sidings during the first Great National Rail Strike in 1911

On the evening of 18 August railway workers from Shildon, and nearby Bishop Auckland, held demonstrations. They marched through the streets in now time-honoured tradition with their union banners flying high, in columns headed by brass bands playing bold, uplifting and defiant march music. This was the powerful music of the working people put to work. A settlement was reached relatively quickly on the national strike action. This did not, however, extend to resolving the underlying dispute between the employees and directors of the North Eastern Railway Company. Railwaymen in the employ of rail companies around the rest of the nation returned to work, leaving only the employees in the principal North Eastern Railway towns and cities of Newcastle, South Shields, Tyne Dock, Gateshead, Darlington, York, Ferryhill, Hull, Shildon and Middlesbrough carrying on the strike and demanding that their specific terms be met. Employees took measures to be deliberately disruptive. Barricades were erected at the NER's station in Leeds. In Darlington the strikers burned straw and attacked and overturned a couple of railway trolleys before police intervened. At Shildon a signal box was attacked; stones were thrown breaking several window panes. Concerned by the prospect of more attacks, particularly on engineering like the Shildon Tunnel, military units were despatched from York to Darlington and Shildon.

This military presence was no small deputation. Fifteen-hundred hundred troops, from the Royal Inniskilling Fusiliers and East Yorkshire Regiments, arrived on a heavy military train from York. Five-hundred of these were sent on to Shildon. Far from placating the railway men, this action further stoked their indignation. It had previously been reported, so was well known, that on 19th August, at Llanelli railway station, two rail workers had been shot dead by troops from the Worcestershire Regiment. Nobody in Shildon wanted to see a repeat of this, yet also they did not want to concede their position. Photographs taken at the time show crowded meetings of workers taking place on the road between the gates of the company's works and the Mason's Arms public house, while others depict the troops occupying strategic positions at the railway station, bridges, and on rooftops monitoring the whereabouts of the strikers and ready to signal action. The number of troops at Shildon was eventually scaled back to 130, or 200 depending upon which of the different reports was more accurate, by the 22nd August. These took positions guarding the signal box, station and approaches to the railway sidings. There continued to be further disturbances. In one instance a crowd attempted to set away some trucks that were standing on a siding. They were quickly driven away by the soldiers. Another incident saw a mineral train, that had been set up to make a run to Teesside, overcome by a crowd of demonstrators who chased off the strike-breaking driver and fireman by throwing stones. Elsewhere a young miner was captured throwing bricks at the locomotive of the military train, only to be released after giving his name and address.

Various reports number the estimated quantity of Shildon strikers at between two-thousand and four-thousand. By Wednesday, 23 August, the North Eastern strike was declared to be over, but the town of Shildon was widely perceived, through the combative conduct of its men, to have blotted its copybook. The Jarrow Express of Friday, 25 August 1911 read:

> "With the exception of Darlington and Shildon the North Eastern men have been a pattern to others. No unseemly conduct has placed a black mark against them. Throughout all the week they have acted in an honourable and gentlemanly manner."

As to whether George Allan played any part in the chaos, we have a very good reason to doubt it. While his comrades were making their case to be heard through skirmishes and disruption, much of which was happening within earshot of his home at Pears Terrace, George had a personal situation of his own to manage. This was one that certainly have removed him from playing a part in the industrial action going on around him, and which would only have added to his distress. What had happened was that Elizabeth Allan, George's wife, the love of his life, had developed a cerebral tumour, causing her suffering and to enter into a coma. This being the pre-National Health Service era, without the treatments and technological wonders of a modern hospital, George would have had no affordable alternative but to attempt to take care of his wife at home. If he could have afforded it, he may have been able to call upon some help from one of the local doctors, Smeddle or Fielden. Whatever aid they could offer at that time, would have been limited. Reports and paperwork give no indication as to the timeline of events leading up to her death, but we do know that she passed away on 20 August. She was only fifty years old. According to the death certificate, George was at his wife's side at the time to witness her death. Of the suffering of both we can only guess. For George it had only been just over a year to the day that he had witnessed the awful wasting death of his younger brother James from tuberculosis. Now his wife too had left him. Though rail men and soldiers were confronting each other yards away from his doorstep, it could all have appeared so distant through the veil his personal grief on that day. Elizabeth's death was formally certified by Dr Smeddle, and subsequently a funeral was arranged to take place at All Saints Church in New Shildon on 25 August, only two days after the conclusion of the strike. The service was conducted by Picton W Francis. She was laid to rest at a depth of 7 feet in a plot that would now await George for the remainder of his own life. An announcement was published on the Darlington and Stockton Times dated 26 August. Elizabeth's personal estate of £328 10s and 6d was passed to George and their eldest daughter Lillie. So far as we can tell, George never sought another in his life, and we know for certain that he would never remarry.

Understandably the remainder of 1911 offers up little evidence as to how George spent his time. One would imagine that he would have spent much of it either privately reflecting upon his loss, or seeking comfort in the company of close family and the distraction of hard work at the works. We speculate that his passion for, and inspiration in, music seems to have been set aside until the pain of loss was sufficiently receded.

Geelong

Throughout 1912, Tom continued to be engaged to accompany the midweek movies being screened at the Mechanics Institute. The silent movie makers continued to produce their carousel of comedies, war dramas and wild west adventures. These were occasionally interspersed by a thought-provoking piece, such as "The Life of a Deported Convict," which was shown on 11 January.

Occasionally he would have the opportunity to provide the same duty at a different venue; such as the evening of Monday, 22 January, when a grand concert was held in aid of the Geelong Fire Brigade in Johnstone Park. On this occasion, Tom's frequent associate, the renowned drummer Mr Twentyman, loaned his piano so that Thomas could accompany "eight up to date films" screened using "Marchant's Latest Urban Kinetiscope." As the event was to benefit the fire brigade, it was preceded by a procession of local brigades. It was a cause Tom had always rallied to during his time in Australia, perhaps made more important to him through his own loss of his business to fire back in his Ballarat days. The band providing the music on this occasion, and whom Tom had only to sit back and watch, was the St Augustine's Champion Band.

On Saturday, 17 February, Tom mustered his own Geelong West Municipal Band, for a grand open-air entertainment to mark the formal opening of long-promised Geelong West Park. The event had been organised by the Mayor. There were two principal elements to the grand opening; an afternoon ceremony at the park itself, and separately an evening entertainment at the Geelong West Theatre. The afternoon garden party attracted around two-thousand residents to the new park, each of whom was greeted by the mayor and mayoress who stood beneath a floral bower at the entrance. The park had been strewn with bunting and other decorations in celebration. Tom and the new Municipal Band entertained, as the guests partook of an afternoon tea in the open air. The boys and girls of the Ashby State School performed maypole dances and demonstrated wand exercises under the supervision of Mr George Clayton. Refreshments were followed by the formal opening ceremony, conducted by the Hon. W H Edgar, a Member of the Legislative Council, the Upper House of the territorial government. Speeches followed the ceremony, during which costs were explained and forecasts were offered, of additional facilities such as tennis courts and a bowling green. Mayor Dickins commented that:

> "It rested with the people to appreciate the benefits of the park and make the concerts there a success. Children should be encouraged to play in the park but it should be enjoined on them that they were not to touch the flowers or walk over the beds. The entertainments to be provided would be clean, and parents could safely let their children come."

On the evening bioscope pictures were shown using Marchant's "recently imported Kinetiscope and Electric Plant," and vocal and there were instrumental renditions of pieces specially arranged by Mr G Steadman. Seating had been prepared for up to 2,000 attendees.

On the evening of Wednesday, 21 February, the Municipal Band assembled at the Geelong West Theatre for another concert. A ticket to attend cost sixpence per adult or three pence per child, with proceeds to be added to the band's funds. Mayor Dickins once again presided, and Tom put in a double-shift, not only conducting the band, but also providing piano accompaniment to more short films, without which no concert now seemed complete. On this occasion these included "Babes in the Wood" and "The Branded Indian." According to the reports in the press the event was well patronised, with gate receipts totalling twelve pounds. The concert wasn't without incident. Unlike today, the small Geelong West Park was enclosed by fences, outside which a small boy had apparently been:

> "...a source of annoyance to patrons by blocking the way, and the absence of the police, whose presence would no doubt mitigate this nuisance, was commented upon."

Above: West Geelong Park and bandstand, at which Tom's Geelong West Municipal Band were simultaneously formed to be a regular entertainment.

The following night it was back to the Mechanics Institute, as Tom accompanied an Irish picture drama entitled "Rory O'Moore" which was billed as the "most thrilling picture ever screened." This pattern of cinematic concerts continued with increasing frequency in Geelong. The evenings often featured the Geelong West Municipal Band, but always a selection of "exciting" cowboy or Indian pictures, "side-splitting" comedy and "beautiful scenic" pictures. Additionally, there would almost always be the inclusion of a guest singer or recital of some sort. Occasionally this was a repeat demonstration of the instrumental versatility of Banveen the human cello. After a while the evenings found competition in drawing the attention of pleasure seeking residents of West Geelong when a purpose built Picture Pavilion was established in Geelong to show movies. Reports also continued to comment upon the misbehaviour of young boys such as this incident from a concert on Saturday, 2 March where:

> "…at the outset Cr H F Christopher warned some small boys who were inclined to be unruly, that the concerts were for the entertainment of the ratepayers, and the slightest disturbance would be met with ejectment from the enclosure. The warning was effective."

We never hear whether Tom's own family attended the concerts and cinematic displays, so we are left to wonder whether Eliza and her sons or daughters were among those, often two-and-a half-thousand persons, sitting back to enjoy the display, admiring Tom conducting his band in their smart uniforms before bringing drama to the moving pictures through his skill at the piano. Unlike today's two-hour 'blockbusters', the films were always short and conveyed condensed stories. "Captain Kate," "Ranger's Stratagem," "The Baron," "The Miser's Heart," "The Wheels of Time," "The Siege of Calais"; a never ending stream of adventure stories or tales of moral virtue. A report on a Thursday night concert on 14th March boasted that the projectionist had run five-thousand feet of film that evening. At the following concert, on the 16th, there was an extra item on the bill. A gold watch was being presented to the cricketer A E Diddicutt, to celebrate his prowess for the Australian side, having helped them see off the English cricket team.

Throughout the Easter weekend in 1912, Tom was engaged almost every night, on his own at the piano, or with the Municipal Brass Band. In those circumstances you would expect that he might be doing well. A point of intrigue, however, is that on Thursday, 13 April a concert was arranged to take place at the Geelong West Open-Air Theatre, with proceeds from the sixpence adult, or three pence per child, entry fees being raised to benefit him personally. Why might this be necessary with all the work he had been doing? As usual, Mr T S Marchant provided his cinematic services, but this time an extra performance was given, by the juvenile dramatic society the Butterfly Pantomime Company. Tom's regular ally, "champion drummer" G F Twentyman, again performed his bombastic "Siege of Paris." As always the newspapers were liberally scattered with mentions of Tom's compositions being performed the length and breadth of the country. So much of this music had been purchased by the bands long ago, and some of those pieces would have been ones that Tom had to sell the rights for during his times of economic hardship. We've have seen no evidence of Tom and Eliza setting up another music shop in Geelong, so it's quite possible that, financially, things weren't as rosy as they appeared.

We are advised, through the Geelong Advertiser, that the benefit concert for Tom had been arranged by the concert committee, and that all the contributors to the spectacle gave their services at no charge. Also, we learn that tickets for the event had been sold by the bandsmen and Tom's friends. The total gate taking that evening amounted to fifteen pounds. Was it done simply as a tribute or mark of respect to their friend and bandmaster, or perhaps to mark the end of the traditional concert season? Might it have been organised in concern that Tom might, once again, be on the verge of financial difficulty? If so, how much difference might fifteen pounds make? Whatever the motive behind it, the concert was reported beyond Geelong, across the bay to Melbourne where Tom had also once resided.

Looking briefly aside, the Cootamundra Herald of New South Wales on Friday, 10 May 1912 contains an interesting letter which, though unrelated directly to Tom's story, still demonstrates the high regard in which he continued to be held among brass band circles. It appears that a journalist from the paper may have misattributed a piece of music, played by one of that area's brass bands, to bandmaster Mr C J Davis. Mr Davis had written to the paper to request a correction:

> "Sir, – allow me space to correct your announcement re the opening number played by the band last night. It would ill become me to allow my name to remain as the composer of such a fine piece of band music. The writer is Mr T Bulch, Australia's most prolific composer and arranger of band music, and for some time conductor of the Albury Town Band. My

qualifications as a musician are small pumpkins indeed placed alongside such an eminent man, and I will be glad if you will make this correction."

Tom probably never read that small tribute to his musical prowess, though, if he had, he would have been heartened by its sentiments.

The press in Geelong keeps us informed that at least one of Thomas's sons continued an interest in playing football that they had seemingly started back in Albury. We don't know which but there is a Bulch named in the Ashby Star squad as playing on Saturday, 20 July 1912.

Tom senior continued his duties at the piano throughout the winter, accompanying the films shown at the Geelong Mechanics Institute. Though it had been quite some time since he had been called upon to adjudicate a band contest, his compositions and arrangements were still helping sort the cream from the milk at band contests elsewhere. At the Scottsdale Competitions in Tasmania that year, his cornet solo "Swanee River," euphonium solo "Faint and Wearily" and bass solo "Bizarre" were selected by the organisers as test pieces for those specific instruments.

In September of 1912, Tom, as he had so many times before, took yet another band under his experienced wing to tutor and conduct as well as the Geelong Municipal Brass Band. This time it was the Geelong Artillery Band, of which he had intimate knowledge having seen them appear regularly at the Mechanics Institute picture house concerts. This adoption was prompted by the resignation of their former bandmaster, Sergeant C Hobday. The Geelong Advertiser cited Thomas's experience of working with a military band in Ballarat as being reflective of his suitability for the role, but went on to point out that the running of the band would not be easy, as older experienced bandsmen were dropping out, requiring a fresh intake of younger players to be recruited. The prospect of additional income earned running the band would have been a welcome opportunity for Tom; yet we have seen in his story so far that, when spreading his talents thinner in this way, problems often followed. If there is any doubt on the matter of spreading his resource thinner, consider too that in that year Tom was also on occasion conducting the orchestra at His Majesty's Theatre in Geelong. An example of this comes on Saturday, 7 September, when he took up the baton over the theatre orchestra for a production of "Wedded But No Wife." This play concerned one Desmond McCartney, the offspring of Lord Illingworth by a clandestine marriage and his journey toward inheritance of that peer's estate.

Above: Geelong Mechanics Institute where Tom put his improvisation skills to good use pursuing a new vocation accompanying silent movies at the piano.

Saturday, 5 October brought another smoke night, this time in celebration of the fiftieth anniversary of the Geelong Garrison Artillery and taking place at their orderly rooms. Between 150 and 170 persons were present, including a number of veterans returned for the celebration. The current serving men greeted the arrival of the old warriors with a hearty three cheers, whilst a placard displayed at the end of the hall read "Welcome to our old comrades, 1862-1912." Toasts were raised and speeches offered in praise of the efficiency and speed through training of the Australian forces generally. One veteran present, Colonel Hall, had been a schoolboy when the battery was founded in 1862 and had enlisted four years later. He proudly reminded those present that they were "units of an Empire that traced its military traditions back to the Norman conquest." Little did any of those realise that in little more than two years time that

Empire would be fighting again, with Australian troops sent to the same country from which those Normans had emerged. Lieut-Col Garrard estimated that some two-and-a-half thousand men had made up the battery since its founding. He went on to say that it was between the ages of fourteen to eighteen years wherein it would be determined whether the young men would make good or bad soldiers and spoke of encouraging the young cadets of the battery. Sergeant W H Searle declared patriotically that he had learned, since enlisting in 1859, that Australians were best at everything, swimming, soldiering or football. Mr G Read Murphy gave an address on "Armies and Fighters of the Past, Present and Future," comparing the capabilities of the Australian aboriginals to the Zulus and the ancient Egyptians, then on through the Greeks, Romans and European armies of the Middle-Ages to the modern world. He predicted that Germany, with its small navy might, keep the British Navy confined to the North Sea leaving Australia to fend for itself, and also that Australia, without a strong navy would be overrun by Japan in a short space of time. Gradually the speech-making gave way to songs and humorous recitations, with bandmaster Tom acting as accompanist. His Artillery Band also rendered a programme of music.

Though the men and veterans of the Geelong Artillery were correct to predict that military trouble was indeed on the horizon, it was still some way distant. For Tom, trouble of a more domestic nature, concerning the affairs of the West Geelong Municipal Brass Band, was brewing. It didn't take long after that night to emerge. When it did, the ever-vigilant Geelong Advertiser was there to report upon the details. Page four of its Saturday, 26 October issue contained the following:

> "GEELONG WEST BAND DISPUTE –
> MR BULCH QUARRELS WITH THE- COMMITTEE.
> HOLDS THE INSTRUMENTS. Trouble has arisen between the park committee and Mr T Bulch, conductor of the Geelong West Municipal Band, over the latter's remuneration. On Tuesday the committee wrote to Mr Bulch, requesting him to return the instruments, &c. to the Geelong West Town Hall by noon of yesterday, but this was ignored. On Monday a meeting of the park committee is to be held to further consider the position. Cr. H F Christopher, secretary of the park committee, made the following statement to an "Advertiser' representative yesterday:- "When it became known that the I.O.R. band was

to disband, steps were taken in Geelong West to accept the band's liability of over £100, and take over the instruments. A committee was appointed, and guarantors were chosen: arrangements were made with a bank to provide the money required. Three signed the guarantee, but the others neglected to do so and this proposal consequently fell through. It was intimated to the committee that the park committee was willing to take the responsibility and this course was eventually adopted. A document was drawn up between the band committee and the persons owning the instruments, which became the property of the Mayor for the time being. Certain moneys were collected towards paying off the indebtedness and the park committee found the balance of about £80. The band was only taken over by the park committee towards the close of last concert season. Mr T E Bulch, the conductor, received 10- per concert during the season from the committee, and was also tendered a benefit concert, which returned him £15. Practically for eight weeks he got £23 10 - nearly £3 per week. This season we had agreed to pay him 15- per concert and to give him the proceeds of two concerts. This was resolved upon at a conference held last Saturday week, and Mr Bulch expressed himself as being perfectly satisfied. But then he wrote a letter, which was couched in anything but respectful terms, demanding better consideration and a reply within 48 hours, and threatening to sever his connection with the park concerts. A special meeting of the park committee was held, and it was decided to send a reply to Mr Bulch, asking for the return of the instruments. uniforms, music, &c. belonging to the Geelong West Municipal Band. The use of the pavilion had been granted to Mr Bulch during the winter months for practice, and the park committee paid for the light. In every way he received the utmost consideration. The position had become untenable, and there was no other course open to the committee but to obtain possession of the instruments and uniforms in the hope of placing the band on a more satisfactory footing. The committee has no animosity whatever towards the band. Mr Bulch has seen fit to ignore our request for the return of the instruments, but we are determined to enforce our rights. This is not intended as a threat. I have no desire to say one word against Mr Bulch or to accentuate the difference that has arisen. On Tuesday the secretary of the band (Mr R H Symonds) waited on me to know if consideration had been given to Mr Bulch's letter; a special meeting was called, as Mr Bulch expressly stated the 23rd inst. This statement was read over to Mayor D'Helin and Cr. Molyneux who stated it fairly represented the facts.

The bandmaster, Mr T E Bulch said that in connection with his benefit concert, he had to practically work it up himself, and the £15 he received did not come out of the committee's funds. He had been paid 10- for playing the piano at each concert: he had sought to get a definite understanding in regard to his remuneration as bandmaster, and the park committee had shut him up by demanding the return of the instruments &c. Since the close of last season, he had not received a copper, although he had given a good deal of his time to bringing the players on. The bandsmen were not paid a penny for their services, and it was high time some arrangement was arrived at. It was not a fact that he had sent a letter to the park committee couched in insolent or aggressive terms. His letter was as under:

"31 Candover-street. Geelong West. 21/10/12. H. F Christopher Esq., Sec. Park Committee. Geelong West. Dear Sir. As bandmaster of the West Geelong Municipal Band, I regret to state that your treatment of us has been anything but satisfactory. We are in the same position to-day financially as 12 months ago. I cannot see my way clear to act the part of a philanthropist any longer, and unless some amicable arrangement be arrived at by the 23rd inst. I will be compelled to sever my connection with the park concerts. Yours &c. T E BULCH. Bandmaster."

He received the following reply, dated 22nd inst. :- "Your letter of yesterday was duly considered at a special meeting of the park committee this evening, and the following resolution was carried unanimously:- "That Mr Bulch be informed by letter that the band instruments, uniforms, music and any other property belonging to the Geelong West Municipal Band be returned to the Town Hall at Geelong West on or before Friday the 25th inst. at the hour of 12 o'clock noon" C W Dickens (chairman and trustee). H F Christopher (secretary). P.S. Also be good enough to return the keys for the pavilion and gate to Cr. Molyneux at once. — H F Christopher, secretary."

Despite the action of the park committee said Mr Bulch. he was determined that the band should not be broken up. He only wanted fair play and decent consideration."

As uncomfortable as it might have been for Tom to have had details of this affair, and his earnings, publicly aired in the local press, for the reflective historian, this gives an excellent insight into the politics between the park committee and the Geelong West Municipal Brass Band. It also reveals where Tom and his family lived at that time, a small, typically Australian, bungalow on Candover Street, where a similar, if not the same, building still stands today. It also explains something of the context of the benefit concert that we revealed earlier, and why the bandsmen and friends of Thomas had put in so much work themselves to sell tickets. Two days after this first article was published, further details emerged, once again in the Geelong Advertiser but this time a counter-explanation in the form of an account exclusively from the perspective of the band's secretary.

"GEELONG WEST BAND DISPUTE. Sir, - With, your permission I wish, to give a few facts with reference to the treatment by the park committee of the band and bandmaster. When the band was formed about twelve months ago, it was decided by a meeting of citizens, held in the Town Hall, that Mr T E Bulch be appointed bandmaster. It was also decided by the players of the band that each and every member should contribute 6d per week towards the bandmaster's salary. We, as bandsmen, were quite willing to do that and did it until the park committee took over the control of the band. At the opening ceremony of the park Mayor Dickins, in addressing the citizens, stated that they had secured "a splendid' asset in the band, and they pledged their support, and it was their intention to allow the band the park free one night each week for their own benefit. Before the first concert took place under the management of the band Mayor Dickins informed the band that the park committee had withdrawn the use of the park to the band to run concerts for their own benefit, but would allow the band 20 per cent of the net profits of each concert held. When the park committee communicated their intentions to the band, we as a band agreed to their proposal; but the 20 per cent was never paid over by the park committee to the band. When the park committee took control of the band at the latter end of last season Mayor Dickins, with a number of councillors, came to the bandroom. Mayor Dickins then told the band that the 6d per week they had contributed towards the bandmaster's salary was to cease from that date, 18/3/12. I asked the Mayor how the bandmaster was to be paid, and he said they (meaning the park committee) would pay him a salary. He did not state what that salary would be. Continuing, he said what a paltry thing 6d a week from a few men was to pay to a man like Mr Bulch. But, sir, paltry as the amount seemed to Mayor Dickins then, it is not quite so paltry as the amount received by Mr Bulch from the park committee since then. The only consideration that the band received from the park committee was a benefit concert tendered to Mr Bulch, which amounted to £15, and for which most of the tickets were sold by bandsmen. When you come to facts, sir, Mr Bulch has fulfilled the important position of bandmaster to the West Geelong Municipal Brass Band for 12 months at a salary of 5/9 per week. The former secretary, Mr D Kincaid, wrote to the park committee asking for some definite understanding regarding the bandmaster's salary, but no definite arrangement could be arrived at. When Mr Kincaid resigned his position as secretary to the band I was appointed to act as secretary for the time being. I wrote to Mayor D'Helin on September 5th, asking for a conference between the council and band committee for September 6th. Mayor D'Helin wrote stating the notice was too short. I again wrote to Mayor D'Helin on the 11th September asking him to appoint an early date for a conference. I received no reply to that letter, but when the park committee fixed the date tor the opening of the concerts Mr Bulch gave him to understand that something would have to be done before starting the concerts. The park committee then arranged a conference in the bandroom for Saturday night, October 12th. At that conference, it was agreed that the band should have two Saturday nights during the forthcoming season to run concerts for themselves. The band committee and Mr Bulch were quite satisfied with that arrangement. But during the week following the opening night this season, Mr Bulch was informed by Cr. Molyneux that the park committee wanted all the Saturday nights for themselves, and as we were issuing tickets for concerts we could have any weeknight other than Saturday. Therefore we concluded that the park committee were again breaking their promise to the band, as they had done with every promise they had made to the band. Hence Mr Bulch's letter to the park committee of October 21st. I interviewed Mr Christopher, the secretary of the park committee, on Tuesday, October 22nd, and asked him if there was anything in what Cr. Molyneux had told Mr Bulch. He said the park committee thought that week-nights other than Saturday nights would do for the band. He also informed me that the park committee had decided at their meeting on Monday night that any bandsman who came to the park concert, in uniform or with his instrument would be admitted free of charge, but if the said bandsman brought his wife or lady friend, such wife or friend would have to be paid for. I think the least the park committee could have done would have been to admit a lady friend or wife of each bandsman, when they were receiving their services gratis. If the park committee had to pay for the services of a band the same as Geelong Municipal did for their concerts in Johnstone Park, it would have cost four guineas per night, which would have amounted to about £70 for the season, and instead of showing a credit balance on last year's concerts there would have been a deficit of about £10. Re your insertion in 'Town Talk" of Saturday's issue, referring to instruments, music, etc. not being returned to the Town Hall as requested by the park committee, I think the request by that committee is very unreasonable – to expect Mr Bulch to spend hours in collecting the property, more especially as he is not a paid servant. The drastic measure taken by the park committee was uncalled for, inasmuch as they have completely ignored Mr Bulch's letter, and directly insulted the band. Neither Mr Bulch not the band committee have refused to return band property, etc. and I consider it would have reflected greater credit on the park committee if they had interviewed the band committee or bandmaster and no doubt their requests would have been complied with. In conclusion, I cannot congratulate the park committee on their management of the band. It is quite evident they did not appreciate a good thing when they had it, and whatever their management may be as far as council matters are concerned, they are a miserable failure in managing a brass band, and will never keep a band unless they alter their mode of management. Thanking you in anticipation. Yours, etc., R H SYMONDS. Secretary. October 26th, 1912."

In this account we see a compelling description of the park committee and local authority's mistreatment of Tom and his bandsmen. If the band secretary's account is true, the band had been fed a diet of manipulation and mistruths on the path to the present stand-off, and it's quite clear how Tom had, once again, found himself in the unwanted position of struggling financially. The park committee, far from being swayed by this argument set out by the band's secretary, decided to increase the intensity of their pursuit of the band's equipment. Tom was served with a notice, from the borough solicitors, demanding the return of the instruments, uniform and accessories. Failure to comply would result in the commencements of legal proceedings. The band committee, in Tom's absence, held a meeting behind closed doors at the St George Hotel, Geelong, to deliberate over the content of the notice. Their decision did not emerge until Monday, 4 October, when the Geelong Advertiser explained that the band would rather disband than obey the park committee. The Advertiser had reported on 31 October that a number of bandsmen were willing to return their instruments, but in a subsequent letter to the newspaper R H Symonds explained that the band had passed a resolution:

> "That the members of the Park Committee be asked to meet representatives from the band in conference so as to try to settle the dispute and that an independent chairman be appointed."

The park committee were in no mood for compromise and refused the request unless all the band property was returned first. As a consequence, the bandsmen resolved, as one, to hand over their instruments with notices of resignation in protest, rather than see their bandmaster further persecuted and harassed with legal proceedings. They stated they would do so immediately after playing a final benefit concert for the aged people of Geelong on the afternoon of 16 November. On this offer they placed one important caveat, which was that the park committee must first pay twelve pounds, representing the twenty percent of the previous concert season's takings that the park committee had agreed at the beginning of that period, plus a further four pounds and four shillings for their first concert of the 1912-1913 concert season. In total a due back-payment of sixteen pounds and four shillings.

If this plan, and caveat, was designed to make the band appear the just party, whilst launching one last attack at the park committee, it was still not well received by that body, and immediate summonses were brought against Tom, Mr Symonds and Mr Kincaid, the latter being the previous band secretary. The summons demanded they produce the musical instruments, or alternatively a hundred-and-ten pounds, five shillings and sixpence, the alleged value of the goods. The newspaper followed the affair closely. The band committee telephoned the park committee's solicitor at midnight on 4 October, to request a stay of the legal proceedings until noon of the Saturday to give the band a chance to collect the instruments before returning them. The Geelong Advertiser interviewed Messrs Dickin and Christopher who remained adamant that they would not put a stop on any action till the instruments had been returned.

By Thursday, 7 November, it was clear that further delay was unacceptable to the park committee. They ordered summons be issued for Bulch and Symonds to appear at Geelong County Court on 10 December, claiming the instruments, uniforms and stands valued at £111, plus a further ten pounds for damages. This court hearing did not, however, take place. On the evening of 16 November, the band met the park committee's demand, returning their instruments to the Town Hall. This action led to an 'out-of court' settlement. At the same time, some within the community announced an intention to attempt to form a citizens committee to try to relieve the park committee of the liability for the instruments and uniforms. The presumed intention of this was to keep a band going, but wrest control of its direction from the park committee. News of the, arguably scandalous, mistreatment of Tom and his bandsmen, by the park committee of West Geelong in not having kept promises made to the band committee and bandmaster and then resorting to legal action when this was made public, was only reported within Geelong itself. The grand vision of a municipal band to entertain the people of West Geelong had turned sour through political mismanagement, and looked to be over. The rest of Australia took little interest in the matter. Still to be resolved, was the matter of the unpaid fees due to the bandsmen. Though the park committee had the equipment back, the bandsmen still pursued what was due to them. Resolution came in late November through the intervention of one Robert J Coxon, who approached the park committee on behalf of the band personnel. The park committee, probably knowing that it was of little use to them and might be worth less if sold, agreed to hand back the instruments and other equipment on production of eighty pounds in cash. Meeting this price would enable a reincarnated West Geelong Band to continue. The park committee also promised that if a band were continued, they would pay the new band of one pound and one shilling for every concert subsequently held in the West Park. Despite the park committee's poor record on keeping to their word on such arrangements, five trustees were appointed to take possession of the instruments on behalf of the ratepayers of West Geelong, and a number of subscriptions were quickly raised towards the eighty pounds. In addition, Tom Bulch was reinstated as pianist for the bioscope concerts at His Majesty's Theatre, and was to receive an improved rate of fifteen shillings per concert. Fundraising toward the band's debt commenced in earnest, with a benefit night for the band being organised for 27 November at the theatre.

On the 9th of December, Tom attended a smoke night held by the Geelong Bicycle Club, to celebrate the opening of that club's new rooms at the old Sailor's Rest building. In the time-honoured tradition, toasts and speeches were made, one of which was proposed by Tom himself. He also fulfilled duties at the piano, culminating in the rendition of "Auld Lang Syne" that brought the night to a close.

The Geelong West Band, still being reported in the press as 'municipal' despite the community takeover, were present on Saturday, 14 December, the first reported occasion since the very public dispute, at the Geelong West Picture Theatre. Tom was there, once again wielding his conductor's baton. The appreciative crowd enjoyed the selections played by the band, as well as the seven-thousand feet of film shown by Mr Marchant, which on this occasion included "Won by a Fish," "Adventures of Dick Turpin," "Sheriff's Round-up" and "The Transit of Venus." For once, Tom was not the accompanying pianist: that duty was performed we are told by the 'efficient' Miss Shugg.

The following week, Tom switched back to conducting the Artillery Band at the annual Christmas entertainment of the Artillery Club. They played selections, and other merry contributions offered were songs from Messrs Larsson and Easeman, the club minstrels, some physical drill from the Artillery team, a maypole demonstration by the Swanson Street State School team and a recitation. After these, Father Christmas appeared to distribute gifts to the children. Tom concluded his year, on new Year's Eve, by conducting the West Geelong Band at West Park as part of the build up to the night's cinematic drama, "The Spider's Web." Even without considering the magic of cinema, it had been a dramatic year in West Geelong. Things now appeared more settled, and Tom's prospects looked to be a little more secure.

New Shildon

Across the world, in New Shildon, the landscape seen from the front window of George's house on Pears Terrace was changing again. His favourite haunt, the Mechanics Institute building on Station Street, had been given up on by its organisation for some years, but there were inklings of hope on the horizon for its members. The North Eastern Railway Company had indicated its support for replacing the building with something more modern. It is thought that the North Eastern Railway company's intention had been to erect a new building during 1911; the biggest clue to this being that this year is boldly carved into a decorative keystone above the main entrance archway. This plan was most likely altered as a consequence of the 1911 industrial action and the Shildon workers' role as being among the most disruptive of employees. But in 1912, the North Eastern Railway did finally commence work. The company had chosen a site on land they owned on the south side of Redworth Road where the Allan family had once lived and the rear of which was overlooked by George's home. The design for this new Institute had been created by the railway company's chief architect, William Bell, and through it would be the last of four new principal institutes built by the company, it's design, incorporating similar architectural elements to the company's main offices at Darlington, ensured that it was the grandest. For now though, George and the other members of the Shildon Institute could only watch the construction of their new home.

The year 1912 also spawned another national strike; this time across the coal industry. As on previous occasions, such as in 1894, the Shildons, Old and New, were impacted deeply, being, as they were, at the heart of the South Durham Coalfield, and hosting both mines and an industry that relied upon a supply of coal. This latest strike commenced in February, with a resultant coal shortage beginning to bite by early March. By that point the availability of rail services were reduced.

The miners were, this time, seeking commitment to a minimum wage. Their strike action ran for thirty-seven economically damaging days before the, then Liberal, Government, pressed by MPs from a rising Labour Party, introduced their Coal Mines (minimum wage) Act of 1912. This milestone Act of Parliament granted coal miners a minimum wage protection for the first time in their history. In his April budget statement, Chancellor David Lloyd-George estimated that the coal strike had cost the nation £400,000; roughly equivalent to around £44.8 million as I write this.

The general national atmosphere and mood in Britain in 1912 was not unlike that in Australia around the same time. There was a certain sense of insecurity. We heard how Tom Bulch had entertained at military veterans evenings, where the old comrades gave and received lectures and speeches outlining Australia's capabilities in the event of invasion. In Britain the public had similar preoccupations. A new fiction form of 'invasion literature' had become popular, with the sense of thrill and unease that it created. One simply has to consider H G Wells's science-fiction classic, "War of The Worlds," published in 1898, but popular at the beginning of the twentieth century, to get a sense of that. However, with real political tensions rising between the European nations, invasion scenarios of a different kind preoccupied the thoughts of the people of Britain. Of course, the 'imperial' nature of the world politically at that time inevitably suggested that any conflict in Europe would most likely have global implications. George Allan needed look no further than the pages of the North Eastern Railway magazine, published by his employers for railwaymen across the region, to get a sense of this tension. The March 1912 issue outlined the likelihood of an invasion of the Yorkshire coast by an unnamed enemy, setting out how the Royal Navy Fleet would immediately be mobilised, and how the rail workers, of all disciplines across the North Eastern Railway, would be called upon to play their part in rushing supplies through for the defensive forces based in either Scarborough or York. The article speculated upon the company management having a secret timetable to be deployed in the event of war, and even predicted a need for ambulance trains.

Despite the gloomy national atmosphere, and the personal tragedy that had befallen him during the previous year in losing his wife, the mother of his three children, George returned to dedicating some spare time to composing music. The May and June 1912 issues of Brass Band News included an announcement of another fine new contest march:

> "Contesting Bands, get my latest Contest March, "Imperioso." Fine test all round, not trash. "La Maestro" and "Senator" (2nd Editions); also "Wizard" very popular, 20 parts 1/1 – ALLAN New Shildon."

By August, there was some considerable buzz around preparations for the annual Shildon Show. A parcel of land that usually played host to merry-go-rounds and other fairground attractions was undergoing a transformation. The local council were in the process of installing a low wall and iron railings around it as part of a conversion to becoming a new recreation ground to sit between the twin towns of Old Shildon and New Shildon. In addition, what was once a private road between the two townships was being upgraded to provide a direct route between the two town centres. The Daily Gazette for Middlesbrough lauded the change as being something that "had been desired for a generation." The improvements had cost a total of around three thousand pounds. The creation of this public park and Central Parade was probably the clearest marker to commence a new era wherein these two, previously separate, towns would begin to be considered as one; a unified Shildon. On Saturday, 28 September 1912, in the presence of thousands of people, Central Parade was formally opened by the Chairman of Shildon Urban Council, Cllr. John Peacock JP. The ceremony was followed by a banquet, at the nearby Masonic Hall, during which speeches and toasts were given with predictions that yet more improvements would be introduced over time; bowling greens and attractions for the children.

As the end of the year approached George advertised, in the small adverts at the back of the Brass Band News December 1912 issue his Christmas Number:

> "GOOD CHRISTMAS NUMBER for Brass Bands. Two choruses, Three hymns, 1/10 for 24 parts. No samples. Money returned if not satisfied. – GEO. ALLAN, Publisher, New Shildon."

These Christmas arrangements that George created in his later years, suggested that either he particularly enjoyed the spirit of this time of year, or else that he sensed the added sales opportunity that an increase in the popularity of Christmas music brought him. With this new music printed, and advertisements for it placed, you would have thought that George might have been able to settle down to enjoy the oncoming festive season with his son and daughters. Once again, though, temperature in the relationship between the NER workers and their managers built up toward a boiling point. This time it was as a result of treatment of a Gateshead driver by the name of Nicol Knox. Knox was a mineral engine driver who, through allegations of drunkenness whilst off duty, had been demoted to the lowlier post of driver of a pilot engine. The company considered him to be a risk to the public if he could not control his drinking outside of work. Knox's colleagues spoke of his thirty-seven years of good conduct, and experience with the company, and argued that a man's pastimes outside of work were no business of the North Eastern Railway. As for the public, they were simply dismayed at the prospect of winter, and possibly Christmas, disruption. The ensuing strike quickly reached the coal distribution yard at Shildon, where, by 8th December, workers agreed to support the fight to have their colleague reinstated. This created a log-jam effect in coal supply, impacting the performance of the rail industry. The company, via its stationmasters, issued a notice in response announcing that, by taking this industrial action, the strikers were effectively terminating their employment and should consequently return their uniforms. It's important to note at this point that though the Shildon railway workers of the General Railway Workers Union and the Amalgamated Society of Railway Servants were striking at this point, George and the men of the Shildon Works were not. Though sympathetic to the cause and ready to 'down-tools' when instructed by their Union branch, the wagon workers were hoping that the company might see sense and reinstate the driver without them having to join in the industrial action. Nevertheless, there were still 1,200 other Shildon railway workers reportedly on strike by Wednesday, 11 December. With the blockage in coal supply, by that same date Shildon Lodge Colliery laid off eight-hundred workers leaving their families with the prospect of struggling to feed themselves in the run-up to Christmas.

On 14 December, however, the strikers tasted victory. The NER Issued a statement explaining that they would reinstate Nicol Knox if a Home Office enquiry proved that he was not drunk on the night in question, and that all workers were to reassume their posts in the meantime, and not harass colleagues that had not joined the strike. Each striker would be fined six days wages. Mr Chester Jones acting as stipendiary magistrate for the Home Office felt, following his inquiry, that there was insufficient evidence to prove that Knox was drunk and as a consequence, the Home Secretary recommended that His Majesty the King offer Knox a free pardon. The outcome of this dispute was reported widely across the United Kingdom, and during the year that followed, to strengthen their collective position the General Railway Workers Union and the Amalgamated Society of Railway Servants merged along with the United Pointsmen and Signalmen's Society to become the National Union of Railwaymen.

Toward the end of 1912, and the beginning of 1913 George had been spending his time composing a new contest march for brass bands. Up until this point, it was felt that "The Wizard" had been his crowning achievement, though "Senator" and "Raby" were also undoubtedly up there among the best that brass bands had available to them. All of these endure even in present times and can be purchased readily. The new piece was to be named "Knight Templar." Once the manuscript was finished and tested it was bundled up and sent by post overseas to Oscar Brandstetter's print works, on Dresdener Strasse in Leipzig, to be set and printed.

Many of George's self-published marches, printed over this later stage of his career, had been printed lithographically. This required that every mark first be first etched onto a sheet made from an alloy of lead and tin using a set of tools designed for the purpose. For example, musical staff lines were created by dragging a five-clawed implement shallowly along a straight edge. Clefs and notes were punched into the metal using specially made punches, whilst the lines that denote the different note values and expression were gouged manually. Consequently, the appearance and quality of the sheet music displayed something of the 'hand' of the printer that had etched it. It was a skilled job requiring great attention to detail as we have already said earlier.

The Brandstetter works was one of many that had developed alternative, and more advanced, ways to represent the musical notation. For his Knight Templar, George had decided that rather than have the march etched from his manuscript for lithographic printing, it would be set out using a complex musical printer's typeface not too dissimilar from that used for the printed word. This process required the assembly of individual cast pieces representing all the component parts of the music; notes, symbols, clefs etc. It was tricky work by the printer, again requiring a great deal of skill and accuracy to ensure all the notes and musical marks were in the correct place on the stave lines. When complete, however, this process enabled the printing of a beautifully superior looking sheet music that was easy for the musician to read.

Above: The facade of the Brandstetter Print Works in Leipzig where George sent manuscripts for pieces like "Knight Templar" to be converted to printed sheet music for sale. Tom used the C G Röder Print Works over the road from this building.

With the new march sent away to Germany to be printed, and railway industrial disputes absent for the moment, on Saturday, 8 February 1913 George Allan would have been able to take a few moments of his available spare time to witness the opening of the brand new Shildon Railway Institute. The construction of the long promised new building, replacing the former Mechanics Institute on Station Street, had finally been completed by the North Eastern Railway. This new building was significantly larger than the old one. The extensive library and billiard tables from the old facility had been transferred to rooms on its first floor. The space inside the roof contained living accommodation for a permanent steward and the ground floor of the three storey building was extended to the west by a single storey grand concert and lecture hall. It was a grand palace for the railway workers of Shildon and their families.

The opening was chaired by Vincent Raven who was at that time the company's Chief Mechanical Engineer. The formal opening ceremony was conducted by Arthur Francis Pease, of the notable Darlington Pease family that had been catalytic and influential in the founding of the first public railway. Pease was now, like his ancestors, a director of this new, more extensive, railway company. As part of that ceremony he accepted a specially made and inscribed gilt silver key, using it to unlock the building and admit all present. The Northern Echo reported upon the opening of the new building in its edition of 10 February, describing how after the doors had formally been opened, the lecture hall was immediately crowded with railway officials and members of this and other various NER region Institutes, as well as other members of the public. It is not reported whether George was present but having been member right through his adulthood it's highly likely that he was. We do know from the report, though, that Dr Samuel Fielden and his wife Jane were present, both of whom were friends of George's and whose Golden Wedding Anniversary he would attend in July that year. Vincent Raven opened the speeches by explaining that, for some years, the wagon works at Shildon had been growing, and consequently the town too. Due to that, and the condition of the old Institute building, the railway company directors had been approached with regard to a new Institute, which had led to the present gathering.

The ceremonial key was then presented to Arthur Pease to keep as a memento, by Mr R W Worsdell, then manager of the works. Pease then offered a speech himself, declaring that he was no stranger to Shildon and that there were already five generations of his family present in the room, referring to several of the portraits of his family ancestors that adorned the walls around him. He reminded everyone that if his father, grandfather and great-grandfather had not been in some way connected with Shildon, their pictures would not have been hanging on the walls. He stated that though he was a director of the North Eastern Railway, there were a number of shareholders equivalent in number to two-thirds of the company's workforce, and a balance had to be maintained between the interests of both workers and shareholders. He observed that this institute was the oldest on the former Stockton and Darlington Railway route and, hoped the building would be a very great blessing to the town, and that there would be many pleasant social gatherings in it for many years to come. In his own speech, Vincent Raven highlighted that he was more connected to the institutes in York, Gateshead and Darlington, some of which were larger, though none of these were better arranged, or more comfortable, than the new Shildon Railway Institute.

A few months after this, the June 1913 issue of Brass Band News finally declared the availability of the march that would, above all others, secure George Allan's name as one of the leading composers of brass band music of his generation. Expressed through his own choice of wording, it read:

> "Knight Templar" a Tip-top New Contest March; splendid, Also "La Maestro" (always in the prizes), "Senator," "Battle Abbey," "Wizard," "Imperioso" &c. 1/3 for 20 parts – George Allan, Publisher, New Shildon."

Through this handful of marches, George Allan, ever considered the gifted amateur, had taken the art of the brass band contest march into new territory. "The Wizard" certainly contained a good share of aural magic, but it would probably principally be the majestic and timeless stirring quality and layered complexity of "Knight Templar" that would ensure that even in the twenty-first century there would barely be a single bandsman in the British Isles who did not know the name of its humble composer. It was destined to become one of the favourite marches of some of the best brass bands in the country. We'll never fully know or understand the full extent to which it was played by bands at contest, for in reports of such occasions the march contest was always considered the poor cousin to the 'main event' of the test piece. If you look, though, for example at the listed entries for "Knight Templar" over the decades on the website brassbandresults.co.uk, which has done a sterling job of becoming the definitive and most thorough reference guide to brass band contesting, you get a real sense of how significant this piece of music is. It has particularly been prevalent as one of the staple marches at the Whit Friday Contests that have taken place annually at twenty-four village locations around Saddleworth and Tameside since about 1870. Casually browsing the list of recorded results, which only seem to have been formally reported from the 1930s onwards, you see bands of the calibre of Black Dyke Mills, Besses o' th' Barn, Grimethorpe Colliery, Fairey and Brighouse & Rastrick winning prize after prize playing this very special march.

When it is played well by a skilled group of bandsmen the march, possibly above all others, despite having originally been scratched onto paper in a lowly terraced two-up two-down house in Shildon by a man more familiar with the glow of the forge and the smell of wagon paint than the fashionable musical institutions and academies of this nation, arguably brings the rousing sound of that band closest to perfection. Purists would argue that the minute intricate technical complexities and detail in modern, non-march, test pieces better demonstrate the ability of a top band; but for connecting band to common listener the rousing emotive qualities and dynamics of a good contest march are unsurpassed. It is a triumph of the music not of the academic, but of the working man. Music wrought during a tense and uneasy time for workers nationally, and in this case a painful period in the life of its composer, still doubtless feeling the loss of his wife.

Above: Euphonium part on an original print of George's "Knight Templar" - one of the finest brass band contest marches ever created and still a favourite at band contests worldwide.

It also strikes me as a shame that though it is still played and heard more frequently perhaps than any other of George's pieces, or indeed those of Tom Bulch, and generally revered, so few know much at all about its composer.

George still had the company of his three children, now quite grown up. His son Bill had, like George, become a bandsman. It's quite likely that, as Tom Bulch had taught his sons, George had most probably done the same. In a time where families had no television around which to gather placidly and compliantly through the long evenings, it would probably have been difficult to grow up in George, or Tom's, household without music being involved somehow. Though the world of brass banding was still almost exclusively a male one, it's probable that George's two daughters would also have had some musical instruction. That summer of 1913 saw the first of George's two girls marry. Daughter Lillie had chosen one Thomas Edward Lewis, then aged twenty-eight, a former hydraulic main worker at the nearby coke works who had progressed to being a fireman there. The Lewis family lived at 5 Granville Terrace, Binchester, a village just outside Bishop Auckland, and one after which George had named a brass band march many years before. They had moved there, though, from a village named Tottenham, which was adjacent to Coundon. It's most likely that Lillie had met Thomas, who was four years older, whilst caring for her grandmother at nearby Coundon Grange.

Thomas had been born on 15 May 1885, in nearby Eldon, to parents Thomas and Hannah Lewis. They themselves had both been born in the area around Mold, Flintshire, North Wales. When old enough, Tom's father had become a coal miner. The young groom's grandfather, John Lewis, had been a brick burner; which was the person responsible for ensuring that the kilns were maintained at the correct temperature at a brick-works. It was probably the availability of work in the Durham coalfield that had brought the Lewis family north to County Durham.

The wedding ceremony was conducted, by vicar Picton W Francis, on 16 July 1913 at All Saints parish church, where George's father had once been a warden. George was present to give away his daughter's hand. Thomas's sister, Annie, a year younger than he, acted as a witness to the marriage. The other two witnesses were George's other daughter Beatrice, and her own sweetheart John Robert Tenwick Appleby, of whom we will hear more soon.

By October, George was promoting festive wares again. He hoped that the readers of Brass Band News might be looking to stock up with new music to play at Christmas so had posted the following advertisement promoting yet another appropriate arrangement that he had created for the new season.

"SPLENDID CHRISTMAS NUMBER (New) – Three Original Choruses and Three Hymns, effectively arranged, not difficult, but good. Just in from printers. 20 parts, 1s 7d; extras 2d. – GEO. ALLAN, Publisher, New Shildon."

It wasn't unusual for composers to prepare Christmas arrangements like this, even though they did not have year-round appeal. Even today we tend to associate the appearance of brass bands, especially the Salvation Army, on our streets with our enjoyment of the atmosphere of the festive season. George appears to have prepared and sold a handful over the years, though as yet we've not been able to find one to try. We know that Tom Bulch also created a Grand Christmas Number back in the mid to late 1880s after he had first arrived in Ballarat. For this year in Shildon, happily, Christmas looked to have been a quiet one.

1913 in Britain, though, had been as tense and politically charged as its predecessor. The Women's Suffrage movement was in full sway, with rallies, pilgrimages and occasional arson attacks in the news. It was, of course, the year in which Emily Davison was trampled to death after running out in front of the King's horse at the Epsom Derby. Interestingly, despite so many of the key events having taken place far from the streets of Shildon, the cause of women's suffrage would have been well known to the folk of New Shildon. The Mechanics Institute had subscribed to the Women's Suffrage Journal from the mid-1870s onward. Elsewhere, there was also trouble in Ireland, with the notorious events of 'Bloody Sunday' occurring on 31 August. Military technology was racing ahead in the mechanised age, with the first of ten-thousand pioneering Avro 504 military aircraft, the first of their kind, taking flight; and HMS Queen Elizabeth, the first oil-fired battleship being launched at Portsmouth. With all this going on, it's easy to wonder how aware anyone might have been of the likelihood of global events erupting as they did the following year.

Geelong

Tom Bulch's first engagement of 1913 was with the Geelong Citizens Band at the Geelong West open air theatre. Once again they were providing selections before and between the short silent films that were being projected on the evening of Saturday, 4 January. About a fortnight later, on the 23rd, the Geelong West Band gave an open air concert at the same venue, again with customary cinematic pictures providing an added draw. During this concert Tom switched to providing piano accompaniment as his younger son, John, known to his friends as Jack, performed a cornet solo. This moment was reported in the press as "one of the choicest items of the evening."

It's clear from this that Tom had ensured that both his sons received sufficient tutelage to become accomplished cornet players. It was now part of an established family tradition. One wonders whether evenings throughout their younger lives were spent with the children huddled round as Tom spoke of their great-grandfather Francis Dinsdale, the railway telegrapher of New Shildon, and their great uncle Edward, from whom he had learned his musical art, as they too learned.

Alas, Tom had begun to find that he was no longer first choice pianist when it came to accompanying the films at the Geelong West theatre. He had been usurped by a new talent, the able Miss Shugg. Mabel Shugg was the nineteen-year-old sister of Henry 'Harry' Rowe Shugg, the young and popular bandmaster of the Geelong Harbour Trust Band. It's not clear why she began to replace Tom, though she seems to have been a serious pianist and there is evidence of her, at a younger age, travelling to Ballarat to participate in the contests there. Perhaps organisers and audiences felt that her youth brought with it a greater appreciation of the musical tastes and styles of that new age. There were still some occasions, such as on the 1st February, where Tom continued to deputise as pianist in her absence. This occasion in particular was convenient, as he also conducted the Citizens Band.

On Saturday, 15 February, the Geelong Fox Terrier Coursing Club held a meeting an Holahan's Field. The club proudly proclaimed to interested parties that they had ninety pairs of rabbits for the dogs to chase down in this celebration of the blood sport. There was also significant prize money at stake. There was a clear expectation that many spectators would gather to watch the proceedings, as Tom and the Geelong West Municipal Band were engaged to play selections of music between the contests.

It would appear to all that the band was being kept busy; yet once again, all was not well. In late February 1913, Tom was replaced as bandmaster of the Geelong West Municipal Band. As at Albury, only a few years previous, this change does not seem to have been a matter of his own choice. His daughter, Adeline Bulch, explained many years later to her family that it had been felt that having reached fifty years of age, and partly on account of his other commitments as a professional musician, that the band wanted to install a younger conductor. This understanding of what happened is borne out in a story in the Geelong Advertiser of 26 February which reads:

> "Yesterday the late conductor of the Geelong West Band, Mr T E Bulch, returned his instruments and music to the trustees who are making a special effort to put the band on a better basis. Mr W Kinkaid is young and enthusiastic, and possess the confidence of the players. Practice is steadily progressing."

The part explaining the new bandmaster 'has the confidence of the players' expressed something of revolution, and implies that perhaps Tom no longer commanded this quality. This, whilst not leaving Tom entirely at a loose end, certainly reduced his appearances throughout the Australian winter of 1913. The next mention of him, in any newspapers, was in the Geelong Advertiser of 6th October, where he was reported as having ably stood-in for Harry Shugg, bandmaster of the Geelong Harbour Trust Band, to conduct the band at a concert in Johnstone Park. Shugg's sister, once again, provided the accompaniment to the moving pictures.

It was through Harry Shugg that Tom received another opportunity to dust off his baton. This was an occasion when Mr A A Hobson, one of Shugg's solo cornet players from the Geelong Harbour Trust Band, secured the opportunity to play for the Latrobe Federal Band at the band contests in Latrobe and Burnie on Boxing Day and New Year's Day. As well as being solo cornetist in Harry Shugg's band, Hobson was the bandmaster of the Portarlington Town Band which was based on the peninsula of land, west of Geelong, reaching out into Port Philip Bay. The Geelong Advertiser explained that Tom would take temporary charge of the band in Hobson's absence.

Thus Tom ended his year as a caretaker bandmaster; surely considering what he should do with himself in the year ahead. Though still revered in Australian banding circles as a composer, he had been sidelined as a bandmaster. Could he ever reattain previous heights with another band.

War

Tom's life continued to be quiet, musically, into 1914, though he occasionally continued to be engaged to provide the piano accompaniment to moving pictures at the Geelong Mechanics Institute. On occasions, such as Saturday 9th May, this involved the probably emotionally painful experience of being in attendance when his former band were also present to play selections under their 'enthusiastic' and 'young' new bandmaster.

The movies themselves, which nowadays would provide a reason for a family or couple's evening out in their own right, were still being seen very much as just one component part of a night of variety entertainment. This example advert from the Geelong Advertiser of 7 May 1914 gives a sense of this.

> "There is to be an innovation at the mechanics Hall next Saturday night, when the management will present a fine programme of pictures and artists. The star picture "Money God," a 4000ft film, shows a bet of £50,000 is made on this declaration, "If this starving man was given a fortune he would be more unhappy in the end than he was before." Some of the scenes: Great Fire at Sea, The Flooding of the Stoke-hold, The Explosion. The other portion of the programme will include H Smith, a tenor; Caviliere, in some of his juggling feats; and Smith and Hyde, in harmonised choruses and ragtime. Selections will be played by the Geelong West Band. Mr T E Bulch at the piano. Prices as per the advertisement."

On Tuesday, 2 June, Tom's son, Jack, was admitted to membership of the Loyal Geelong Lodge of the Manchester Unity. Then a week later on 9 June Thomas himself was accepted as a member of the Southern Star Lodge of the Manchester Unity. The Manchester Unity, or Independent Order of Oddfellows Manchester Unity Friendly Society Limited, to give it its full title, was, and still is today in a way, a fraternal order founded in Manchester in 1810. It was in part created to fill a purpose that was once filled by the Trade Guilds. As we've mentioned before, such organisations were set up to protect their members and communities in the absence of a welfare state or national health service. Members would pay a subscription, and would be involved in fundraising. Any funds belonging to the society could be deployed to support members in times of need. The Manchester Unity had reached Australia in 1840 where a branch was established in Melbourne, across the bay from Geelong. We had seen through his life how Tom had involved himself, and his bands, in fundraising for many causes. In a way it's unsurprising to learn of his joining the Manchester Union, but it's possible to see also that, at this time in his life, and now deprived of his bandmaster's salary, he may have had one eye on the future, and his own vulnerabilities, and predicting his own future needs.

Throughout the Australian winter months of 1914, Tom was an ever-present at the piano at the Saturday night variety and movie events at the Geelong Mechanics Hall. These merry evenings saw him accompany artists like Scottish comedian Arthur Douglas; Freda Cuthbert, performing her Salome Dance; magician and conjurer Sylvesto; Jim Mack, the lightning man on the ball; Stan Cornish, hand-balancing tables, chairs and other items of furniture; and Tom Brown with his repertoire of eccentric songs, American mat dance and banjoline.

On 16 July, Tom received a mention in the Evening Echo of Ballarat relating to a 'historic picture' of Bulch's Model Band that had been presented in 1887 to a Mr Jamieson for his services as the first Secretary of the band. The picture was being presented back to the band, by Jamieson, for safekeeping. Tom's achievements in Ballarat were briefly recalled in the body of article. Had he read it, he may well have been delighted, to know that his achievements were still recognised; yet at the same time slightly horrified to contemplate that he was being considered part of history. Though Jamieson reportedly prized the picture very much, he said he realised that it would be of special interest to the City of Ballarat Band, and was assured by the current President, Mr Trekardo, that it would be valued.

On Saturday, 18 July, at the Mechanics Hall, the Geelong West Band, as part of their contribution to the evening's entertainment, were to play "Semiramide," the own choice contest piece they would be playing at the upcoming Ballarat competitions. As he sat at the piano that evening you have to wonder how hearing this might leave Tom feeling; given his historic connection to the Ballarat contest and his circumstance as the ousted bandmaster. Tom may have been feeling sore that evening, but three days later something happened that would shake-up everyone's understanding of their place in the world. On 28 July 1914, almost a month after a Bosnian-Serb nationalist assassinated the Austro-Hungarian heir, Archduke Franz Ferdinand, international diplomatic tensions reached boiling point. The Triple Entente of France, Russia and the United Kingdom faced-off against against the Triple Alliance of Austria, Germany and Italy. The peoples of the worldwide empires, and allies, of these powerful nations held their breath, with a sense that everyone could be affected by what looked to be about to happen.

Though the various nations declared commencement of war in stages, over a number of days, beginning with Austria against Serbia, the 28 July seems to have been the pivotal point and the date upon which the Great War, the 'war to end all wars,' officially began. The United Kingdom of Great Britain and Northern Ireland, signalled to all imperial subjects across the world that, by default of their being British subjects and part of this extended family, they too were now at war with other nations. This, of course included the states of Australia and New Zealand.

Australia already had a form of military conscription before this war broke out. Compulsory military training had been introduced in 1911, yet the Defence Act of 1903 provided that unexempted males could only be called upon for home defence in times of war. There was widespread hope that this war would prove to be a brief one, and conclude before Christmas of 1914. Despite the optimism, many everyday things quickly changed. The War Precautions Bill was introduced by Australia's Federal Parliament on Wednesday, 28 October, "to enable the Governor-General to make regulations and orders for the safety of the Commonwealth during the present state of war." This legislative act authorised the court-martial of anyone communicating with, or assisting the enemy, as well as securing the safety of and communications between railways, docks, harbours and public works. It also included powers to prevent the spread of reports that might be likely to cause public panic or alarm, principally through applying a form of censorship. Further powers that were introduced covered national security objectives such as prohibiting the ingress of 'aliens,' generally or to certain places, or requiring such 'aliens' to register their details and for their movements to be tracked. Additionally such persons might be deported or restricted to residing and remaining in certain districts. Any 'alien' in contravention of the act faced a one-hundred pound fine, six months imprisonment, or possibly both. Any person found assisting or abetting 'aliens' was also punishable to the same extent.

At about the same time, the Australian Senate debated over what treatment should be afforded to naturalised Commonwealth citizens, particularly those of German or Austrian heritage. The need for secrecy was stressed, especially over information concerning the movements of Commonwealth troops, with special emphasis on those being transported by sea, which could be easy targets for enemy navy. The Senate felt that drastic powers needed to be employed. During the debates a Senator Stewart made the case that naturalised citizens, formerly of other nations, should be assumed to be loyal to the Commonwealth. Senator Pierce, in stark contrast, felt that other nations did not recognise the right of such as the Commonwealth to naturalise their citizens, and that this particularly applied to Germany and Austria. He went on to add that in the event of an invasion by those powers, these enemy nations would expect citizens of shared heritage to obey them or face death. Therefore former nationals of those countries should be prevented from leaving Australia and should further be detained preventing them from moving freely from place to place. As these announcements and discussions were published in the daily newspapers, a wave of paranoia permeated communities. In Australia, and Britain, neighbours watched anyone with any suggestion of foreign heritage, pondering on their background, nationality, loyalty and intent. Anyone foreign may well be colluding with enemy nations and could present a threat to the safety of their family.

Looking back to when the young Tom Bulch first arrived in Ballarat, you'll recall that he was mistakenly identified in the press as being a German musician. This was largely an assumption on account of his unusual surname. It wasn't just an unusual surname, it was almost unique. Further fuel was added to the misunderstanding on account of much of Tom's music having been printed in Leipzig, Germany. Remembering how Tom had entertained at revelries of the German sub-community at Albury it becomes clear now that any friendships with German nationals now would be seen as a likely collusion. The political developments of 1914 set the scene for a troubling time for the Bulch family. We can imagine a dark mood in Geelong as neighbours, that perhaps did not know them so well, watched them with suspicion as they walked along the street, peering and murmuring at them from behind the veils of curtains and blinds.

Tom continued to compose, though some of his focus seems to have drifted from brass band to music that could be played at home. An article in the Geelong Advertiser of 21st November 1914 announced two new pieces:

> "GEELONG COMPOSER. Mr T E Bulch, who under the name of Henry Laski, has composed "My Polly," "Darling Dolly," and "Flowers of Australia," has just published two tuneful works – Valse "Noralla," and "Dance of the Dandy Coons." The valse is melodious and easy to play: the other is a lively coon dance, with a catchy melody. Both have received commendations from leading musicians, and are on sale at all music sellers. The price is: piano, 2/- nett; violin part, 3d; cornet part, 3d."

Setting aside the clear racist implications of Tom having penned a 'coon dance', which was part of an institutionalised trend in the musical genres at that time, it's good to see that Tom, like George Allan, was still self-publishing music. The front cover of "Dance of the Dandy Coons," predictably featuring two very smartly dressed dancing black men, states that it was published by Bulch & Co. Geelong. Australia. It also informs us that by this time Tom had acquired an export agent for his sales in America. This was Mr H A Richardson of Los Angeles, California. The newspaper article is useful in reconfirming to us that Tom was the true identity behind Henry Laski. Confirmations of identity like this have been useful in establishing these facts.

One other point of note about these compositions is that they had, again, been printed in Leipzig; though not by the C G Roder company that had printed many of his brass band publications. For these advertised pieces, Tom had engaged the Oscar Brandstetter printing house. This was the same business that George Allan was using at around that same time. The printer's mark on each page of "Dance of the Dandy Coons" identifies it as having been the third piece Brandstetter had printed for Bulch & Co. Tom may have wished he had thought better of sending his manuscripts to Germany to be printed, as the details printed on each sheet of his published music, along with his falsely German sounding surname certainly fuelled the suspicions over his allegiances during the war. The wartime newspapers provide no insight as to what happened next, but his grandson Eric Tomkins told us, from accounts given by his mother, that the family music shop became known as "the German music shop," and was shunned by those who had previously patronised it. Eric also tells us that the authorities investigated Thomas's nationality and that he had to be proven to be of English descent. As to the timing of these incidents, we can't be sure, but Eric also told us that Tom's earnings from his music were affected.

Shildon

The year 1914 would also have been just as bewildering for George Allan in Shildon. Even before the war broke out there continued to be troubling news appearing in the press. Some regarding disturbances and violence in Ireland, with tensions between Unionists and Nationalists not being helped by the passing of the Home Rule Bill on 25 May presenting Ireland with some powers of self-government. Other news told of the Suffragettes continuing their campaign of civil disruption. There were arson attacks on the Britannia Pier, Great Yarmouth and Bath Hotel in Felixtowe during April, then marching on Buckingham Palace, during May attempting to deliver a petition to the King, an action that was thwarted by the police. In that same month, activists from the Women's Suffrage movement also damaged a number of portraits of prominent figures such as Henry James and the Duke of Wellington.

Shildon, though, would have seemed far away from much of this. The daily work routine continued; Saturday football matches against regional rivals such as Spennymoor Town, Carlisle United, Blyth Spartans and Newcastle City in the North-Eastern League continued to be the subject of idle chatter in the pubs and bars. Something else was changing in Shildon that also would have been evident at George's workplace. Shildon had been selected as an end point for an experiment in rail freight. The North Eastern Railway had, the previous year, been given approval to electrify the mineral route of the former Clarence Railway, once a rival to the Stockton & Darlington Railway, which commenced at Shildon and ran out to the coal port of Newport on the north bank of the mouth of the River Tees. Electric locomotives had been successfully trialled on Tyneside earlier that century, giving the railway company the confidence to develop a full scale pilot on this Shildon to Newport route. If it proved more efficient for transporting coal, then it was likely that this electric technology could replace steam on a wider scale. The basic infrastructure for electrification was being installed, and one of the engine sheds on the Shildon works site was prepared to receive the fleet of new cleaner quieter electric locomotives that required no fireman and produced no steam.

In March of 1914 the North Eastern Railway made another announcement that may have been unsettling to George and his colleagues at Shildon. This appeared in the Newcastle Journal, and concerned a purchase of land at Faverdale, just outside nearby Darlington. The rail company intended to centralise all of their coach building, wagon building and repair operations, from Shildon and York, to Darlington. The new site would be a huge, state of the art, industrial complex. Three-thousand men from Shildon, George among them, would be displaced by this bold plan. It would see five new workshops, five-hundred feet long, built for the smiths shop, press shop for steel wagon making, sawmills and erecting shops, and would cost an estimated quarter of a million pounds. The plan would also most likely have resulted in the decline of Shildon as a town, as workers would uproot and follow the work to Darlington. George and his neighbours would surely have been deeply concerned by this news. Most had now firmly rooted their lives in Shildon. Though there were still mines and collieries on land surrounding the town, the economy was principally built on the prosperity brought by rail works and the owners of shops and small businesses would surely have had to ponder on their livelihoods should the wagon workers leave town.   Soon after, on Wednesday, 25 March, a Local Government Board inquiry was held into Darlington's plans, which included a number of other boundary expansions for the town. The Mayor of Darlington, Alderman J G Harbottle, was called as a witness to give evidence in support of the proposals. He stated that there were signs of very great developments, particularly in respect of the Railway Company, and that the development applications should be granted. He pointed out that the development of the new Railway Works itself would not extend the town beyond its current boundaries, but the provision of houses for the additional workers would. One Mr Hornsby, representing the North Eastern Railway, then read out a letter from Vincent Raven, the Chief Mechanical Engineer of the North Eastern Railway. This stated that he knew nothing of the intentions that had been expressed through articles in the press, and furthermore that the company officials knew nothing of the scheme to centralise operations and had furthermore not given information of this nature to anyone. He expressly stated in the letter that there was no immediate prospect of the company moving either the carriage works operations away from York, or the wagon operations from Shildon. This declaration by Raven proved something of a bombshell to the proceedings, with many councillors having believed the story that had appeared in the press. After some further discussion, the inquiry was adjourned till the following day.

At the same time, and at a separate meeting elsewhere in Darlington, Arthur Pease, the director of the North Eastern Railway who the previous year had formally opened Shildon's new Railway Institute, who was also an Alderman of Darlington, was giving a speech somewhat contradicting Vincent Raven's letter of testimony. In his speech he declared that the North Eastern Railway Company had every intention of gradually increasing their works at Darlington, though he did add that there would be no sudden increase.

The inquiry continued the following day with various officials and Councillors being called upon to give evidence. This included statements that the Darlington development had been proposed because the North Eastern Railway had been declined permission to extend their premises at Shildon, and at other sites. Thus the company desired to move more work to Darlington where they had recently built large offices at Stooperdale, and Faverdale, and had widened the thoroughfare of Brinkburn Road. Councillor Bates was convinced they would not have done that if they had no future developments in view. Councillor C H Leach from the Darlington Rural Council, however, testified that this particular body had petitioned against the developments.

The debate continued in the newspapers on into April, with repeated predictions that wagon manufacturing would transfer to Darlington leaving only repair work at Shildon. A report of a further meeting on Friday, 8 May appeared to confirm that intention. Throughout all this, George could well have been wondering how much longer he could remain at his home in Pears Terrace, which of course was not just the place from which he walked to and from work at the beginning and end of every shift. It was also integral to his publishing business, the address being printed as the correspondence address at the top of all the sheet music he had issued thus far. To have to move to Darlington could prove most disruptive.

He placed one of his usual small advertisements in June's Brass Band News:

> "CELEBRATED CONTEST MARCHES – "Knight Templar," "La Maestro," "Senator" and others. Winners. Price 1/3 for 20 parts. – ALLAN, Publisher, New Shildon."

On this occasion there was no new title to promote. It appears that he had neither had the time, nor the will, to compose and publish a new composition since the previous year. Just over a month later, as had happened in Australia the declaration of war with Germany and Austria was issued, and here too, day to day lives began to change significantly.

As the country was now at war, the organising committee for the annual Shildon Show decided it inappropriate to go ahead. The celebration, along with its almost obligatory brass band contest, was cancelled. Notices issued in the press optimistically pointed out that the cancellation would only be for this year, as if the war should soon be over. One week later, with just a week to go before the show, the same committee issued a small notice in the press changing the decision. They explained that it would still go ahead, but be greatly reduced from its usual splendour, with just the horticultural section and the band contest taking place.

As soon as war was declared, reservists from across the nation were called up for active service, with instructions to report directly to their units or ships. The armed forces were quickly further expanded by including those that were already signed up to be part of the Territorial Force, or "Home Army" that had been formed in 1908. Then invitations were issued for civilians to volunteer for the Service Battalions of Kitchener's Army; units expected to exist solely for the duration of the war. Some of the Service Battalions were comprised of recruits from a like background, offering the encouragement to the men that they would be serving and fighting alongside their colleagues from the same neighbourhood or workplace. These became known as "Pals" Battalions. The North Eastern Railway, keen to show willing, applied to set up one such the North Eastern Railway Battalion attached to the Northumberland Fusiliers. Once that permission was granted, they extended an invitation to their workforce to apply. They stressed, though, that the company still had an important role to play at home, and that only such volume of men as could be spared would be permitted to enlist.

Railwaymen that remained with the North Eastern Railway, particularly those in engineering and mechanics, quickly saw different types of work coming their way. Carriage workers at York found themselves building new types of utility carriage for such as Ambulance Trains to bring casualties from the battlefront. Workers in Gateshead were challenged to build gun trolley carriages, upon which large guns could be mounted and transported around as portable coastal defences. Shildon works would also see unusual work coming its way as contribution to the war effort. For those that chose or were compelled to stay behind, there was a danger through social stigma. Neighbours might consider them shirkers, and, at the instigation of Admiral Charles Fitzgerald at the beginning of the war, an organisation of mainly young women roamed freely, distributing white feathers as a token of accusation of cowardice and contempt to any able bodied man that had not signed up for the armed forces. To be presented with these was deemed symbolic of great shame, even though many of the young men were still required at home to keep the nation moving and the great furnaces fuelled. Mindful of this, the North Eastern Railway initially issued men in its reserved occupations with armbands to wear when not in work clothes. These stated that they were required by the "RAILWAY SERVICE" in bold black lettering. They were superseded in December of 1914 by enamelled Railway Service lapel badges.

By the time way broke out, George Allan had celebrated his fiftieth birthday, and would be considered broadly too old for either conscription or volunteer duty. By the time the war was reaching its conclusion in 1918 powers had been passed by Parliament to expand conscription eligibility to able bodied men up to the age of fifty; but essentially George's age and his reserved occupation ruled him out of participation in the military forces.

It wasn't just the railwaymen of Shildon that were called away to the war. As it wore on, the army found many uses at the front for men whose expertise lay in underground workings; many of the town's young coal miners were recruited into the engineering battalions, for their physical strength, resilience and expertise.

As we know, George was no longer running a brass band by that year, but for those that were we can get a sense from reports by writers such as Pedal See, the Brass Band News's correspondent for the South Durham area, that the egress of men from Shildon to join the war had an immediate depleting effect on bands during that first year. In November he wrote:

> "The Shildonites are only moderately situated at present. Some of their men have volunteered for active service, and this seems to have put them in a difficult position."

In December he continues:

> "A good number of our Durham bandsmen have shown true patriotism by enlisting, and so proving their determination to destroy our great German enemies. The Shildon bands have been more lively these last four weeks. They were very busy playing at an engagement on the 7th of November, this being the only engagement fulfilled for some time. But bands can always make work for themselves if they are determined to be busy."

The war would have an effect upon George's activities and business. Despite being in no danger of being mistaken for an foreign national, as had happened to Tom Bulch, George too had been using German printing companies to produced the printed sheet music that was the means of him selling his work. This was something he would have no choice but to cease doing at once. Unauthorised correspondence with 'the enemy' was an offence, with severe consequences. The Oscar Brandstetter company even had an office in London which closed permanently as a result of the war. Any as yet unfulfilled orders for sheet music would remain unfulfilled. There was as much public paranoia in Britain as in Australia concerning the presence of German 'spies'. George would have had to make alternative arrangements for his music, or hope that the war would soon be over.

Interesting to consider, at this point, whether either George or Tom, might have had any new composition in production when the war was declared; perhaps something printed but never returned. We will probably never know; though we do know that when George placed his annual Christmas advertisement in the December issue of Brass Band News it was for music that he had already advertised in previous years. This advert continued to appear in the January 1915 issue:

> "My Grand Christmas Number.- "Star of the East," "The World Awakes," &c, Three Hymns and Three Choruses, twenty parts. 1s 7d,; extras. 2d. Allan, Publisher, New Shildon."

Geelong

With his father no longer being the master of a brass band, and being a noted musician in his own right, Thomas Edward Bulch junior still sought to keep his musical skills honed. Despite his father having been removed as bandmaster, he remained as cornetist with the Geelong Municipal Band. He had turned twenty-seven years of age in November 1914, and now he, his wife Ivy Mae, and their three children Thelma, Eric and Frederick were living in a house on Walker Street in West Geelong. It would have been a busy little home with the three young children, the youngest of which was only two years old. As well as being a bandsman, Tom junior had also taken work as a dredge-hand, which entailed operating dredging machinery aboard a dredger vessel, keeping the waterways and harbour around Geelong free from debris and blockages.

With the war intensifying, and not looking as though it would be brought to as quick a conclusion as people had hoped, the social pressure on any young man of fighting age to enlist would have been intense. In Australia, as in Britain, there was a stigma upon any person not occupied in reserved occupations who was late to accept the call to join the boys in the military forces. Many needed no persuasion at all and were keen to play their part in defending the Commonwealth.

Tom junior would have been very much aware of the military traditions in the Bulch family. His father having been the bandmaster of the 3rd regiment in Ballarat, not once but twice, and his grandfather a volunteer rifleman back in Britain. He'd have grown up around military personalities, and, of course, served his own basic training. The call being almost irresistible, he enlisted in March 1915. Whether he had experienced any of the national identity issues that had befallen his father is untold excepting one incident that we will address in a few moments. It is interesting to note that his enlistment papers include a written addition, under his name and locality, that he was a "Paternal Born British subject." His own nationality was, of course, clearly presented as being Australian.

Above: Thomas Edward Bulch junior in his Australian Imperial Forces uniform having enlisted to serve during WWI. He became a Sergeant Bugler in the 23rd Battalion AIF

Another interesting detail was that Tom junior did not enlist into the local garrison in Geelong. For some reason, perhaps on account of his father's military connections there, he chose to travel to Ballarat to enlist with what had now become the 23rd Battalion. The procedural details on his enlistment papers suggest that enlisting may not have been entirely straightforward. He first attempted to sign up on 19 March, but there was an additional requirement that the Town Clerk in Geelong provide an attestation as to his national identity. The implication here is that Tom senior was not the only member of the Bulch family who had been regarded with suspicion. It wasn't until 29 March that he was able to sign the oath to serve his "Sovereign Lord the King in the Australian Imperial Force" from that day until the end of the war. Tom junior's enlistment papers describe him as being five feet and nine inches in height, weighing nine stones and three pounds, with a chest measurement of thirty-five and a half inches and being of fair complexion with blue eyes and fair hair. His religious denomination was captured as being Church of England. In terms of his distinguishing features, it was noted that he had three molars missing from his right lower jaw and one from the left. Now a Private, he was assigned to a training battalion; but by the 6th of May his wish to join the 23rd Battalion had been fulfilled and he had joined his unit as an infantryman and bandsman. The latest intake of the Battalion was mobilised quickly and left Melbourne on 10 May 1915 aboard His Majesty's Australian Transport ship Euripides. This vessel was a triple-screw steamship that had been built by Harland and Wolff at Belfast for the Aberdeen Line. The ship, initially launched on 29 January 1914, had made its maiden voyage to Australia in July 1914. She was one of twenty-eight vessels that had been requisitioned by the Australian government to be fitted out as a troopship, and was equipped to carry 136 officers, 2204 other ranks and stabling for twenty horses on each voyage. One of the other men aboard that vessel, Private John Reid, of the 23rd Battalion, a fellow bandsman who knew Tom junior, began a diary that related something of the voyage. He wrote:

> "The 23rd and 24th Battalions left Victoria on TSS Euripides on Saturday 8th May at 3pm but did not leave the bay until 11am on Monday the 9th. We did not touch land again until we reached Albany and then did not go within 5 miles. I was fairly sick nearly all the way, but got better as we sighted land.

The band played on the sun deck on sighting land. We left the bay the same night. Our next port was Colombo on Tuesday 25/5/15 at 7:30am. Some of us took French leave. A splendid city with lovely buildings and gardens. About forty were arrested. Three deaths reported up to now. Left at 5:30am on the 27/5/15. Rained heavily on the 26th. We played "Goodbye Little Girl" in the rain. Cheers from the city."

"Next port was Suez. We stayed until we could get through the Canal. The journey up the red sea was very hot. The trip through the canal was very interesting. Soldiers mostly camped all along. Put in at Port Said for a day and a night. Reached Alexandria where we landed on 12th June. We were eleven weeks camped at Heliopolis near Cairo. I spent a very interesting time on the whole. We were in Egypt for eleven weeks."

On 24 July, the Geelong Advertiser announced that of the men and boys of the Geelong Municipal Band, fifteen had either already enlisted or expressed that they intended to do so, and it went on to list Tom junior among the named recruits. It explains how the losses from the band ranks had been accepted in the right spirit by the bandmaster, Percy Jones, who had since been attempting to fill the vacant seats in the band with members brought up from the junior band.

With his son headed away from the rest of the family to fulfil his military service, the year continued to be quiet, musically, for Tom senior, though he did fulfil an engagements to provide musical services occasionally. One such occasion was the Jubilee Smoke Social of the Ancient Order of Foresters that took place on 21 August 1915 at the Geelong West Fire Brigade Hall. Tom, and a number of other gentlemen, added music and harmony to the evening, between and after the toasts that were being proposed by the countless officials present. On Saturday 11 September 1915 a notice was published in the Ballarat Star announcing the death of one of Tom's few direct relatives in Australia. This was his niece, Olive May, the daughter of his ill-fated brother Frank who had followed him to Australia. The notice reads:

"Reed. The friends of Mr Walter Reed of 263 Victoria Street are respectfully invited to follow the remains of his late dearly-beloved wife, Olive May Reed (nee Bulch), to the place of her interment, the Ballarat New Cemetery. The funeral cortege will move from her mother's residence, Mrs J Wakeling; 119 Skipton Street, near Dawson Street, on Monday 13th day of September, 1915, at 1 o'clock. Melbourne and Geelong papers please copy."

The request for the Melbourne and Geelong papers to repeat the article was probably an educated one, given that this area was now where Olive May's few blood relatives from the Bulch line were resident. Olive had been born to Frank, and his wife Isabella, in Ballarat in 1885, not long after the couple had arrived. She may have been conceived back in New Shildon, but was born an Australian. After Frank Bulch had perished in the gold mining accident, his wife Isabella had remained in the Ballarat area, and had later remarried to Ralph William Wakeling in 1889. This was entirely understandable and practical given the difficulty of raising a family as a single parent, then even more so than now. The couple raised Olive May, alongside nine other children that Isabella bore William Wakeling. Olive would have had no recollections of her natural father. She later was married, to Walter Reed, but had now died aged only about thirty. It is worthy of note that, where the newspaper gives Olive's mother's name as Mrs "J" Wakeling, this is a probable misinterpretation of her own handwriting. A sample of her handwriting captured on her son, Ralph Murchison Wakeling's, military enlistment papers, when he too answered the call to the war, shows when she wrote a capital letter I by hand, it did look rather like a letter J.

Though Tom senior was no longer a master of a band, he was still active in composing for bands, and in doing so was now very much inspired by events in the war. This may have been through his having once been bandmaster of the 3rd Battalion Militia military band. He had often been inclined to compose martial pieces over the decades, and an article in 'Every Week,' published in Bairnsdale, Victoria on 23 Sept showed how this trend continued. It reads:

> "Last Sunday afternoon the Municipal Band performed in the Rotunda. Several new numbers were rendered in good style. The attendance of the public was meagre owing to the weather conditions not being favourable for the performances. During the afternoon the war was brought to mind by the playing of several of Mr T Bulch's compositions, notably the "General Joffre" and the "Heroes of Gallipoli" marches."

The Gallipoli campaign, now so ingrained into the national consciousness of Australia, had commenced on 17 February 1915. In the battles of which it comprised, the allied forces of the Triple Entente sought to weaken the Ottoman grip on the straits of the Dardanelles. The first assault on Ottoman forts at the entrance to those straits failed entirely and cost many lives. This outcome necessitated a second amphibious assault on the Gallipoli peninsula, which took place in April 1915. It is this endeavour to which Tom was referring in his piece "Heroes of Gallipoli." A great many troops from Australia and New Zealand were involved in this assault, alongside others from India, Newfoundland and the United Kingdom itself. What's interesting about this choice of a composition title is that, on 30 August 1915, Tom's son was one of the troops assigned to reinforce the Mediterranean Expeditionary Force at Gallipoli. Whether his father had expected it, or not, when producing and publishing this march, his own son was to become one of those "Gallipoli heroes." Tom junior hadn't taken part in the main April, or later August, offensives, but he had joined the battle, and had risked his life there. It's certain, though, from the production timescale, that the piece was composed before Tom junior was posted, and inspired by news of the April landing attempts. John Reid's diary tells of the 23rd Battalion's move to that front at Gallipoli:

> "We boarded the SS Haverford on Sunday 29th August and got to Limnos Island on 2nd September. On the way the SS Southend was torpedoed in sight of our ship. This was a notorious incident and gave our brigade a name. We were at Limnos three days and boarded the ship Partridge on Saturday 4th. Moved for the front as ordered."

> "We arrived at our destination about 1pm on Sunday morning, the bullets flew all around us as we were landing but only strays. We took over Lone Pine on Monday 7th Sept."

He goes on to say:

> "The 23rd and 24th Battalions experienced the worst bombardment on the peninsular on Saturday 29th November. On the Saturday snow had fallen and it was bitterly cold. The casualties of the two battalions were 243. The evacuation of Gallipoli started on 18th December."

Overall, the Gallipoli campaign was destined to fail. Despite being outmanned, the Turks held the defensive advantage and stood firm. During the campaign, the combined deployed force of just less than half a million men of the British Empire, including 65,000 from Australia and New Zealand, aided by under 30,000 French, were stopped from progressing by the 315,000 strong force of the Ottoman Empire. It was thus considered a victory by the Ottoman Turks when the Allies were forced to withdraw from the peninsula at the beginning of 1916. Casualties on both sides had been extremely heavy, with the Empire losing over 160,000 men through battle casualties and just short of a further 3,800 through disease. There were also 90,000 evacuated through illness or injury. For young Private Bulch it must have been a horrendous experience.

We are left to consider, then, that while the Municipal Band in Bairnsdale, Victoria played his father's "Heroes of Gallipoli" young Tom was right there, experiencing what it was like to be such a 'hero'. How strange and poetically tragic, a moment.

The other new march played in Bairnsdale that day, "General Joffre," was Tom senior's tribute to Joseph Jacques Césaire Joffre, a French general who had been Commander-in-Chief of the French forces on the Western Front. He had become extremely popular in his time, earning him the nickname Papa Joffre, and may have become enough of a folk-hero, through the press reports reaching Australia, for Tom to have selected him as the inspiring candidate for this brass band march's title. Overall, Joffre came to be known more for his political machinations such as pushing for the purge and dismissal of generals unsuccessful in battle. Yet he is also remembered for regrouping and rallying the retreating allied forces in mid 1914, to turn the situation around and defeat the Germans at the strategically important first battle of the Marne in September that year. There is a strong probability that this is the deed that proved the inspiration for the "General Joffre" march.

Whatever the case, these were new marches, inspired by events of the day and showing that Tom Bulch was not yet done composing brass band music. They also demonstrate that bands were not finished buying his music either. A report of the monthly meeting of the Oakleigh Brass Band from October 1915 includes a breakdown of accounts, which included three shillings and two pence paid to Mr Bulch for music purchased.

Within the month they were playing "Heroes of Gallipoli" in the local public gardens, along with Tom's "South Street Parade." The Bendigo Citizen's Band of Victoria and Randwick Brass of New South Wales were among others that invested in "General Joffre." The latter of these played it one time at the Coogee Rotunda along with Tom's "Noralla" and "South Street Parade". On 9 November, the Gippsland Mercury told that:

> "Maffra Brass Band is expected to again give a good account of itself at Hospital Demonstration on Saturday next. The band which is augmented by other district bandsmen will play compositions by an ex bandmaster of Sale, T E Bulch. These pieces – "General Joffre" and "Heroes of Gallipoli" – are becoming popular."

As well as these new pieces, the war seemed to have breathed new life into Tom's old descriptive military fantasia "The Young Recruit." It was played widely in the early years of the war, possibly in with the hope and expectation that young men might be inspired to enlist and serve the Empire. It had been a popular choice for bands to include in their concert programmes ever since it had been published, but now that a global conflict really was drawing in all those young recruits from families across the country, the piece saw a resurgence in interest.

The absence of the men through military duty proved a cause for anxiety for the women of all those families, among whom were Tom junior's wife Ivy May and their children and also mother Eliza. Australians with loved ones overseas would scan the papers daily for news. In October a story appeared that was so troubling as to compel Eliza to write for confirmation:

> "To the Ministry of Defence. Dear Sir, It is reported throughout Geelong that a Transport with the 23rd Battalion on board, was torpedoed on its way to the front and also that my son, Bandsman Thomas E Bulch No.1149.23 Batt. Band, 6th Inf. Bge. was on board and drowned and as we have had no word from Headquarters would you kindly let us know if there is any truth in this report. Hoping to have an early reply as we are all terribly anxious. I remain yours respectfully. E A Bulch. 1 Anakie Street, Geelong W."

This letter was received by the Ministry on 29 October, who issued a note of acknowledgement the next day, and then on 1st

November issued a letter of reply commencing with the opening salutation "Dear sir." This is an understandable mistake as Eliza had not indicated she was writing as Tom's mother.

> "In reply to yours (undated), I beg to inform you no official report has been received here concerning your son No. 1149 Private Thomas Edward Bulch, 23rd Battalion, consequently it may be assumed he is with his unit. Next of kin will be promptly advised upon receipt of any report. His postal address is:- No. 1149 Private T E Bulch, 23rd Battalion, 6th Infantry Brigade, Australian Imperial Force, Alexandria, Egypt. Yours faithfully,"

This reply, though likely soothing to Eliza's anxieties, appears to be contradictory to other evidence on Thomas's military records which suggests that he had not arrived in Egypt until 10 January 1916. This was the date on which he arrived in Alexandria having previously embarked upon a transport ship from "Mudros," or Moudros, a port town on the Greek island of Lemnos close to the Gallipoli peninsula. It's possible, though, that the 6th Infantry Brigade were based, generally, in Alexandria with troops continually being ferried between the Dardanelles and Egypt. Perhaps the records of soldiers whereabouts weren't entirely accurate, or the records officer simply wanted to relieve Eliza's anxiety over the true location of her son. We don't have any information as to whether there was any direct correspondence between Tom junior and the family, though, that is quite possible given that a mailing address had been provided by which he could be contacted. We can be sure that the Bulch family, as a whole, would still have spent an anxious Christmas and New Year hoping that Tom was safe. They would share that experience with so many families around the world whose sons swelled the ranks on both sides of the conflict. Despite the misery of constant anxiety, they might also have considered themselves fortunate, for many other families had already been informed of the death of their menfolk and were facing their first, or perhaps second, Christmas knowing that they were never returning.

Shildon

The year 1915 in Shildon would have been equally sombre for those with family members away at the front. That initial optimism at the outset of the war that it might be over quickly had evaporated. Stories were published and read concerning truces, and subsequent fraternisation, between the two sides over the Christmas 1915 and the New Year, but both sides commenced 1915 by entrenching themselves deeper into what looked set to become an even more enduring and bloody war.

We already saw how George Allan's usual printing arrangements for his compositions had been inconvenienced by the war, and it is possibly the reason that we see no evidence of him publishing new brass band music to sell. We have spotted one interesting incident which suggests that Shildon had another budding brass composer at this time; possibly a younger person, who may have been tutored by George in the New Shildon Saxhorn Band, or even Tom Bulch, or his successors, in the New Shildon Temperance Band. Toward the winter of 1914, the Brass Band News, began running march and melody contests inviting amateur composers to submit their best efforts. Such a contest could, if viewed cynically, appear as a thinly veiled effort to find new material to publish, or reveal new up and coming composers that might be brought on board to freshen up the Wright and Round catalogue of music. Readers having submitted their efforts at each time of asking, might find in each monthly issue, a very brief critique of the pieces entered for consideration; though the composers were never named. The best pieces would earn a prize and consequently also become property of Wright and Round, to do with as they pleased. The rules stated clearly that any composers that had previously been published were not eligible to enter, ruling out the likes of George and his published contemporaries, unless of course they were to adopt a pseudonym. The piece that caught our interest was mentioned in the March 1915 issue. A composition named "Shildonian" had been submitted, earning judge's comments which were not especially encouraging. "A moderate effort again. Melodies and form are correct, but a perusal fails to interest us much. Melodies are not copies, yet they do not show originality."

From this we're left to wonder whether Shildon spawned another amateur brass composer of which we know nothing. There were certainly other bandsmen, including members of the Bulch family that remained after Tom emigrated, staying with the Temperance Band. There were George's son Bill, and Harry Gibbon, the stores worker at the wagon works that took charge of both the Temperance Band and Male Voice Choir and plenty of others besides.

Early in the spring, in its March issue, the Brass Band News local correspondent for the district, 'Pedal See,' tells us that the Shildon Wesleyan Band and nearby Leasingthorne Colliery Band had begun to assist each other by loaning each other musicians to occupy the seats at concerts that were vacant through men being away at the war, or already lost in battle. In April he follows up by saying:

> "I hope the Shildonites have not fallen through altogether. It is no use giving up because of being shorthanded as nearly every band in the country has suffered from that complaint. The point now is to get out of these difficulties as soon as possible."

Then in June:

> "No news of the Shildonites of late, I hope they have not gone dead. Please drop me a line some of you."

In July we hear that the Shildon musicians had taken not just to loaning players for concerts but also rehearsing with the Leasingthorne band and their conductor Mr Sellars. Both bands were reported, later in the year, as having been unable to attend any contests since 1914. This shortage of musicians was, of course, not limited to Shildon, and knowledge of the sorry state of bands across the nation may have been another determining factor in George's decision not to publish new marches. He may have felt there was little point. Many of the bands that were his regular customers would have been in similarly sorry states, with doubts over their future viability and probably not investing in new music.

Work may have been another distracting factor. Industrial production across Britain had been stepped up to equip the war, and the production centres of the North Eastern Railway were no exception to this. The wagon works, at which George was employed, may well have demanded more of him and his fellow workers than at any other time in their lives. New types of freight were required to be transported by rail, including gunpowder for arms manufacture, and of course munitions themselves. The strategic importance of the railway network would also not have been lost upon both the British and their enemies. Shildon, hosting one of the worlds largest sidings and marshalling yards, as well as its rail engineering centre, was certainly a possible target. It was clear to the civilians of the North East of England that they were certainly not out of reach of the war. In December the previous year, the first Zeppelin airships had begun crossing the North East coastline indiscriminately dropping bombs; and though these rarely had great effect it was still a deadly prospect.

Just along the line from Shildon, a new building had been erected at the Darlington Railway Works which would become known as the National Projectile Factory, or less formally the Shell Shop. Staffed mainly by local women this was a hazardous place of employment and throughout its period of operation, explosions would occasionally occur killing groups of the women.

Despite the backdrop of war, the North Eastern Railway had, in September of 1915, also commenced experimentally running their new electrified locomotives on the former Clarence Railway line between Shildon and Newport near Middlesborough. These new locomotives, designed by Vincent Raven, who had been present at the opening of Shildon's new Railway Institute, were stationed in an engine shed on the Shildon Works site. They would regularly have run along the line that passed only a few feet from George's house. While he had grown up accustomed to the sound of steam locomotives shunting in and out of the works this entirely different sound of the electric locomotives setting out on their daily coal runs had become a new normal. They were immensely successful in efficiently transporting greater quantities of coal, and on account of this and his other engineering successes toward the war effort, Vincent Raven, later that year, left the employment of the North Eastern Railway to become the chief engineer of the munitions works at London's Woolwich Arsenal. He later, during 1917, would receive a knighthood, for his engineering endeavours.

Another change George would have noticed in his workplace was that where once the works had been the exclusive preserve of the men of New Shildon, the North Eastern Railway had, by necessity been backfilling many roles vacated by men, away serving their country, with local women. Photographs, taken by the works photographer, show how women ably fulfilled tasks like cleaning the Shildon based locomotives, new electric ones included. They also took on engineering and maintenance tasks. To the old hands like George and his comrades, too advanced in years to be called up for war, and who had been employed at the works for decades, working alongside the women for the first time would have seemed strange indeed.

The daily newspapers brought updates of happenings at the various fronts around the world, news of local men killed or wounded in battle and of the collective efforts of community groups, associations and trades unions to raise funds and collect goods to maintain the war relief effort.

By November George breaks his silence by advertising the following:

> "Two splendid Christmas numbers – Each contains three choruses and three hymns. Twenty parts 1s 9d – extras 2d each. Allan, Publisher, New Shildon."

The advertisement shows a slight price increase on his prices from the previous year. There is no claim that these are new compositions, which suggests that they could have been unsold stock from previous years. It's not clear why he chose to advertise these but not his contest marches during 1915. Perhaps the idea of, and sentiments surrounding, Christmas brought some kind of optimism and hope, and even the possibility that, as had happened the previous year, there might be a brief pause in the hostilities in which the leaders of the two sides might come to their senses.

On 11 December 1915, George's Son, Bill, who had by then been working as a painter rather like his father, enlisted into the Army Reserve of the Durham Light Infantry. He was aged twenty-one years and nine months at the time and, like so many young men, enlisted on short service. This meant that he would serve in the army for the duration of the war, but be demobilised once it was declared over. On his recruitment forms, he gave his father, George, as next of kin, with his contact address of 2 Pears Terrace, New Shildon. Bill's height was recorded as five feet ten-and-a-half inches, with a chest measurement of thirty-five inches. He gave his own personal address as being Boot & Son, Canada Camp, Richmond, Yorkshire. He was accepted into the army reserve awaiting mobilisation.

Though the Bulch family in Australia already knew their son was away facing the dangers of battle, that anxiety of having an enlisted son was just beginning for the Allans.

Hornsea

On 21 February 1916, Private William Willoughby Allan underwent a military medical examination. His physical development was assessed as 'good', his vision in both eyes was deemed somewhat defective and classified as 6/12 and it was noted by the medical officer that he had "defective teeth." In terms of distinguishing features he had two vaccination marks on his left arm from injections received in infancy. Overall, he was determined medical category "A," meaning he was fit for military service. Following his recruitment he received a series of standard inoculations. He had already been mobilised and assigned to the Durham Light Infantry's 21st Training Reserve Battalion.

This unit was based at a camp especially established for the purpose, at Hornsea, near Hornsea Mere, just above the mouth of the River Humber on England's north-east coast. Its new recruits were sent there to be trained before being allocated to units on the the front lines. The provision of basic military and machine gun training to these men required that a regular staff be based permanently at the camp. However it transpired, young Bill soon found himself assigned to camp staff, training troops to serve at the front. So far as his military records attest, he did not receive a front line posting .

It was a bleak winter in early 1916, with the heaviest snow falling between 26 February and 14 March, producing significant challenges to the North Eastern Railway who needed to keep trains running. Men of the Durham Light Infantry who were stationed on the British mainland were often called upon to help clear the lines and rescue trains at notoriously difficult locations such as Bleath Gill near Kirkby Stephen where the drifts reportedly reached thirty feet high. The primary duty of the Training Reserve Battalion, however, was to keep ensuring a supply of competent and compliant soldiers for the battlefront.

On 1 July 1916, Bill was promoted to acting unpaid Lance-Corporal, the lowest rank of non-commissioned officer in the British infantry. This usually occurred when a soldier was appointed as second in command of a section, but also sometimes happened if a soldier was a designated specialist of some sort such as a clerk, driver, machine gunner or mortarman. Back at home, by the middle of the year, Bill's father, George, found a solution to his problem of not being able to send his handwritten musical manuscripts to Germany to be printed. He also appears to have found new inspiration to create music. With the help of a new printing company he published two new marches, which he then once again advertised in the small advertisements section of the September 1916 issue of Brass Band News.

Bandmasters hoping for stunning new contest marches to test their bands at contest might have been disappointed, and surprised, to find he had taken a slightly different direction. His advertisement was as follows:

> "'Home Guards' and 'Dragoon' marches. Easy and good. Suitable for long parades. Price 1s 1d each – Allan Publisher, New Shildon."

As with his old bandmate Tom Bulch then, he'd been inspired to produce two less challenging military-themed pieces. Perhaps, with "Knight Templar" and "The Wizard," he felt he'd reached a pinnacle in contest marches. It's far more likely, though, that these easier marches were reflective of times and the state in which the brass bands found themselves. Either having been forced to join forces, or else rely on the younger players that were not yet old enough to serve their country, there were probably very few brass bands sufficiently equipped to play challenging contest marches.

On 1 September 1916, as part of a reactive reconstruction following the introduction of a national conscription scheme in January which had created a large increase in the influx of new recruits, the 21st Durham Light Infantry become the 87th Infantry Reserve Battalion and Bill Allan was reassigned to that unit as a consequence. Continuing to be stationed in England with a Training Reserve Battalion made it relatively easy for Bill to stay in contact with his sweetheart, Henrietta Willerton. Henrietta was born in July 1895 in the mining village of Esh Winning. She was the only daughter of Henry and Esther Willerton. Henry was employed as a gas stoker for the colliery company that operated Shildon Lodge Colliery, which was overlooked by the family's home at 6 Bolckow Street. There was an appropriate coincidental connection in that address, for Henry was born in Middlesbrough, the town that had thrived and grown through the endeavours of the Victorian industrialist Henry Bolckow, after whom that street had been named. Henrietta's mother, Esther, was born in the nearby village of Aycliffe. During 1916, Henrietta turned twenty-one years of age. The young couple made a decision that they should be married before the end of the year. An article in the Auckland Chronicle of 23 November 1916 tells us something of the wedding:

> "There was a quiet wedding on Saturday afternoon at St John's Church, the bride being Miss Henrietta Willington, daughter of Mr and Mrs Willington of Bolckow Street, and the bridegroom Pte. Willoughby Allan of Pears Terrace, New Shildon. Miss Nellie Robson was bridesmaid and Mr A Stephenson best man. The vicar officiated."

Bill, and his father George, would have been quite used to having their surname misspelt. Throughout George's life, newspapers were littered with references wherein his name had been spelt Allen rather than Allan. For once, it was Bill's bride's family name that had been misspelt by the reporting journalist. On 30 December, Bill's promotion to being a fully paid Lance Corporal in the Training Reserve Battalion was completed. The change was formally noted on his military service records. Bill was not, however, the only soldier promoted during 1916. On 1 January 1916, Tom Bulch junior was promoted to to the rank of Sergeant Bugler, and became the bandmaster of his band which were attached to the Army Medical Corps. This was something his father would surely have been most proud to learn.

France

As Thomas Edward Bulch senior had learned how to be a bandsman through the tutelage of men like his grandfather from the previous generation of bandmasters, that tradition had been passed on by him to his son who was now mentoring the bandsmen of his battalion. Thus a kind of family lineage had been created that was beyond being purely genetic. The musical spirit and legacy of Francis Dinsdale, bandmaster of New Shildon had been handed into the custody of this young ANZAC Sergeant.

As explained previously, we know a little about Sergeant Tom Bulch's war experiences through documented records of where the 23rd Battalion was deployed, and also through the 1915-16 war diary of Private John Anderson Reid of that battalion, which was preserved, transcribed and made available online as part of the Australian War Memorial website. The diaries outline in brief the main day to day events that defined the lives, and deaths, of men in the battalion. We also learn that Private Reid was under Sergeant Tom Bulch's charge.

After the withdrawal from Gallipoli, the 23rd Battalion had retreated to the Canal Zone in Alexandria, where they stayed until March. Then, as part of the 1st ANZAC Corps under General Birdwood, they embarked on another troopship, bound for France, to join the British Expeditionary Forces at the front. The troopships arrived at Marseille on March 19. There Tom and his comrades-in-arms disembarked and proceeded by train to the battlefields. These Australian troops were billeted in the St Omer-Aire-Hazebrouck region of French Flanders, which was known informally as the "Nursery." On 1st April, Australian reconnaissance parties entered the front line of this battle for the first time. On that particular day the 23rd Battalion were away from the front. Private Reid declared it a 'splendid day' in his diary and noted that the band played music in a village, marched to the parade ground, practised their gas helmets, saw a squadron of twelve aeroplanes fly overhead, and had a kit inspection before tea. After that they played football. He also noted that the men of the battalion had not been paid since leaving the Canal Zone and Alexandria, a factor causing some discontent. The musical performances at the village near where they were based seems to have been a daily affair, and possibly maintained to keep morale high. On Tuesday 4 April the men were told that they were going to advance to the firing line in two days time, and were lectured by their Colonel on what their job there would be.

By 7 April, the 23rd Battalion began taking over duties at sectors of the front lines. Private Reid's diary tells that the men were up at seven in the morning, and breakfasted before getting their packs and blankets ready to move out. They had lunch at eleven o'clock in the morning and then marched out, arriving at Haverskerque by seven o'clock in the evening. The next day they marched through Merville, and Sailly-sur-la-Lys, to a small village near the front that was to be their resting destination.

They reached this objective by three o'clock in the afternoon. Later they observed from the ground as two Zeppelin airships passed overhead. Here, closer to the front-line, we are told that the effect of the artillery guns of both sides was far more audible. The following day the enemy guns refocussed, and the men of the 23rd were heavily shelled. Despite this they fared quite well, and on the next day, 10 April, they advanced to take up positions on the firing line. From that point in the diary, the recollections are of rainy days and nights, sporadic shelling and the men entertaining themselves by reading each other old letters and writing new ones to send back home.

In mid-April, the Australian 1st and 2nd Divisions were committed again into the line at Fleurbaix, just south of the key strategic manufacturing town of Armentières, which had a population of about 30,000 and is situated on the Lys River near the Belgian border. They relieved the British 2nd Corps and had command of the area south-east of Armentières. Tom was attached to the headquarters staff here. This particular location had been the scene of extremely bloody fighting during 1914, as the German and Franco-British forces had made several attempts to outflank each other during that first year of the war. On 21 April, which was Good Friday, the 23rd Battalion relieved the 24th Battalion, and reportedly had a rotten trip in doing so, on account of the duck boards being so slimy that the men slipped all the way there. The days that followed included further bombardments and aircraft activity. Private Reid mentions Tom in his diary entry for 30 April, in which he says he'd helped the cook that day, who had subsequently asked him to stay and help out, and that Sgt Bulch was going to see about it. Tom must have done this, as Private Reid continued to make references to cooking throughout his May diary entries. This did not, however, spare him from the ongoing rounds of shelling by the enemy. On 1 June, according to Private Reid's account, the 23rd Battalion band was reunited with its instruments, which arrived in good form along with some new music. Reid wrote:

> "Have a lot of Bulch's new music amongst it, some very good pieces. Had a blow tonight. Hughes and Fisher inspected us."

The reference to 'having a blow' was a bandsman's term for spending time playing and rehearsing music. It's touching to think that so simple a pleasure could bring cheer to the men at the front. In early June rumours reached the trenches of good progress having been made by the Russians and the death of the Kaiser. The latter in particular proved to be nothing more than a rumour, offering false hopes of a swift return home to the men in the trenches.

Back in Australia, on 17 June, the Herald of Melbourne reported that the following men had enlisted at the Brunswick Recruiting Depot on the preceding Thursday, then giving four names, of which Tom's brother John Southey Paterson Bulch, known to friends and family as Jack, was one. For a brief moment, both of Thomas Edward Bulch's sons were in uniform in the active service of their country, together. But it was really only to be a very brief time, for soon tragedy struck.

As the month had worn on in France, the shelling over the battlefield intensified. On 19 June, the Germans launched a heavy bombardment into the area where Sergeant Tom Bulch and his unit were serving, and he was injured by shrapnel from at least one exploding shell. Private Reid's diary on that day states:

> "Heavy shelling to both sides for 2 hours, 8 casualties. Serg Bulch fractured skull."

Tom was removed from the front and admitted to No. 2 Casualty Clearing Station with wounds to his head, hand and knee. On inspection of his helmet and head-wound, it was discovered that a fine sliver of shrapnel had pierced the helmet and entered his head. It's recorded that that this was the wound that caused his death, which occurred on the following day, 20 June 1916. News of this reached Private Reid, at the front, on the 21st. He recorded it in his diary. Almost immediately, the Red Cross Sister that managed the ward wrote a letter to Tom's wife, back in Australia, enclosing a lock of his hair. The letter would not reach Australia for some weeks, but when it did the grieving family arranged for it to be published in the Geelong Advertiser where it appeared on 22 August. It read:

> "Amid the many calls on the services at the clearing hospitals in France, some of the nurses find time to pen notes of sympathy to bereaved relatives. The following has been received by Mrs Bulch, of Geelong West, whose husband, Sergt. Bulch, a well-known bandsman, fell in action:- France 21 6 16. – Dear Mrs Bulch – I am very sorry to tell you that your husband was

brought in here to No. 2 casualty clearing station, severely wounded in the head, right hand, and left knee and quite unconscious, and though everything possible was done for him he passed away peacefully at 3 o'clock yesterday (Tuesday) morning, June 20th. He will be laid to rest in a part of the cemetery reserved for our brave troops, and a little wooden cross bearing the name and date marks each resting place. I enclose a lock of his hair you may like to have. With much sympathy, – Yours sincerely L F Jolley. Sister in charge."

Geelong & Melbourne

News of Tom's death had reached Victoria well before the letter. A number of newspapers around Victoria, and beyond, all reported Sergeant Bulch as among that week's confirmed war dead, though the Herald of Melbourne went a step further, printing a photograph of the young soldier alongside the following report:

"Relatives of Sgt T E Bulch have been notified that he has been killed in France. He joined the Australian Imperial Force as a private in a band and after spending some months in the trenches at Gallipoli he was promoted to bandmaster with the rank of Sergeant Bugler. Sergeant Bulch was the eldest son of Mr T E Bulch the well-known bandmaster and composer, and was born in Ballarat. He was 27 years of age and leaves a widow and two children. His only brother is in camp training."

On 8 July 1916, the Preston Leader of Victoria stated:

"Sergt. T E Bulch of 37 Victoria Road, Northcote, died of wounds in France on June 20. He was bandmaster for the 23rd Battalion and was attached to the Army Medical Corps."

The Australasian reported this on 15 July 1916

"Bulch. - Anzac Hero Bulch. – Killed in action on the 20th June, in France, Sergeant T E Bulch, dearly loved husband of Ivy, loving father of Thelma and Freddy, aged 27 years. Late of Geelong."

The Border Morning Mail and Riverina Times included in its obituary that Thomas was the son-in-law of Mr R B Cozens of

Albury. A few days later on the 20 July the same paper reporting on the Albury Town Band reads:

> "A more gratifying incident of the past year which could not be omitted from this report is the fact that four members of the band have gone to serve their country at the front, and were granted leave of absence. They were each made the recipient of suitable presentations prior to their departure, and we hope to have the pleasure of welcoming them back when peace is declared at no distant date. The bandsmen referred to are:– Charles Engel, Alex Morris, Percy Edwards, Leslie Pogson. Many ex-members of the band have also joined the colours, among them being Sergeant Tom Bulch, whose death has lately been reported, and the news of which has been received with deep regret by his old comrades here."

Tom was buried at Bailleul Cemetery in France; Plot 2 Row E. According to an account related by his sister, Adeline, to family, his helmet was sent for damage inspection to better understand how it had been penetrated, and was one of many later acquired by the British Museum. Tom's meagre personal effects were later returned to his wife, and consisted of an identity disc, a charm, card case, badges, a cotton bag and some letters and cards. This was typical of such lists of returned possessions. Soldiers owned, and carried, little beyond their military equipment. Tom's death must also have come as a terrible blow to his father and mother. We know, already, that Eliza had previously been anxious enough to write to the army about Tom's whereabouts and wellbeing. The family's mood would not have been improved any by the knowledge that their other son, Jack, was now to face similar dangers. Prior to enlisting he had worked as a pastry cook, but had taken an interest in the military and been a senior cadet with the 70th Infantry Battalion.

On enlisting, Jack, a bandsman like his brother, had been assigned to the 16th Reinforcements Military Band at Royal Park in Melbourne. He and his intake of troops had been scheduled to be sent to Europe on 2 October 1916. First, though, he had a personal engagement to fulfil. On 4 September, Jack Bulch was best man at the wedding of his friend Albert Henry Riddell of Footscray, Victoria who was marrying his sweetheart Elsie Louise Gratwick at St John's Anglican Church, Footscray. Both bridegroom and best man wore their military uniforms and the reception after the service was held in a marquee decorated in the 24th Battalion's colours. Towards the end of the speeches, a Mr Phillips proposed the toast of the 24th Battalion Reinforcements to which Albert was assigned. That Battalion would leave soon, bound for action:

> "The bridegroom and Private Bulch in responding to the toast thanked them for all their good wishes, and assure them all that they were out to win and do their best fearlessly with the hope that in the near future peace would be declared, but not before they had had time to strike a well-aimed blow at the Kaiser."

The article continues:

> "The happy couple motored to Footscray station and later left for Mordialloc, a charming little seaside resort, where they are staying till Private A H Riddell's leave expires."

At Mordialloc, that newly married couple spent their only time together. Albert Riddell was transported first to England, and then to France to serve at the front. He never returned to Australia. On 30 May 1918, he was severely wounded to the head chest and leg by shrapnel from a shell and died from his wounds.

Private John Bulch boarded the troopship, the Nestor, as planned and scheduled on 2 October, bound for Plymouth, England. There he disembarked on 16 November 1916 and stayed for the remainder of the year, awaiting allocation to the battlefront.

Of his father, Thomas Edward Bulch senior, no further news was published during the year 1916. There were no mentions of evenings at the piano accompanying the silent films, of smoke evenings, band meetings, new compositions or charity fundraising benefits. There are a handful of pieces that are reported in the papers for the first time during 1916, which include "En Avant," "Our Heroes Return," "To Arms" and "Torchlight Parade," though it is possible that these may be a little older. There were, as always, many reports of pieces he had created in years gone by being played by bands across the country, but of personal news there is nothing. We can be sure that he and Eliza were not inactive, but he seems to have withdrawn from the limelight. On 30 December 1916, he probably spent his birthday reflecting quietly on his fifty-four years of life, the loss of his son and whatever the remainder of his life might hold.

At some point between late 1916 and early 1917 Tom and Eliza moved away from Geelong, back to Melbourne, to take residence at 127 Stewart Street, Brunswick East. This was a small house that still stands today next to a tiny Gospel Church. The reason for this move is not documented, but we do know from the account of his life by grandson Eric Tomkins that Thomas continued his music publishing business from home, much as George was doing was in Shildon. Tom was definitely still selling his music as there are mentions in reports of band meetings. One example from the Windsor and Richmond Gazette of Feb 1917 that tells us that the Windsor Municipal Band bought two shillings and sixpence worth of music from him during the previous year.

There is one further thing that we do know, from official records, about Tom Bulch's activities in 1917. On 2 May, possibly motivated by his grief for his lost son, and wanting to make a contribution, Tom, once again, enlisted for home service in the Australian Imperial Force "only for such period as services be required." His enlistment application appears to be written in his own hand as the handwriting matches the signature quite closely, and the details are quite precise, explaining that he was born in the parish of Thickley in or near Bishop Auckland in the county of Durham, England and that he is a natural-born British citizen. Interestingly he gives his age as forty-five years and three months, or as he expressed it, three twelfths. We know this to be incorrect. He would have fifty-five five years of age, which would highly probably have been considered too old to be accepted into the Australian Army. He probably lied about this to ensure that he appeared eligible. He also details his previous military service with the 3rd Battalion Militia, in Ballarat, stating that he resigned.

An extra handwritten question has been added to the form which reads "Have you ever been convicted" to which the answer is "No." He gives his height as five feet, seven and a half inches tall and weight as ten-and-a-half stone. Complexion is recorded as 'dark', eyes 'brown', hair 'dark, and religion as Church of England. He received an immediate medical examination at Langwarrin, near the top of the Mornington peninsula south of Melbourne. Quite surprisingly, no issues were identified relating to his age being ten years older than he had stated, though had anyone considered his first period of service they would have understood that he would have had to be very young to have been bandmaster of the 3rd Battalion Militia in his mid-teens. The deception accepted, Tom was immediately made Sergeant Bandmaster of the Langwarrin Army Camp Band. Perhaps this was his motivation for re-enlisting. Perhaps he missed being in charge of a band so much that he felt to offer his services in a military capacity might be the way to satisfy that need. Or perhaps there was another motive.

Langwarrin Camp had, between 1914 and 1915, been a camp housing up to five-hundred German internees in generally poor conditions. It was a camp comprised mainly of tents, with inadequate washing and bathing facilities. What huts there were there had been built by the internees at their own expense, mainly on account of the tents being so thin that they leaked in bad weather. Whatever improvements there had been built by the hands of those same people. It had closed as an internment camp in 1915, with most internees being transferred to Holsworthy in New South Wales. However, a number of the former internees had stayed behind to work at the nearby venereal diseases hospital. It was effectively a prison camp and, as such, would have given Tom an opportunity to come face to face with Germans, Austrians and Turks; people whose nations were responsible for the death of his son. Perhaps this was part of his motive.

Those internees were not, however, prisoners of war in the sense of being serving military personnel captured in battle. Prior to the war, these internees had been citizens of the state of Victoria; the types of people Tom had entertained at socials and smoke evenings in years gone by. As well as any feelings of grief and anger, Tom might have remembered that misunderstandings over his own family origin earlier in the war might well have seen he and his children detailed there. By the time Tom had arrived at Langwarrin, the number of internees there had reduced significantly such that, by the end of the year, only 326 remained.

On 20 June 1917, Tom and Eliza, placed a 'memoriam' notice in The Age newspaper of Melbourne commemorating the anniversary of their son's death. It was accompanied by the following two lines of verse: "There is a link death cannot sever, Love and remembrance last forever." The notice also refers to their other daughters and son; Adelina, Myrtle, Alice and Jack, whom it notes is on active service. A further notice was placed on behalf of Sgt Bulch's wife Ivy and their two children Thelma and Fred. In the Geelong Advertiser on the same date, Sgt Tom Bulch's sister Alice placed her own memoriam notice.

> "In fond and loving memory of our dear brother, Sergeant Thomas E Bulch, died of wounds at No. 2 Casualty Clearing Station, France, June 20th 1916 aged 27 years. The supreme sacrifice. Dear to our memory, dear to my heart, Love for my brother will never part, I miss him, I mourn him, in silence unseen, and dwell on his memory of days that have been. – Inserted by his loving sister and brother-in-law, Alice and Norm, and Little Keith"

Though Tom and Eliza had lost their son to war, a photograph of Tom junior, in his military uniform, was always displayed in their home. Grandson, Eric, recalls that when he was very young it was hung over Tom's piano. He remembers how the pocket button of his uncle's uniform was undone in the photograph, and that as the photograph had been taken before Tom's promotion to sergeant, the couple had arranged to have Sergeant's stripes added to the picture. Tom had been promoted in the field, so the couple never had the opportunity to see the stripes on his uniform for themselves.

On 2 July, Tom's other son, Private Jack Bulch, commenced his journey from England, via the port at Folkestone, to Le Havre on the French coast, as part of a detachment to reinforce the 22nd Battalion at the front. He, and his comrades-in-arms aboard that transport, were to spend the remainder of the year on rotation between the horror of frontline trenches and the brief respite of the rearwards positions.

In early 1917 the Germans, whose numbers had thinned significantly through losses during the Battle of Verdun, had pulled back to the Hindenburg Line. This was a defensive position they had prepared during the winter, and which ran from Arras to Lafaux on the River Aisne. As part of the ANZAC 2nd Division, the 22nd Battalion were part of an allied initiative to break this defence. Before Jack arrived, the 22nd had played their part in the Battle of Bullecourt, and continued engagement through a number of offensive operations during the summer.

In the run up to October, the 22nd Battalion had been given time to prepare for what would be called the Battle of Broodseinde, fought against the 4th German Army near Ypres. On the night before 4 October, the Australian 2nd Division, Jack and his mates included, were brought up to the front line. As they made their journey the heavens opened and rain poured down. Once in position, the Division was subjected, from five-thirty in the morning onward, to a heavy bombardment by the German artillery. This caused many casualties, but ceased when an Allied preparatory bombardment commenced at six o'clock.

Above: Tom's other son, John Southey Paterson Bulch, known to friends as 'Jack', pictured after enlisting in the Australian Imperial Forces

This was the Australians' signal to advance. Along with the Australian 1st Division, they formed the main attack. Firing as they moved the Australians overran the German 45th Reserve and 4th Guard, many of whom were hiding out in ruins on the battlefield. Finally they reached the village of Broodseinde, their objective. Here the Australians met sniper, and machine-gun, fire and consolidated under cover in an old British trench line some 180 metres short of the village. Overall the Australians and New Zealanders in the week long battle suffered 3,500 casualties, but Jack Bulch was not among them. This, and the other engagements he took part in, must have been nothing short of both horrendous and terrifying. Though he was a survivor, the experiences he was subjected to must surely have left mental scars.

On 18 December, Jack was appointed to the rank of Lance Corporal, the same rank as Bill Allan. Unlike Bill, Jack had earned his promotion in the field. Bill was to be be spared the horrors of front line action.

Shildon

In New Shildon, away from the daily tragedies of front-line action in the war, life continued much as usual. George Allan continued his daily work at the North Eastern Railway works, which continued to produce additional items to support the war effort, alongside the usual building and maintaining freight and coal rolling stock. The Defence of the Realm Act, Regulation 7B, passed in December 1916 and applicable to all the railway companies of Britain, had ensured that those companies were playing their part in supporting the continuation of the hostilities. Nearby, at Darlington, the company had created a specialist war munitions factory. In Shildon's workshops, those skilled engineers that had not been drawn away to battle were also allotted work producing munitions items. These included machined nose-caps for six inch high-explosive shells and diaphragms and diaphragm discs for 18-pounder ammunition. It's not recorded whether George, the former blacksmith turned wagon painter, was involved in this war production, or whether he'd continued to work on the wagons that would, among other things, carry supplies to the front. He'd certainly have been reminded daily of the war. It's also thought likely that the significant Shildon railway sidings were used to store storage of truckloads of munitions and parts, awaiting delivery to the Empire's battlefronts.

Despite the daily reminders of war, an occasional happy event befell the Allan family. On Valentines Day, 14 February 1917, in the midst of one of the bitterest and harshest of winters, George made the short journey up the hill from his house, passing the Railway Institute and then along All Saints Road to his parish church. His role on that most appropriately chosen day was to give away his daughter's hand in marriage.

Beatrice Allan had met, and fallen in love with, a young man named John Robert Tenwick Appleby. John was a schoolmaster who had trained for education in York, but whose family had lived at North Terrace, Brusselton. This was, and still is, a tiny village just outside Shildon that was once famed for its powerful static steam engine that, almost a century previous, had hauled chains of coal trucks up the Brusselton Incline, and lowered them down the other side for the Stockton & Darlington Railway. Robert, as he preferred to be known, had enlisted into the Royal Army Medical Corps on 4 November 1915, giving his mother, Mary Hodgson, as his next of kin. He had originally signed up for home service only; but on 6 April 1916, and possibly under some pressure, he had further volunteered for overseas service opening up the possibility of serving at the front. So far, he had not received an overseas posting. He had, however, already risen via the rank of Corporal, to Sergeant. The couple's wedding was taking place during a period of home leave for Robert. The Daily Gazette for Middlesborough included a brief report the following day:

> "Shildon War Wedding. At All Saints Church, New Shildon, yesterday, Sergt. J R Appleby, of Brusselton, was married to Miss Beatrice Allan, of Pears Terrace, New Shildon. The bridegroom was on the teaching staff at All Saints School prior to enlisting and is now stationed with the R A M C at Tidworth. The bride is a member of All Saints Choir. The bridesmaid was Miss Crooks and Mr Stabler of Brusselton was best man. A silver teapot was given from All Saints Church Choir and a silver butter dish from the day school children. The vicar (the Rev. P W Francis) and the curate (the Rev J W Graham) officiated."

Reverend Graham was, at that time, also anticipating a happy day. His thirty-five-year-old wife Edith was pregnant with a son. 1917 would, however, turn out to be as bitter for him personally as the winter weather it had brought. His son would indeed be born on the 7 April that year, but his wife Edith would experience complications and die a week later on the 15 of April.

At around that same time, George's new son-in-law, Robert, was transferred back to the Royal Army Medical Corps Reserve on account of his progressive short-sightedness and being affected by a 'disordered action of the heart' which had additionally rendered him unsuitable for front line service. His newly assigned 'W Reserve' classification meant that Robert was able to return home, where he resumed his old job at All Saints School until such time as he might be called back to service. He immediately moved-in with his wife, Beatrice, and father-in-law George, at 2 Pears Terrace where he would continue to live until his eventual full discharge from the Army Reserve after the war in 1919.

As the war went on, food supply shortages bit more and more into everyday lives. Shildon, being a railway town, was somewhat fortunate in that the railway company, and the Railway Institute there, had provided workers with allotment land for many years, upon which they could grow food and keep small animals and poultry. The land immediately to the rear of the Railway Institute itself was divided up into such plots. In 1917 the North Eastern Railway increased their provision of allotment land and made new additional provisions such as the provision of allotment books and the free delivery of seed potatoes to any station on their railway network. Through his job at the works, George would have qualified for one of the designated plots in Shildon. With the bitter winter gradually becoming a memory, this increased amount of food grown by the railway workers offered some green shoots of hope for the future.

1917 was a year in which George also found a new vocation for his musical capabilities as we are informed that this was the year in which he became the conductor of the orchestra for the New Shildon All Saints Amateur Operatic Society. This group was the lesser acclaimed of the two operatic societies in the Shildons. The more highly regarded was the Shildon Amateur Operatic Society, whose regular conductor was George's acquaintance, Harry Gibbon. Both of these amateur operatics societies would rehearse and stage productions, many of which would be presented to the public at the town's own Hippodrome Theatre.

Lance Corporal Bill Allan also returned to Shildon for the Christmas of 1917, having been granted leave from his company for the festive season. By this time, it appears that the importance of both George Allan, and Tom Bulch, in their respective musical circles was fading. George had almost entirely ceased to advertise his published music in the small adverts of the brass press. Whether that was on account of the war, or of a general disillusionment, is hard to know. Similarly, in Australia, Tom had largely become no longer newsworthy. The first reference to him that I found in the Australian newspapers, during 1918, appears in the Ballarat Star where, at a meeting of the Citizens Military Band on Wednesday, 1 May, the band's secretary was noted as having read out correspondence from Tom Bulch who had also forwarded some sheet music for their attention. Tom's grandson, Eric, tells us that Tom continued to write and publish music from his home at 127 Stewart Street, Brunswick, throughout the war. This understanding is supported by new pieces being reported in these years, such as "Boys of ANZAC," "The Battle of Jutland," "Jamie Stewart's Birthday: Scotch Patrol," and "Bombardique." Otherwise though, like George, Tom and his work had become eclipsed by world events and the lives of his offspring.

Melbourne

On 16 January 1918, Thomas Edward Bulch, army number V65140, after 260 days of home service, resigned from his post as the bandmaster sergeant at Langwarrin Camp. A certificate of attestation was added to his military records by the 3rd Military District putting on record his clean conduct during his service. By that point in the war, there was probably little to be done at Langwarrin. It had been gradually run-down by the military authorities, and this may have influenced Tom's decision to stand down, despite the war not yet being concluded.

Before we leave Langwarrin, however, we pause briefly to tie up the end of a loose thread from earlier in Tom's story. 1918 also saw one of Tom's old friends arrive at Langwarrin, that being fellow former Shildonian, and bass playing bandsman from Tom's Ballarat bands, George Malthouse.

George Malthouse, it seems, had led a perpetually troubled life. You might recall that as a young boy, at six years of age, he had been separated from his brothers and sent to board with another family miles away from New Shildon. After relocating to Australia with his mother, stepfather and brothers, George had met and married Elizabeth Finch. Though he spent much of his spare time as one of Tom's bandsmen, he worked as a cabinet maker, a miner and a railway labourer, and his wife bore him seven children. But the couple's marriage had not been a happy one. Troubled George frequently turned to drink, and when doing so would assault his wife and frighten his children. Elizabeth later testified that George gave her black-eyes on several occasions, threatened her with an axe and an iron bar. From 1910 he was the subject of several court appearances in relation to his violent conduct and imprisoned twice. Elizabeth divorced him in 1911, referring to the assaults, and George's having taken to visiting houses of 'ill-fame', whereafter his mental health further suffered and he was admitted to Melbourne's Royal Park Psychiatric Hospital.

Above: Langwarrin Camp, where Tom served briefly in WWI and where George Malthouse spent some of his final days.

By 1916 George's mind had improved sufficiently for him to have been discharged. He soon sought to enlist and, as Tom Bulch had done, he lied to the recruiting officers about his age, claiming to be only forty-four years old. It quickly became apparent that he was in no condition to bear the rigours of military life and the Army discharged him on account of his mental weakness. George might well have attempted to turn to the army so that the discipline might save him from his inclination to alcohol. Released from the Army, he seems to have quickly rediscovered alcohol and by December was once again appearing in court on account of his drunkenness.

George Malthouse's tragic downward spiral eventually brought him to the Military Hospital at the camp at Langwarrin in 1918 where he passed away at the end of September. We don't know whether Tom and George Malthouse crossed paths at Langwarrin, but if they had it would surely have hurt Tom, with his temperance sensibilities, to have seen how far his old bandmate had fallen, how much pain he had caused, and that his journey through life had ended so sadly and wastefully.

1917 had seen the United States of America enter the Great War, bringing a change to the seemingly never ending conflict. The United States was never formally an 'ally' of the Triple Entente, but became an 'associated power'. By the Summer of 1918, that nation was shipping ten-thousand troops a day to France. In anticipation of the increasing American influence, the Germans commenced a Spring Offensive of surprise bombardments and mass offensives, seeking to divide the British and French armies. They had limited successes, but eventually retreated back to the River Marne with little strategic gain. In Germany itself, anti-war sentiment was strengthening and industrial output declined significantly.

20 June 1918, brought a further memoriam notice, published in Melbourne's Argus newspaper. This was placed, again, by Ivy, Tom junior's wife:

> "Bulch. – In memory of my dear husband and our loving father, Sergeant T E Bulch, died of wounds in France, June 20 1916. Sadly missed."

Nine days later, on 29 June, there was another death in the extended Bulch family. This time one that would have elicited much less grief for Tom, and his brothers and sisters back in Britain. Their stepmother, Margaret, the former widow of

Cuthbert Harrison and who had been born Margaret Brass, had passed away at the age of seventy-four, at what had once been the Bulch family home at 48 Adelaide Street, New Shildon. None of the Bulch siblings would have forgotten how, shortly after she had married Tom's father, he, whether prompted by Margaret or not, had disinherited them all in favour of Margaret and her daughters. Margaret's burial, recorded in the Parish Magazine of All Saints Church, took place on the 3rd July, with the service being performed by Mr Rees. She was buried in plot 658 at a depth of seven feet. Probate of her will did not take place until 30 January 1919, whereupon the last remnants of Tom's's legacy were passed on to Margaret's daughters Mary Jane Harrison and Alice Harrison, both of whom were spinsters at the time. We believe that her only son, Fredrick, once a wagon painter like George Allan, had died in 1909. The estate was valued £362 1s and 4d. If the news reached Tom and Eliza at Brunswick, Victoria, it would be forgivable if they felt little regret at her passing. Margaret had given Tom's father comfort in his later years, but would most likely have earned little appreciation among the wider family.

Peace

In France, Lance Corporal Jack Bulch was still living out a hard life at the battlefront, and contracted a sickness which saw him posted to a military hospital on 27 June. His malaise was only temporary, and by the 3rd of July he was discharged and sent back to duty. The allied armies began a counter-offensive against the Germans on the 8 August; an operation which became known as the Hundred Days Offensive and included the Battle of Amiens. The German generals steadily began to realise that they would no longer be able to win the war militarily. The allied armies broke through the defensive Hindenburg Line in September, fuelled by a seemingly inexhaustible supply of oil which had been acquired largely through American intervention in the war. An open revolt erupted in Germany, which led to the abdication of the Kaiser as head of state, and the declaration of a new Republic on 9 November. At eleven o'clock on the 11 November 1918 an armistice declaration was signed, finally bringing an end to this hitherto bloodiest of conflicts.

That declaration was not yet the signal for troops to lay down their arms and return home to their wives, sweethearts and families. There was still work to be done to tie up the loose threads of the war. In England, Bill Allan was retained for a few months longer to D Company of the Durham Light Infantry's Machine Gun Corps Training Battalion, whilst Jack Bulch patiently remained with his unit in France.

We learn from the Geelong Advertiser, of 27 November 1918, that people of Geelong, encouraged by the Mayor and Mayoress, had been collecting, and arranging transport of, relief packages of foodstuffs to send to their Australian boys and men at the front. We know also that Jack had been the recipient of a parcel of such goods as that same report explains how he had written back to the Geelong West Soldier's Comforts Club to express his appreciation.

The cessation of hostilities enabled communities to plan celebrations in anticipation of seeing their surviving loved ones return home. In Victoria the Essendon Citizens Military association met on the 6th of December to plan a number of initiatives, including the erection of an Honour Board at the Town Hall referring to a Brigadier General Elliott, a significant local heroic figure, and organising a band contest to which they invited Tom Bulch to be the judge. He, in turn, wrote back to accept and set out his terms of engagement.

Back in Shildon, Bill Allan was, again, given leave to return home to Henrietta for Christmas. For him, home was no longer George's house at 2 Pears Terrace. Bill's military papers had been updated to registered his home address as being his in-law's home 6 Bolckow Street. It's almost certain that he'd have spent at least some time with his father, George. Whilst relishing this brief serenity of the festive season away from the Army, he must have anticipated a permanent return home, and hoped it would not, now, be long in coming. If he had, he would have been right. On the 13 January 1919, Bill was ordered to attend the Ripon Dispersal Centre, Rugeley, to be demobilised from the army. His military service papers were updated to reflect that his conduct throughout his service years had been clean, and he was reclassified as an army reservist, to be recalled should his country require him again.

Many at that time regarded the Great War of 1914 to 1918 as having been the war to end all wars, anticipating that the unprecedented scale of aggression, devastation, horror and bloodshed would signal a new era in which such folly could never, and would never, be repeated. This notion that humanity had somehow learned a great lesson would prove naive when, less than two decades later it was, arguably, surpassed in terms of the creativity of destruction and terror, by the second such war that sprang once again from the roots of the first. Bill Allan would, indeed, don the military khaki again; though on that second occasion it would be the uniform of the Home Guard as part of Shildon Works's own home defence unit.

Jack Bulch had to wait just a little longer for his discharge. He, and his unit, had been relocated back across the English Channel on the 16 May 1919 where they were camped temporarily until arrangements could be made to get them all back to Australia. Jack was ordered to embark the troop-ship Chemnitz on the 7 July 1919. That particular ship had been sailing under a German flag until the surrender, whereafter it was handed over to the allied forces and prepared for use as a military transport ship. Once that was done it was designated for use in returning the Australian forces to their homeland. Having been launched in 1901, she was a 7,542 gross ton vessel, 428.2 feet in length with a beam measuring of 54.3 ft. She had one funnel, two masts, a twin screw propellor and a top speed of thirteen knots.

While Jack was resting easy at last with his comrades, and possibly getting in some band practice with them, Dunn's Gazette of 24 June 1919 shows that Tom and Eliza registered the business name of "Bulch and Co." at 127 Stewart Street, Brunswick as a music publishing business. A matter of interest is that Eliza appears to have taken care of Tom Bulch's copyright affairs. An item in the Commonwealth of Australia Gazette of 17 July 1919 shows Eliza having been granted copyright on the name of Bulch's Brass Band Journal. It reads:

> "Proceedings under the Copyright Act 1912. List of Applications for the registration of the copyright in literary (including musical and dramatic) and artistic works and the performing rights in musical and dramatic works under the Copyright Act 1912. 1st April to 30 June 1919. Literary Copyright Applications."
> "7587. Eliza Ann Bulch trading under the name of style of Bulch & Co., 127 Stewart Street Brunswick, Vic – Journal: "Bulch's Brass Band Journal." 16th June, 1919"

The troopship Chemnitz's voyage back to Melbourne was documented photographically by one of the returning soldiers by the name of Holloway. From his candid snapshots we get a visual impression of how the experience must have been for those battle-weary young men. Decks are crowded with ANZAC troops, with little to keep them occupied or entertained during the long voyage. Occasionally officers would inspect the men, possibly to give them a routine with a view to keeping order. A military Padre accompanied them holding services out on the open deck on Sundays. In most of the photographs, the men appear relaxed and casual, though in actuality many would most likely still be traumatised by their experiences and could well have been experiencing mental difficulties. The joyous news of Jack's imminent return reached Australia, prompted his sister to place a notice in the Geelong Advertiser of 9 August 1919 which read:

> "Mrs N B Johnson of 'Noralla', Albert Street, Geelong West has been notified that her brother Cpl. Jack Bulch is returning by the Chemnitz, due to arrive on August 24th."

Worthy of note, there, that the couple had chosen to name their house after the waltz Tom Bulch had composed in their honour. It was not, however, until 5 September that the Chemnitz finally arrived at port in Melbourne. On arrival at the jetty, the men of the 22nd Battalion lined-up on deck, overlooking rows of motor transports that waited on the harbour side to take them all to their barracks. As much as they may all have wanted to head straight home to their families, they would not yet be fully released from military duty. We do know, though, that although Jack didn't receive his full discharge until 20 October 1919, he was allowed to go home to Geelong before that date. The Geelong Advertiser tells of his homecoming on the evening of Monday, 10 September:

> "The Geelong City Band turned out in force last night to welcome home Cpl. J Bulch, a former member, who returned home by the late train. As the train pulled in they played "Home Sweet Home," and later gave Cpl. Bulch a rousing welcome. At his sister's (Mr Johnson's) residence, Albert Street, West Geelong, where they marched and serenaded the returned soldier, who was a member of the City Band for six years."

If ever there was a demonstration of the camaraderie felt by men and boys who played music together in a brass band this must surely offer a tremendous example. It's likely that, of the men of that band that went to war, not all would have returned, and so to see one safely back on home soil this way would be a joyful occasion. We know nothing of any reunion between Jack and his father, though there would certainly have been one, and that too would most likely have been a happy moment. The war was now in the past, though could never be never entirely forgotten by the Bulch family as it had taken Tom junior from them forever.

Melbourne & Sydney

Tom Bulch found himself gradually returning to judging a few band contests in peacetime. One opportunity arose through the Essendon Citizens Military Association, who engaged Tom to judge at their Band Contest and Sports Meeting on the Queens Park, Moonee Ponds which took place in March 1920 and was reported in Melbourne's Herald newspaper on the 27th of that same month. Seven bands competed on that occasion, hoping to capture the Sutton Shield. As was now the long established custom with Australian contests, points were awarded for quality of marching as well as musical perfection. For this reason, Tom was accompanied by fellow judge, Captain H J Grainger, for his expertise in knowing what made a good marching band. The band from Moonee Ponds were top in the street marching, but on musical performance finished second to Ascot Vale in the Sutton Shield, and were followed by the Malvern band in third place.

A few days later there was a Bulch family wedding to attend. On 5 April 1920, Tom's daughter, Myrtle May Bulch, was married in Sydney to Charles Tomkins. Charles was the son of a family from Havelock Street, Ballarat. The newly-wedded couple initially set up home in the district of Greenwich, North Sydney, New South Wales. Consequently, as happens with many families over time, Tom's sons and daughters were becoming increasingly widely distributed. We're told, by Myrtle and Charles's son Eric, that when the young couple moved to Sydney, Tom and Eliza went with them. The family briefly remained in Greenwich, but not long afterward moved to a rented house in Sydney's Mascot suburb situated south of the city's centre and just to the north of Botany Bay.

Above: Tom and Eliza's three daughters, Alice Bertha, Adeline Maud and Myrtle May Bulch photographed around 1915 - a fourth daughter sadly died in infancy.

This moving to be with Charles and Myrtle proved timely, as another side effect of ending of the Great War was a fully understandable general fatigue with anything military throughout the population. People broadly, if not entirely, wanted to embrace a new peace-time aesthetic. Consequently, many of Tom's military-themed marches he'd been selling in Brunswick lost their appeal, and sales had declined making it harder to get by. There were still many references to his older compositions being played in concert, or at contest, by bands throughout the 1920s; so they did remain a significant part of the banding culture for a good while longer. As Tom's services as a bandmaster were no longer in demand, he relied upon teaching and selling music to make a living. It made sense for the family to consolidate, so Charles Tomkins arranged accommodation for the whole family.

The music publishers W H Paling & Co, who were based in Sydney, offered Tom a lifeline. They invited him to work for them as an arranger and transposer of music. As his own business had been running flat it made sense for him to accept the post.

After a while of living with his daughter and son-in-law, Tom and Eliza acquired their own home at 86 King Street, Mascot, a move likely made possible through the security of having taken the job with Paling & Co. We sense, throughout his life though, that Tom much preferred to be his own boss.

Ever adaptable, he became an expert in preparing and arranging music for the pianola; the remarkable mechanical self-playing pianofortes that required 'programming' through the production of perforated paper rolls. The holes in the paper denoted when certain keys were required to be struck in order to construct the tune. Such machines had been around for many decades but were being quite aggressively marketed in the early twentieth century. At a time when recorded music was still thin-sounding, a pianola would produce natural and full sounding music automatically, making it sound as though a skilled musician were present. They still, of course, required the work of a skilled musician to create the first programmed imprint. Over time, Charles and Myrtle later moved away slightly to the St Leonard's district to be closer to Charles's workplace.

Twilight

Back in Shildon, in 1920, George Allan, continued sharing his home with his daughter and his son-in-law. By now he was midway through his sixth decade and continuing his daily labours at the railway works. Despite the end of the war, the times and the local and national economies were far from stable, and his working conditions and pay fluctuated. On 2 April 1920, he was given a pay-rise to four shillings and ten pence, which then on 4 June was again increased to five shillings and fourpence, only to be reduced again in August of 1921 to four shillings and fourpence; a rate lower than where it had started the previous year. George continued to publish music, but it was quite infrequent and extremely rarely advertised.

On the 20 April 1921 Bill and Henrietta gave George his first granddaughter. They named the little girl Dorothy Allan. In that same year we also learn that George and Tom's old Shildonian bandmate, and Tom's successor as conductor of his Bulch's Model Band, James Scarffe had moved to Melbourne to conduct the Malvern Tramway Band. That same year a memorial was installed and unveiled at the Railway Institute, detailing the names of members of that organisation that had served, and in thirty cases given their lives, during the Great War. This tribute comprised of three brass panels, and featured the North Eastern Railway company crest, for almost all those remembered upon it were employed by the company. It was a time for deep reflection, and on his visits to the Institute, George would have seen those names and remembered those men he'd likely have seen there or at the works.

On 18 October 1922, the world of music was further revolutionised when the British Broadcasting Company was formed by a number of wireless radio manufacturing companies including the Marconi company. The BBC wasn't the first company in Britain to broadcast, as Marconi themselves held that honour, broadcasting that from their factory in Chelmsford from June 1920. Interestingly they opened their broadcasting by treating the somewhat limited public audience to a performance by the Australian singer Dame Nellie Melba, whom Tom Bulch and his band had welcomed to Albury decades earlier. In those early days, new radio companies broadcast only scheduled live performances rather than recorded music. This, however, afforded composers like George and Tom an entirely new opportunity. Throughout the decades past, to hear bands playing any music that they had composed, the composer would need to be present at the contest or concert when it was being played. This new wireless era meant that George might spot in the published and printed broadcast schedules that one of his pieces was due to be played, and then he might hear the band play it via the wireless radio set. Though he may not have known this at first, it was certainly something he could look forward to.

On 14 May 1923, George's son, Bill, joined him at the railway wagon works, moving straight in to work alongside his father as a wagon painter. Shildon's railway works had always had a reputation for this, with family connections and a good reputation generally always assuring a man work. The remembrance ceremony in November saw the unveiling of the town's main war memorial, as a band from nearby colliery village of Eldon provided music; then in December George advertised his grand Christmas numbers from this, and the previous four years, in the Brass Band News.

> "CHRISTMAS MUSIC. No. 1: "Star of the East," &c. No. 2: "Glad Voices," &c. No. 3: "Greenlands," &c. No. 4: "Hosanna."

&c. No. 5: "Walworth." &c. Each contains 3 Choruses and 3 Hymns. Per Number, 2s 7d (23 parts). – ALLAN, Publisher. New Shildon"

In 1921, Jack Bulch had married his sweetheart, Linda Irene Riddell, a pianist who thus shared his own interest in music. By 1923 they the couple had given Tom and Eliza another granddaughter, Irene Alberta, strengthening the Australian branch of the Bulch family. By this time Alice and her husband also had a son, Keith, born in 1915; Myrtle May and her husband had two sons, John Charles and Eric Stanley; and Thomas Edward junior had left behind children, Thelma Evelyn, and two sons, Eric Leslie and Fredrick Norman, now in the care of his widow Ivy Mae. Were it important to him, Tom could be assured that, despite his own advancing years, a new dynasty of the Bulch family had been founded in Australia.

Tom seemed to have begun to start taking life a little easier, if only in terms of finding attention in the press. Jack and his new wife seem to have taken on the task of providing musical entertainment. They were in attendance at a reception after the wedding of Mr Edward Howard Barclay to Miss Katie Nissen on the 17 March, at a house called "Emoh" on Paisley Street, Footscray. There, along with a Mr T Riddell, who played violin, Jack and his wife completed an entertaining trio on cornet and piano respectively. Whether this was done as a favour for friends or whether the couple made themselves available for this kind of engagement is uncertain. We suspect the former as we found no further stories of this happening.

Where Tom did appear in the press throughout this late era of his life, other than the numerous mentions of bands playing his compositions and arrangements as part of their programmes, it was usually as part of a retrospective. One article in the Albury Banner and Wodonga Express of 2nd November 1923, summarises the history of the Albury Town Band recollecting Thomas's appointment there, which we covered earlier, describing him as "one of the best-known bandsmen in Australia." That piece goes on to point out that his arrival was the cause of the introduction of the Easter Monday competitions in Albury, which ended the year after Thomas left Albury. It is a clear indication of the importance that Tom placed on encouraging bands to compete to improve their playing and professionalism. The article goes on to explain that Mr D B

Pogson, who replaced Tom as part of his his acrimonious removal, was in poor health at the time of his arrival in Albury, and lived only twelve months. He was succeeded by his son who returned from America to take on the post.

There's evidence, from the early 1920s, that Thomas hadn't finished composing. New pieces, such as the selection "Sons of the Empire," and waltz "Queen of the Rink," began to be reported as being performed alongside some of his evergreen older titles that remained popular; "Austral," "Tasma," "Sydney By Night," "The Empire," and "Reminiscences of Weber" to name but a few. Now also in his autumn years, Tom, was afforded that luxury of occasionally being able to enjoy bands playing his music from the comfort of his home. The first Australian radio broadcast had taken place in August 1919, when Ernest Fisk, of Amalgamated Wireless Australasia Limited, arranged for a broadcast of the National Anthem after a lecture. Wireless Australasia was a joint venture between the Marconi company, who were pioneering radio in Britain, and its rival company Telefunken. By 1921, amateur organisations were being granted broadcast licenses and the airwaves across Australia opened up. Again, the broadcast music was generally performed live, with any and every missed note or error exposed to the listening public. By the middle of the nineteen-twenties, Tom, listening in Sydney, would have been able to hear the likes of the Kogarah Municipal Band playing his intermezzo "Miranda" on 1 February 1925, or the Newtown Band play his march "Newtown" the previous day. On Monday, 2 March, he could have listened to the Mordialloc Citizens Band rendering his "Les Fleurs D'Australie" or "Austral." Through the power of wireless radio broadcasting, his music was reaching new audiences. Contemplating this technological advance for a few moments, you have to wonder what that experience must have been like for a composer denied such opportunity for most of their musical career, and whether a judge, critic and perfectionist, like Tom, found each broadcast performance of his pieces a pleasure and wonder or an irritation.

In terms of other ways his time was spent in his later years, we're told that Tom, who had an interest in horse racing, would occasionally attend race meetings at Randwick with his son-in-law, Charles. Even this involved music. It was still common for the race meetings to feature a brass band, which would provide music between the races to keeping the racegoers entertained.

Of course this, in particular, drew Tom's attention. He'd often hear the bands play one or more of his own pieces, and would remark not only upon the performance by the band, but also how he might have improved upon the composition himself. Such is the curse of the perfectionist as a creator, never being quite satisfied with what they have produced.

As his years advanced, his grandson tells us that Tom's health was gradually failing him, and that this caused him to eventually retire from his job with Paling & Co. In spite of this, he never gave up his love for music, composition or publishing new works. He fell back upon his abilities as a music teacher. Where he had once taken on whole bands as students, he now took on individual students from the surrounding local community and taught them piano, violin or cornet. Grandson Eric remembers seeing a brass plaque on the door of his grandparents' house, pronouncing Tom's trade as a music teacher. A string of letters after his name set out his qualifications both in teaching music and a Diploma from the London College of Music. As this latter body was founded in 1887, this qualification must have been acquired through examinations taken in Australia during his adulthood. We understand that this was a service which that particular college offered.

In between teaching and composing, Tom and Eliza also kept a vegetable garden to the rear of their house, which they maintained well as a steady source of fresh food. Tom kept the remnants of his music publishing business in a shed to the rear of their home. The publishing business had ceased when the couple left Brunswick, Melbourne. Now these reams of unsold sheet music and lead type for the printing press sat dormant. This information does give us a clue as to how Tom may have countered the issue of not having been able to send his handwritten manuscripts to Germany during the war. It appears that he had adapted, once again, and begun to print music himself. Tom's music was still available to buy. Rights to some of it had been bought over the decades by the bigger publishing companies, and a music shop in Mascot stocked his self-published works on his behalf. His son, Jack, also retained a good selection of it where he and his wife lived in Coburg. This too was offered for sale. It's a fair expectation, though, that his works were not as widely distributed or available as had been the case when he enjoyed better health.

On 24 October 1925, it was announced, in the Geelong Advertiser, that Sergeant Thomas Edward Bulch's name was been among the many received to be included on a planned Peace Memorial that would be built in Geelong to commemorate sons of the district lost in the war. An appeal was lodged requesting that friends, employers and parents submitted any other names that might otherwise be missing from the list, so as to ensure that every lost man should be represented when the memorial was built.

1925 proved also to be a significant year for George Allan. According to the London and North Eastern Railway Company's wage books, George retired from his railway engineering job on the 17th of February, after forty-three years in the service of the company. The 1921 Railways Act, had merged Britain's plethora of railway companies into four larger companies, often referred to as the Big Four, making the LNER his employer for his last few years as a wagon painter.

Following this retirement, George made a decision to give up his house on Pears Terrace, making a move to live with his daughter Beatrice and her husband Robert, at 4 Osbourne Terrace, Leeholme; a village less than three miles away from the clash and clatter of Shildon's rail works. This part of Leeholme would have been a quieter spot, though still offered an industrial vista as the house overlooked the southern edges of the working colliery there. It's unclear whether there was a health factor influencing George's decision to relocate; though his wife had been gone fourteen years previous, and his children were now grown up with lives, homes and families of their own. It might have made economic sense to move. Three people could live together more affordably than one. Shildon was still close, so he could maintain his conducting commitments to the All Saints Amateur Operatic Society.

George's retirement did present an opportunity to dedicate more time to composing new music. He created, and published, a number of fine new pieces in that era, all of which featured his new Osbourne Terrace, Leeholme, address beneath their titles. These included the fabulous contest march "Belmont," almost a rival for his greatest works, as well as "La Rustica," "Pendragon" and "The Diplomat".

1925 also presented George with a rare opportunity to return to the contest adjudicator's tent. The 27 September 1925 was the date of the Centenary Celebration of the beginning of the world's first public steam-hauled passenger railway, which had famously started from Shildon when George Stephenson's Locomotion No. 1 was attached to a train of coal wagons brought by horse and rope from Witton Park among the hills to the west. Some of the wagons, and a specially built single carriage, contained passengers that day, making this a world first. The train had set out from the Masons Arms crossing, via Darlington and Yarm, to coal staithes on the River Tees, to be transported to markets by ship. The passing of a hundred years since this occasion warranted a grand celebration, which is just what the local authorities in the region had planned.

The Shields Daily News of 20 June 1925 set out the timing of the entertainments for these 1925 Stockton and Darlington Railway Centenary celebrations. The Duke and Duchess of York were due to arrive by train at Darlington's Bank Top Station at a quarter to three in the afternoon on 1 July to witness the proceedings. On the following day, a procession of 'old and modern locomotives' would parade along a section of the old Stockton and Darlington Railway route. Later, at half past five, in Stanhope Park, a band contest would take place featuring only Darlington bands. It had been organised by the Darlington Corporation, whom, the newspaper said, were offering valuable prizes for both March contest, in which bands could choose which piece to play, and the more complex test piece "Les Huguenots." The report goes on to explain that the adjudicator was to be George Allan of Leeholme, Bishop Auckland. There is some indication in this that, though he had stepped back from being a bandmaster and judge for some years, he was still held in sufficient high regard by the local brass band community. After the band contest had taken place, George awarded the top prize for the test piece to the Cockerton Band, as best on the day, followed in second and third place by the bands of Darlington Forge and Darlington British Legion respectively.

There was further loss, too, for George in 1925. On 28 September, his mother, still resident at the former Allan family home of 68 Adelaide Street, New Shildon, passed away. According to her death certificate, Hannah passed away aged eighty-eight through 'senile decay,' at home, with her son John Robert Allan, of Bryonia, Central Parade, Shildon, in attendance. She was buried on the thirtieth at All Saints Church in New Shildon. There is an implication that she was buried with her husband, John James Allan, as records indicate she was buried at a depth of only five feet.

Despite George being still musically active, he was no longer newsworthy, and no further reports of his activities or musical compositions appear in newspapers. However, some earlier researchers into his life have passed on a couple of, mainly second-hand, verbal accounts that offer a little additional insight. A few decades ago, an old Shildon bandsman named Jack Kitching had a brief exchange with Bob Wray, a bandsman himself, and enough of a fan of George's music to look a little deeper into his life. Kitching, a cornet player in Shildon Town Band, related that, as he himself had started playing with brass bands in around 1926 or 1927, he had not been personally acquainted with George. His music teacher, however, a gentleman named Bob Collinson, had told Jack what a good grasp of musical theory George had possessed, and how he had helped Collinson from time to time with his musical problems.

Another personal account from George's later years came from a bandsman who played with Leasingthorne Colliery Band in the 1950s; some years after George's death. He had been told that when George was living at Leeholme after his retirement, he would take his march compositions along to the Leasingthorne Colliery Band to hear them played through. Leasingthorne was the village adjacent to Leeholme and within sight, across the fields from the front windows of George's house. The Leasingthorne Band may have rehearsed in Leeholme, at its Welfare Hall, which has recently been replicated at the Beamish Museum. The bandsman relating that news claimed that he had heard it from William "Kettle" Hughes, the musical director of Leasingthorne Band from 1923 to 1953. Hughes, was a stocky euphonium player who at one time ran a pub in nearby Coundon. If the account is correct, it would explain how George tested his later marches and compositions before publishing them.

We were not entirely surprised by this news, as we do have evidence of the Leasingthorne Colliery Band playing George's music, and not just the pieces he created whilst at Leeholme. For example, a newspaper report from the Hull Daily Mail of 15 August 1926 tells us that at around nine o'clock on that evening, the Leasingthorne Colliery Prize Band played a rendition of George's most famous contest march "Knight Templar" broadcast live from the BBC's Newcastle radio studio. If they were able to perform that piece well, they would certainly have been the calibre of brass band that George would respect and trust to test his music.

The dawn of the radio era exposed George, and his music, to new and wider audiences. Bands hearing that broadcast of "Knight Templar," for example, would be able to hear how fine a march it was, and perhaps desire to buy it and have their band give it a try. In return, the broadcasts also gave him opportunities to hear his own works played by new bands. Other examples include a broadcast on 7 August 1923, where the North Seaton Workingmen's Brass Band played "Belmont," and another on 24 March 1924, where the Aldershot Prize Silver Band performed "Boscombe" from the Bournemouth Radio station's studio.

Al Fine

It's probable that, between 1925 and 1930, George Allan and Tom Bulch did a great deal more than we are able to account for. They certainly don't seem to be the types of men to have settled for inactivity. Despite being retired, in most respects, they were probably young enough to remain mentally sharp.

The challenge we have, though, is that records of the activity of the two during this last decade of their lives are extremely scarce, leaving us little to work with other than the remembrances of family members that spent some of these autumn years with them.

Bob Wray, the admirer of George Allan whom I mentioned earlier, had conducted some research into George Allan, back in the mid nineteen-eighties, which he was kind enough to share with me when he learned we had started our own research. At that time George's grand-daughter Dorothy Allan was still alive and resident in Shildon. Dorothy never married and remained childless. In those years, the Shildon Town Band, which she tells us evolved from the Shildon Wesleyan Band, was still a going concern. Dorothy explained that George had no conducting relationship to either the Wesleyan or Shildon Town bands. But Bob was able to discover, whether from Dorothy or otherwise, that George had been conductor of the orchestra for the New Shildon Amateur Operatic Society in their productions of, among others, "The Gondoliers," "Merrie England" and "Iolanthe." Dorothy did say, of George, that when she was very young she found him to be "a very kind and quiet man" and explained that her mother, Henrietta, held him in "high esteem." She also recalled that though George had been born into a musical family, her remembrance, from family discussions, was that he was largely self taught.

Above: George Allan in later years, during his time as conductor of the New Shildon All Saints Amateur Operatic Society

Toward the end of Dorothy's own life, there was a revival of interest in her grandfather's music within the town as during the nineteen-nineties, under the auspices of the Shildon Town Band and their musical director Graeme Scarlett, a George Allan Memorial Band Contest was inaugurated. Though it only ran for a brief few years, bands from across the region gathered in Shildon to compete for a trophy dedicated in his name. Alas, the venture was expensive to organise, particularly with the imperative to offer appealing prizes, and the motivation to keep it up gradually faded. Surplus funds from the final year of the venture were spent installing the memorial stone, opposite the Town Square in Shildon, which was a trigger for my own commencement of researching this story. Though the George Allan Memorial Band Contest is no more, it has played its part in a chain of ensuring his ongoing remembrance and legacy. We shall return to the contest in a short while, but for now we need to consider George's own end.

Throughout his life, George had, in many respects always been a few steps behind Tom Bulch. He was born later, became a bandmaster later, become a published composer later, married later, a home owner later, a contest judge later and had even commenced to make his name as a music publisher after Tom. Yet he was the first of the two to bring a conclusion to his story. On 16 March 1930, just a few days before his sixty-sixth birthday, George passed away at his home at 4 Osborne Terrace, Leeholme. His ending had been caused by a combination of chronic bronchitis and an aortic regurgitation with chronic nephritis. According to the death certificate, his son Bill was with him at the time of his death. An announcement was printed in the Northern Echo and Evening Despatch:

> "Allan. At 4 Osbourne Terrace, Leeholme, on 16th. George aged 66 years beloved husband of the late Elizabeth Allan (formerly of Shildon). Internment will take place at All Saints' Churchyard, Shildon on Wednesday at 3 o'clock. Cortege leaving residence at 2.20 p.m."

He left an estate totalling £1,658 3 shillings and 11 pence, to be divided between his three children, William Willoughby Allan, Lillie Lewis and Beatrice Appleby. In terms of equivalent value in 2020, George's estate would now be close to £96,000. Though he had not become incredibly wealthy from his music and work, he was certainly not impoverished. The Auckland and County Chronicle newspaper of 27 March 1930 described the burial:

> "The internment took place at Shildon All Saints Churchyard last Wednesday of Mr George Allan, 4 Osbourne Terrace, Leeholme. Mr Allan was a native of Shildon, and worked at the LNER shops for over 40 years. He retired five years ago and

came to live with his daughter. He was the bandmaster of the Saxhorn Brass Band and also the conductor of the Shildon All Saints Operatic Society from its inauguration until two years ago. During later years he spent a great deal of time in composing band music, for which there was a great demand, and his pieces have won first prizes with first-class bands in all parts of the country. Mr Allan had reached the age of 63 years and was held in the highest respect in the Shildon District. The Rev. Mr J Llewellyn conducted a service in All Saints' Church and also performed the last rites. The chief mourners were, Mr & Mrs T E Lewis (son-in-law and daughter), Mr and Mrs J R T Appleby (son-in-law and daughter), Mr and Mrs W W Allan (son and daughter-in-law), Mr W Allan, Spennymoor, (brother), Mr and Mrs J R Allan, Shildon (brother and sister-in-law), Mr E Allan, Darlington (brother), Mrs Birtle, Middlesbrough (sister-in-law), Mr W Allan (nephew), Mrs Birkbeck (his brother's wife) and Mrs Middlemass (sisters-in-law)."

George was buried on 19 March 1930 at a depth of five feet suggesting that he was buried in a shared plot with his wife Elizabeth. It's difficult to confirm this though as the local authorities purged the cemetery of old and loose gravestones during the nineteen-nineties leaving most of the older rows of graves unmarked. Additionally, though records exist, at the Durham County Archives, concerning the dates of interment there is now no record of specific burial locations.

After his father's death, Bill Allan, doubtless influenced by his father's teaching, continued to represent the Allan family within the banding community of Shildon. He was a baritone horn player with Shildon Town Band. He did not share his father's desire to compose or conduct. He continued to live and work in Shildon, and when the Second World War broke out his former military experience was brought back to the fore as he served as a sergeant in the Home Guard as part of the No. 9 Shildon Works Company. In January of 1942, his company were winners of the 15th Durham Shooting Competition, resulting in Bill being photographed with the competing marksmen of his company and their captain along with the works manager and assistant works manager. His time as an instructor with the the Durham Light Infantry and Machine Gun Corps would have been useful in training the men of the Home Guard. He remained in Shildon until his own passing in March 1976. George's daughters, Lillie and Beatrice, moved to Spennymoor with their husbands, living until 1970, and 1962, respectively.

We have no idea at all whether Tom Bulch received news of George Allan's passing, and can only speculate. By the time of George's death, there was very little Bulch family presence in Shildon so it's quite likely that the event probably wasn't relayed to Tom in Sydney. Likewise, nothing appeared, that we know of, in the British banding papers that might have been exported, making it unlikely that Tom would hear about it that way.

Above: Tom Bulch in his later years in the garden to the rear of his house in Sydney with his grandchildren

Tom's own health had been in decline throughout his autumn years, though he refused to relinquish his passion for music. Grandson, Eric, has written of how Tom continued to take pupils and teach music, and would closet himself in the lounge of their house in Mascot with students. He remembers Tom also spending much time composing at the piano, and one specific occasion when he and his brother had been playing boisterously around his grandfather's house, whereupon Tom came out from the lounge and said "Piano! Piano!" Not understanding, the boys asked their father, Charles Tomkins, what was meant. Charles, thought to have once been a member of Tom's band in Ballarat, knew the Italian terms for musical expression that were part of Tom's everyday vocabulary, and explained that he meant "Softly! Softly!." It had been his plea that they might play quietly so that he might be less disturbed.

Eric also shared a photograph with us, of Tom in the back garden of his Mascot home, with his grandchildren. It's a tender family intergenerational moment depicting Tom, clean shaven and grey haired, slender and aged, in shirt and waistcoat and seated in a wheeled chair - not quite a wheel-chair - but suggesting that by that time his mobility may have become impaired.

In 1926, the planned Geelong and District Peace Memorial was opened, in that city's Johnstone Park, commemorating soldiers who had served in the Great War. It was unveiled, on October 31st, by Lord Somers, then Governor of Victoria. An estimated 10,000 citizens thronged to the memorial to see it. The Foyer appeal, initiated to generate the money to build it, had raised £23,000. As the Foyer itself had cost only £15,000, the remainder was invested in providing homes for the widows of soldiers. There were ten marble plaques installed, each listing the names of soldiers and nurses; Tom's son, Sergeant Thomas Edward Bulch, among them.

Tom's own end came while he, like George, was at home. It was not a sudden ending; he had been in poor health for while. This is evident in part through a newspaper report that appeared on August 20th 1930 in the Herald of Melbourne:

> "Mr T E Bulch, one of the best known bandmasters in Victoria for nearly half a century, is seriously ill in Sydney. He was a founder of Bulch's Model Band in Ballarat, and was for some years bandmaster of the old 3rd Battalion Militia Band."

There was to be no recovery from this illness, and Tom finally passed from this life on 13 November 1930, almost eight months after George's death in Shildon. The Sydney Morning Herald reported the news on Saturday, 15 November as follows:

> "Bulch – November 13th 1930 at his residence 84 King Street, Mascot. Thomas Edward Bulch beloved husband of Eliza M Bulch and father of Adeline, Myrtle (Mrs. Tomkins), Alice (Mrs. Johnson), Corporal Jack Bulch and the late Sergeant T E Bulch AIF, aged 67 years. Melbourne papers please copy"

The Herald of Melbourne followed on the Monday, 17 November:

> "The death is announced of Mr Thomas E Bulch at his residence in Mascot (Sydney). Mr Bulch was a well known composer and band contest adjudicator, and many of his marches are very popular. In 1887 the late Mr Bulch was bandmaster of the old 3rd Battalion Band at Ballarat. A dispute with the commanding officer caused the band to resign as a body and form what was known as Bulch's Model Band, the parent of the present Ballarat City Band. Mr Bulch had been in ill health for some time prior to his death. He is survived by a widow, son and three daughters."

Tom was buried, in the presence of his family, at the East Suburbs Cemetery, Botany on the 15th of November. His music had defined him in life, and he continued to compose right up to the time of his death. His last, unpublished, work in manuscript in his own hand was a tutorial book entitled "Bulch's Virtuoso Cornet School" which he had been compiling in the months leading up to his death. This handwritten manuscript was donated to the Latrobe University, and is now part of the Arthur Stirling Collection, which contains many of his published works and a handful of manuscripts, retained for posterity and research purposes. That collection later found its way into a larger collection curated by Dr John Whiteoak, of Monash University, where it is preserved with a huge collection of heritage brass band music.

More than a year after his death, on 26 December 1930, and just before what would have been Tom's sixty-eighth birthday, an obituary was published in the Australian Band and Orchestra News. This gave a brief career history, concluding with the following words:

"His work will remain in the minds of those who knew him as a musician and a man. His coming to Australia gave new life to band work, and thus has passed a great benefactor to the musical world."

One year later, in the Sydney Morning Herald of Friday, 13 November 1931, Tom's wife, Eliza, placed a memoriam notice.

"BULCH – In loving memory of my dear husband and our father, Thomas Edward, who passed away November 13 1930. Always remembered. By his wife, daughters Adelina, Myrtle, son-in-law, Charlie Tomkins."

Of particularly sad note, here, is that Myrtle died barely six months later, leaving Charles Tomkins a widower. The Sydney Morning Herald, again, on 4 May 1932, communicated this to friends family and neighbours.

"Tomkins. – May 3, 1932 Myrtle May, beloved wife of Charles Tomkins of 46 Nicholson Street St Leonards and second daughter of Mrs and the late T E Bulch of King Street Mascot, aged 41 years"

In the same publication it reads elsewhere

"Tomkins - The Relatives and Friends of Mr Charles Tomkins of 46 Nicholson Street, St Leonards, Mrs E Bulch and family, of King Street, Mascot, are kindly invited to attend the funeral of his beloved wife, their daughter and sister, Myrtle May; to leave our Funeral Parlour, 294 Lane Clove Road, Crow's Nest, this Wednesday, at 2:15 o'clock for the Church of England Cemetery, Botany."

After Myrtle's untimely death, Charles moved into Eliza's home so that, whilst he was working, she might look after her grand-children. Eliza, Tom's love and closest supporter throughout his life in Australia, held out only a few more months before joining her husband. The Sydney Morning Herald proclaiming her passing thus:

"Bulch – April 30th 1933, at 136 King Street, Mascot. Eliza Ann, widow of the late Thomas E Bulch, and loving mother of Adelina, Thomas (deceased), Myrtle (Mrs. Tomkins deceased), Alice (Mrs. Johnson) and Jack aged 68 years."

Hers had not been an easy life, choosing to love and support her musician, and businessman, husband. Though little is written of her direct involvement, there are clues throughout her story that she endured hardships for her love, such as the loss of her first child, and the financial collapse of their business bringing financial worries, and the regular relocations as her husband pursued work around Victoria and New South Wales. And yet her part in this story is perhaps undersold. There is much to suggest that without her by Tom's side, and her enduring support for his lifetime goals, he might not have achieved what he did. That she took on the copyright tenure of some of his self published works suggests that she had been so much more than a passive onlooker in her husband's affairs.

Eliza's death presented Charles with the challenge of looking after the children on his own. However, their Aunt Adeline, Myrtle's sister, stepped in to assist until Charles remarried in 1935. Through this upbringing, the youngsters were brought up exposed to stories of their grandfather's heyday, and achievements, and the family's adventures throughout this musical journey. After Charles remarried, Adeline Bulch stayed on at her parents Mascot home. Prior to the war she had been engaged to a sweetheart who had been killed during the conflict. Greatly affected by this, and perhaps through an undying loyalty, she chose never to marry another. In 1950 her sister, Alice, asked Adeline to move in with her, and her husband, in Geelong; an offer which Adeline accepted. She remained there until her own death in 1971.

Alice Bulch had married Norman Brownbill Johnson, owner of a successful printing and bookbinding business in Geelong. The union had prompted Tom to compose the waltz "Noralla," which had later become the name of the family's home. Their son, Keith, following a Bulch family tradition, became what his cousin Eric described as "a competent violinist"; something of which his grandfather would almost certainly have been proud. Alice remained at Albert Street, in Geelong West, not far from the park that her father's band had frequented, until she drew her own last breath in 1964. John Southey Paterson Bulch, known through his lifetime as Jack, survivor of the battlefields of Europe in the First World War, was thus the last of Tom's children when he too eventually succumbed to a heart attack whilst on holiday with his second wife in Tweed Heads in 1972.

Da Capo al Coda

To what end, then, all this creativity and strife if, as with any performance, the curtain must inevitably fall and the stage be cleared of its players and stalls emptied of admiring listeners? Must the theatre always be left empty, and desolate, with only the settling creak of timbers and the faint whistle of a breeze through cracks beneath doors? Every story ends; even our own, as unpalatable as that thought may be. What might we imagine of a world without us, and what, if anything, might we expect to leave behind us after we are gone?

For many of us, as with so many of those other children born in the clattering smoke and steam fragranced streets of 1860s New Shildon, this might amount to little or nothing. So many people, so many cogs, that when locked together fulfilled great deeds, yet when disassembled and considered individually barely register in the collective memory. The babes snuffed out in infancy, through avoidable illnesses, or tragic accident, drowned through misadventure or crushed tragically by the rail machinery, machine workings or rolling stock, as reported all too frequently in press of the day. Those mechanics and engineers, who toiled day in, day out, on sustenance wages, designed to be just enough to keep them alive to serve their profitable purposes; making the wagons to pump coal, goods and livestock around the railway arteries of the nation. Those women that strove through every minute of their lives to make ends meet, keep homes safe, keep their men well enough to work and who bore their children; most likely the one meaningful thing they might hope to leave behind.

When, should you be so inclined, you seek to visit what remains of those ordinary men, women and children of New Shildon you find that even the churchyard, the final resting place for so many, has been cleared. The gravestones, of those who might have afforded one, taken away, deemed dangerous, leaving only a field under which they might lie anywhere. Francis Dinsdale, the grand champion and godfather of brass band music in New Shildon. Those Bulch family members that remained in Shildon till their final day; Tom's mother, father, infant brothers and sisters. The Allans, George's mother and father, brothers and sisters. George himself, and his wife Elizabeth. All there. All hidden, undetectable, uncelebrated.

Yet, for some, in peculiar ways, life does not end with the last breath. A last reward for those with a creative mind and soul is that they leave echoes, that may ring on for many, years after their corporeal existence has ended. It is heartening too that the story we have been following shows that this is not solely the gift of those born into greatness. Greatness, and a lasting legacy, can be achieved whatever your starting station in life. Just as architects and master builders leave behind them their works, painters their pictures, scientists the discoveries they have uncovered and shared and teachers the knowledge they have passed on; the musical composer and teacher may also create a legacy beyond their living years.

Consider Francis Dinsdale, the man who was inspired to found a brass band in Shildon to help bring his community closer together. We should bear in mind that, in the late 1850s, this was innovative music, a relatively daring venture and certainly a form of pop-music of the day. Francis himself had clearly received tuition, from Robert de Lacy in mentoring a band, but the basic skills much earlier from other musicians and teachers. As a bandmaster he then taught, and inspired, others in his hometown; his own sons included. They then developed their teaching and mentoring to pass that skill on to the very next generation which, as we now know, included the young George Allan, Tom Bulch; as well as others, Samuel Lewins, John Malthouse, James Scarff to name only but a few of which we know. In their lifetimes, all of those dispersed to teach those same skills, in their own way, to their own bandsmen. George taught and guided the Saxhorn Band; his own son among them. Sam Lewins did the same with the Bathurst District Band. John Malthouse and James Scarff the City of Ballarat Brass Band, and others across the state of Victoria. Tom Bulch, master and tutor of so many bands. His own sons, one of whom we know at least became bandmaster of his military battalion and whom, had he lived, would surely have followed his father in like manner.

Project this forward through time, beyond their deaths, and consider in the generations that followed how many bandsmen today might be able to trace the inheritance of their musical knowledge and learning back to that one inspired railway telegrapher in 1850s New Shildon. Each generation adding its own musical chromosomes to the DNA of that learning process, to the benefit of the generation following. Though it's not a unique legacy to leave, for it was mirrored throughout communities across the Victorian world and beyond, it's surely a truly powerful one.

Above all, the brass band movement has been one that has granted opportunity to the working classes, that owned it and made it their own. That it began as a working class movement is, in my opinion, largely why so little effort has been invested in who these men were, and what they did for their communities. It has been a world never considered sufficiently high-art enough to warrant the attention bestowed elsewhere upon the greatest figures of classical music or jazz. Yet, to do what Tom Bulch did, exchanging a life destined for the blacksmith's or fitters shop to become a dedicated influencer in a music scene that embedded itself deeply into the identity and psyche of a worldwide empire, was a bold move requiring a great deal of confidence and considerable bravery. Many of the more noted brass composers of the day emanated from more comfortable backgrounds.

Consider the pages of the brass and military banding press of the day, wherein pages are adorned with advertisements placed by those bandmasters able to afford advertising their services to all who might wish to employ them, wherever they might be. George Allan, by contrast, was limited in means through his meagre income as a blacksmith's striker and later wagon painter, and thus not afforded the luxury of being able to travel far from the occupation that sustained him. He was limited to advertising his own published music in the small advertisements toward the rear of the music papers. Despite his clearly demonstrated capability, he was denied the status of great contemporaries such as James Ord Hume and William Rimmer who were both, in their time, able to travel to Australia to tour and to judge brass band contests there.

Arguably we should not pity George too much in that respect. As Tom showed, it was about the choices you made. George chose the security and stability of his job, and life close to his extended family. There was much about his life that may have made it a happy one, free of jealousy over the comparative achievements of other composers. Tom, conversely, knew much hardship throughout his lifetime, through having taken the chance to dedicate his life to music. He probably knew from the outset that it would not be an entirely a stable path to tread.

In the cases of all these young Shildon bandsmen, their involvement in music opened so many doors, presenting them with opportunities they would almost certainly never have otherwise been afforded. The opportunity to experience events from which they might otherwise have been excluded; to make social connections that might otherwise have been closed to them and to travel to places they might otherwise not have seen. All things considered, banding probably gave them all a greater control over their own destinies, and some freedom to choose the extent to which they took advantage of that. Both men also chose to put their abilities to work for the good of their communities. As we have seen, Tom's bands acted in support of countless local charitable appeals and causes from orphanages and hospitals to industrial disaster relief efforts, with a consequent result being that many lives were improved slightly. Similarly there is much evidence of George putting his band at the heart of his community, as his mentor Francis Dinsdale had done before him. Despite his credentials as a contest judge and composer of prize winning marches, he does not seem to have been as keen as Tom in the pursuit of superiority through band contesting.

Then there is the grand legacy of the fine music created by these two inspired and talented men. Can anyone ever be said to have truly left us when we are able to hear the sounds that once only existed as thoughts reverberating around their minds; unique and individual patterns of idea that encapsulate something of the personalities of each that is otherwise really difficult to put into words? It would be fair to say that, of the pieces of music they created that we have become aware of, over four hundred and fifty in total, the greater majority are now never played; having long been relegated to the bottoms of cabinets in band libraries. Australian band historian Jack Greaves wrote that:

> "By today's standards Bulch's compositions are in the main 'old hat' but to several former generations of Australian bandsmen his numerous musical works were widely known and played. Indeed, it would be extremely doubtful if any band library of yesteryear did not contain a large number of his compositions."

When Tom Bulch, and later George Allan, started composing music, it was for a young scene that was desperate for music to claim for itself, rather than having to repurpose that music which was composed for the generations before them. This was often music to dance to, and new dance crazes came and went, rendering those discarded styles obsolete and quaint. Marches, fantasias, and selections fared somewhat better, having a more perennial appeal yet, even then, so many have become buried under subsequent waves of new brass band music produced by further generations of worthy composers. In banding circles, the older music is often, almost derogatorily, being referred to by by bandsmen as 'yellow music' in part due to the colour of the aged, and ageing still, paper and march cards on which they are printed. Some pieces that have endured are those which retain some special significance in their own right, or those which, through their own excellence, remain relevant as an enduring and time honoured test of a great band. An example of the former category is that there is a band in the village of Ashbourne, in Derbyshire, who still occasionally perform George Allan's march "Ashbourne." Similarly, Tom Bulch's old band in Ballarat, now the City of Ballarat Brass Band, keep some of Tom Bulch's marches alive as a tribute to his contribution as founder of the band and one of the leading figures in the development of the brass movement in Victoria and Australia. Elsewhere in Australia there are bands that have existed for many generations for whom Tom composed a piece titled in their honour.

In the second category, for the music that remains brilliant and which in some respects has been barely surpassed such that it can still be heard over a century later at national and international brass contests, look no further than Allan's "Knight Templar," "Senator" and "The Wizard." A brief search for these titles on the website www.brassbandresults.co.uk reveals the scale on which these pieces have been played by some of Britain's finest bands over the decades, and how often those performances have resulted in the claiming of honours. Despite their age there is an astounding vitality to the music that is ageless. This is possibly one of the reasons why such pieces have been adopted, not to say adapted in the sense of the range of instruments involved, more recently by one or two of the marching display bands of high schools in the United States, particularly in California. Those young students know little of George, his life, the commonality with the Tom Bulch story or Shildon's place in the world; but they recognise an impressive and challenging piece of music that sounds great and is enjoyable to play when the musician has the skills to do so.

We also cannot discount the indirect contribution of Tom Bulch to the shape of Australia's unofficial anthem, "Waltzing Matilda." Without the march "Craigielee," drawn from Scots musical tradition through Barr and Tannahill's folk song with its memorable musical hooks, that later anthem would almost certainly have sounded different, and might not have even found its way into the heart of the Australian consciousness. For so long as that song continues to be played and sung, then just like Banjo Paterson, the other names in the chain Tom Bulch, James Barr, Archibald Milligan and Christina MacPherson will never truly have left us completely.

It is probable that, among the more obscure and seemingly forgotten pieces, there are probably a few waiting to be rediscovered that still deserve to be heard today. For example, the march "Whitworth" composed under the name of Robert Malthouse but which bears hallmarks of Bulch's works, has been revived recently by the Spennymoor Town Band which absorbed the nearby Whitworth Band that the piece was named after some decades ago. The band played it whilst marching through the city of Durham en route to the 2019 Durham Miner's Gala, having prior to that been unaware of its story.

Why should we perhaps make more of an effort to celebrate Thomas Edward Bulch and George Allan? They were after all but two of a whole generation of such brass band composers many of whom are largely uncelebrated. To me, having followed their stories now painstakingly from end to end, the answer to this lies in the uniqueness of that story. If I have interpreted the writings of brass band historians such as Roy Newsome and Dennis Taylor correctly, then, despite his amateur status, George Allan should be considered as being among the best brass composers of his generation. Of the contemporaries and influencers Newsome names in his excellent book "Brass Roots," he considers Allan to be among a second tier of only nine composers and certainly one of the top seventeen. Of those notable figures he is the only English brass composer to have emerged from anywhere north of Yorkshire and Lancashire, and certainly the only one from County Durham.

But what makes this story so particularly unique and worthy of celebration is that County Durham did not produce one such man. It produced two, the second of whom, Tom Bulch, Roy Newsome would almost certainly have known more about had he seen out his career in England instead of Australia.

Furthermore it wasn't just County Durham that gave the world these men, but two streets mere metres apart in New Shildon. That common starting point, and the parallel lives they led, ending in the same year, are what makes the stories of Tom Bulch and George Allan worth knowing. Two men, so clearly different in personality, in style, in outlook to life, with different priorities and who followed different paths that nonetheless remained interwoven in wonderful ways almost to the very end.

Though much has changed in Shildon, in Ballarat, Melbourne, Albury, Geelong and Sydney, there are themes and messages within this story, and values and ideas worth passing down through generations. Seeds of hope for those who feel they have been dealt little to spring them on their way to success; and a message that though our time is short there are ways to ensure an enduring presence after the last bars of your own tune have been played out.

The oldest streets of what was once New Shildon are barely present today – just stubs remain of Strand Street, and Chapel Street with their modest accommodation into which large families were crammed. The British School is now a place to learn to dance. The old Mechanics Institute a tiny sunless square of shrubs and benches. The former railway works is now an industrial estate with no rails to be seen. Yet the ghosts of the sheds in which generations of men of New Shildon laboured to produce locomotives and rolling stock for the railway companies that owned them can still be seen. As you wander in their midst you can almost imagine the clamour and clattering rhythms of industry that provided the background to the imaginings of music that left this place on its way out to the world, and hear the faintest distant reverberation of two young cornetists at practice as the evening turns to dusk.